Byzantine Rome and the Greek Popes

Byzantine Rome and the Greek Popes

Eastern Influences on Rome and the Papacy from Gregory the Great to Zacharias, A.D. *590–752*

Andrew J. Ekonomou

LEXINGTON BOOKS

A division of
ROWMAN & LITTLEFIELD PUBLISHERS, INC.
Lanham • Boulder • New York • Toronto • Plymouth, UK

LEXINGTON BOOKS

A division of Rowman & Littlefield Publishers, Inc.
A wholly owned subsidiary of The Rowman & Littlefield Publishing Group, Inc.
4501 Forbes Boulevard, Suite 200
Lanham, MD 20706

Estover Road, Plymouth PL6 7PY, United Kingdom

British Library Cataloguing in Publication Information Available

Library of Congress Cataloging-in-Publication Data

Ekonomou, Andrew J., 1948–
  Byzantine Rome and the Greek popes: Eastern influences on Rome and the papacy from
Gregory the Great to Zacharias, 590–752 a.d. / Andrew J. Ekonomou.
    p.cm.
1. Papacy—History—To 1309. 2. Church history—7th century. 3. Church history—8th
century. I. title.
  BX1070.E36 2007
  270.2—dc22   2006029690

ISBN-13: 978-0-7391-1977-8 (cloth : alk. paper)
ISBN-10: 0-7391-1977-X (cloth : alk. paper)
ISBN-13: 978-0-7391-1978-5 (pbk. : alk. paper)
ISBN-10: 0-7391-1978-8 (pbk. : alk. paper)
ISBN-13: 978-0-7391-3386-6 (electronic)
ISBN-10: 0-7391-3386-1 (electronic)

Printed in the United States of America

⊗™ The paper used in this publication meets the minimum requirements of American
National Standard for Information Sciences—Permanence of Paper for Printed Library
Materials, ANSI/NISO Z39.48–1992.

To the memory of my grandparents
Anastasios and Anthe Chakiris
and
Emmanuel and Katina Ekonomou

~

Contents

Abbreviations

AA.SS.	*Acta Santcorum*
BHG	*Bibliotheca hagiographica graeca*
BHL	*Bibliotheca hagiographica latina*
Dölger	F. Dölger, *Regesten der Kaiserurkunden des Oströmischen Reiches von 565–1453*, Vol. I
Jaffé	Ph. Jaffé, *Regesta Pontificum Romanorum*
Mansi	J. D. Mansi, *Sacrorum Conciliorum Nova et Amplissima Collectio*
MGH	*Monumenta Germaniae Historica*
MGH, AA	*Auctores Antiquissimi*
MGH, SRM	*Scriptores Rerum Merovingicarum*
MGH, SSrL	*Scriptores Rerum Langobardicarum et Italicarum*
LP	L. Duchesne, ed., *Liber Pontificalis*
PG	J. P. Migne, ed., *Patrologia cursus completus series Graeca*
PL	J. P. Migne, ed., *Patrologia Latina*
Reg.	Pope Gregory I, *Registrum epistularum*

~

CHAPTER I

Cum Illi Graeci Sint, Nos Latini[1]

Rome and the East in the
Time of Gregory the Great

Greeks were not strangers to Rome. When they arrived from the East in the middle of the sixth century to occupy the imperial palace on the Palatine Hill, they came back to a city that was familiar to them. But enthusiasm at their arrival was not entirely unrestrained. While Rome rejoiced in its liberation from the barbarians, it could not completely shed a lingering suspicion inherited from antiquity that its emancipators, although calling themselves Romans, were still Greeks. The gift of freedom might yet be an artful deception that no one could trust. Although much had changed in the five centuries since Vergil had written Rome's creation epic, the Latins who remained in the beleaguered city could not resist the temptation to see specters of the Argives in the Byzantines from Constantinople;[2] *timeo Danaos et dona ferentes* was an admonition that lingered deep within their psyche.[3]

Although Rome had a long fascination for things Greek, the allure of Hellenism paradoxically carried with it a dark counterpart in Roman contempt for the very same things that made the East appealing. While mimicking Greek customs and practices, Romans were nonetheless wary of vacuous Hellenic theorizing and Greek tendencies toward verbal trickery rather than genuine understanding.[4] By the end of the second century B.C., Hellenic education and culture had infiltrated Rome's upper classes. Although Roman intellectuals were fully bilingual, their use of Latin in affairs of state remained a matter of principle.[5]

Rome's pagan authors had often been scathing in their attacks on Easterners. Juvenal had satirized Antioch's Orontes river discharging "its language and morals and slanting strings" into Rome's Tiber, and he had lamented the infectious and ubiquitous "hungry Greekling" forever hawking his seemingly endless store of knowledge.[6] Plautus invented the word *pergraecari*, meaning to live dissolutely, in order to contrast Roman moral superiority over Greek tendencies to debauchery.[7]

Christian writers centuries later were no less vitriolic. Tertullian was strident in his condemnation of the East's love for argumentation, conjecture, and the "useless affectation of stupid curiosity." For him such "sublime speculations," expressed in verbal trickery and an "artful show of language," inhibited rather than illuminated the search for truth. A disciple of Greece could not also be a disciple of heaven.[8] When Julian, bishop of Eclanum, refused to accede to Pope Zosimus's condemnation of Pelagius, Augustine produced a polemic containing citations from a host of Latin Fathers ranging from Irenaeus of Lyons to Ambrose of Milan. He then sarcastically taunted his adversary demanding to know whether his sources were less authoritative merely because they were Latins instead of Greeks.[9] Writing in the middle of the fifth century, Salvian of Marseilles complained bitterly that in their moral depravity the Romans of his day were even closer to the Greeks than their fathers had been.[10] Apparently the Christianization of the empire had not extirpated the undercurrent of suspicion and even disdain that still flowed between Latin West and Greek East.[11] Nor had the Justinianic reconquest of Italy effaced it. The discontented citizens of Rome petitioned the emperor to recall Narses, whom they accused of subjecting them to slavery, declaring that it would have been better for them to continue serving the Goths rather than the Greeks.[12] When Vacis, Witigis's commander, reproached the Romans for their faithlessness, he did not hesitate to remind them that the Goths could at least defend them while the only Greeks who had ever come to Italy were "actors of tragedy and mimes and thieving sailors."[13]

Paul the Deacon reflected a sense of differentiation between Latin West and Greek East in the latter part of the sixth century when he called attention to the fact that Maurice was the first of Greek birth to become emperor.[14] Italian antagonism toward the Greeks was not limited to Rome. Writing to the Lombard king Agilulf in 607, the Patriarch of Aquileia questioned whether the Istrian schism could ever be healed in the face of the cruelties shown by the Greeks who, through the exercise of force from Ravenna, had established a more compliant patriarchate at Grado.[15] The Ravennates showed a similar contempt for the Greeks. Agnellus reminded his fellow citizens of the venom they had drunk from the mouth of the Byzantine serpent and vowed never to yield to the Greeks' swollen sense of pride.[16] In times of necessity, however, the ancient animus revealed its latent ambivalence and cautiously relented.[17] Rome's ties to the East had a history characterized by such ambivalence, and that same unease and tension, which simultaneously drew Rome to and repelled it from the East, was to mark its Byzantine years.

Genuine anti-Eastern sentiment must, however, be distinguished from the mere repetition of well-established literary *topoi* to which Western authors routinely resorted when they wrote about the East. Although from the time of Tertullian the West harbored an innate distrust of Greek theological speculation because of its likelihood to lead to heresy, that did not necessarily translate into a wholesale rejection of things Eastern.[18] Western ambivalence toward the East was largely the result of a justified apprehension that oriental infatuation with philosophy generally resulted in doctrinal error. It was not the Greek language, for example, that was objectionable, but rather those who spoke it. Thus the rhetoric of inherited anti-Eastern *topoi* that permeates Western sources from the pre-Christian period onward must never be taken to mean that all things Greek were somehow tarnished and objectionable.[19] Quite the contrary, even before the end of the sixth century, the East was becoming warmly and increasingly embraced in Byzantine Rome.

⌁

The future pope Gregory the Great was ten years old when, in the winter of 550 along with his parents and relatives, he was driven from Rome by the Ostrogothic king Totila and sent with the rest of the population south to the Campanian countryside. The city was left entirely deserted for the first time in its history.[20] Justinian I's grandiose plan to restore the Roman Empire to its ancient grandeur had resulted in disaster and desolation for the Italian peninsula.[21] Time and again Rome was besieged. Death, starvation, and famine were commonplace.[22] If the city was not suffering from Gothic depredations, it was being afflicted by the plundering of the imperial army and profiteering by Byzantine commanders.[23] Senators were reduced to begging; their clothing was that of rustics.[24] Rome could put little faith in imperial forces that often resorted to acts of betrayal and treachery, especially when their pay was not forthcoming.[25] The city that Belisarius claimed the whole world hailed as the "greatest and most noteworthy" had been reduced to a mere shadow of its former splendor.[26] Procopius had reason to lament the forlorn condition that had befallen the senate and people of Rome.[27] When Narses finally captured Rome in 552 and sent the keys of its gates to the emperor, he was handing over a city that was very nearly the apple orchard that Totila had threatened to make of it.[28]

Despite Procopius's dismal portrait of Roman devastation, the beneficial consequences of Justinian's reconquest were extolled in both the East and the West. Agathias proclaimed that Sicily, Rome, and Italy had cast off the yoke of foreign domination and were restored to their ancient way of life.[29] In his panegyric to Justin II, Corippus depicted Rome, "the nourishing parent of empire and liberty," as a suppliant holding out her arms and naked breasts to her imperial liberators.[30] Western sources also praised the return of imperial rule to Rome. Narses's victory had returned Italy to its "pristine joy."[31] Even the *Liber Pontificalis*, which rarely showed any sympathy toward the East, recorded that "all Italy was rejoicing."[32]

Italian sympathies during the Gothic wars appear to have been largely in favor of the Byzantines. In a speech to the senate contrived by Procopius, Totila berates the aristocracy for having conspired with the alien Greeks to attack their own homeland, and he attempts to generate support for the Ostrogoths by recounting imperial injustices.[33] But Ostrogothic appeal to Rome's historic aversion for the treacherous and "unmanly" Greeks seems to have failed to engender support for their cause.[34] Pope Vigilius not only supported the Byzantine war effort but seems to have exhibited a special animus toward the Goths.[35] It appears that the Italians did favor the imperial side, thus reflecting a tradition that continued to see, or at least want to see, unity in the Roman world.[36]

Along with the return of imperial rule, Rome experienced an influx of Byzantine functionaries, especially military personnel, who were sent from the East to implement Justinian's grand scheme for Rome's rebirth.[37] With the defeat of the Goths, Justinian had vowed to "restore to Rome what was Rome's."[38] The Pragmatic Sanction of 554 declared that Rome would regain her ancient place as a center for literature, medicine, and law. The aristocracy, or what remained of it, was given the unfettered right to travel between Rome and Constantinople. Moreover, it provided that funds from the imperial fisc would be used to preserve and repair Rome's ruined public buildings.[39] Realities, however, fell far short of the emperor's eloquent pronouncements and pious promises.[40] Unlike Constantinople, Byzantine Rome was never afforded a system of public education financed by the government.[41] Except for rebuilding the Ponte Salaria in 565 and the erection of a column and statue to the emperor Phocas in 608, the Byzantine administration engaged in no other building projects in Rome. As far as its public edifices were concerned, Rome had fallen to the level of a provincial town.[42] The emperor, moreover, determined that Italy would pay for the privilege of having been restored to the empire. Soon the peninsula was invaded by squads of imperial fiscal agents specially charged with the collection of taxes and other financial impositions. It did not take long for these dreaded *logothetes* to make themselves universally despised in the province.[43] Once again indigenous Roman hostility toward the Greeks began to surface. Instead of being treated like the "ancient home of the Roman Empire,"[44] the Byzantine administration relegated Italy to the status of a "remote backwater, the North-West Frontier of a beleaguered empire."[45] By 602, the Roman senate had lost whatever power and prestige it had and ceased to meet.[46] The most ambitious of the city's remaining senatorial aristocrats decided to abandon Rome and try to recover their former glory around the imperial court in Constantinople.[47]

The period of peace following the end of the Gothic wars lasted less than twenty years. Sometime in 568 or 569 the Lombards began to move from Pannonia into the Veneto, progressively insinuating themselves into Byzantine Italy until they had succeeded in driving a wedge through the center of the peninsula and ultimately threatening Rome itself.[48] Imperial military efforts to check the Lombards had proved ineffective. An expedition sent against them by the emperor Justin II in 576 resulted in a disastrous defeat on the Po River plain.[49] The invaders continued to press southward and, although bypassing most towns at the time, returned to take them some ten years later.[50] By 577 or 578 they were pressing hard upon Rome, threatening the city for the first time since their entry into Italy some ten years earlier.[51] In a display of generosity that was inconsistent with the emperor's apparent inclination toward avarice, but which nonetheless showed some solicitude for Rome's suffering, Justin II sent a large quantity of grain from Egypt to relieve the city's privation.[52] At the same time an embassy headed by the patrician Pamphronius, who was probably prefect of the city, was dispatched from Rome to Constantinople to seek imperial military assistance against the Lombards.[53] The delegation met with the future emperor Tiberius II, then Justin II's Caesar, who declined to send military forces owing to the need to maintain troop strength in the East in connection with the war against the Persians. Tiberius did, however, give Pamphronius the substantial amount of 3,000 pounds of gold to bribe the Lombard leaders into allying themselves with the Byzantines and possibly even joining them against the Persians. If, as Tiberius thought more likely, the Lombards refused to be bribed, Pamphronius was told to use the gold to buy an alliance with the Franks and thus enlist them to fight the Lombards.[54] Tiberius's financial generosity to the Roman embassy, together with Justin II's earlier efforts to relieve the city's hunger, reflect a concern for Rome on the part of the imperial government that was manifested by tangible assistance and not merely by moral posturing.

But Byzantine bribes were not sufficient either to buy off the Lombards or to induce the Franks to turn against them. Sometime in early 579 the Roman Senate dispatched yet another embassy to Constantinople seeking imperial aid.[55] The delegation consisted of both secular officials and clerics designated by the pope. Once again, however, Tiberius, now the reigning emperor, replied that troubles with the Persians prevented him from sending a force of any size to Italy. The emperor did, nonetheless, agree to send a small army from the men whom he had available.[56] This force does not appear to have arrived until late 579 or early 580 since, when Pope Benedict I died in July 579, Rome was under siege and his successor Pelagius II was consecrated pope in November of that year without receipt of the emperor's prior approval.[57] But even this contingent seems to have met with little or no success for John of Biclar records that in the year 579 the Romans waged a "pitiable war" against the Lombards.[58]

By now it had become painfully obvious that the Lombards were not going to be easily or rapidly defeated and that the empire needed to prepare itself for a prolonged struggle. The Byzantines had come to the conclusion that their best course of action was to consolidate the positions they presently occupied in such a way as to assure access between Rome and the Liguiran coast on the west side of the peninsula and the region around Ravenna on the east.[59] Moreover, the repeated defeat of imperial forces was sufficient proof that military intervention, even if small segments could be diverted from the East, was not going to succeed. Byzantium's principal weapon against the Lombards became, under Tiberius II, first gold and then diplomacy. With the accession of Maurice in 582, bribes were replaced by diplomacy alone.[60]

⁓

When the Lombards first entered Italy, the child who had been routed from Rome by the Ostrogoths was nearly thirty years old. Gregory had grown up as an imperial subject in a city that, thanks to Justinian and the grace of God, had at last received the gift of peace.[61] A scion of Rome's senatorial aristocracy, and supposedly descended from the ancient *gens Anicius*, which included Pope Felix III, Gregory was held to be unsurpassed by anyone in the city in the arts of grammar, rhetoric, and dialectic.[62] The most that can be said with any degree of assurance, however, is that Gregory received a private education that was commensurate with that of a "Roman patrician" of his time.[63] An anonymous monk of Whitby wrote in the eighth century that Gregory was called the "golden-mouthed" by the Romans because of his eloquence.[64] The irony in this obvious allusion to John Chrysostom is that Gregory's education in the Greek authors was weak, at least in comparison with Latin writers, although it was not totally lacking. In a letter to the bishops of Alexandria and Antioch, Gregory offers a critical commentary on Sozomen's *Historia Ecclesiastica*. Elsewhere, he shows a knowledge of Greek mythology and the Greek poets.[65] Gregory's familiarity with Greek texts probably came from Latin translations or from recollections of examples used in his grammatical lessons as a child.[66] On the other hand, Rome's *doctor eximius*, as Ado of Vienne described him, seems to have been fully schooled in Western thought. Augustine was indisputably his religious master and model.[67] Among the profane authors, Gregory appears to have had a familiarity with such writers as Macrobius, Cicero, Seneca, and Juvenal.[68]

If the Rome of Gregory's youth and early manhood was far from that of Cicero or Vergil, or even from the city that Boethius and Cassiodorus had known in the brief period of its resplendence, it remained for him "the chief among cities and the mistress of the world."[69] Whether he was drawn to Rome because of his ancestral ties or his early intellectual formation, Gregory was fiercely devoted to his native city. The anguish that Gregory expressed for Rome's safety in a letter to the archbishop of Ravenna in 592 was but a small indicator of the solicitude for the city's care that weighed so heavily upon him from his early days.[70]

In 572 or 573, Gregory became prefect of the city thereby undertaking a variety of important and burdensome responsibilities.[71] Chosen to serve in this position by a combination of bishops and leading citizens of Rome, Gregory exercised jurisdiction over legal disputes, maintained the city's defenses, and provided for feeding and provisioning the population.[72] During his prefecture, the Lombards had completed the first phase of their expansion into Italy by taking Pavia in 572. The only Lombards present in central Italy before 575 had been installed by the Byzantines as federates and would still have been imperial allies.[73] It may therefore have been the absence of any threat posed to Rome at this time that caused the imperial government to permit the prefect wide latitude in conducting the city's affairs, contrary to its normal practice of restricting the powers of civil authorities and concentrating power in the military.[74] Nonetheless, Gregory's tenure as prefect appears to have been relatively short, for sometime in 574 or 575, he renounced all civic responsibilities and retired to a monastery that "he had established . . . inside the walls of the city of Rome," placing himself under the supervision of an abbot.[75] Gregory's monastery, dedicated to St. Andrew, was actually his paternal home situated on the Caelian Hill directly across from the Palatine Hill where Rome's Byzantine rulers now lived.[76] The form of monasticism that Gregory adopted was thus based not on the eremitic life of the desert, but on an urban model established originally by Athanasius at Alexandria and developed further by Basil the Great in Asia Minor.[77] As he undertook the religious life, Gregory was following a tradition whose roots lay in the East.

It was probably at this point in his life that Gregory gave up the name Vigilius, by which he had been known since birth, and took the name Gregory. This was consistent with the tradition that as a monk he was rejecting the world by not only renouncing his goods and affairs but also by changing his secular name and assuming a spiritual identity.[78] Significantly, this outward manifestation of a break with the world, which was to become de rigueur in Western hagiography, had its origins in Eastern monasticism.[79] Nor was his choice of the name Gregory without design. One of the very few Eastern fathers whom Gregory mentions by name is the renowned Cappadocian Gregory Nazianzen, to whom he specifically refers in the *Liber Regulae Pastoralis*.[80] Nazianzen, too, was an aristocrat who had been forced into the active life with its burdens and duties (in his case ordination to the priesthood) and, like his Latin counterpart, he had turned away from worldly affairs to live a life of solitude on his ancestral estates. Throughout his life Gregory Nazianzen struggled, as Gregory the Great was to do, between his own desire to renounce the world and the demands of the Church. Finally, Gregory Nazianzen had, like Gregory the pope, abhorred much of pagan learning as the work of the devil that aimed not at illumination but at obfuscation. Yet, he had not hesitated to extract from the classics what was useful for the exposition of Christian precepts while avoiding the unprofitable parts.[81] Gregory of Rome had followed identically the model created by Nazianzen.[82]

It is quite likely that Gregory had had access to Nazianzen's writings in Latin translation. In the short cultural efflorescence that Rome experienced early in the sixth century, the works of Greek authors, both sacred and profane, were translated into Latin by persons of exceptional proficiency in both languages. Epiphanius Scholasticus had translated Theodoret as well as the ecclesiastical histories of both Socrates and Sozomen.[83] Cassiodorus had praised the linguistic versatility of the Scythian monk Dionysius Exiguus.[84] These texts doubtless found their way into the papal library begun by Pope Agapetus around 535. The library building was incorporated by Gregory into his monastery on the Caelian Hill, and its codices ultimately moved by him to the Lateran.[85]

Gregory's time in the monastic community on the Caelian Hill was to last only a few years. In 578 he was plucked from the solitude of St. Andrew's by Pope

Benedict I and ordained one of Rome's seven regionary deacons.[86] Given the fact that he had been prefect of the city and was now an important administrative official of the Roman church, Gregory may well have been part of the delegation of clerics and laymen sent East in early 579 to seek imperial assistance against the Lombards.[87] In any event, Gregory was to remain in Constantinople for six years as papal envoy to the imperial court. He left behind a city both under siege and under water.[88] Traditional classical education had declined nearly to the point of extinction.[89] The Eastern fathers could not be read in the original Greek; even intellectuals of Gregory's caliber had to rely on translations.[90] Pope Agapetus's grand design for a papal library lay in ruins.[91] Venantius Fortunatus's claim that Vergil was still read in the Forum of Trajan was the fond delusion of an Italian expatriate who had already been at Poitiers for half a century and could not have known the city's true condition.[92]

As for Gregory himself, there is nothing to indicate that on the eve of his departure for Constantinople he harbored any particular animosity toward the East. His entry into the religious life had been inspired by one of the most illustrious of the Cappadocians, and he had modeled his type of monasticism after forms established by Athanasius and Basil. Gregory had become attracted to Eastern forms of monasticism through the writings of Rufinus of Aquileia, who had promoted the oriental eremitic tradition with his Latin translations of Basil the Great's monastic rules as well as various homilies on the ascetic life by Basil and Gregory Nazianzen.[93] Dionysius Exiguus's Latin translation of Gregory of Nyssa's Περί κατασκευῆς ανθρώπου (De conditione hominis) would also have been available to him and may in fact have been in Pope Agapetus's library that Gregory transported to the Lateran.[94] In addition, he was probably familiar with the writings of Gregory of Tours, Athanasius of Alexandria's widely circulated Life of Antony, as well as the works of John Cassian, all of which would have further stimulated his fervor for Eastern monastic ideals and practices.[95] As for the imperial government, the emperors had shown their solicitude for Rome's welfare by providing food and gold at critical times. If Gregory's latent Latin hostility toward the Greek East came to the surface when he returned to Rome sometime in 585, it was his years in Constantinople that had dredged it up.

❧

When Gregory came to Constantinople sometime in 579 as Pope Pelagius II's papal representative to the imperial court, he beheld a city that contrasted radically with the ramshackle agglomeration of decaying monuments, collapsing buildings, and demoralized people he had left behind in Rome.[96] As papal *apokrisiarios*, Gregory represented the interests of the Roman church at the imperial court. *Apokrisiarii* were generally chosen from the diaconate, since this order of clergy was usually the best educated and hence the most likely to be able to engage successfully in lengthy and delicate negotiations with imperial authorities.

The Roman *apokrisiarios* maintained his residence at the Placidia Palace, which was originally constructed by Galla Placidia, and was situated in the area of Armatiou within the city's tenth district between the Gate of the Plataea and the Monastery of the Pantokrator.[97] On the northeastern side of the Augusteum, the great square built originally by Septimius Severus and remodeled by Constantine the Great, stood Justinian's magnificent basilica of Haghia Sophia, which had arisen in dazzling splendor after being burned in the Nika riots, and had been consecrated anew less than two decades earlier.[98] Attached to the Great Church were some six hundred clergy who performed the holy offices in an "ecclesiastical theatre" rich in the ceremony and ritual that late antiquity had inherited from the ancient world.[99] The reigning emperor, Tiberius II, had built a magnificent public bath in the city's Blachernae district along with many new churches and *xenodochia* or homes for travelers and the aged. He had adorned the *triclinium* or dining room of the imperial palace with gold and provided spacious stables for his horses.[100] His successor Maurice was to found some forty churches and spend lavish sums to rebuild his native city of Arabissus in Cappadocia.[101] The monumental statues that adorned the Senate were still standing in the early eighth century.[102] It had to appear to Gregory that while his beloved Rome crumbled no expenditure was spared to embellish Constantinople and the East.[103]

Nor does it appear that the emperors hesitated to draw heavily upon the imperial treasury to defend Constantinople from the enemies that threatened it on virtually all sides. If, as appears probable, Gregory was part of the delegation of clerics and laymen who had come from Rome to Constantinople in 578 seeking aid from the emperor against the Lombards, he would have heard directly from Tiberius II that the emperor "was preparing a very large army and was already sending horse transport ships to the East" to fight the Persians.[104] During the entire period of Gregory's *apokrisiariat*, the empire seems to have been continuously engaged in campaigns against the Persians.[105] But imperial troubles were not confined to the East. In the winter of 574/575 Tiberius had made a treaty with the Avars under the terms of which the Byzantines paid them 80,000 *nomismata* annually. After the Avars captured Sirmium, this sum had been raised by 20,000 gold pieces. When Maurice refused the Avars's demand for a further increase, they captured Singidunum (Belgrade), as well as other cities in Illyricum, and threatened to destroy the Long Walls, which crossed Thrace from Selymbria on the Sea of Marmara to the Black Sea. Later, the Avars enlisted the Slavs (*Sklavini*) to join them against the Byzantines.[106]

It is not, therefore, surprising that Rome's appeal for assistance against the Lombards met with tepid responses from the emperor. In 584, Pelagius II wrote to his *apokrisiarios* outling in detail the calamities that Rome was experiencing at the hands of the Lombards and asking Gregory to entreat Maurice to send military force to relieve Rome's suffering.[107] But Maurice had long since determined that he would combat the Lombards not so much by force of imperial arms as by attempting through diplomatic means to enlist the Franks to fight them.[108] It became quickly apparent to Gregory that imperial preoccupation with the Persians to the east and the Avars and Slavs to the north was going to attract more of the emperor's attention in terms of the deployment of military force than the Lombard menace to Rome and the imperial territories on the Italian peninsula. With the dagger poised at the empire's heart from two directions, neither Tiberius, nor Maurice after him, was likely to be overly concerned with the Lombards in the west. In effect, Rome and Italy were largely on their own.[109]

If Gregory's principal task was to plead Rome's cause before the emperor, there seems to have been little left for him to do once imperial policy toward Italy became evident. Papal representatives who pressed their claims with excessive vigor could quickly become a nuisance and find themselves excluded from the imperial presence altogether. Eutychius's return as patriarch of Constantinople in 577, after having been driven out by Justinian, raised the practical difficulty as to whether the acts of John III Scholasticus, who had occupied the see in the intervening twelve years, were valid. When the archdeacon of Rome launched into a complicated exposition on how church law would resolve the dilemma, the emperor gave him a sharp rebuke and told him not to "trouble himself about the exact letter of the canons."[110] It appears that Gregory astutely determined that his best course of action was not to engage in a fruitless collision with imperial policy, but rather to cultivate acquaintances and friendships with the elite who might, through their influence with the emperor, better advance Rome's interests. He would quickly come to know and to despise the serpentine ways of Byzantium.[111]

Gregory was able to enter into Constantinople's aristocratic circles by cultivating his own predilection for rigorous asceticism and personal piety, thereby establishing himself as a spiritual model for the imperial elite. At some point, he was joined by monks from his monastery in Rome, and the Placidia Palace became virtually another St. Andrew's. There Gregory was able to escape from the world and adopt a regimen of religious practices by which he became "filled with the exhalation of daily compunction."[112] By emulating the tradition of the Eastern holy man, Gregory was to establish himself as a sort of *abba* to the city's aristocracy.[113] His dedication to self-perfection and pursuit of inner purity invested him with a spiritual force that attracted a broad spectrum of Constantinople's upper class, especially aristocratic women.[114] His subsequent correspondence as pope attests to the wide contacts Gregory established with persons of rank in Constantinople ranging from the emperor, for whose eldest son he stood as godfather, all the way down the aristocratic hierarchy including the empress, the emperor's sister, the patriarch of Constantinople, the powerful bishop of Melitene, who was the emperor's kinsman and close adviser, the imperial physician, various clerics of the church of Constantinople, and a host of aristocratic noblemen and noblewomen, who included both Greeks and Roman transplants now living in the royal city.[115] But while Gregory may have become spiritual father to a large and important segment of Constantinople's aristocracy, this relationship did not significantly advance the interests of Rome before the emperor. Although John the Deacon relates that Gregory labored diligently for the relief of Italy, in reality his tenure as papal representative appears to have accomplished few, if any, of the things for which Pelagius II had sent him to the imperial city.[116]

The affair with Patriarch Eutychius would cause Gregory to leave Constantinople with a bitter taste for the theological speculation of the East that would extend to an almost virulent dislike of the Greek language and a deep suspicion toward the disingenuous Orientals. Sometime between 565 and 577, on the eve of Gregory's arrival in Constantinople, a debate seems to have again arisen in the East on the nature of the resurrected body. The Fifth Ecumenical Council, which Eutychius had attended as patriarch of Constantinople in 553, had anathematized Origen's proposition that the resurrected body would be ethereal and possibly even spherical.[117] Eleven years later, Eutychius was deposed and exiled for having refused "to subscribe to a notion of Justinian's that the body of our Lord was incapable of corruption."[118] During the tenure of his successor, John III Scholasticus, a treatise published by the Alexandrian John Philoponos had appeared and resuscitated the debate and, when Eutychius returned to the patriarchate under Justin II in 577, he seems to have joined in the dispute.[119] John of Ephesus, a Monophysite with a strong bias against Eutychius, accused the patriarch of teaching that human bodies "do not attain to the resurrection but others are created anew which arise in their stead."[120] Eutychius's disciple and biographer, however, contended that the patriarch was misunderstood by *stulti homines* and that, consistent with Basil, Gregory Nazianzen, Gregory of Nyssa, and Dionysios the Areopagite, he was simply repeating the proposition that after the resurrection the body and soul will be found together divested of their heavy outer garment (the body) and crowned with the lighter and more beautiful garment of immortality.[121]

We do not know what prompted Gregory to weigh into this robust debate, which was apparently far more animated than his pallid record reflects.[122] The climax of this raging quarrel, according to Gregory and the Western sources, took place before Tiberius II himself on which occasion Gregory vanquished Eutychius by a simple citation to the words of Christ, *Palpate et videte, quia spiritus carnem et ossa non habet, sicut me videtis habere*, thereby proving that, like the body of Christ after His resurrection, the human body would be corporeal and palpable. The emperor was so overcome by the simplicity and force of Gregory's appeal to Scripture that Eutychius's writings were ordered to be burned and his heresy extinguished forever. A repentant Eutychius recanted on his deathbed.[123]

Western accounts of Gregory's affair with Eutychius are largely fanciful or at best gross overstatements. The patriarch was neither the fool portrayed by John of Ephesus nor the heresiarch painted by Gregory. In a thousand-line epic poem composed by Paul the Silentiary on the occasion of the re-consecration of Haghia Sophia in 562, Eutychius is described as a "reverend serenity" who was sympathetic to the afflictions of others, generous in almsgiving, opposed to bribery and simony, holy in temperament, and having a peerless knowledge of both the Old and New Testaments.[124] Even if allowance is made, as it must, for the hyperbole inherent in classical panegyric and its stereotyped forms of praise, the real Eutychius was neither an impious heretic nor the archetype of holiness. But even that assessment misses the point. Gregory used the Eutychian affair for a variety of purposes. First, he attempted to show that a simple appeal to the Bible, which for him was the ultimate repository for all virtues and the final defense against all vices, was able to achieve what all the treatises and disputations of the religious philosophers could not.[125] On another level, Roman orthodoxy had triumphed over the East's unremitting tendency to lapse into heresy through vain speculation; it was the Papacy and not the patriarchate of Constantinople that stood as the true bastion of doctrinal purity. Lastly, Gregory could record at least one achievement of an otherwise fruitless *apokrisiariat*.

The Eutychian affair reflects not simply the continuing fecundity of religious discourse but also the sustained vitality of learning in general which existed in Constantinople and the East in the last quarter of the sixth century. Although Justinian I closed the Athenian academy in 529, the University of Constantinople, which had two chairs of grammar and rhetoric in both Greek and Latin and two chairs of law both in Latin, continued to function until in or soon after the reign of Phocas in the early seventh century.[126] The Alexandrian school of John Philoponos and his successors, which included a faculty in medicine, continued throughout the sixth and seventh centuries, migrating to Antioch in 718 and then to Baghdad ca. 850.[127] The Eutychian affair also shows that Rome was, by comparison with the East, an intellectual wasteland. Although Gregory is supposed to have quickly settled the debate, the claim that he had to do so by relying on Scripture alone reflects the educational poverty of the former imperial capital where, dependent upon Latin translations of whatever meager Eastern sources were available, intellectuals like Gregory retreated to an almost complete reliance on Scripture alone in their writings. In his *Liber Regulae Pastoralis*, for example, except for a reference taken from Pliny the Elder and the allusion to Gregory Nazianzen, Gregory's nearly five hundred citations to authority all refer to the Bible: 261 are drawn from the Old Testament and 237 from the New Testament. He refers to no commentator on the Scriptures, and appears to have had no knowledge of John Chrysostom's six-chapter work Περί ιερωσύνης on the same subject.[128] By taking refuge in the sole authority of the Bible, Gregory could conceal his own educational shortcomings. The "supreme distrust of abstract thought" and theological speculation that prevented Gregory from opening himself up "to the theology of the monks of Chrysopolis," may have been in part based upon a genuine belief that it was through the Bible alone that God speaks to human beings.[129] But we should not ignore the likelihood that Gregory's *esaltazione della Bibbia* was also a convenient way of concealing his ignorance of a vast body of literature that he simply had not had at his disposal.[130]

The unfortunate result of this was to cause Gregory to misunderstand and even despise the vibrant and often turbulent ways in which the East acted out its theological debates. Precisely such an episode occurred while Gregory was in Constantinople when Tiberius II dispatched forces to suppress a band of Satan worshipers in Heliopolis near Palestine. In the process, the emperor uncovered a hotbed of heathenism in Antioch, practicing both human sacrifice and devil worship, and allegedly including Gregory, patriarch of Antioch, and Eulogius, the future patriarch of Alexandria. The offenders were arrested and transported to Constantinople where a trial was held at the Placidia Palace, Gregory's residence as papal *apokrisiarios*. As a result of bribery, the guilty were acquitted. The corrupt verdicts set off riots in the city involving some 100,000 persons. The mob attacked the patriarchal palace, believing that Eutychius had shielded the guilty, and then stormed the Placidia Palace where the trial had taken place. It required the emperor's personal intervention to restore order.[131] Even if allowance is made for John of Ephesus's exaggeration in recounting the incident, doubtless the product of his virulent anti-Chalcedonian beliefs, it may have been occurrences such as this that soured Gregory on the raucous manner in which Easterners conducted themselves in matters of religion. When Gregory left Constantinople bound for Rome in 585, he carried with him a prism, perhaps in many ways distorted, through which he would forever after see the East. The *souvenirs assez mêlés* which Gregory brought back from his sojourn in the imperial city would have a significant impact on Rome and the Papacy as the sixth century drew to a close.[132]

⌁

When Pelagius II died in February 590, among the first victims of the plague then raging in Rome, Gregory was once again seized from the monastery on the Caelian Hill, to which he had retreated after his return from Constantinople, and by popular acclamation elected pope. The imperial *iussio* approving his election arrived from the emperor the following September.[133] After four decades of Byzantine rule, the East was inexorably insinuating itself into the city on the Tiber.[134] Even Gregory would succumb, perhaps unwittingly, to the *lux orientis*. For although his years in Constantinople may have in many ways resurrected a hostility toward the Orient that was an ineradicable part of Gregory's Roman heritage, there were aspects of the East, not the least of which was an uncompromising loyalty to the concept of an *imperium Romanum* and *res publica Christiana*, that drew him there in spite of himself.[135] Once the political bonds had been reformed, both Rome and the Papacy would quickly begin to experience, even before the sixth century came to a close, its influence in other ways as well.

The increasing insinuation of oriental elements that began during the last decades of the sixth century, and was to continue throughout the seventh and eighth, was not the result of an intentional or systematic program on the part of the emperors in Constantinople, or through them the exarchs of Ravenna, to "Byzantinize" Italy. The Justinianic reconquest and the reintroduction of Eastern rule in the Italian peninsula was not accompanied by a conscious effort to "Easternize" those territories newly gathered back into the imperial fold, but rather to rule and tax them. While the reconquest may well have created a political situation that facilitated and even encouraged the infusion of Eastern motifs into Rome and the Papacy, it was not, in and of itself, the cause of what began to take place as the sixth century was drawing to a close.[136]

The Byzantine reconquest had not done much to improve the distinct decline in the knowledge of Greek in Rome during the second half of the sixth century. John the Deacon tempered his fulsome description of early Byzantine Rome as a "temple of wisdom," where the pope's companions paraded about in togas like the Latin *Quirites* of old, with the mournful observation that the only thing it lacked was its ancient skill in translating from the Greek.[137] Throughout his pontificate Gregory complained about the lack of persons in Rome with sufficient command of Greek to be able adequately to translate Greek texts into Latin.[138] On one occasion he appears to have tried to remedy the situation by the ingenious maneuver of ordaining a Greek-speaking Isaurian named Epiphanius as a deacon of the Roman church and then prohibiting him from leaving the city.[139] But Roman proficiency in Greek, although certainly wanting in the late sixth century, seems not to have been as dismal as Gregory suggests. As early as 592 there were persons with sufficient knowledge of Greek in Rome to review the proceedings of an ecclesiastical court in Greece and advise the pope on what had transpired.[140] In 595, Gregory, or more likely someone on his behalf, was able to scrutinize a Greek codex sent from Constantinople, which contained charges of heresy against an Isaurian priest, and determine that the accused had indeed succumbed to Manichaeism.[141] Two years later, Gregory was able to give advice to an abbot of a monastery in Jerusalem who had written him in Greek describing his spiritual struggle.[142] In 598, there were persons in Rome with a sufficient knowledge of Greek to interpret Basil, Gregory Nazianzen, and Epiphanius, whose works patriarch Eulogius of Alexandria had sent to Gregory at his request.[143] By 600, Gregory was able, without any apparent difficulty, to understand and reply to a letter written in Greek from Zittanus, *magister militum* of Sicily, which complained about certain religious institutions refusing to comply with the requirements of civil law that applied to them.[144] Thus, a familiarity with John the Deacon's "Cecropian maiden" seems not to have entirely vanished from Rome.[145]

Although knowledge of the Greek language seems to have undergone at least a slightly increased vitality as the sixth century came to a close, there does not appear to have been a corresponding increase in the number of Greek books in Rome for the same period. In response to a request from patriarch Eulogius of Alexandria that Gregory send him the acts of all the martyrs that Eusebius of Caesarea had compiled during the time of Constantine, the pope confessed that, except for a one-volume book on the subject, no library in Rome possessed such a work.[146] But Gregory's inability to find anything in Rome, in either Greek or Latin, about Eudoxius of Constantinople is far more illustrative of the dearth of Greek texts in the city. Eudoxius, bishop of both Antioch and Constantinople, had been condemned for his Arian views by the first canon of the Second Ecumenical Council in 381.[147] In 596, two centuries later, Gregory wrote to patriarch Kyriakos of Constantinople wanting to know who Eudoxius was and why the patriarch had condemned him in his synodal letter. Gregory had apparently scoured whatever synodical texts he had available in Latin as well as certain patristic writings and could find no mention of Eudoxius.[148] Nor had he been able to find anything about him in any of the Greek histories, which he had available only in Latin translation.[149] Since his Latin sources had proved unavailing, Gregory asked both the patriarchs of Alexandria and Antioch to provide him with Greek texts on the subject.[150] Thus, while Rome seems to have had a fairly good number of Latin translations of Greek works, Greek texts on so basic a subject as the proceedings of the Second Ecumenical Council seem to have been altogether absent.

While Gregory lamented Rome's lack of persons proficient in Greek and went to great lengths to acquire Greek texts that might be useful in illuminating a problem, as he did in the Eudoxian matter, he himself repeatedly and adamantly professed ignorance of the Greek language.[151] At times his insistence could be strident, as it was in a letter he wrote in 601 to bishop Eusebius of Thessalonika in the matter of the monk Andreas. It appears that Andreas, who was cloistered in a Roman monastery, had composed certain works in Greek that contained various falsehoods and had made it appear that Gregory was their author. Fearing that the writings may have been disseminated in Thessalonika, Gregory directed Eusebius to search for and destroy them since, as he protested, he neither knew Greek nor had he ever written anything in Greek.[152] At other times his purported ignorance of Greek could be petulant, as it was when he refused to reply to a letter from Dominica, a Roman noblewoman who had moved to Constantinople and who, although a Latin, had the effrontery to write him a letter in Greek.[153]

Gregory's ambivalence toward Greek may well have been part of his Augustinian heritage. The great African bishop had professed an ignorance of Greek and, while professing a passion for Latin literature, had openly admitted a hatred of Greek letters.[154] Moreover, Latin rather than Greek was for Gregory a symbol of the universality and integrity of the empire and of the catholic faith; it was the language of solid doctrinal orthodoxy centered upon Rome and the Papacy in a tradition that stretched from Peter to Leo.[155] Greek, on the other hand, was the dangerous vehicle of high theological speculation. Latin fathers since Tertullian insisted that its subtle nuances and circuitous phraseology led to confusion, doctrinal heresy, and, worst of all, the dangerous potential for lapsing into paganism.[156] In his distaste for Greek philosophical speculation and his suspicion of the Greek language, therefore, Gregory was acting in a manner fully consistent with traditional Western Christian views of the East.

With the same singularity he had shown in condemning the all too flexible Greek tongue, Gregory indiscriminately painted all Easterners as bribers, simoniacs, heretics, and heresiarchs.[157] In their excessive zeal to extirpate heresy they were likely to succumb to false doctrines themselves.[158] Nor was the church of Constantinople above perpetrating outright fraud. Gregory warned his friend Count Narses to carefully examine Constantinople's texts of the Council of Ephesus for possible interpolations. Since Constantinople had falsified a certain portion of the text of the Council of Chalcedon, it is likely that its texts of the Ephesine synod were similarly suspect.[159] Roman texts, Gregory told Narses, were indisputably authentic, for just as the Latins lacked Greek cleverness, so also did they lack the East's inclination toward deceit.[160] But Gregory unleashed his most scathing attack on the church of Constantinople in a letter to his Eastern suffragans who had been summoned to a synod in Constantinople in May 599.[161] He warned them that although the emperor himself was pious and orthodox and would not suffer anything illicit to be done, the bishops needed to be scrupulously careful about Constantinople's ecclesiastics, who operated exclusively through blandishments, bribes, threats, and cajolery, and who were no better than wolves.[162] While Rome may have lost all its worldly possessions for the sake of the empire, with the help of God and St. Peter, the East had still not robbed it of its faith.[163]

The faith, to which Rome was so tenaciously attached, was somehow purer when expounded by the Latin fathers. While Gregory extolled the unanimous spirit that both oriental and occidental patristic writers had shown in condemning the Agnoetic heresy, he could be confident that the East's position was doctrinally sound only because he had found Western fathers who concurred in anathematizing it. Thus the East's doctrinal pronouncements were valid only if they found support in Western sources.[164] Similarly, the propriety of religious customs and practices was determined by the Western norm. When the empress Constantina requested that Gregory send her the head or some part of the body of St. Paul so that she could place it in a church she was building in honor of the saint in Constantinople, the pope expressed horror at the prospect of even touching a saint's body, much less lifting or dismembering it. Gregory was "greatly astounded and could hardly believe" the Greek practice of disturbing the bodies of saints, declaring that the West deemed it a sacrilege to do so.[165]

But Gregory's protest may have been inspired more by a reluctance to part with so precious a relic as the head of St. Paul than by his professed abhorrence of Eastern practices. He himself had authorized the translation of the body of St. Donatus, and he had related the story of the disinterment and reburial of the body of bishop Herculanus of Perugia.[166] In fact, the translation of saints' bodies had occurred in the West on numerous occasions. St. Martin's body was brought from Candes to Tours in 395 and moved again sixty-four years later.[167] The body of St. Severinus had been transported by his disciples from Noricum to Italy.[168] Ambrose had translated the relics of Saints Gervase and Protase and others to Milan, and Jerome himself related that the remains of Ignatius of Antioch were returned to his native city from Rome.[169] Gregory's astonishment, therefore, seems somewhat contrived especially since, as papal *apokrisiarios*, he had to have known that in the middle of the fourth century Constantine the Great had translated the bodies of Saints Andrew, Luke, and Timothy to Constantinople for interment in the Church of the Holy Apostles. Nor could he have been ignorant of the fact that Theodosius I had himself carried the head of John the Baptist into the Church of the Hebdomon.[170]

Eastern customs were beginning to appear in Rome in Gregory's time. When someone complained that instead of resisting the influence of the church of Constantinople, whose practices were creeping into the rituals of the Roman church, Gregory was acquiescing in them, the pope launched into a vigorous effort to prove that Rome's liturgical dispositions did not slavishly follow those of Constantinople but were derived from its own ancient traditions. But Gregory's protest strongly suggests that churches in both Rome and Sicily, which were under Rome's ecclesiastical jurisdiction, were increasingly following Eastern ritualistic forms and that Gregory was either trying to curtail them or to invest them with a Roman provenance. In response to the charge that the Roman church was following Constantinople in saying *Allelueia* during the mass outside of the fifty days between Easter and Pentecost, Gregory replied that, while Rome followed that practice, it had derived it not from Constantinople but from the church of Jerusalem through Jerome and Pope Damasus. As for the accusation that Roman subdeacons were allowed to proceed without tuncis at mass as they did in Constantinople, Gregory responded that again Roman practice did not mimic Constantinople's but was of ancient origin. As for saying the *Kyrie Eleison*, Gregory distinguished Greek from Roman practice by noting that while the Greeks say it in unison, in Rome it was only recited by the clerics with the addition of *Christe Eleison*, which the Greeks never said. Finally, Gregory observed that in the Roman church the Lord's Prayer, and not a prayer composed by some "scholastic" as in the East, was recited after the imprecation over the divine gifts in accordance with the custom of the apostles.[171]

If the East had begun to influence the ritual practices of the Roman church, Gregory himself was at least in part responsible for it. The plague that had killed Pelagius II still had Rome in its grip on the eve of Gregory's enthronement in April 590. In order to assuage the wrath of God and relieve the city's suffering, Gregory, still a deacon, exhorted the people to "celebrate the sevenfold litanies . . . [that] . . . the stern Judge may acquit us of this sentence of damnation which He has proposed for us." He divided the population into seven categories, corresponding to the seven regionary divisions of the city, and directed each group to assemble in a specific church located in that region. Each group was then ordered to form a procession and, while singing psalms and chanting *Kyrie Eleison*, to pass through the streets to the church of St. Maria Maggiore on the Esquiline, where all the processions were to converge.[172]

Gregory's sevenfold litany was based on similar liturgical processions he had doubtless witnessed on many occasions while serving as *apokrisiarios* in Constan-

tinople. Although popular liturgical processions did not appear in Roman sacramentaries until the seventh century, such processions were "the usual response
to unusual danger in the liturgy of Constantinople."[173] The *Typikon* of the Great
Church of Constantinople prescribed sixty-eight public liturgical processions
during the year of which seventeen were related specifically to civic needs such
as earthquakes, sieges, and plagues.[174] Such litanies, which would always have
taken place out-of-doors in the city streets, featured processional chants and the
Kyrie Eleison.[175] The convergence of the seven liturgical processions at a church
dedicated to the Virgin Mary was also directly influenced by Constantinople. In
the early sixth century, the Constantinopolitan patriarch Timothy I augmented
the city's established custom of conducting liturgical processions by adding the
practice of holding litanies on Friday evenings at the church of the Theotokos at
Chalkoprateia.[176] By the end of the sixth century, "devotion to the Virgin Mary
as the protectress of the city was intimately tied to Constantinopolitan processional practice."[177]

Byzantium's growing fervor for the cult of the Virgin Mary seems also to have
had its effect on Gregory for he ordered the seven processions to meet not at St.
Peter's, the church dedicated to Rome's historic protector and whose basilica
would have been the naturally expected terminus, but instead at the church
of St. Maria Maggiore.[178] Both Gregory's veneration of the Theotokos and the
fact that it was a product of his years in Constantinople may be inferred from a
twenty-four-line epigram dedicated to the Virgin Mary and painted onto a picture of her holding the child Jesus that was affixed to Gregory's paternal home
in Rome. The poem, titled *Andreae oratoris de Maria virgine ad Rusticianam car-
men*, seems to have been originally composed by one Andrew the Suppliant and
invoked the protection of the Virgin Mary on Rusticiana and her family. Rusticiana was among the Roman noblewomen who had moved to Constantinople after
the reconquest and had known Gregory when he was there as *apokrisiarios*.[179]

The introduction of Eastern liturgical customs and practices into the Roman church is symptomatic of a growing oriental presence in Rome even before
the sixth century came to a close. Apart from public officials, such as a certain
Count Theophanios in nearby Centumcellae (Civitavecchia), there was a thriv-
ing population of Eastern merchants among whom was a Syrian trader named
Cosmas whom Gregory helped to obtain relief from his creditors.[180] A society of
Egyptians from Alexandria had apparently accumulated enough wealth to build
a chapel in Rome sometime in 589 dedicated to their patron saint Menas, an
Egyptian martyred in Phrygia in 296.[181] The Roman medical community seems
to have been dominated by Easterners. Alexander of Tralles, who had accompanied Belisarius to Italy and lived in Rome for ten years around the middle of the
sixth century, may have been responsible for founding a Greek medical school
in the city.[182] Gregory consulted a close friend, who had studied medicine in
Alexandria, about the condition of his colleague Bishop Marinianus of Ravenna,
who was vomiting blood.[183] A tomb in the basilica of St. Lawrence on the via Ti-

burtina, which contains the remains of an Eastern couple named Dionysios and Rhodina, bears the inscription *"quod medicina dedit."*[184] It is clear that whatever medical skill Rome possessed at this time was a product of Greek learning.[185]

Members of the religious community, however, probably accounted for the greatest number of Easterners present in Rome in the time of Gregory the Great. While there may not have been any exclusively Greek monasteries in Rome in Gregory's time, we know that Eastern monks were cloistered in Roman monastic communities.[186] The venerable monk Eleutherios had lived for years at St. Andrew's monastery on the Caelian Hill, and the Greek monk Andreas, who was exposed as an aphthardocetist, had resided in Rome at the monastery of St. Paul.[187] It is likely that at least some of the beneficiaries of the gold, which the Constantinopolitan noblewoman Theoctista sent Gregory for the relief of the three thousand consecrated virgins living in Rome, included Greek nuns whom Theoctista wanted to assist.[188] The Roman convent, whose abbess was a certain Constantina, may have been largely a community of Eastern women.[189] We have already encountered the Isaurian deacon Epiphanius, whom Gregory ordained and then prohibited from leaving Rome probably because he was Greek-speaking.[190] But it also appears that Gregory held him in sufficiently high esteem to send him on a mission to sort out charges against a bishop who claimed he had been wronged.[191] A priest/monk named Athanasius from a monastery in Iconium was in Rome for three years appealing an accusation of heresy made against him in Constantinople.[192] Ultimately, Gregory acquitted him and another Eastern cleric, John of Chalcedon, of the charges.[193] In 597, Gregory lamented the departure for Constantinople of two clerics, a priest named George and a deacon named Theodore, who had apparently been with him for some time in Rome.[194] At least one Easterner, the acolothus Olympos, rose within the household of Pelagius II to the position of first sacristan to the pope.[195]

During the early part of the sixth century, Rome experienced a considerable increase in the number of persons with names of African association. This was due in part to the presence of refugees from the Vandal persecutions in North Africa and also reflected the consequences of the Laurentian schism. Eventually these Africans and their descendants entered the ranks of the Roman church.[196] The same phenomenon occurred at the end of the sixth century, except that the influx came from the East and was a result of the Byzantine reconquest.[197] Although Easterners appear to have been admitted to the clergy of the Roman church in the last years of the sixth century, they were a distinct minority. This conclusion is, however, based on the lists of subscribers to synodal proceedings and involves the precarious practice of attempting to deduce ethnic identity from personal names. Whether a name is Greek or Latin is not a consistent or reliable indicator of ethnic identity, and we must be careful not to draw a conclusion about a person's ethnicity solely from a personal name. Names can be selected for reasons that have nothing to do with ethnic origins. They might be chosen for religious or symbolic reasons, to emphasize one's family, acquire prestige, identify with a saint or patron, or display humility or profession.[198] Papal names provide a good example of the danger inherent in equating a name with nationality. In the early Middle Ages, popes of Latin origin, such as Anastasios I and II (Άναστάσιος), Symmachus (Σύμμαχος), and Agapetus (Άγάπιτος) took typically Greek names.[199] Pope Gregory the Great (Γρηγόριος), although having a distinctively Greek name, was certainly not Greek.[200] Some names were taken by both Latins and Greeks. Leo I was from Tuscia, while Leo II was a Greek Sicilian.[201] John I, II, and III were Latins, but John V, VI, and VII were Easterners.[202] There are some names, such as Felix and Benedict, that are characteristically Latin and that no Eastern pope assumed.[203]

Although three Roman synods took place during Gregory's pontificate, the list of subscribing clerics survives only from a synod convened to enact certain monastic reforms in April 601.[204] There are twenty-three subscribing bishops, excluding the pope who was Latin. Sixteen have indisputably Latin names.[205] Three bishops, who occupied respectively the sees of Tarento, Falaria, and Velitrae, are named John (Ioannes). Since they signed third, fourth, and seventh, they were senior prelates and almost assuredly Latin. Paulus and Angelus, who signed fourteenth and sixteenth, were bishops respectively of Nepi and Terracina; although their names suggest an Eastern origin, their seniority indicates that they also were probably Latin. Apart from them, only two bishops, Constantinus (or Constantius) of Narni and Anastasius of Tiburtina (Tivoli), have names generally indicating an Eastern provenance. The fact that they sign last is significant since it shows that they had the lowest seniority and had thus been only recently consecrated. Taken together with their Eastern names, it is evident that very few Easterners, in this case less than 1 percent, had succeeded into the hierarchy of the Roman church at the beginning of the seventh century.

The percentage was higher for the priesthood. The synod of April 601 contains the names of thirty-three subscribing priests of whom twenty-five have names that are distinctively Latin.[206] There are five whose names can imply either a Western or an Eastern origin: four are named John (Ioannes) and there is one Leo. John of Saints John and Paul and John of St. Vitale are sufficiently high in seniority as to suggest they were Latin, while John of St. Chrysogonus and John of St. Silvester are low enough that they may have been recently ordained and hence Easterners. Leo, who signed thirty-second, was probably Greek. Andromacus, Andreas, and Agapetus, whose names are typically Eastern and who subscribed respectively twenty-first, twenty-seventh, and twenty-eighth, were sufficiently low in the clerical hierarchy as to suggest recent ordination which, combined with their oriental names, is strong evidence that they were Greek. At most, therefore, six of the thirty-three priests, or 18 percent, were probably from the East.

Written between 593 and 594 while Gregory was pope and after his apocrisiariat in Constantinople, the *Dialogues* best reflect the impact that the East exercised on Rome and the Papacy in the late sixth century.[207] The spirit of monasticism flowed deep within Gregory and had surfaced before he left Rome for Constantinople in 579. While in the imperial city, Gregory had lived the life of an ascetic, establishing himself as an *abba* to the aristocracy on a model patterned closely on that of the quintessential oriental holy man.[208] He had heard, read, and absorbed the miracle stories of the many Eastern saints and confessors that formed a "common fund" of tales and teachings prevalent throughout the Mediterranean.[209] Gregory's Eastern sources had included Rufinus's *Historia monachorum in Aegypto* as well as his *Historia Ecclesiastica*, Palladius's *Lausiac History*, Athanasius's *Life of Antony*, Pope Pelagius I's Latin translation of the *Apophthegmata Patrum*, Theodoret of Cyrrhus's *History of the Monks of Syria*, Aeneas of Gaza's *Theophrastes*, the *Paradise of Heraclides*, and various other similar texts.[210] Indeed, the format of the *Dialogues*, in which Gregory repeats the responses he had given to questions posed by his deacon Peter, may have been borrowed from Palladius's *Dialogues on the Life of St. John Chrysostom*, a work that is set in Rome and is structured as an exchange between an Eastern bishop and a Roman deacon.[211] But what is particularly striking is that Gregory's format follows closely the *abba*/pupil relationship of Eastern texts, especially the *Apophthegamata Patrum*, where the disciple asks his spiritual father to "speak a word" and then listens attentively to what his master says.[212] As with its Eastern model, the *Dialogues* takes on the form of this "one-way street."[213]

When he returned to Rome, Gregory determined that Italy would share in this rich tradition, and that, like the East, it would be able to boast of the achievements of its own thaumaturges. But Italy's wonder-workers would be better than those of the East because they were living and performing their miracles in the present, or had done so in the very recent past, and not only in times long gone.[214] The *Dialogues* gave Italy holy men who were part of an unmistakable hagiographical tradition whose roots lay in the Egyptian desert and the Syrian caves. They cultivated the same virtues and combated the same vices as their counterparts who battled in the oriental wilderness. Gregory's holy men fled from the world and lived a life of solitude where silence was prized over useless talk.[215] They were both ignorant of and despised secular learning.[216] Their lives were devoted to continual prayer and psalmody.[217] They labored ceaselessly to overcome the temptations of the flesh.[218] Obedience and humility were among the highest virtues.[219] They battled and expelled demons, tamed the wild beasts, and had the gift of prophecy and discernment.[220] Compunction, the gift of tears and weeping, is a theme that pervades the *Dialogues* just as it does the *Apophthegmata Patrum*.[221] The *vitae patrum* of the Latin West, which would provide the Occident with a rich source of material for many subsequent hagiographies, had arisen in the spiritual ethos of the monks of the Thebaid and the cells of Nitria.[222]

Finally, Gregory would create in Benedict of Nursia an Italian Antony, giving the afflicted peninsula and the entire West a superhuman figure whose sanctity could match that of "the patriarch of Eastern monks."[223] The parallels between Gregory's life of Benedict and the life of Antony leave little doubt that Gregory had Athanasius's text in Latin translation before him when he wrote.[224] Through Gregory's *Dialogues*, Benedict becomes Antony, assuming nearly all of the latter's traits, enduring the same spiritual combat, experiencing the same spiritual growth, and attaining the same extraordinary holiness.[225] What is significant is that Gregory patterned Italy's quintessential holy man not on an existing Western model, specifically St. Martin of Tours, but rather upon an oriental archetype. The Roman church thereby acquired its *modèle de l'idéal ascétique* from the hagiography of the Greek-speaking East, not the Latin-speaking West. When it came to creating a paradigm of holiness for his beloved Italy, the erstwhile papal *apokrisiarios* looked eastward to a world that he admired but, at the same time, distrusted because of its tendency to engage in theological speculation and thus fall into doctrinal heresy. It was, nonetheless, to an oriental tradition, where "holy men, and particularly monks, had won the trust of God by defeating the 'wild beasts' of sin with prayers, vigils, fasting, discomfort, and humiliation," that Rome's *consul dei* turned to create the father of Western monasticism.[226]

❦

In describing and evaluating the extent to which Rome and the Papacy experienced the impact of the East in the closing decades of the sixth century we have relied heavily upon Gregory the Great. The state of the evidence, however, allows us to do little else. Gregory was a prolific writer who composed more than any pope before him. His works fill five volumes of the *Patrologia Latina* and comprise some three thousand separate documents.[227] As fourteen books of letters will attest, few matters escaped his attention; nothing was too trivial for his watchful papal eye. Eastern sources have little to say about Italy or the Papacy in this period. After 574 the name of the bishop of Rome disappears from the rubrics that precede each year in Theophanes's *Chronographia* and does not reappear for a century and a half.[228] Theophylact Simocatta mentions Rome in passing only twice.[229] Menander gives it scarcely more attention.[230] And so, we must rely largely on Gregory.

But in doing so we must be cautious about his occasional outbursts of anti-Eastern vitriol. In his attitude toward the contemporary Greek East, as well as the classical Greek and Roman past, Gregory reflects the tension of an age that had to bear the heavy burden of Justinian's grand design of *renovatio*.[231] The emperor's efforts to restore the glory of imperial Rome to an empire that was now Christian inevitably led toward an antagonism between concepts and ideologies that were often not susceptible of an easy synthesis. The evolution of the Greco-Roman world to the Byzantine ideal of a Christian theocracy often produced a tension between a desire to revive and maintain classical traditions while simultaneously crusading for the Christian faith that frequently led to a rhetoric containing familiar and persistent anti-classical and anti-Greek *topoi*.[232] Tertullian, the father of Latin Christianity, had told Westerners that they no longer needed to look only to the Greek East for sources able to expound the Christian faith: "If you are near Italy, you have Rome, where we too have an authority close at hand."[233]

That Gregory succumbed to the same anti-Eastern and anti-Greek *topoi* should therefore come as no surprise.

Moreover, Gregory was unconditionally devoted to Rome. He grieved at the lavish sums that the emperors spent to embellish Constantinople and other places in the East while his beloved Rome crumbled in desolation.[234] It so chafed him to see Rome's old aristocrats fleeing eastward to luxuriate in Byzantium's splendors that he reproached Boethius's widow Rusticiana for having consigned her native city to oblivion in order to savor the delights of Constantinople.[235] The East's proclivity to lapse into heresy, which he had witnessed firsthand in the Eutychian affair, had made a deep impression on him. As Leo's successor he had inherited the burden of defending doctrinal orthodoxy; it was a charge that rested heavily upon him. Gregory rankled at the thought that "the chief of cities and mistress of the world" had yielded her place of honor to the upstart *urbs regia* on the Bosphorus and that Rome was becoming "ever more marginal, geographically and politically, to the emperors' policies."[236] Simply stated, Gregory was unutterably jealous.[237]

An uncritical reading of Gregory the Great is bound to lead to the conclusion that late sixth-century Rome consciously sought to draw a curtain between itself and the East in order to protect its native *Latinitas* from a foreign and corrupting *Graecitas*.[238] If there was a growing estrangement between Rome and Constantinople, there was not a great deal of evidence of it in late sixth-century Rome. In fact, a growing cultural rapprochement would seem to characterize their relationship far more accurately. Even before the sixth century came to a close, a good number of Easterners, including merchants, physicians, and ecclesiastics (both men and women) were present in Rome. Greeks were making their way into the clergy and hierarchy of the Roman church. Although knowledge of Greek had experienced a period of decline, there were still persons in Rome who were proficient in it. The Roman church had absorbed Constantinopolitan liturgical customs and practices into its forms of worship and intercession. While not a serious rival to St. Peter, the Virgin Mary, whose cult was growing in Byzantium, had made an imprint as one of Rome's protectors. For its monastic patriarch, Rome looked to the Orient, not Gaul, modeling Benedict of Nursia after Antony of Egypt. In the great testament of its holy men, Rome imitated the monks of Scetis; Italy's ascetics were clothed in a spirituality whose roots lay deep in the Egyptian desert. For protection against the Lombards, Rome still appealed to the emperor regardless of whether he was as Maurice, "most pious and a despiser of wickedness," or as Phocas, "a tyrant, bloodthirsty, and impious."[239] The ties that bound Rome to Constantinople in 600 were growing more secure since, despite all the differences that had arisen over the previous three centuries, Romans and Byzantines still shared allegiance to a universal Christian empire whose emperor, unlike the kings of the barbarians, ruled free men and not slaves.[240]

Gregory himself not only reflected but was in many ways responsible for Rome's ambivalent attitude toward the East. While he might take his doctrine

from Tertullian and Augustine, he modeled his monasticism on Gregory Nazianzen and his mysticism on Dionysios the Areopagite.[241] Although he protested
that the Roman church did not follow obsequiously the liturgical dispositions of
Byzantium, he introduced Rome to the sevenfold litany borrowed unapologeti-
cally from the *Typikon* of the Great Church of Constantinople. Though lavish-
ing St. Peter's basilica with silver and gold in the manner of his predecessors,
he introduced observances to the Theotokos that he had seen in the East and
that were hitherto unknown in Rome.[242] While excoriating Greek as the pliable
vehicle of heretics and heresiarchs, he scoured the empire for persons competent
to speak and translate it. Finally, first as a monk and then as "teacher, protector,
sustainer, and father of the believers entrusted to his care," Gregory patterned
himself on the Eastern ideal of a bishop.[243] If the "vocation of the *consul dei* was
an eminently Roman one," then it fell squarely in line with a long tradition of
Western ambivalence toward the East that had begun in pagan times and had
survived the Christianization of the empire.[244] Constantinople had influenced
Gregory far more than he ever admitted. Rome, too, was slowly and perceptibly
beginning to experience the impact of the Orient. Once again the tide from the
East was swelling the Tiber's waters.

Notes

1. St. Augustine, *PL* 44: 648. "What then shall we do, since they are Greek and we [are] Latin?"

2. Procopius, *de bello Gothico*, VII, xvii, 3–7, trans. H. B. Dewing (Repr. Cambridge, MA, 1992), pp. 293–95.

3. P. Vergili Maronis, *Opera*, ed. R. A. B. Mynors (Oxford, 1969), p. 128.

4. Erich S. Gruen, *The Hellenistic World and the Coming of Rome*, Vol. 1 (Berkeley, 1984); especially chapter 7, "Philhellenism: Culture and Policy," p. 250ff.

5. Gruen, id., pp. 257, 259.

6. Juvenal, *Saturae XIV*, ed. J. D. Duff (Cambridge, 1962), p. 9.

7. Plautus, *Mostellaria*, trans. Jean Collart (Paris, 1970), p. 35; Plautus, *Curculio*. ed. F. Leo (Berlin, 1958), p. 320. For further evidence of pagan Rome's antipathy to the Greeks, including disparaging comments by Martial, Livy, and Cicero, see L. Bréhier, "Les colonies d'Orientaux en Occident au commencement du moyen-âge," *Byzantinische Zeitschrift* 12 (1903): 3.

8. Tertullian, *Ad Nationes*, Book II, Chapter IV; *Apology*, chapters 46 and 49, in Alexander Roberts and James Donaldson, eds., *The Ante-Nicene Fathers*, Vol. 3 (Peabody, MA, 1994), pp. 51–52, 54, 132–33.

9. "St. Augustine, against Julian." trans. Matthew A. Schumacher, in *The Fathers of the Church*, Vol. 35 (New York, 1957), xii; *PL* 44: 648; Peter Brown, *Religion and Society in the Age of Augustine* (London, 1972), p. 225.

10. Salvian, *De Gubernatione Dei* 7, 88 in MGH *Auctorum Antiquissimorum*, 1, 1., ed. C. Halm (Berlin, 1877), p. 100.

11. Oriental merchants in Rome were active enough to arouse the anger of local tradesmen so that in 440 Valentinian III expelled the successful *"graeci negotiatores."* They were later allowed to return following a famine. L. Bréhier, id., 3.

12. *LP*, I. p. 305; Paul the Deacon, *Historia Langobardorum*, MGH SSrG, pp. 87–88.

13. Procopius, *de bello Gothico*, V, xviii.

14. Paul the Deacon, *Historia Langobardorum*, in MGH SSrG (Hanover, 1878. Repr. 1987), p. 123.

15. *Epistolae Langobardicae Collectae* in MGH *Epistolae Merowingici et Karolini Aevii*, Vol. 3, eds. E. Dümmler, W. Gundlach, et al. (Munich, 1994), p. 693.

16. Agnellus qui et Andreas, *Liber Pontificalis Ecclesiae Ravennatis* in MGH SSrL c. 140. Agnellus takes particular joy in describing how the Ravennates slaughtered the Greeks and threw their bodes in the River Po so that for six years no one would eat any fish taken from the stream. Id., c. 153.

17. Such was the case with the Christian soldier who told a military tribune, whose wife had been sick for many years, that a certain person recently arrived in Ravenna from Rome, actually St. Apollinaris, had cured his son without the use of any medicine. The tribune inquired whether the healer was of Roman stock—*Romanus genere est?*—to which the soldier answered that he did not know, but that the man rather appeared to be a Greek. *Nescio: plus tamen Graecus esse videtur.* The suspicious tribune asked the soldier to bring him secretly to his home so that he might inquire further. *Secrete perduc eum in domum meam, ut cognoscam vera esse, quae dicis. Passio S. Apollinaris. Acta Sanctorum*, Iul. V, 345. For a fuller account of this "deep-seated suspicion of Greeks" on the part of the Romans and Italians from antiquity through the eighth century, see T. S. Brown, *Gentlemen and Officers: Imperial Administration and Aristocratic Power in Byzantine Italy* A.D. 554–800 (Rome, 1984), pp. 146–47. Latin suspicion of the Greek East seems to have been reciprocated. During his trial in Constantinople in the mid-seventh century, the imperial *sacellarius* asked Maximos Confessor, an eastern monk who had been in the vanguard of Rome's opposition to Monothelism, why he loved the Romans and had hatred for the Greeks. *Mansi*, X, 10. *Quare diligis Romanos, et Graecos odio habes?*

18. Brown, *Gentlemen and Officers*, pp. 146–47.

19. Brown, id.; Patrick Amory, *People and Identity in Ostrogothic Italy, 489–554* (Cambridge, 1997), p. 234n192; R. A. Markus, *Gregory the Great and His World* (Cambridge, 1997), pp. 83–96.

20. Procopius, *de bello Gothico*, VIII, xxii. 19; Amory, id. (Cambridge, 1997), p. 11.

21. Amory describes the Gothic wars as "one of the most drawn-out and horrifying wars of the early Middle Ages." Id., p. 167.

22. Procopius, *de bello Gothico*, VI, iii. 18–21; VII, xvii. 7–12.

23. Procopius, *de bello Gothico*, VII, ix. 1–6; 8–15; VII, xvii. 10. Bessas, one of the commanders of the imperial garrison in Rome, hoarded grain and sold it to the aristocracy at inflated prices. It appears that he gave more attention to his war profiteering than to the defense of the city. Id. VII, xix. 14; xx. 1–3.

24. Procopius, *de bello Gothico*, VII, xx. 26–28.

25. Procopius, *de bello Gothico*, VII, xx. 4; xxxvi. 7.

26. Procopius, *de bello Gothico*, VII, xxii. 17.

27. Procopius, *de bello Gothico*, VII, xvii. 25. Rome's recovery by the Byzantines was seen by Procopius as the first step in what was to be "still worse suffering" to come. It was "no splendid and glorious victory but the bringer of a tragic irony." Averil Cameron, *Procopius and the Sixth Century* (London, 1985), p. 237.

28. Procopius, *de bello Gothico*, VIII, xxxiii. 27; VII, xxii, 7; Theophanes, *Chronographia*, p. 333. Agnellus of Ravenna confirms Procopius's picture of devastation when he records that the Romans were "everywhere reduced to nothingness." *MGH SSrL*, c. 95, p. 338; Nikephoros Kallistos Xanthopoulos, *Ecclesiasticae Historiae*, PG 147: 254.

29. Agathias, *Historiarum Libri Quinque*, ed. R. Keydell, *Corpus Fontium Historiae Byzantinae*, *Series Berolinensis*, 2 (Berlin, 1976), prooimion, 30.

30. Corippus, *In laudem Justini Augusti minoris*, ed. and trans. Averil Cameron (London, 1976) 2, l. 124 and l, ll. 288–90.

31. *Auctarii Havniensis Extrema*, ed. T. Mommsen, *MGH AA*, ix (Berlin, 1892), c. 3, pp. 337–39.

32. *LP*, I, 305; L. Duchesne, *Les Premiers Temps de l'État Pontifical* (Paris, 1911), p. 2.

33. Procopius, *de bello Gothico*, VII, xxi. 12ff.

34. Procopius, *de bello Gothico* VIII, xxiii. 25.

35. John Moorhead, "Italian Loyalties during Justinian's Gothic War," *Byzantion* 53 (1983): 575, 579.

36. Id., pp. 589; 596. Patrick Amory asserts that the evidence does not support the view that Italian sympathies during the Gothic wars were largely with the Byzantines. Id., p. 166.

37. Charles Pietri, "La Rome de Grégoire," in *Gregorio Magno e il suo tempo*, XIX Incontro di studiosi dell'antichità cristiana in collaborazione con l'École Française de Rome. Rome 9–12 May 1990 (Rome, 1991): 29.

38. John of Lydia, *On Powers or the Magistracies of the Roman State*, trans. and ed. A. C. Bandy (Philadelphia, 1983), p. 219.

39. Justinian, *Novellae*, 802, App. VII, clauses 22, 25, and 27 in *Digest, Codex, Novellae= Corpus Iuris Civilis*, vol. iii, *Novellae*, ed. R. Schöll and G. Kroll (Berlin, 1954).

40. André Guillou, *Culture et Société en Italie Byzantine (Vie–IXe siècles)* (London, 1978), VI, 294.

41. André Guillou, id., VI, 293–94.

42. Bryan Ward-Perkins, *From Classical Antiquity to the Middle Ages: Urban Public Building in Northern and Central Italy* A.D. *308–850* (Oxford, 1984), p. 48.

43. R. Guilland, "Les Logothètes: Études sur l'histoire administrative de l'Empire byzantine," *Revue des Études Byzantines* 29 (1971): 5, 7. The most notorious and despised of the *logothetes*, especially among the soldiers, was one Alexander, who earned the epithet of Ψαλίδιος or "Snips" for having apparently mastered the art of paring down gold coins in such a way as to preserve their shape. Procopius, *Anecdota*, xxvi, 30. For a history of the office of *logothete* in the Byzantine Empire's civil and ecclesiastical administration, see Iacovos G. Pililis, *Titloi, Offikia kai Axiomata* (Athens, 1985), p. 75ff.

44. Amory, id., p. 12.

45. T. S. Brown, "The Background of Byzantine Relations with Italy in the Ninth Century: Legacies, Attachments and Antagonisms," *Byzantinische Forschungen* 13 (1988): 27, 29.

46. E. Stein, "La disparition de Sénat à la fin du VIe siècle," in *Opera Minora Selecta* (Amsterdam, 1968), pp. 386–400.

47. T. S. Brown, "Transformation and Continuity in Byzantine Italy: Society and Administration ca. 550–ca. 650," in *From Late Antiquity to Early Byzantium*, ed. Vladimir Vavrinek (Prague, 1985).

48. Paul the Deacon, *Historia Langobardorum*, MGH SSrG, p. 89ff.; Bede, *Anglo Saxonis Chronica sive De Sex Huius Seculi Aetatibus* in *Opera Historica Minora*, ed. Joseph Stevenson (London, 1841), p. 193; Ado of Vienne, *Chronicon*, PL 123: 23, 111. The *Liber Pontificalis* first mentions the Lombard invasion of Italy during the pontificate of Benedict I (575–579), *LP*, I. 308.

49. John of Biclar, *Chronicle*, MGH AA v. xi, ed. T. Mommsen (Berlin, 1894), p. 214; L. Hartmann, *Untersuchungen zur Geschichte der Byzantinischen Verwaltung in Italien (540–750)*, (Leipzig, 1889), pp. 8, 109. The imperial forces were commanded by Badu-arius, Justin II's son-in-law, who was killed in the fighting. Theophanes incorrectly identi-fies him as the emperor's brother. Theophanes, *Chronographia*, p. 364.

50. Thomas S. Burns, "The Alpine Frontier and Early Medieval Italy," in *The Fron-tier: Comparative Studies*, ed. W. W. Savage and S. I. Thompson (Norman, Oklahoma, 1979), pp. 51–68; but see *LP*, I, 308. *Multitudo castrorum se tradidissent Langobardis ut temperare possent inopiae famis.*

51. Bernard Bavant, "Le Duché Byzantin de Rome: Origine, Durée et Extension Géographique," *Mélanges de l'École française de Rome. Moyen Age-Temps Moderne* 91 (1979), pp. 41, 47.

52. Paul the Deacon, *Historia Langobardorum*, p. 118–19; *LP*, I. 308 (Justin II is incor-rectly identified as Justinian).

53. The Pamphronius who led this delegation in 577–578 may have been the same person whom Narses had sent in 562 to encourage the Franks, then camped along the River Athesis near Verona, not to attack the Byzantine forces. In the Frankish mission, Pamphronius is described as ον εν τοις βασιλέως πατράσιν; in connection with his em-bassy to Constantinople he is described by the closely similar terms αξίωμα βασιλέως πατήρ. Menander, Frag. 3, 1, pp. 44–45; Bernard Bavant, id., p. 47n36.

54. Menander, Frag. 22, p. 196–97.

55. E. Stein, *Studien zur Geschichte des byzantinischen Reiches vornehmlich unter des Kaisern Justinus II und Tiberius Constantinus* (Stuttgart, 1919), p. 114n4.

56. Menander, Frag. 24, p. 216–17.

57. *LP*, I, 309. After notifying the emperor that a pope had died and that his successor had been chosen, the Romans were required to petition for issuance of an imperial *iussio* authorizing the new pope to be consecrated. *Liber Diurnus Romanorum Pontificum*, ed. Theodor von Sickel (Vienna, 1889 Repr. Darmstadt, 1966), LVIII *De Electionem Pontificis ad Principem*, p. 47–49. Beginning with the election of Pope Hono-rius I (625–638), the prerogative for granting such approval was transferred from the emperor to the exarch of Ravenna. *Liber Diurnus*, LX, pp. 50–54; L. Hartmann, id., p. 31.

58. John of Biclar records that this occurred in the second year of the reign of the emperor Tiberius. *Chronicle*, p. 215.

59. Bernard Bavant, id., pp. 50–53.

60. Walter Goffart, "Byzantine Policy in the West under Tiberius II and Maurice," *Traditio* 13 (1973): 73, 75, 80–81, 117–18.

61. *LP*, I, 299.

62. Paul the Deacon, *Vita S. Gregorii Magni*, *PL* 75: 42; John the Deacon, *Vita S. Gregorii Magni*, *PL* 75: 63; Gregory of Tours, *Historia Francorum*, X.1; Bede, *Historia Ecclesiastica*, II.1; I. Schuster, "Les ancêtres de saint Grégoire et leur sépulture de famille à Saint-Paul de Rome," *Revue bénédictine* 21 (1904): 113–23; A. Ferrua, "Gli antenati di San Gregorio Magno," *Civiltà Cattolica* 115, 4 (1964): 238–46; J. T. Milik, "La famiglia di Felice III Papa," *Epigraphica* 28 (1966): 140–42. Marrou points out that there is no textual support for the tradition that Gregory was a descendant of the Anicii, and that his link to this family is probably a fabrication of the Renaissance. H.-I. Marrou, "Autour de la bibliothèque du Pape Agapit," *Mélanges de l'École française de Rome* 48 (1931): 125, 130–31.

63. R. A. Markus, *Gregory the Great and His World* (Cambridge, 1997), p. 35.

64. *The Earliest Life of Gregory the Great by an Anonymous Monk of Whitby*, trans. Bertram Colgrave (Lawrence, KS, 1968), pp. 117–19.

65. *Reg.* VII, 31; *Reg.* V, 53a (the legend of Atlas); *Moralia* ix. 12 (Hesiod, Aratus, and Callimachus). In the light of this evidence, the statement that Greek writers were totally foreign to him requires some modification. See Erich Caspar, *Geschichte des Papsttums*, Vol. 2 (Tübingen, 1933), p. 347. Aber auch als Römer stand Gregor inbesondere griechischer Bildung fremd.

66. Pierre Riché, *Education and Culture in the Barabarian West*, trans. John J. Contreni (Columbia, SC, 1976), p. 147; R. A. Markus, id., p. 35n7.

67. Ado of Vienne, *Chronicon*; *PL* 123: 23, 111; E. H. Fischer, "Gregor der Großer und Byzanz. Ein Bildung zür Greschichte der päpstlichen Politik," *Zeitschrift der Savigny-Stiftung für Rechtsgeschichte, Kanonische Abteilung* XXXVI, 36 (1950): 15, 18. In response to a request from the Praetorian Prefect of Italy for a copy of his *Moralia*, Gregory suggested that he would do better to taste Augustine's fine flour than his own rough bran. *Reg.* X, 16.

68. Th. Delforge, "Song de Scipion et vision de s. Benoit," *Revue bénédictine* 69 (1959): 351–54; *Reg.* I, 33 (Seneca); *Reg.* V, 40 (Cicero); *Reg.* I, 5 and 6 (Juvenal). For an extensive collection of Gregory's allusions to Western authors, see Pierre Courcelle, "Grégoire Le Grand à l'École de Juvénal," *Studi e materiali di storia delle religioni* (1967), pp. 170–74.

69. *The Earliest Life of Gregory the Great by an Anonymous Monk of Whitby*, id., 125 (*urbium caput est orbisque domina*); Henri de Lubac, "Saint Grégoire et la Grammaire," *Recherches des Sciences Religieuses* 48 (1960): 195.

70. John the Deacon, *Vita*; *PL* 75: 217; Claude Dagens, "Saint Grégoire le Grand, Consul Dei," *Gregorio Magno e il suo tempo*, Vol. I, pp. 33, 36.

71. The only evidence that Gregory served as prefect of Rome is an almost casual reference he makes to having occupied this post in a letter to Constantius, bishop of Milan in September, 593. *Reg.* IV, 2.

72. Justinian, *Novellae*, id., clause 12; Louis Bréhier and René Aigrain, eds. *Histoire de l'Église*, Vol. 5 (Paris, 1947), p. 20.

73. Bernard Bavant, id., pp. 45–46.

74. Thomas Hodgkin, *Italy and Her Invaders* (Oxford, 1895–1899), p. 289.

75. Gregory of Tours, *Historia Francorum*, X.1; *Earliest Life of Gregory the Great by an Anonymous Monk of Whitby*, id., 73. "He lived for a long time in a monastery." Bede, *Historia Ecclesiastica*, II.1; cf. John the Deacon, *Vita, PL* 75: 231.

76. R. A. Markus, id., p. 10.

77. Susanna Elm, *Virgins of God: The Making of Asceticism in Late Antiquity* (Oxford, 1994), p. 354.

78. Amory, id. (Cambridge, 1997), p. 87: "People could, and did, change their names, at marriage, baptism, *taking monastic vows*, and conversion" (emphasis added).

79. René Nouailhat, *Saints et Patrons: Les premiers moins de Lérins* (Paris, 1988), p. 90.

80. *Liber Regulae Pastoralis*, trans. as *St. Gregory the Great: Pastoral Care* by Henry Davis (Westminster, MD, 1950), p. 89.

81. Rosemary Radford Ruether, *Gregory of Nazianzus: Rhetor and Philosopher* (Oxford, 1969), pp. 32, 141–142; 146; 156–158; *PG* 37: 1581.

82. *Moralia*, xviii. 45, 73 (salvation comes through Christ, not philosophy); *In I Librum Regum*, V. 84 (use of secular knowledge to obtain spiritual knowledge); *Moralia, Dedicatory Letter to Leander of Seville, MGH Epp. I, Ep.* v. 53a.1 (despises worldly affairs and seeks instead a life of quiet contemplation and spiritual fulfillment). Gregory's admiration for Nazianzen may also have been influenced by the high regard that Augustine had for him. His eloquent profession of the faith was so admired in the West that Augustine even numbered him among the pantheon of Latin fathers. Augustine. *Contra Julianum, PL* 44: 649.

83. *A Select Library of Nicene and Post-Nicene Fathers*, Second Series, Vol. 2, eds. P. Schaff and H. Wace (Repr. Peabody, MA, 1995), p. 227.

84. *PL* 70: 1137; Caspar, id., p. 307.

85. H.-I. Marrou, id., p. 164ff.

86. John the Deacon, *Vita*, i. 25; Paul the Deacon, *Vita*, 7; Gregory of Tours, *Historia Francorum*, X.1.

87. See p. 5, supra.

88. At the time Pelagius II became pope in 579, the Lombards were besieging Rome and rains created massive flooding. *LP*, I, 309.

89. F. Ermini, "La scuola in Roma nel VI secolo," in *Medio Evo Latino, Studi e Ricerche* (Modena, 1938) pp. 55, 64.

90. Guillou, id., II, 15–17.

91. H.-I. Marrou, id., p. 124ff.

92. Charles Pietri, "Le Rome de Grégoire," in *Gregorio Magno e il suo tempo*, Vol. I, id., p. 31.

93. M. M. Wagner, *Rufinus the Translator: A Study of His Theory and Practice as Illustrated in His Version of the Apologetics of St. Gregory Nazianzen* (Washington, D.C., 1945); Berschin, id., pp. 46, 49.

94. Marrou, id., p. 167.

95. Petersen, *The Dialogues of Gregory the Great in Their Late Antique Cultural Background*, id., pp. 68, 159.

96. The Rome of Gregory the Great was but a feeble specter of the splendid city whose awesome sights inspired Zacharias of Mytilene to describe its prosperity, opu-

lence, and grandeur ca. 500. Thomas S. Burns, *A History of the Ostrogoths* (Bloomington, Indiana, 1984), p. 68; *Homiliae in Hiezechielem Prophetam*, ed. M. Adriaen, CCSL 142 (Turnholt, 1971), p. 312; see also Pierre Batiffol, *Saint Grégoire le Grand*, 5th ed. (Paris, 1931), p. 32.

97. Paul the Deacon, *Vita, PL* 75: 44; John the Deacon, *Vita, PL* 75: 72; see also Bede, *Historia Ecclesiastica*, II.1; Bede, *Anglo Saxonis Chronicon*, p. 192; *Earliest Life of Gregory the Great by an Anonymous Monk of Whitby*, p. 75; Ado, *Chronicon*, id., 111; *Moralia*, Dedicatory Letter to Leander of Seville, p. 1; J. Pargoire, "Apocrisiaire," in *Dictionnaire d'Archéologie Chrétienne et de Liturgie*, Vol. I, Pt. 2 (Paris, 1924), cols. 2537–55. Stratos, id., appendix, map of Constantinople. The Placidia Palace had been occupied by Pope Vigilius in 547 and was to be the residence of Pope Constantine I when he visited Constantinople in 711. *Mansi* IX, 50, 52; *LP*, I, 390. In the middle of the seventh century, it housed the representatives of Pope Martin I who were prohibited from saying mass there by the Byzantine authorities. *Mansi* X, 879. Later, in more happy times, it was occupied by representatives of Pope Agatho who came to Constantinople to attend the Sixth Ecumenical Council in 680–681. *LP*, I, 351. See also A. Emereau, "Apocrisiarius et apocrisiariat," *Echos d'Orient* 17 (1914–1915): 289–97.

98. Theophanes, *Chronographia*, p. 350; Andreas N. Stratos, *Byzantium in the Seventh Century*, Vol. I, trans. Mark Ogilvie-Grant (Amsterdam, 1968), pp. 393ff.

99. Mark Whittow, *The Making of Byzantium, 600–1025* (Berkeley, 1996), p. 128.

100. Theophanes, *Chronographia*, p. 350; John of Ephesus, id., p. 204; Leo Grammatikos, *Chronographia*, ed. Immanuel Bekker, Corpus Scriptores Historiae Byzantinae (Bonn, 1842), p. 127.

101. Leo Grammatikos, *Chronographia*, p. 128; John of Ephesus, *Third Part of the Ecclesiastical History*, trans. R. Payne Smith (Oxford, 1860), pp. 361–63. For a detailed description of Maurice's extensive constructions in Constantinople and the East, see Michael Whitby, *The Emperor Maurice and His Historian: Theophylact Simocatta on Persian and Balkan Warfare* (Oxford, 1988), pp. 19–21.

102. Averil Cameron and Judith Herrin, trans. and eds., *Constantinople in the Early Eighth Century: The Parastaseis Syntomoi Chronikai* (Leiden, 1984), pp. 38, 117–21.

103. Hodgkin's description of the pique that Gregory must have felt at seeing the disparity between imperial treatment of Rome and Constantinople remains vivid and compelling a century after it was written: "we can well believe that a Roman noble, one who had seen from his childhood the triumphal arches, the fora and the palaces of Rome, glorious even in their desolation, viewed with some impatience the pinchbeck splendours of the new Rome by the Bosphorus, already, it is true, near three centuries old, but still marked with somewhat of the ineffaceable brand of a parvenu among cities." Hodgkin, id., p. 295.

104. Menander, id., Frag. 23. 1, pp. 198–99; Frag. 24, p. 217. Stein believes that for Tiberius the Persian War took precedence over every other imperial interest. Für den Kaiser Tiberius Constantinus war es ein Axiom, dem er bis zu seinem Tod treu geblieben ist, daß der Perserkrieg vor allen anderen Staatsinteressen unbedingt den Vorrang habe. Id., p. 117.

105. Theophanes, *Chronographia*, p. 373 (581/2), pp. 373–75 (582/3), pp. 375–76 (583/4), pp. 377–79 (585/6).

106. Menander, id., Frag. 25.1, pp. 217–19; Theophanes, *Chronographia*, pp. 342n7, 374–76.

107. *PL* 72: 703–5.

108. See Gregory of Tours, *Historia Francorum*, X.3; John of Biclar, *Chronicle*, p. 217; Goffart, id., pp. 75, 117–18.

109. Michael Whitby, *The Emperor Maurice and His Historian: Theophylact Simocatta on Persian and Balkan Warfare* (Oxford, 1988), p. 11; see Whittow, id., p. 298ff.

110. John of Ephesus, id., pp. 143–144.

111. Paul Goubert, *Byzance avant l'Islam*, Vol. II, Pt. 2 (Paris, 1955), p. 143.

112. *Moralia, Dedicatory Letter to Leander of Seville*, id., p. 2. Gregory's reference to compunction or πένθος, a doctrine much esteemed in the East, places him within an oriental ascetic tradition that finds its fullest expression among the desert fathers of Egypt. See David Burton-Christie, *The Word in the Desert* (Oxford, 1993), p. 185ff. Gregory would return to this doctrine in the *Dialogues*. See p. 20ff., infra.

113. See Peter Brown, "The Rise and Function of the Holy Man in Late Antiquity," *Journal of Roman Studies* 61 (1971): 80–101.

114. Philip Rousseau, "The Spiritual Authority of the 'Monk-Bishop': Eastern Elements in Some Western Hagiography of the Fourth and Fifth Centuries," *Journal of Theological Studies* 23, Pt. 2 (1971): 380, 383; see Abba Sisoes in Benedicta Ward, trans. *The Sayings of the Desert Fathers* (Kalamazoo, 1975), 216n17; *Reg.* VII, 23 (Gregory instructs the emperor's sister Theoctista on the virute of compunction); *Reg.* VII, 27 (Gregory is asked to provide the noblewomen Gordia and Theoctista, as well as their husbands, *de anima sua aliquid admonere*); *Reg.* XI, 27 (Gregory consoles the emperor's sister Theoctista for an attack that has been made on her religious beliefs).

115. *Reg.* III, 61; V, 30, 36–37; VI, 16, 64; VII, 6, 30 (Emperor Maurice); *Reg.* IV, 30; V, 38, 39 (Empress Constantina); *Reg.* I, 5; VII, 23; XI, 27 (Theoctista, the emperor's sister); *Reg.* III, 62; V, 43; IX, 4 (Domitian, bishop of Melitene); *Reg.* I, 4 (John the Faster, patriarch of Constantinople); *Reg.* VII, 15 (George and Theodore, deacons of the church of Constantinople); *Reg.* VII, 25 (Theodore, the emperor's physician); *Reg.* I, 6; III, 63; VI, 14; VII, 24 (Narses, a count); *Reg.* III, 65 (Theotimos, a physician); *Reg.* I, 28 (Aristobolos, a translator); *Reg.* I, 6; VII, 22, 27 (the noblewomen Gregoria, Eudokia, and Hesychia); *Reg.* I, 6; III, 27; VII, 26, 27 (the noblemen Alexander, Andreas, Marinos, and Christodoros); *Reg.* II, 24; III, 63; IV, 44; VIII, 22; XI, 26; XIII, 24 (the Roman women Dominica and Rusticiana); *Reg.* XIII, 33 (Eusebia, Rusticiana's daughter); and *Reg.* VIII, 22; XI, 26; XIII, 24 (Strategios, son of Eusebia and grandson of Rusticiana).

116. John the Deacon, *Vita*, PG 75: 75.

117. P. Schaff and H. Wace, eds., *A Select Library of the Christian Church: Nicene and Post-Nicene Fathers*, 2d Series, Vol. 14 (Peabody, MA, 1995), p. 391. Origen had taught that the resurrected body would maintain its earthly form (εἶδος), but that its material substratum (τό ὑλικόν ὑποκείμενον) would be different. J. N. D. Kelly, *Early Christian Doctrines* (San Francisco, 1978) pp. 471–72.

118. John of Ephesus, id., p. 2.

119. John Philoponos (ca. 490–ca. 570) was a Monophysite and pupil of the Neoplatonist philosopher Ammonius. His theological works, which belong to his later years, include the *De Opficio Mundi*, which is a commentary on the *Hexaemeron*, and the

Διαιτητής or "Arbiter." Philoponos's Christology approached that of Severus of Antioch. He was condemned as a tritheist at the Sixth Ecumenical Council. F. L. Cross, ed., *Oxford Dictionary of the Christian Church*, 3rd ed., ed. E. A. Livingstone (Oxford, 1997), p. 896. The treatise referred to here is not extant, but was effectively restated in a work by patriarch Timothy of Constantinople at PG 86: 61 C D, and is alluded to by Nikephoros Kallistos at PG 147: 424–26.

120. John of Ephesus, id., pp. 147, 186. John claimed further that Eutychius became so obsessed with this doctrine that he aroused the anger of the entire city, inciting both his opponents and Chalcedonian allies to regard him as a "heretic and simpleton." Id., pp. 147–48.

121. Eustratios, *Vita Eutychii*, PG 86/2: 2373–76.

122. *Moralia*, 14, 74; John the Deacon says merely that Gregory disputed with Eutychius about what form the body would assume at resurrection. PL 75: 73ff. Paul the Deacon incorrectly characterizes the dispute as representing a "new heresy" (*novam haeresim*) propounded by Eutychius. PL 75: 45.

123. Paul the Deacon, *Vita*, PL 75: 45; Bede, *Chronica*, id., p. 308; Bede, *Anglo Saxonis Chronicon*, id., p. 192; Bede, *Historia Ecclesiastica*, id., II.1. It has been argued that the first two lines of Gregory's epitaph, which read *Suscipe, terra, tuo corpus de corpore sumptum/ reddere quod valeas vivificante deo*, recall Gregory's debate with Eutychius on the nature of the resurrected body. Gabriel Sanders, "L'Épitaphe de Grégoire Le Grand," in *Gregorio Magno e il suo tempo*, Vol. I, pp. 251, 271–75. No Eastern source says anything about Gregory's alleged refutation of Eutychius, a debate before the emperor, the burning of Eutychius's books, or a deathbed recantation. According to the *Vita Eutychii*, Tiberius sent his best doctors to treat Eutychius during his last illness. When it became evident that the patriarch's case was hopeless, the emperor himself visited him, received his blessing, and heard from the dying man a prediction of his own imminent death, which occurred precisely as foretold. PG 86/2: 2379–82.

124. Mary Whitby, "Eutychius, Patriarch of Constantinople: An Epic Holy Man," in Michael Whitby, Philip Hardie, and Mary Whitby, eds., *Homo Viator: Classical Essays for John Bramble* (Bristol, 1987) pp. 297, 301, 305–7.

125. *Moralia*, 6, 15; Raoul Manselli, "Gregorio Magno e la Bibbia," in *La Bibbia nell'alto Medioevo*, Settimane di Studio del Centro Italiano di Studi sull'alto Medioevo (Spoleto, 1963), pp. 67, 77.

126. John Malalas, *Chronographia*, xviii, p. 187; Barry Baldwin, "Latin in Byzantium," in *From Late Antiquity to Early Byzantium*, ed. Vladimir Vavrinek (Prague, 1985), p. 237, 239–40.

127. H.-D. Saffrey, "Le Chrétien Jean Philopon et La Survivance de l'École d'Alexandrie au VIe siècle," *Revue des études grecques* 67 (1954): 396–410.

128. Guillou, id., pp. II, 14; 16–17.

129. F. Homes Dudden, *Gregory the Great: His Place in History and Thought*, Vol. II (London, 1905), p. 289; M. Frickel, "Deus totus ubique simul. Untersuchungen zur allgemeinen Gottgegenwart im Rahmen der Gotteslehre Gregors des Grossen," *Freiburger theologische Studien* 69 (1956): 1; Claude Dagens, *Saint Grégoire le Grand. Culture et expériences chrétiennes* (Paris, 1977), p. 437.

130. Raoul Manselli, id., p. 78.

131. John of Ephesus, id., p. 209ff.

132. Claude Dagens, "L'Église universelle et le monde oriental chez saint Grégoire le Grand," *Istina* 20 (1975): 457, 475.

133. *LP*, I, 309, 312; Gregory of Tours, *Historia Francorum*, X.1; John of Biclar, *Chronicle*, id., p. 217; *Continuatio Prosperi Havniensis* in MGH AA, Vol. IX, ed. T. Mommsen (Berlin, 1892), p. 270.

134. Lynn T. White, "The Byzantinization of Sicily," *American Historical Review* 42 (1936): 1, 7.

135. *Reg.* I, 59, 73; II, 4, 10, 28, 47; III, 61, 64; IV, 25; V, 30, 36–38; VI, 64; IX, 68, 100, 101, 105, 112, 136; XII, 7; XIII, 5, 7, 31, 39–40; T. S. Brown, id., p. 145; E. H. Fischer, "Gregor der Große und Byzanz. Ein Beitrag zur Geschichte der päpstlichen Politik," *Zeitschrift der Savigny-Stiftung für Rechtsgeschichte, Kanonische Abteilung* XXXVI, 36 (1950): 15, 90. An der Idee des *imperium romanum*, der *republica christiana*, hält Gregor unentmegt fest; see also Amory, id. (Cambridge, 1997), pp. 166, 169, 176, 185, 235, 268, 310.

136. Pierre Riché, "Le Grec dans les centres de culture d'Occident," in Michael W. Herren and S. Brown, eds., *The Sacred Nectar of the Greeks: The Study of Greek in the West in the Early Middle Ages* (London, 1988), p. 146.

137. John the Deacon, *Vita*, PL 75: 92–93; see Jeffrey Richards, *Consul of God: The Life and Times of Gregory the Great* (London, 1980), p. 27.

138. *Reg.* X, 21; cf., *Reg.* I, 28; VII, 27.

139. *Reg.* V, 35.

140. *Reg.* III, 7.

141. *Reg.* VI, 14.

142. *Reg.* VII, 29.

143. *Reg.* VIII, 29.

144. *Reg.* X, 10.

145. John the Deacon, *Vita*, PL 75:93.

146. *Reg.* VIII, 28.

147. P. Schaff and H. Wace, *A Select Library of the Christian Church*, p. 172; see J. N. D. Kelly, id., p. 281ff.

148. *Reg.* VII, 5.

149. *Reg.* VII, 31.

150. Id.

151. Reg. VII, 29.

152. *Reg.* XI, 55. The monk was condemned as an aphthardocetist by a council of the Roman Church over which Gregory presided in November, 601. Although the proceedings of the council have not survived, it appears that the principal witness against Andreas was Probus, abbot of the monastery of St. Andrew that Gregory had founded. *Mansi* X, 489ff.

153. *Reg.* III, 63. There is a substantial body of literature on the subject of Gregory's knowledge of Greek. See, namely, Joan M. Petersen, "Did Gregory the Great Know Greek," in *Studies in Church History* 13 (1976): 121–34; Joan M. Petersen, "'Homo omnino Latinus'?: The Theological and Cultural Background of Pope Gregory the Great," *Speculum* 62/3 (1987): 529–51; G. J. M. Bartelink, "Pope Gregory the Great's Knowledge of Greek," trans. Paul Meyvaert in *Gregory the Great: A Symposium*, ed. John C. Cavadini (Notre Dame, 1995), pp. 117–36. (The notes to this article contain an extensive bibliog-

raphy on the subject.) The current consensus among scholars appears to be that Gregory "had no more than a tenuous, even quite negligible, knowledge of Greek." Bartelink, id., p. 117. Although Greek words appear throughout his writings, they were "part of the traditional legacy of Latin" and reflect further that "Christian usage included many Grecisms." Bartelink, id., p. 130n7. For only a few examples of Gregory's usage of Greek words or their Latin cognates, see *Reg.* I, 42; II, 50; IV, 24; IX, 8, 35, 63, 67; XIII, 5, 9, 12, 26; XIV, 2 (xenodochium); IV, 44 (angariis); V, 16; VI, 63 (xenia); VII, 23 (monastrias); IX, 48 (podagra); IX, 48 (monomachus); IX, 200 (orfano); IX, 229 (cartofilacium); IX, 234; X, 16; XII, 8, 9; XIII, 20 (chartularius); XI, 2 (hierochomion); XI, 17 (diaconiae); XIV, 12 (filacta); XIV, 15 (amphimallum); *Homilia in Hiezechielem*, Vol. II, VI, 2; VIII, 14 (φυλλάτειν); *Moralia*, 31, 43 (cerastes); *Moralia* 31, 47 (cenodoxorum); *XL Homiliarum in evangelium libri duo*, Homily 6 (eleos); Homily 11 (gerontas; presbyteros); Homily 19 (platea; odos); Homily 30 (paraclete); Homily 40 (paralysis). For additional Greek "neologisms" which Gregory used in his letters, see Dag Norberg, *In Registrum Gregorii Magnii Studia Critica* (Uppsala, 1937). Bruzzone has identified a great many Latin cognates of Greek words that appear in the *Dialogues*. See, namely, *Dial.* III, 18, 2 (clibanum); I, 4, 8 (flebotomum); II, 7, 3 (melotem); II, 11, 2 (psyatio); III, 14, 9 (sportas); III, 4, 2; IV, 25, 1 (leo). Antonella Bruzzone, "Sulla lingua dei 'Dialoghi' di Gregorio Magno," *Studi Latini e Italiani* 5 (1991), p. 195. If the true test of whether Gregory knew Greek is his ability to construe a sentence, that is, whether he knew grammar and especially morphology (see A. C. Dionisotti, "Greek Grammars and Dictionaries in Carolingian Europe," in Michael W. Herren and Shirley Ann Brown, eds., *The Sacred Nectar of the Greeks: The Study of Greek in the West in the Early Middle Ages* [London, 1988], pp. 2–3), then as Petersen has shown, Gregory's knowledge of Greek "was neither extensive nor always reliable." Petersen, 'Homo omnino Latinus'?, id., p. 550.

There is a less extensive body of literature on the related subject of how Gregory was able to communicate in Constantinople as papal *apokrisiarios* if he did not know Greek. Petersmann makes the compelling argument that Latin was still widely spoken among the aristocracy in Constantinople in Gregory's time. Hubertus Petersmann, "Quid S. Gregorius Magnus Papa Romanique Eius Aetatis de Lingua Sua Senserint," in *Gregorio Magno e il suo tempo*, Vol. 2, pp. 137–48. Justinian I venerated it as the πάτριον φωνήν, *Novellae*, 7, 1, 30, and John of Lydia says that, although it had been allowed to degenerate into a "haggish and base idiom," it was still used to conduct public business. Id., pp. 145–46. Moreover, the Byzantine army of this period appears to have been bilingual. Although Maurice's *Strategikon*, composed during the latter part of his reign or during that of Phocas, is written in Greek, words of command were given in Latin, generally in Greek letters. Military punishments were to be read out in both Greek and Latin, and heralds were supposed to be able to speak Greek, Latin, and, if possible, Persian. *Das Strategikon des Maurikios*, ed. George T. Dennis, trans. Ernst Gamillscheg, *Corpus Fontium Historiae Byzantinae* 17 (Vienna, 1981). For commands, see, namely, III. 2.7; III 3.4; III. 5.29; for the order on reading military punishments, see I. 8.2-3; for the linguistic abilities of heralds, see XII. B.7.3-4.

154. Augustine. *Contra litteras Petiliani*, PL 43: 292; Augustine, *Confessions*, PL 32: 670. *Quid autem erat causae cur graecas litteras oderam*; S. Salaville, "La connaissance du grec chez saint Augustin," *Echos d'Orient* 21 (1922): 387–93.

155. Cf., Leo the Great. *Sermon* 82, *PL* 54: 422ff.; see M. Fuhrmann, "Die Romidee der Spätantike," *Historische Zeitschrift* 207 (1968/69): 533; Petersmann, id., supra.

156. Pierre de Labriolle, *Histoire de la Littérature Latine Chrétienne*, Vol. 2 (Paris, 1947), p. 810; H. Steinacker, "Die römische Kirche und die griechischen Sprachkenntnisse des Frühmittelalters," *Mitteilungen des Instituts für Österreichische Geschichtsforschung* 62 (1954), pp. 28, 61.

157. *Reg.* V, 37; *Reg.* VII, 24; *Reg.* IX, 136; *Reg.* XI, 28. Despite Gregory's broad accusation, simony was not unique to the Eastern churches and seems to have been a problem in the West as well. A Roman synod, over which Gregory himself presided in 595, prohibited persons from giving anything in exchange for ordination, but provided that afterwards persons admitted to holy orders might be given tokens of appreciation. *Mansi* X, 475; Karl J. Hefele, *A History of the Councils of the Church*, Vol. IV (Edinburgh, 1895; repr., New York, 1972), pp. 426–27.

158. *Reg.* XI, 27.

159. *Reg.* VI, 14. The alleged falsification to which he was referring was probably Canon 28, which gave Constantinople pre-eminence over all patriarchates after Rome. Gregory's apprehension about the accuracy of Constantinople's texts of the Council of Ephesus appears again in a letter to patriarch Anastasius of Antioch. He warns the patriarch that he has had occasion to examine such texts and found them to be heretical. He suggests that Anastasius consult texts of the Ephesine synod maintained by the churches of Alexandria and Antioch, or better yet Rome, if he wishes to be sure that he is relying on documents that are doctrinally sound. *Reg.* IX, 136.

160. *Reg.* VI, 14.

161. In the east, Rome's ecclesiastical jurisdiction extended to Illyricum and Greece, including Thessalonika, Thebes, Corfu (Kerkyra), Dyrrachium, Nicopolis, Corinth, Prima Justiniana and Larissa, as well as the island of Crete, whose bishop was located at Gortyna. *Reg.* III, 7; V, 63; VII, 7; VIII, 10; XIV, 7.

162. *Reg.* IX, 157.

163. *Reg.* V, 45.

164. *Reg.* X, 14; cf., *Reg.* X, 21.

165. *Reg.* IV, 30.

166. *Reg.* XIV, 7, *Dialogues*, III, 13.

167. *Libri historiarum* 1.48, pp. 32–43; *De virtutibus S. Martini*, 1.6, p. 142.

168. *Vita S. Severini*, 44–46, pp. 112–17.

169. *Vita Ambrosii*, 14, pp. 70–73, 90–91; 32, pp. 94–95; Jerome, *De viribus illustris liber* 16, ed. W. Herding (Leipzig, 1924), p. 21.

170. *Contra Vigilantium* 1.5, *PL* 23: 358; Paulinus of Nola, *Carmina* 19, 349–51; Dudden, id., Vol. I, p. 281n2; Sozomen, *Historia Ecclesiastica* 7.21, 1–5, pp. 333–34. Others, however, argue that "regardless of any ecclesiastico-political motives Gregory may have had for refusing the empress' request, his justification for his refusal was no mere excuse. He presented a thoughtful description of traditional—and contemporary—Roman practice." John M. McCulloh, "The Cult of Relics in the Letters and 'Dialogues' of Pope Gregory the Great: A Lexicographical Study," *Traditio* 32 (1976): 145, 181. There does appear to have been at least one precedent justifying Gregory's refusal. When, in 519, Justinian I had asked Pope Hormisdas for relics of the apostles and of St. Lawrence, the papal *apokrisiarii*

in Constantinople were constrained to reply that it was against Roman practice to send corporeal remains of the saints and that they could only oblige the emperor with a noncorporeal relic. *Epistulae imperatorum pontificium aliorum*, ed. O. Guenther, *Corpus Scriptorum Ecclesia Latina* 35 (2 pts. in 1 vol.) (Vienna, 1895–1898), 2: 679–80.

171. *Reg.* IX, 26; see also John the Deacon, *Vita, PL* 75: 94–95.

172. Gregory of Tours, *Historia Francorum*, X.1; Paul the Deacon, *Historia Langobardorum*, III, 24; Paul the Deacon, *Vita, PL* 75: 47; John the Deacon, *Vita, PL* 75: 80–81; Gregory the Great, "Denuntiatio Pro Septiformi Letania," *Corpus Christianorum Series Latina*, Vol. 140A, Appendix IX, pp. 1102–4. The accounts of Gregory's sevenfold litany are essentially consistent, although there are variations. All sources agree that the seven groups consisted of clergy, abbots and monks, abbesses and nuns, men, married women, widows, and children. John the Deacon and Gregory the Great, in a form for a sevenfold litany written for use on a later occasion, include the poor with the children. Only three accounts, that of Gregory of Tours, John the Deacon, and Gregory's form for a later litany, identify the churches at which each group was to assemble. The identities of those churches in the accounts of John the Deacon and Gregory the Great differ from those set down by Gregory of Tours. Both John the Deacon and Gregory of Tours relate that the processions all converged at the church of St. Maria Maggiore; neither Paul the Deacon nor Gregory the Great mentions this. The account of the sevenfold litany of April, 590 given by Gregory of Tours is probably the most reliable since it is based on the eyewitness evidence of his deacon Agiulf, who was in Rome at the time. Gregory of Tours, *Historia Francorum*, X.1.

173. John F. Baldovin, *The Urban Character of Christian Worship: The Origins, Development and Meaning of Stational Liturgy* (Rome, 1987), p. 190.

174. J. Mateos, ed., *Le Typicon de la Grande Église*, Orientalia Christiana Periodica, 165–66, 2 vols. (Rome, 1962–1963); Baldovin, id., p. 196.

175. Baldovin, id., pp. 166, 207.

176. Frag. 56-Epitome 494, ll. 16–17 in Theodore Lector, *Ecclesiastical History*, ed. G. C. Hansen (Berlin, 1971), p. 140. Τάς κατά παρασκευήν λιτάς εν τῶ ναῶ της Θεοτόκου εν τοις Χαλκοπρατείοις Τιμόθεος επενόησε γίνεσθε.

177. Baldovin, id., p. 197. Gregory may still have been in Constantinople or have just departed for Rome when in 587 or 588 the emperor Maurice introduced the feast of the Assumption of the Virgin Mary (Κοίμησις τῆς Θεοτόκου) into the ecclesiastical calendar by ordaining that litanies and laudations were to be held at the Church of the Theotokos at Blachernae. Theophanes, *Chronographia*, p. 387. Nikephoros Kallistos specifies that these celebrations were to take place on August 15. Nikephoros Kallistos, *Ecclesiasticae Historiae*, PG 147: 291–92. It seems clear that Gregory was both aware of and influenced by Maurice's institution of this feast, for as early as July, 591, he wrote to the rector of the papal patrimony in Sicily expressing his desire that an oratory, recently built there by some monks in honor of the Virgin Mary, be dedicated in the month of August since he was determined that the feast days of the saints be observed. *Reg.* I, 54.

178. See *Reg.* VIII, 22.

179. See *Reg.* II, 24; IV, 44; VIII, 22; XI, 26; XIII, 24. It is possible that Rusticiana gave the picture to Gregory, who brought it back with him to Rome and placed it on his paternal home, which he had converted to a monastery years earlier, in order to invoke

the Virgin Mary as a protectress. This is so because the last line of the poem, which originally read *protegat illa tuum Rusticiana genus*, was changed to *protegat illa tuum gregori presule genus*. Giovanni Baptista de Rossi, *Inscriptiones christianae urbis Romae septimo saeculo antiquiores*, Vol. 2, Pt. I (Rome, 1888), p. 109n3.

180. *Dialogues* IV, 28. Count Theophanios is also mentioned in *XL Homiliarum in evangelium libri duo*, Homily 36; *Reg.* IV, 42.

181. De Rossi, id., pp. 454–55. For a discussion of the genesis and expansion of the cult of St. Menas in Egypt and elsewhere in the East, see Paul Peeters, *Les Tréfonds Oriental de l'Hagiographie Byzantine* (Brussels, 1950), p. 32ff.

182. F. Brunet, *Oeuvres Médicales d'Alexandre de Tralles*, Vol. I (Paris, 1933), pp. 16, 28; Gaetano Marini, *I papiri diplomatici* (Rome, 1805) (no. 120 for the year 572 reads, in pertinent part *Eugenius . . . filius Leonti medici ab schola graeca*).

183. *Reg.* XIII, 42; *Reg.* XI, 21.

184. De Rossi, id., p. 107.

185. Brunet, id., p. 190.

186. According to the history of the Roman monastery of St. Sabas, Eastern monks, who had been driven out of Palestine by Origenists, arrived in Rome during the time of popes Benedict I (575–579) and Pelagius II (579–590) and settled into a monastery on the Little Aventine. PG 89: 535. Chitty contends, moreover, that the Life of St. Gregory of Agrigentum, PG 98: 549–716, proves that the monastery of St. Sabas on the Little Aventine dates from the time of Gregory the Great and thus reflects that there was an Eastern monastic community in existence in Rome prior to the end of the sixth century. Chitty, id., p. 166n128.

187. Joan M. Petersen, "'Homo omnino Latinus'?" id., p. 542; *Dialogues* III, 33; *Mansi*, X, 490ff.; *Reg.* XI, 55.

188. *Reg.* VII, 23. Gregory thanked Theoctista profusely for helping the *ancillis Dei quas vos Graeca lingua monastrias dicitis*. John the Deacon also records Gregory's gifts for relief of the *ancillis Dei*. *Vita*, PL 75:97. See E. Dekkers, "Saint Grégoire et les moniales," *Collectanea Cisterciensia* 46 (1984): 23–36.

189. *Reg.* VI, 12.

190. *Reg.* V, 35; *XL Homiliarum in evangelium libri duo*, Homily 39.

191. *Reg.* III, 2.

192. *Dialogues*, III, 40; *Reg.* III, 52; V, 44; VI, 14; VII, 4.

193. *Reg.* VII, 6.

194. *Reg.* VII, 15.

195. Olympos's tomb on the via Latina bears the inscription *pontificum qui primus vestiarius esse*. De Rossi, id., p. 107.

196. P. A. B. Llewellyn, "The Roman Church during the Laurentian Schism: Priests and Senators," *Church History* 45 (1976): 417–27. Llewellyn's analysis of the names of the clerical signatories to the synods convened by Pope Symmachus reveals a high proportion of African-associated names, indicating that these refugees and their descendants made their way "firmly into the ranks of the Roman Church." Llewellyn, "The Names of the Roman Clergy, 401–1046," id., p. 359.

197. Kajanto has shown that Rome experienced a 6 percent increase in the number of inhabitants with Greek or barbarian names from the fifth to the sixth centuries while

undergoing a decrease of six percent in Latin names for the same period. I. Kajanto, *Onomastic Studies in the Early Christian Inscriptions of Rome and Carthage* (Helsinki, 1963).

198. Amory, id., p. 87–88; P. A. B. Llewellyn, "The Names of the Roman Clergy, 401–1046," id., p. 355.

199. *LP*, I, 218, 258, 260, 287.

200. *LP*, I, 312.

201. *LP*, I, 238, 359.

202. *LP*, I, 275, 285, 305, 366, 383, 385.

203. Llewellyn, "The Names of the Roman Clergy, 401–1046," id., p. 360. Conversely, there are typically Eastern names such as Agathon, Sissinius, Constantine, and Zacharias that no pope of Western origin took. In these cases, ethnic identity may be more reliably deduced from name selection.

204. *Mansi* X, 488–489. We know only that twenty-four bishops and thirty-five priests attended the Roman synod of 595. Except for the six canons it promulgated, nothing else survives. *Mansi*, X, 475; Bede, *Anglo-Saxonis Chronicon*, id., p. 193; Bede, *Chronica*, id., p. 309; Ado of Vienne, *Chronicon*, PL 123: 111–112; Hefele, id., pp. 426–427; Dudden, id., p. 261ff. Only the recitation of the condemnation of the aphthardocetist Greek monk Andreas survives from the Roman synod of November, 601. Hefele places this synod in October, 600. *Mansi* X, 489ff; Hefele, id., p. 430.

205. *Mansi* X, 488–89. Marinianus, Romanus, Pelagius, Luminosus, Balbinus, Martianus, Dominicus, Fortunatus, Proculus, Gratiosus (Generosus), Dominicus, Felix, Candidus, Uribonus (Urbanus), Secundinus, and Homobonus.

206. *Mansi* X, 488–89. Laurentius, Speciosus, Deusdedit, Crescens, Vibulus, Spectatus, Felix, Justus, Maurus, Victor, Aurelius, Felix, Bassus, Albinus, Antonius, Romanus, Aventius, Deusdedit, Rusticus, Petrus, Speciosus, Placidus, Donus, Candidus, and Fortunatus.

207. Umberto Moricca, "Gregorii Magni Dialogi, Libri IV," in *Fonti per la Storia d'Italia* (Rome, 1924), xlviii.

208. See p. 20ff., supra.

209. Joan M. Petersen, *The Dialogues of Gregory the Great in Their Late Antique Cultural Background* (Toronto, 1984), pp. xxi, 20.

210. Francis Clark, *The Pseudo-Gregorian Dialogues*, Vol. II (Leiden, 1987), pp. 585–86.

211. Grégoire Le Grand, *Dialogues*, Vol. I, trans. Adalbert de Vogüé (Paris, 1978) pp. 113–14, 115n9; PG 47: 5–82.

212. See, namely, Abba Daniel, 2, PG 65: 153BC; Abba Anoub, 1, PG 65: 345B.

213. De Vogüé, id., p. 79.

214. *Dialogues* III, 16 (*recentia*); 19 (*praesenti infirmitati hominum . . . nuper*); 31 (*nostris . . . temporibus*); 4 (*diebus nostris*); 17 (*nostris modo temporibus*); 25 (*modernos patres*); 26, 32 (*nuper*).

215. Compare *Dialogues* I, Prologue; 1 with Arsenius, 44; Apphy, 1; Theodore of Pherme, 5; Isidore of Pelusia, 1; Isaac, 2; Carion, 1.

216. Compare *Dialogues* III, 37 with Arsenius, 5–6; Euprepius, 7.

217. Compare *Dialogues* I, 10; III, 14; IV, 15–17, 20, 49 with Epiphanius, 3; Agathon, 9; John the Dwarf, 35; Syncletica, 27.

218. Compare *Dialogues* IV, 12 with John the Dwarf, 1, 34.

219. Compare *Dialogues* I, 5; 9 with John the Dwarf, 20, 22; Isidore of Pelusia, 5; Rufus, 2; Joseph of Panephysis, 5; Sisoes, 10.

220. Compare *Dialogues* I, 4, 10; II, 15; III, 3, 14 with Longinus, 4; Macarius, 20; Pityrion, 1; Poemen, 129, 161; Theodore of Pherme, 4; Agathon, 5; Evagrius, 1; Nicon, 1.

221. Compare *Dialogues* III, 33; IV, 57, 58, 60–61 with Poemen, 29, 209; Joseph of Panephysis, 3; Dioscorus, 2; Euprepius, 6. Hausherr asserts that the great success which the *Dialogues* achieved in the East was due largely to the sections in which Gregory dealt with the doctrine of compunction, a concept much esteemed not only among the desert fathers but also by a long line of Eastern patristic writers including Origen, Athanasius, Basil the Great, Gregory Nazianzen, Gregory of Nyssa, John Chrysostom, Ephraim, Evagrius, and John Climacus. Irénée Hausherr, "Penthos: La Doctrine de la Componction dans l'Orient Chrétien," *Orientalia Christiana Analecta* 132 (Rome, 1944).

222. Baudouin de Gaiffier, "Les héros des Dialogues de Grégoire le Grand inscrits au nombre de saints," *Analecta Bollandiana* 83 (1965): 53–73.

223. Francis Clark, id., p. 587.

224. Both come from noble families, reject secular learning, and seek escape from the world in order to avoid falling into its abyss. *Dialogues*, II, Prologue; *Vita Antonii*, 1–2. Both progressively distance themselves to even remoter locations and depend upon friends to provide them with bodily sustenance. *Dialogues* II, 1, 1–8; *Vita Antonii*, 8. Each faces and conquers the temptations of the flesh by bodily mortifications and the sign of the Cross. *Dialogues* II, 2, 1; *Vita Antonii*, 5–7. While Antony retreats to a mountain fortress in the desert and drives out reptiles and creeping things, Benedict finds refuge in the mountain fortress of Cassino where he drives out images built to the cult of Apollo. *Dialogues* II, 8, 10; *Vita Antonii*, 12. Each one is heard battling the demons, who emit terrifying shrieks as they are vanquished. *Dialogues* II, 10, 12; *Vita Antonii*, 13. Both attain the gift of prophecy and discernment. *Dialogues* II, 11, 3; 13, 3; 14, 1–2; *Vita Antonii*, 62, 86, 88. Both have contacts with and give advice to rulers; Benedict admonishes Totila to refrain from iniquity, and Antony tells Constantine to give attention to justice and the poor. *Dialogues* II, 15, 1; *Vita Antonii*, 81. Each is found weeping bitterly in his cell, Benedict because of a vision of impending Lombard devastations and Antony because of the impending assaults of the Arians. *Dialogues* II, 17, 1; *Vita Antonii*, 82. Both decline to perform acts of healing, protesting that they are merely human beings and incapable of such miracles. *Dialogues* II, 32, 1–3; *Vita Antonii*, 48. Finally, each foretells his own death. *Dialogues* II, 37, 1; *Vita Antonii*, 89.

It is also likely that Gregory was familiar with the life of Pachomius, which had been translated by Dionysius Exiguus during St. Benedict's lifetime, a generation before Gregory, and was addressed to the pious virgin Proba, of whose sister Galla, Gregory writes in the Fourth Dialogue. P. A. Cusack, "The Temptation of St. Benedict: An Essay at Interpretation through Literary Sources," *American Benedictine Review* 27 (1976): 143, 151; see also H. van Cranenburg, *La vie latine de s. Pachome traduite en grec par Denys le Petit* (Brussels, 1969), pp. 39, 48.

225. Maximilian Mähler, "Evocations bibliques et hagiographiques dans la vie de Saint Benoit par Saint Grégoire," *Revue Bénédictine* 83 (1973): 398, 402, 429.

226. Guglielmo Cavallo, ed., *The Byzantines*, trans. Thomas Dunlap (Chicago, 1997), p. 11. It is perhaps the ultimate irony that, despite his strong anti-Greek prejudices, no

Western saint has been honored in Byzantium as much as Gregory. F. Halkin, "Le pape S. Grégoire le Grand dans l'hagiographie byzantine," *Orientalia Christiana periodica* 21 (1955): 109. But Eastern veneration for Gregory is not based on his apocrisiariat in Constantinople or his pontificate, neither of which is mentioned in any documents of the church of Constantinople. H. Delehaye, "S. Grégoire Le Grand dans l'Hagiographie Grecque," *Analecta Bollandiana* 23 (1904): 449. Gregory is instead commemorated as a saint in the Eastern church (March 12) exclusively, and not surprisingly, on the strength of the *Dialogues*, for which he has been accorded the eponym ο Διάλογος ("the Dialogist"). Ὡρολόγιον τό Μέγα (Great Horologion), (Athens, 1973), p. 266. Gregory's *kontakion* incorporates the revered epithet by which he is commonly known in the East: "The God-inspired lyre of the Church,/Truly the divinely-inspired tongue of wisdom./Let us with great esteem praise Dialogos,/Who imitated the zeal of the Apostles,/Clearly following in their paths./To him we say, Hail Father Gregory." Ὁ Ἐνιαύσιος Στέφανος τῆς Ὀρθοδόξου Ἀνατολικῆς Ἐκκλησίας (The Annual Cycle of the Eastern Orthodox Church), 2nd ed. (Athens, 1986), p. 188.

227. E. Dekkers, "Saint Grégoire et les moniales," *Collectanea Cistercensia* 46 (1984): 23.

228. Following Benedict I in 574, Theophanes mentions no pope until Gregory II in 724. Theophanes, *Chronographia*, id., pp. 365, 558

229. Theophylact Simocatta, id., pp. 77; 228.

230. Menander, id., pp. 197 (Frag. 22), 217 (Frag. 24).

231. See Amory, id., p. 144ff.

232. Averil Cameron, *Christianity and the Rhetoric of Empire: The Development of Christian Discourse* (Berkeley, 1991), p. 194.

233. Tertullian, *De Praescriptione Haereticarum*, 36 in Alexander Roberts and James Donaldson, eds., *The Ante-Nicene Fathers*, Vol. 3 (Repr. Peabody, MA, 1994), p. 260.

234. *Homiliae in Hiezechielem Prophetam*, id., p. 312.

235. *Reg.* VIII, 22.

236. *The Earliest Life of Gregory*, id., p. 125; Aidan Nichols, *Rome and the Eastern Churches* (Collegeville, MN, 1992), p. 134.

237. Judith Herrin, *The Formation of Christendom* (London, 1987), p. 181.

238. Claude Dagens, "Grégoire le Grand et le monde oriental," *Rivista di Storia e Letteratura Religiosa* 17 (1981), pp. 243, 247.

239. *Reg.* V, 36–37; *Reg.* XIII, 31, 39; see *Chronika 14, Die Byzantinischen Kleinchroniken*, Vol. XII/1, ed. Peter Schreiner, *Corpus Fontium Historiae Byzantinae* (Vienna, 1975), p. 133. (Maurice is described as ευσεβέστατος καί μισοπόνηρος; Phocas is called τύραννος καί αιμοβόρος καί δυσεβής.)

240. *Reg.* XI, 4.

241. Homily 34, *XL Homiliarum in evangelia libri duo*.

242. *LP*, I, 312.

243. Vera Falkenhausen, "Bishops," in *The Byzantines*, Guglielmo Cavallo, ed., trans. Thomas Dunlap (Chicago, 1997), p. 172. When Gregory admonished King Aethelbert to follow Augustine's advice as if it were the voice of God, he was displaying yet another attribute of an imperial bishop. Henry, Archdeacon of Huntingdon, *Historia Anglorum*, ed. and trans. Diana Greenway (Oxford, 1996), III. 9, p. 154.

244. Walter Berschin, *Griechisch-lateinisches Mittelalter. Von Hieronymus zu Nikolaus von Kues* (Bern and Munich, 1980), trans. by Jerold C. Frakes as *Greek Letters in the Latin Middle Ages* (Washington, D.C., 1988), p. 88.

~

CHAPTER II

Corpora Nostra Cum Inimicis Nostris Abibunt, Corda Nostra Cum Christo Manebunt[1]

The Impact of the Barbarian Invasions of the East on Rome and the Papacy in the Early Seventh Century

The Swiss monastery of Einsiedeln preserves a manuscript written sometime between 687 and the beginning of the ninth century that describes a journey taken along the walls of Rome by a pilgrim who visited the city during Holy Week.[2] Part of the itinerary describes the pilgrim's progress as he moved from the Porta Sancti Petri in a southerly direction toward the Porta Sancti Pauli and the road toward the seaport town of Ostia. From the church of San Lorenzo *in Damaso* next to the Pompeiian theater, the traveler proceeded along a covered walkway to the eighth century church of San Angelo *in foro Piscium* next to the theater of Marcellus. The colonnaded portico then led him to *ad Elephantum*, whose name was derived from a picture of an elephant and a giant that adorned the facade of a house near the Ponte Rotto. In the bend of the river before him lay the *schola Graecorum*, a stretch along the bank of the Tiber located at the foot of the Aventine Hill along the Via Ostia, which since the time of Constantine the Great had been the Greco-Oriental quarter of Rome.[3]

The *schola Graeca*, which was also known as the *ripa Graeca* or Greek bank, had derived its name from the fact that this segment of the Tiber was heavily populated by Easterners, including Greeks, Syrians, and Egyptians. With the reappearance of imperial power, this quarter quite naturally became the center of Byzantine Rome.[4] By the sixth century the Greek community had established its own church in the district and dedicated it, not surprisingly, to the Theotokos, naming it Santa Maria *in Cosmedin*, Latinizing the Greek word κοσμίδιον, which derives from the word κόσμος meaning, among other things, "pure" or "elegant."[5] Churches with the same name were founded by Greek communities in both Ravenna and Naples.[6] Even a place on the Aventine, which overlooks the *ripa Graeca*, was named *ad Balcernas* or *Blachernas* after the famous district of the same name in northwestern Constantinople.[7] Through the centuries, this enclave of Easterners came to dominate the city's commercial activities and to control its trading links with the Orient and Africa.[8] A corporation of merchants from Gaza, who had established themselves at Ostia where eastern goods destined for Rome initially arrived, inscribed their praise to the emperor Gordian III (238–244) on the Porta Traiana in gratitude for his imperial patronage.[9] An Egyptian traveling to Rome in the fifth century, most likely on some commercial matter, encountered a violent storm on the Tyrrhenian Sea and cried out for deliverance to the God of St. Martin.[10] Eastern domination of Rome's mercantile activities appears to have sufficiently aroused the anger of native entrepreneurs such that in 440 the emperor Valentinian III expelled the "Greek traders" from the city, only to have them recalled later following a famine.[11] Even Gregory the Great interceded on behalf of the Syrian merchant Cosmas, who was being harassed by his creditors.[12]

In addition to dominating the city's mercantile establishment, Easterners also came to Rome in large numbers to practice medicine. Various inscriptions on tombs dating from the third century forward reflect that the deceased were doctors.[13] Gregory the Great consulted a close friend, who had studied medicine in Alexandria, about the condition of his colleague Bishop Marinianus of Ravenna.[14] The father of Boniface IV (608–615) was the "doctor John," which suggests that the pope may well have been of Eastern descent.[15]

Along with merchants and medical practitioners, imperial functionaries came to Italy from the East in increasing numbers after the Justinianic reconquest. The government of the peninsula was entrusted to an exarch, who resided in Ravenna and who wielded the highest power in both civil and military matters.[16] In ecclesiastical affairs, it was the exarch who, from the time of Honorius I, was vested with authority to confirm papal elections and permit the consecration of a pope.[17] The exarchs of Italy were without exception Greeks dispatched from the court at Constantinople. They answered directly to the emperor and their authority over Italian affairs was equal to that of the emperor himself.[18] They were assisted in the execution of their administrative responsibilities by an extensive civil and military bureaucracy consisting of officials who, by the seventh and eighth centuries, were increasingly drawn from the local population.[19] Easterners, however, occupied prominent positions in both spheres. A rare inscription surviving from seventh century Rome refers to a *Theodorus Grecus*, whose title, *vir clarissimus*, indicates that he was probably among the host of lesser officials who would have been chosen by the exarch to assist him in the execution of his duties.[20] Another early seventh century epitaph, dating from the year 619, survives on the tomb of one *Theodorus Grecus Vizanteus* in the Roman church of St. Cecilia. The deceased, who also was a *vir clarissimus*, was an imperial judge in Rome during the reign of the emperor Heraclius and thus part of the ducal administration of the city.[21] If the inscription is a reliable indicator of his virtues, Theodore's fidelity, friendship, kindness, and duty made him a particularly effective imperial servant. While it is not at all surprising that he is described as *Grecus*, the adjective *Vizanteus* is indeed remarkable since it represents a rare use of this word by Easterners in early seventh century Rome to describe themselves not simply as Greeks but as Byzantines.[22]

Easterners in the military apparatus included the exarch Plato's son-in-law Theodore Chila (Χίλα), indicating that he was the commander of a unit of one thousand men, who was called as a witness against Maximos Confessor at the latter's trial in 653 or 654.[23] Others included the *chartularios* Maurikios, who assisted the exarch Isaac in plundering the Lateran Episcopium in 640; the *magister militum* and *sakellarios* Donos, who was dispatched by Isaac to Rome in the early 640s to suppress Maurikios's rebellion; the imperial chamberlain Theodore Pellurios, who assisted the exarch Theodore Kalliopas in arresting Pope Martin; and the *spatharios* Zacharias, whose unsuccessful attempt to arrest Pope Sergius nearly resulted in his own death.[24]

But it was not traders, doctors, or imperial officials who were most attracted to Rome or who came there from the East in the greatest numbers. It was instead the Christian faithful who flocked to Rome to venerate the holy places, where Peter and Paul, the chiefs of the apostles, had met their deaths and where so many of the martyrs of the early church had shed their blood.[25] From the time of Pope Damasus through the pontificate of Leo the Great and culminating with the reign of Gregory I, the Roman church drew heavily upon its Petrine origins to exalt its claim to pre-eminent spiritual dignity as the head of the world.[26] Gregory the Great maintained close contacts with Eastern bishops, priests, and monks, sending them apostolic relics and thereby solidifying their vision of Rome as the fountain of correct doctrine and the defender against heresy.[27] Rome's claims in that regard found ready acceptance among Eastern ecclesiastics and monastics. Eulogius, patriarch of Alexandria, praised Rome as the guardian of apostolic teaching.[28] Sophronios, patriarch of Jerusalem, wrote that Rome was "the apostolic See [and] foundation of orthodox doctrine."[29] In his *Spiritual Meadow*, which was written in Rome in the early seventh century, the Palestinian monk John Moschos expressed the reverence and esteem that many Eastern monks had for the Papacy, including specifically popes Leo, Agapetus, and Gregory.[30] The *Verba Seniorum* relates the story of two Eastern monks who, unable to obtain satisfaction in their entreaties to the patriarchs of Alexandria, Antioch, and Jerusalem, traveled to Rome to appeal to the pope as the "head of all."[31] From at least the fourth or fifth centuries, a tradition developed among the Eastern religious community that the pope was not just another patriarch nor Rome simply another ancient patriarchate. While all else might fail, there was always the Roman pontiff, who, speaking through Peter, could be relied upon both to express orthodox doctrine and to protect the true faith from the heretics.[32]

Those who came to Rome from Syria, Palestine, and Egypt in the eastern part of the empire could travel by land to Alexandria, then across the North African littoral to Carthage, and thereafter by sea to Sicily and on to Italy. They might also have proceeded by ship following the ancient trade routes between Alexandria and Rome that made intermediate stops in Sicily, Sardinia, and Naples.[33] Mercantile vessels, which would have also carried passengers, maintained connections between the East and the Italian peninsula and adjacent islands throughout the seventh century. Nor were those routes ever seriously threatened even with the coming of the Arabs.[34] The relative ease of travel between East and West made early seventh century Rome a cosmopolitan city, where the native Latin population combined with "Greek functionaries, Greek merchants, [and] Greek monks" to give the city a diverse ethnic composition.[35] Nowhere is this better documented than in the story of St. Cummian, an Irish monk who arrived in Rome around 633 to research the correct calculation of Easter, and who wrote to Abbot Seginus of St. Columba that he was staying at a hostel along with a Greek, a Jew, a Scythian, and an Egyptian.[36] By then, however, Easterners coming to Rome were not predominantly merchants looking to exploit the commercial opportunities that had seen the community along the *ripa Graeca* prosper since antiquity. They were instead refugees fleeing the Persian invasions, or seeking sanctuary from the Christological battles between Monophysites and Chalcedonians to which the Monothelite controversy had added another dimension, or finally looking for shelter from the onslaught of the Arabs.[37] To each of these groups the see of St. Peter extended its solace and protection.

⌇

The foreign irruptions into imperial territory, which were to convulse the eastern Roman world during the seventh century, though temporarily held in check by Maurice's treaty with the Persians in 591, burst open with renewed vigor in 603.[38] During the previous year the army had become disillusioned by the emperor's avarice and angry at his orders to spend the winter in foreign territory. As a result it had rebelled and "put up the centurion Phocas as their leader, and having raised him on a shield [the traditional method of recognizing one as emperor] they acclaimed him as leader."[39] Phocas, to whom Theophanes repeatedly refers as the "usurper" and whom Theophylact Simocatta calls the "tyrant,"[40] was thereafter crowned emperor by the patriarch of Constantinople at the church of St. John the Baptist at the Hebdomon and, either two or three days later, entered the city "with no one at all opposing, but everyone acclaiming him."[41] Maurice and his sons were brutally slaughtered while the empress and their daughters were put in the monastery of Nea Metanoia, after which they too were executed.[42]

By 604, when Gregory the Great died, the eastern part of the empire was suffering from external attack and internal bloodshed. The Avars had taken all the country north of Thessalonika and the major part of the imperial forces had already been transferred from the Balkans to the East. Christian cities in Illyricum had been devastated and their inhabitants killed or taken captive; Justiniana Prima is not heard of after 602.[43] The Persians had captured the fortress at Dara just over the old Roman frontier and three years later they took Amida to the northwest.[44] Phocas continued to execute prominent persons whom he suspected of conspiring against him.[45] In 605 or 606, he ordered the deaths of nearly a dozen of the highest-ranking imperial officials.[46] By the time Phocas's reign ended in 610, the Persians had crossed the Euphrates and taken Zenobia.[47] While Theophanes's statement that they had overrun Galatia and Paphlagonia and had advanced as far as Chalcedon is premature and in anticipation of events to come, it reflects the mentality of fear and apprehension that gripped the East by the end of the first decade of the seventh century.[48] The terror and turbulence that characterized the reign of Phocas in the eastern part of the empire is perhaps best expressed in the *Miracles of St. Demetrios*, which records that in his time:

> the devil raised the whirlwind of hatred in all the East, Cilicia, Asia, Palestine and all the lands from there to Constantinople: the factions, no longer content simply to spill blood in public places, attacked homes, slaughtered women, children, the aged, and the young who were sick; those whose youth and frailty impeded their escape from the massacre, [saw] their friends, acquaintances, and parents pillaged, and after all that, even set on fire so that the most wretched inhabitant was not able to escape.[49]

Although it continued to experience destructive incursions by the barbarians, Italy escaped the turmoil and depredations that the East experienced during the seventh century. In 601, a combined force of Lombards, Avars, and Slavs invaded and ravaged Istria, and by 603 they had reached and destroyed Cremona and Mantua.[50] Gregory continued to grieve over Rome's afflictions at the hands of the Lombards and how their swords had brought suffering to Italy each day for thirty-five years.[51] He too recognized, however, that matters in Constantinople were in disarray when, in a letter to the noblewoman Eusebia, the pope encouraged her to turn her mind away from the "alarming and perplexing difficulties of the royal city" to which she had referred in her letters.[52] Although he was aware that all was not well in the capital, both Gregory and his immediate successors effusively embraced the regime in Constantinople. The pope had quickly established a cordial relationship with the new and apparently accommodating exarch Smaragdos,[53] and there was every reason to hope that the emperor Phocas would prove more tractable than his obdurate predecessor had been.

Gregory acclaimed the accession of Phocas as an act of divine dispensation. He rejoiced at his assumption of the pinnacle of imperial power and encouraged the people of the empire, who up to then had suffered serious afflictions, to cheer the advent of the restorer of liberty. The former centurion, whom Eastern sources regarded as an insensate and bloodthirsty assassin,[54] was hailed by the Roman pontiff as a most pious and clement lord.[55] Nor did Gregory fail to heap praises upon the new empress Leontia. After expressing his unbridled joy at the return of the "light yoke of imperial authority," he likened her to the emperor

Marcian's consort Pulcheria, whom the Council of Chalcedon had heralded as the new Helena.[56] In May 603, portraits of the imperial couple arrived in Rome where they were acclaimed by "all the clergy and the senate" and ordered by the pope to be placed in the oratory of St. Caesarius in the imperial palace on the Palatine.[57] In July of that year Gregory dispatched his deacon Boniface, who in three years would become Pope Boniface III, to Constantinople as *apokrisiarios*, thus filling a vacancy in that position that up to then everyone had declined to undertake owing to a "fear of oppression and hardship."[58]

Gregory's fulsome overtures to Phocas were undoubtedly calculated to assure the new emperor of Italian loyalties and thereby to obtain a more favorable treatment for both Rome and the Papacy than Maurice had been inclined to show. The splendor that Rome had radiated around the year 500 had faded out by the time Gregory died in 604, and the city needed all the imperial favor it could muster in order to deal with the situation it faced at the turn of the century.[59] When Sabinian, Gregory's former *apokrisiarios* in Constantinople, became pope in September of that year, the city was suffering from a serious famine and in a few years plagues and floods would follow.[60] The new pope did not ingratiate himself with the Romans when, instead of doling out wheat from the church's granaries, he put it on sale. The disgruntled citizens showed their disdain for him by creating such chaos at his funeral that the cortege had to be diverted outside the city walls.[61]

The presence of Easterners in Rome, which we saw increasing in Gregory's time, continued to escalate as the new century dawned. The fact that Sabinian's election was "not without disturbance" is said to have been "confirmed by all the Latins and the Greeks." When Severinus Binius attempted to reconcile a discrepancy regarding the length of Sabinian's pontificate, he noted that while the *Liber Pontificalis* said it was one year, five months, and nine days, "all the ancient writers and the Greeks" had recorded that it was one year, five months, and nineteen days.[62] A writer with the distinctively Eastern name of Onnophrius, who may well have been living in Rome at the time, recorded that Sabinian accused Gregory of false teaching and suggested that his books should be burned.[63]

Gregory's death was followed by a general decline in his prestige and may well have been responsible, at least in part, for the growth of Eastern influences on the Roman church and the Papacy that became evident from as early as the time of Sabinian. Between his death in 604 and the ninth century, Gregory is referred to only four times: once at a Roman synod in 610, on each of the epitaphs of popes Boniface IV and Honorius I, and once again at a Roman synod in 679 in connection with the English church.[64] Taio of Saragossa wrote bishop Eugenius of Toledo from Rome in 642 that, although he had perused Gregory's writings and found them comparable in greatness to the works of Socrates, Plato, Cicero, and Varrus, they were largely ignored around the Lateran.[65] Following Gregory's death, imperial favor smiled upon Rome and the benefits that Gregory sought so fervently to secure from Phocas were soon to be forthcoming.

The tumultuous state of affairs in the East accounted no doubt for the fact that the Papacy remained vacant for nearly a year following the death of Sabinian in February, 606.[66] While the Persians prowled before the gates of the city menacing the empire from without, the emperor "heaped greater damages on the republic" from within.[67] It was apparent that Phocas's attention was directed more toward torturing, maiming, and killing everyone whom he suspected of participating in a plot to overthrow him rather than authorizing the consecration of a new pope.[68] At last the imperial *iussio* was issued, and in February 607 Gregory's former *apokrisiarios* was consecrated pope as Boniface III.[69] The new pontiff, who appears to have established an exceptionally good relationship with the emperor while in the capital, was probably chosen by the Roman electors since they had reason to believe that he would be acceptable to Phocas.[70] His kindness and eloquence, and especially his patience, may well have been determinative factors both in Gregory's decision to send him to Constantinople as *apokrisiarios* and in the decision of the Roman electors to choose him as pope, since his mild temperament would have been well suited to deal with Phocas's notorious brutality.[71]

But another and perhaps more compelling reason for his election lay in the fact that Boniface III appears to have been of Eastern ancestry. His father is identified in the *Liber Pontificalis* as *Iohanne Cataadioce*, although the manuscripts contain several variations including *Cataantioche, Cataadioc, Catadioce, Cataaudiace,* and *Cataaudioce.*[72] The prefix "cata," which is derived from the Greek word κατά meaning "down," "through," or "from," when taken together with the variation "antioche" or Antioch, indicates that he may have migrated from Antioch to Rome sometime in the latter part of the sixth century. Both the sack of Antioch by the Persians in 540 and a general economic decline in North Syria between Aleppo and Antioch around 550 may well have contributed to John's migration to Rome at or about that time.[73] Other variant suffixes of his surname such as "dioc" and "dioce" seem to be Latin forms of the Greek word διοικητής, or tax collector, meaning that he could also have been an official of the imperial fiscal administration.[74] When either of these possibilities is combined with the fact that he was named John, which as we have seen was popular among Easterners, it is highly likely that the pope's father was an Easterner who was part of the civil service of the exarchate. Boniface himself was most likely born in Rome, probably around 570, and thereafter entered the Roman church where he served as Gregory's *apokrisiarios* in Constantinople where he was sent doubtless because he knew Greek. When he became pope in 607 he would have been in his mid-thirties. Ascribing John with an Antiochene provenance would also explain the name of the church of St. Boniface the Martyr located near the Aventine in the Greco-Oriental quarter of Rome. The church was founded by Boniface III in honor of the saint who had achieved martyrdom in the time of Diocletian at Tarsus in Cilicia very near his own father's native city of Antioch. The martyr's body had been returned to Rome, buried by his former mistress

Aglaea, and then translated by the pope to a church dedicated to his memory and built where the city's Eastern population lived.[75] Boniface III's unmistakable oriental provenance makes him, rather than the Palestinian pope Theodore (642–649), the first among the seventh-century oriental popes, thereby placing an Easterner on the papal throne as early as 607, or thirty-five years earlier than traditionally thought.[76]

Phocas acted quickly in showing his favor toward the Roman church and the new pontiff. At Boniface's request and in the same month that he was consecrated pope, the emperor issued an imperial proclamation declaring the church of Rome as "the head of all the churches."[77] Phocas's decree may well have been motivated more by a desire to humiliate the patriarch of Constantinople than to exalt the Papacy. During the previous year, he had sent a contingent to Haghia Sophia, where the former empress Constantina and her daughters had sought asylum, with orders to forcibly remove them. Patriarch Kyriakos had opposed the emperor's attempted abduction, thereby incurring an enmity from which he was spared imperial vengeance only by his own death in late 606.[78] Nor was Phocas's decree particularly extraordinary from an ecclesiological point of view. Justinian I had long ago declared that in accordance with the canons of the ecumenical councils the pope of Rome was "the first among all the priests."[79] For Rome and the Papacy, however, all that was unimportant; Phocas was at last raising them from the deep shadows of Maurice's long neglect.

Within nine months, Boniface III was dead and once again events in the East distracted imperial attention from Rome and delayed the consecration of a new pope for just over ten months. Phocas's atrocities continued unabated as he relentlessly slaughtered his suspected adversaries. The savagery reached the point where even his son-in-law Priscus, commander of the elite imperial guardsmen, urged the exarch of Africa to send his son, who would become the emperor Heraclius, to Constantinople in order to stem the tyranny. Perhaps because such an invasion was already being planned, ships carrying grain did not depart from Africa for the capital in 607–608. The city began to experience serious food shortages and its suffering was compounded by the onset of a plague.[80] Farther east, the Persians continued their incursions into Roman territory, advancing to such an extent that by 609 they held the imperial fortresses at Kitharizon, Satala, Nikopolis, and Theodosioupolis.[81] When the imperial *iussio* was finally issued, Boniface IV, the last of the popes who had been among Gregory's intimates, was consecrated Roman pontiff.[82]

During the time of Boniface IV, Phocas continued to show partiality toward both Rome and the Papacy. His persisting beneficence may have been prompted by the possibility that he had been favorably impressed by the new pope, whom he may well have known in Constantinople. It is quite possible that the Boniface to whom Gregory referred as his deacon and *responsalis* papal representative in the capital in mid-603 was the future pope Boniface IV.[83] If, as his epitaph recites, Boniface's qualities resembled those of his distinguished predecessor, it is not unlikely that he had earned the emperor's admiration.[84] On August 1, 608, only three weeks before Boniface's consecration, the exarch Smaragdos presided at the dedication of a Corinthian-style column placed in the heart of the Forum that soared fourteen meters and was surmounted by a gleaming bronze statue of the emperor Phocas. The base of the column was inscribed with a tribute to the emperor's clemency and piety, and praised his efforts to bring peace to Italy.[85] It was the only public monument that the Byzantine administration would erect in Rome during the seventh century.[86]

But the emperor was to bestow an even greater gift on Rome. At the request of Boniface IV, Phocas issued an imperial *iussio* on May 13, 609, allowing the Pantheon to be converted into a Christian church.[87] Agrippa's most beautiful monument, whose impressive rotundity had stood for centuries as a mocking reminder to Christian Rome of its pagan past, was at last to be purged of its demons and dedicated to the Holy Mother of God and all the martyrs.[88] Perhaps because it was the first example of a temple in Rome being converted into a Christian church, neither the pope nor the emperor spared anything in sanctifying it to Christian use.[89] Phocas presented the church with many gifts, and Boniface caused twenty-eight cartloads of martyrs' bones to be collected from various cemeteries around the city and transported to the new Christian church.[90]

In 610, Boniface IV convened a synod of bishops in Rome to deal with the issue of whether monks, if found worthy, could be ordained and exercise the functions of a priest on an equal basis with the regular clergy.[91] The pope had already shown his favor toward monastics by converting his house into a monastery,[92] so not surprisingly the synod concluded that the "office of binding and loosing" could indeed be exercised by meritorious monks. In placing monks and clerics on a parity, the synod produced a verbal example to illustrate its conclusion: just as the Lord's messenger is called an ἄγγελος or "angel" in Greek and a *nuntius* or "bearer of news" in Latin, so both monks in their way and priests in theirs could be God's envoys.[93]

The use of Greek in the illustration reflected not only a working knowledge of the language by the synod's participants, but also a belief that those who would hear or read the council's decisions had a sufficient understanding of at least rudimentary Greek to be able to grasp what the example meant to convey. In addition, the fact that a synod was having to deal with an apparent insistence on the part of monastics for parity with the regular clergy in admission to holy orders suggests rather strongly that monks were increasingly becoming a force in the Roman church. The participants in the synod of 610 could not possibly have imagined just how influential monastics were to be at another Roman synod that would take place in less than forty years. Nor could they have anticipated that it would be Greek and not Latin monks who would wield that influence. It is to the convulsions that rocked the eastern part of the empire and drove those monastics, along with the regular ecclesiastical hierarchy, to flee westward to Rome that we now turn our attention.

◄

To John of Ephesus the Slavs and their Avar masters were "an accursed people." Between 578 and 584 he records that they "overran the whole of Greece, and the country of the Thessalonians, and all Thrace and captured the cities, and took numerous forts, and devastated and burned, and reduced the people to slavery."[94] Other Eastern sources confirm John of Ephesus's account of Slavic devastations. Menander lamented that "Greece was being plundered by the Slavs," and Nikephoros Kallistos related that the Avars were pouring into the Balkans and all of Greece, destroying cities and fortified places and acting with unbridled cruelty.[95] Michael the Syrian recorded that the Slavs "roamed like a lion on the prowl, assembling by the thousands and pillaging without end."[96] During this same time, they had twice made incursions up to the Long Walls west of Constantinople, reduced Anchialus, and taken Singidunum (Belgrade) burning and destroying as they went.[97] In 584, the Avar Chagan breached the peace treaty he had concluded with Maurice and, arming his Slav tributaries, invaded Thrace, where the barbarians devastated the countryside as they marched toward the capital.[98] But between the summer of 584, with Komentiolos's victory over a force of Avars and Slavs near the river Erginia, and the spring/summer of 587 with an imperial victory at Adrianople, the barbarians withdrew from Thrace and imperial forces had repulsed the immediate threat to Constantinople.[99] By the spring of 588, however, the Avars were demanding an increase in tribute from Byzantium. When the emperor refused, they began to make fresh preparations for invasion.[100] From then on imperial efforts were directed more toward repelling the continuous threat they posed to Constantinople rather than in any realistic efforts to drive the Slavs out of the territories they had already taken.[101] From the last quarter of the sixth century forward, the Slavs had begun to settle permanently in the northern Balkans. They ceased their mere plundering and began to establish themselves firmly on imperial soil in that region, taking effective possession of the country.[102]

Phocas's effort in 604 to contain the Slavs in the territories, which they had already occupied in the northern Balkans, by increasing the tribute paid to them was a failure.[103] From that point "great masses of Slavs" began to establish themselves in northern Greece, forming communities which the Byzantines called *sclavinies*.[104] From there they spread south taking all the country around Thessalonika and beginning their advance into peninsular Greece.[105] During the remaining years of the reign of Phocas and the early years of Heraclius, the Slavs spread throughout Greece proper and, crossing the gulf to Patras and the isthmus to Corinth, they penetrated the Peloponnesus and thereafter by means of their *monoxyla*, which were boats hollowed out from a single tree trunk, ultimately arrived in Crete in 623.[106]

Slavic penetration of Greece, including the Peloponnesus, continued throughout the seventh century.[107] Although the Avars ceased to be a force in the Balkans after their unsuccessful siege of Constantinople in 626, the Slavs continued to pour into the Balkans, largely shattering imperial authority from the Danube in the north to Cape Tainaron at the southern tip of the Peloponnesus.[108] Isidore of Seville recorded that the "Slavs took Greece from the Romans,"[109] and the abbreviator of Strabo, writing between 670 and 680, noted that "the Scythian Slavs now hold all Epirus and almost all of Greece, together with the Peloponnesus and Macedonia."[110] When, in 723, Bishop Willibald of Eichstätt sailed from Syracuse in Sicily across the Adriatic to Monemvasia in the Peloponnesus, he described the great fortress town as lying "in Slavinian territory."[111] A few years later, in 730, a life of St. Pancratius of Taormina mentioned Avars (meaning probably Slavs) as inhabiting the countryside around Athens.[112] When in the tenth century the emperor Constantine VII Porphyrogenitos described Greece and the Peloponnesus during the seventh and eighth centuries, he said that "the entire country was Slavicized and had become barbarian."[113] Patriarch Nicholas III Grammatikos (1084–1111) asserted that for the 218 years between 589 and 807 no Byzantine official set foot in the Peloponnesus.[114]

The enormous numbers of Slavs who invaded and occupied peninsular Greece from the seventh century onward, as well as the extent of their geographical distribution in the region, created a demographic crisis of massive proportions. Literally hundreds of thousands of native Illyrians, Thracians, and Greeks were killed or deported. Between 614 and 619, the Avars engaged in massive deportations of Greeks from the Balkans to Danubian Pannonia.[115] The Slavs established themselves on the lands of those whom they had either slain or exiled. Based on a toponymic analysis, it appears that Slavic settlements in Greece were most numerous in Epirus and western Greece, the western and central Peloponnesus, and Thessaly, and that they were the least extensive in Attica, Argolis, Boetia, Corinth, and Phokis.[116] Thus, the parts of Greece most Slavicized were Thessaly, the western Peloponnesus, and Epirus, while the least affected regions were those in central Greece, including Attica, and the eastern part of the Peloponnesus.[117]

Since the Slavs were an agricultural and pastoral people, they tended naturally to occupy the countryside rather than the towns and cities.[118] Thus, at least a portion of the indigenous Greek population, which was not killed or led into captivity, sought refuge in the coastal towns and cities and on the offshore islands.[119] Corinth appears to have remained in imperial hands despite Slavic invasions into Greece in the late sixth century since, between 591 and 595, Gregory the Great carried on an uninterrupted correspondence with the city's bishops.[120] Thessalonika, spared in the Slavic siege of 586 by the intervention of its patron, Saint Demetrios, remained a Roman island encircled by a Slavic sea. Although it accommodated large numbers of Greek refugees, it was an isolated outpost reduced to reliance on its own defenses with no expectation of help from Constantinople.[121] Athens also appears to have remained an imperial possession. Pope Zacharias wrote St. Boniface that Theodore, the future archbishop of Canterbury, had once been "a learned philosopher at Athens."[122] If so, Theodore, who was sixty-six years old when he went to Britain in 668, had to have studied in Athens in the early years of the seventh century.[123] Moreover, the emperor Constans II stopped in Athens in 662 on his way to Rome.[124] It is probable that the barbarians never took Corinth, Patras, Nauplion, Argos, Chalcis, Thebes, or Athens and that Byzantine administration remained uninterrupted in these places.[125]

For that portion of the native Balkan population who escaped death and deportation or chose not to seek refuge in the coastal towns and cities or off-shore islands, salvation appears to have lain in flight to safer parts of the empire, especially southern Italy and the city of Rome. According to the *Chronicle of Monemvasia*, a short document written sometime before 932, the inhabitants of Patras in the northern Peloponnesus relocated en masse to Rhegium in Calabria just across the straits from Messina. A part of the population of Laconia, whose chief city was Sparta, went to Sicily where they became known as *Demenitai*, a corrupt form of the word Lacedaemonians. Other Laconians retreated to the extreme end of the Peloponnesus where, under the leadership of their bishop, they built the fortress town of Monemvasia from which the *Chronicle* derives its name. Finally, the inhabitants of Argos fled to the island of Orobe, most likely one of the Sporades to the east of Amorgos, while the Corinthians sought refuge on Aegina.[126] Thus, according to the *Chronicle*, at least two Greek communities, those of Patras and a part of the people of Laconia, appear to have abandoned Greece altogether and relocated in Sicily and southern Italy.[127]

During Phocas's reign the Avaro-Slavic invaders had virtually devastated the population of Illyricum and killed, captured, or driven off its people.[128] Salona, the administrative center of Dalmatia, was destroyed in 614 thereby effectively ending imperial control and influence in the western part of the Balkan peninsula. The fall of Salona was soon followed by the destruction of many other Dalmatian cities as well as the fall of towns such as Singidunum (Belgrade) and Sardica (Sofia) in the interior.[129] It may well have been partially as a result of these disturbances in the western Balkans that persons such as Venantius, father of the Dalmatian pope John IV (640–642), came to Rome in the early seventh century to serve in the imperial service as legal adviser. There, his young son entered the ranks of the Roman church.[130]

The Avaro-Slavic invasions of the Balkans, including peninsular Greece and the Peloponnesus, did not, however, result in massive movements of the native population from those regions to Sicily, southern Italy, or Rome. While at least some of the indigenous population of the Balkans did relocate to Italy in order to escape the barbarians, there is no source from which we can deduce definite numbers or that would lead us to conclude that there was an immense westward exodus.[131]

Those who fled to Italy would have included imperial officials who, as representatives of the government in Constantinople, would have been particularly vulnerable to the likelihood of death or captivity.[132] They may also have included merchants and traders, who would have had both the means of transportation and the financial wherewithal to make the journey westward, as well as contacts in Italy which would have provided them with at least temporary accommodations.[133] But probably the greatest number of refugees were those in religious orders, whether clerical or monastic, who may have had more reason to fear death and captivity at the hands of the heathen Avars and Slavs than even the imperial civil servants.[134] When imperial authority in the Balkans collapsed, leadership of the communities appears to have devolved upon the local church hierarch; it was a bishop who led part of the Laconians to found Monemvasia and probably a bishop who led the citizens of Patras to Calabria.[135] Nor was the fact that the refugees fled to Italy and Sicily particularly remarkable. Apart from the obvious fact that these locations offered the nearest safe havens,[136] they were the logical destinations for bishops, priests, and monks fleeing the Balkans. Both Salona in Dalmatia and Prima Justiniana in Illyricum were under the ecclesiastical jurisdiction of the bishop of Rome, as was all of peninsular Greece, the Peloponnesus, and the island of Crete including, in particular, the cities of Thessalonika, Larissa, Athens, Corinth, Patras, and Gortyna (Crete).[137] But after all, there was nowhere to go but west for those with the ability to flee the Balkans. Constantinople and the East were, as we shall see, the last places to which one could turn for refuge in the early seventh century.

◈

While the Avars and Slavs were ravaging the Balkans killing, capturing, or routing the native population from their homes, farther east the Persians breached the peace that had been concluded with the empire, when in 603 they moved against the citadel of Dara (Anastasiopolis), which they captured the following year.[138] According to Michael the Syrian, the Persians "harmed no one who was not Roman; but wherever those [Romans] were found, they were massacred."[139] A temporary respite following the capture of Dara was followed by a major Persian breakthrough into imperial territory beginning in 608. By August 610, the Persians had crossed the Euphrates, first taking Zenobia and thereafter Mardin, Amida, Theodosioupolis, Constantina, and Edessa.[140] Meanwhile, in 609 Heraclius, *strategos* of Africa, rebelled against Phocas and sent his son, who was also named Heraclius, toward Constantinople "with ships and a large force of barbarians."[141] The younger Heraclius reached the capital early in October 610, defeated Phocas in battle, killed him, and burned his body.[142] On the same day Phocas was executed, the youthful Heraclius was proclaimed emperor and invested with the imperial diadem by patriarch Sergius in the church of Haghia Sophia.[143] There was, however, no cause for rejoicing in the empire. The new emperor "found the affairs of the Roman state undone, for the Avars had devastated Europe, while the Persians had destroyed all of Asia and had captured the cities and annihilated in battle the Roman army."[144] Still worse was to come.

Following Heraclius's accession, the Persians invaded Syria, taking Apamea and Emesa, and on October 8, 611, they captured the great metropolis of Antioch.[145] Caesarea in Cappadocia also fell to them in 611, along with "many tens of thousands of captives."[146] By 613, the barbarians had occupied Damascus, taking "a multitude of captives" and "creating confusion in the land."[147] They then turned their forces southward and headed for the Holy City of Jerusalem.

Even if we take into account the sources' tendency toward exaggeration and hyperbole, Persian advances into imperial territory appear to have been accompanied by a remarkable savagery that included wholesale slaughter, burning, and deportation on a massive scale.[148] The violent and barbaric tone of the war is no better illustrated than in the taking of Jerusalem in 614. According to a contemporaneous eyewitness account written by Strategios, a monk of the lavra of St. Sabas in Judaea, the siege of Jerusalem began on April 15 and lasted for twenty days.[149] On the twenty-first day, the Persians breached the city's defenses and burst in with unbridled fury, slaughtering the native population and burning and desecrating Christian churches and holy places with a special vengeance.[150] Those in priestly and monastic orders seem to have incurred the brunt of Persian hostility. This may have been the result of the fact that during the siege the invaders had been unsuccessful in suborning two Phoenician monks into becoming traitors and exposing the city's weaknesses.[151] A toll of the carnage taken when the killing ended on May 20 amounted to 66,509 dead; their bodies were collected from monasteries and churches, extracted from cisterns, and taken down from towers and fortifications.[152] Patriarch Zacharias of Jerusalem was led off to Persia, as was the True Cross.[153]

Following the capture of Jerusalem, the Persians continued their advances into imperial territory. To the north, after taking Cappadocian Caesarea, they crossed Anatolia and in 615 came as far as Chalcedon directly across the Bosphorus from Constantinople.[154] To the south, they invaded Egypt in 616 and three years later took Alexandria where, upon entering the city, they put 80,000 young men to death.[155] By 620, the Persians had occupied all of Egypt, Libya, and Ethiopia.[156] By the end of the first decade of the seventh century, the Persians had "seized all the Romans' lands in Mesopotamia, Syria, Cilicia, Palestine, Egypt, and the African coast." In the process, they had captured their riches, and enslaved or massacred most of the population.[157] Those who remained in the lands taken by the Persians groaned under the "yoke . . . of bloodthirstiness and taxation."[158]

Since almost all accounts of the Persian invasions are by those in clerical or monastic vocations, it is tempting to suppose that sympathy for their Christian coreligionists naturally inclined such authors to emphasize, perhaps excessively, the tribulations experienced by priests and monks. Although there may be more than a small measure of such bias in the texts, it is nonetheless highly probable that monastics and ecclesiastics did in fact experience the worst of Persian vengeance.[159] Both bishops and monks were in their own ways leaders in the Christian communities whose competing influence and authority the Persians could hardly be expected to tolerate. The Christian bishop not only taught the believers entrusted to his care, but protected them from their adversaries.[160] It was to their patriarch that the people of Jerusalem looked for consolation in the face of the Persians invaders, and it was the patriarch who sought to negotiate an acceptable surrender of the city.[161] It was also toward the monks, those irrefragably holy "friends of God," to whom the people of late antiquity turned in the times of their greatest peril. Through their purity of spirit, they had achieved an intimacy with the Lord, and it was this friendship with God that invested them with a power surpassing that of any patron to whom one could appeal in moments of crisis.[162] The Persians, therefore, showed little restraint in their efforts to curtail the influence of bishops, priests, monks, and consecrated virgins.[163]

The record of Persian atrocities directed against monastics includes killings marked by an uncommon brutality. On May 15, 614, the barbarians broke into the lavra of St. Sabas in the Judaean desert and slaughtered forty-four monks. Their bodies were later taken up, washed, and buried by passing Christians who came upon the carnage.[164] At Henaton near Alexandria, the Persians attacked six hundred monasteries, killing all but the few monks who went into hiding. The monasteries were plundered and left in ruins. At Nikiu in Egypt they massacred seven hundred monks.[165] Advanced age brought no reprieve. Stephen the Syrian, a monk over one hundred years old, was summarily slain.[166] Even those who seemed to pose no threat were killed. A monk named Leontios was slain "because he refused to leave his cell and interrupt his seclusion."[167]

Great numbers of Christian religious persons were led off to captivity, such as the nearly one thousand nuns whom patriarch John of Alexandria later ransomed.[168] Others were determined to stay in place. George of Choziba and his disciple Antony remained committed "in life or in death to the land of their renunciation"; instead of leaving the desert, they sought refuge in even more remote locations.[169]

Still other monks chose to flee the Persian invaders. Dorotheos, hegumen of Choziba, and Nicomedes, hegumen of St. Sabas, sought refuge to the south in Arabia.[170] But it appears that most monastics who sought refuge in flight moved westward toward Egypt. The Persian invasions in Syria and Palestine brought "great numbers" of refugees to Alexandria.[171] There they were given shelter by such persons as patriarch John, whose legendary acts of charity toward those who arrived in the city from the East earned him the surname the "Almsgiver" as well as a glowing biography by Leontios, bishop of Naples.[172] Among those who sought refuge in Egypt in the face of the Persian invasions was John Moschos, a monk at the monastery of St. Theodosios in Judaea and later at the New Lavra of St. Sabas. The invaders drove him first to seek refuge in Antioch and, after it fell in 611, he departed for Jerusalem. The capture of the Holy City in 614 led him to Alexandria later that year. As the Persians threatened Egypt, Moschos departed for Rome, where he spent the remainder of his life.[173]

John Moschos was accompanied in his flight to Alexandria by his friend Sophronios, who was born in Damascus in the late sixth century. In Damascus, Sophronios became professor of rhetoric and it was there that his erudition earned him the epithet the "sophist." Sophronios entered the monastery of St. Theodosios where he met Moschos, whom he accompanied to Antioch and finally to Egypt as the Persians advanced into Palestine. He departed with Moschos in 614 for Rome as the Persians pressed into Egypt. Sophronios lived in Rome at least until 619 when he returned east bearing the body of Moschos home for burial as he had promised his friend he would do.[174]

The Persian invasions also had the effect of reigniting the Christological controversy between Monophysites and Dyophysites that had festered unresolved since the victory of the latter at the Council of Chalcedon in 451. The dispute on the nature of Christ had not been settled to the satisfaction of either side despite Justinian's determined efforts to reach an accommodation at the Council of Constantinople in 553. To the extent that the Persians showed any tolerance toward the Christian population, they supported the Monophysites against the Chalcedonians. This was based upon the well-founded assumption that the Monophysites, who had suffered at the hands of the imperially supported Chalcedonians, would tend to see the Persians more as liberators than as oppressors and thus be more likely to encourage the native and predominantly Monophysite population to cooperate with rather than to resist them. Moreover, the Persians viewed the Chalcedonians as potential collaborators with Constantinople.[175] In either case, the Monophysites could not have been more pleased with the Persians' religious policies. For them, it was preferable to live under the regime of tolerant heathens rather than that of persecuting and heretical Christians.[176]

The Persians extended a considerable degree of toleration, at least toward the Monophysite Christians, in the areas they occupied.[177] Beginning around 610, the Persians "expelled all the Chalcedonian bishops from all the land of Mesopotamia and Syria." Christian churches and monasteries in those regions were given over to the Monophysites.[178] Soon their conquests of imperial territory had progressed to such an extent that the Persian king decreed that "Chalcedonians be expelled from all places in the East, and he permitted orthodox [Monophysite] bishops to take over their sees." Michael the Syrian was exultant as he recorded that:

> The episcopal sees everywhere were taken over by our [Monophysite] bishops and the memory of the Chalcedonains disappeared from the Euphrates to the East. The Lord made their iniquity fall upon their head: that which they had achieved through the intervention of the Roman emperor was repaid to them through the intervention of the Persians, kings of Assyria.[179]

Athanasios the Camel Driver, the Monophysite patriarch of Antioch who was restored to his see by the Persians after they took the city in 611, was equally joyous when in his synodical letter to his fellow Monophysite patriarch

Anastasius of Alexandria he wrote, "that the world today rejoices in peace and love because the Chalcedonian darkness has passed away."[180] The Monophysite bishops of Syria, who had earlier been routed by the Chalcedonians and taken refuge in Egypt, returned to their churches. It was now the Chalcedonians' turn to flee to Alexandria where, for example, Thomas, the Monophysite bishop of Hierapolis (Mabbug), had been compelled to go at the time of the persecutions by Maurice.[181] But Chalcedonians fleeing to Egypt were not as likely to find the kind of warm reception there as Syrian and Palestinian Monophysites had earlier experienced.[182] Except for Alexandria, where patriarch John the Almsgiver had extended help to fleeing Syrian Chalcedonians,[183] the Egyptian hinterland was largely Monophysite. For many fleeing Chalcedonians, Egypt was only a temporary stop in a longer journey. As with John Moschos and his friend Sophronios, they would eventually make their way to Rome far from the Persians and the Christological battles.[184] But the predominantly monastic and fiercely Chalcedonian refugees who made their way to Rome in advance of the Persian onslaught would soon be joined by more exiles from the East, driven westward by yet another wave of barbarian invaders.

ᴥ

The fall of Alexandria to the Persians in 619 and the loss of Egypt during the course of the following year severed Constantinople's grain supply and led to a "severe famine . . . in the state."[185] The population of the capital, which from the time of Constantine had received the privilege of a free bread distribution, was now required to pay for each loaf. Soon the bread distribution was suspended altogether.[186] The onset of a severe plague compounded the suffering already caused by the shortage of commodities. Widespread death and hunger resulted in severe hardship.[187] The desperate state of affairs in which Constantinople found itself in the later years of the first decade of the seventh century had to have affected the direction taken by refugees fleeing the Persian invaders in the East. The city's precarious condition would have been a significant factor in causing them to press westward toward Africa (Carthage) and Italy rather than toward the beleaguered capital. Nor, as we have seen, did the Balkans offer them a safe harbor from the barbarians.[188] Indeed, by 621, neither Constantinople nor the entire eastern part of the empire could offer sanctuary to anyone for they themselves were on the brink of total collapse.[189]

Heraclius began Byzantium's long campaign against the Persians on the Monday following Easter Sunday in 622.[190] In the same year, far to the south, Mohammed moved to Medina and founded Islam as a political state that, unlike previous Arab federations, subscribed to an ideology that did not confess allegiance to Constantinople.[191] During the course of the previous two years, Heraclius had concluded a peace with the Avars and, as a result, was able to transfer his armies from Europe to Asia in preparation for the attack on the

Persians.[192] The initial assault, which began in the autumn of 622, resulted in strategically important though not spectacular successes. The emperor was able to capture key positions to which he intended to return the following year and utilize as launching points for deeper incursions into Persian-occupied territory. Far more important, Heraclius's successes raised morale among the troops and in the capital, proving that the empire was far from moribund and that the Persians were not invincible.[193]

Heraclius returned to Constantinople in March 623. A mere three months later the Avars mounted a surprise attack on the capital.[194] They ravaged and plundered the suburbs, including the area of Blachernae, and sent the startled emperor into an "ignominious flight" during which he barely managed to enter the city clutching the imperial crown under his arm. After destroying a few more villages in Thrace, they retreated into their own lands, but not until they were promised a substantial annual tribute of 200,000 *nomismata* and were given members of the imperial family as hostages.[195] It was not until the Feast of the Annunciation of the Theotokos on March 25, 624, that Heraclius again departed for the East.[196] As he had done when he had started his campaign against the Persians in 622, the emperor again entrusted the care and government of the city to patriarch Sergius.[197] Following four more years of war, Heraclius at last dispatched news of the final defeat of the Persians to Constantinople, where the proclamation of victory was read from the pulpit of Haghia Sophia on the Sunday of Pentecost.[198] Even the Monophysites, their enthusiasm for Persia on the wane, rejoiced momentarily at the triumph of the Roman, albeit Chalcedonian, emperor.[199] Later that year, or possibly as late as 631, Heraclius made a jubilant return to the capital where he was acclaimed with olive branches, lights, tears of joy, and hymns of thanksgiving to God. He had fulfilled a "mystical allegory": for just as the Lord had created the world in six days and had rested on the seventh, so, it was proclaimed, the Roman emperor had defeated all Persia in six years and in the seventh had returned to Constantinople to take his rest.[200] It would be a brief repose.

✦

Mohammed first began to attract attention around 618 when he left the interior of Arabia and came into the northern part of that country and on into Palestine in order to trade.[201] But neither he nor his kind had a good reputation in the region. It was said that Mohammed had ingratiated himself with a rich woman of noble ancestry, misappropriated her possessions, and deceived her into believing that he was a prophet.[202] Beginning around 611, a band of raiders had come over from Arabia into Syria where they "pillaged and devastated the lands, massacred many people, and set fire without pity or mercy."[203] Arab attacks in Syria and Palestine, which Heraclius's victory over the Persians had once again made imperial territory, continued throughout the second decade of the seventh century.[204] Incursions into southern Syria, which became increasingly prevalent in 633, were followed the next year by an Arab sortie into Palestine, where on February 4, 634, a small contingent of imperial troops was defeated at Dathin near Gaza.[205] At Ajnadayn, on July 30, 634, an imperial army commanded by Heraclius's brother suffered a major and unexpected defeat.[206] The Arabs began freely to pillage the region around Caesarea, severing communications between towns and spreading fear and insecurity throughout Palestine.[207] During the year 634, the situation in Syria and Palestine had seriously deteriorated. When Sophronios, who had returned to Jerusalem and become patriarch, wrote his synodical letter at the beginning of the year, he had referred to the "audacious Saracens" and the cruelty and savagery they had shown in ravaging the countryside.[208] But by the end of the year, when he delivered his Christmas sermon, circumstances had reached a state of desperation: confined within the walls of the city, Sophronios lamented that "restrained and terrified by fear of the Saracens" he could not even visit and venerate the place where Christ was born.[209]

The empire was now powerless to arrest the Arab advance.[210] Damascus and Emesa fell in 635.[211] In September 636, imperial troops sustained a disastrous and decisive defeat at the battle of Jabiya-Yarmuk, which resulted in the total rout of the Roman army and an Arab breakthrough that led the way toward the imminent collapse of the remainder of Syria.[212] Thereafter, Byzantium lost Apamea and Aleppo in rapid succession.[213] Antioch, the capital of Roman Syria, fell in 636 or 637.[214] Michael the Syrian despaired that the evils that the land and people had suffered were too numerous to relate.[215] The emperor Heraclius, assessing the devastation that surrounded him, departed for Constantinople, turning back toward Antioch and sadly sighing, "Live in peace, Syria!"[216]

On Epiphany, January 6, 637, patriarch Sophronios of Jerusalem delivered a sermon of gloom and foreboding: the Holy City was encircled by the Saracens who had "overrun the land, sacked the towns, devastated the fields, set fire to villages, overturned holy monasteries, and poised themselves to seize the whole world."[217] By July, Jerusalem was under a siege that would last six months. In December 637 or January 638 the patriarch negotiated the city's surrender on a promise of immunity for all of Palestine.[218] But the terms of capitulation were not as generous to the vanquished as this might suggest. Christians were henceforth forbidden to build new churches or monasteries, or to repair or make improvements on any such existing structures.[219] Nearly eight years to the day that patriarch Modestos had received a triumphant Heraclius into Jerusalem the calif Omar "entered the Holy City dressed in filthy garments of camel hair and, showing a devilish pretence, sought the Temple of the Jews—the one built by Solomon—that he might make it a place of worship for his own blasphemous religion."[220] Caesarea, the last of the major Byzantine positions in Palestine, capitulated between 639 and 641.[221]

The Arab conquests in the East resurrected the same kinds of tensions between Chalcedonians and Monophysites that had been ignited by the earlier

Persian invasions. When the Monophysite bishop Epiphanios sought refuge in Cilicia, against which the Arabs moved after the fall of Syria, the imperial commander Gregorios summoned him to inquire about his beliefs. When Epiphanios replied that he did not "divide Christ in two" as did the synod of Chalcedon, Gregorios gave him the option of renouncing his heresy and receiving "a great dignity from the emperor" or facing the sword. Epiphanios chose death, but not before predicting that Gregorios would soon die in the same way. The bishop's prophecy was fulfilled the next day.[222] The attitude of an inhabitant of Emesa on the eve of the Byzantine defeat at Jabiya-Yarmuk reflects the resentment frequently felt by the native Monophysite population toward their imperial masters. Speaking to a leader of the Arab invaders, he declared, "[W]e like your rule and justice far better than the state of oppression and tyranny in which we were. The army of Heraclius we shall indeed, with your amil's [general's] help, repulse from the city."[223] These same tensions, which resulted in substantial defections by the native Monophysite population to the Arab camp and thus inhibited imperial efforts to develop effective defenses against the intruders, also obtained in Egypt, toward which the invaders turned their sights after Syria and Palestine had fallen into their hands.[224]

When Heraclius recovered Egypt from the Persians around 631, he immediately expelled the Monophysite patriarch Benjamin I, whom the Persians had supported, and replaced him with the Chalcedonian Cyrus, whom he translated to Alexandria from Phasis in the Caucasus. In addition to making him patriarch, Heraclius named Cyrus prefect of Egypt, thereby taking the unprecedented step of uniting in a single person both the highest ecclesiastical and civil authority.[225] Under Cyrus, Monophysite sources claim that the Dyophysites instituted severe persecutions and attempted by various artful and deceitful means to persuade them to renounce their beliefs and become Chalcedonians.[226] It was only when Cyrus purloined the church's gold and silver and fled to Constantinople that the persecutions ended and the Monophysites regained their churches and monasteries.[227] But it was, in fact, Cyrus's bungled attempt to negotiate a peace with the Arabs (resulting in his own death in 642 allegedly from chagrin at the debacle he had created) that allowed the barbarians to occupy Alexandria in 644. The Byzantines briefly recaptured the city in 645, but then lost it and the whole of Egypt forever in 646.[228] Patriarch Benjamin returned to Alexandria to reclaim its holy places for the Monophysites.[229]

To the opponents of Chalcedon, the Arab victories in Egypt, similar to their successes in Syria and Palestine, were the product of divine retribution for imperial adherence to the Dyophysite heresy.[230] The memory of Arab deceit and depredations, including the customary references to wholesale massacre and pillage, and even the heavy burden of taxation, which John of Nikiu lamented "was heavier than the yoke which had been laid on Israel by Pharaoh," could be more easily borne when joined with the sight of Chalcedonians routed from Egypt's churches and monasteries.[231] When pressed to provide an example of the "many Egyptians" who renounced Christianity and "accepted the doctrine of the detestable beast Mohammed," the Monophysite bishop of Nikiu could only cite the case of John, a monk from a monastery in Sinai, and he had been a Chalcedonian.²³²

Following their victory in Egypt, the Arabs pursued their successes against the empire by moving westward across the Mediterranean shore raiding and plundering imperial towns that dotted the coastline.²³³ Sometime between the end of 646 and the beginning of 647, while struggling to contain the Muslim menace, imperial troubles were exacerbated by the rebellion of Gregory, exarch of Africa.²³⁴ The Arabs took advantage of the confusion caused by Gregory's insurrection to launch an assault on Sufetula, thereafter freely pillaging and looting the countryside of Byzacena.²³⁵ After defeating Gregory, who managed to escape and make peace with the emperor, the Arabs exacted a substantial tribute from the imperial province and withdrew, at least for the moment.²³⁶

The disasters suffered by the Christian population as a result of the Arab invasions were at least as severe as the Persian atrocities. Patriarch Sophronios's negotiation of an immunity seems to have been insufficient to prevent Arab soldiers from breaking crosses on the heads of Christians during religious processions or from tearing down places of worship.²³⁷ Patriarch Cyrus of Alexandria equated the ferocity of the Persians with the audacity of the Arabs.²³⁸ Stephen, bishop of Dor in Palestine, deplored the Arab desecration of Christian holy places.²³⁹ The Arabs appear to have attempted to coerce Christians on pain of death to renounce their faith and accept Islam.²⁴⁰ Sixty Byzantine soldiers refused to apostasize from Christianity and were slain in 640.²⁴¹ Monks were marked out for especially cruel treatment.²⁴² An anchorite who was walking along the shore of the Red Sea was attacked by a band of Arabs who cut off his head. A monk named Ianthos, who had fled into the wilderness, was confronted by Arabs intent upon killing him. A repentant Arab confessed to having approached a monk with the intention of robbing and possibly even killing him, only to remain frozen in the act of assault for two days and two nights until released by his putative victim.²⁴³ Christian sources, such as the seventh century pseudo-Methodios of Patara, repeatedly refer to Arab atrocities against those in religious vocations and of Muslim disrespect for "priests whose holy altars they defile."²⁴⁴ Even if these stories were exaggerated, the effect upon their listeners would have been nothing less than abject terror.

But not all were prepared to die for their faith. Having established a monument to martyrdom and secured the salvation of their departed brothers, Christian religious, both monastics and ecclesiastics, felt that they could now justify their departure from the East to continue their toil for the faith elsewhere. Unlike the masses who were rooted to the soil and without contacts abroad, monks and clerics turned toward the West as they had done when pursued by the Persians. Constantinople offered them no refuge; in 653–654 the citizens of the capital could look across the Bosphorus and see a Muslim army camped on the opposite shore.[245] As it had been for John Moschos and Sophronios, the ultimate destination for those who could flee would once again be Rome.

⌒

The early decades of the seventh century witnessed a reversal of the "avalanche of ascetics to the East" that followed the Gothic invasions of 408 to 410 in the West.[246] For many of the same reasons that had driven persons such as Pelagius and his circle to Palestine in the fifth century, monastics and ecclesiastics two hundred years later retraced the footsteps of those who, fleeing Rome, had then sought both physical refuge and religious sympathy in the East.[247] The Gothic invasions of the early fifth century had resulted in mass devastation in the West, making large parts of Europe insecure and unsafe. Two centuries later, the Avaro-Slavic invasion of the Balkans, and the Persian and later Arab occupation of Syria, Palestine, and Egypt, had resulted in the same kind of extensive destruction and often wholesale slaughter in the East. For monks and clerics, who had suffered as much and perhaps even more than the remainder of the population and who had the contacts and the ability to facilitate flight, Constantinople could offer little, if any, refuge since it was often under siege, suffering from plague, or experiencing famine. As the Arabs pressed across the North African littoral toward Carthage, soon it too would collapse. As a practical matter, between 620 and 640 Rome and Italy were the last remaining safe havens in the empire.[248]

The Persian and Arab invasions had added new fuel to the fire that had blazed between Monophysites and Dyophysites since the victory of the latter at Chalcedon in 451. Just as the turbulence that had been generated by Pelagianism resulted in the persecution of its adherents and their flight eastward in the fifth century, so also in the seventh century the virulent quarrels between Monophysites and Chalcedonians were exacerbated as the invading Persians and Arabs, seeing the adherents of Chalcedon as imperial loyalists and hence potential collaborators with Constantinople, bestowed preferences and privileges on the Monophysites.[249] As Chalcedonians were routed from churches and monasteries, their only place of refuge was in Rome, which was and would forever remain fiercely Dyophysite in its Christology.[250]

Those who sought shelter in Rome in the early decades of the seventh century were, as we shall see, highly educated and intellectually articulate. They had for generations been feasting in the lush pastures of the East and, as John Moschos described it, "plucking the finest flowers of the unmown meadow."[251] Their arrival in Rome would also reverse the "brain drain of ascetic emigrants to the Holy Land" that had impoverished the city as the fifth century dawned.[252] But there is nothing to indicate that the early-seventh-century movement of what were predominantly Chalcedonian monastics and ecclesiastics from the East to Rome and Italy consisted of either "wave after wave of terrified orientals" or "great shifts of

population from East to West."²⁵³ Although the barbarian invasions and the reinvigorated controversy between Monophysites and Chalcedonians did account in
large measure for the unrest and even panic that swept Easterners westward toward
Rome in the early seventh century, the West was not inundated with "great crowds
of fugitives" nor did it experience the onslaught of "thousands of refugees [from]
across the sea."²⁵⁴ Those who arrived in Rome and Italy as a result of the political
and religious tumult in the early-seventh-century East were few in number. They
were *la minoranza di una minoranza*—the minority of a minority.²⁵⁵ But while their
numbers may have been quite small, their influence on Rome and the Papacy in
the early seventh century was disproportionately immense.²⁵⁶ Their first opportunity to exercise that influence would be in the battle against Monothelitism.
Amidst an atmosphere that warmly welcomed them, the small force of monks and
clerics who came to Rome at this time would combine their zeal for Chalcedon,
their intellectual acumen and high learning, and the spiritual authority of the Roman church and the Papacy to mobilize the battle and win the war against the last
of the great Christological controversies to confront the church.

Notes

1. Strategios Monachos, *La Prise de Jérusalem par les Perses en 614*, trans. Gérard
Garitte, in *Corpus Scriptorum Christianorum Orientalium*, Vol. 203 (Louvain, 1960), p.
30. ("Although our bodies shall go away with our enemies, our hearts shall remain with
Christ.")

2. Roberto Valentini and Giuseppe Zucchetti, eds., *Codice Topographico della Città
di Roma*, Vol. 2, in *Fonti per la Storia d'Italia* (Rome, 1942), pp. 155–207. The itinerary
and description of the walls of Rome are contained in the fourth part of the codex and
are believed to have been written sometime after the pontificate of Honorius I (625–638)
and before the extensive reconstruction of Rome undertaken by Leo IV (847–855). Id.,
p. 156.

3. Id., pp. 169–171.

4. G. Marchetti-Longhi, id., p. 183.

5. Easterners appear to have lavished substantial donations on St. Maria *in Cosmedin*. An eighth-century inscription in the portico records a gift of extensive properties in
the vicinity of Rome to the church's *diaconia* or ministry to the poor by no less a person
than Eustathius, the last known Byzantine duke of Rome (ca. 752–756), and his brother,
the *vir gloriosissimus* Georgios. Angelo Mai, *Scriptores Veterum Nova Collectio*, Vol. V
(Rome, 1831), pp. 216–17; see also B. Bavant, *Le Duché Byzantine de Rome*, id., p. 86.

6. Roberto Valentini and Giuseppe Zucchetti, id., p. 171n4; cf., *LP*, I, 507.

7. Ferdinand Gregorovius, *History of the City of Rome in the Middle Ages*, Vol. II,
trans. Mrs. Gustavus W. Hamilton (London, 1907), p. 408; L. Bréhier, id., p. 4; G.
Marchetti-Longhi, id., p. 184.

8. G. Marchetti-Longhi, "Il Quartiere Greco-Orientale di Roma nell'Antichità
e nel Medio Evo," in *Atti del IV Congresso Nazionale di Studi Romani*, Vol. I (Rome,
1938), pp. 169, 182; O. Bertolini, "Discussione sulla lezione Pertusi" in *Centre e Vie*

di *Irridiazione della Civiltà nell'Alto Medioevo, Settimane di Studio Del Centro Italiano di Studi sull'Alto Medioevo,* 18–23 April 1963 (Spoleto, 1964), pp. 160–61; Carlo Battisti, "Appunti sulla storia e sulla diffusione dell'Ellenismo nell'Italia meridionale," *Revue de linguistique romane* 3 (1927): 1, 85. Sepulchral inscriptions also attest to the presence of large numbers of Eastern merchants in Rome in Late Antiquity. See, namely, E. Curtius and A. Kirchoff, eds., *Corpus Inscriptionum Graecarum, Inscriptiones Christianae,* Vol. 4 (Hildesheim, 1977), No. 9612, pp. 533–34 (Abednesoubous, a wine merchant from the Syrian village of Arrhorum); No. 9640, pp. 537–38 (Ioannes Adoun, from the Syrian village of Cobroea); No. 9656, p. 540 (Flavius Paulus Heraclidous, an Egyptian); No. 9787, p. 561 (reflecting that the deceased, whose name has been effaced, was from the Syrian village of Adana).

9. Ioannes Franzius, ed., *Corpus Inscriptionum Graecarum, Inscriptiones Italiae,* Vol. 3 (Hildesheim, 1977), No. 5892, p. 772.

10. *PL* 61: 1079–80.

11. L. Bréhier, "Les Colonies d'Orientaux en Occident au commencement du moyen-âge," *Byzantinische Zeitschrift* 12 (1903): 1, 3.

12. *Reg.* IV, 42. For a survey of the history of Syrians in the West, including Rome, see Paul Scheffer-Boichorst, "Kleinere Forschungen zur Geschichte des Mittelalters IV–VI: Zur Geschichte der Syrer im Abendlande," *Mitteilungen des Instituts für Österreichische Geschichtsforschung* 6 (1885): 521–50.

13. E. Curtius and A. Kirchoff, eds., id., No. 9578, p. 528 ("Ablabis . . . doctor"); No. 9669, p. 542 ("Dionysios . . . doctor and priest"); No. 9792, p. 562 ("Alexander . . . Christian doctor"); De Rossi, id., p. 107.

14. *Reg.* XIII, 42.

15. *LP,* I, 317.

16. Paul Goubert, *Byzance Avant l'Islam,* Vol. 2 (Paris, 1965), p. 49; L. M. Hartmann, *Untersuchungen zur Geschichte der Byzantinischen Verwaltung in Italien (540–750)* (Leipzig, 1889), pp. 4–34. The earliest reference to an exarch of Italy occurs in a letter sent in 584 by Pope Pelagius II to Gregory while the latter was his *apokrisiarios* in Constantinople. *PL* 72: 704.

17. Hartmann, id., p. 31. The *Liber Diurnus* provided a form for announcing the death of a pope to the exarch (No. LIX) as well as a form for advising the exarch of the name of the person who had been elected to succeed him and asking for exarchal confirmation of the candidate (No. LX). Theodor E. Von Sickel, ed., *Liber Diurnus Romanorum Pontificum* (Darmstadt, 1966), pp. 49–54.

18. Hartmann, id., p. 31. The exarchs of Italy for the seventh century were Kallinikos (596–603) (*Reg.* IX, 142, 155); Smaragdos (603–608) (*Reg.* XIII, 34); John Lemigios or Thrax (608– 616) (*LP,* I, 319); Eleutherios (616–619) (*LP,* I, 319, 321); Isaac (625–643) (*LP,* I, 328, 331–32); Theodore Kalliopas (643–645) (*LP,* I, 332); Plato (ca. 645–ca. late 649) (*LP,* I, 337); Olympios (ca. late 649–652) (*LP,* I, 337–38); Theodore Kalliopas (653–666) (*LP,* I, 338; *Mansi* X, 849, 851); Gregorios (ca. 666) (Paul the Deacon, id., IV, 38); Andrea Dandolo, *Chronica* in L. A. Muratori, *Rerum Italicarum Scriptores,* Vol. 12, Pt. 1 (Bologna, 1728), p. 92; Theodore II (678–687) (*LP,* I, 332: *Mansi* XI, 195ff.); and John Platyn (687–ca. 701) (*LP,* I, 369, 372).

19. T. S. Brown, *Officers and Gentlemen,* p. 77.

20. Charles Diehl, *Études sur l'Administration Byzantine dans l'Exarchat de Ravenne (568–751)* (Paris, 1888), p. 278n4. Such subordinate officials would have included *consiliarii, scholastici, adsessores, domestici,* and *cancellarii*. Hartmann Grisar, *History of Rome and the Papacy in the Middle Ages,* trans. Luigi Cappadelta (London, 1912), p. 65.

21. See A. Guillou, "L'Italia Bizantina dall'Invasione Longobarda alla Caduta di Ravenna" in *Storia d'Italia: Longobardi e Bizantini* (Turin, 1980), p. 242.

22. Ottorino Bertolini, *Roma di Fronte a Bisanzio e ai Longobardi,* in *Storia de Roma,* Vol. IX (Bologna, 1941), Plate XII (I).

23. *PG* 90: 113–14; cf., *LP*, I, 337.

24. *LP*, I, 328; 331; 338; 373–374. For the duties and functions respectively of the *chartularios, sakellarios,* and *spatharios,* see Pililis, id., pp. 205ff.; 58ff.; and 292ff.

25. Henry Chadwick, *The Early Church,* rev. ed. (London, 1993), pp. 82, 163.

26. Leo the Great, Sermon 82, I, *PL* 54: 422–423; Chadwick, id., pp. 161, 237ff.

27. *Reg.* XI, 1; 20, 28.

28. *Reg.* VII, 37.

29. *Mansi* X, 896BC.

30. John Moschos, *The Spiritual Meadow (Pratum Spirituale),* trans. John Wortley (Kalamazoo, 1992), p. 120–21 (Pope Leo I); pp. 122–24 (Pope Agapetus); pp. 124, 165 (Pope Gregory).

31. *PL* 73: 968–69.

32. J. J. Taylor, "Eastern Appeals to Rome in the Early Church: A Little Known Witness," *Downside Review* 89 (1971): 142–46.

33. *Reg.* VI, 61; *Reg.* VII, 37; *Reg.* VIII, 28; *Reg.* IX, 176; *Reg.* X, 21; *Reg.* XII, 16; *Reg.* XIII, 43.

34. Robert S. Lopez, "The Role of Trade in the Economic Readjustment of Byzantium in the Seventh Century," *Dumbarton Oaks Papers* 13 (1959): 69–85. Lemerle agrees with Lopez that the seventh century did not experience a cessation of commerce between East and West, although he contends that the volume of such trade was reduced. Paul Lemerle, "Les Répercussions de la Crise de l'Empire d'Orient au VIIe siècle sur les Pays d'Occident," *Caraterri del secolo VII in occidente, Settimane di Studi del Centro Italiano de Studi sull'Alto Medioevo,* 23–29 April 1957 (Spoleto, 1958): 729.

35. Ernesto Seston, "La Composizione Etnica della Società in Rapporto allo Svolgimento della Civiltà in Italia nel secolo VII," in *Caratteri del secolo VII in occidente, Settimane di Studio del Centro Italiano di Studi sull'Alto Medioevo,* 23–29 April 1957, Vol. 2 (Spoleto, 1958): 651.

36. *PL* 87: 970–71, 977–78.

37. Silvano Borsari, "Le migrazione dall'Oriente in Italia nel VII secolo," *La Parola del Passato* 6 (1951), p. 133.

38. Whittow, id., pp. 72–73.

39. Theophanes, *Chronographia,* p. 412.

40. Theophanes, id., pp. 413–414; 418–419; 423–424; Theophylact Simocatta, *History,* trans. Michael and Mary Whitby (Oxford, 1986), p. 225.

41. *Chronicon Paschale 284–628 A.D.,* trans. Michael and Mary Whitby (Liverpool, 1989), p. 142.

42. Theophanes, id., p. 414, 418; Theophylact Simocatta, id., p. 234; *Chronicon*

Paschale, pp. 143–44, 146.

43. John, bishop of Nikiu, *Chronicle*, trans. R. H. Charles (London, 1916), pp. 175–76; A. P. Vlasto, *The Entry of the Slavs into Christendom* (Cambridge, 1970), pp. 5–6.

44. Theophanes, id., p. 422; *Chronicle of Michael the Syrian*, Vol. II, trans. J.-B. Chabot, (Paris, 1901), p. 378; Georgios Cedrenos. *Historiarum Compendium*, ed., Immanuel Bekker (Bonn, 1838), p. 711.

45. *Chronicle of Michael the Syrian*, id., p. 378.

46. Theophanes, id., p. 423; Georgios Cedrenos, id., p. 711; *Chronicon Paschale*, id., pp. 145–146.

47. Theophanes, id., p. 424; Georgios Cedrenos, id., p. 711; *Chronicle of Michael the Syrian*, id., p. 378.

48. Theophanes, id., p. 425 and p. 425 n3.

49. Paul Lemerle, trans. and ed., *Les Plus Anciens Receuils des Miracles de Saint Démétrius et la Pénétration des Slaves dans les Balkans*, Vol. I (Paris, 1979), pp. 112–13 (original Greek text); p. 109 (French translation by Lemerle). The English translation is by the author.

50. Paul the Deacon, *Historia Langobardorum*, id., pp. 156–157.

51. *Reg.* XIII, 39.

52. *Reg.* XIII, 33.

53. *Reg.* XIII, 34.

54. John, bishop of Nikiu, id., p. 167; 175; Peter Schreiner, ed., *Die Byzantinischen Kleinkroniken, Corpus Fontium Historiae Byzantinae*, Vol. XII/1 (Vienna, 1975), p. 133. Georgios Monachos describes Phocas as "treacherous," "exceeding all in evil," "mad," and "God-killer." *PG* 110: 824. Leo Grammatikos calls him a "drunkard," "joyous in blood," "wicked," "womanizer," "savage and bold in speech," and "merciless and bestial in manner." Leo Grammatikos, *Chronographia*, ed. Immanuel Bekker, *Corpus Scriptorum Historiae Byzantinae* (Bonn, 1842), p. 143. These graphically contemptuous epithets reflect the extent to which the literary evidence shows that the emperor was detested in the East.

55. *Reg.* XIII, 32; 39.

56. *Reg.* XIII, 40. Helena was, of course, the mother of Constantine the Great and one of the most honored and respected Christian holy women. *AA.SS.* Aug. III, 548–654 (1737).

57. *Reg.*, Appendix VIII, p. 1101.

58. *Reg.* XIII, 39.

59. Ottorino Bertolini, *Rome di Fronte a Bisanzio e ai Longobardi*, id., pp. 288–89.

60. *Reg.* III, 54; *LP*, I, 315, 317.

61. *LP*, I, 315.

62. *Mansi*, X, 495.

63. *Mansi*, X, 496. On the eastern provenance of the name Onnophrius, cf., *Histories of the Monks of Upper Egypt and the Life of Onnophrius by Paphnutius*, trans. Tim Vivian (Kalamazoo, 1993).

64. *Mansi* X, 506–7; *LP*, I, 317n4, 326n19; *Mansi* XI, 180.

65. *MGH, AA* xiv, ed. F. Vollmer (Berlin, 1905), pp. 287–90.

66. *LP*, I, 315.

67. Georgios Cedrenos, id., p. 711; Nikephoros, Patriarch of Constantinople. *Short History*, trans. Cyril Mango, *Corpus Fontium Historiae Byzantinae*, Vol. XIII (Washington, D.C., 1990), p. 35.

68. Theophanes, id., p. 423.

69. *LP*, I, 316.

70. *Mansi* X, 501.

71. De Rossi, id., pp. 126, 141.

72. *LP*, I, 316 n1.

73. See Whittow, id., pp. 41, 63.

74. Hartmann, id., p. 103.

75. See, Ωρολόγιον τό Μέγα (Athens, 1973), pp. 222–23.

76. Although the scholarly consensus is that Pope Boniface III was of Eastern ancestry, most historians have continued to see Theodore as the first among the seventh-century Eastern popes. See Richards, *The Popes and the Papacy in the Early Middle Ages, 476–752* (London, 1979), pp. 245, 269ff.; Gregorovius, id., p. 105; Horace K. Mann, *The Lives of the Popes in the Early Middle Ages*, Vol. I, Pt. 1 (London, 1925), pp. 264–65; Bertolini, id., p. 291; Lemerle, "Les Répercussions de la Crise de l'Empire d'Orient au VIIe siècle sur les Pays d'Occident," id., p. 725.

77. *LP*, I, 316; Ado of Vienne, *Chronicon*, id., p. 112; Franz Dölger, *Regesten der Kaiserurkunden des Oströmischen Reiches von 565–1453* (Hildesheim, 1976), No. 155, p. 17.

78. Theophanes, id., p. 422.

79. Justinian, *Novella*, 131, c. 2, t. 14. πρώτον εἶναι πάντων τῶν ἱερέων.

80. Theophanes, id., p. 424.

81. Whittow, id., p. 74.

82. *LP*, I, 317.

83. *Reg.* XIII, 41, 43–44. It is likely that both Boniface III and Boniface IV were papal *apokrisiarii* in Constantinople. Caspar contends that the early successors of Gregory I had all occupied this position at one time or another, and he includes among them Sabinian and both Bonifaces. See Caspar, id., Vol. 2, p. 517.

84. See De Rossi, id., p. 128. According to the *Liber Pontificalis*, Boniface IV was "of the Marsi by origin, from the province of Valeria, son of Iohanne (John) the doctor." *LP*, I, 317. The Marsi were an ancient people of central Italy who from the first century A.D. cultivated a close relationship with the Romans. Along with the Peligni, Vestini, and Marrucini, they inhabited a region east of Rome, corresponding to present-day Abruzzo, which was known as Valeria from the Via Valeria that traversed it. *Enciclopedia Italiana*, Vol. 22 (Rome, 1937), p. 316; id., Vol. 34, p. 913. It is possible that Boniface's father emigrated from Valeria to Rome in the sixth century where he studied medicine under Eastern physicians whom, as we have seen, dominated the city's medical establishment. See, supra, p. 43. Since he was a doctor and because his name was Iohanne (John), which was quite popular among Easterners at the time, it is tempting to suggest that he had an Eastern provenance.

85. Bertolini, *Roma di Fronte a Bisanzio e ai Longobardi*, p. 292. In 609, Phocas erected a similar column to the east of the Church of the Forty Martyrs in Constantinople. When he heard that a monk had predicted he would soon die, the emperor "made so much haste in the erection of the statue that, as his contemporaries have told, he caused still more

deaths." Cameron and Herrin, trans. and eds., *Parastaseis Syntomoi Chronikai*, id., pp. 155–57. While his reason for constructing a column in Constantinople may well have been to impress his image on public spaces "in an attempt to counter his growing unpopularity" in the capital, he would not have had any such motive for doing so in Rome, where he had always been well received. *Chronicon Paschale*, id., p. 148 and p. 148n415.

86. Bryan Ward-Perkins, id., p. 48.

87. *LP*, I, 317; Ado of Vienne, *Chronicon*, *PL* 123:112; De Rossi, id., p. 211. The sources are not in accord on whether the *iussio* was issued in 609 or 610. See Dölger, id., No. 156, p. 17.

88. Bede, *Historia Ecclesiastica*, II, 4; Gregorovius, id., p. 106ff.

89. Paul the Deacon, *Historia Langobardorum*, MGH, pp. 160–161; Bede, *Chronica*, id., p. 310; *LP*, I, 317n2.

90. *LP*, I, 317; AA.SS. Maii VI (1737), p. 75.

91. *Mansi* X, 504.

92. *LP*, I, 317. Boniface's partiality toward monks had irritated the regular clergy. The *Liber Pontificalis* pointedly noted that his successor Deusdedit "greatly loved the clegy" and that he "restored the *sacerdotes* and clergy to their original places." *LP*, I, 319.

93. *Mansi* X, 505.

94. John of Ephesus, id., p. 432.

95. Menander, id., Frag. 21, pp. 192–93: Nikephoros Kallistos. *Ecclesiasticae historiae*, PG 147: 355.

96. *Chronicle of Michael the Syrian*, id., p. 362.

97. Evagrius. *The Ecclesiastical History*, ed. J. Bidez and L. Parmentier (London, 1898), p. 228.

98. Theophanes, *Chronographia*, p. 376; Georgios Monachos, *Chronicon Syntomon*, PG 110: 814.

99. Theophylact Simocatta, *History*, id., I.7.1–4; ii. 16.12–17.13.

100. Id., vi.3.9–4.4.

101. For a summary of the efforts undertaken by the emperor Maurice to combat the Avars and Slavs during the last ten years of his reign, see P. Lemerle, "Invasions et migrations," *Revue historique* (1954), pp. 291–92.

102. George Ostrogorsky, *History of the Byzantine State*, rev. ed., trans. J. M. Hussey (New Brunswick, NJ, 1969), p. 81. In February 601, Maurice sought to replace the ailing bishop of Prima Justiniana in Illyricum. Although Gregory protested the emperor's uncanonical approach to the matter, he agreed that the see needed strong leadership "lest it perish from the enemies," a clear reference to the Slavs, who by then had effectively taken over the region. *Reg.* XI, 29.

103. Dölger, id., No. 152, p. 17; Ostrogorsky, id., p. 85.

104. Antoine Bon, *Le Péloponnèse Byzantin Jusqu'en 1204* (Paris, 1951), p. 35.

105. Vlasto, id., p. 5.

106. Bon, id., p. 35. Charanis maintained, on the strength of the authenticity of the *Chronicle of Monemvasia* and such corroboration as is provided by John of Ephesus and Michael the Syrian, that the Avaro-Slavic penetration of the Peloponnesus began during the reign of Maurice, and that by 587 the barbarians had become masters of its western and central areas. Peter Charanis, "On the Slavic Settlement of the Peloponnesus,"

Byzantinische Zeitschrift 46 (1963): 91, 95, 100. Vasmer also contends that the Slavs had penetrated as far as the Peloponnesus in the sixth century. Max Vasmer, *Die Slaven in Griechenland* (Leipzig, 1970), p. 14. Ostrogorsky, on the other hand, argued that the Slavs did not penetrate southern Greece until early in the seventh century. George Ostrogorsky, "The Byzantine Empire in the World of the Seventh Century," *Dumbarton Oak Papers* 13 (1959): 3–4. Bon, with whom Lemerle appears to be in accord, also maintained that the Slavs did not establish themselves in the Peloponnesus until the first half of the seventh century. Bon, id., pp. 54–55; P. Lemerle, "Une Province Byzantine: Le Péloponnèse," *Byzantion* 21 (1951): 341, 344.

107. Bon, id., p. 37; Dimitri Obolensky, *Byzantium and the Slavs* (Crestwood, NY, 1994), pp. 31–32.

108. Nicolaus Cheetham, *Medieval Greece* (New Haven, 1981), p. 17.

109. *PL* 83: 1056.

110. *Chrestomathiae ex Strabonis geographicarum libro VII* in *Strabonis rerum geographicarum libri XVII*, 2 vols. (Amsterdam, 1707), II, 1251–52; Bon, id., p. 36n5.

111. *MGH Scriptores* xv, Pt. 1 (Hanover, 1887), p. 93.

112. Vasmer, id., p. 15; cf., *AA.SS.* Apr. I (1675), 237–43.

113. Constantine VII Porphyrogenitos. *De Thematibus*, ed. A. Pertusi (Vatican City, 1952), p. 91.

114. P. Lemerle, "Invasions et migrations," id., 303.

115. Peter Charanis, "Ethnic Changes in the Byzantine Empire in the Seventh Century," *Dumbarton Oaks Papers* 13 (1959): 25, 39; John V. A. Fine Jr., *The Early Medieval Balkans* (Ann Arbor, 1983), p. 36; Paul Lemerle, *Les Plus Anciens Receuils des Miracles de Saint Démétrius*, Vol I, id., 5 [284], p. 222.

116. Vasmer, id., pp. 20–76, 85–110, 113–174.

117. Charanis, id., p. 40.

118. Lemerle, "Une Province Byzantine: Le Péloponnèse," id., p. 344.

119. Ostrogorsky, *History of the Byzantine State*, p. 94.

120. *Reg.* I, 26; *Reg.* V, 57, 62. Fine contends that Corinth remained Byzantine from ca. 600 to as late as 662. Id., p. 61.

121. Paul Lemerle, id., pp. 183–85.

122. Ephraim Emerton, trans., *The Letters of St. Boniface* (New York, 1940), p. 143.

123. Bede, *Historia ecclesiastica*, iv. I.

124. *LP*, I, 343.

125. Ferdinand Gregorovius, *Geschichte der Stadt Athen im Mittelalter*, I (Stuttgart, 1889), p. 85. Gregorovius doubtless based his conclusion regarding continued imperial presence in these cities on the tenth century text *De Administrando Imperio* of the emperor Constantine VII Porphyrogenitos. See p. 31n136, infra.

126. P. Lemerle, "La Chronique Improprement Dite de Monemvasie: Le Contexte Historique et Légendaire," *Revue des Études Byzantines* 21 (1963): 5–49. The text of the *Chronicle* is printed at pages 8–11 of Lemerle's article. Lemerle notes that while there is a place known as Demenna in Sicily, it is not a corruption of Lacedemon. Id., p. 14. See also Charanis, id., p. 159.

127. But see p. 54n136, infra.

128. See, supra, p. 45n43.

129. George Ostrogorsky, *History of the Byzantine State*, p. 93.

130. *LP*, I, 330. During his pontificate, John IV showed particular solicitude for the sufferings of his Dalmatian confreres by ransoming captives and building a church to house the relics of Dalmatian martyrs whom he had transported to Rome. *LP*, id.; De Rossi, id., p. 425.

131. Compare P. Lemerle, "La Chronique Improprement Dite de Monemvasie," id., p. 48 with K. Lake, "The Greek Monasteries in South Italy, I," *Journal of Theological Studies* 4 (1903): 345, 348 and Lynn T. White, *Latin Monasticism in Norman Sicily* (Cambridge, MA, 1938), p. 16ff. In his tenth-century treatise *De Administrando Imperio*, the emperor Constantine VII Porphyrogenitos recorded that at the time of the emperor Nikephoros I (802–811) the Slavs then in the Peloponnesus revolted against "their neighbors, the Greeks," and "moved against the inhabitants of the city of Patras and ravaged the plains before its wall and laid siege to itself." The besieged Patrans sought assistance from "the then military governor [who] was at the extremity of the province in the city of Corinth." Constantine VII Porphyrogenitos, *De Administrando Imperio*, ed. and trans. G. Moravcsik and R. J. H. Jenkins, *Corpus Fontium Historiae Byzantinae*, I, 2nd ed. (Washington, D.C., 1967), pp. 228–33. Based on this text there was not the total exodus of native Greeks from either Patras or Corinth in the late sixth century that the *Chronicle of Monemvasia* recites since Greeks continued to occupy these cities as late as the early ninth century in sufficiently large numbers so as to be able to repel a major Slavic siege. It is possible, of course, that there was indeed a substantial westward exodus of the inhabitants of Patras and Corinth, but that the *Chronicle of Monemvasia* exaggerated the numerical proportions of the flight. In any event, the opinion of Gregorovius cited above that cities such as Patras and Corinth remained uninterruptedly in imperial hands throughout the Slavic invasions appears to find support in Constantine VII's text.

132. *LP, I*, 330 (Venantius, the Dalmatian *scholasticus* and father of the future pope John IV).

133. Peter Charanis, "The Chronicle of Monemvasia and the Question of the Slavonic Settlements in Greece," id., p. 159 (suggesting that the fleeing Laconians were principally merchants who settled in Messina).

134. Fine, id., p. 41.

135. P. Lemerle, "La Chronique Improprement Dite de Monemvasie," id., p. 14.

136. Peter Charanis, "Ethnic Changes in the Byzantine Empire in the Seventh Century," id., p. 42.

137. *Reg.* II, 19; IV, 20; VI, 25, 26 (Salona); *Reg.* III, 6, 7; V, 8; VIII, 10; IX, 157; XI, 29; XII, 10 (Prima Justiniana); Jean Darrouzès, *Notitiae Episcopatum Ecclesiae Constantinopolitanae*, Vol. I (Paris, 1981), pp. 260–361, 365 (Thessalonika, Larissa, Athens, Corinth, Patras, and Gortyna in Crete).

138. Leo Grammatikos, *Chronographia*, id., p. 145; Theophanes, *Chronographia*, id., pp. 414, 420, 422.

139. *Chronicle of Michael the Syrian*, id., p. 378.

140. Theophanes, *Chronographia*, id., p. 424; *Chronicle of Michael the Syrian*, id., p. 378; Whittow, id., p. 73. Among Western sources, Isidore of Seville recorded that in the time of Phocas "the Persians incited most severe wars against the republic by which the Ro-

mans were greatly harmed and lost many provinces up to the river Euphrates." *Chronicon, PL* 83: 1056. Bede also recites that in Phocas's time "the Persians waged most heavy wars against the republic and took many Roman provinces." *Chronica*, id., p. 310. Paul the Deacon wrote that the "Persians also waged a very severe war against the empire [and] took away many provinces of the Romans." *Historia Langobardorum, MGH*, id., p. 161.

141. John, bishop of Nikiu, id., p. 176; Theophanes, *Chronographia*, id., p. 426; *Chronicon Paschale*, id., p. 149; Paul the Deacon, *Historia Langobardorum, MGH*, id., p. 161.

142. Theophanes, *Chronographia*, id., p. 428; *Chronicon Paschale*, id., p. 152; John, bishop of Nikiu, id., p. 177; *Parastaseis Syntomoi Chronikai*, id., p. 156.

143. Theophanes, *Chronographia*, id., p. 428; *Chronicon Paschale*, id., p. 152; Nikephoros, *Short History*, id., pp. 43–45. According to John of Nikiu, Heraclius was crowned in the church of St. Thomas the Apostle and resisted elevation to the purple. Id., p. 178.

144. Theophanes, *Chronographia*, id., p. 429.

145. Theophanes, *Chronographia*, id., p. 428; *Chronicle of Michael the Syrian*, id., p. 400; John of Nikiu incorrectly ascribes the capitulation of Antioch to the time of Phocas. Id., p. 176.

146. Theophanes, *Chronographia*, id., p. 429. Michael the Syrian confirms the Persian capture of Cappadocian Caesarea but places it in 613. Id., p. 400.

147. Theophanes, *Chronographia*, p. 430; C. House, *Vita sancti Georgii Chozibitae auctore Antonio Chozibitae*, Ch. VII, 30, *Analecta Bollandiana* 7 (1881): 95–144. Michael the Syrian records the fall of Damascus as occurring in 615. Id., p. 400.

148. See Whittow, id., pp. 1–14; Clive Foss, "The Persians in Asia Minor and the End of Antiquity," *English Historical Review* 90 (1975): 721, 728. Foss supplements the literary evidence of Persian atrocities with examples of coin hoards and the burial of treasure reflecting fear on the part of the native population. The chronology of the coin hoards as well as the mint closings show that the Persian menace was severely felt by the mid-600s and grew in intensity for the remainder of the decade. Id., p. 734.

149. Strategios Monachos, *La Prise de Jérusalem par les Perses en 614*, id., pp. 13–15.

150. Strategios, id., p. 14. An anonymous source describes bodies cut from head to heart and from shoulders to stomach. One person was severed in half at the waist; another's intestines were spilling out; yet another was so dissevered that he resembled a sheep at a butcher's shop. The social order was turned on end as servants ruled and rulers were reduced to servitude. *PG* 86/2: 3235–38.

151. Strategios, id., pp. 7, 10.

152. Strategios, id., pp. 52–53. Strategios's count of the dead is probably more accurate than that of either Theophanes or Michael the Syrian, both of whom record that 90,000 lost their lives. Theophanes, *Chronographia*, id., p. 431; *Chronicle of Michael the Syrian*, id., p. 400. Andrea Dandolo's figure of 90,000 is doubtless based on Eastern sources. *Chronica*, id., p. 92; cf., *The Secular History of Dionysius of Tel-Mahre* in *The Seventh Century West-Syrian Chronicles*, trans. Andrew Palmer (Liverpool, 1993), p. 128, which recites a figure of 90,000 killed.

153. Theophanes, *Chronographia*, id., p. 431; *Chronicle of Michael the Syrian*, id., p. 400; *Chronicon Paschale*, id., p. 156. In a letter to his flock following the capture of Jerusalem, patriarch Zacharias lamented the fate which the city had suffered saying "All have been afflicted . . . all still agonize . . . Today we find ourselves in severe circumstances." *PG* 86B: 3234.

154. *Chronicon Paschale*, id., p. 159 and p. 159n442: Theophanes, *Chronographia*, id., p. 432.

155. Severus of Asmounein. *History of the Patriarchs of the Coptic Church of Alexandria*, ed. and trans. B. Evetts, *Patrologia Orientalis*, Tome I, Fasc. 2 (Paris, 1904), pp. 485–86.

156. *Chronicle of Michael the Syrian*, id., p. 401; Nikephoros, *Short History*, id., p. 45; Andrea Dandolo, *Chronica*, id., p. 92; Whittow, id., p. 76.

157. *Chronicle of Michael the Syrian*, id., p. 401.

158. Theophanes, *Chronographia*, id., p. 435. With the notable exception of Jerusalem, Kaegi disputes source accounts of the extent of Persian devastation in Syria and Palestine maintaining, instead, that there was "no generalized destruction" by the Persians in those areas. Walter E. Kaegi, *Byzantium and the Early Islamic Conquests* (Cambridge, 1992), p. 45.

159. Peter Schreiner, ed., "Chronik 24 (Chronik von Jerusalem)" in *Die Byzantinischen Kleinchroniken, Corpus Fontium Historiae Byzantinae* XII/1 (Vienna, 1975), p. 197.

160. Vera von Falkenhausen, "Bishops," in Guglielmo Cavallo, ed. *The Byzantines*, trans. Thomas Dunlap (Chicago, 1997), p. 172; see also the funerary inscription of Metrophanes, metropolitan of Smyrna in S. G. Mercati, "Inno anacreontico alla SS. Trinità di Metrofane, arcivescovo di Smirne," *Byzantinische Zeitschrift* 30 (1930): 60.

161. *PG* 86B: 3228.

162. Peter Brown, *The Making of Late Antiquity* (Cambridge, MA, 1978), p. 64.

163. Strategios Monachos, id., p. 6.

164. Letter of Antiochos Monachos to Eustathios, abbot of the monastery of Attalina in Ancyra. *PG* 89: 1421–24.

165. Severus of Asmounein, id., pp. 485–86.

166. C. House, "Vita sancti Georgii Chozibitae auctore Antonio Chozibitae," id., Ch. VII, 31. The north wall of the chapel at Choziba contains "a reliquary with the skulls of fourteen martyred monks from the period of the Persian conquest in 614." A. Ovadiah and C. G. de Silva, "Supplement to the Corpus of the Byzantine Churches in the Holy Land," *Levant* 13 (1981): 213.

167. *Life of St. Theodore of Sykeon* in Elizabeth Dawes and Norman H. Baynes, trans., *Three Byzantine Saints* (Crestwood, NY, 1977), p. 124.

168. *Life of St. John the Almsgiver* in Dawes and Baynes, *Three Byzantine Saints*, p. 204; see also Theophanes, *Chronographia*, id., p. 431. According to Pseudo-Sebeos, an Eastern source, the Persians captured and exiled 35,000 persons. Bernard Flusin, *Saint Anastase le Perse et l'Histoire de la Palestine au début du VIIe siècle*, Vol. II (Paris, 1992), p. 165. Strategios Monachos records that following the fall of Jerusalem, the Persians exiled 3,000 children aged seven years or less to Persia. Id., p. 39.

169. Derwas Chitty, *The Desert a City* (Crestwood, NY, 1995), p. 155.

170. Chitty, id., p. 156; C. House, id., Ch. VIII, 34.

171. *Life of John the Almsgiver*, in Dawes and Baynes, *Three Byzantine Saints*, pp. 202, 205, 213–14.

172. *PG* 93: 1620.

173. Henry Chadwick, "John Moschos and his friend Sophronios the Sophist," *Journal of Theological Studies* 25 (1974): 41, 49; Bernard Flusin, id., p. 65.

174. Christoph von Schönborn, *Sophrone de Jérusalem: Vie Monastique et Confession Dogmatique* (Paris, 1972), pp. 55–56, 69–71; Aidan Nichols, *Byzantine Gospel: Maximus the Confessor in Modern Scholarship* (Edinburgh, 1993), p. 9; Bernard Flusin, id., p. 65. Although most authorities accept 619 as the year in which Sophronios returned to the East to bury John Moschos, arguments have been advanced suggesting that this did not occur until 634. See Enrica Follieri, "Dove e quando morì Giovanni Mosco?" *Rivista di Studi Bizantini e Neoellenici*, n.s. (1988) 3–39; cf., Henry Chadwick, "John Moschos and His friend Sophronios the Sophist," id., p. 52, and Derwas Chitty, *The Desert a City*, p. 160.

175. John Meyendorff, *Imperial Unity and Christian Divisions* (Crestwood, NY, 1989), pp. 340–41.

176. Gilbert Dagron, Pierre Riché, and André Vauchez, *Évêques, Moines et Empereurs (610–1054)*, Vol. IV, in *Histoire du Christianisme des origines à nos jours* (Paris, 1993), pp. 16–17.

177. Kaegi, id., p. 45.

178. *The Secular History of Dionysius of Tel-Mahre* in *The Seventh Century in the West-Syrian Chronicles*, trans. Andrew Palmer (Liverpool, 1993), p. 125.

179. *Chronicle of Michael the Syrian*, id., pp. 379–80.

180. Severus of Asmounein, id., p. 481.

181. Id., p. 381. Thomas had fled to the monastery of Henaton near Alexandria where he wrote a critical text of the Gospels and the entire New Testament. Id.

182. The observation that in Egypt "ogni melchita diviene uno straniero, ogni jacobita un cittadino" ("each melkite [Chalcedonian] became a stranger, each jacobite [Monophysite] a citizen") neatly epitomizes the situation. Mario Scaduto, *Il Monachesimo Basiliano nella Sicilia Medievale* (Rome, 1982), p. xix.

183. PG 93: 1654.

184. The Roman church had been and would continue to remain firmly committed to Chalcedon's Christological formulation. That definition, which was articulated by Pope Leo I in his *Tome* or doctrinal statement, "asserted in the strongest language the permanent distinction of the two natures in the incarnate Lord." Henry Chadwick, *The Early Church*, id., pp. 201–2; PL 54: 756 (*Tome* of Leo I).

185. Nikephoros, *Short History*, id., p. 49; Georgios Monachos, *Chronicon*, Vol. II, C. de Boor and Peter Wirth, eds. (Stuttgart, 1978), p. 669.

186. *Chronicon Paschale*, id., p. 164 and p. 164n618.

187. Nikephoros, *Short History*, id., p. 49; Georgios Monachos, *Chronicon*, id., p. 669.

188. See supra, pp. 22–31.

189. See Whittow, id., pp. 76–77.

190. Theophanes, *Chronographia*, id., p. 435; Georgios Monachos, *Chronicon*, id., p. 670; Georgios Cedrenos, *Historiarum Compendium*, id., p. 717; Leo Grammatikos, *Chronographia*, id., p. 149; George of Pisidia, *Expeditio Persica I*, in *Poemi. I. Panegirici Epici*, ed. and trans. A. Pertusi (Ettal, 1959), p. 91.

191. Whittow, id., p. 88.

192. Theophanes, *Chronographia*, id., pp. 434–435; Georgios Monachos, *Chronicon*, id., p. 669; Georgios Cedrenos, *Historiarum Compendium*, id., p. 717.

193. Andreas Stratos, *Byzantium in the Seventh Century*, Vol. I, trans. Marc Ogilvie-Grant (Amsterdam, 1968), p. 144. Vasiliev maintains that in the spring of 622 "Heraclius

crossed into Asia Minor, where he recruited a large number of soldiers and trained them for several months." A. A. Vasiliev, *History of the Byzantine Empire*, Vol. I, 2nd ed. (Madison, 1952), p. 197. Baynes places the first imperial movements against the Persians in the autumn of 622. Norman H. Baynes, "A Note on the Chronology of the Reign of the Emperor Heraclius," *Byzantinische Zeitschrift* 26 (1926): 55–56.

194. Stratos, id., p. 143; *Chronicon Paschale*, p. 165. Theophanes places the Avar surprise on Constantinople in 617. *Chronographia*, pp. 433–34. Norman Baynes follows Theophanes's chronology, "The Date of the Avar Surprise, A Chronological Study," *Byzantinische Zeitschrift* 21 (1912): 110–28, although Cyril Mango, adhering to the date set forth in the *Chronicon Paschale*, believes Baynes "was misguided in moving it to 617." See Theophanes, *Chronographia,* id., p. 434n1.

195. Nikephoros, *Short History*, pp. 52–53; Theophanes, *Chronographia*, p. 434; *Chronicon Paschale*, p. 165; Leo Grammatikos, *Chronographia*, p. 151; Whittow, id., p. 77.

196. Theophanes, *Chronographia*, p. 438; *Chronicon Paschale*, p. 166; Whittow, id., p. 78.

197. Georgios Monachos, *Chronicon*, p. 670; Georgios Cedrenos, *Historiarum Compendium*, p. 718; Leo Grammatikos, *Chronographia*, p. 150; *Chronicon Paschale*, p. 167.

198. *Chronicon Paschale*, p. 182.

199. Severus of Asmounein records that "by the grace of Christ, he marched against them [the Persians], and slew Chosroes, their misbelieving king, and ruined his city and made it a wilderness, and carried away its wealth and captives in triumph to Constantinople." Id., p. 489; see also *Chronicle of Michael the Syrian*, id., p. 410.

200. Theophanes, *Chronographia*, pp. 457–458; Georgios Monachos, *Chronicon*, p. 672; Georgios Cedrenos, *Historiarum Compendium*, p. 735; Leo Grammatikos, *Chronographia*, p. 154. Pertusi, in the commentary to his edition of George of Pisidia, maintains that Heraclius returned to Constantinople before January 1, 629. George of Pisidia, id., pp. 233–34. Nikephoros records that Heraclius's return to the capital took the form of a triumph: "He brought four elephants, which he paraded at the Hippodrome contests to the delight of the citizens, and celebrated [several] days of triumph and distributed largesse to everyone." Id., p. 67. Mango places Heraclius's return to Constantinople around the middle of 631. Id., p. 186.

201. *Chronicle of Michael the Syrian*, p. 401.

202. Theophanes, *Chronographia*, pp. 464–65; Georgios Cedrenos, *Historiarum Compendium*, pp. 738–39.

203. *Chronicle of Michael the Syrian*, p. 401.

204. Theophanes, *Chronographia*, p. 466; Nikephoros, *Short History*, pp. 65–66.

205. Theophanes, *Chronographia*, p. 467; Nikephoros, *Short History*, p. 69.

206. Theophanes, *Chronographia*, p. 468. The Chronicle of Fredegarius, a Western source composed around 658/660, reported that "150,000 Roman soldiers were slain." Fredegarius, *Chronicles*, ed. B. Krusch. *MGH Scriptores Rerum Merovingicarum*, Vol. 2 (Hanover, 1888), p. 153.

207. Kaegi, id., pp. 98–100.

208. Theophanes, *Chronographia*, p. 468; *PG* 87: 3197.

209. *PG* 87: 3205.

210. Theophanes, *Chronographia*, p. 467; *Chronicle of Michael the Syrian*, p. 413; Nikephoros, *Short History*, p. 69; Dagron, id., p. 25.

211. Theophanes, *Chronographia*, pp. 469–70; Whittow, id., p. 86; Dagron, id., p. 25.

212. For details of the battle of Jabiya-Yarmuk and an assessment of its significance, see *Kaegi*, id., pp. 110–46. According to the *Chronicle of Fredegarius*, Arab forces numbered 200,000 men, and the battle resulted in the loss of 52,000 imperial soldiers. Id., pp. 153–54. Kaegi calls the number of both soldiers and casualties "wildly exaggerated." Id., p. 125. Michael the Syrian recorded sadly that the "Romans were cruelly cut to pieces and abandoned this region." Id., p. 420.

213. Dagron, id., p. 25.

214. Georgios Cedrenos, *Historiarum Compendium*, p. 751.

215. *Chronicle of Michael the Syrian*, id., p. 421.

216. Id., p. 424; Georgios Cedrenos, *Historiarum Compendium*, p. 745. Cyril Mango believes that Heraclius's "famous exclamation would more naturally have taken place after the battle of Yarmuk." Theophanes, *Chronographia*, p. 468n8.

217. Sophronios, *In Theophaniam* (CPG 7643), ed. A. Papadopoulos-Kerameus, Ἀνάλεκτα Ἱεροσολυμιτικῆς Σταχυλογίας, V (St. Petersburg, 1898), pp. 151–68 = *Clavis patrum graecorum*, I–V, ed. M. Gerard, *Corpus Christianorum* (Turnhout, 1974–1987), No. 7643.

218. Theophanes, *Chronographia*, p. 471.

219. D. J. Constantelos, "The Moslem Conquests of the Near East as Revealed in the Greek Sources of the Seventh and Eighth Centuries," *Byzantion* 42 (1972): 325, 349.

220. Id., p. 471; Georgios Cedrenos, *Historiarum Compendium*, p. 746; *Chronicle of Michael the Syrian*, pp. 435–26; Bernard Flusin, id., pp. 358–59.

221. Theophanes, *Chronographia*, p. 475; *Chronicle of Michael the Syrian*, p. 430; Whittow, id., p. 86.

222. *Chronicle of Michael the Syrian*, pp. 422–23, 431.

223. Ralph-Johanes Lilie, *Die Byzantinische Reaktion auf den Ausbreitung der Araber*, (Munich, 1976), p. 9n46.

224. Kaegi, id., p. 215.

225. Severus of Asmounein, id., p. 489; Dagron, id., p. 26n72. Cyrus is alleged by Monophysite sources to have flaunted his dual role by wearing a red shoe as evidence of his imperial authority and a black shoe representing his ecclesiastical power. *Chronicle of Michael the Syrian*, pp. 432–33.

226. Severus of Asmounein, id., p. 491.

227. *Chronicle of Michael the Syrian*, p. 433.

228. Whittow, id., p. 86; Dagron, id., p. 27.

229. John of Nikiu, id., p. 200.

230. Severus of Asmounein, id., pp. 492–93; John of Nikiu, id., p. 202.

231. John of Nikiu, id., pp. 179, 181–82, 184, 188, 195.

232. Id., p. 201.

233. *Chronicle of Michael the Syrian*, p. 441.

234. Theophanes, *Chronographia*, p. 477; *Chronicle of Michael the Syrian*, p. 441.

235. Stratos, id., Vol. 3, p. 71.

236. Theophanes, *Chronographia*, p. 478; *Chronicle of Michael the Syrian*, p. 445; Stratos, id., Vol. 3, p. 72.

237. Christos Papadopoulos, Ἱστορία Ἐκκλησίας Ἱεροσολύμων (Jerusalem, 1910), p. 264.

238. *Mansi* X, 1006.

239. Id., 895.

240. *Doctrina Iacobi nuper baptizati*, ed. N. Bonwotsch, *Abhandlungen der Königlich Gesellschaft der Wissenschaften zu Göttingen*. Philologisch-Historische Klasse, n.s. vol. 12, n3 (Berlin, 1910): 88.

241. H. Delehaye, "*Passio sanctorum sexaginta martyrum*," *Analecta Bollandiana* 23 (1904): 289–307.

242. Arab attacks on Christian monastic communities had occurred as early as the sixth century. According to St. Nilos, the Arabs were entirely uninterested in producing crafts or engaging in agriculture, preferring instead to live "a beastly and bloodthirsty life." St. Nilos, *Narrationes*, PG 79: 589ff.; see also the testimony of Ammonios in F. Combefis, ed., *Illustri Christi Martyrum Lecti Triumphi* (Paris, 1660).

243. John Moschos, *Spiritual Meadow*, id., pp. 15, 80, 109.

244. Constantelos, id., p. 331; see also Sebeos, *Histoire d'Héraclius*, trans. F. Macler (Paris, 1904), p. 104.

245. Whittow, id., p. 87.

246. Peter Brown, *Religion and Society in the Age of Saint Augustine* (London, 1972), p. 224.

247. There is admittedly no direct evidence of the emigration of laypersons to Rome as a result of the Persian and Arab invasions of the East in the early seventh century. Jean-Marie Sansterre, *Les moines grecs et orientaux à Rome aux époques byzantine et carolingienne*, I. Texte, (Brussels, 1983), p. 20. While conceding the absence of direct evidence, Sansterre nonetheless contends that there is "indirect testimony" of such lay emigration. However, the only examples he gives in support of his contention are those of popes Theodore, Agathon, Conon, and John VI, all of whom were ecclesiastics. Id., pp. 20–21.

248. See B. Flusin, Vol. II, id., p. 356, describing the flight of monks from Jerusalem sometime between 630 and 651 bearing the head of their patron St. Anastasius the Persian, which they would carry to Rome and deposit in the monastery of Aquas Salvias. See infra, p. 205.

249. Sansterre, id., p. 17. The Arabs did not permit the election of a Chalcedonian patriarch in Alexandria for ninety-one years, in Jerusalem for sixty-seven years, and in Antioch for forty years. Constantelos, id., p. 355.

250. See Henry Chadwick, id., p. 68, describing Rome as the ultimate safe harbor of the "zealots for the doctrine of Chalcedon."

251. John Moschos, *Spiritual Meadow*, id., p. 3.

252. Peter Brown, *Religion and Society in the Age of Saint Augustine*, p. 223.

253. K. Lake, "The Greek Monasteries in South Italy, I," *Journal of Theological Studies* 4 (1903): 348; Lynn T. White, *Latin Monasticism in Norman Sicily* (Cambridge, MA, 1938), p. 16.

254. Lake, id., p. 348. In support of his argument that the events of the first decade of the seventh century forced "thousands" of refugees westward, White cites the single example of John Moschos. Id., p. 17. White's propensity to exaggerate the numbers of Eastern immigrants to Rome in this period appears to be notorious. See Sansterre, id., II, Bibliographie, notes, index et cartes, p. 73n77. It is now generally conceded that the vol-

ume of immigrants was not nearly what most scholars had earlier this century conceived it to be. Sansterre, id., I, p. 18 ("l'ampleur du mouvement ne doit pas être exagérée.").

255. Silvano Borsari, "Le migrazione dall'Oriente in Italia nel VII secolo," *La Parola del Passato* 6 (1951): 133, 138. While the refugees who fled to Rome were predominantly clerics and monastics, Scaduto's observation that they were "exclusively ecclesiastics" surely goes too far. Scaduto, id., p. xix.

256. It is insufficient to account for the influence which the relatively small numbers of Eastern immigrants exercised on Rome and the Papacy in the early seventh century by asserting that "[I]n a city relatively thinly populated, such an immigration would not have to be massive to be significant." Sansterre, id., I, p. 21. Even assuming a relatively small population, such an assertion fails to take into account the substantial impact which the immigrants' high level of learning and culture had on a city which was by comparison intellectually destitute.

CHAPTER III

~

Diligo Romanos ut Unam Habentes Fidem; Graecos Autem ut Eadem Qua Ego Lingua Loquentes[1]
The Monothelite Controversy

The sun was setting when the ship from Rome arrived in Constantinople and sailed into the Sea of Marmara one summer evening in 654. The two impe- rial officials and ten palace guards who had been sent to meet the vessel and take custody of the prisoners it had brought from Italy must have been bewildered that such a force had been dispatched to arrest what turned out to be nothing more than a barefoot, half-clothed monk in his mid-seventies and his two disciples. The old monk had been born in the imperial city of a distinguished family.[2] He had been exceptionally well educated at the hands of private masters, acquiring skills in grammar, philosophy, and especially oration.[3] Entering the imperial civil service during the reign of Heraclius, he had served as ministerial secretary to the emperor until renouncing the world and entering the monastery of Chrysopolis across the straits from the capital.[4] He had left Constantinople over twenty years earlier to take up the battle against what was to be the last of the great Chris- tological heresies to plague the Church.[5] Now he was returning in shackles and under guard to face the wrath of Heraclius's grandson, the emperor Constans II.

Within a few days, the elderly abbot was led into the royal palace where, humiliated by being compelled to stand all day before the senators, he was re- lentlessly interrogated about his alleged acts of sedition and treason against the empire, the most egregious of which was his flagrant refusal to comply with the *Typos*, an edict which Constans II had issued in 648 decreeing an end to all talk about the energies and wills of Christ.[6] Driven into a rage by the old man's re- calcitrance, Troilus, the imperial *sakellarios*,[7] shouted that the *Typos* did not deny what the old man professed but rather ordered "a silence in order to arrange a peace." But the accused, as defiant as his accuser, hurled back a quotation from Scripture that equated silence with denial.[8] The aged monk would not relent, nor would the emperor allow his edict to be openly defied. On the following day, the venerable Maximos, who was to earn the eponym of confessor for the faith, was banished to Bizya in Thrace to meditate upon his stubbornness.[9] But even there he did not cease to agitate.

In June 653, the Romans had been compelled to witness the spectacle of their ailing pope Martin I arrested by the exarch Theodore Kalliopas and the imperial chamberlain Theodore Pellurios as he lay on a bed before the altar of the basilica of the Savior on the Lateran.[10] As would happen to Maximos a year later, Martin too had been led off in chains to Constantinople to stand trial for his refusal to comply with the *Typos*.[11] The Romans had chosen Eugenius, a local cleric, to succeed their hapless pontiff, and envoys were about to depart for the capital to petition the emperor to issue the *iussio* for his consecration.[12] Instigated no doubt by Maximos, his faithful disciple Anastasios the Monk frantically wrote the monks of Cagliari in Sardinia, urging them to hasten to Rome and warn the papal *apokrisiarii* that they should be prepared to resist the pressure that would be put on them to obtain Eugenius's acquiescence to the *Typos* as a condition precedent to issuance of the *iussio*.[13] Suspecting that he might encourage dissent if he were allowed too long a leash, Maximos was brought closer to Constantinople and confined to the monastery of St. Theodore in the suburb of Rhegium where he could more easily be watched.[14]

The stratagem did not succeed. Maximos continued to be a rallying point for those who opposed Constans II's religious policies. Condemned at last by a synod in Constantinople, which included among its bishops Peter, patriarch of Constantinople, Macedonius, patriarch of Antioch, and Theodore, *locum tenens* of the patriarchate of Alexandria,[15] the frail but indefatigable monk and his two companions were first taken by the prefect of the praetorian guards and beaten with ox tails. Their tongues were then cut out and their right hands severed so that they might neither speak nor write their treasonous doctrines.[16] Thus mutilated, the three were paraded through each of the twelve quarters of the capital and then sent off to Lazica, a remote region on the east coast of the Black Sea at the foot of the Caucasus.[17] Maximos and his fellow prisoners arrived in Lazica on June 8, 662. Placed in a litter made of tree branches, the elderly monk now nearing eighty-three was carried from the ship and locked in the fortress of Schemaris. With the aid of two pieces of wood attached to what remained of his tongue, he managed to mumble the prophecy of his impending death which, as he predicted, came on August 13, 662. It was said that each night thereafter, three lamps would miraculously come to light, spreading their radiance over the confessor's tomb at the monastery of St. Arsenios.[18]

※

Heraclius entered Jerusalem on March 21, 630, bearing the True Cross, which he had recovered "untouched by the profane and murderous hands" of the Persians.[19] As the Cross was elevated so that it could be seen by the multitude, patriarch Modestos and his clergy "offered to God a hymn of thanksgiving."[20] The *apolytikion*, or dismissal hymn of the feast, glorified the Lord for having saved His people by granting victory to the Christian king over his barbarian adversaries.[21] The triumph over Persia was thus seen as the result of God's intervention in aid of His own empire. A consequence of this was that henceforth the ecclesiastical establishment would exercise significant influence in political affairs.[22] Nor did such an arrangement appear to trouble the emperor. Indeed, the Persian war had signaled a kind of personal epiphany for Heraclius. He confided to his panegyrist George of Pisidia that up to then he had spent his years in slothfulness, but that he was now determined to devote the remainder of his days to serving God.[23]

The opportunity to make good his pledge came quickly. From Jerusalem, Heraclius continued his triumphal journey to Syrian Edessa, arriving there sometime between 630 and 633.[24] After he had taken up residence in the palace, the local priests and monks arrived to pay their respects. The emperor was astonished by the large numbers of monastics and, inquiring about their faith, quickly, but hardly with any surprise, learned that they were Monophysites. The piety of the monastic throng must have made a deep impression on Heraclius for, although he was a Chalcedonian, the emperor lamented to his entourage, "How can we leave such admirable people out of our realm?" He determined at once to make peace between the Chalcedonians and the Edessene Monophysites by implementing the maxim that "power must shine forth not so much through fear as in love," a precept which the emperor's court poet and panegyrist George of Pisidia recites was another revelation Heraclius had received from the Persian experience.[25]

On the day of a great feast, the emperor went to the Great Church of Edessa, then in the hands of the Monophysites,[26] and distributed largesse to the people, thereafter entering the sanctuary to receive Holy Communion from metropolitan Isaiah. But the bishop, either because of zeal for his beliefs, as Michael the Syrian described it, or because he was an "uneducated idiot" as Dionysius of Tel-Mahre put it, refused to give Heraclius communion unless he first anathematized the Council of Chalcedon and the Tome of Leo.[27] Forgetting for the moment his own axiom about the exercise of power, the emperor went into a rage, driving out the Monophysite bishop and his clergy and handing over the cathedral of Edessa to the Chalcedonians.[28]

The imperial anger slowly cooled. Sometime later at Hierapolis, Heraclius attempted once again to come to terms with the Syrian Monophysites. For twelve days, the emperor sat in discussions with Athanasios Camelarios, the Monophysite patriarch of Antioch, and eleven of the principal bishops of Syria. At the conclusion of their discussions, Heraclius asked that the bishops set forth their position in writing. After reading their document and once more praising the zeal with which they defended their doctrines, the emperor gently reasoned that they could surely not find fault with a formulation which "confessed two natures united in Christ, [and] one will and one operation according to Cyril [of Alexandria]."[29] But for the stubborn Syrians this was nothing more than Nestorianism combined with the heresy of Leo. When at last they refused to give the emperor communion or even consider accepting his compromise formulation, Heraclius lost all patience, declaring that he would sever the nose and ears and pillage the home of anyone who did not accept the Council of Chalcedon.[30]

Chalcedon's proclamation of "the two indivisible and unconfused natures in Jesus Christ our God"[31] had obviously failed to arrive at a confession of the faith that would be accepted throughout the empire. During the succeeding one hundred years, the Chalcedonian Christological formulation had drifted unmistakably toward an interpretation more in line with that of Cyril of Alexandria and hence closer to the Monophysite point of view. The *Henotikon*, issued by the emperor Zeno in 482, attempted to resolve the dogmatic impasse that followed Chalcedon by seeking to appease the Monophysites. But by essentially capitulating to the Monophysite position, it had created a breach with Rome.[32] In 551, the emperor Justinian I attempted to arrive at a "mediating position" which, known as neo-Chalcedonianism, was ambiguous on the critical question of whether the incarnate *Logos* had one or two natures.[33] Justinian's equivocal position regarding the natures of Christ was adopted by the Fifth Ecumenical Council in 553 which, accordingly, did no more to resolve the pivotal point of divergence between Monophysites and Dyophisites than had Chalcedon or anything that had followed it.[34]

The crises that confronted the empire at the beginning of the seventh century made it more important than ever to arrive at a conceptual accord among the two opposing Christological positions that would lead to a dogmatic unity indispensable for the very survival of the realm. Heraclius had to arrive at a religious accommodation that would achieve the political goal of rallying the oriental and still Monophysite churches of Syria, Palestine, and Egypt to the aid of Constantinople against the barbarian invaders.[35] Although the situation presented a conundrum that seemed incapable of being resolved, the emperor desperately needed a solution in order to preserve "the unity of his tottering empire."[36] Heraclius had hoped that the Christological formula he had proposed to the Syrian bishops might meet Monophysite objections to Chalcedon's "in two natures" by glossing that definition with the addition of words that spoke of Christ's "one will," thereby introducing reassuring language more familiar to them.[37] But the emperor's conciliatory compromise, which was regarded by both sides of the controversy as nothing more than the promulgation of doctrinal heresy for political reasons, turned out to be an abysmal failure.[38] It both infuriated the strict Chalcedonians and earned the ridicule of the Monophysites, who chortled mockingly that "[I]t is not we who have communicated with Chalcedon, but rather Chalcedon with us by confessing one nature of Christ through the one energy."[39] But the shame which Theophanes records the emperor felt at the reception accorded to what came to be known as Monothelitism was far less than the anathemas it earned at the Sixth Ecumenical Council for all those who had had a role in propagating it.[40] Among the first of those execrated was patriarch Sergius of Constantinople, Monothelitism's principal architect and the one whom the Council declared had been "the first to write on this impious doctrine."[41]

Sergius had become patriarch of Constantinople on April 18, 610, only six months before Heraclius arrived from Africa to dethrone Phocas.[42] He had previously been a deacon at Haghia Sophia as well as guardian of the harbor, thereby suggesting that he had already achieved a position of importance in the city since this office indicated involvement in the regulation and reception of commodities into the capital, especially grain for the bread dole.[43] Sergius had officiated at Heraclius's coronation in October 610, at the marriage of the new emperor to his fiancée Eudokia, and at the baptism of the imperial couple's daughter Epiphaneia the following August.[44] When the empress Eudokia died in 612 and Heraclius announced his intention of marrying his niece Martina, the patriarch "put earnest pressure on him by letter and admonished him to repudiate his connection with this woman," since the proposed union clearly came within the prohibited degrees of kinship. Sergius seems by then to have already achieved a close relationship with Heraclius for, although the emperor proceeded with his marriage plans, he wrote the patriarch, recognizing both the soundness of his advice and acknowledging that Sergius had already paid him "the obligation you owe me as high priest and friend."[45] Sergius seems to have relented enough in his reservations about the union to crown Martina Augusta and to baptize their son Heraklonas, but the first two sons of the marriage were both born with defects: the elder had "a paralyzed neck which he could not turn in any direction" and the younger was deaf.[46] Heraclius would henceforth pay far closer attention to the patriarch's admonitions.

By the time Heraclius departed on his first campaign against the Persians in 622, Sergius's prestige had risen to such a degree that the emperor entrusted the care of Constantinople and of his own son jointly to the Theotokos and the patriarch, investing Sergius and the patrician Bonosos with responsibility for conducting "the business of state."[47] Four years later, the city was to face the greatest threat to its existence since its foundation by Constantine the Great three centuries earlier, and Sergius would play a crucial role in its deliverance. A foretaste of the cataclysmic events that were to occur in 626 took place in May of that year when Sergius succeeded in appeasing a crowd that had risen against one John Seismos, a high city official who had incurred the mob's anger by favoring the soldiers over the general population, including the imperial guards units, in connection with the bread dole.[48] But the protests of the citizens over the bread distribution were nothing in comparison with the events that unfolded the following month.

In the beginning of June, the Persian army appeared at Chalcedon on the Asian shore of the Bosphorus directly across from Constantinople. While awaiting the arrival of the Avars on the capital's west flank, the Persians set fire to Chalcedon's homes and churches.[49] On June 26 an Avar vanguard of reportedly about 30,000 men appeared along the Long Walls to the west of the city from where it steadily advanced toward the capital. Rejecting all imperial offers of conciliation short of total capitulation, the Avars arrived at Constantinople's walls on July 29. The attack on the city began two days later, when the Avar forces, now 80,000 strong and armed with a vast array of war machinery, massed before the Gate of Philoxenou.[50] The barbarian offensive, which began on July 31 and lasted for six days thereafter, reached its climax on August 7, when imperial forces defeated the Avars in a decisive naval battle that resulted in such slaughter that "the sea was dyed with much blood."[51]

Contemporary accounts of the Avar siege give Sergius a great deal of the credit not only for bolstering the city's morale during the crisis, but especially for the prayers and intercessions that he offered on its behalf to the Theotokos, who emerged from the episode as the special protector of Constantinople from that moment until the city fell to the Turks in 1453.[52] The most effusive praise for his efforts appears in the epic poem *Bellum Avaricum* by Sergius's private secretary George of Pisidia, whose often fulsome verses extolling the patriarch's role in the siege were doubtless owing, in large measure, to the bishop's patronage.[53] As the Avars appeared on the horizon, George recites, the citizens considered sending an embassy led by Sergius to persuade Heraclius, who was in the East fighting the Persians, to return and defend the city. But because they feared that such a mission would expose the patriarch to excessive danger and risk the loss of the empire's two celestial bodies, it was decided that he remain in the capital.[54] During the siege, Sergius participated in every important decision taken in response to the Avar threat. This included participating in an imperial council held at the darkest point of the siege on August 2, where, in the presence of the royal prince and the senate, it was decided to send an embassy to the Avars to sue for peace.[55]

But his greatest contributions to the salvation of the city were the invocations he offered to the Mother of God, which succeeded in convincing the Theotokos to champion the imperial cause.[56] Sergius began by setting icons of the Virgin at each of the western gates of the capital as safeguards against an Avar intrusion.[57] Then, taking up an icon of the Theotokos as well as her robe, the treasured relic of the Virgin's church at Blachernae, the patriarch conducted a procession of priests and monks around the city's walls offering litanies "beseeching God for his speediest help."[58] Through ceaseless prayers and vigils, Sergius was able to enlist the help of God's Mother in vanquishing the barbarians. Although the Virgin was credited with sinking the Avar fleet in the final battle on the Golden Horn, it was, the Byzantines insisted, the patriarch's tireless efforts that had persuaded her to do so.[59]

It was hardly astonishing, therefore, that Heraclius believed he had found in Sergius the *eminence grise* who would produce a solution to the riddle that had eluded two ecumenical councils and nearly every emperor since Marcian. If Sergius could bring superhuman assistance to Byzantium's aid against the invaders from the West, surely he could find a way to bring the obstinate Monophysites to the city's cause against the invaders from the East. It appears that the wily patriarch had anticipated the need to reach such a *modus vivendi* far sooner than the emperor, for as early as 615, with the Persians camped uncomfortably close at Chalcedon, he had begun to set his hand toward solving the enigmatic Christological quarrel between Monophysites and Chalcedonians and the political implications which flowed from it. Eventually, Heraclius joined in these initiatives.[60] But while both emperor and patriarch had begun to reach out to the Monophysites even before 626, we shall see that their energies thereafter were redoubled. The shock resulting from the near loss of Constantinople itself had convinced them of the absolute urgency of achieving a religious accommodation that would weld the Monophysites to the imperial side and thereby suppress the internal strife that threatened the very existence of the empire.[61] They could hardly have imagined that the doctrinal bases for frustrating their painstaking efforts to make religion, through Monothelitism, the servant of politics would be articulated at a synod of predominantly Latin bishops assembled in Rome through the combined efforts of two Easterners, one of whom was an aged and intractable Constantinopolitan monk named Maximos and the other a Greco-Palestinian, who assumed the Papacy as Theodore I.

Between the time the Persians appeared at Chalcedon in 615 and before the fall of Alexandria in 619, Sergius had begun corresponding with a number of predominantly Monophysite bishops in an effort to reach some common ground upon which an accommodation on Christology might be achieved. Whether his efforts to create a "bridge toward the Monophysites" were truly motivated by political considerations or whether he was a crypto-Monophysite surreptitiously planning to overturn the Council of Chalcedon remains an intriguing question. Both Theophanes Confessor and Anastasios Sinaites appear to have believed that since Sergius was of Syrian origin and the son of Jacobite parents he sympathized with the Monophysites and probably espoused Monothelitism even before he began to canvass opinions as to its doctrinal soundness. It seems that both writers suspected a conspiracy between Sergius and another Syrian, Athanasios Camelarios, the Monophysite patriarch of Antioch, to obtain Heraclius's approval of Monothelitism as a first step toward reversing Chalcedon and sanctioning Monophysitism as orthodox doctrine. Theophanes and Anastasios Sinaites both record that the emperor was approached by Athanasios, who falsely confessed that he was a Chalcedonian, only so that Heraclius would confirm him in the see of Antioch. Once he had obtained that assurance, Athanasios broached the subject of Christ's wills and energies with the emperor. At that point, the emperor consulted with Sergius, whose reply "confessed and propounded in writing one natural will and one energy in Christ." This delighted Athanasios, and by implication Sergius as well, since "if only one energy was recognized, one nature would thereby be acknowledged."[62]

The patriarch's overtures at a Christological accommodation solicited authoritative opinions from his correspondents on the question of Christ's energy and will, and appear to have used as their point of departure the Λόγος Δογματικός, or dogmatic pronouncement, of his predecessor patriarch Menas of Constantinople (536–552) in which Menas had offered his views on the subject to Pope Vigilius.[63] Sometime before 619, Sergius appears to have sent Menas's pronouncement to Theodore, bishop of Pharan in the Sinai, with a request, communicated through the Egyptian Monophysite bishop Sergius Macaronas of Antinoe, that Theodore provide the patriarch with his opinion on the issue of Christ's will and energy in light of Menas's writings.[64] Theodore seems to have assured Sergius, through the bishop of Antinoe, that there was indeed patristic support for the doctrine that Christ possessed a single energy or operation.[65] In addition to Theodore of Pharan, Sergius wrote to George Arsas, alleged by Maximos Confessor to have been a Paulician, asking that he provide him with similar citations.[66] Finally, the patriarch sent Menas's pronouncement, along with Theodore of Pharan's acquiesence in the single energy concept, to Paul Monophthalmos, a prominent Monophysite and leader of the Severan sect, hoping to elicit a favorable response from him as well. In the meantime, Paul had left Cyprus, where he had been residing, and traveled to Theodosiopolis in Armenia where he had engaged in discussions on the subject of Christ's energies with Heraclius shortly after the emperor's first sortie against the Persians in April, 622.[67] But neither Sergius's efforts nor the talks with Heraclius had persuaded the obstinate Monophysite. Sometime in 623, the emperor ordered Paul confined to Cyprus, declaring in an edict issued at the same time to archbishop Arkadios of Cyprus, that henceforth orthodox doctrine forbade any profession that Christ possessed two energies.[68] By doing so the emperor, guided no doubt by Sergius's skillful hand, had taken a momentous step away from Chalcedon, and had opened the door to the possibility of arriving at a formula in which the *Logos* could be said to possess one energy.[69] Paul Monophthalmos and the difficult Monophysites might yet be brought around.

By 626, events had progressed to the point where it appeared that an accommodation between Chalcedonians and Monophysites might be achieved on the basis of Monoenergism, a doctrine that recognized Christ's two natures but professed His single energy or operation.[70] While in Lazika in the western Caucasus, Heraclius had engaged in discussions with Bishop Cyrus of Phasis, who seemed to be amenable to the Monoenergistic formulation. After Sergius provided Cyrus with various patristic references in support of the single energy doctrine, including Menas's dogmatic pronouncement, the bishop of Phasis not only embraced Monoenergism but would become one of its most fervent and successful proponents.[71] Cyrus's conversion to Monoenergism would give Sergius a productive ally in his unionist efforts toward the Monophysites. Further support would come in 626, when a council assembled in Constantinople gave the new doctrinal creation its first *imprimatur* by a synod of bishops.[72]

The Armenian Monophysites adopted Monoenergism at a synod held in Theodosiopolis in 633.[73] At about the same time, or perhaps a few years earlier, Sergius and Heraclius had attempted to reach a similar accommodation with the Syrian Monophysites through Athanasios Camelarios, the Jacobite patriarch of Antioch, but it is uncertain whether an agreement based upon the compromise formulation was ever achieved.[74] Monoenergism experienced its first significant triumph during the early summer of 633 in the same year that the Arab conquest of the East began with Arab raids into Palestine.[75] Two years earlier, Cyrus of Phasis, who as we have seen had espoused the new Christological formula at a crucial point in its life, was transferred from the obscurity of the western Caucasus and enthroned as patriarch of Alexandria.[76] Having proved both his loyalty to the imperial cause and shown his skill in fashioning an ecclesiastical bridge between Chalcedonians and Monophysites, Cyrus appeared eminently suited to the critical mission of establishing the religious unity of Egypt.[77]

Cyrus could hardly contain his exuberance when he announced to Sergius that at an archieratical divine liturgy celebrated at the cathedral of Alexandria on June 3, 633, the entire clergy of the Theodosian segment of the Egyptian Monophysites, as well as the highest civil and military figures and a vast crowd of the faithful, had received communion from his hands and confessed the truth of Monoenergism. He praised the divine illumination that had led both the emperor and Sergius to this doctrine and, as for himself, hoped only that they would find no fault in his implementation of what was, of course, their great accomplishment.[78] But the patriarch's self-effacement concealed what had indeed been a remarkable achievement. The agreement, which was contained in a document consisting of nine chapters, affirmed Cyril of Alexandria's language confessing "one incarnate nature of the divine *Logos*," which was so cherished by the Monophysites, with the gloss that what Cyril meant was "one hypostasis composed of two natures." It added, however, Chalcedon's affirmation that the Logos consisted *in* two natures, but that Christ "acted divinely and humanly through one divino-human [theandric] energy, as the divine Dionysios said."[79] The compromise with the Theodosian Monophysites thus retained the ancient rallying cry of the Monophysite movement as articulated by Cyril of Alexandria, affirmed the "in two natures" language of Chalcedon, and proclaimed a single theandric energy based upon the authority of the hallowed Areopagite, without offering any refinements or explanations that might be problematic for the Monophysites.[80]

Cyrus's Monoenergist compromise, which he assured Sergius had brought joy "even to the heavenly beings," was not as well or as widely received among the Egyptian Monophysites as it appeared.[81] Although it seems to have been embraced by the greater part of the urban clergy of Alexandria and the influential Monophysite bishops Cyrus of Nikiu and Victor of Fayum, the hard-line Monophysites outside of Alexandria condemned the capitulation of their coreligionists, attributing their departure from the true faith to the lure of "bribes and honors . . . persuasion and deceit." The bishops of Nikiu and Fayum were reviled for having succumbed to Cyrus's "fishing line of error." For those unyielding adherents to Monophysitism, Monoenergism was simply Chalcedon in disguise. It would have been better, wrote Severus of Asmounein, for the apostates to have hidden or, following the example of Menas, brother of the Jacobite patriarch Benjamin, to have had their teeth knocked out and been placed in a sack filled with sand and cast into the sea, rather than to have surrendered their faith.[82]

Although Theophanes ridiculed the Egyptian settlement as a "union written in water," the catholic faith had suffered a severe blow as Monophysites derided Chalcedon "in taverns and baths," chortling that the Chalcedonians had come "to their senses and returned to the truth when they united with us in the one nature of Christ by way of the one energy."[83] Intentionally or not, the Alexandrian compromise had raised the fundamental problem of "maintaining, within the 'hypostatic' union an existentially real, and therefore *actively* created humanity" in Christ.[84] Constantinople's "ingenious politico-religious construction" threatened the very essence of Chalcedonian orthodoxy.[85] Although the rapture of reunion had for the moment stilled the voices of Chalcedon's champions, its defenders would not long remain as "mute as fish."[86]

The late-fifth-century monastery of St. Theodosios stands on the top of a hill west of Bethlehem containing the cave where the Magi are said to have rested after adoring the Christ child.[87] Sophronios returned to St. Theodosios from Rome in 619 to bury the body of his friend John Moschos and seems to have remained there until the late 620s, when, harassed by the increasing Arab raids, he and a retinue of monks fled westward along the Mediterranean shore until they reached Byzantine Africa in the early 630s.[88] Maximos Confessor seems to have left the monastery of Chrysopolis, across the straits from Constantinople, sometime around the famous siege of 626, sojourned for a time in Crete,[89] and in 627 or 628 left for Africa, where he was present for Pentecost in 632, having preceded the arrival of Sophronios and his group.[90] According to Maximos's Syriac life, however, he had been raised at the Judean monastery of St. Chariton and thus may have known Sophronios, who was living close by at St. Theodosios, well before the two met in Africa in the early 630s. The Syriac life, which is decidedly hostile to Maximos, recites that he, his disciple Anastasios, and "the other brethren with him," fled from Palestine in the face of the Arab invasions and, like Sophronios, traveled westward along the Mediterranean coast until they reached Africa. On the way, they are said to have spent time at an African monastery known as Hippo Diarrhytus, whose abbot and eighty-seven monks were Nestorians.[91] In any event, between about 632 and 641, Africa became the *situs* of a substantial monastic community consisting of exiled Eastern monks who included Maximos, Sophronios (until his departure for Alexandria in 633), and members of Sophronios's brotherhood, whose name *Eukratades* was taken from the eponym of their venerable spiritual father John Moschos.[92]

During their time together in Africa, Maximos and Sophronios formed a close relationship. Maximos referred to Sophronios as his "blessed lord, father, and master," and the degree of devotion forged at this time surfaced years later in the vigor with which Maximos defended Sophronios against charges made by the exiled patriarch Pyrrhus of Constantinople that Sophronios had departed from orthodox doctrine.[93] Strangely enough, it was the very defense of orthodoxy that drew Maximos and Sophronios together, for, as Maximos later wrote, it was during this time that the two discussed "the perversities relating to the faith [that] were being made up."[94] Until 633, there seems to have been no opposition voiced by the Chalcedonians against Sergius's Monoenergist doctrine.[95] In a letter to John Kubikularios written in 626, Maximos alluded to Christ's energy in a way that suggests that the formulation Sergius was proposing, and with which Maximos had to have been familiar, posed no particular problem.[96] It was only when Maximos encountered Sophronios in Africa sometime in 632 or early 633, and was instructed in the implications of the Monoenergist Christology, that he came to realize the danger that it posed for Chalcedonian orthodoxy. Maximos's failure to apprehend the peril which Monoenergism presented to Chalcedon seems to have been the product of sheer ignorance resulting from a lack of authoritative patristic texts on the subject. Sophronios, however, arrived in Africa armed with two codices in which he had assembled some six hundred citations from the fathers demonstrating the errors of Monoenergism.[97] Maximos was enormously impressed with the quantity of Sophronios's books and reveled in the enlightenment he was able to derive from them. Empowered by the authority of the fathers, Maximos wrote to Peter the Illustrious in Egypt that, with the aid of Sophronios's codices, he was able as never before to understand and articulate the doctrinal errors presented by Monoenergism. He encouraged the pious layman to seek out both Sophronios and his texts through which he was sure to be enriched in "divine things."[98] For by early 633, Sophronios had left Africa bound for Alexandria prepared to confront Cyrus and challenge the novel doctrine with which the patriarch had embraced the Egyptian Monophysites.[99]

Sophronios appears to have arrived in Alexandria before consummation of the agreement between Cyrus and the Monophysites since the patriarch, probably out of respect for his learning and devotion, allowed Sophronios to read the nine chapters of the act of union before they were promulgated. Sophronios was aghast at Cyrus's lapse into what he said was Apollinarianism.[100] But the patriarch was unmoved by his objections, citing patristic texts of his own in support of Monoenergism. In any event, Cyrus insisted, a matter of words should not be an impediment to the salvation of souls. Neither Sophronios's prostration at his feet nor his flood of tears were sufficient to move the patriarch.[101] Sophronios left Alexandria frustrated and desperate, hoping to find a more receptive ear for his entreaties in the patriarch of Constantinople. Little did he suspect that his puta-tive ally in the capital had been the chief architect of the doctrine Sophronios was about to ask him to condemn.

Sophronios's remonstrances with Sergius about Monoenergism and Cyrus's act of union with the Egyptian Monophysites based upon that formula seem to have achieved at least some success for the Chalcedonian cause. In an effort to end what the patriarch of Constantinople described as a battle over words, while at the same time recognizing the possible danger of heresy, in August 633, he agreed to issue his *Psephos*, or authoritative opinion, which approved the Alexandrian settlement but henceforth forbade any discussion of whether Christ possessed one or two energies.[102] In this way, Sergius hoped to assuage Sophronios and the Chalcedonians by avoiding language that hinted at a slide toward Monophysitism while simultaneously prohibiting talk of two energies, which scandalized many as both lacking patristic support and leading to the possibility that Christ might have had two opposing wills.[103] Sergius appears to have believed that his concession had appeased Sophronios, for he declared that Sophronios had consented to it and that he had set sail from Constanti-nople satisfied with the patriarch Sergius's promise that he would commit his declaration to writing and send it on to Sophronios in Jerusalem.[104] Sergius then hastened to inform Heraclius, who was still in the East, of the accommodation he had made to Sophronios in the *Psephos*, advising the emperor that he had done so in order to suppress the great disturbances that discussions over Christ's energies and operations had created.[105] For his part, the emperor was pleased to accede to any religious compromise that would yield political solidarity between his Chalcedonian and Monophysite subjects. Based on Sergius's assurances that the *Psephos* would achieve such a result, Heraclius placed his *imprimatur* on the patriarch's pronouncement by issuing his *Keleusis*, or imperial rescript, approving its contents.[106]

At about the same time Sergius wrote to assure Sophronios that all further discussions regarding Christ's one or two energies were to be forbidden, the pa-triarch of Constantinople communicated with Pope Honorius I advising him of the accommodation that he had reached in the face of Sophronios's objections to Monoenergism. Sergius invited the Roman pontiff to examine his statements, correct what might be erroneous, and advise him of his opinion on what he had written.[107] It was the first time since Sergius had begun his initiative toward reaching an accommodation with the Monophysites nearly twenty years earlier that he informed a Roman pope of his efforts or solicited the Papacy's views on their doctrinal soundness.[108] Honorius's reply praised Sergius for eschewing all reference to energies, since such language, the pope warned, had no support in Scripture, among the fathers, or at any of the church councils and indeed, if pursued further, would surely lead to Nestorianism or Eutychianism.[109] As far as the pope was concerned, orthodox doctrine knew nothing of energies and recognized instead "one will of our Lord Jesus Christ."[110] Honorius's apologists would forever after argue that the unsuspecting pontiff, convinced that the entire debate was a childish quarrel over words better left to grammarians than theologians, had fallen into a trap intentionally set by the scheming patriarch of Constantinople.[111]

Maximos Confessor took great pains to prove that Honorius had been doctrinally sound, and that his apparent lapse into heresy was simply an error in translation.[112] Indeed, he appears to have gone so far as to send his disciple Anastasios to Rome to interview those who may have been in a position to know what the pope had meant by the expression *unam voluntatem*. Despite clear and unambiguous language professing that Christ possessed one will, Anastasios reported that he had determined Honorius had been free of all doctrinal error. He had apparently spoken with those who had written Honorius's letter to Sergius since it appears that the pope's secretary, Abbot John Symponos, had entrusted the task of rendering the pope's Latin into Greek to certain scribes, who had admitted their errors in translating to Anastasios. John Symponos himself also confirmed that Honorius had never subscribed to the "one will" doctrine, but that such an erroneous impression had been given by those who had translated the pope's Latin into Greek.[113] But Maximos's effort was useless. Honorius may have hoped that he had forever closed the door on any discussion of energies, but his careless phrase had moved the centuries' old Christological debate into what would be yet another dimension. Monoenergism had died but Monothelitism had been conceived, and an inattentive Roman pope, rather than a conniving patriarch of Constantinople, had been its procreator.[114]

Sophronios returned to Jerusalem, where he was elected patriarch, apparently pleased that Monoenergism had been suppressed.[115] Cyrus of Alexandria's efforts to bring about unity with the Egyptian Monophysites was warmly lauded by Pope Honorius, although the formula by which it had been achieved was disapproved.[116] Both Rome and Constantinople had agreed to abandon henceforth all talk of whether Christ possessed one or two energies. For a brief time in late 633, it appeared that the Christological quarrels that had consumed the Church for centuries had finally been resolved. But the calm was not to endure for long. Between the time he had departed from the capital and was enthroned as patriarch of Jerusalem in early 634, Sophronios appears to have continued to brood over the matter of Christ's energies. Although he recognized that both the *Psephos* and the *Keleusis* had forbidden all discourse that inclined toward "counting" energies, he seems to have been troubled by an inability to reconcile a Christology that confessed Christ's two natures with a rejection of the idea that the *Logos* possessed a single energy. Sophronios articulated this unease in the synodical letter that he sent, as was the custom, to his fellow patriarchs as an expression of his doctrinal orthodoxy.[117] Although couched in conciliatory terms that carefully avoided any talk of one or two energies, the letter nonetheless insisted that each of Christ's two natures must correspond to its own essential and natural energy, and that accordingly, Christ's dual natures necessarily gave rise to an energy, divine and human, proper to each nature.[118] Without ever once in the course of his lengthy letter saying that Christ possessed two energies, Sophronios simply asserted that there are in Christ as many energies as there are natures, and that each such nature has its own corresponding energy.[119]

Whether Sophronios's views were his own pronouncements or were also approved and promulgated by a synod of bishops in Jerusalem remains uncertain.[120] Sergius considered the synodical letter both a breach of Sophronios's promise and a violation of both the *Psephos* and the *Keleusis*. Honorius seems to have been moved by its logic, but he retreated from endorsing it, repeating instead his appeal to desist from all talk of energies.[121] If Honorius's letter to Sergius had articulated the conceptual framework that would take shape as Monothelitism, then Sophronios's synodical letter became the manifesto of Dyothelitism, although never once did the patriarch of Jerusalem utter a single word about Christ's wills.[122] Once more, however, political events in the East would impact upon the formulation of religious doctrine. As the great cities of Syria and Palestine tumbled successively into Arab hands, the same reasons that had caused Constantinople to reach out to the dissident Monophysites of those regions during the Persian invasions rekindled the impetus to achieve a Christological *modus vivendi* with them in the face of the Islamic threat. Yet again, the embattled emperor looked to his beleaguered patriarch to untangle the Christological imbroglio, and once more Sergius set his hand to the task.

The prospects for achieving a solution were bleak. Despite nearly two decades of persistent efforts, Constantinople's politics of religious unification had failed miserably.[123] Except for winning over the urban clergy of Alexandria and scattered bishops and monks in Palestine and Syria, Monophysites had resolutely resisted the Monoenergist compromise.[124] Sophronios had stirred the sluggish Chalcedonians, who now awakened to the dangers lurking within Sergius's formula. Meanwhile, the Islamic advances into imperial territory begged for an accommodation among the subjects of the Christian empire that would unite them in resisting the "stinging bites of the Arabian wolves."[125] By 636, Sergius appears to have arrived at a Christological formula that he had reason to believe would be acceptable to both sides. Consistent with the *Psephos* and *Keleusis*, it abandoned all talk of energies and fastened instead upon Christ's *single* will, thus employing a concept articulated by no less a Chalcedonian than Pope Honorius and which the patriarch was therefore certain would be agreeable to Dyophysites. On the other hand, by eschewing altogether any formulation that attempted to define Christ's energies and focusing instead upon his *unitary* will, Sergius hoped to please Monophysites both by using language of reassuring familiarity and by making it appear that he was categorically rejecting Sophronios's synodical letter, which by now had become a shibboleth for the Chalcedonians.[126] Sergius seems to have presented his proposal, which came to be known as the *Ekthesis* or Exposition, to Heraclius after the emperor returned from the East, probably after the disastrous Byzantine defeat at Jabiya-Yarmuk in 636.[127] The emperor appears to have entertained reservations about the *Ekthesis*, doubtless accounting for the fact that he withheld approving it for nearly two years.[128] It was not until some-time in September or October 638 that the *Ekthesis* was finally published, and shortly thereafter, in late November or early December 638, approved at a synod in Constantinople and affixed to the wall of the narthex of the Great Church of Haghia Sophia as the expression of imperial orthodoxy.[129]

Monothelitism was now the official faith of the empire. By the end of the year, with the exception of the emperor, the principal antagonists in the long Christo-logical battle that had resulted in its promulgation were all dead: Sophronios had succumbed in March, Honorius in October, and Sergius in December.[130] Sergius, bishop of Joppa, would, with the assistance of the civil authorities, uncanonically install himself as patriarch of Jerusalem and ordain a Monothelite hierarchy that would split the Palestinian church between the few remaining Chalcedonians and those who adhered to the new creed espoused by Constantinople.[131] Eusta-thios, the imperial military commander dispatched to Italy to notify the exarch Isaac of the *Ekthesis* and to convey the emperor's directive that the exarch obtain the pope's adherence to it, would find the chair of St. Peter empty.[132] Pyrrhus, the new patriarch of Constantinople and Sergius's handpicked successor, would quickly convene a synod in January 639 and reaffirm Monothelitism as official imperial doctrine.[133] Chalcedon was dangerously close to extinction. If its Chris-tological confession was not to be relegated to a mere footnote in the history of the Church, it desperately needed an articulate advocate of Sophronios's impres-sive intellectual caliber and literary skills. The patriarchates of the East offered no hope of a successor to him. Constantinople and Jerusalem were firmly in the hands of Monothelites. At Antioch, Athanasios Camelarios had been succeeded by the Monophysite John Sedra.[134] Cyrus of Alexandria, who had engineered the Monoenergist compromise with a segment of the Egyptian Monophysites, had no difficulty in making the subtle shift to Monothelitism.[135] Benjamin I, the rival Monophysite patriarch of Alexandria, presided over the vast body of Monophysites in Egypt who had resisted the accord. In Rome, the Papacy was vacant and would remain so for well over a year and a half.[136] The pope who was to succeed Honorius would soon show his resistance to the *Ekthesis*, but for the moment the church of Rome lay silent. It was far to the West in distant Africa that the voice of Sophronios could still be heard as the vigorous and brilliant Constantinopolitan monk Maximos Confessor now began with uncompromising persistence to sound Chalcedon's cry.

Maximos was perfectly situated to launch his polemic against the *Ekthesis* and the Monothelitism that it espoused. He enjoyed the support and protection of the African exarch George, who had shown resistance in obeying Constanti-nople's directives in other areas and who saw an opportunity to further his own political goals by facilitating and promoting Maximos's opposition to the official religious policy being proclaimed in the capital.[137] It was during these years in Africa that the Monothelites later accused Maximos of having conspired against Constans II by foretelling the African exarch's victory over the emperor, and the Monophysites reviled his stirrings for Chalcedon as evidence that he was "no true monk."[138] But, as a result of the safety of his geographical position and the political patronage of the exarch, beginning around 640 Maximos was able to start an energetic campaign against the Monothelite heresy.[139] Significantly, it was at this time that Maximos articulated the method that he would utilize to examine theological questions and to determine whether a particular belief could be authenticated and validated and hence whether it did or did not express doctrinal truth. Drawing upon his early monastic training at Chrysopolis, the discussions that he had had years earlier with Sophronios, as well as upon the voluminous patristic texts which he had received from him, Maximos concluded that doctrinal truth was received through succession from the fathers and councils, and that the only acceptable method of arriving at such truth was "to confess the voices of the fathers."[140] Accordingly, any attempt to determine whether a particular doctrine was correct required that one begin by confirming whether it found support in any of the councils, beginning with Nicaea in 325, and among the early fathers of the Church. It was their exposition of Scripture alone, as handed down through succeeding councils and subsequent patristic authorities, that formed the seamless garment known as holy tradition.[141] If a particular doctrine could withstand an examination that proved its fidelity to holy tradition, then it could safely be accepted as truth. If not, then it was novel and innovative and must be rejected as heresy.[142] When sometime in 640 Maximos wrote the Cypriot deacon Marinos labeling the doctrine announced in the *Ekthesis* as καινή, or new, he signaled unmistakably that Monothelitism had been subjected to the test for theological truth and had failed.[143] It was a position from which he never retreated.

While Maximos was mobilizing ecclesiastical opinion against the *Ekthesis* from Africa, envoys from Rome had arrived in Constantinople sometime in the spring of 640 to petition for issuance of the *iussio* authorizing the consecration of Severinus as pope. When they were told that before the *iussio* could be issued the candidate would have to subscribe to the *Ekthesis*, the *apokrisiarii* hesitated, saying that they could not speak for the future pope but would have to allow him to examine the document and make his own decision whether or not to accept it. Issues of faith, they politely protested, could not be resolved by force, but rather by reference to whether they were consistent with the teachings of the apostles and the councils.[144] Maximos later claimed that the envoys presented their position with such faith and sincerity that the imperial officials relented, and the *iussio* was issued without a formal acceptance of the *Ekthesis* by the Roman church.[145] But it may well have been the arrival of a generous portion of the loot that the exarch Isaac had plundered from the papal residence on the Lateran and sent to Heraclius in Constantinople, rather than the piety of the papal envoys, that had softened imperial resolve over Roman acceptance of the *Ekthesis*.[146] Consecrated on May 28, 640, Severinus wasted little time in convening a synod that condemned the *Ekthesis*, thereby sending Constantinople a clear message that the church of Rome was not prepared to capitulate to pressure from the East and compromise doctrinal truth for political expediency.[147] Although Severinus was dead by August 640, he had lived long enough to take the momentous step of placing the enormous prestige of the Apostolic See on the side of Chalcedonian orthodoxy. Across the Mediterranean, Maximos no doubt realized what an important ally he had gained.

Severinus's successor, the Dalmatian John IV, was equally resolute in his rejection of the *Ekthesis*. It appears that he also refused to accept it as a condition to the issuance of the *iussio* authorizing his consecration as pope, and that, as in the case of Severinus, the emperor dropped his insistence. In addition to permitting the consecration to proceed, moreover, Heraclius wrote the pope regretting the dissension that had arisen over the *Ekthesis*, whose authorship he ascribed entirely to Sergius, and emphasizing that he had had no part in its formulation.[148] It is impossible to determine with any certainty whether Heraclius was distancing himself from the *Ekthesis* since he had begun to entertain doubts about its political efficacy or because of his personal convictions about the doctrine it espoused, or perhaps both.[149] The issue, however, shortly became moot when on February 11, 641, the emperor who had ruled Byzantium for three of the most tumultuous decades of its existence, died of dropsy, bringing to the throne a brief period of joint rule by his sons Constantine III and Heraklonas.[150]

In January 641, before Heraclius died, John IV had convened a local Roman synod that condemned the *Ekthesis* and "proclaimed two natures and energies in our Master and God Jesus Christ."[151] Shortly thereafter, the pope composed an apology on behalf of his predecessor Honorius directed to Constantine III, which endeavored both to explain the errors of Monothelitism and to provide a justification for Honorius's apparently errant phraseology.[152] John IV urged the new emperor to remove the *Ekthesis* from the narthex of the Great Church of Haghia Sophia as offensive to both the *Tome* of Leo and the teachings of Chalcedon.[153] At about the same time, the pontiff expressed his sentiments against the *Ekthesis* to patriarch Pyrrhus, whom he attempted to enlist in the battle against Monothelitism.[154] The pope dispatched Rome's synodal pronouncement against the *Ekthesis*, as well as his apology for Honorius, to Constantinople, wisely choosing as his envoy the archdeacon Barsika, a Syrian who had achieved a high position in the papal service and who was doubtless fluent in Greek.[155] But by the time Barsika had reached the capital, the brother-emperors were dead and had been succeeded by Heraclius's ten-year-old grandson, who ascended to the purple on November 9, 641, as Constans II.[156]

Although Barsika had to linger in Constantinople some ten months after Constans had been enthroned, waiting for a reply to the pope's communications, his return to Rome in the summer of 642 must have been filled with joy because of the news he was carrying. The new emperor had written to reassure the pontiff that he subscribed to the doctrine that Christ possessed two natures and two wills, and that he was entirely in accord with the Council of Chalcedon.[157] But by the time Barsika arrived in Rome, John IV was dead and his successor was in place.[158] The Romans had moved quickly to elect a new pope. They had departed from the custom of choosing a Latin drawn from the ranks of the diaconate and who had spent time in the capital as papal *apokrisiarios*. Instead, they settled upon Theodore I, a Greek[159] from Palestine whose father, also named Theodore, had been a bishop in Jerusalem.[160] The new pope's father had been an auxiliary bishop of the Jerusalem patriarchate and may have been ordained by Sophronios himself or by his predecessor Modestos. As a Chalcedonian, he had most likely been displaced from his see by one of the uncanonical bishops ordained by Sergius of Joppa after Sophronios's death and, as a result, had fled to Rome along with his son the future pope in the late 630s.[161]

Anticipating the worst from Constantinople, the papal electors, who included the high Roman clergy, had put aside their personal interests, ambitions, and apprehensions and had chosen a candidate who in every respect appeared best suited to lead the battle against the heresy that had spread throughout the East and was threatening to engulf the entire Church.[162] If, as it appeared, it had once more become Rome's burden to defend orthodoxy against Eastern lapses into heresy, the Papacy had to be occupied by a pontiff with certain definable qualities and abilities.[163] It was especially important that the new pope have the skill needed to disentangle the subtle linguistic machinations for which the Greeks were famous and which, true or not, the Romans believed had snared the unfortunate Honorius. A knowledge of Greek such as that possessed by a native speaker who knew its idiomatic niceties, was therefore essential.[164]

The prospect of choosing a Greek as pope must have resurrected in the Romans a host of historic suspicions that many Westerners had harbored for centuries against the East. Occidental skepticism of oriental proclivity to engage in theological speculation and thereby lapse into heresy, and worst of all paganism, was not easily overcome. To a great extent, however, the influx of Easterners into Rome as a consequence of the political convulsions and religious controversies that had plagued the eastern part of the empire in the early seventh century had softened those ancient hostilities. The Greek abbot John Symponos had risen to become Pope Honorius's "secretary of state" and personal assistant.[165] Honorius had also entrusted various significant missions to Easterners. The Syrian subdeacon Sergius was dispatched to deal with the matter of certain excommunicated Sardinian clerics, and the Greek deacon Kyriakos, doubtless because of his knowledge of Greek, was given the delicate task of investigating certain allegedly scandalous acts committed by Peter, bishop of Syracuse.[166] During Honorius's pontificate, an Easterner named Epiphanios had risen to the highly responsible position of *defensor* of the papal patrimony in Tuscia.[167]

Roman reluctance to elect a pope of undisputed Eastern provenance such as Theodore may also have been moderated by the choice two years earlier of John IV, who, although from Dalmatia and not by origin a Greek or Syrian, had nonetheless been the first pope born and raised in a land east of Italy since Pope Zosimus (417–418) over two hundred years earlier.[168] Pope John had also had confidence in the diplomatic skills of Easterners, choosing the Syrian Barsika as his *apokrisiarios* to Constantinople and thus conferring upon him the potentially explosive mission of notifying the emperor that the Roman church rejected the *Ekthesis* and the heresy that it espoused. Easterners such as these and probably many others had proven themselves both doctrinally sound and highly capable, loyal, and efficient representatives of the Roman church. Theodore's election was unquestionably a consequence, at least in part, of their impressive records.

But a flawless facility in Greek and an absolute fidelity to the Apostolic See, though necessary, were not sufficient to meet the challenge of Monothelitism. The new pope needed a thorough command of the relevant Scriptural passages, patristic literature, and conciliar texts to meet the intellectual demands of responding to the Monothelites. Both Theodore and his father had lived in Jerusalem while Sophronios was campaigning vigorously against the Monothelites. As one of Sophronios's bishops, Theodore's father was an integral part of the Christological debate and indeed had taken such an active part in it that he was expelled from his see by a Monothelite usurper. The future pope, nurtured in the household of a Chalcedonian bishop and obviously showing an inclination toward an ecclesiastical career, had to have been conversant with the theological discussions that virtually dominated religious discourse at the time. It is hardly likely that Theodore was unaware of Sophronios's seminal synodal letter to Honorius and Sergius or his famous and extensive anti-Monothelite florilegium.[169] Sophronios had willingly shared these same patristic texts with Maximos when the two had met in Africa in 632 or 633. They had greatly inspired the truculent Eastern monk, and had provided him with the authoritative sources so vital in framing the intellectual response to the Monothelites. There is every reason to believe that these texts were freely made available to Theodore, and that the future pope was as motivated and enlightened by Sophronios's spirit and his works as Maximos had been before him.

Finally, the Roman church needed a leader with the enthusiasm and the will to fight. Theodore's own father had suffered persecution at the hands of the Monothelites and, together with his son, had had to flee his homeland. There could be no better champion for Chalcedonian orthodoxy than one who had become an exile as a result of his commitment to it. The exigencies of the times had caused the Roman electors to cast aside what surely had to have been grave doubts and great suspicions about electing a Greek as pope. But they had settled on the ideal pontiff. Theodore had an impeccable knowledge of the language in which his Eastern adversaries would conduct the debate; never again would the Papacy suffer the sort of embarrassment that had resulted from Honorius's linguistic carelessness. In addition, he had acquired from Chalcedon's greatest advocate a knowledge of the scriptural, patristic, and conciliar texts necessary to meet the intellectual challenge of Monothelitism. Lastly, he had the fervor for battle of one who has himself been the victim of persecution. The Roman church saw in Theodore its best hope of a pontiff capable of leading the battle against the doctrinal deviation into which the churches of the East had once again succumbed. Its faith in him would not be misplaced.

Theodore weighed into the battle against Monothelitism with an intensity that seemed to free the Papacy of the shame of subservience that had hung about it like a pall since Pope Vigilius had trembled before Justinian I in Constantinople a century earlier.[170] Replying to the letter that Constans II had sent John IV, the new pope praised the emperor's profession of fidelity to Chalcedon but warned him in no uncertain terms of his duty to ensure henceforth that the orthodox faith was observed and kept unsullied.[171] The Monothelite patriarch Pyrrhus had been deposed and exiled to Carthage in 641 for alleged complicity with the empress Martina in plotting the death of Constantine III.[172] Pyrrhus had been succeeded by Paul II, to whom Theodore now wrote praising the affirmation of orthodoxy contained in the new patriarch's synodal letter, but expressing concern that, in light of his profession, Paul II had not ordered the removal of the *Ekthesis* from the narthex of Haghia Sophia.[173] Theodore appears also to have been concerned that the proper formalities be observed in connection with the deposition of Pyrrhus, urging both the new patriarch and the Constantinopolitan bishops to convene a synod and canonically pronounce his removal.[174] In an unprecedented expression of papal assertiveness toward the church of Constantinople, Theodore suggested that he send his *apokrisiarii* Sericus and Martin to the capital to oversee such a synod and make sure that Pyrrhus's deposition was properly performed.[175] The pope's offer was almost certainly declined.

After he had dealt with the emperor and the hierarchy of the church of Constantinople, Theodore turned his attention toward the situation in his own homeland. In another unusual assertion of papal authority over matters within the jurisdiction of an Eastern patriarchate, the pope took the extraordinary measure of naming Bishop Stephen of Dor as apostolic vicar for Palestine with plenary authority to depose the uncanonical Monothelite bishops who had been ordained by Sergius of Joppa.[176]

The Roman pontiff's bold initiatives against Monothelitism appear to have inspired others to openly join in the combat. Sergius, bishop of Cyprus, wrote Theodore that a synod of Cypriot bishops held on May 29, 643, had endorsed Rome's efforts against the Monothelites.[177] In July 645, Maximos and the former patriarch Pyrrhus, who had fled the capital for Africa, engaged in a celebrated disputation over Monothelitism held at Carthage under the auspices of the Byzantine exarch.[178] After he had been convinced of its doctrinal error, Pyrrhus sailed to Rome, renouncing the Monothelite heresy, acknowledging his previous misstatements as well as those of his predecessors, and submitting to the pope a signed profession of Chalcedonian orthodoxy not as a patriarch but rather as a simple priest. Theodore then showed his magnanimity by seating Pyrrhus on a throne near the altar and acknowledging him as rightful patriarch of Constantinople. But by the time he had left Rome and arrived in Ravenna, Pyrrhus had renounced his pledge of orthodoxy.[179] The outraged Roman pontiff at once convened a synod of bishops, which condemned Pyrrhus and solemnly pronounced his deposition from the see of Constantinople.[180] In a dramatic scene played out upon St. Peter's tomb, Theodore mingled ink with drops of the Holy Sacrament and with his own hand signed Pyrrhus's anathema.[181]

The African church, inspired unquestionably by Maximos's zeal, took up the anti-Monothelite cause with particular vehemence. Sometime early in 646 the African bishops of Byzacena, Numidia, Mauretania, and Carthage each convened a synod, which "anathematized Sergius, Cyrus, and Pyrrhus and proclaimed two wills and energies in Jesus Christ our Savior and God."[182] In a letter to Pope Theodore, the African bishops expressed alarm that Monothelitism had still not been extinguished, citing Pyrrhus's recantation and the fact that Paul II still refused to remove the *Ekthesis* from Haghia Sophia.[183] Stephen, bishop of Byzacena and primate of the African church, wrote the emperor urging him to defend Chalcedon and to take immediate measures to bring Paul II into the orthodox confession.[184] Another letter from the African episcopacy urged Paul to desist from his adherence to heresy, citing anti-Monothelite texts from Ambrose and Augustine.[185] A final letter from Victor, bishop of Carthage, to Pope Theodore urged the pontiff to renew his efforts to suppress Paul's recalcitrance.[186] Together Theodore and Maximos had generated a storm of protest against Monothelitism that spanned the length of the empire from Palestine through Cyprus and into Africa.

Theodore seized the opportunity suggested to him by Victor of Carthage and promptly dispatched his *apokrisiarii* to Constantinople carrying the pope's appeal that Paul "correct his falsehood and return to the orthodox faith of the catholic church."[187] The patriarch's reply, which cited texts from Gregory of Nyssa, Athanasius, Cyril, and Honorius, persisted in proclaiming "one will of our Lord."[188] When it was clear that Paul was not about to abandon his adherence to Monothelitism and that Constans II was obviously unwilling to compel him to do so, Theodore convened a Roman synod that, sometime in 648, declared the patriarch deposed.[189] Rome and Constantinople were now in schism and at open war over which Christological formulation the Christian empire would confess.

What had begun as a political initiative designed to ensure that the empire's Monophysite subjects remained faithful to Byzantium in the face of the Persian and later the Arab invasions had ended ironically over three decades later in a breach between the Chalcedonians and the distressing spectacle of a Greek pope excommunicating the patriarch of the imperial city. But once again political developments would dictate religious policy. After the Arabs had taken Egypt in

646, they moved westward into Africa and north into Anatolia pressing relentlessly toward Constantinople.[190] The emperor desperately needed peace within the Church in order to concentrate his efforts against the invaders, rather than occupying himself in mending the division between the Papacy and the church of Constantinople. Following the example of his grandfather Heraclius, Constans II turned to his patriarch Paul II to find a means to still the discord. The emperor was determined to preserve the unity of imperial ideology amidst the seemingly interminable quarrels over religious doctrine.

Paul's solution was the *Typos* or Decree Concerning the Faith.[191] Issued by Constans II as an imperial edict in 648, the *Typos* proposed to create peace between Rome and Constantinople by imposing silence.[192] It prohibited all discussions over "one will and one energy, or two energies and two wills" in Christ. At the same time, and in an obvious effort to appease the West, it ordered that the *Ekthesis* be removed from the narthex of Haghia Sophia. Finally, it provided severe penalties for anyone who violated its injunction against further Christological debate of any kind; offending clerics would be defrocked, monks would be excommunicated and banished, and aristocrats would lose their offices, dignities, and possessions.[193]

If the emperor and his patriarch had thought that a decree of silence would end Rome's determination to see Monothelitism affirmatively rejected, they had underestimated the tenacity of the Greco-Palestinian who now sat upon St. Peter's throne.[194] Moreover, Pope Theodore had in the meantime gained an important ally. Arab incursions into Africa had driven Maximos and his retinue of monks across the Mediterranean to Sicily, where they had briefly sojourned, before moving on to Rome, probably in late 646.[195] Their alliance would unite Sophronios's two most distinguished heirs and bring together a formidable force for Chalcedonian orthodoxy. Regrettably, however, that zeal would also prevent them from appreciating Constans's anxiety about the need to maintain imperial unity. Theodore and Maximos either could not or would not see the *Typos* as the instrument of peace and political unity that the emperor intended it to be. While they focused upon preserving doctrinal purity, the emperor's concern lay with keeping the empire intact. These competing and apparently irreconcilable interests threatened the stability if not the existence of the *imperium Romanum Christianum*. Whether East and West would still be one after the last great battle for Chalcedon had ended remained to be seen.[196]

Notes

1. *PG* 90: 127. ("I delight in the Romans because we have one faith and in the Greeks, however, because they speak the same language as do I.")

2. *PG* 90: 70. An unsympathetic early Syriac life of Maximos Confessor, written by one Georgios (or possibly Gregorios) who was an active Monothelite, claims that he was the son of a Samaritan linen maker and a Persian slave girl, and that he was given over

to be raised by Palestinian monks at St. Chariton's monastery near Jerusalem. Sebastian Brock, "An Early Syriac Life of Maximus the Confessor," *Analecta Bollandiana* 91 (1973): 314–15, 321.

3. *PG* 90: 70; *AA.SS.* Aug. III (1737) 118.

4. *PG* 90: 74.

5. *PG* 90: 79ff.

6. *Mansi* X, 1029–32; *LP* I, 337; Dölger, id., No. 225, p. 26. Violations of the *Typos* carried severe consequences. Clerics were subject to deposition, monks to excommunication and exile, aristocrats would lose their public offices and dignities as well as having their property confiscated, and members of the lower classes were subject to flogging and banishment. See Friedhelm Winkelmann, "Der monoenergetisch-monotheletische Streit," *Klio* 69 (1987): 515, 537 (No. 106).

7. Although the *sakellarios* was originally responsible for imperial fiscal and economic matters, the position eventually developed into one with significant political power as well. See Pililis, id., pp. 58–61; L. Bréhier, *Les institutions de l'empire byzantin* (Paris, 1970), p. 210.

8. Psalms 19: 3.

9. *PG* 90: 109C–129D. The date of Maximos Confessor's first trial has been disputed. One authority contends that it could not have begun before the end of August nor after the middle of December, 654. E. Montmasson, "Chronologie de la Vie de saint Maxime le Confesseur (580– 662)," *Echos d' Orient* 13 (1910): 149, 153. More recently, it has been placed as early as June 654. J.-M. Garrigues, "Le martyre de saint Maxime le Confesseur," *Revue Thomiste* 76 (1976): 410, 414. For an analysis and discussion of the various manuscripts relating to the life, trial, exile, and death of Maximos Confessor, see Robert Devreese, "La vie de saint Maxime et ses recensions," *Analecta Bollandiana* 46 (1928): 5–49.

10. A Greek life of Martin I, written between 730 and 740 during the reign of Leo III, presents a vivid picture of the dreadful clamor created within the church by the imperial soldiers who came to arrest the pope. In a metaphor of poetic quality, it compares the sight and sound of the candles rolling onto the pavement as they are cut down by the soldiers' swords to the roar of the winter wind as it tears the leaves from trees and sends them hurtling to the earth. Paul Peeters, "Une vie grecque du Pape S. Martin I," *Analecta Bollandiana* 51 (1933): 225, 256.

11. *LP* I, 338; Jeffrey Richards, *The Popes and the Papacy in the Early Middle Ages 476– 752* (London, 1979), p. 188.

12. *LP* I, 341.

13. *PG* 90: 133B–136C.

14. Garrigues, id., p. 439.

15. Devreese, id., p. 39.

16. Theophanes, *Chronographia*, p. 484.

17. *Mansi* XI, 73–76; *PG* 90: 169C–172B; Garrigues, id., 447n73.

18. *PG* 90: 171C–178A; Garrigues, id., p. 450; Devreese, id., p. 43.

19. Nikephoros, *Short History*, id., pp. 67, 185; Theophanes, *Chronographia*, pp. 459, 459n3; Strategios Monachos, id., p. 54.

20. Nikephoros, *Short History*, id., p. 67.

21. Ωρολόγιον τό Μέγα, id., p. 171.

22. Ostrogorsky, id., p. 106; Vasiliev, Vol. I, id., p. 194.

23. George of Pisidia. *Expeditio Persica III*, id., p. 131, ll. 345–46.

24. *The Chronicle of Zuqnin*, A.D. *725* in *The Seventh Century in the West-Syrian Chronicles*, trans. Andrew Palmer (Liverpool, 1993), p. 57; cf., id., p. 68; Theophanes, *Chronographia*, p. 459; *Chronicle of Michael the Syrian*, p. 411. Edessa was an important trans-Euphrates fortress whose fall had resulted in the Persian breakthrough after 611. Whittow, id., pp. 81, 86. Before the Persian invasion, it was an opulent city of "gardens, mills, shops and public baths." *Chronicle of Dionysius of Tel-Mahre* in *The Seventh Century in the West-Syrian Chronicles*, id., p. 140. The city's wealth can be deduced from the fact that the quantity of silver, which was stripped from its cathedral and shipped to Persia, amounted to an impressive 112,000 pounds. Id., pp. 133–34.

25. *Chronicle of Michael the Syrian*, p. 411; George of Pisidia, *Expeditio Persica II*, id., p. 101, ll. 90–91.

26. Theophanes, *Chronographia*, 460n4.

27. *Chronicle of Michael the Syrian*, p. 412; *Chronicle of Dionysius of Tel-Mahre*, id., p. 140.

28. *Chronicle of Michael the Syrian*, p. 412; *Chronicle of Dionysius of Tel-Mahre*, id., p. 140; Theophanes, *Chronographia*, p. 459.

29. *Chronicle of Michael the Syrian*, p. 412.

30. Id. This Monophysite version of the encounter between Heraclius and the Syrian bishops at Edessa by Michael the Syrian contrasts sharply with the versions set forth by the Greek chroniclers. See Theophanes, *Chronographia*, p. 460; Georgios Cedrenos, *Historiarum Compendium*, p. 736; Leo Grammatikos, *Chronographia*, p. 155; Georgios Monachos, *Chronicon*, p. 673.

31. *The Synodicon Vetus*, trans. John Duffy and John Parker (Washington, D.C., 1979), p. 81.

32. Jaroslav Pelikan, *The Emergence of the Catholic Tradition (100–600)*, Vol. I (Chicago, 1971), pp. 274–75.

33. *PG* 86: 997–1003; Pelikan, id., pp. 275–76.

34. *Mansi* IX, 377ff.; Pelikan, id., p. 277; see also J. N. D. Kelly, *Early Christian Doctrines*, rev. ed. (New York, 1978), p. 343.

35. Dagron, et al., eds., *Évêques, Moines et Empereurs (610–1054)*, id., p. 40; Hans Urs von Balthasar, *Liturgie Cosmique: Maxime le Confesseur*, trans. L. Lhanmet and H.-A. Prentout (Paris, 1947), p. 36.

36. Henry Chadwick, "John Moschos and His Friend Sophronios the Sophist," id., p. 52.

37. Henry Chadwick, "A Review of Rudlof Riedinger's *Concilium Laterananse a. 649 celebratum*," *Journal of Ecclesiastical History* 38 (1987): 448.

38. Georges Florovsky, *The Byzantine Fathers of the Sixth to Eighth Century*, trans. R. Miller, A. Döllinger-Labriolle, and H. Schmiedel (Vaduz, 1987), p. 206.

39. Theophanes, *Chronographia*, p. 461.

40. Philip Schaff and Henry Wace, eds., *A Select Library of the Christian Church: The Nicene and Post-Nicene Fathers*, 2nd series, *The Seven Ecumenical Councils*, Vol. 14 (Peabody, MA, 1995), pp. 342–43.

41. Id., p. 343.

42. Theophanes, *Chronographia*, p. 425.

43. *Chronicon Paschale*, p. 149, 149n419.

44. *Chronicon Paschale*, p. 152; Theophanes, *Chronographia*, p. 428; Nikephoros, *Short History*, p. 37.

45. Nikephoros, *Short History*, p. 53.

46. Id., p. 53; Theophanes, *Chronographia*, pp. 430–31, 431n2.

47. Theophanes, *Chronographia*, p. 435; Georgios Monachos, *Chronicon*, p. 670; Georgios Cedrenos, *Historiarum Compendium*, p. 718; Leo Grammatikos, *Chronographia*, p. 718; Theodore Synkellos, *Short History of the Arrival of the Persians and Avars* in *Analecta Avarica*, ed., Leo Sternbach (Cracow, 1900), p. 334, ll. 6–8; cf., *Chronicon Paschale*, p. 167. Nikephoros, *Short History*, p. 55.

48. *Chronicon Paschale*, pp. 168–169, 169n456.

49. Theophanes, *Chronographia*, p. 447; *Chronicon Paschale*, p. 170; George of Pisidia, *Bellum Avaricum* in *Poemi. I. Panegirici Epici*, ed. and trans. A. Pertusi (Ettal, 1959), p. 194, l. 461; Theodore Synkellos, *Homily on the Avar Siege of Constantinople* in *Analecta Avarica*, id., p. 300, ll. 25ff. For a detailed analysis of the sources and events surrounding the Avar siege of Constantinople in 626 as well as the best reconstruction of its chronology, see F. Barisic, "Le siège de Constantinople," *Byzantion* 24 (1954): 371.

50. *Chronicon Paschale*, pp. 171ff.; George of Pisidia, *Bellum Avaricum*, id., p. 186, ll. 217ff.

51. Nikephoros, *Short History*, p. 61; *Chronicon Paschale*, pp. 178–79; Theodore Synkellos, *Homily*, id., p 310, ll., 40ff.; George of Pisidia, *Bellum Avaricum*, id., pp. 196–97, ll. 441–74.

52. Norman H. Baynes, "The Supernatural Defenders of Constantinople," *Analecta Bollandiana* 67 (1949): 165–77; Averil Cameron, "The Virgin's Robe: An Episode in the History of Early Seventh-Century Constantinople," *Byzantion* 49 (1979): 42–56.

53. George of Pisidia, *Bellum Avaricum*, id., pp. 12–13,176, l. 13.

54. Id., p. 168, ll. 128–32. The emperor did dispatch a portion of his army to Constantinople to aid in its defense. Theophanes, *Chronographia*, p. 446; George of Pisidia, *Bellum Avaricum*, id., p. 187, ll. 280–83.

55. George of Pisidia, *Bellum Avaricum*, id., p. 190, ll. 311–27; *Chronicon Paschale*, pp. 175–76; Theodore Synkellos, *Homily*, id., p. 306, ll. 20–25. The participation in this embassy of Theodore Synkellos, described as "most dear to God," would appear to bolster the credibility of his two accounts of the Avar siege. The other members of the mission included the patricians George, Theodosios, and Athanasios, and Theodore, a customs officer. *Chronicon Paschale*, p. 175

56. Nikephoros, *Short History*, p. 61.

57. *Theodore Synkellos, Homily*, id., p. 304, ll. 5–16.

58. Id.; Theodore Synkellos, *Short History*, id., p. 334, ll. 18–23. The *Chronicon Paschale*, id., p. 180.

59. George of Pisidia, *Bellum Avaricum*, id., p. 182, l. 137; Leo Grammatikos, *Chronographia*, p. 151.

60. Meyendorff, *Imperial Unity and Christian Divisions*, pp. 336–37.

61. Paul Lemerle, "Les répercussions de la crise de l'empire d'Orient au VIIe siècle sur le pays d'Occident," in *Le monde de Byzance: Histoire et Institutions* (London, 1978) pp. IV, 724.

62. Meyendorff, *Imperial Unity and Christian Divisions*, id., p. 338; Theophanes, *Chronographia*, pp. 460–61; Anastasios Sinaites, *Sermo III*, PG 89: 1153. See also J. L. Van Dieten, *Geschichte der Patriarchen von Sergius I. bis Johannes VI.* (610–715) (Amsterdam, 1972), pp. 1–56.

63. *Mansi* X, 528CD; XI, 525CD; 529E–532A. Sergius's inquiries may have been accompanied by Menas's pronouncement in order to make it appear to the orthodox that, while trying to arrive at an accommodation with the Monophysites, he was not prepared to sacrifice Chalcedon. Venance Grumel, "Recherches sur l'histoire du monothélisme," *Echos d'Orient* 28 (1929): 19.

64. *PG* 91: 332BC.

65. *Mansi* XI, 568. The patristic text to which Theodore was referring may very well have been Dionysios the Areopagite's allusion to Christ's θεανδρικήν ενέργειαν, or "theandric energy," which he made in a letter to the monk Gaius. Dionysios the Areopagite, *Epistola IV*, PG 3: 1073–74. Theodore of Pharan's early expression of support for the doctrine that Christ possessed a single energy or operation resulted in his condemnation at the Lateran Council of 649 as the originator of Monoenergism, the precursor to Monothelitism. *Mansi* X, 893, 957–61.

66. The Paulicians were a sect of dualists who professed matter to be evil and who denied the reality of Christ's body and of the Redemption. Their name was probably derived from their admiration for Paul of Samosata, heretical bishop of Antioch. Paul Lemerle, "L'Histoire des Pauliciens d'Asie Mineure d'après les sources grecques," *Travaux et Mémoires* 5 (1973): 1–144. Maximos contended that John the Merciful, patriarch of Alexandria, had actually taken Sergius's letter from George Arsas's hand on the eve of the Persian irruption into Egypt in 619. PG 91: 334A.

67. *PG* 91: 331C–334A; *Mansi* XI, 561AB; 525B; 529A–D; *Synodicon Vetus*, id., pp. 107–9.

68. *Mansi* XI, 559; Dölger, id., No. 182, p. 20.

69. V. Grumel, "Recherches sur l'histoire du monothélisme," *Echos d'Orient* 27 (1928): 269ff.

70. Meyendorff, id., p. 339.

71. *Mansi* XI, 560D–561D; 525B–528C.

72. *Synodicon Vetus*, Nos. 128 and 129, pp. 108–9.

73. Sebeos, *Histoire d'Héraclius par l'évêque Sebeos*, trans. F. Macler (Paris, 1904), p. 91ff.; Grumel, id., p. 258.

74. Theophanes, *Chronographia*, p. 461. Monophysite sources insist that the Monoenergist formula was a purely imperial initiative (see Dölger, id., No. 203, p. 23), and that Athanasios Camelarios refused to agree to any compromise with the emperor remaining consistently intransigent in the face of imperial pressure. *Chronicle of Michael the Syrian*, pp. 402–12. Chalcedonian sources, on the other hand, make Athanasios a participant both in promulgating Monoenergism (which they conflate with and do not distinguish from Monothelitism which appears slightly later) and, along with Sergius of Constantinople, in tricking the emperor into succumbing to the heresy. Georgios Monachos, *Chronicon*, p. 673; Georgios Cedrenos, *Historiarum Compendium*, pp. 736–37; Leo Grammatikos, *Chronographia*, p. 155; cf., Grumel, id., pp. 276–77.

75. Whittow, id., p. 86.

76. Severus of Asmounein, *History of the Patriarchs of the Coptic Church of Alexandria*, id., p. 489.

77. Meyendorff, id., p. 345.

78. *Mansi* XI, 561D–565D. The Theodosians or Severans were one of the principal sects among the Monophysites and derived their name from a certain Theodosios, who had been their leader in the midddle of the sixth century. Karl Hefele, *Histoire des Conciles*, Vol. III, Pt. 1 (Paris, 1909), p. 339.

79. *Mansi* XI, 565D. Dionysios's expression was probably acceptable to most Monophysites since it was consistent with their Christology. Meyendorff, in fact, goes so far as to assert that no one suspected that the author of the *Corpus Aeropagiticum* was himself probably a Severan Monophysite. Id., p. 338n10; cf., *PG* 3: 1072B.

80. *Mansi* XI, 564C–568B; Hefele, id., pp. 340–41. The statement in the *Synodicon Vetus* that the agreement with the Egyptian Monophysites was promulgated at a synod is not reported in any other source. Id., No. 130, p. 109.

81. *Mansi* XI, 564A.

82. Severus of Asmounein, id., pp. 491–92; Meyendorff, id., p. 347.

83. Theophanes, *Chronographia*, p. 461.

84. Meyendorff, id., p. 348.

85. Schönborn, id., p. 79.

86. George Papadeas, trans., *The Akathist Hymn to the Theotokos* (Athens, 1972), p. 37.

87. E. Weigand, "Das TheodosioskLöster," *Byzantinische Zeitschrift* 23 (1914): 167–216.

88. Schönborn, id., p. 72, 72 n70.

89. *PG* 91: 49C.

90. Diehl contends that Maximos did not reach Africa until sometime in the beginning of 640. Charles Diehl, *L'Afrique byzantine. Histoire de la domination byzantine en Afrique* (Paris, 1896), p. 548; cf., *PG* 91: 460. But Devreesse subsequently proved that Maximos was present in Africa by the early summer of 632, since he witnessed the forced baptism of Jews and Samaritans pursuant to imperial command on the Sunday of Pentecost that year. Robert Devreesse, "La Fin Inédite d'Une Lettre de saint Maxime: Un Baptême Forcé de Juifs et de Samaritains à Carthage," *Revue des Sciences Religieuses* 17 (1937): 25–35.

91. Brock, id., pp. 315–21.

92. *PG* 91: 461A; John Moschos, *The Spiritual Meadow*, id., p. xvi; Chitty, id., 167n144. The *Eukratades*, which derives from the Greek ευκρατόν, meaning "abstinent" or "continent," earned their name from their refusal to drink wine, preferring instead a common monastic concoction consisting of pepper, cumin, and anise dissolved in water. *PG* 99: 1716B. Cf., John Moschos, *The Spiritual Meadow*, id., p. 133; see Schönborn, p. 56n13.

93. *PG* 91: 533A; 332–33. Maximos appears to have been acquainted with Sophronios even before they met in Africa, since during the early summer of 632 he wrote Sophronios, who was either still in Jerusalem or possibly already en route westward, expressing his reservations about Heraclius's forced baptism of Jews and Samaritans then residing in Africa. Devreesse, id., pp. 34–35.

94. *PG* 91: 142A.

95. Andrew Louth, *Maximus the Confessor* (London, 1996), p. 14.

96. *PG* 91: 401CD.

97. *PG* 87/3: 3147–4014; cf., Eutychius, *Annales*, *PG* 111: 1109.

98. *PG* 91: 532–33.

99. *PG* 91: 143.

100. For a description of this early Christian heresy, whose origin is attributed to Apollinarius of Laodicea, see Kelly, *Early Christian Doctrines*, pp. 189–195.

101. *Mansi* XI, 533B–536D; *PG* 91: 143; Hefele, id., pp. 342–43.

102. *Mansi* XI, 529–37; *PG* 91: 592BC–596AB.

103. Hefele, id., p. 345.

104. *Mansi* XI, 536D. Maximos appears to have joined Sophronios in regarding Sergius's *Psephos* as an acceptable resolution of the Monoenergist controversy. Despite efforts by Pyrrhus, the future patriarch of Constantinople, to elicit his opinion on the meaning of various parts of Sergius's pronouncement in an exchange of correspondence that took place toward the end of 633 and the beginning of 634, Maximos declined to engage in any extensive commentary. *PG* 91: 589–97; V. Grumel, "Recherches sur l'histoire du monothélisme," *Echos d'Orient* 28 (1929): 31–34. Both his praise for Pyrrhus and his reference to Sergius as "the new Moses" would prove embarrassing in years to come. *PG* 91: 589C–592B; 592C.

105. *Mansi* XI, 536E–537A. τον ἐκ τῆς τοιαύτης κινήσεως αρξάμενον θόρυβον; V. Grumel, "Recherches sur l'histoire du monothélisme," *Echos d'Orient* 27 (1928): 13.

106. *Mansi* XI, 537 AB; Dölger, id., No. 205, p. 23 (identified as the Ἴδικτον); Georgios Cedrenus, *Historiarum Compendium*, p. 737; Theophanes, *Chronographia*, p. 461 (the editors of this text of Theophanes's *Chronographia* incorrectly refer to the *Keleusis* issued by Heraclius in 634 as the *Ekthesis*, which was an entirely different document issued in 638. Id., p. 463n7; see infra, p. 93). The *Keleusis* appears to have been more in the nature of an imperial rescript in reply to the patriarch's petition for the emperor's approval of what he had professed in the *Psephos*, rather than an imperial order or command, since there is no evidence that violation of the *Keleusis* carried any penalties or sanctions. Cf., G. W. H. Lampe, *A Patristic Greek Lexicon* (Oxford, 1961), p. 741, where κέλευσις is also defined as an "imperial rescript."

107. *Mansi* XI, 529A–537B; Grumel, "Recherches sur l'histoire du monothélisme," *Echos d'Orient* 28 (1929): 19–22, 272–74; Hefele, id., pp. 343–47.

108. The conspicuous absence of any opposition from strict Chalcedonians (which would have certainly included Rome) until Sophronios raised his objections in 633 doubtless reassured Sergius that his proposed solution to the Christological quarrel between Dyophysites and Monophysites was consistent with Chalcedonian orthodoxy. Neither he nor the emperor had acted in secret; their initiatives were open and notorious, and their successes in Armenia, Egypt, and perhaps even Syria were loudly acclaimed. Moreover, when he was confronted with dissent from the Chalcedonian camp, he not only abandoned his formula, but sought advice on going forward from no less a committed adherent to Chalcedon than the pope of Rome. Sergius's letter to Honorius has been seen as a clever attempt by the patriarch to seduce the pope into heresy and make him an unsuspecting partner in Constantinople's political machinations. Hefele, id., pp. 346–47; von Schönborn, id., p. 92. Such a conclusion is, however, founded upon little

else than characterizing the tone of that letter and speculating on Sergius's motives. The facts, however, are just as consistent with a patriarch genuinely concerned with achieving "theological integrity." Meyendorff, id., p. 349.

109. *Mansi* XI, 537–44; *PL* 80: 470–74; Jaffé, id., No. 2018, p. 224.

110. *Mansi* XI, 539–40; *PL* 80: 472. *unam voluntatem fatemur Domini Jesu Christi*; Eutychius, *Annales*, PG 111: 1110.

111. P. Goubert, "La Discussione," in *Caratteri del Secolo VII in Occidente*, Vol. II, *Settimane di Studio del Centro Italiano di Studi sull'Alto Medioevo* (Spoleto, 1958), p. 805.

112. PG 91: 243.

113. *PL* 129: 572. Richards incorrectly asserts that John Symponos "translated Honorius's letter from Latin to Greek." Id., p. 182. Apart from the fact that the sources clearly reflect this task was not performed by John himself, it is most unlikely that a Greek monk, who had achieved the position of the pope's "secretary of state," would have committed such an egregious translation error. Nevertheless, it was on the basis of the Greek translation, which was read at the Sixth Ecumenical Council, that Honorius was condemned as a heretic. Schaff and Wace, eds., *Nicene and Post-Nicene Fathers*, Vol. 14, "The Seven Ecumenical Councils," id., p. 343; Hefele, id., p. 350.

114. Eutychius of Alexandria, *Annales*, PG 111: 1108, 1110. Eutychius, a ninth-century Chalcedonian patriarch of Alexandria, recorded that it was Honorius who conceived the doctrine of Monothelitism, thereby "creating a division of opinion within the church"; Meyendorff, id., p. 353; Anton Thanner, *Papst Honorius I. (625–638)* (St. Ottilien, 1989), p. 132; H. G. Beck, *Kirche und theologische Literatur im byzantinischen Reich* (Munich, 1959), p. 458; Paul Verghese, "The Monothelite Controversey: A Historical Survey," *Greek Orthodox Theological Review* 13 (1968): 196–211.

115. Theophanes, *Chronographia*, p. 468.

116. Hefele, id., p. 350.

117. PG 87/3: 3168A; *Mansi* XI, 461; Rudolf Riedinger, "Die Epistula synodica des Sophronios von Jerusalem im Codex Parisinus Graecus 1115," *Byzantiaka* 2 (1982): 143–54; Rudolf Riedinger, "Die Nachkommen der Epistula synodica des Sophronios von Jerusalem a. 634," *Römische Historische Mitteilungen* 26 (1984): 91–106.

118. PG 87/3: 3169D.

119. Grumel, "Recherches sur l'histoire du monothélisme," *Echos d'Orient* 28 (1929): 26.

120. The *Synodicon Vetus* records that Sophronios, "the honey-tongued champion of truth," convened a synod in Jerusalem, which proclaimed two wills and energies in Christ, and that thereafter Sophronios sent his synodical letter to that effect to Sergius and Honorius. Id., p. 111. Theophanes also records that Sophronios convened a synod of bishops in Jerusalem, which "anathematized the monothelite doctrine," and that his synodical letter to that effect was sent "to Sergius of Constantinople and John [IV] of Rome." *Chronographia*, p. 461. Since John IV became pope in 640, at least one and possibly two years *after* Sophronios had died, Theophanes was obviously mistaken. Sophronios died on either March 11, 638 or 639. See von Schönborn, id., 97n136. Hefele doubts that Sophronios could have assembled a synod of Palestinian bishops in the face of the encircling Arab menace, and that the sources which report such an assembly may have confused his issuance of a synodical letter, known as τά συνοδικά, with the gathering of bishops at his

enthronisation as patriarch, which was known as a συνοδικόν. *Id.*, p. 369.

121. *Mansi* X, 896D; Meyendorff, id., p. 356.

122. Grumel, id., *Echos d'Orient* 28 (1929): 27.

123. Grumel, id., *Echos d'Orient* 29 (1930): 19.

124. Id., pp. 18–19.

125. *PG* 91: 443.

126. *Mansi* X, 741.

127. *Mansi* X, 992–97; Dölger, id., No. 215, p. 25.

128. *Mansi* XI, 9. Years later Heraclius would write Pope John IV disavowing any part in preparing the *Ekthesis* and attributing his consent to its publication to pressure he received from Sergius. But the emperor may have been conveniently distancing himself from a document that by 640 or 641 had generated an acrimonious response from the Roman church. Dölger, id., No. 215, p. 25.

129. Id., X, 999–1001; Dölger, id., No. 211, p. 24.

130. Theophanes, *Chronographia*, p. 472 (Sophronios died on March 11, 638); *LP*, I, p. 324 (Honorius died on October 12, 638); Nikephoros, *Short History*, p. 75 (Sergius died on December 13, 638).

131. Rudolf Riedinger, ed., *Acta Conciliorum Oecumenicorum*, Ser. IIa, Vol. I (Berlin, 1984), pp. 46–47; Flusin, id., pp. 360–61.

132. *Mansi* X, 1004–5; Winkelmann, id., No. 54, p. 527.

133. *Mansi* X, 1001–4; *Synodicon Vetus*, No. 132, p. 111; Theophanes, *Chronographia*, p. 461.

134. *Chronicle of Michael the Syrian*, p. 419.

135. *Mansi* X, 1004–1005; cf., Bede, *Chronica*, Theodor Mommsen, ed., in *MGH Auctores Antiquissimi*, Vol. XIII (Berlin, 1898), p. 312.

136. *LP*, I, p. 328. Severinus, who succeeded Honorius, was consecrated pope on May 28, 640, nineteen months after his predecessor died.

137. *PG* 91: 460–509; Stratos, id., Vol. III, pp. 59–60; Nichols, id., p. 17.

138. During his trial in 654, Maximos was accused of having seen "a vision in his sleep that in the heavens there were factions of angels in the east and west; and those in the east shouted, 'Constantine Augustus, you shall conquer'; but those in the west cried, 'Gregory Augustus, you shall conquer.' And the voice of those in the west overcame the voice in the east." George C. Berthold, trans., *Maximus Confessor: Selected Writings* (New York, 1985), p. 18. Hefele maintains that Gregory and George are in fact the same person. Hefele, id., 402n5. Confusion between these two names appears to have been common. See footnote 2, supra. Severus of Asmounein erroneously places the beginning of Maximos's polemic for Chalcedon in the period between 677 and 686 during the time of the Alexandrian Monophysite patriarch John III. Id., Vol. 5, Fasc. 1, p. 11.

139. See *PG* 91: 228–45 (letter to the Cypriot presbyter Marinos on Pope Honorius's orthodoxy); *PG* 91: 152B–153B (on the definition of the energies and wills in Christ); *PG* 91: 89–112 (letter to Bishop Nikander on Christ's two energies); *PG* 91: 268ff. (brief thesis against Monothelitism); *PG* 91: 169–173 (ten chapters on Christ's two wills); *PG* 91: 68A (commentary on Matthew 26:29 dealing with Christ's double natures and wills); *PG* 91: 276–80 (reply to questions from the monk Theodore with citations from various fathers of the Church).

140. *PG* 91: 1304D, 224D.

141. *PG* 91: 260B, 245A; Jaroslav Pelikan, "The Place of Maximus Confessor in the History of Christian Thought," in F. Heinzer and C. von Schönborn, eds., *Maximus Confessor. Actes du Symposium sur Maxime le Confesseur* (Fribourg, 1982), pp. 387–89.

142. Nichols, id., p. 53; cf., Gregory Nazianzen, *Theological Orations*, V. 25, *PG* 36: 161ff.

143. *PG* 91: 69–89.

144. O. Bertolini, *Roma di Fronte a Bisanzio e ai Langobardi, Storia di Roma*, Vol. IX (Bologna, 1941), pp. 317–18.

145. *Mansi* X, 677–78; *PL* 129: 583D–586B (letter to the Abbot Thalassios).

146. *LP* I, pp. 328–29.

147. *Mansi* X, 679–80, 1005; Jaffé, id., No. 2039, p. 227; cf., *Liber Diurnus* LXIII, *Promissio Fidei Episcopi*, id., p. 72.

148. *PG* 90: 125AB; *PL* 129: 615D; Dölger, id., No. 215, p. 25.

149. Bertolini, id., p. 325.

150. Theophanes, *Chronographia*, p. 474; Nikephoros, *Short History*, p. 77. Later postscripts to his death notice mentioned none of the great achievements of his long and eventful reign, recording only, with a certain satisfaction, the morbid details of his final illness (which were attributed to his incestuous marriage to his niece Martina), and that he had been tricked into the Monothelite heresy by the patriarchs of Antioch and Constantinople. Georgios Cedrenos, *Historiarum Compendium*, p. 752; Georgios Monachos, *Chronicon*, p. 673; Leo Grammatikos, *Chronographia*, p. 155.

151. *Synodicon Vetus*, No. 137, p. 115; *Mansi* X, 697–698; Theophanes, *Chronographia*, p. 461; Jaffé, id., p. 227; Hefele, id., p. 393.

152. Eutychius, *Annales*, *PG* 111: 1108–9.

153. *Mansi* X, 682–86; *PL* 80: 602–7; *PL* 129: 561–66.

154. *Mansi* XI, 9.

155. Eutychius, *Annales*, *PG* 111: 1111. Barsika's Syrian ethnicity can be deduced from an examination of proper names of Syrian origin which are obvious cognates of the name Barsika, such as Bardayson, a third-century philosopher from Edessa; Barses, a fourth-century bishop of Edessa; Barbahlul, a tenth-century Syrian lexicographer; and Gregory Barhebraeus, a thirteenth-century Syrian chronicler. See Theophanes, *Chronographia*, p. 95; Palmer, *The Seventh Century in the West-Syrian Chronicles*, id., p. 274. Cf., John of Barkaina, whom Heraclius appointed as general of the imperial army following his departure from Syria after the battle of Jabiya-Yarmuk in 636. Nikephoros, *Short History*, pp. 71, 188–89; *Chronicle of John, Bishop of Nikiu*, id., pp. 178–80, 184.

156. Dölger, id., p. 26; Theophanes, *Chronographia*, pp. 475, 476n1.

157. *PG* 111: 1111AB; Dölger, id., No. 221, p. 26.

158. John IV had died on October 12, 642. *LP* I, p. 330.

159. The *Liber Pontificalis* describes Theodore as *natione Grecus* thus using the ablative form of the noun *natio* signifying that he was by nationality, race, or ethnicity a Greek and not that he was physically born in Greece, in which case it would have used *natus*, the perfect passive participle of *nascor*. In his English translation of the *Liber Pontificalis* through the reign of Pope Constantine I published in 1989, Raymond Davis incorrectly rendered *natione* as "born in" throughout the text. Raymond Davis, *The Book of the Pontiffs*

(Liverpool, 1989). He corrected this error in his subsequent book, which began with Pope Gregory II, by translating *natione* as "of __ origin," inserting Roman, Greek, or Syrian as the case might be. Raymond Davis, *The Lives of the Eighth-Century Popes* (Liverpool, 1992). The proper translation of *natione* is of utmost significance since the so-called Greek popes were not necessarily born in the East, but were instead the sons (or possibly even grandsons) of persons born there who moved to the West during the course of the seventh century.

160. Based upon a canon of Boniface III, the election of a new pontiff could not take place until three days after his predecessor had been buried. *LP* I, 316. Since John IV died on October 12 and was probably buried three days later on October 15, Theodore could not have been canonically elected until after October 18. The fact that he was *enthroned* on November 24 (*LP* I, 331) suggests both his speedy selection by the Roman electors and a quick confirmation by the exarch Isaac (625–643), who by then would have exercised the power to ratify the papal election in Ravenna rather than having to refer it to Constantinople for approval. *Liber Diurnus*, id., LIX (*Nuntius ad Exarchum de Transitu Pontificis*), pp. 49–50; LX (*De Electione Pontificis ad Exarchum*), pp. 50–54.

161. Flusin, id., p. 362. If Theodore I was between thirty and thirty-five years old when he was elected pope, then he was probably born between 607 and 612 and was between twenty-two and twenty-seven years old when Sophronios returned to Jerusalem and became patriarch in 634. If, as is likely, Theodore's father was driven from his bishopric by one of Sergius of Joppa's Monothelite bishops after Sophronios died in March 638, then the two Theodores arrived in Rome in late 638 or early 639. Thus, Theodore I had been in Rome less than four years when he was chosen pope in 642.

162. Bertolini, id., p. 327.

163. Tellenbach remarks that historically "the defense of orthodoxy against deviation or open heresy by the eastern churches in many dogmatic and liturgical controversies became the task of the *ecclesiae Occidentis*" or western churches. Gerd Tellenbach, "L'Italia nell'Occidente nel Secolo VIII," in *I Problemi dell'Occidente nel Secolo VIII*, Volume 2, *Settimane di Studio del Centro Italiano di Studi sull'Alto Medioevo*, 6–12 April 1972 (Spoleto, 1973): 387.

164. Jules Gay, "Quelques Remarques sur les papes Grecs et Syriens avant la Querelle des Iconoclastes (678–715)," *Mélanges offerts à M. Gustave Schlumberger* (Paris, 1924), pp. 40–54.

165. *PL* 129: 571; Richards, id., p. 179.

166. Jaffé, id., No. 2015, p. 224; No. 2029, p. 226.

167. Id., Nos. 2031; 2036, p. 226.

168. *LP* I, p. 223. Unlike Theodore, John IV appears to have followed the *cursus* of the Roman church, rising to become archdeacon and thus pope presumptive. The two men named Iohannes, one of whom was *primicerius notariorum* or head of the papal chancery and the other *consiliarius* or papal counselor following the death of Pope Severinus and the enthronement of John IV, were also probably of Eastern origin. Jaffé, id., No. 2040, p. 227.

169. Riedinger, ed., *Acta Conciliorum Oecumenicorum II*, 1, 40, id., p. 20ff.; *Mansi* XI, 461– 510; *PG* 87: 3148–3200. See von Schönborn, id., p. 100ff.

170. Bertolini, id., p. 333; Grisar, id., p. 25ff.

171. PG 111: 1111C–1112A. It is unlikely, as Eutychius of Alexandria recorded in the ninth century, that Pope Theodore anathematized Heraclius, Sergius, Honorius, and patriarch Paul II, who had succeeded Pyrrhus in 641, by name, and impossible that he condemned Peter, who became patriarch of Constantinople in 654, five years *after* Theodore had died in 649. Id., 1111.

172. Theophanes, *Chronographia*, p. 461; cf., Nikephoros, *Short History*, p. 83; *Synodicon Vetus*, No. 138, p. 115; John of Nikiu, *Chronicle*, id., p. 199.

173. *Mansi* X, 702; *PL* 87: 75; Jaffé, id., No. 2049, pp. 228–29.

174. *Id.*; *Mansi* X, 705–6; *PL* 87: 80–81; Jaffé, id., Nos. 2050, 2052, p. 229.

175. *Mansi* X, 702. "Sericus" appears to be a scribal error for "Sergius," although Bertolini believes that Theodore actually suggested Barsika. Id., p. 330. Martin, the other proposed envoy, would succeed Theodore as pope. *LP* I, p. 336.

176. *Mansi* X, 891; Bertolini, id., p. 333. Stephen of Dor, a confidante of Sophronios, had traveled to Rome in 634, most likely to deliver the patriarch's synodal letter to Pope Honorius. von Schönborn, id., p. 92ff. He had returned to receive his commission as apostolic vicar for Palestine from Pope Theodore, and would come back a third time to participate in the Lateran Council in October, 649. Hefele, *A History of the Councils of the Church*, id., pp. 94, 101–2.

177. *Mansi* X, 913–916.

178. PG 91: 288–353; Nikephoros, *Short History*, p. 85; Theophanes, *Chronographia*, p. 462; *Synodicon Vetus*, No. 138, p. 115.

179. Ado of Vienne, *Chronicon*, PL 123: 113.

180. Stratos contends that Pope Theodore had no right to depose Pyrrhus since no ecclesiastical canon or conciliar decision gave the Roman pope, even though he was "first among equals," the authority to depose a coequal patriarch. Andreas N. Stratos, "Ό Πατριάρχης Πύρρος," in *Studies in Seventh-Century Byzantine Political History* (London, 1983), VIII, 18.

181. *Mansi* X, 610; Jaffé, id., No. 2054, p. 229; Theophanes, id., p. 462; *Synodicon Vetus*, id., No. 138, p. 115; *LP* I, p. 332.

182. *Mansi* X, 918; Hefele, id., p. 426; *Synodicon Vetus*, Nos. 133–136, pp. 111–13; Theophanes, *Chronographia*, pp. 461–62 (Theophanes does not mention the synod held by bishop Victor of Carthage).

183. *Mansi* X, 919–22; *PL* 87: 81–86.

184. *Mansi* X, 925–28.

185. Hefele, id., pp. 91–92.

186. *Mansi* X, 943–950; *PL* 80: 637–644; *PL* 87: 85–92.

187. *LP* I, p. 333.

188. *Mansi* X, 1019–25; *PG* 87: 91–99; Hefele, id., pp. 430–32.

189. *LP* I, p. 333; Jaffé, id., p. 230.

190. Theophanes, *Chronographia*, p. 478; Whittow, id., p. 86.

191. *Mansi* X, 1029–1032 (τύπος περί πίστεως).

192. Western sources uniformly place responsibility for the *Typos* upon the patriarch rather than the emperor. Drawing a parallel between it and the *Ekthesis*, they record that just as Sergius had misled Heraclius so Paul had deceived Constans and "boldly presumed to contravene the definitions of the Fathers . . . [and] to mask his error with deceptions such as to induce the clement emperor to issue a *Typos*, which would destroy catholic

dogma." *LP* I, p. 336; cf., Bede, *Chronica*, id., p. 313; Ado of Vienne, *Chronicon*, *PL* 123: 114.

193. Id.; Hefele, id., pp. 432–34.

194. J. M. Hussey, *The Orthodox Church in the Byzantine Empire* (Oxford, 1986), p. 19.

195. *PG* 91: 112; 443–46.

196. See Meyendorff, *Imperial Unity and Christian Divisions*, pp. 365–67.

~

CHAPTER IV

Reverendissimi Abbates, Presbyteri, nec Non Monachi Introeant[1]
The Lateran Council of 649

Theophylaktos arose from his seat in the magnificent and monumental basilica that Constantine the Great had built early in the fourth century on the Lateran as a cathedral for the bishop of Rome and that he had lavishly embellished with ornaments of gold and silver and dedicated to Christ the Savior.[2] As principal notary of the Apostolic See and chief of the papal chancery and library, the Greek cleric was second only to the pope within the administrative hierarchy of the Roman church and, together with the archpriest and archdeacon, performed the duties of the Papacy when the see was vacant.[3] Standing in the vast cathedral before an assembly of 105 bishops drawn entirely, except for one, from the Western parts of the empire, Theophylaktos formally announced the convocation of what would come to be known as the Lateran Council of 649, invoking as he did both the name of Jesus Christ and the regnal year of the "august and most pious lord Constantine [Constans II]."[4] He then called upon the pope to deliver the opening address. Reading from a prepared text, the pontiff excoriated the Monothelite heresy espoused by the patriarchs of Constantinople and Alexandria, savaged the Ekthesis and Typos, and, claiming to respond to pleas that Rome invoke its apostolic authority to put an end to these errors, said that he had convened the council to condemn the heretical doctrines of those "who had presumed to entwine novelties among the immaculate faith."[5] After brief speeches containing more of the same from the bishops of Aquileia and Cagliari, and from representatives of the conspicuously absent archbishop of Ravenna, the assembled bishops uttered in unison a few sentences assenting to what their colleagues had said. The council then recessed for two days.[6]

Theophylaktos convened the second session of the Lateran Council on October 8, 649, by acknowledging the presence of the Palestinian bishop Stephen of

Dor, who had acted as papal vicar in Palestine with plenary authority to depose the Monothelite clergy installed by Sergius of Joppa, and who was again in Rome this time seeking permission to present the council with a *libellus* or small tract that he had composed against Monothelitism.[7] Recalling the pledge that he had made to Sophronios on Mount Calvary, Stephen told the bishops that his presence at the synod fulfilled the vow he had made to the patriarch of Jerusalem that he would happily travel from one end of the Earth to the other to proclaim the true faith.[8] The Palestinian prelate then handed his tract to the papal notary Anastasios, who freely translated the Greek text into Latin for the assembled prelates.[9] The pope read a perfunctory reply approving Stephen's speech.[10]

Theophylaktos then informed the assembly that a delegation of Greek abbots, priests, and monks, including both those who had lived in Rome for years and those who had only recently arrived, were outside the basilica seeking permission to appear and be heard by the council. After the pope read out his approval, four Eastern abbots accompanied by "other venerable men" were admitted to the synod.[11] They, too, had composed a "most humble tract" against Monothelitism which they sought to have presented.[12] At the insistence of the bishop of Aquileia, the Greek monastics handed their tract to the papal notary Theodoros, who, as his Eastern colleague Anastasios had done with Stephen of Dor's *libellus*, unfalteringly rendered the Greek text prepared by the monks into Latin for the benefit of the Western bishops.[13] Thirty-six subscriptions were appended to the monastic tract; the thirty-fourth read simply "Maximos, monk."[14]

The brutal and efficient suppression of a revolt by the *chartularios*[15] Maurikios against the exarch Isaac in 644 did not augur well for opponents of imperial policy, whether political or religious, in mid-seventh-century Byzantine Rome.[16] Maurikios's uprising, which was based on the flimsy pretext that Isaac intended to usurp the emperor's authority,[17] appears to have been endorsed by the highest level of Roman society, including its civil authorities, who together with the imperial troops garrisoned in the city and the inhabitants of the neighboring towns all swore oaths supporting the insurrection.[18] But an army dispatched to Rome by the exarch under the command of the *magister militum* Donos terrorized the citizens into renouncing their pledges to Maurikios and the rebellion was quickly quelled. Abandoned by his influential supporters, Maurikios and his confederates were seized from the church of St. Maria *ad praesepe* where they had sought refuge, bound in irons, and sent to Ravenna. At the twelfth milestone from the city, Maurikios was decapitated and his head sent to Isaac, who gleefully displayed it on a pole to the populace as an example to anyone who might entertain thoughts of challenging imperial authority.[19]

Pope Theodore's open condemnation of Monothelitism followed by his bold and unprecedented act of presuming to depose patriarch Paul II of Constantinople only two years later were therefore taken at great personal risk, and reflected the Palestinian pontiff's uncompromising resolve to challenge the empire's officially approved religious doctrines in spite of the terrible repercussions that Maurikios's abortive rebellion had shown would assuredly descend upon opponents of imperial policy and authority.[20] At the same time, however, the breadth of support that Maurikios was able to generate in and around Rome revealed a growing resentment toward Byzantine political domination independent of the religious issues raised by the Monothelite controversy.[21] The shrewd and determined pope appears to have correctly gauged an increase in the strong undercurrent of Roman rancor against such heavy-handed use of imperial force emanating from Ravenna since the Maurikios incident, and to have sensed that enthusiastic acceptance of imperial political authority exercised with such brutality was perceptibly waning.[22] It is important to note, however, that the discontent which manifested itself in thirteen major revolts in Italy and Sicily prior to the fall of the exarchate in 751 were all "imperial in character" in the sense that the rebels never departed from their allegiance to the ideal of the Christian Roman Empire. At no time did any such uprising "spring from hostility to the imperial ideal" nor set out to establish "an independent Italian kingdom."[23] In any event, Pope Theodore judged that the time was now particularly propitious to press Rome's position against Constantinople on the Monothelite question with even greater vigor. For his part, the courageous pontiff was fully prepared to accept the awesome consequences of such a daring initiative.[24]

Pope Theodore was far too astute to believe that Rome could ever successfully hope to challenge Monothelitism by simply denouncing it *ex cathedra* as heresy based on nothing more than the Papacy's claim to be *caput omnium* or head of all in matters of doctrine.[25] Nor were theatrics, such as signing the deposition of the patriarch of Constantinople in ink mingled with the Blessed Sacrament, however breathtaking, alone likely to carry the cause of Chalcedon's Christology.[26] If the Roman church was to succeed in championing the orthodox position against Monothelitism, it had to confront its opponents with solid arguments grounded in Scripture, sanctioned by the councils, and approved by the Fathers. The intellectual poverty displayed by Theodore's immediate predecessors had to be replaced with a revitalized theological knowledge and skill sufficient to pierce the subtlety of the East and expose its apparent truth for the heresy it really was.[27]

Theodore would certainly have failed to restore the Papacy to the place where it might truly speak with Leonine authority in this regard if he had had to rely entirely on the native Roman clergy to sustain his efforts.[28] Its inability to grasp even the fundamental issues presented in the Monothelite controversy reflected the wretched condition to which education and learning had fallen in mid-seventh-century Rome in religious as well as secular matters.[29] But Maximos's flight from Africa to Rome along with his monastic retinue substantially raised the prospects for Theodore's success and assured that the case for Chalcedon would be articulated in a manner that would pose a genuine challenge to Mono-thelitism that the church of Constantinople could not summarily dismiss.[30] For the first time in well over a century, the church of Rome would be in a position to debate theological issues with Byzantium from a position of equality in both intellectual substance and rhetorical form. The irony was that Rome would experience its revitalization not by drawing upon its own pitiable resources, but rather through the collaboration of a Greco-Palestinian pope and a Constanti-nopolitan monk employing a style of theological discourse whose tradition was purely Eastern.[31]

Pope Theodore and Maximos likely exchanged letters on the subject of convening a synod under the auspices of the church of Rome to condemn Monothelitism even before Maximos arrived in Rome in 646.[32] When, in late 646 or early 647, patriarch Pyrrhus of Constantinople solemnly renounced Monothelitism before the assembled clergy and people of Rome, it seemed that the whole heretical edifice might swiftly begin to come tumbling down without the need for such an assembly.[33] But his subsequent relapse into heresy after he had left Rome and gone no farther east than Ravenna, followed by the refusal of his successor Paul II to condemn the *Ekthesis* and "return to the faith of the catholic church," rekindled Pope Theodore's inclination to convene a council since it had become painfully obvious that the church of Constantinople was determined to continue to embrace a heretical Christology.[34] That inclination appears to have turned into a firm decision when in 648 the emperor Constans II issued the *Typos* prohibiting, upon the imposition of severe penalties, any discus-sions over "one will and one energy, or two energies and two wills" in Christ.[35] Thus, although discussions had been under way to convene a synod and formally condemn Monothelitism while Maximos was still in Africa, it was not until 648 that Theodore and Maximos set themselves irreversibly to the task of system-atically preparing the case against the Monothelite heresy to be presented at a council of bishops summoned by the pope to appear at the Lateran basilica in Rome.[36] While the political climate in Rome was admittedly volatile and fraught with danger, it appeared to be as favorable a time as could be expected to launch such an initiative. In any event, the clear and present threat that the *Typos* now posed to Chalcedonian orthodoxy pushed the collaborators over the precipice, giving them no alternative but to act.[37]

Maximos and his monks assumed authority for all aspects of planning, prepar-ing, and scripting the proceedings of the Lateran Council of 649.[38] While Pope Theodore was also instrumental in formulating the plans and preparations for this synod, there is little direct proof of the pope's involvement.[39] When Maxi-mos was asked by the *sakellarios* Troilus, during his first trial in Constantinople in June 654, where it was that he had condemned the *Typos*, he replied that he had done so "at the synod of Rome in the Church of the Savior [Constantinian basilica]." At the mention of the Roman synod, a certain Demosthenes cried out that that council had "no force since the one who summoned it [Pope Martin

I] had been deposed."[40] Although Maximos contested Demosthenes's claim that the pope had been canonically removed from office, he insisted that whatever had happened to Martin did "no prejudice to what has been established as orthodox according to the sacred canons, which are consistent with the authoritative writings set down by Pope Theodore of blessed memory."[41] Maximos's reply may simply have meant that Pope Theodore's opposition to Monothelitism had been doctrinally sound regardless of the canonicity of Martin's deposition and the ensuing validity of the Lateran Council. But his specific reference to Pope Theodore and his "authoritative writings" in the context of a colloquy in which the principal subject was the Roman synod which had condemned Monothelitism suggests rather strongly a connection between certain anti-Monothelite documents assembled and prepared by Theodore and the ensuing synod where the views expressed in those writings were approved.[42]

Demosthenes's violent outburst at the mention of the Roman synod of 649 reflected the deep rancor that the council engendered in Constantinople. That virulence extended to Maximos and Pope Martin and indeed to whomever imperial authorities believed had played any part in it. Theodore's loyalty to the emperor was already under suspicion as a result of the claim, which surfaced at Maximos's trial in 654, that the pope had participated in transmitting a message to Gregory, the rebellious exarch of Africa, in which Maximos had foretold Constans's defeat at Gregory's hands.[43] Only Theodore's active role in promoting and organizing the imperially-detested synod can account for the reference by later orthodox writers to his ἄθλησις,[44] or athletic-like exertion for the faith and for the pair of lines which graphically denounce his Monothelite antagonists as "Man-eating wolves, beasts I say/Tearing off and eating the flesh of Theodore."[45]

The synod that Theodore and Maximos planned to convene was to be in the nature of a general or ecumenical council and not merely a local or provincial assembly of the Roman church summoned to address a doctrinal or disciplinary issue of regional concern.[46] Writing to the Cypriot priest Marinos, Maximos referred to the Lateran Council as the "sixth synod, which through the divine inspiration of God set forth with all pure piety the doctrines of the holy Fathers," thereby expressly placing it on a level equal to that of the five ecumenical councils which were claimed to have preceded it.[47] Moreover, the papal encyclical, which accompanied the dissemination of the council's acts and decrees at the conclusion of the assembly, purported to express the faith of the universal church by having exercised the collective power of the episcopate to define and declare orthodox belief and to condemn false teaching.[48] By asserting that it had acted with universal authority, the Lateran Council claimed to have transcended the status of a mere provincial synod and, as such, to have bound the whole church to its decisions after the manner of a general council.[49] But this claim faced an apparently insurmountable problem.

The council planned by Theodore and Maximos would obviously have to be convened by the pope rather than the emperor. Although Maximos might employ the full force of his eloquence to proclaim that the Roman church was the ultimate repository of the true faith,[50] no council ever claiming to speak for and bind the entire church on matters of doctrine had ever been convened except by the emperor.[51] Although the emperor and the episcopate shared the duty of defining and spreading the correct faith, as God's representative on Earth the emperor alone had the right to convene a general church council and to confirm and promulgate its decisions.[52] Moreover, even Athanasius, while bitterly opposed to Constantius's Arianism, never denied that the right to convene a general council belonged to the emperor alone even though he was a heretic.[53] Nor had the Papacy ever denied the emperor this absolute prerogative. When Pope Julius I convened a Roman synod to rehabilitate Athanasius, who had been condemned by a synod at Tyre (335), the Antiochians protested that calling a synod without imperial consent was a prohibited innovation in ecclesiastical practice. Although the pope tried to defend his action on other grounds, he never denied that the emperor alone had the right to summon a general synod.[54] In addition, only the emperor or his representatives had presided at general councils, directed the debates, and confirmed the decisions.[55] Finally, no council claiming to be ecumenical had failed to formally promulgate its acts and decisions before the emperor, and to acclaim his role as guardian of the faith, usually couched in such ornate superlatives as "most truly pious and beloved of God."[56]

The Roman synod proposed by Theodore and Maximos was to fail the test of ecumenicity on every basis that had been deemed indispensable to support such a claim since the Council of Nicaea over three centuries earlier. It would be summoned by the pope rather than by the emperor; the fact that Constans II was a Monothelite, and thus a heretic in Roman eyes, would not excuse this radical departure from accepted practice. The pope, rather than the emperor or his representatives, would preside and, if not actually direct, at least acquiesce in the conduct and order of the proceedings.[57] Although the acts of the council would be sent to the emperor in Constantinople for ratification, the gesture would be one of form without substance for he was bound to repudiate them.[58] Nor would simply referring to the regnal year of the "august and most pious lord Constantine" be an adequate substitute for the flamboyant but important acclamation extolling the emperor for having put down the heretics and kept pure the faith, thereby acknowledging his traditional collaborative role along with bishops in connection with councils of ecumenical stature.[59]

Maximos was fully aware that the role he was proposing for the pope constituted a direct challenge to the emperor's historic authority in ecclesiastical affairs. However, the reprehensible compromise which Constantine had made with the Arians and Justinian's blatant pretensions to exercise sacerdotal functions demanded an end to traditional notions of the emperor's jurisdiction in matters of belief.[60] By placing the pope in the position historically occupied by the emperor and insisting on the council's ecumenical nature, Theodore and Maximos were claiming nothing less than a revolutionary role for the Papacy.

No longer was the Roman church content to collaborate with God's representative on Earth by yielding to him, albeit a heretic, the exclusive prerogative of summoning a general council, even while reserving to bishops alone the right to determine matters of faith at such assemblies. By presuming to arrogate to the pope the exclusive "guardianship of orthodoxy," Theodore and Maximos boldly challenged the emperor's authority to supervise and direct divine matters, thereby denying him a prerogative that had belonged to and been exercised by every emperor since Constantine.[61] Having effectively denied the emperor his traditional role in matters pertaining to the faith, Rome could now act alone to impose its exclusive authority over the entire church. Simply stated, the Roman church had become the equivalent of the universal church.[62]

The paradox was that this radical ecclesiology was an innovation conceived not by the native Roman clergy but rather by a Greco-Palestinian pope and a monk from Constantinople. Under their enormous influence and as a result of their unrestrained zeal to fight Monothelitism, the Papacy would, in the mid-seventh century, articulate an ecclesiological theory of unprecedented proportions. Although it would shortly retreat from that position by recognizing the emperor's traditional and historic role in connection with the convocation of the Sixth Ecumenical Council in 680,[63] the synod planned by Theodore and Maximos set the Papacy to thinking of the Universal Church not as the sum of individual churches as the East did, but as synonymous with the Roman Church.[64] Moreover, the germ of an ecclesiological conscience that would come to conceive of papal authority in juridical terms had been planted.[65] Although wholly foreign to the East, these novel importations had ironically been the product of Eastern minds bent on combating a heresy of Eastern origin.[66]

While Rome's challenge to the emperor's role with regard to summoning an ecumenical council was shockingly innovative, Theodore and Maximos knew that if their proposed synod had any hope of purporting to speak authoritatively on the issue of Monothelitism, its methodology had to adhere strictly to the established norms for defining the ancient and unchanging faith of the church.[67] On this point even the intractable Maximos realized that there was no room for innovation. Despite his unprecedented ecclesiological claims on behalf of the Papacy, Maximos had consistently taken the position that the only way to arrive at changeless truth in matters of doctrine was to scrupulously avoid the presumptuous invention of novel formulas and terminologies based upon one's own thoughts and ideas.[68] Any attempt to define the orthodox faith depended entirely upon what had been ordained "by the divinely inspired fathers of the catholic church and the five ecumenical councils."[69]

But correctly ascertaining the testimony of those divine witnesses, and arriving at orthodox teaching in the process, was a complicated exercise.[70] It was not sufficient merely to have access to the relevant patristic texts and sources, or to be able to cite Scripture, or the canons and proceedings of a council. Although a substantive knowledge of the Bible and the Fathers as well as conciliar decisions was certainly indispensable, the heretics also claimed to "confess the voices of the Fathers," yet what they espoused was doctrinally erroneous.[71] The ability to arrive at orthodox truth required skill in the profane arts such as rhetoric and grammar.[72] Moreover, a proper interpretation of Scripture and the Fathers was predicated upon the skill to discern not simply the literal meaning of a word or phrase, but its spiritual (Maximos would say mystical) sense as well.[73] Divining orthodox truth, therefore, depended not only upon an uncompromising fidelity to "our holy fathers and teachers,"[74] but upon possessing the necessary learning and education to penetrate a patristic, conciliar, or biblical text with sufficient acumen so as to ensure that it was being interpreted in a fashion truly consistent with what the Fathers had taught.[75]

The high degree of erudition required to achieve this end was, as we have seen, woefully lacking in the native Latin-speaking clergy of the mid-seventh-century Roman church. But it was present in Easterners such as Pope Theodore, in the monastics who had fled the Persians and Arabs and made their way to Rome earlier in the century, and in the small coterie of monks who, along with Maximos, had only recently arrived by way of Africa. They brought with them from the East an unbroken legacy of learning that, though shattered almost beyond recognition in the West, Byzantium had preserved in nearly pristine form from antique times.[76] The Lateran Council of 649 would owe "its essential inspiration and theological structure" entirely to that quintessentially Greek inheritance.[77]

Byzantium's inheritance of learning and education from the Greco-Roman world, though stretched to a fine filament, remained intact despite the convulsions that rocked the empire during the tumultuous decades of the seventh century.[78] The major cities of the East all continued to be centers for the pursuit and dissemination of knowledge, although their antique luster had admittedly diminished. While the claim that Byzantium experienced a literary renaissance in the time of Heraclius is probably an exaggeration, erudite and learned men continued to teach and write and to produce works of admirable quality.[79] At the same time, however, secular education was yielding perceptibly to the increasing social influence of the church and the demands of theology. By the middle of the century, the East had effectively begun to abandon the pursuit of profane studies.[80] Education and learning now focused not on producing histories and panegyrics or serious works on secular subjects, but on examining the Scriptures, the councils, and the writings of the Fathers as the church came increasingly to require "literate and cultured men for its high offices."[81]

Damascus in the late sixth century could justifiably claim to rival the other centers of learning of the late antique world. It was there that Sophronios, later patriarch of Jerusalem and author of the florilegium that would form the basis of the anti-Monothelite Christological arguments at the Lateran Council of 649, received his early education acquiring both the titles of sophist and professor of rhetoric.[82] Even before his departure for Egypt, along with his inseparable companion John Moschos, Sophronios had been schooled in a city with a cultural tradition that would continue to generate persons whose literary creations were a testament to the magnificent results of employing ancient Greek learning in the service of Christianity.[83] Eventually, Persian incursions into Syria and Palestine drove Sophronios and Moschos to Alexandria, where they arrived sometime before 607.[84] But it was not only the barbarians who caused them to travel to Egypt. Sophronios and Moschos were inspired to go to Alexandria by a desire to complete their *paideia*, which, since neither had yet taken monastic vows, could only mean the further pursuit of secular studies.[85]

Even during the late empire, Alexandria maintained its position as one of the East's pre-eminent centers of learning. Severus of Sozopolis had studied there and Gregory Nazianzen visited the city to consult its renowned library.[86] Its medical school, to which Gregory the Great made reference, surpassed all others in the empire.[87] The famed Alexandrian school of the Monophysite neo-Platonist John Philoponos (c. 490–c. 570) remained in existence without interruption throughout the sixth century and even after the Arab conquest of Egypt.[88] When Sophronios and Moschos arrived in Alexandria early in the seventh century, they encountered an intellectual milieu that in large measure still retained its antique vitality. During the nearly seven years they spent in the city, they became acquainted with a number of notable figures including Theodore the Philosopher, a penurious scholar whose lectures they attended, and Zoilos the Reader, an equally impoverished philosopher who practiced calligraphy.[89] The companions also came to know Cosmas the Lawyer, who probably instructed them in rhetoric, and whose voluminous collection of books exceeded that of anyone else in Alexandria.[90] The incumbent patriarch of Alexandria, John the Merciful, with whom they formed a close liaison, was an accomplished poet who wrote a panegyric in honor of St. Tychon of Cyprus.[91] Perhaps their most famous acquaintance was Stephen the Sophist, an illustrious Alexandrian who wrote commentaries on Aristotle and Plato as well as Galen and Hippocrates. His erudition in philosophy and medicine, not to mention arithmetic, geometry, astronomy, and music, resulted in an invitation to teach in Constantinople during the reign of Heraclius.[92]

The impressive quantity of books that they took with them on their travels is an important indicator of the commitment to acquire ever more knowledge exhibited by Sophronios and Moschos. Maximos commented on the "copious number of divine books" which Sophronios always maintained in his possession, and Moschos records that when they were told by a maid that they could not at the moment see Stephen the Sophist because he was taking his midday nap, they quietly retreated to await his rising "for we had our books with us."[93] Eventually, as we have seen, Sophronios and John Moschos made their way to Rome where

Moschos completed his sole work, the *Leimonarion* or *Spiritual Meadow*, in which he recounted anecdotally, after the manner of the *Apophthegmata Patrum*, his personal observations of the "spiritually beneficial deeds of the fathers."[94]

Sophronios's literary output was prodigious. His dogmatic works include the famous synodal letter, which ignited the Monothelite controversy by challenging patriarch Sergius's *Psephos* and the imperial *Ekthesis* that followed it, and his letter to bishop Arkadios of Cyrpus.[95] Sophronios's homilies consist of sermons on the Nativity of Christ, the Annunciation, the Elevation of the Cross, the Ypapante or Presentation of Christ in the Temple, and the Epiphany, as well as sermons on the Apostles Peter and Paul and St. John the Baptist.[96] Hagiographical works include a panegyric on Saints Cyrus and John, a life of the Alexandrian patriarch John the Merciful, and an encomium on the life of St. John the Evangelist.[97] Among his liturgical compositions are *troparia* or hymns for the Great Hours of Christmas ("Make ready, O Bethlehem"), Epiphany ("Today the nature of the waters is sanctified"), and Holy Friday, and the *stichera* or stanzas chanted at Epiphany during the Great Blessing of the Waters.[98] By far his most impressive work is a collection of twenty-three anacreontic poems on subjects ranging from the major events in the life of Christ to encomia on St. Paul and the martyrs Stephen and Thekla.[99] Their metrical scheme, in which each stanza has four lines which rhyme alternately to each other and where every line has three feet of trochaic meter followed by a long syllable or spondee, mimics precisely the scheme created by the ancient Greek poet Anacreon, whose name became associated with this particular verse form.[100] Although doubt has been raised about Sophronios's authorship of several of the epigrams, those positively attributed to him reflect his ability to produce "passable classicizing elegiacs," thereby making him probably the last author of the classical epigram "before the onset of the Byzantine Dark Ages."[101] Poem 20 of the *Anacreontica* titled "On His Desire for the Holy City and the Sacred Places" is especially noteworthy because in it Sophronios reveals his special reverence for Mount Calvary, thereby corroborating Stephen of Dor's testimony before the Lateran Council of 649 that it was there that the patriarch made him swear that he would always remain steadfast in his fidelity to Chalcedon.[102]

Although learning and education in Greece suffered lethal blows as a result of the Avar and Slavic invasions of the late sixth and early seventh centuries, classical culture was never completely extinguished in the major cities of the peninsula, all of which appear to have escaped barbarian occupation.[103] Synesios's boast that Athenian scholars despised all others had to undergo significant modification, even before the arrival of the invaders, as a result of Justinian I's decision to close the Academy in the sixth century.[104] But the situation could not have been as dismal as it might appear if Theodore of Tarsus, the future archbishop of Canterbury, studied in Athens as a young man, probably around the year 620.[105] The pursuit of learning in Athens seems to have been continuous throughout the seventh century due in large measure to the fact that the city remained in imperial hands.[106] Nor was the active pursuit of knowledge lacking in the decades that followed. An eighth century hagiographical text records the sojourn there of a pilgrim who, although he had come to Athens with the principal intention of worshiping at a particular church dedicated to the Theotokos, also met and conversed with "philosophers and rhetoricians."[107]

Thessalonika also appears to have resisted successive attempts to capture it on the part of the Avars, Slavs, and Bulgars in the seventh century. The abortive effort of one Mauros, a lieutenant of the Bulgar Kouber, to take the city by ruse sometime in 640 indicates that Thessalonika was in imperial hands during the reign of Heraclius.[108] Moreover, Constans II's dream that he was in Thessalonika on the night before the naval engagement with the Arabs at Phoenix in 655 reflects that the city remained in imperial hands past mid-century.[109] Finally, the presence of John II, archbishop of Thessalonika, at the Sixth Ecumenical Council in Constantinople in 680/681, and Justinian II's campaign against the Slavs and Bulgars that brought him to Thessalonika in 688/689 show that the city was continuously held by the empire throughout the seventh century.[110] As a consequence of its ability to resist barbarian occupation, Thessalonika retained its ancient position as an important intellectual center during this period. Its schools and masters continued to attract numerous students, thereby permitting the city to retain a virtually uninterrupted tradition of transmitting Greek culture that lasted at least as late as the eleventh century.[111]

Although classical education and culture persisted in the major cities of the East throughout the seventh and eighth centuries, the growing influence of the church in society and its determination to eradicate any vestiges of suspected paganism was becoming palpable. Ecclesiastical ascendancy in matters of learning, for example, often gave strange twists to ancient literary traditions. In an effort to minimize the valor of pagan heroes, and eventually to extinguish their memory altogether, some Christian writers resorted to intentional distortion. Achilles was portrayed by Leo the Deacon not as a Hellene but as a Scythian, and John Malalas depicted the ancient Myrmidons as Bulgarians.[112] Thus, while education in the East never entirely forgot its "classical parentage," profane learning was increasingly becoming harnessed and subordinated to the needs of sacred studies.[113] This evolution over the course of the seventh century was nowhere more apparent than in the capital itself.

When, among his many other atrocities, Phocas closed the University of Constantinople in the early seventh century, he ended the uninterrupted existence of an institution which had been established by Constantine the Great and which, by the time of Theodosios II in 425, had become the most important center of learning in the empire.[114] Heraclius revived the university as an "ecumenical academy" following his accession in 610, and thereafter it flourished as a center for the teaching of all disciplines with the exception of theology. The study of philosophy, geometry, astronomy, music, and mathematics was under the direction of Stephen the Sophist who, as we have seen, moved from Alexandria to Constantinople at the emperor's request sometime around 612.[115] Medical and surgical works of the early seventh century Paul of Aegina suggest that Byzantium was the nexus between "the classical medical school of Galen and later developments in Italy and the Arab world."[116] In Heraclius's time, lectures on medicine were also given in Constantinople by the *protospatharios* Theophilos. Moreover, the university once again achieved prominence as a center for legal studies.[117] As Theophilos's title reflects, the institution's professors were all imperial officials holding rank in the official hierarchy. It is not surprising, therefore, that while the University of Constantinople offered a broad range of studies in secular subjects, its principal aim was to provide knowledgeable civil servants for the empire's burgeoning bureaucracy.[118]

A reinvigorated intellectual creativity complemented the revived university. Sometime around the beginning of Heraclius's reign in 610, Theophylact Simocatta arrived in Constantinople from Alexandria, probably to pursue a career in the law. The fact that he attained the ranks of *ex-praefectus* and *antigrapheus* suggests success in this endeavor, but Theophylact is remembered not for his legal or administrative achievements but as "the last in the succession of secular classicizing historians of late antiquity."[119] His *Universal History*, whose ambitious title spans only the life and reign of the emperor Maurice, is replete with allusions to real and mythological persons and events, thereby betraying a rhetorical and literary training firmly within the antique Hellenic tradition.[120] In addition, a text in logic and the various types of argument titled the Προπαρασκευή was composed during the first third of the seventh century by Theodore of Raithu, thus revealing the continued vitality of studies in the use of dialectical reasoning based upon categorical definitions.[121]

The most outstanding literary figure of the Heraclian era was without doubt George of Pisidia. Born in a mountainous region in southern Asia Minor, George came to Constantinople during the reign of Heraclius and was probably educated at the patriarchal school that had been established by Sergius. Ordained to the diaconate, he became first *skevophylax* or sacristan of the Great Church of Haghia Sophia thereafter rising to the position of *referendarios* or private secretary to the patriarch, with whom he shared an intimate friendship.[122] His theological studies resulted in a mastery of both the Old and New Testaments as well as the writings of Basil and Origen. As far as secular learning was concerned, George was equally proficient. His works reflect a thorough knowledge of Greek tragedy, mythology, and epic poetry with frequent and extensive references to Homer, Hesiod, Aeschylus, Sophocles, Euripides, Aristotle, Herodotos, Plutarch, and Dio Chrysostom among others.[123]

George of Pisidia enjoyed enormous prestige among later Byzantine poets such as Manuel Philes and theorists like Gregory of Corinth.[124] The eleventh-century aesthete Michael Psellus set himself to the task of comparing George's works with those of Euripides in order to determine which of the two was the superior poet.[125] Psellus praised George's iambs for their combination of "euphony and grandeur," finding that his verses "leap forth as if shot from a sling, completing with vigor the thought of his poem together with the feet and the meter."[126] Although the badly damaged conclusion of Psellus's manuscript has led to conflicting interpretations regarding which poet he determined to be the better, the remainder of the text reflects that Psellus believed George would have been the best heroic poet known to him if his heroic lines had not been so short and few.[127] George seems clearly to have shared the same high opinion of himself as did Psellus.[128]

George's literary skills did not escape imperial attention. It was not without design that Heraclius took the celebrated poet with him on his first Persian expedition in 622/623. The predictable result was a thousand-line poem praising the emperor's heroic feats against the Persians.[129] This was followed by the *Heracliad*, a panegyric on the emperor written in the antique style which at one point calls upon Rome itself, rich in the tradition of heroes, to declare whether any Roman ever was Heraclius's equal.[130] The remainder of his works, which include an encomium on the patrician Bonos, a poem on the Avar War, a short improvisation on the occasion of the announcement of the restitution of the Holy Cross, and the *Hexaemeron*, a two-thousand-line poem in iambic trimeter exalting the harmony of Creation and the wisdom of the Creator, justify the assertion that George of Pisidia was indeed "the best poet of his time."[131]

The checkered career of Ananias of Shirak epitomizes better than any single text the condition of secular education and learning in the seventh-century Byzantine East. In his ceaseless search for knowledge, Ananias embarked on an odyssey that took him from his home in Armenia to Greece, where he studied with one Eliazar, thereafter returning to Armenia where he studied under a certain Christodotos. When he had learned all that Christodotos had to teach, Ananias departed for Constantinople to study mathematics. On the way, he met a deacon of the church of Constantinople named Philagrios, who was taking a group of youths to the capital to be instructed in theology. Eventually, Ananias left Constantinople to study with Tychichus of Trebizond. Tychichus, who had taught for some time in the capital, told Ananias that he too had traveled extensively in search of knowledge, visiting Jerusalem and even Rome. But Tychichus reserved special praise for Alexandria, which he called "the metropolis of all sciences," and Athens, which he said for him would always be "the city of philosophy."[132]

The life of Ananias of Shirak reveals both the continuing vitality of profane learning in the East and, as a corollary, the large place afforded to the exercise of human reason in a broad range of disciplines that did not require resort to divine revelation.[133] But by the end of Heraclius's reign in 641, secular learning was "reduced to a very thin trickle" as the needs of religion and theology pushed profane letters nearly to obscurity.[134]

Theophanes attributed the eclipse of secular learning to the iconoclastic measures undertaken by Leo III in 725/726 that, he recorded, resulted in the "extinction of schools and of the pious education that had lasted from St. Constantine the Great until our own days."[135] Other chroniclers, such as Georgios Monachos, also ascribed the demise of secular studies to the iconoclastic Isaurian emperor, who was blamed for burning a famous school in Constantinople's Chalkoprateia district and driving out its teachers and students.[136] Nikephoros, however, assigned responsibility for the decline of learning in the capital to the anarchy that prevailed after the final fall of Justinian II in 711.[137] Although the disorder following Justinian II's deposition and Leo's subsequent iconoclastic policies may both have contributed to the decline in secular learning by the early eighth century, the role of the church was probably an even greater factor. During the course of the seventh century, the church assumed a pivotal function with respect to all aspects of education, including the transmission of "literacy and literary culture."[138] Beginning in the middle years of the seventh century, for example, the Psalter came into regular use as the basic reading primer in both Constantinople and the provinces.[139] Georgios Choeroboskos, who wrote treatises and commentaries on grammar, prosody, spelling, and declension, based his works entirely on the Psalter.[140] Thus, while the church had always exercised exclusive control over the teaching of theology and religion, whether in patriarchal or episcopal schools or monasteries distinct from the university, during the course of the seventh century it extended its influence and control over all learning.[141] Inevitably, secular studies came to be tolerated only to the extent that they served a religious goal or promoted theological ends.

As education and learning came increasingly to be occupied with matters related to religion, it became necessary to further develop and refine the tools needed in order to engage in theological research, writing, and argumentation. Ever mindful of and indebted to its past, Byzantium turned once again to the rhetorical styles, techniques, and conventions of classical Greece for guidance and direction.[142] Drawing upon that inheritance, the East would reinvent and impress into the service of religion an ancient device of pagan ancestry that had been used in Christian polemical writing since the fourth century. Since then it had never ceased to be an implement in the arsenal of religious discourse, although from the time of Justinian I it had been increasingly employed in the broader process of what has been termed the "redefinition of knowledge" that was taking place during the late sixth century in the eastern part of the empire.[143] By the middle of the seventh century, it would achieve its first great triumph in the Christological battle over Monothelitism. But although of Eastern provenance, it was to realize its success as a weapon in the church's last great debate over the nature of Christ not in the East but in the West, through the painstaking toil of Greek monastics at a gathering of mainly Latin bishops in the Lateran basilica in Rome.

Since pre-Christian times Greek writers had composed anthologies or *florilegia* consisting of select passages drawn from the works of noted authors that they then presented as a single collection that literally resembled a bouquet of flowers representing the finest parts of a writer's entire literary output.[144] Consistent with its inherent disposition to imitate its classical past, Byzantium continued this literary tradition.[145] The education of Constantinople's civil officials was for generations based upon texts that consisted of extracts from the works of ancient authors.[146] Christian writers in the East, schooled in the literary tradition of classical Greece, also seized upon the concept of compiling collections of select passages taken from Scripture, the writings of the Fathers, or the acts of church councils, and utilizing them for various religious purposes.[147] Procopius of Gaza used selected biblical excerpts to support his commentary on the Octateuch.[148] His example was followed by a host of other Eastern biblical exegetes whose appeal to scriptural, patristic, and conciliar texts to support their particular interpretations often consisted of lengthy strings of citations that came to be known as *catena*.[149] Eventually, the use of such catena became the standard method of Biblical commentary in the East.[150]

Florilegia were also put to polemical use in the doctrinal controversies that arose within the church.[151] St. Basil freely admitted that the purpose of his work *On the Holy Spirit* was "to attack our opponents in the endeavor to confute those 'oppositions' advanced against us which are derived from 'knowledge falsely so-called.'"[152] In order to refute his adversaries, the great Cappadocian father first cited a variety of texts derived from Holy Scripture in support of his position, and then followed these biblical passages by an appeal to the writings of the "blessed men of old," whose works he had found "worthy of credit both on account of their early date [and] because of the exactness of their knowledge."[153] Following St. Basil's example, Cyril of Alexandria further developed and refined the *florilegium* as a weapon in theological debate.[154] By the beginning of the fifth century, it was considered insufficient to support an argument in favor of a particular doctrinal position by appealing solely to Scripture. Biblical passages had to be augmented by citations to authoritative patristic texts. As a result, adversaries in doctrinal disputes meticulously scrutinized the writings of the fathers, extracting χρήσεις or proof texts, which they then assembled into *florilegia* intended to prove the orthodoxy of their own beliefs and the heresy of their opponents.[155]

The compilation of *florilegia*, which seems to have intensified during the course of the sixth century, appears also to have brought with it a certain amount of abuse and intellectual dishonesty. The Monophysite bishop John of Ephesus soundly condemned them as "lacerations, which those who considered themselves to be philosophers tore from the living body of the writings of the holy fathers in the idea that it established and confirmed their heresy."[156] John's criticism was not without merit. Exclusive reliance on περικοπές, or selected texts and passages, had the effect of restricting and reducing, if not distorting, the range of potential knowledge. It became accepted practice merely to cite an excerpt in order to substantiate one's position; extracts took the place of the original work, which no one ever seems to have considered reading in its entirety, even if it was available, in order to ascertain its true spirit and meaning.[157]

The practice of assembling *florilegia* intensified in the late sixth century. Whether writing the biography of a religious figure, as in the case of Eustratios's *Life* of patriarch Eutychius, or launching an attack on one's ecclesiastical rival, intellectuals in late-sixth-century Constantinople, where Maximos Confessor was born and educated, frantically engaged in the pursuit of compiling proof texts aimed at establishing that they were orthodox and their opponents were heretics. With his undisguised disdain for Chalcedonians, John of Ephesus records that when Justinian I sent patriarch Eutychius into exile in 565, the deposed bishop "occupied himself in his monastery in tearing up and arranging books of lacerations [florilegia] as proof from the fathers" of his doctrines.[158]

With the dawn of the seventh century, florilegia would enter upon their virtual apotheosis as weapons in theological debate, beginning what has been described as their "golden age."[159] Eastern monastics seem to have pursued the composition of florilegia with uncommon vigor during the course of the next two hundred years. Sophronios most likely composed his extensive anti-Monothelite florilegium at the Palestinian monastery of St. Theodosios, where he took his vows as a monk, or at the lavra of the Aeliotes in the Sinai, where he and John Moschos spent a decade of their lives.[160] The anonymous seventh-century Syrian florilegium known as the Garden of Delights was doubtless a monastic product.[161] Antiochus Monachos compiled his Pandect, which was a collection of extracts from the Old and New Testaments along with passages from Ignatius of Antioch and other church fathers, at the Great Lavra of St. Sabas in Palestine in the seventh century as well.[162] Around the year 700, the Cypriot monastic Anastasios the Sinaite composed his Erotapokriseis or Questions and Responses, another text in the tradition of exegetical florilegia.[163] Toward the middle of the eighth century, while cloistered at St. Sabas in Jerusalem, John of Damascus compiled his monumental Hiera or Sacra Parallela, an encyclopedic florilegium containing between five and six thousand citations that was the most extensive anthology of biblical and patristic texts assembled up to that time.[164]

It is scarcely surprising, therefore, that Maximos Confessor and the Eastern monks who articulated the bases of Monothelitism's error at the Lateran Council in mid-seventh-century Rome should set themselves to the task of assembling florilegia designed to prove, by an appeal to scriptural, patristic, and conciliar authorities, that the doctrine of Christ's one will violated the "tradition of the Fathers [which] has been preserved by an unbroken sequence of memory to our own day."[165] The inconspicuous but looming omnipresence of these fervent and intractable monastics from the East would mould and shape every aspect of the synod, bringing to it a tradition of Greek education and learning that stretched back irrefragably to antique times.

ᕫ

Pope Theodore died on May 14, 649, in the midst of preparations for the Lateran Council.[166] Maximos had lost the ally with whom he had closely toiled in the struggle against Monothelitism for nearly three years. Theodore's death deprived Maximos of his most educated and articulate collaborator, and left the Papacy vacant at one of the most critical times in the church's history. If the forthcoming Roman synod was to present Constantinople with a challenge to its heresy that it could not dismiss as trifling, the new pope had to be in many respects another Theodore. It was not enough that he emulate his predecessor's courage and resolution against the Monothelites. The new pontiff also had to be someone whom the East could not ignore as intellectually inconsequential. But any such candidate was certain to be denied the *iussio* authorizing his consecration. Faced with this dilemma, the Roman electors, pressed no doubt by Maximos, boldly eschewed the course of caution. On July 5, 649, less than two months after Theodore had died, a deacon from the Umbrian hill town of Todi named Martin was consecrated pope without imperial approval.[167] The battle cry against Constantinople had at last been sounded.[168]

Although ethnically Italian, Martin had been profoundly influenced by the East and Easterners. He appears to have been closely attached to Pope Theodore, who had ordained him to the diaconate, thereafter serving as his *apokrisiarios* in Constantinople.[169] As a deacon, Martin would have been among the most educated clerics of the Roman church and, as such, intimately familiar with the issues presented in the Monothelite controversy. Moreover, as *apokrisiarios* he would have had to possess a high degree of diplomatic finesse in order successfully to navigate Byzantium's serpentine waters.[170] Pope Theodore appears to have had confidence both in Martin's intellectual acumen and political adroitness since he wrote patriarch Paul offering to designate him as his personal representative at a proposed synod to be held in the capital for the purpose of formally deposing patriarch Pyrrhus, who had lapsed into Monothelitism after professing the orthodox position and as a consequence incurred Rome's anathema.[171] Theodore's offer to appoint Martin as his legate in this highly delicate affair also reflects that the future pontiff was fully proficient in Greek.

The linguistic Hellenization of the eastern part of the empire, which had begun at the start of Heraclius's reign, was completed by about the middle of the seventh century when the emperor died.[172] By the late 640s, Greek had become the official language of the imperial court, the church, the legal and administrative apparatus, and the military organization.[173] The complex Latin forms of imperial address disappeared as *imperator, augustus,* and *caesar* were all replaced by the single word *basileus,* the royal title of the ancient Greek kings.[174] Imperial edicts and decrees were henceforth drawn up only in Greek, while administrators ceased to use their Latin titles and became instead logothetes and eparchs. Even the refined and somewhat affected form that Greek had displayed in the late sixth century yielded to increasing vulgarization as it became the language of the people.[175] At mid-century, a knowledge of Latin in Constantinople, even among the educated members of society, was not only rare but a "complete anachronism."[176] Under these circumstances, it is inconceivable that Pope Theodore would have dispatched Martin as his *apokrisiarios* to the capital and sought to entrust him with a mission that required the utmost delicacy in ecclesiastical politics if he were not fluent in Greek and thus fully at ease in Byzantium's linguistic milieu.

In addition to his education, diplomatic skills, and knowledge of Greek, Martin showed an inclination toward religious zealotry, which seems to have been nurtured, if not acquired, during his days as Pope Theodore's *apokrisiarios* in Constantinople, through his association with members of a society known as the Spoudaei. The fervor to fight Monothelitism, which Martin was to gain from his close relationship with this confraternity of Eastern religious enthusiasts, added to the other qualities that made him an ideal successor to Pope Theodore.

The Spoudaei seem to have come into existence sometime during the fourth century in various parts of the East including Egypt, Jerusalem, Antioch, Cyprus, and Constantinople. They were known to have supported John Chrysostom in his battles against the Arians while he was still in Antioch by engaging in processions, vigils, chants, and various ascetic practices. The Spoudaei appeared in Constantinople around 450, where they assiduously participated in the various divine offices celebrated in the capital's churches, to which they attached themselves as auxiliaries or fellowships. Their piety and devotion is exemplified by St. Auxentios, a fifth-century member of the Spoudaei who, according to his *Life* by Simeon Metaphrastes, enjoyed a great reputation in Constantinople for his religious zeal and pursuit of personal virtue.[177]

While in Constantinople as Pope Theodore's *apokrisiarios*, Martin became acquainted with a certain Theodore and his brother Theodosios, who were members of the Spoudaeite fellowship attached to the Great Church of Haghia Sophia.[178] The future pope seems to have formed an exceptionally close liaison with these religious zealots that survived his years as *apokrisiarios* and continued into his pontificate. When he became pope, Martin probably introduced his Constantinopolitan *apokrisiarios* Anastasios to Theodore and Theodosios, both of whom became Anastasios's close friends. Anastasios's vocal opposition to Monothelitism led patriarch Paul II to impose an interdict on the celebration of mass by the papal *apokrisiarii* at the Placidia Palace where they resided.[179] While detained for nearly a year on the Aegean island of Naxos awaiting trial in Constantinople, Martin wrote Theodore two impassioned letters whose content belies a deep personal bond of longstanding duration.[180] The Spoudaei, who were ardent anti-Monothelites, adopted Martin as a paradigm for those who espoused the orthodox faith. Sometime in 668 or 669, Theodore wrote a work entitled the *Hypomnesticon*, which was intended to inspire the Spoudaei of Constantinople in their struggle against Monothelitism by setting forth the tribulations of the pope and others as examples to be emulated.[181]

Martin's election quickly filled a void that threatened to upset years of planning. It gave Rome a pontiff who, although by birth a Westerner, bore the heavy imprint of the East in all the attributes that would be needed in the fight against Monothelitism. It also provided Maximos with a vigorous and capable collaborator. On both counts, the intransigent old Greek monk, who had surely played a major part in choosing Martin as Pope Theodore's successor, would not have had it any other way.[182]

Preparations for the forthcoming Roman synod continued through the summer and early fall of 649. Although it is inconceivable that news of the impending council did not reach Constantinople, the empire was far too occupied with crises in the East to divert its attention to events taking place in Rome. In late 647, a large Arab fleet invaded Cyprus for the second time. An imperial army under the *cubicularios* Kakorizos succeeded in driving the Arabs to the offshore island of Arados, but not before the invaders had ravaged and plundered extensively. Since the Arabs could not take Arados and winter was setting in, they returned to Damascus, but came back in 648 or 649 with a substantial force that succeeded in burning Arados and razing its walls. Later in 649, an Arab force invaded Isauria in Asia Minor, inflicting significant casualties among the imperial troops and taking five thousand prisoners.[183]

In Rome, meanwhile, nearly three years of meticulous planning was about to come to fruition. Nothing had been left to chance; no detail had gone unaddressed. There would be no surprise or spontaneity; no extemporaneous speeches or unfettered debates would be permitted.[184] Every part of the proceeding had been carefully scripted.[185] Each speaker had rehearsed what he had been assigned to say long before Theophylaktos arose to announce the opening of the synod on October 5, 649.[186] Although Martin of Todi occupied the apostolic throne, and the scores of bishops present had been formally called together by his authority,[187] everyone there knew that what was about to take place had been the product of the firm but shadowy hand of the "zealous God-bearing Maximos" of Constantinople and his retinue of zealous and devoted Eastern monks.[188] It was, therefore, hardly unexpected that the Lateran Council would turn out to be, in form as well as substance, a manifestly Byzantine affair.

⌇

The bishops who attended the Lateran Council of 649 were, with the single exception of the Palestinian Stephen of Dor, all from dioceses located in Italy, Sicily, Sardinia, Corsica, and Africa.[189] There were no hierarchs from any other parts of the West, including Transalpine Europe and Spain, or from Greece or Crete, despite the fact that all these areas were under Rome's ecclesiastical jurisdiction.[190] Nearly one-fourth of the bishops present, nevertheless, had names reflecting an eastern origin or ancestry, or like Pope Martin, although not ethnically Easterners, had been influenced by the intellectual traditions of the East so that they were well educated and had a good knowledge of Greek.[191] Predictably, it was from among ethnic Easterners and those native Latins who had experienced the impact of Eastern learning and who also knew Greek that Maximos, no doubt in consultation with the pope, chose the bishops who were to have speaking roles at the synod.[192] The most prominent part was, not surprisingly, undertaken by Pope Martin, followed by Bishops Maximos of Aquileia and Deusdedit of Cagliari in Sardinia.[193] Bishops Maurus of Cesena, representing the absent archbishop of Ravenna, Sergius of Tempsa, Benedict of Ajaccio in Corsica, and Leontios of Naples each made what amounted to procedural statements concurring, for example, in the suggestion that certain texts be read to the assembly.[194] Based upon the order in which they subscribed to the synodal acts, the prelates who played prominent roles at the council, with the exception of Leontios of Naples, also ranked highest in seniority among the bishops present.[195] Thus, by the middle of the seventh century, the most senior bishops of the churches under Rome's jurisdiction in Italy included Easterners and Westerners with strong links to the intellectual traditions of the East.

The remaining ninety-eight bishops who attended the council were little more than spectators. They played no substantive role in the synodal proceedings and spoke, purportedly in unison, only five times.[196] On three of those occasions they merely agreed to proposals that certain texts be read.[197] The fourth time they professed their adherence to the faith of the fathers and the declarations of the five ecumenical councils and condemned those who departed from either.[198] At the end of the final session of the council, they recited the Creed, adding a confession that Christ possessed two wills and energies, and ended by announcing, again en masse, the synod's canons and the usual anathemas.[199] Despite their negligible role in the proceedings, however, the presence of so large a number of bishops was important in at least two respects.[200] It reinforced Maximos's claim to the council's ecumenicity by bolstering the synod's "horizontal" aspect. It was not enough that the assembly adhere to a mode of argumentation that sought to derive doctrinal truth by examining the writings of the fathers and the councils and thereby determine whether Monothelitism was consistent with what they had handed down "vertically" so to speak. In order to be ecumenical, the synod also had to arrive at a *consensus omnium* or universal consensus regarding what was correct doctrine and what was not. Its "horizontal" aspect thus required the presence of a sufficiently large assembly of bishops so that the council's doctrinal pronouncements might at least appear to have been formulated by a substantial segment of the episcopate.[201] Moreover, a sizable assembly of even "silently attentive supernumeraries" contributed to the politico-ecclesiastical weight of the council and at least gave some credence to the claim that the episcopate from Africa to Palestine was solidly behind the Roman church in its struggle against Monothelitism.[202] The sad but undeniable truth was that however much they may have wanted to understand the theological arguments and patristic *florilegia* that were paraded past them, the vast majority of bishops at the synod were so uneducated and intellectually ill-equipped that they simply could not grasp the subtleties and nuances that the Easterners had woven.[203] In the end, they would subscribe mechanically to the canons that had been prepared by others and that they only vaguely understood.[204] It was enough for them to know that Monothelitism departed from Chalcedon. As for the details of how and why, they were content to leave that to Maximos and his monastic entourage.[205]

The participation of the Palestinian bishop Stephen of Dor and a delegation of thirty-seven Greek monks, as well as the presentation of a letter from archbishop Sergius of the autocephalous church of Cyprus, all of which occurred at the synod's second session on October 8, 649, added another vital element to the Lateran Council. Stephen of Dor, as we have seen, had written a tract in Greek that, with papal approval, was translated into Latin and read to the synod by the notary Anastasios.[206] Stephen called upon the assembled prelates to imitate his mentor Sophronios of Jerusalem and adhere to the orthodox faith with the same tenacity and fervor that the late patriarch had shown. He castigated the doctrinal depravity espoused by the *Typos*, and told the bishops that "all the orthodox priests and people of the East" were depending upon Rome, whose authority was based on its Petrine foundation, to champion the faith as it had been defined "by the glorious fathers of the church and the five ecumenical councils."[207] The monastic *libellus*, which had also been composed in Greek, was, with papal leave, translated into Latin and presented to the council by the notary Theodoros immediately after Stephen's tract had been read. The monks also urged the synod to anathematize the principal exponents of Monothelitism such as Cyrus, Sergius, and Pyrrhus, and to condemn the *Typos*, whose promulgation they attributed, as had Stephen of Dor, not to "our most pious emperor," but rather to patriarch Paul, who had deceived the emperor into issuing it.[208] Finally, the notary Exsuperius translated for the council a letter that had been written to Pope Theodore seven years earlier by archbishop Sergius of Cyprus. The Cypriot prelate had, like Stephen of Dor, extolled Rome's spiritual authority by virtue of its Petrine origin, and recalled how Pope Leo's *Tome* and Theodore's own writings had correctly set forth the faith of the holy fathers by confessing Christ's two wills.[209]

The presentation of the *libelli* of Stephen of Dor and the Greek monastics as well as the letter of Sergius of Cyprus was, like everything else at the Lateran Council of 649, arranged by Maximos by design. The anti-Monothelite confessions of even a great number of western bishops would not alone have been sufficient to make the council a truly ecumenical assembly. But, by adding to them the voices of such figures as Sophronios of Jerusalem, as transmitted through Jerusalem's principal suffragan the bishop of Dor, together with representatives of Eastern monasticism and the Cypriot church, what Constantinople might have otherwise dismissed as a mere provincial synod now took on the appearance of a universal council.[210] It was not only the West that was condemning Monothelitism, but a broad and influential segment of the East as well.

By far the most visible among those who were not bishops was Theophylaktos, *primicerius notariorum* of the Roman church and head of the papal chancery and library, and the regional notaries Anastasios, Theodoros, Paschalios, and Exsuperius, who served as Theophylaktos's assistants in the pontifical *scrinium*. During the course of the synod, the notaries were responsible for retrieving the copious codices and texts that related to the matters at issue at a particular point in the proceedings, and reading the relevant excerpts to the assembly.[211]

Since the vast majority of the texts, whether heretical or orthodox, were written by authors of Eastern provenance, the notaries had to be able to render simultaneous translations from Greek into Latin for the majority of the bishops who knew no Greek.[212] The foregoing reflects in several ways the radical transformation that the papal secretariat had experienced as a result of the influence of the East during the first half of the seventh century. The paucity of books in the papal library around the year 600 contrasts sharply with the numerous codices, most of them in Greek, that stocked its shelves fifty years later.[213] Moreover, functionaries fully proficient in both Greek and Latin now staffed the papal chancery, contrasting markedly with Gregory the Great's lament about the lack of good Greek translators in Rome at the turn of the previous century.[214] Finally, the obviously Eastern ethnicity of the chief of the papal chancery and three of his assistants reveals that by the middle of the seventh century Greeks had come to dominate the increasingly important administrative apparatus of the Papacy.

But it was not only in the papal *scrinium* where Greeks and the Greek language predominated. Until only recently, it was generally accepted that the acts and proceedings of the Lateran Council were originally written in Latin and later translated into a Greek version which was disseminated in the East.[215] But a close comparison of the Greek and Latin texts reveals precisely the opposite: the acts and proceedings of the Lateran Council of 649 were set down initially in Greek, and the Latin version was a translation of the original Greek text.[216] This conclusion was arrived at by observing, for instance, the repeated use of anomalous verbal constructions in the Latin manuscripts which, when compared with the correct use of the equivalent words or phrases in the Greek sources, suggested that the Latin text had been written by persons fully proficient in Greek but severely deficient in composing polished Latin.[217] Based upon these as well as other grammatical and verbal aberrations, it became clear that the authors of the Latin text of the synodal proceedings, though masters in Greek composition, were not native Latin speakers and appeared to have learned Latin as a second language.[218] That conclusion, although astonishing, was, of course, entirely correct.[219]

The Lateran Council was the result of the collaborative efforts of a Greco-Palestinian pope and a monk from Constantinople along with his coterie of Eastern monastics. None of them was a native Latin speaker, and all of them, although fully proficient in Greek and probably even Syriac, had doubtless learned whatever Latin they knew after they had fled to the West. The council's proceedings had been scripted by these Easterners, and the vast majority of the conciliar and patristic texts upon which they relied were, as we shall examine in greater detail, of Eastern provenance. It is, therefore, not surprising that they would have composed the speeches and the synodal acts in their native Greek tongue and then translated what they had written into the passable but imperfect Latin which they had had to quickly learn in their new environment.[220]

It was, however, in the methodology by which it set out to challenge Monothelitism that the Lateran Council reflected most clearly the impact of the East. That methodology consisted of a tripartite approach that combined elements of purely Eastern provenance directly traceable to oriental concepts imported to Rome and brought to bear upon the synod by Maximos Confessor and his monastic collaborators.

The Monothelite controversy provided Maximos Confessor with the opportunity to develop and further refine a theological method that he had already used against Origenism and for which he was indebted to Dionysios the Areopagite.[221] Maximos's unquestioning reliance on the voices of the fathers as evidence for the orthodox faith is directly traceable to this shadowy and elusive figure from the East, upon whose writings he composed an extensive commentary and who was for him nothing less than the θεοφάντωρ or revealer of God.[222] According to Dionysios, God modeled the terrestrial realm upon the celestial kingdom establishing a hierarchical order of authority on earth that was a reflection of a similar ordering in heaven.[223] Authority in the celestial kingdom flowed downward from God through the ranks of the heavenly beings commensurate with their proximity to the Deity.[224] On earth, it was imparted "to those below Him according to their merit," coming ultimately to reside in persons who were "holy and inspired" and in whom "all sacred knowledge is completely perfected and known."[225] For Dionysios, therefore, a true knowledge of God could only be achieved by turning to those who, in the rigorous but "inspired, hierarchical harmony," were "truly beautiful, wise, and good."[226] It was thus from Dionysios that Maximos obtained the first principle that formed the basis of his methodology for revealing doctrinal truth. Correct teaching, for Maximos, derived from the authority of the fathers and the councils, and arriving at orthodox doctrine required an examination of scriptural, conciliar, and patristic texts to determine whether a particular belief did or did not find support in those sources.[227] In the same way that the authorities of heaven were for Dionysios "harmoniously and unfailingly uplifted toward the things of God," so for Maximos the fathers of the catholic church were divinely inspired.[228] Like the hierarch in Dionysios's *Ecclesiastical Hierarchy*, the fathers possessed the sacred gift of the knowledge of God and, by passing it on through holy tradition "from mind to mind," they had "generously poured out on everyone the shining beams of inspired teaching."[229] Dionysios's legacy to Maximos, and through him to seventh-century theological discourse regardless of whether one was in Rome or Constantinople, was, therefore, the indisputable principle that doctrinal orthodoxy could only be determined by an appeal to the fathers.[230]

Moreover, it was vital that the search for doctrinal truth proceed κατα τάξιν, which is to say in a systematic manner, by ordered facts, and through structured argument. Thus, any examination of the writings of persons who professed to speak with the authority of the fathers had to be pursued in a tightly organized and methodical fashion, reflecting, once again, Dionysios's injunction that divine knowledge could only be obtained by adhering to the "sacred rules of order" which was obtained in both the celestial and the terrestrial realms.[231] Thus, at the first session of the Lateran Council, bishop Deusdedit of Cagliari urged the synod to examine the writings of Cyrus, Sergius, Pyrrhus, and Paul so that their deviation from the "immaculate faith" could be exposed κατα τάξιν or in an orderly fashion.[232] Thereafter, Pope Martin proposed that the council conduct its inquiry by means of an orderly examination into the matters at issue so that a just determination could be made regarding what was and what was not consistent with the fathers. To that end, he announced that the papal notaries were prepared to present the council in an orderly fashion with the appropriate textual expositions.[233] At the conclusion of the synod, and after setting forth the position of the principal proponents of Monothelitism, the pope declared that he would proceed εν τάξιν, or in an orderly way, to prove how the views of his adversaries were consistent with those of the heretics rather than the orthodox fathers.[234]

Thus, the final ingredient in the formula for arriving at doctrinal truth required the application of natural argumentation and reasoning to those patristic texts which had been systematically assembled and methodically presented so that what was orthodox could be proved and what was heretical could be exposed.[235] Dionysios had asserted that human minds had the capacity to think, and that although human souls were on a lower level than celestial intelligences, they nonetheless possessed the power of reason, which they were capable of exercising "in their own fashion and as far as they can."[236] In the famous letter to his brother Gregory of Nyssa concerning the difference between essence (ουσία) and hypostasis (υπόστασις), Basil the Great had shown how the principles of logic and reasoning could be employed to elucidate Christian truth and, by doing so, had legitimated their use in that endeavor.[237] Drawing upon this Eastern patristic tradition, Maximos also believed in the importance of dialectical reasoning and the utility of the rules of logic and argumentation in the search for Christian doctrinal truth.[238] Consistent with Dionysios and Basil, Maximos was firmly committed to the proposition that human reason had the capacity to distinguish between teaching that represented "the pious, right, true and saving word of the apostolic faith," and that which departed from tradition and, by becoming infected with innovation, fell outside the chain of recognized authorities and was doctrinally unsound.[239]

Maximos departed radically from Dionysios, however, to the extent that he disputed the emperor's historically exclusive prerogative of convening an ecumenical council of the church. For Dionysios, the terrestrial sociopolitical order was an expression of God's will reflecting on earth the "unseen things of God."[240] The visible hierarchical arrangement of society that God had ordained on earth was for him a "ministerial colleague" of the divine hierarchy.[241] This meant that "order and rank here below are a sign of the harmonious ordering toward the divine realm."[242] Since the terrestrial hierarchy "bears in itself the mark of God," it was positively wrong in Dionysios's eyes "ever to do anything or even to exist against the sacred orderings of him who is after all the source of all perfection."[243]

Dionysios had severely criticized the monk Demophilus for having departed from his assigned place in the hierarchical order and presumed to exercise a role beyond that which God had prescribed for him. Such a disturbance of the divine ordering of society was tantamount to a blatant violation of God's θεσμός or law and, as such, an act of arrogance that represented the very essence of evil.[244] It is inconceivable that Maximos was unaware of this fundamental tenet of Dionysian sociopolitical philosophy and highly probable that he simply chose to ignore it since it was altogether incompatible with his intensely anti-Monothelite agenda. If so, it represents an instance of eclecticism that shows that Maximos was at best inconsistent and at worst not entirely honest intellectually where the war against Monothelitism was concerned.

Considering the extent to which elements of Eastern origin influenced the Lateran Council of 649, and in particular the Eastern provenance of those who scripted the proceedings, it is not at all extraordinary to find that the vast majority of patristic *florilegia* presented during the course of the synod came from the writings of the Greek fathers rather than the Latin ones. In his opening address to the council on October 5, Pope Martin referred to five texts written by Greek fathers and to only two texts written by Pope Leo.[245] During the third session on October 17, the pope responded to the arguments made in eleven excerpts taken from Theodore of Pharan's letter to bishop Sergius of Arsinoe by citing only Eastern patristic sources.[246] Similarly, Martin's explanation of how Cyrus of Alexandria and Sergius of Constantinople had misconstrued Dionysios's fourth letter against Gaius appealed only to a text from Cyril of Alexandria.[247] The addresses made at the synod's fourth session on October 19 contained references to two letters of Gregory Nazianzen and a work by Anastasios Sinaites.[248]

But it was at fifth and final session on October 31 that the council's overwhelming reliance on *florilegia* culled from the writings of the Greek fathers as compared with their Latin counterparts was most evident. As the session opened, Pope Martin announced that he had directed that sacred books containing the venerated testimonies of the holy fathers be brought to the assembly so that by examining them the synod would be able to know what the approved fathers had taught and, by contrast, what was censurable in the teaching of the heretics.[249] At that point, bishop Leontios of Naples requested that, before the testimonies were presented, the synod be read that portion of the proceedings of the Fifth Ecumenical Council where it had identified the fathers whose "words and teachings were to be received and confessed by all Christians." In this way, Leontios reasoned, the present assembly could distinguish between the approved fathers of the church and those who claimed to be orthodox but who, in fact, had succumbed to innovation and departed from tradition.[250] The pope readily approved Leontios's suggestion, whereupon Theophylakos produced the relevant excerpt from the Fifth Ecumenical Council and handed it to the notary Anastasios, who read it to the synod.[251] Of the twelve fathers whom the Fifth Council had specifically identified as the principal "holy fathers and doctors of the church," eight were Greek and only four were Latin. The list, however, was admittedly not exclusive for the council recognized that, beyond those whom it had named, there were "other holy and orthodox fathers."[252]

With the preliminaries neatly out of the way, Theophylaktos produced the "excerpted testimonies of the holy fathers" and handed them to his assistant Exsuperius, who then began the lengthy process of reading the *florilegia* to the synod.[253] Extracts from fifty-eight works of twenty-one orthodox fathers were read to the council: sixteen of the authors were Greek and only five were Latin; forty-three of the texts were written by Easterners, only fifteen by Westerners.[254] In addition to the *florilegia*, which were actually read at the council's fifth session, it appears that extracts from other orthodox patristic works, contained in a manuscript titled the *Florilegium dyotheleticum*, which dates to the thirteenth century, were also presented to the assembly, although there is no evidence of how or when this was done.[255] The prologue to the *Florilegium dyotheleticum* recites that the document contains "other texts which were brought before this holy and apostolic synod of fathers consistent with those which had been previously presented, and that positively show that it is impossible to contend that there is one energy in the deity and humanity of our Lord Jesus Christ."[256] Here again, Eastern patristic texts preponderate heavily against their Western counterparts. The *Florilegium dyotheleticum* contains excerpts from eighty-one works of sixteen authors. Seventy-four works are of Eastern origin; only seven are from the West. Twelve of the fathers are Greek; only four are Latin.[257]

After the orthodox patristic texts had been read, the synod unanimously pronounced its adherence to what the fathers and the five ecumenical councils had taught, and condemned all those who contradicted them.[258] For Maximos, however, simply anathematizing the heretics was not enough. It was necessary to "uncover the disgraceful and confront them to their face so that we may expose the uncleanliness of their heresy to all."[259] When the synod requested that the writings of those "heretical infidels" who had departed from the teachings of the approved fathers and the church councils be read, Theophylaktos immediately produced the relevant *florilegia* and delivered them to his assistant Theodoros, who read a Latin translation of the original Greek text to the council.[260] Excerpts from the works of thirteen authors were presented to the synod: all of them were Easterners.[261]

The orthodox and heretical *florilegia* read at the fifth session of the Lateran Council were part of the extensive collection of proof texts that Sophronios of Jerusalem had assembled and shared with Maximos Confessor while they were together in Africa in 632 or 633.[262] The Roman synod of 649 was not, however, the first occasion on which Maximos had combined his impressive inheritance of Eastern learning and erudition with his legacy from Sophronios in order to craft weapons in the fight against Monothelitism. Indeed, the striking similarity between various aspects of the Lateran Council and Maximos's anti-Monothelite writings that preceded it provide further evidence of the influence that he exerted on the Roman synod.[263]

In late September, 641, patriarch Pyrrhus of Constantinople was driven from his see as a result of his involvement in the struggle for the succession to the throne that followed the death of Heraclius. Pyrrhus fled to Africa where he was almost immediately confronted by members of the local monastic community, one of whose leaders was Maximos, regarding his position on the *Ekthesis*.[264] In July, 645, Pyrrhus and Maximos engaged in a famous debate on Monothelitism conducted in Carthage under the auspices of the exarch Gregory.[265] The *Disputation with Pyrrhus* was in many ways a dress rehearsal for what would take place in Rome four years later.[266] Maximos began by framing the debate as a struggle between tradition on the one hand and "new dogma" on the other. Monothelitism, he contended, had departed from the "patristic and apostolic teaching which has come to us from the beginning" and embraced, instead, doctrines that were innovative and hence outside the chain of recognized authorities.[267] Four years later, he would establish the same conceptual framework for the Lateran Council, arguing, through the speeches of Pope Martin and bishops Maximos of Aquileia and Leontios of Naples, that the Monothelites had concocted "novel inventions" and, through the letters of the African prelates, that these innovations had caused them to stray from apostolic authority and patristic doctrine.[268]

During the disputation with Pyrrhus, Maximos naturally appealed to the substantial corpus of *florilegia* that he had in his theological arsenal in order to prove the error of Monothelitism. Among the many texts that he cited were Gregory Nazianzen's first and second orations *Concerning the Son* and his *Letter to Cledonius*, Gregory of Nyssa's oration *On Resurrection Sunday*, Hilary of Poitiers's treatise *On the Trinity*, Cyril of Alexandria's *Commentary on the Gospel of John* and *Apology Against Theodoret*, Pope Leo's *Letter to the Emperor Leo*, and Dionysios the Areopagite's *Letter Against Gaius*.[269] These identical excerpts would be presented to the Lateran Council in 649.[270] In another pre-Lateran polemic against Monothelitism entitled the *Tomus Spiritualis*, Maximos appealed to the same works by Gregory Nazianzen, Cyril of Alexandria, and Pope Leo that he had cited in the debate with Pyrrhus, but here he added citations to Athanasius's *On the Trinity* and *On the Incarnation*, Gregory of Nyssa's *Book II Against Eunomius* and his treatise *Against Apollinaris*, Cyril's *Thesaurarum*, Ambrose of Milan's *Second Letter Against Gratian*, Severian of Gabala's "*Father let this pass from me*," and three works by John Chrysostom including his *Sermon on the Apostle Thomas*.[271] Among the heretics, Maximos noted the errors of Themestius as set forth in his *Sermons Against Colluthus*, Theodore of Mopsuestia in his *Second Book on Miracles*, Polemon in his *Sixth Letter to Timothy*, Apollinaris of Laodicea in his treatise *On the Incarnation* and his *Sermon on Epiphany*, Nestorius in his *Second Book Concerning Epiphanius*, and without citing any specific work, he condemned generally Nestorius's pupil Paul the Persian.[272] These same orthodox and heretical texts would reappear, either exactly or with some linguistic variations, at the Roman synod.[273] Of the one hundred sixty-one textual citations read at the fifth and final session of the Lateran Council of 649, twenty-seven appear verbatim in Maximos's *Tomus Spiritualis*: sixteen are taken from the writings of the orthodox fathers and eleven from the works of those identified as heretics. Easterners predominate disproportionately over those from the West.[274]

Finally, the council's formal pronouncements, which were expressed in twenty canons, similarly reflect Maximos's influence.[275] Canons X and XI, which specifically address the matter of Christ's two wills and two energies and thus speak to the core issue dealt with by the synod, parallel almost exactly the language that Maximos had used in his disputation with Pyrrhus in Carthage.[276]

At the conclusion of the Lateran Council, Pope Martin disseminated a general epistle to the universal catholic church, including bishops, priests, deacons, abbots, and monks everywhere, announcing the decisions of the Roman synod.[277] There can be little doubt that it too was the literary product of Maximos Confessor and his monastic followers.[278] The encyclical repeated yet again Maximos's mantra that the council had reached its decisions based upon the authority of holy tradition faithfully received from the fathers and the councils that had preceded it. It emphasized that the synodal canons were based upon a scrupulous examination of orthodox patristic texts and a careful comparison of those sources with the writings of the heretics in an effort to "differentiate light from darkness" and thereby distinguish the "clear doctrine of the fathers from the madness of false heretical beliefs."[279] Maximos labored one last time to prove that the deliberations of the Lateran Council were both procedurally and substantively in conformity with the five general councils that preceded it and thus authoritatively their equal. In what was doubtless an effort to augment this claim to universality, the synodal acts were widely distributed. In the West, they were sent to bishop Amandus of Maastricht along with a papal directive that the bishop arrange with King Sigibert III to convene a synod of Frankish bishops for the purpose of expressing adherence to what the Roman synod had promulgated.[280] As for the East, Pope Martin dispatched four of the thirty-six Greek monks who had appeared at the second session of the Lateran Council with their anti-Monothelite tract as envoys to bishop John of Philadelphia, papal vicar for Palestine, bearing the conciliar acts.[281] The pronouncements of the Roman synod were also made known to bishop Theodore of Esbas in Arabia, bishop Anthony of Bacatha, archimandrite George of the monastery of St. Theodosios, bishop Pantaleon of Dor, bishop Paul of Thessalonika, as well as the churches of Jerusalem and Antioch.[282]

But neither Maximos's insistence on the Lateran Council's ecumenicity nor the broad circulation of its acts was ever sufficient to raise its official status beyond that of a provincial episcopal assembly. The emperor's absence and opposition confirmed beyond cavil that convening ecumenical councils was and would remain an exclusively imperial prerogative.

৵

The Lateran Council of 649 had not diminished by one particle Rome's unequivocal commitment to the concept of a single, undivided Christian empire under the authority and protection of an emperor ordained by God. The imperial ideology espoused by Pope Gregory I had lost none of its vitality in the half century between his pontificate and the Roman synod of 649. But the issue of how and at whose initiative the faith would be defined—a problem festering since Pope Leo I and the acceptance of his Christological formula at Chalcedon—still lay unresolved. Could the emperor accept a church defined by others than himself while at the same time preserving his own dignity as Christ's delegate on earth? The furies had been unleashed. Could Constans II force them back into the darkness? He certainly would try. Within four years of the day the council adjourned on October 31, 649, Martin and Maximos would both be arrested and brought to Constantinople to stand trial for defying the emperor and transgressing the *Typos's* command of silence on the question of Christ's wills and energies.[283] The Lateran Council's claim to be "holy sixth synod" would represent nothing more than the determined aspiration of its shadowy spiritual father.[284] Although its condemnation of Monothelitism would be vindicated at the true Sixth Ecumenical Council a little over thirty years later, the real importance of the Roman synod of 649 lies in the fact that it ushered in the period of Rome's "Greek intermezzo," reflecting the many ways in which the East was making its presence in the city on the Tiber ever more palpable as the seventh century moved along.[285]

Notes

1. *Mansi* X, 903. ("The most reverend abbots, presbyters, and monks may come in.")
2. Richard Krautheimer, *Rome: Profile of a City, 312–1308* (Princeton, 1980), pp. 21–24.
3. G. B. de Rossi, *Codices Palatini Latini Bibliothecae Vaticanae*, Vol. I (Rome, 1886), p. 66; *Liber Diurnus LIX, LX, LXI, LXII, and LXIII*, id., pp. 49–59.
4. Jaffé, id., No. 2057, p. 230; Rudolf Riedinger, ed., *Concilium Lateranense a. 649 celebratum* (Berlin, 1984), p. 3.
5. *LP* I, pp. 336–37; Hefele, id., pp. 436–37; Riedinger, *Concilium*, pp. 9–23.
6. Riedinger, *Concilium*, pp. 23–29.
7. Id., pp. 36–37. The texts refer to the sessions of the Lateran Council of 649 as *secretaria* since synods or councils were frequently held in buildings adjacent to the Lateran's Constantinian basilica that were referred to by that name. Hefele, id., p. 435n7. See also *Mansi* X, 891; Bertolini, id., p. 333; Hefele, id., pp. 94; 101–2.
8. Riedinger, *Concilium*, p. 41.
9. Id., pp. 38–47.
10. Id., p. 49.
11. The abbots included John, of the monastery of St. Sabas; Theodoros, of an unidentified monastery in Africa; Thalassios, of the Armenian monastery of Renatus in

Rome; and Georgios, of the Cilician monastery located at Aquas Salvias outside the walls of Rome. Id., p. 49. See infra, pp. 205ff.

12. Id., p. 51. *humillimum libellum.*

13. Id., pp. 51–55.

14. Id., p. 57.

15. The *chartularios*, or *comes vestiarii* in the West, first appears in the fifth century, at which time his responsibilities are primarily those of clothing and provisioning the army. By the eighth century the duties of the position were expanded to include various financial responsibilities related to philanthropic and benevolent institutions such as *xenodochia* or hostelries and *gerocomia* or homes for the elderly. See Pililis, id., pp. 205–7.

16. Gregorovius, id., pp. 139–40n2.

17. The inscription on Isaac's sarcophagus in the church of San Vitale in Ravenna reflects that in fact the exarch, who successfully governed Byzantine Italy for eighteen years, showed particular loyalty to Constantinople during his long tenure and indeed, along with his erstwhile confederate Maurikios, had greatly pleased the emperor Heraclius when he sent him a portion of the spoils plundered from the Lateran *episcopium* during the pontificate of Severinus. *LP* I, p. 329. For the Greek text of the inscription on Isaac's sarcophagus, see Gregorovius, id., p. 141n1.

18. *LP* I, p. 331. By the seventh century, the term *iudices*, whom the *Liber Pontificalis* identifies as having supported Mavrikios's rebellion, meant "official in the broadest sense and judge in the literal sense." By the late seventh and early eighth centuries, social standing came to be so equated with military rank that "*iudices* became a collective term for the highest stratum of society." T. S. Brown, *Gentlemen and Officers*, p. 12.

19. *LP* I, p. 331–32.

20. *Mansi* X, 610; 878; *LP* I, p. 332; Jaffé, id., Nos. 2054 and 2055, p. 229.

21. O. Capitani, "Le relazioni tra le vite di Teodoro I e Martino I del *Liber Pontificalis* e gli Atti del Concilio Lateranense del 649: nuove prospettive," *Studi e richerche sull'Oriente cristiano* 15 (1992): 5, 7.

22. T. S. Brown, *Gentlemen and Officers*, p. 158. Id., p. 159.

23. Id., p. 159.

24. Capitani, id., pp. 7–8; Ottorino Bertolini, "Riflessi politici delle controversie religiose con Bisanzio nelle vicende del sec. VII in Italia," in *Caratteri del secolo VII in Occidente*, Vol. 2, Settimane di Studio del Centro Italiano di Studi sull'Alto Medioevo, 23–29 April 1957 (Spoleto, 1958), pp. 758–59.

25. *PG* 91: 137–38; J. J. Taylor, "Eastern Appeals to Rome in the Early Church: A Little Known Witness," *Downside Review* 89 (1971): 142–46.

26. *Mansi* X, 610; Jaffé, id., No. 2054, p. 229; Theophanes, *Chronographia*, p. 462; *Synodicon Vetus*, No. 138, p. 115.

27. Rudolf Riedinger, "In welchen Richtung wurden die Akten der Lateransynode von 649 übersetzt, und in welcher Schrift war der lateinische Text dieser Akten geschrieben," in *Martino I Papa (649–653) e il suo tempo*, Atti del XXVIII convegno storico internazionale, Todi, 13–16 October 1991 (Spoleto, 1992), p. 149.

28. Cf., Judith Herrin, *The Formation of Christendom* (London, 1987), p. 252.

29. Pietro Conte, *Il Sinodo Lateranense dell'ottobre 649: La Nuova Edizione degli Atti a*

Cura di Rudolf Riedinger (Vatican City, 1989), pp. 127–28; Riedinger, "In welcher Rich-tung wurden die Akten der Lateransynode von 649 übersetzt," id., p. 153.

30. Mansi X, 896BC.

31. Conte, id., p. 116; Averil Cameron, "Byzantium and the Past in the Seventh Cen-tury: The Search for Redefinition," in Changing Cultures in Early Byzantium (Aldershot, 1996), pp. 268–69.

32. Rudolf Riedinger, "Zwei Briefe aus den Akten der Lateransynode von 649," Jahr-buch der Österreichischen Byzantinistik 29 (1980): 37, 43.

33. LP I, p. 332; Theophanes, Chronographia, p. 462.

34. Id.; Rudolf Riedinger, "Die Lateransynode von 649 und Maximos der Bekenner," in Maximus Confessor. Actes du Symposium sur Maxime le Confesseur, Fribourg, 2–5 Sep-tember 1980 (Fribourg, 1982), pp. 111–21..

35. Mansi X, 1029–1032; Dölger, id., No. 225, p. 26; see also Ambrogio Piazzoni, "Arresto, Condanna, Esilio e Morte di Martino I," in Papa Martino e il suo tempo, id., pp. 189–91.

36. Georg Jenal, "Monaci e vescovi al tempo di Martino I (649–653)," in Papa Mar-tino e il suo tempo, id., p. 178; A. Grillmeier, "Rudolf Riedinger's Concilium Lateranense: A Review," Theologie und Philosophie 60 (1985): 289–93, esp. 290.

37. Capitani argues that the Typos did not arrive in Rome until after Pope Theo-dore's death on May 14, 649, although he admits that even before the pope knew about it he had decided on a confrontation with Constantinople regarding Monothelitism. O. Capitani, "Le relazioni tra le vite di Teodoro I e Martino I del Liber Pontificalis," id., p. 502.

38. See infra, p. 134ff.

39. Riedinger, "In welcher Richtung," id., p. 150; Gilbert Dagron, et al., eds., Histoire du Christianisme. Évêques, Moines et Empereurs (610–1054), Vol. 4, (Paris, 1993), p. 43; Bernard Flusin, Saint Anastase le Perse et l'histoire de la Palestine au début du VIIe siècle, Vol. 2, (Paris, 1992), p. 362; Judith Herrin, The Formation of Christendom, p. 252; Georg Jenal, id., pp. 180–81; Erich Caspar, Geschichte des Papsttums, Vol. II, (Tübingen, 1933), p. 559; Johannes Pierres, Sanctus Maximus Confessor: Princeps Apologetarum Synodi Lateranensis Anni 649 (Rome, 1940), p. 8.

40. PG 90: 111D–112D; George C. Berthold, trans., "The Trial of Maximus," in Maximus Confessor: Selected Writings, id., p. 26.

41. PG 90: 127D–128D. The Greek text's use of the word γραφέντα when referring to Pope Theodore's writings denotes an authoritativeness in content which is consistent with the fact that they were, as we have seen, taken from Sophronios's florilegium of patristic sources and intended to set forth the orthodox position against Monothelitism. See supra, p. 127ff.

42. In a letter to Pope Theodore that was read at the Lateran Council, archbishop Sergius of Cyprus refers to certain anti-Monothelite writings that the pope had composed. Since Sergius's letter had been written "seven years earlier," that is, in 642, it appears that Theodore had been expressing his opposition to Monothelitism in written works (γεγραμμένα) long before the Roman synod assembled in 649. Riedinger, Concilium, pp. 60–65.

43. PG 90: 111D–112D.

44. References to athletic feats or struggles of athletic magnitude in order to achieve the virtues through rigorous ascetic practices are commonplace in monastic literature. See, namely, Athanasius, *The Life of Antony and the Letter to Marcellinus*, trans. Robert C. Gregg (New York, 1980), p. 39; Theodoret of Cyrrhus, *A History of the Monks of Syria*, trans., R. M. Price (Kalamazoo, 1985), p. 3; Theodoret of Cyrrhus, *The Life of St. Simeon Stylites*, trans. Robert Doran, (Kalamazoo, 1992), p. 71; Palladius, *The Lausiac History*, trans. Robert T. Meyer (New York, 1964), p. 18.

45. *Καί ἄθλησις του οσίου πατρός ἡμων Θεοδόρου πάπα Ρώμης*, in Theoharis Detorakes, "Βυζάντιο καί Ευρώπη: Άγιολογικές Σχέσις (527–1453)," in *Byzantium and Europe*, First International Byzantine Conference, Delphi, 20–24 July 1985 (Athens, 1987), pp. 85, 89. Detorakes, id., 89n18. The only "Theodore, pope of Rome" to whom these references can possibly apply is Theodore I. The only other Roman pontiff who took the name Theodore was Theodore II, who reigned for twenty days in December, 897. Pope Theodore I is recognized as a saint by the Eastern church; Theodore II is not. Horace K. Mann, *The Lives of the Popes in the Middle Ages*, 2nd ed., Vol. IV (London, 1925), pp. 88–90.

46. The fifth canon of the Council of Nicaea (325) expressly directed that provincial synods be convened twice a year so that the assembled bishops might inquire into whether the orthodox faith was being observed by the regional clergy and laity and, if not, to correct deviations and punish offenders. Schaff and Wace, eds., *Nicene and Post-Nicene Fathers*, Vol. 14, *The Seven Ecumenical Councils*, id., p. 13; see also Francis Dvornik, "Emperors, Popes and General Councils," *Dumbartoan Oaks Papers* 6 (1951): 3.

47. *PG* 91: 137–138. The fact that Maximos considered the Lateran synod to be the Sixth Ecumenical Council can also be inferred from Theophylaktos's opening remarks in which he says that the council was being convened in order to affirm the faith as set forth both by the fathers of the catholic church and by the Fifth Ecumenical Council. The specific reference to the Fifth Ecumenical Council (Constantinople II), which had nothing to do with Monothelitism, can only mean that Maximos regarded the present assembly as its successor insofar as its authority to speak on doctrinal matters and bind the whole church. Riedinger, *Concilium*, pp. 8–11.

48. Riedinger, *Concilium*, p. 411.

49. Id., p. 413; Hermann Josef Sieben, *Die Konzilsidee der Alten Kirche* (Paderborn, 1979), pp. 515–16. Although Pope Theodore's predecessors Severinus and John IV had both convened Roman synods that condemned Monothelitism, neither of those assemblies ever made pretensions to ecumenical status or to speak for the universal church. For Pope Severinus see *Mansi* X, 679–80; Jaffé, id., No. 2039, p. 227; cf., *Liber Diurnus* LXIII, *Promissio Fidei Episcopi*, id., p. 72. For Pope John IV, see Theophanes, *Chronographia*, p. 461; *Synodicon Vetus*, No. 137, p. 115; cf., *Liber Diurnus* LXIII, *Promissio Fidei Episcopi*, id., p. 72.

50. *PG* 91: 137–38.

51. Nicaea (325) had been convened by Constantine I; Constantinople I (381) by Theodosios I; Ephesus (431) by Theodosios II; Chalcedon (451) by Marcian; and Constantinople II (553) by Justinian I. Schaff and Wace, eds., *Nicene and Post-Nicene Fathers*, Vol. 14, *The Seven Ecumenical Councils*, id., pp. 3, 161, 191, 243, 296.

52. Leo I. *Epistola* No. 162, *Mansi* V, 338ff.; J.M. Hussey, *The Orthodox Church in the Byzantine Empire* (Oxford, 1986), p. 302; Dvornik, id., p. 17.

53. Dvornik, id., pp. 11–12.

54. *PG* 25: 281–308.

55. Dvornik, id., p. 3.

56. See, namely, the acclamations to Theodosios I at the Second Council of Constantinople and to Marcian at the Council of Chalcedon. Schaff and Wace., eds., id., pp. 170, 265.

57. See, namely, Riedinger, *Concilium*, id., pp. 49, 61, 67, 120, 146, 165, 197, 207.

58. *Mansi* X, 790; Hefele, id., p. 450.

59. Id., p. 3; Schaff and Wace, eds., id., p. 265.

60. *PG* 90: 117AD; J. M. Garrigues, "Le martyre de saint Maxime le confesseur," *Revue Thomiste* 76 (1976): 410, 412.

61. *PG* 90: 117BC; *PG* 119: 949B; Riedinger, *Concilium*, pp. 8–9; Hussey, id., pp. 302–3.

62. Yves M.-J. Congar, "Conscience ecclésiologique en Orient et en Occident du VIe au IXe siècle," *Istina* 6 (1959): 187, 202–3.

63. *PL* 87: 1161.

64. The difference between East and West in this regard finds expression in their respective liturgical practices. In the eastern liturgies, the celebrant prays "for the stability of the holy churches of God," while in the West he prays for the unity of "the Church." Cf., "The Liturgy of St. John Chrysostom," "The Liturgy of St. Basil," and "The Liturgy of the Presanctified Gifts," in Ιερατικόν, 3rd ed. (Athens, 1987), pp. 106, 158, 203; Congar, id., 202n51. For a discussion of "the One and the Many" in the ecclesiological traditions of East and West, see Aidan Nichols, *Theology in the Russian Diaspora. Church, Fathers, Eucharist in Nikolai Afanas'ev* (Cambridge, 1989), pp. 177–87.

65. Congar, id., pp. 203.

66. See Aidan Nichols, *Byzantine Gospel: Maximus the Confessor in Modern Scholarship*, (Edinburgh, 1993), pp. 47–48; Vittorio Croce, *Tradizione e ricerca. Il metodo teologico di San Massimo il Confessore* (Milan, 1974), p. 69.

67. *PG* 100: 428; Jaroslav Pelikan, *The Christian Tradition: A History of the Development of Doctrine. The Spirit of Eastern Christendom (600–1700)*. Vol. 2, (Chicago, 1974), p. 16.

68. *PG* 91: 224–25; *PG* 90: 873.

69. *PG* 91: 128; see also *PG* 91: 160, 180BC, 465, 1089A.

70. *PG* 91: 432CD

71. *PG* 4: 213; *PG* 91: 224D; Pelikan, id., p. 17.

72. *PG* 90: 693.

73. *PG* 90: 521, 792; Pelikan, id., pp. 17–18.

74. *PG* 91: 1033.

75. *PG* 4: 197; *PG* 91: 245; *PG* 99: 376; Pelikan, id., p. 19.

76. Pierre Riché, *Education and Culture in the Barbarian West*, trans. John J. Contreni (Columbia, SC, 1976), p. 346; J. M. Hussey, *Church and Learning in the Byzantine Empire, 867–1185* (Oxford, 1937), p. 29; J. M. Hussey, *The Byzantine World* (New York, 1961), p. 145.

77. Aidan Nichols, *Byzantine Gospel: Maximus the Confessor in Modern Scholarship* (Edinburgh, 1993), p. 13; F. X. Murphy and P. Sherwood, *Constantinople II et Constantinople III* (Paris, 1973), pp. 178–79.

78. George Ostrogorsky, *History of the Byzantine State*, rev. ed. (New Brunswick, NJ, 1969), p. 328.

79. Giorgio di Pisidia. *Poemi. I. Panegirici Epici*, ed., trans., and comm. Agostino Pertusi (Ettal, 1959), p. 12.

80. Cyril Mango, *Byzantium: The Empire of New Rome* (London, 1980), p. 137.

81. J. F. Haldon, *Byzantium in the Seventh Century* (Cambridge, 1990), pp. 426–27.

82. Von Schönborn, id., pp. 55–56; Riedinger, *Concilium*, p. 41; for the significance and meaning of the title "sophist," see P. Festugière, *Antioche païenne et chrétienne* (Paris, 1959), 105n6; for the identification of Sophronios the Sophist with Sophronios the patriarch of Jerusalem, see Ihor Sevcenko, *La civiltà bizantina dal IV al IX secolo* (Bari, 1977), p. 137ff.

83. In Byzantine hymnography and church poetry alone, Damascus produced St. Andrew of Crete, author of the *Great Canon*, as well as St. John of Damascus and St. Cosmas of Maiuma, whose *Octoechos* and *Triodion* provide the basic structure of the hymnody of the Eastern church. Chitty, id., p. 180; von Schönborn, id., p. 54; E. Bouvy, *Poètes et Mélodes. Études sur les origines du rythme tonique dans l'hymnographie de l'Église grecque* (Nîmes, 1886).

84. John Moschos. *The Spiritual Meadow*, trans. John Wortley (Kalamazoo, 1992), p. xix.

85. H. Delehaye, ed., *Propylaeum ad Synaxarium Ecclesiae Constantinopolitanae* in *AA.SS. Novembris* (Brussels, 1902), c. 527; von Schönborn, id., pp. 57–58.

86. Georgina Buckler, "Byzantine Education," in Norman H. Baynes and H. S. B. Moss, eds., *Byzantium* (Oxford, 1969), p. 201.

87. *Reg.* XIII, 42.

88. H.-D. Saffrey, "Le Chrétien Jean Philopon et La Survivance de l'École d'Alexandrie au VIe siècle," *Revue des Études Grecques* 67 (1954): 396–410. John Philoponos's theological works, which belong to his later years, include *De opficio mundi*, a commentary on the *Hexaemeron*, and the Διαιτητής, or Arbiter. Philoponos, whose Christology was close to that of Severus of Antioch, was condemned as a tritheist at the Sixth Ecumenical Council. E. A. Livingstone, ed., *Oxford Dictionary of the Christian Church*, 3rd ed. (Oxford, 1997), p. 896.

89. John Moschos, *The Spiritual Meadow*, id., c. 171, pp. 139–40.

90. Id., c. 172, p. 141.

91. Von Schönborn, id., p. 65; Elizabeth Dawes and Norman H. Baynes, trans., *Three Byzantine Saints* (Crestwood, NY, 1977), p. 195. Leontios, bishop of Neapolis in Cyprus, wrote a biography of John the Merciful as well as the lives of St. Spyridon of Trimithuntos and the fool for Christ St. Simeon of Emesa. Id., p. 195; Lappa-Zizicas, ed., "Epitomé de la Vie de S. Jean l'Aumônier," *Analecta Bollandiana* 88 (1970): 274.

92. Id., c. 77, pp. 59–60; Paul Lemerle, *Byzantine Humanism*, trans. Helen Lindsay and Ann Moffatt (Canberra, 1986), pp. 88–89; Cyril Mango, *Byzantium: The Empire of New Rome*, (London, 1980), p. 136.

93. John Moschos, *Spiritual Meadow*, c. 77, p. 159; PG 91:533–34.

94. Id., p. 4.

95. PG 87: 3148–3200; *Cod. Mus. Brit. Orient.* 8606ff. 127a–140b.

96. BHG 807: 3201–12; BHG 808: 3287–3302; BHG 844: 3321–53; BHG 1098:

3217–88, 3356–64; *BHG* 3301–9; *BHG* 1939.

97. *BHG* 475–79: 3380–3676. The life of John the Merciful is lost, while the encomium on John the Evangelist exists only in a fragment.

98. *The Festal Menaion*, Mother Mary and Bishop Kallistos Ware, trans. (London, 1969), pp. 224, 316, 348; von Schönborn, id., pp. 108–9.

99. *Sophronii Anacreontica*, ed. M. Gigante (Rome, 1957).

100. *The Compact Oxford English Dictionary*, 2nd ed. (Oxford, 1991), p. 48.

101. Alan Cameron, "The Epigrams of Sophronios," *Classical Quarterly* 33 (1983): 284, 291–92.

102. *Sophronii Anacreontica*, id., p. 124 ("When to the place of the skull [Mount Calvary] I come, thrice-suffused am I with spiritual exhilaration."); ("Επι τρίστοον παρέλθω ολομαργαραργυρόχρουν περικαλλέος τε παύλαν κρανίου τόπον προσέρπων"); Riedinger, *Concilium*, p. 41.

103. Ferdinand Gregorovius, *Geschichte der Stadt Athen im Mittelalter* (Stuttgart, 1889), pp. 85–88.

104. Steven Runciman, *Byzantine Civilization* (Cleveland, 1967), p. 179; Buckler, id., p. 201.

105. Referring to Theodore in a letter to St. Boniface written on 1 May 748, Pope Zacharias calls him "the Greco-Roman Theodoros, once a learned philosopher at Athens." Ephraim Emerton, trans., *The Letters of Saint Boniface* (New York, 1940), p. 143; Nicolas Cheetham, *Medieval Greece* (New Haven, 1981), p. 18.

106. Constans II wintered in Athens with his troops in 663 while en route to Italy. *LP* I, p. 343.

107. *Life of St. Stephen of Surozh*, ed., V. Vasilevskij, *Russko-visantijskija izsledovanija*, II (St. Petersburg, 1893), p. 75, cited in Peter Charanis, "Ethnic Changes in the Byzantine Empire in the Seventh Century," *Dumbarton Oaks Papers* 13 (1959): 41n109.

108. Paul Lemerle, ed., *Les Plus Anciens Recueils des Miracles de Saint Démétrius*, Vol. II. Commentaire (Paris, 1981), pp. 144–62.

109. Ioannis Zonaras, *Epitome Historiarum*, Vol. III, id., p. 316; Andreas N. Stratos, "The Naval Engagement at Phoenix," in *Studies in 7th-Century Byzantine Political History* (London, 1983), XII 229–47.

110. Rudolf Riedinger, ed., *Concilium Universale Constantinopolitanum Tertium*, Vol. II, Pt. 2 (Berlin, 1992), pp. 778–79; Theophanes, *Chronographia*, p. 508.

111. See Michael Psellus, *Epistolae ad Eustathum Thessalonicae* in T. L. F. Tafel, *Historia Thessalonicae* (Tübingen, 1835), appendix.

112. M. C. Sathas, "La Tradition Hellénique et La Légende de Phidias," *Annuaire des Études Grecques* 16 (1882) pp. 122, 124, 125n1, 126n1.

113. J. M. Hussey, *The Byzantine World*, id., p. 148; Jean-Pierre Mahé, "Quadrivium et cursus d'études au VIIe siècle en Arménie et dans le monde byzantin," *Travaux et Mémoires* 10 (1987): 159–94; Louis Bréhier, "Notes sur l'histoire de l'enseignement supérieur à Constantinople," *Byzantion* 3 (1926): 73, 87.

114. Runciman, id., p. 180. In the early fifth century, the University of Constantinople "had ten Chairs of Greek and ten of Latin grammar, five for Greek and three for Latin rhetoric, with one for philosophy and two for law." Ostrogorsky, id., p. 56. The capital's public library possessed some 120,000 volumes. Bréhier, id., p. 88; see also P. Speck, *Die*

Kaiserliche Universität von Konstantinopel (Munich, 1974).

115. On Stephen the Sophist's installation as a professor at Constantinople, see H. Usener, *De Stephano Alexandrino Commentatio* (Bonn, 1880).

116. Hussey, *The Byzantine World*, pp. 148–49.

117. K. Vogel, "Byzantine Science," in J. M. Hussey, ed., *The Cambridge Medieval History*, Vol. IV, Pt. II (Cambridge, 1967), p. 264ff., 289. The rank of *protospatharios*, meaning the first *spatharios* or bodyguard of the emperor, eventually developed into an honorific title. Cyril Mango and Roger Scott, eds., *The Chronicle of Theophanes Confessor* (Oxford, 1997), p. 693.

118. Bréhier, id., p. 94.

119. The *History* of Theophylact Simocatta, trans. Michael and Mary Whitby (Oxford, 1986), pp. xiii–xiv, 7n1.

120. In the Dialogue between Philosophy and History, Theophylact refers to Theseus's escape from the Cretan labyrinth; the third-century B.C. scholar and poet Callimachus; the boar and centaurs conquered by Heracles; Anytus, Socrates's accuser; the Heraclidae, mythical descendants of Heracles who led the Dorians in reestablishing Greek control in the Peloponnesus and elsewhere in Greece; the poet Hesiod; a metaphor from Plato's *Phaedrus*; a tale from Homer's *Odyssey*; and Tethys, the sister-wife of Ocean. Id., pp. 3–5 and notes. Theophylact describes the tragic end of Maurice and his family as "An *Iliad* of woes" in which the "Erinyes are chorus for my speech." He also refers to "the Muses of praise, Athens of the white cloak." Id., p. 229. For more detail on the use of such imagery in Byzantine literature, see J. Trilling, "Myth and Metaphor at the Byzantine Court," *Byzantion* 48 (1978): 249–63.

121. F. Diekamp, ed., *Analecta Patristica*, Orientalia Christiana Patristica 117 (Rome, 1938), pp. 173–222.

122. Giorgio di Pisidia, *Poemi. I. Panegirici Epici*, id., pp. 12–13.

123. Id., pp. 37–38.

124. On Manuel Philes and his imitation of George of Pisidia, see Paul Maas, *Kleine Schriften*, ed. W. Buchwald (Munich, 1973), p. 264; on Gregory of Corinth, see D. Donnet, "Précisions sur les oeuvres profanes de Grégoire de Corinth," *Bull. Inst. Hist. Belge de Rome* 37 (1966) 81, 85–86.

125. Michael Psellus, *The Essays on Euripides and George of Pisidia and on Heliodorus and Achilles Tatius*, ed., Andrew R. Dyck, *Byzantina Vindobonensia* XVI (Vienna, 1986).

126. Id., pp. 49; 51.

127. Id., p. 51.

128. Giorgio di Pisidia, *Poemi. I. Panegirici Epici*, id., p. 14.

129. Id., *Expeditio Persica I, II, and III*, pp. 84–136.

130. Id., *Heracliad II*, ll. 1–4, p. 251. George of Pisidia's classical training finds full expression in the *Heracliad*. For example, drawing upon the similarity of names between the emperor Heraclius and the Greek hero Heracles, George develops the comparison by likening each of Heracles's twelve labors with an equal number of achievements by Heraclius against the Persians. See Herbert Hunger, "On the Imitation (ΜΙΜΗΣΙΣ) of Antiquity in Byzantine Literature," *Dumbarton Oaks Papers* 23–24 (1969/1970): 17, 23–24.

131. Giorgio di Pisidia, *Poemi. I. Panegirici Epici*, id., pp. 48, 163–170 (On the Patrician Bonos), 176–200 (On the Avar War), 225–230 (On the Restitution of the Holy Cross).

132. F. C. Conybeare, "Ananias of Shirak (A.D. 600–c.650)," *Byzantinische Zeitschrift* 6 (1897): 572–84.

133. Mahé, id., p. 194

134. Mango, *Byzantium: The Empire of New Rome*, id., p. 137.

135. Theophanes, *Chronographia*, p. 560.

136. Georgios Monachos, *Chronicon*, p. 742.

137. Nikephoros, *Short History*, p. 121.

138. Haldon, id., p. 428.

139. Id., p. 427. It was doubtless from the Psalter that St. Theodore of Sykeon learned to read when he attended a town school in the countryside of Galatia in Asia Minor in the seventh century. Hussey, *The Byzantine World*, p. 146.

140. Mango, *Byzantium: The Empire of New Rome*, p. 136; Lemerle, *Byzantine Humanism*, pp. 87–88.

141. Bréhier, "Notes sur l'histoire de l'enseignement supérieur à Constantinople," id., p. 86; Runciman, *Byzantine Civilization*, p. 180.

142. Lemerle, *Byzantine Humanism*, p. 353.

143. Averil Cameron, "Byzantium and the Past in the Seventh Century: The Search for Redefinition," in *Changing Cultures in Early Byzantium* (Aldershot, 1996), V 250–71.

144. Henry Chadwick, "Florilegium," in *Reallexikon für Antike und Christentum*, Vol. 7, ed. T. Klauser, et al. (Stuttgart, 1950), cols. 1131–43; see also M. Richard, "Florilèges grecs," in *Dictionnaire de Spiritualité ascétique et mystique*, Vol. 5 (Paris, 1962) 475–512, and N. G. Wilson, "A chapter in the history of scholia," *Classical Quarterly* 17 (1967): 244–56.

145. Hunger, id., pp. 21, 38.

146. Averil Cameron and Judith Herrin, eds., Constantinople in the Early Eighth Century: The *Parastaseis Syntomoi Chronikai* (Leiden, 1984), pp. 40, 69–70.

147. Th. Scherman, *Die Geschichte der dogmatischen Florilegium vom V.–VIII. Jahrhundert, Texte und Untersuchungen zür Geschichte der Altchristlichen Literatur*, N. F., Bd. 13 (Leipzig, 1905).

148. Chadwick, "Florilegium," id., cols. 1151–52; see also S. Leanza, ed., *Procopii Gazaei Catena in Ecclesiasten necnon Pseudochrysostomi Commentarius in eundem Ecclesiasten*, Corpus Christianorum, Series Graeca 4 (Turnhout, 1978), for Procopius's use of patristic excerpts in biblical exegesis.

149. Such writers, all of whom were of Eastern provenance, include Andreas the Presbyter, Ioannis Drungarios, Makarios Chrysokephalos, Markellinos, Niketas of Herakleia, Nikolaos, Oekumenios, Olympiodoros, Philotheos, and Polychronios. M. Faulhaber, "Katenen und Katenenforschung," *Byzantinische Zeitschrift* 18 (1909): 383–84.

150. See, namely, Françoise Petit, ed., *Catenae Graecae in Genesim et in Exodum. I: Catena Sinaitica*, Corpus Christianorum, Series Graeca 2 (Turnhout, 1977); R. Devreesse, "Chaines exegetiques grecques," in *Dictionnaire de la Bible*, Supp. Vol. 1 (1928) 1084–1233.

151. Gustav Krüger, *History of Early Christian Literature*, trans. Charles R. Gillett (New York, 1897), p. 2.

152. Schaff and Wace, eds., *A Select Library of the Christian Church: Nicene and Post-Nicene Fathers*, 2nd Series, Vol. 8, "Basil: Letters and Select Works," (Repr. Peabody, MA,

1995) 2, 16. Henry Chadwick considers St. Basil's treatise *On the Holy Spirit* to be the first clear use of the *florilegium* in a dogmatic dispute within the church. Id., col. 1157.

153. Schaff and Wace, id., p. 45. The church fathers to whom St. Basil refers include Irenaeus of Lyons, Clement of Rome, Dionysios of Rome, Dionysios, patriarch of Alexandria, Eusebius of Caesarea, Origen, the historian Julius Africanus, Athenagoras the Hymnographer, Gregory Thaumaturgos, Firmilian of Caesarea, and Meletios. Id., pp. 45–47.

154. Chadwick, id., cols. 1158–59.

155. Id., col. 1158; see, namely, Robert Hespel, *Le florilège Cyrillien refuté par Sévère d'Antioche* (Louvain, 1955).

156. John of Ephesus, *Third Part of the Ecclesiastical History*, id., p. 63.

157. The composition and use of *florilegia* would eventually degenerate into a kind of intellectual mannerism reducing the search for knowledge into a mere exercise in technique where the works of the ancient authors became nothing but "a vast store of props at the service of a learned and complicated rhetoric." Lemerle, *Byzantine Humanism*, p. 352. The fourteenth-century philosopher Joseph Rhakendytes criticized it as a vacuous "pasting together" of masses of quotations. Hunger, id., p. 30; Averil Cameron, "Byzantium and the Past in the Seventh Century: The Search for Redefinition," id., V 254–55.

158. John of Ephesus, id., p. 146.

159. Cameron, id., V 254–55; see M. Richard, "Les florilèges diphysites du Ve et du VIe siècle," in Grillmeier-Bacht, *Des Konzil von Chalkedon* I (Würzburg, 1951), pp. 721–48.

160. Von Schönborn, id., p. 62; John Moschos, *The Spiritual Meadow*, id., c. 67, p. 50.

161. Chadwick, "Florilegium," id., col. 1151.

162. PG 89: 1689D–1692B; Chitty, id., p.159.

163. PG 89: 312–824; Gilbert Dagron, et al., eds., *Histoire du Christianisme des origines à nos jours*, Vol. 4, *Évêques, Moines et empereurs (610–1054)*, id., pp. 53–56; M. Richard, "Florilèges grec," in *Dictionnaire de Spiritualité*, Vol. 5 (Paris, 1964) cols. 475–512. Anastasios the Sinaite also composed a text on logic entitled the *Viae Dux*. PG 89: 36–309. For further studies on Anastasios the Sinaite, see S. N. Sakkos, Περί Ἀναστασίου Σιναιτόν (Thessalonika, 1964) and Evangelos Chrysos, Νεότεραι ἔρευναι περί Ἀναστασίου Σιναιτόν Kleronomia 1 (1969) 121–44.

164. PG 95: 1044; see also K. Holl, *Die Sacra Parallela des Johannes Damascenus, Texte und Untersuchungen*, 16, 1 (Leipzig, 1897); K. Holl, *Fragmente vornicänischer Kirchenväter aus den Sacra Parallela, Texte und Untersuchungen*, 20, 2 (Leipzig, 1899); A. Ehrhard, "Zu den Sacra Parallela des Johannes Damascenus und dem Florilegium des Maximos, *Byzantinische Zeitschrift* 10 (1901): 394–415. John of Damascus also wrote a text on dialectical reasoning entitled the *Dialectica*. B. Kotter, ed., *Die Schriften des Johannes von Damaskos I*. (Berlin, 1969), pp. 47–146.

165. Basil the Great, *On the Holy Spirit*, id., p. 50.

166. *LP* I, p. 333.

167. *LP* I, p. 336; Jaffé, id., p. 230; cf., *Mansi* X, 852; *PL* 87: 106.

168. Erich Caspar, *Geschichte des Papsttums*, Vol. II (Tübingen, 1933), p. 553; Bertolini, *Roma di Fronte a Bisanzio e ai Longobardi*, id., p. 337.

169. Paul Peeters, "Une vie grecque du Pape S. Martin I," *Analecta Bollandiana* 51 (1937) 225, 253; Hefele, Vol. 5, id., pp. 70–71.

170. J. Pargoire, "Apocrisiare," in *Dictionnaire d'Archéologie Chrétienne et de Liturgie*, Vol. I, Pt. 2 (Paris, 1924), cols. 2537–55; Vera von Falkenhausen, "I Bizantini in Italia," in Guglielmo Cavallo, et al., eds., *I Bizantini in Italia* (Milan, 1982), p. 20.

171. *Mansi* X, 702; *LP* I, p. 332.

172. Haldon, id., pp. 403–4. John of Nikiu makes a point of noting that Heraclius was acclaimed emperor in 610 by "all with one voice in the Greek language." *Chronicle*, id., p. 177.

173. Averil Cameron, "The Eastern Provinces in the 7th Century A.D.: Hellenism and the Emergence of Islam," in *Changing Cultures in Early Byzantium* (Aldershot, 1996) IV 287, 310; Gilbert Dagron, "Aux origines de la civilisation byzantine: langue de culture et langue d'état," *Revue historique* 241 (1969): 23–56; H. Zilliacus, *Zum Kampf der Weltsprachen im Öströmischen Reich* (Helsingfors, 1935), p. 36ff.

174. Ostrogorsky, id., p. 106.

175. Charles Diehl, *History of the Byzantine Empire*, trans. George B. Ives (Princeton, 1925), p. 49.

176. Cameron, "The Eastern Provinces in the 7th Century A.D.," id., IV 310.

177. *PG* 114: 1380–81; S. Petrides,"Le Monastère des Spoudaei à Jerusalem et les Spoudaei de Constantinople," *Echos d'Orient* 4 (1900): 225–31; S. Petrides, "Les Spoudaei de Jerusalem et de Constantinople," *Echos d'Orient* 7 (1904): 341–48.

178. Jaffé, id., Nos. 2078 and 2079, p. 233.

179. *LP* I, p. 336; Bede, *Chronica*, MGH *Auctores Antiquissimi*, id., pp. 312–13. Anastasios was later exiled to Trebizond, from where he was recalled in 662 to stand trial in Constantinople. As with Maximos, he was mutilated by having his tongue excised. He died in 666. Robert Devreesse, "Le Texte Grec de l'Hypomnesticum de Théodore Spoudée," *Analecta Bollandiana* 53 (1935): 49–50, 58–59.

180. For details regarding Pope Martin's detention on Naxos from August 653 to June 654, see J. Dakoronia, "Ὁ ἔπι ἕν ἔτος περιορισμός του Πάπα Μαρτίνου Ἀ εις Νάξον," in *Epeteris Hetaireias Kykladikon Meleton* 8 (1969–70) 395–411. In his first letter to Theodore (*Quoniam agnovi*), Martin swears unwavering devotion to the orthodox faith "even unto death," while protesting that he is innocent of the scurrilous accusations that he has conspired with the Arabs and blasphemed the Virgin Mary. *Mansi* X, 849; *PL* 87: 197; Jaffé, id., No. 2078, p. 233. In the second letter (*Noscere voluit*), the pope describes his arrest and tortuous voyage from Rome to Naxos, during the course of which he appears to have suffered a variety of personal indignities and privations at the hands of his imperial captors. *Mansi* X, 851; *PL* 87: 199; Jaffé, id., No. 2079, p. 233.

181. Robert Devreesse, "Le Texte Grec de l'Hypomnesticum de Théodore Spoudée," id., 49–80. The rubric at the beginning of the Greek text reads, "A short history reciting the events relating to the blessed Martin, pope of Rome, and the holy Maximos and those with him." Id., p. 66.

182. Rudolf Riedinger, "Die Lateransynode von 649 und Maximos der Bekenner," in *Maximus Confesssor. Actes du Symposium sur Maxime le Confesseur*, id., p. 119.

183. Theophanes, *Chronographia*, pp. 478–79; *The Seventh Century in the West-Syrian Chronicles*, id., pp. 58, 68, 108, 176–78.

184. Gilbert Dagron, et al., eds., *Histoire du Christianisme. Évêques, Moines et Empereurs (610–1054)*, Vol. 4, id., 43n162.

185. Pietro Conte, *Il Sinodo Lateranense dell'ottobre 649: La Nuova Edizione degli Atti di Cura di Rudolf Riedinger* (Vatican City, 1989), p. 145. (papa, vescovi e notari interressati abbiano letto le rispettive parti); Riedinger, "In welcher Richtung wurden die Akten der Lateransynode von 649 übersetzt, und in welcher Schrift war der lateinische Text dieser Akten geschrieben," id., p. 150.

186. Riedinger, *Concilium*, id., p. 3; Theophanes, *Chronographia*, p. 479 ("In the same year [AM 6141, AD 648/649] a council was held in Rome against the Monotheletes (*sic*)."); *AA.SS.* Aug. III (1737) 97, 192 (the *Acta Sanctorum* incorrectly records the presence of 150 bishops, an obviously erroneous scribal inversion of the digits zero and five); Bede, *Chronica, MGH Auctores Antiquissimi*, Vol. XIII, id., p. 313 (Bede's account, which makes no reference at all to Maximos, correctly notes the presence of 105 bishops, but says that the synod took place on October 9, 649, incorrectly intimating that it lasted only one day); *Chronicle of Michael the Syrian*, id., pp. 431, 443–44 (Michael the Syrian, who places the blame for "perverting the spirit" of Pope Martin into subscribing to the "heresy of two wills and two operations" in Christ to "Maximos of Hacfin [Nasfin]" of Tiberias in Palestine, records the presence of 109 bishops, when in fact there were 105); Anastasios Sinaites, *Sermo III*, PG 89: 1155 (Anastasios, who incorrectly places the Lateran Council in the time of the emperor Heraclius, records only that there were "many holy bishops" in attendance). The Venetian chronicler Andrea Dandolo is incorrect on so many points that his account is almost wholly unreliable. Apart from confusing Monothelitism with Monophysitism, he records that Martin's pontificate lasted from 643 to 650, rather than from 649 to his exile in 653, and that 200 bishops attended the Lateran Council. Andrea Dandolo, *Chronica*, in L. A. Muratori, *Rerum Italicarum Scriptores*, Vol. 12, Pt. 1 (Bologna, 1728), pp. 94, 97.

187. Paul Peeters, "Une vie grecque du Pape S. Martin I," *Analecta Bollandiana* 51 (1932): 225, 254.

188. *Synodicon Vetus*, id., p. 117; (του θεοφόρου Μαξίμου τω ζήλω); *AA.SS.* Aug. III (1737) 97, 102, 123 ("likewise through the most wise Maximos they achieved everything with the reason and power of the Holy Spirit."); Conte, id., p. 145; Theophanes, *Chronographia*, p. 462; Johannes Pierres, *Sanctus Maximus Confessor: Princeps Apologetarum Synodi Lateranensis Anni 649*, id., p. 8.

189. Riedinger, *Concilium*, pp. 3–7.

190. Herrin, id., p. 254; for episcopal sees under Rome's jurisdiction in the East, see Jean Darrouzès, *Notitiae Episcopatum Ecclesiae Constantinopolitanae*, Vol. I (Paris, 1981), pp. 260–61, 265.

191. In order of seniority, the bishops with clearly Eastern names included Maximos of Aquileia, Sergius of Tempsa, Epiphanios of Albano, Maximos of Pesaro, Maximos of Trocala, Theodosios of Cotrona in Calabria, Scholasticos of Fana, Elias of Lilibeo in Sicily, Eusebius of Atella, Theodore of Rosellano, Andreas of Hydrontum, Anastasios of Narni, Theodore of Tindari and Maximos of Messina, both Sicilians, Leontios of Naples, Kallionistos of Adriana, and Leontios of Fabentia. Nine bishops named John (Iohannes) attended; their dioceses included Pestum, Tropea in Calabria, Taranto in Puglia, Carina, Rhegium in Calabria, Vicosabina, Unnogoria, and Gabala. Riedinger, *Concilium*, pp. 3–7.

192. Conte, id., p. 142.

193. Id., pp. 11–23, 117–19, 143–45, 147–51, 183–93, 337–43, 359–65 (Pope Martin); pp. 27, 51, 235–45, 345–53 (Maximos of Aquileia); pp. 29, 59, 153–55, 353–59 (Deusdedit of Cagliari).

194. Id., pp. 23, 65, 119 (Maurus of Cesena); 141 (Sergius of Tempsa); 193–95 (Benedict of Ajaccio); 253 (Leontios of Naples).

195. Pope Martin subscribed first, followed by bishops Maximos of Aquileia, Deusdedit of Cagliari, Maurus of Cesena, and Sergius of Tempsa who signed respectively second, third, fourth, and fifth. Bishop Benedict of Ajaccio signed eighth, and bishop Leontios of Naples was eighty-seventh. Id., pp. 391–93.

196. The assembled prelates are referred to in the text of the synodal proceedings collectively as either "the holy synod" or "all the most holy bishops." Id., pp. 29, 119, 195, 315, 365.

197. Id., pp. 29, 119, 195.

198. Id., pp. 315–21.

199. Id., pp. 365–89.

200. Herrin characterizes the size of the Lateran Council of 649 as "one of the largest ever assembled in Rome." Id., p. 253. Others assert that it attracted "only a small number of bishops." Dagron, et al., id., p. 43.

201. Hermann Josef Sieben, *Die Konzilsidee der Alten Kirche* (Paderborn, 1979), pp. 307ff., 515–16.

202. Caspar, id., p. 555; Jenal, id., p. 185.

203. Jenal, id., pp. 185–86; Conte, id., pp. 127–28; Riedinger, "In welcher Richtung," id., p. 153.

204. Riedinger, *Concilium*, pp. 390–403.

205. Jenal, id., pp. 185–186. It has been contended that the bishops played a far more active role at the Lateran Council than the text of the synodal proceedings reflects, and that this included personally reading the conciliar and patristic *florilegia* and discussing them in synod before finally adopting the anti-monothelite position. For this distinctly minority view, see Elena Zocca, "Due Papi di Fronte al Monotelismo," in *Papa Martino I e il suo tempo*, id., pp. 138–39.

206. See supra, p. 114.

207. Riedinger, *Concilium*, pp. 36–47.

208. Id., pp. 49–57.

209. Id., pp. 60–65.

210. Pietro Conte, "Il *consortium fidei apostolicae* tra vescovo di Roma e vescovi nel secolo VII, con appendice filologica e canonica," in M. Maccarrone, ed., *Il primato di Pietro nel primo millenio. Ricerche e testimonianze*. Atti del symposium storico-teologico, Rome, 9–13 October 1989 (Vatican City, 1991), pp. 363–431.

211. Id., p. 36.

212. Id., pp. 39–47, 51–55, 61, 120–25, 133–39, 141, 146–47, 157–63, 165–73, 197–205, 208–11, 257ff., 321ff.

213. *Reg.* VII, 5, 31; VIII, 28; see, infra, p. 14ff.

214. *Reg.* X, 21; cf., *Reg.* I, 28; VII, 27.

215. Erich Caspar, "Die Lateransynode von 649," *Zeitschrift für Kirchengeschichte* 51 (1932) 75–137; Erich Caspar, *Geschichte des Papsttums*, Vol. 2 (Tübingen, 1933), pp. 553–86.

216. Rudolf Riedinger, "In welcher Richtung," id., p. 152. Riedinger's conclusion is now universally accepted. See, namely, Herrin, id., p. 253; Jenal, id., pp. 179–80; J.-M. Sansterre, "Concilium Lateranense a. 649 celebratum, edidit Rudolf Riedinger: A Review," *Byzantion* 55 (1985): 596–597.

217. Rudolf Riedinger, "Die Lateranakten von 649," *Byzantina* 13 (1985): 517–34. For example, instead of translating the phrase ἡμᾶς ἐνδιδάσκει as *nos docet*, the translator uses the cumbersome phrase *docere nos demonstratur*, which, by joining the present infinitive of the verb *doceo* with the third person singular passive form of the main verb *demonstro*, fails to clearly and accurately render the Greek verb form into Latin and reflects an unfamiliarity with polished Latin prose composition. Riedinger, id., p. 524–25. Similarly, rather than translating the verb ἐκήρυξαν as *monstraverunt*, the translator uses the unwieldy expression *tradidisse monstrantur*, joining the perfect infinitive of the verb *trado* with the third person plural passive form of the verb *monstro*, once again unnecessarily complicating the translation of the Greek verb and at the same time employing a Latin construction who no one proficient in the language would have used. *Id.*, p. 527. Riedinger points out numerous similar examples. Id., pp. 522–33.

218. Id.

219. See, namely, Rudolf Riedinger, "Grammatiker-Gelehrsamkeit in den Akten der Lateran-Synode von 649," *Jahrbuch der Österreichischen Byzantinistik* 25 (1976) 57–61.

220. Caspar, id., pp. 557–59; Riedinger, "Die Lateranakten von 649," id., p. 520; Rudolf Riedinger, "Sprachschichten in der lateinishcen Übersetzung der Lateranakten von 649," *Zeitschrift für Kirchengeschichte* 92 (1981) 180–203; Herrin, id., p. 253; Nichol, id., p. 13; Sansterre, id., p. 596. Riedinger makes a compelling argument that the letter *Magnum et indeficientem*, sent by the African bishops Columbus, Stephen, and Reparatus to Pope Theodore in 646, was originally composed in Greek by Maximos and his monks while they were still in Africa, and that it was thereafter translated into Latin for use at the Lateran Council where it was read to the assembled bishops. Riedinger, "Zwei Briefe aus den Akten der Lateransynode von 649," id., pp. 37–43.

221. Nichol, id., p. 25; Croce, id., p. 12; see also AA.SS. Oct. IV (1780) 865–987; Jaroslav Pelikan, "The Odyssey of Dionysian Spirituality," in Colm Luibheid, trans., *Pseudo-Dionysius: The Complete Works* (New York, 1987), pp. 11–24.

222. PG 4: 264, 337, 360, 393, 405; PG 91: 1312–13, 1080, 1260; Averil Cameron, "Byzantium and the Past: The Search for Redefinition," id., p. V 268; H.-G. Beck, *Kirche und theologische Literatur im byzantinischen Reich* (Munich, 1974) pp. 436ff.

223. Dionysios the Areopagite, *The Celestial Hierarchy*, trans. Colm Luibheid, trans., *Pseudo-Dionysius: The Complete Works* (New York, 1987), pp. 146–47; R. Roques, *L'Univers dionysien. Structure hiérarchique du monde selon le Pseudo-Denys* (Paris, 1983).

224. Id., pp. 160–61.

225. Dionysios the Areopagite, *The Ecclesiastical Hierarchy*, trans. Colm Luibheid, trans., *Pseudo-Dionysius: The Complete Works* (New York, 1987), p. 197.

226. Id., pp. 196–97.

227. PG 91: 465 ("We do not invent new formulas . . . but we confess the statements of the fathers."); PG 91: 117B, 1304D; see supra, pp. 16–18.

228. PG 91: 160.

229. Dionysios the Areopagite, *The Ecclesiastical Hierarchy*, id., pp. 199, 205; PG 91: 245A.

230. Cameron, "Byzantium and the Past in the Seventh Century," id., p. V 268–69.

231. Dionysios the Areopagite, *The Celestial Hierarchy*, id., p. 146; *The Ecclesiastical Hierarchy*, id., p. 206.

232. Riedinger, *Concilium*, p. 28.

233. Id., p. 36.

234. Id., p. 338. Dionysios's view that the hierarchical structure of the celestial kingdom is mirrored on earth, and that maintenance of the same τάξις, or order, that obtains in heaven should be observed in the arrangement of terrestrial relationships, was the cornerstone of Byzantine political philosophy. In the Prologue to his *Book of Ceremonies* composed in the tenth century, the emperor Constantine VII Porphyrogenitos insisted on the importance of governing the empire in an orderly manner, since maintaining such order and decorum (ρυθμώ καί τάξει) in the exercise of imperial power reflected the harmony with which God had ordered the universe (τό πάν). To the end, he set down in great detail the particulars of imperial ceremonies so that by rigidly observing them the evil of disorder (αταξία) could be avoided, and imperial power would, consequently, appear "more majestic, increase in prestige, and thus inspire the admiration of both strangers and our own subjects." Constantine VII Porphyrogenitos, *Le Livre des Cérémonies (De Ceremoniis)*, Vol. I., trans. Albert Vogt (Paris, 1967), pp. 1–2.

235. PG 90: 152C; PG 91: 344A, 425A.

236. Dionysios the Areopagite, *The Divine Names*, in Colm Luibheid, trans., *Pseudo-Dionysius: The Complete Works* (New York, 1987), pp. 106–7.

237. Basil the Great, *Epistle 38*, in Schaff and Wade, eds., *Basil: Letters and Select Works*, Vol. 8, id., pp. 137–41.

238. PG 91: 363–649; see especially, PG 91: 544–576 (Epistle 15 to Cosmas the Deacon).

239. PG 90: 144C, 149A; PG 91: 584, 1304D; Nichol, id., pp. 50–51.

240. Dionysios, *Letter 9 (To Titus)*, in Ronald F. Hathaway, *Hierarchy and the Definition of Order in the Letters of Pseudo-Dionysius* (The Hague, 1969), p. 155; René Roques, "La Notion de Hiérarchie selon le Pseudo-Denys," *Archives d'histoire doctrinale et littéraire du Moyen Age* 17 (1949), pp. 183, 187.

241. See René Roques, *L'univers dionysien: structure hiérarchique du monde selon le Pseudo-Denys* (Paris, 1983), p. 42.

242. *Celestial Hierarchy*, id., pp. 146–147.

243. Id., p. 154.

244. PG 3: 724D; René Roques, "La Notion de Hiérarchie selon le Pseudo-Denys," id., p. 220. Dionysios's conception of hierarchies was based on the model of Plato's πόλις, and thus presupposed a monarchical governmental structure. Roques, *L'univers dionysien*, id., p. 82.

245. Riedinger, *Concilium*, pp. 12–18 (Basil, *On the Holy Spirit*; Ps.-Basil, *Against Eunomius* IV; Cyril of Alexandria, *Thesaurarum 32* and *On the Holy Trinity*; Dionysios, *The Divine Names*; Leo I, *Letter to emperor Leo* and *Letter to bishop Flavianus of Constantinople*).

246. Id., pp. 121–30 (Cyril of Alexandria, *Explanation in Twelve Chapters*; Gregory Nazianzus, *Letter 101 Against Cledonius*; Dionysios, *The Divine Names* and the *Fourth Letter Against Gaius*; Basil, *Homily on the Giving of Thanks*).

247. Id., pp. 142–45 (Cyril of Alexandria, *Letter 46 Against Successus*).

248. Id., pp. 182–93, 234–45 (Gregory Nazianzen, *Letter 23 Against Nectarius* and *Oration 30*; Anastasios Sinaites, *The Guide of Life*).

249. Id., pp. 252–53.

250. Id. The fact that Maximos, and no doubt Martin and probably Theodore before him, believed it necessary to identify by name those who comprised the approved fathers of the church (and by omission from that list those who did not) was a sad commentary on the deplorable state of religious learning among the episcopate in mid-seventh-century Italy. See, *Mansi* XI, 234; *PL* 87: 1161.

251. Id., pp. 254–55.

252. Id., pp. 254–57. The list consisted, in order, of the following persons: Athanasius of Alexandria, Hilary of Poitiers, Basil the Great, Gregory Nazianzen, Gregory of Nyssa, Ambrose of Milan, Augustine of Hippo, Theophilus of Alexandria, John Chrysostom, Cyril of Alexandria, Pope Leo I, and Proclus of Constantinople.

253. Id., pp. 258–315. *deflorata sanctorum patrum testimonia.*

254. Id. The Greek fathers included Basil the Great, Gregory of Nyssa, Cyril of Alexandria, Gregory Nazianzen, Amphilochius of Iconium, Athanasius of Alexandria, John Chrysostom, Theophilus of Alexandria, Severian of Gabala in Syria, Dionysios the Areopagite, Justin the Philosopher and Martyr, Epiphanius of Constantia in Cyprus, Cyril of Jerusalem, Ephraim of Antioch, John of Scythopolis, and Anastasios of Antioch. The Latin fathers consisted of Ambrose of Milan, Augustine of Hippo, Hippolytus the Martyr of Rome, Pope Leo I, and Hilary of Poitiers. *Mansi* X, 1071–1108; G. B. de Rossi, *Codices Palatini Latini Bibliothecae Vaticanae*, Vol. I (Rome, 1886), LX, VIII–LXX; Maurice Geerard, ed., *Clavis Patrum Graecorum*, Vol. IV (Turnhout, 1980), p. 175.

255. The *Florilegium dyotheleticum*, Cod. Vat. gr. 1455 (a.1299)ff. 165r–176r, appears to have been first noted by Jean Darrouzès in an article published in 1960. Jean Darrouzès, "Notes de littérature et de critique," *Révue des Études Byzantines* 18 (1960) 179–94; see also Riedinger, *Concilium*, p. XI and p. XI, n5. It was not, however, published until Riedinger's edition of the acts and proceedings of the Lateran Council of 649 appeared in 1984. Id., pp. 425–36.

256. Id., p. 425. Translation from the Greek text by the author.

257. The Greek fathers include Cyril of Alexandria, Athanasius of Alexandria, Gregory of Nyssa, Anastasios of Antioch, Gregory Nazianzen, John Chrysostom, Proclus of Constantinople, Justin Martyr and Philosopher, Basil the Great, Epiphanios of Constantia in Cyprus, Amphilochius of Iconium, and Theophilus of Alexandria. The four Latin fathers consist of Pope Leo I, Ambrose of Milan, Hilary of Poitiers, and Pope Hormisdas. Id., pp. 425–436; Pietro Conte, *Il Sinodo Lateranense dell'ottobre 649: La Nuova Edizione degli Atti a Cura di Rudolf Riedinger* (Vatican City, 1989), p. 75.

258. Riedinger, *Concilium*, pp. 314–21.

259. Id., pp. 318–19.

260. Id., pp. 320–21.

261. Lucius, the Arian bishop of Alexandria; Apollinaris of Laodicea; Polemon, a disciple of Apollinaris of Laodicea; Severus of Antioch; Theodosios of Alexandria; Themistius, an Alexandrian deacon who was a member of the sect known as the Agnoetae; Colluthus; Julian of Halicarnassus; Theodore of Mopsuestia; Nestorius; Paul, a Nestorian deacon from Persia; Theodulos the Nestorian; and Ibas of Edessa. Id., pp. 320–35; *Mansi* X, 1113–24; de Rossi, id., LXX–LXXI; Geerard, ed., *Clavis Patrum Graecorum*, Vol. IV., id., p. 75.

262. See supra, Chapter III, p. 88.

263. Johannes Pierres, *Sanctus Maximus Confessor: Princeps Apologetarum Synodi Lateranensis Anni 649* (Rome, 1940), pp. 8, 11.

264. Nikephoros, *Short History*, p. 83; *Synodicon Vetus*, p. 115.

265. Stratos, Vol. III, id., pp. 60–61.

266. PG 91: 288.

267. PG 91: 287; cf., Gregory of Nyssa, *Contra Eunomium 4*, in *PG* 45: 653; Gregory Nazianzus, *Oration 5*, in Schaff and Wace, eds., "Cyril of Jerusalem, Gregory Nazianzen, Vol. 7, id., p. 327.

268. Riedinger, *Concilium*, pp. 12, 48, 234, 252, 314, 326, 350, 406 (novelties and innovations); 68, 98, 102, 168 (departure from apostolic and patristic authority). Riedinger makes a compelling showing that the four letters of the African bishops presented at the second session of the Lateran Council were originally written in Greek by Maximos or his monks while they were in Africa, and that they were brought to Rome where they were translated into Latin for use at the synod in 649. Rudolf Riedinger, "Zwei Briefe aus den Akten der Lateransynode von 649," *Jahrbuch der Österreichischen Byzantinistik* 29 (1980), pp. 37–43.

269. PG 91: 295–96, 311, 315–17, 325, 344–45, 352.

270. Riedinger, *Concilium*, pp. 426–27, 431–32, 434; De Rossi, id., LXIX.

271. PG 91: 160–61, 164–65, 168–69.

272. PG 91: 169–173.

273. Riedinger, *Concilium*, pp. 426–27, 431; de Rossi, id., LXIX–LXXXI.

274. Pierres, id., pp. 30–51.

275. Riedinger, *Concilium*, pp. 368–89.

276. PG 91: 287ff; Caspar, id., p. 558; Pierres, id., pp. 12–27.

277. Riedinger, *Concilium*, pp. 404–21.

278. Riedinger, "Zwei Briefe aus den Atkten der Lateransynode von 649," id., pp. 50–59.

279. Riedinger, *Concilium*, pp. 410–11.

280. Id., pp. 422–24.

281. *Mansi* X, 805–14; cf., Riedinger, *Concilium*, p. 57.

282. *Mansi* X, 815, 817, 819–24, 827–32, 833–44.

283. LP I, p. 338; PG 90: 109C–129D.

284. PG 91: 137; see Caspar, id., p. 559; Jenal, id., p. 170.

285. Riedinger, "In welcher Richtung wurden die Akten der Lateransynode von 649 übersetzt," id., p. 164.

CHAPTER V

~

Ὁ Δε Γε Κώνστανς Ἀπῆλθεν Ἐν Σικελία Βουλόμενος Ἐν Ρώμη Τήν Βασιλείαν Μεταστήσαι[1]

The Italian Expedition of Constans II: Prelude to the Greek Popes, 649–678

The Romans were as prepared to forget Pope Martin as Constans II was relieved to see him removed to the remote northern shores of the Black Sea.[2] From his place of exile in the Tauric Chersonese on the southern part of the Crimean peninsula, the pope wrote to his friends in Constantinople shortly after his arrival in May, 655 asking that they send him wheat, wine, and oil. He lamented that his own flock—oblivious of how the Thessalonians had succored Paul in his affliction—treated even strangers in Rome better than their suffering pontiff.[3] A few months later Martin's despair had turned to astonishment at the extent to which the Romans ignored his misfortunes, failing to display, as he wrote his friends in Constantinople, even a "grain of salt's worth of care" toward him. Although he would never cease to pray for the Roman church, the hapless pontiff could not accept that those for whom he had so greatly sacrificed showed no concern for whether he lived or died.[4] But the shabby treatment that the Romans showed Martin as he starved and shivered on the Crimea in the fall of 655, though obviously painful for the pope to accept and apparently impossible for him to understand, was not intended as a personal rebuff by a churlish and ungrateful flock.

Both Rome and Constantinople had grown weary of the decades of religious warfare brought on by the Monothelite controversy. Since the Lateran Council of 649, Martin had become the focal point of Roman resistance to Eastern doctrinal heresy, providing the church in Italy with a sense of religious solidarity centered upon the figure of the pope of Rome.[5] But the pronouncements of the Roman synod of 649, which directly defied an imperial edict prohibiting any discussion of Christ's wills and energies, had transcended the ecclesiastical arena elevating a religious quarrel into a challenge to Byzantine political authority that the imperial government could not ignore.[6] Martin's arrest and removal to Constantinople, although momentarily shocking to Roman sensibilities, had nonetheless succeeded over time in lowering the religious fever of the empire's Italian subjects. At the same time, it provided them, as well as those in the capital, with a period during which to reflect dispassionately upon political realities.

The relative ease with which the Arabs penetrated into North Africa during the late 640s, routing the imperial army and driving the exarch to seek refuge in Constantinople, revealed to the invaders not only the region's wealth, but its military vulnerability as well.[7] Successful naval sorties from their base in Alexandria against the imperial islands of Cyprus in 649 and 650, and Cos, Crete, and Rhodes in 653 and 654, further intensified their appetite for plundering the empire's riches.[8] The disastrous defeat of the imperial fleet by an Arab armada at Phoenix off the coast of Lycia in 655 provided undeniable proof that Arab naval strength posed a serious challenge to Byzantine control of the eastern Mediterranean.[9] Inspired by their successes in the East, it did not require any extraordinary foresight to envision that the Arabs would soon turn their attention westward, pressing across the Mediterranean littoral to repeat their earlier victories in Africa and targeting Carthage as a base from which to launch their ships on expeditions against the riches of Byzantine Sicily and the imperial territories in southern Italy.[10]

The Lombards had exploited the rancor caused by the religious breach between Rome and Constantinople to renew their aggression against both imperial and papal territories in Italy.[11] Before his death in 652, Rothari had captured imperial cities along the Ligurian shore from the ancient city of Luni along the Via Aurelia west of Carrara up to the territory of the Franks.[12] In northeastern Italy, he attacked the fortress of Oderzo, between Treviso and Cividale di Friuli, continuing the protracted history of warfare with the exarch Isaac that had at times brought the Lombards uncomfortably close to Ravenna.[13] Rothari's seizure of its patrimony in the Cottian Alps renewed the Papacy's fear, which had existed in every pope since Gregory the Great, that it was perilously close to becoming just another Lombard bishopric.[14]

If Byzantine Italy was to escape the calamitous consequences of Arab and Lombard aggression and remain within the imperial fold, then the division caused by the Christological quarrel between Rome and Constantinople had to be healed. By 654, it seems that both sides had come to the conclusion that the time was ripe to begin the process of reconciliation.[15] Since the memory of Martin merely revived the differences that drew East and West apart, it is not at all surprising that in the time of rapprochement that was about to begin, the unfortunate pontiff would be conveniently, if regrettably, forgotten. Indeed, nearly three-quarters of a century would pass before a Roman pope referred again to Martin I.[16] For the present, the emphasis would be on promoting concord and suppressing dissension as Rome and the Papacy, temporarily estranged from the imperial bosom, reassumed their historic roles as loyal subjects of a solicitous emperor.[17]

~∽

Byzantium's renewed solicitude toward Rome was not, however, wholly unre-strained nor did it succumb to acts of political folly. The fourteen-month vacancy in the Apostolic See between Martin's arrest in the early summer of 653 and the consecration of his successor in the late summer of 654 was probably a combina-tion of imperial punishment for the Lateran Council, and a lingering reluctance among the more militant Romans to choose a new pope while the one whom they considered the rightful pontiff still lived.[18] When at last the exarch Theo-dore Kalliopas, who had presided over Martin's arrest and deportation, gave his consent for the consecration of a new pope, it was no surprise that the candidate whom he approved was in nearly all respects the opposite of his strident and intractable predecessor.[19] From the Eastern perspective, the Roman popes had, since the days of the pliable Honorius, so escalated their intransigence on mat-ters of faith as to create a religious chasm between East and West that threatened to result in a breach of the empire's political hegemony as well. Constantinople was not about to countenance another Martin.

The elderly presbyter who ascended the throne of St. Peter in August, 654, as Eugenius I appeared perfectly suited to collaborate with the Byzantines in their undisguised goal of taming an unruly Papacy and, in the process, of keeping Italy and Sicily, with their precious grain supplies, securely within Constantinople's control.[20] Described by his biographer as "kind, gentle, meek, courteous to all, and of distinguished holiness," Eugenius seemed to have the requisite submissive-ness and malleability that imperial authorities were seeking in a Roman pontiff as the process of healing the religious and political wounds caused by the Mono-thelite controversy got under way.[21] The fact that he was drawn from among the priesthood of the Roman church, rather than the more educated diaconate or the religiously fervent monastics, suggests that Eugenius had not participated in the doctrinal disputes of the recent past. Moreover, his willingness to be elected pope while Martin was still alive indicated a disposition to sacrifice strict canoni-cal regularity for political accommodation with Byzantium.[22] Finally, although he was a Roman by birth, he appears to have come from the region around the Aventine, which over the centuries had developed into the Greco-oriental quar-ter of the city, thereby indicating an association with Easterners that may have added to his attractiveness as far as the imperial authorities were concerned.[23]

The years of Eugenius's pontificate from 654 to 657 witnessed the beginning of the detente that both East and West were seeking. Following the death of patriarch Pyrrhus I in June, 654, Peter was ordained as his successor.[24] Roman *apokrisiarii* had arrived in Constantinople to greet the new patriarch and were preparing to receive Holy Communion with him as a first step in the process of bridging the gap that had been caused by Pope Theodore's excommunication and deposition of patriarchs Pyrrhus I and Paul II some five years earlier.[25] Sig-nificantly, the legates were not carrying the customary synodic letter for the new patriarch, probably because the Papacy was still vacant in June, 654, or, more likely, because a written profession of the faith was almost certain to be subject to scrutiny and possible objection.[26] It seemed far more conducive to rapprochement that doctrinal issues be left unclear or better yet ignored. Encouraged, however, by the gesture from Rome, patriarch Peter went a step further, sending the *apokrisiarii* back to Rome bearing his synodic letter for Pope Eugenius, who had been consecrated in August 654. But Peter's *synodikon* so dissimulated on the issue of Christ's wills and energies that the zealots in Rome, who had not given up the Dyothelite cause, raised a furor over its contents while the pope was celebrating mass in the church of St. Maria *ad praesepe*. Eugenius was obliged to promise that he would not accept the patriarch's letter, but the distinct impression is that he did so more to quiet the unseemly disturbance that was preventing him from completing the liturgy than to provoke Constantinople or from any conviction that Peter's profession was problematic.[27] The fact that Eugenius incurred no adverse consequences from imperial authorities as a result of his promise not to accept the patriarch's *synodikon*, and that he completed his pontificate without incident until his death two years later, reflects Byzantium's determination to restore the bonds with Rome which the Monothelite controversy had severed on grounds that avoided the religious issues that had driven them apart.[28] Perversely, the way of reconciliation that both sides would now adopt was precisely that which the *Typos* had ordained nearly a decade earlier.[29]

When Pope Gregory II expressed outrage at Leo III's edict against images and warned the emperor that if he tried to pursue him he need only slip three miles south of Rome into Campania to escape imperial apprehension, the pope threatened to seek refuge in a region that since the eighth century B.C. had been colonized by Greeks during the period of overseas Hellenic expansion that had seen the establishment of Greek settlements throughout the western Mediterranean and especially in Sicily and southern Italy.[30] Although the focal point of Campania's Hellenic heritage was centered upon the Greek city of Naples, the influence of the East had radiated far into the surrounding countryside so that by the mid-seventh century, both Greek and Latin cultural traditions spanned Campania from Salerno in the south as far as the walls of Rome in the north.[31] When Eugenius died in June, 657, and the vigilant exarch Theodore Kalliopas promptly gave his consent to the election of Vitalian of Signia (Segni) in northern Campania to succeed him, he was authorizing the ordination of a pope from a region that had experienced the impact of the East from antique times. Moreover, the fact that the new pope's father was named Anastasios, thus indicating an Eastern provenance or at least an unmistakable identification with the East, must have given further confidence to his belief that he had authorized the enthronement of a pontiff who would be sympathetic to the reinvigorated

Byzantine administration and its program of reconciliation.[32] Neither the exarch nor the emperor would be disappointed in the choice.[33]

Vitalian hastened to show the Papacy's loyalty to Constantinople. He at once dispatched papal *apokrisiarii* to the capital bearing a letter addressed to the emperor Constans II and his sons and coemperors Constantine, Heraclius, and Tiberius formally informing them of his ordination.[34] Following a warm reception, the legates returned to Rome having obtained imperial reaffirmation of the historic privileges of the Apostolic See, as well as a set of golden gospel books embellished with precious stones as a gift from the emperor to the throne of St. Peter.[35] While in Constantinople, the *apokrisiarii* also delivered the new pope's customary *synodikon*, containing a profession of his faith, to patriarch Peter.[36] They probably returned to the West also carrying Peter's reply to Vitalian's *synodikon* for, although the pope's letter to the patriarch is lost, the patriarch's letter to Vitalian survived long enough to be read at the thirteenth session of the Sixth Ecumenical Council in 680/681.[37]

We may well wonder what it was in Vitalian's letter that caused patriarch Peter to say that it reflected a spiritual unity between him and the pope that delighted him, especially since it was based solely upon Peter's reply to Vitalian that the patriarch was declared a Monothelite and anathematized.[38] In what was probably an effort to palliate the sting caused by Eugenius's tepid rejection of patriarch Peter's *synodikon* three years earlier and, suffused with the spirit of detente that was abroad in the empire, Vitalian's *synodikon* to Peter may have stretched Rome's tolerance of Monothelitism to the brink of compromising its doctrinal orthodoxy. Although the pope's orthodoxy would later be unsuccessfully challenged, he escaped the censure that befell Peter largely because of imperial gratitude for his loyalty.[39] For the moment, however, his doctrinal flexibility and apparent willingness to be accommodating earned him the distinction of being the first Roman pontiff since Honorius to be inscribed on the diptychs of the church of Constantinople.[40] For the churches of the East the presence or absence of one's name on the diptychs was both a mechanism for resolving past conflicts and an important public indicator of the state of ecclesiastical politics at any given moment. The inclusion of Pope Vitalian among those who merited the special prayers of the church of Constantinople represented a symbolic recognition of his legitimacy and thus a highly significant gesture of benevolence toward the Papacy.[41] The imperial plan of reconciliation between Rome and Constantinople appeared to be progressing favorably.

For his part, Pope Vitalian showed great respect and admiration for the East and Easterners. When in 664 the kings of Kent and Northumbria sent an envoy to Rome asking the pope to designate a successor for the see of Canterbury, which had long remained vacant following the death of archbishop Deusdedit, Vitalian's first choice was a certain Hadrian, who at the time was abbot of a monastery on the island of Nisida in the Gulf of Naples.[42] Hadrian, a Greek-speaking aristocrat from Libya Cyrenaica, had like so many others fled Africa in the face of the Arab invasions of the early 640s and sought refuge in Campania.[43] There he entered a monastery where he eventually acquired skill in ecclesiastical and monastic administration as well as a mastery of Latin. Hadrian had already at-tracted the attention of the emperor Constans II, whom he probably met during the latter's Italian expedition, and had been dispatched to Gaul on two imperial embassies, which were possibly intended to forge a Frankish-Byzantine alliance against the Lombards and the Arabs.[44] Together with his extensive knowledge of both sacred and secular literature, the erudite Easterner appeared eminently suited to serve as primate of the English church.[45]

When Hadrian excused himself as unworthy of such a lofty assignment, Vi-talian turned to Andreas, another Easterner, who was chaplain to a Neapolitan convent that may have been identical with the nunnery of SS. Nicander and Marcian.[46] If so, Andreas was affiliated with an institution that had been substan-tially patronized by St. Patrizia, an aristocratic Constantinopolitan woman who had visited Naples during Constans II's reign and had been so impressed with SS. Nicander and Marcian that she eventually died and was buried there.[47] Andreas, however, declined the offer on grounds of ill health, whereupon the pope again pressed Hadrian to accept the position. Hadrian persisted in his refusal, but asked to be given time to recommend another candidate. The choice ultimately fell upon yet a third Easterner as Vitalian agreed with Hadrian's suggestion that he ordain a Greek monk named Theodore as archbishop of Canterbury.[48]

Theodore, a native of Tarsus in Cilicia, had spent considerable time in Con-stantinople to which he had fled as a refugee from either the Persian or Arab invasions of his homeland in southeastern Asia Minor.[49] While in the capital, he acquired expertise in Roman civil law, astronomy, poetry, the calculation of the church calendar, music, philosophy, rhetoric, medicine, and both sacred and secular literature either through study at the university, Sergius's patriar-chal school, or in the company of George of Pisidia, Theophylact Simocatta, and Stephen of Alexandria.[50] Toward the middle of the seventh century, his opposition to Monothelitism caused him to immigrate to Rome, where he probably took up residence with his countrymen at the Cilician monastery of St. Anastasios at Aquas Salvias.[51] Theodore appears to have been among the Greek monks who subscribed to the *libellus* presented by a delegation of Eastern monastics at the second session of the Lateran Council of 649.[52] Despite his opposition to Monothelitism and his participation in the Roman synod of 649, Vitalian had no concern about ordaining him to the see of Canterbury.[53] Nor is there any basis for Bede's claim that the pope made it a condition of Theodore's ordination that Hadrian accompany him to Britain "so that he [Theodore] not introduce into the church over which he was to preside anything contrary to the true faith after the custom of the Greeks."[54] Theodore's flight from Con-stantinople and his participation in the Lateran Council of 649 were more than sufficient indicators of his opposition to Monothelitism and hence his doctri-nal orthodoxy. Nor was it likely that Hadrian, a transplanted Greek-speaking monk from Byzantine Africa who had undertaken two diplomatic missions on behalf of the Monothelite emperor Constans II, would have been in the best position to ensure that Theodore not deviate from the customs and practices of the Roman church.[55] But Bede's groundless suspicions, based in part upon the fact that until his ordination as archbishop Theodore continued to wear the Eastern monastic tonsure,[56] nonetheless reflected a persistent undercurrent of uneasiness among a large segment of Western ecclesiastics about the orthodoxy of their Eastern brethren. The fact that Pope Vitalian, who appears to have been determined to select the best candidate available for Canterbury, could overcome that deeply ingrained suspicion and select a candidate based solely upon his piety and erudition and regardless of his Eastern ethnicity reflects a significant turning point in papal attitudes toward the East. In fact, it appears that Vitalian never even considered a candidate of Western provenance to serve as primate of the English church.[57]

The entourage that accompanied archbishop Theodore from Rome as he traveled through Francia on his way to Canterbury between 668 and 669 included a certain chanter named John, who was also probably an Easterner and most likely among those principally responsible for what Bede describes as the spread of the knowledge of sacred music throughout England.[58] John's skill in ecclesiastical chant was an integral part of a papal liturgical rite which, under the auspices and encouragement of Pope Vitalian, began to grow and develop around the middle of the seventh century alongside the traditional rite observed in the Roman church. The old Roman or urban rite, which had achieved its final shape around 600, reflected a primitive simplicity that made it seem terse and abrupt with a sense of "unemotional sobriety" that was almost juridical in its restraint.[59] Vitalian's pontificate (657–672) witnessed the early stages in the development of a distinctively papal rite which, in sharp contrast to the old Roman *ordo*, was a grandiose and dazzling spectacle modeled on the ceremonial of the imperial court, focused on the person of the pontiff, accentuated by a particular type of Eastern chant, and characterized by a strict and immutable etiquette which, in the awesome and magnificent impression it was intended to create, was redolent of the opulence and splendor of Byzantium.[60]

Vitalian's particular contribution to this emerging papal rite was the creation of a new *schola cantorum* or school of chant designed to provide specialized training in the music peculiar to its elaborate ceremonial.[61] Known as *Vitaliani*, after the name of their founder, these chanters were separate and distinct from those who sang at the celebration of the old Roman or urban rite in the presbyteral *tituli* or quasi-parish churches of the city.[62] The *Vitaliani* sang only in the presence of the pontiff at the stational masses offered in the patriarchal basilicas that were located in each of the seven regions of Rome.[63] Vitalian's *schola cantorum* developed from what was at first a small Lateran choir into an elaborate *collegium* whose organizational structure, in imitation of its Byzantine model, was as complex as the papal liturgy at which its members chanted. As the pontifical liturgy grew in splendor and detail over the course of the third quarter of the seventh century, so also did the *schola cantorum* attached to it. Eventually, it came to consist of a subdeacon known as the *prior* or *primus* under whom there were three other subdeacons called respectively the *secundus, tertius,* and *quartus.* The *quartus,* who served as senior chanter and choirmaster and was officially known by the Byzantine title of *archiparaphonista* (αρχιπαραφονίστα), directed the choir or *paraphonistae,* which consisted of clerics in minor orders and acolytes, as well as young pupils who, in a combination of Greek and Latin terms unique to this body, were called *infantes paraphonistae.*[64]

It was not only in the introduction of a papal rite evoking the ceremonies of the court in Constantinople that the liturgical practices of the Roman church were to experience the impact of the East as a result of Pope Vitalian's attachment to Byzantium. Beginning about the time of his pontificate, the pope and papal court began to celebrate the solemn Easter vespers, a service long performed in Constantinople but unknown in Rome until after the mid-seventh century.[65] That the observation of the Paschal vespers was the direct result of Vitalian's intervention is attested to by bishop Amalar of Metz, who remarked that their solemnization in Rome was prescribed by the Apostolicus, a papal title that the *Liber Pontificalis* uses only with reference to Pope Vitalian.[66] In addition to the observance of the Easter vespers, it was probably during Vitalian's reign that the Roman church also began the practice of administering the sacrament of baptism at Epiphany.[67] While this practice was common in the East, earlier Roman popes had opposed it. However, the *Ordo Romanus XV,* which was compiled in 675 by John, archchanter of St. Peter's and abbot of the adjacent monastery of St. Martin, reflects that by the time of Vitalian's immediate successor Pope Adeodatus (672–676), it was accepted practice in the Roman church.[68] Given Vitalian's predilection for Eastern liturgical pomp and practices, there is every reason to believe that baptism at Epiphany was first introduced in Rome during his pontificate.

The rise of a papal rite patterned on the ceremonial of the imperial court, the creation of a school of chant specifically intended to train singers in the Byzantine court music (*diaphonia basilika*) proper to this new and majestic ritual, and the observance of services and sacramental practices common in the East but hitherto unknown in Rome reflect the beginnings of a "liturgical byzantinization" of the Roman church that can only have occurred under a pope who appreciated the importance of the city's bonds with Byzantium and was determined to see them strengthened.[69]

Vitalian's initiatives also symbolize the return of peace between pope and emperor and an overt rejection of the disposition to emphasize the differences between Rome and Constantinople that had poisoned their relations and driven them apart, especially as a result of the Monothelite controversy.[70] The Roman church, which under Gregory the Great prided itself on being impervious to Eastern ecclesiastical practices, now embraced them with alacrity regarding them not as efforts to supplant its own traditions but rather to enrich and complement them.[71]

The adoption of oriental liturgical practices was also an unmistakable barometer of the broader cultural influences and changes that Rome and the Papacy were about to experience.[72] While Greek monastic domination of the Lateran Council of 649 had given Rome a generous sampling of the East, its result had been division from Constantinople rather than cohesion with it. Under Vitalian, however, Rome and the Papacy would begin to undergo a voluntary and peaceful adoption and imitation of Byzantine practices and ideas whose effect would be to unite East and West rather than to separate them.[73] The evolution from an urban to a papal rite, as well as the adoption of other Eastern liturgical observances, was therefore also a statement that Rome and the Papacy were prepared to accept, though not entirely capitulate, to a wide range of Byzantine attitudes and values.[74] Reconciliation with the empire would soon bring Rome "the great epoch of its Greek domination."[75] It would also bring the emperor himself.

⌘

In 653 the peace treaty, which had been concluded three years earlier between the imperial ambassador Prokopios and the caliph Muawiya, expired, thereby causing the Arabs to resume their incursions into Byzantine territory with raids on Cyprus, Rhodes, Cos, and Crete.[76] By late 653 or early 654, while Pope Eugenius I reigned peacefully in Rome, the inhabitants of Constantinople could see an Arab army massed along the shores directly opposite the capital.[77] The Arab raiders had been intent not only on accumulating booty, but in acquiring timber with which to construct a fleet of ships to launch a major naval armada against Constantinople.[78] With preparations at last completed, the Arab fleet set sail from Phoenician Tripolis in 655 bound for the imperial capital.[79] The Byzantine fleet, under the command of Constans II, lay in wait for the Arab ships off the promontory of Chelidonia at the foot of Mount Phoenix, a cypress-covered peak in the province of Lycia in southeastern Asia Minor. On the night before the battle, the emperor dreamed that he was in Thessalonika. This was taken as a portent of evil since a seer, who was consulted for an interpretation of the vision, related that Thessalonika was a pun on the words "θές ἄλλω νίκην" or "give to another the victory," meaning that the Arabs would prevail in the forthcoming battle.[80] The engagement indeed turned out badly for Byzantium as the "sea became red with the blood of the Romans."[81] Sensing the impending disaster, Constans is said to have fled in disguise to Constantinople in order to save himself, while twenty thousand of his men lay floating dead upon the waters and all the empire's ships "rose up from the earth in a cloud of dust."[82] Neither Theophanes nor the Greek historians whose accounts of the battle of Phoenix depended upon him would ever forget or forgive what they considered to be the emperor's ignominious and unpardonable flight.

Compounding the cowardice he is reputed to have displayed at Phoenix, Constans was also accused of having arranged the murder of his brother Theo-

dosios either because he suspected him of plotting to usurp the throne or because of his belief that Theodosios had joined an orthodox conspiracy opposed
to the emperor's Monothelite religious policy.[83] The fratricide was made even
more heinous by the charge that, before murdering him, Constans compelled
patriarch Paul to ordain Theodosios a deacon and, knowing that his brother
was to be slain, shamelessly received Holy Communion from his hands. As a
result, the emperor was forever after plagued with the vision of Theodosios
beckoning him to partake from a chalice of blood with the words "Drink, O
brother."[84]

The disfavor which the Greek sources uniformly show toward Constans was
principally the result of what they considered to be his vigorous espousal of
Monothelitism which, unlike his grandfather Heraclius, who was supposedly
mislead into embracing it by others, these writers were convinced that Constans
adopted and promoted of his own volition.[85] The emperor's outrageous treatment of Maximos and Martin provided more than enough for these virulently
orthodox sources, led by Theophanes, to add cowardice and fratricide to the
shameful misdeeds he was already believed to have committed against these two
hallowed champions of the true faith.[86] But no crime could compare in wickedness to the accusation that Constans was preparing to abandon Constantinople
and to transfer the imperial capital back to Rome.[87] Theophanes appears to have
correctly concluded that nothing was more likely to fuel the hatred with which
his ninth-century Constantinopolitan audience was disposed to regard Constans
than the charge that he intended to forsake their sacred city and return the seat
of the empire to her arch rival in the West.

By the turn of the sixth century, the idea was firmly rooted in Byzantine
mentality that Constantinople, the new Rome of the East, was young and vibrant while the old Rome of the West was falling hopelessly into decay, senility,
and death.[88] The city was in the process of being transformed and sanctified
into the new Jerusalem through the construction of churches and other sites
designed to recreate a Holy City on the Bosphorus.[89] A century later Constantinople had acquired a host of exalted epithets including "great miracle
and thunderous roar of the universe," "torch of piety," "workshop of virtue,"
"paradisaical meadow," "heaven on earth," "father of fathers and mother of
mothers," and the "savior and treasury of all the righteous."[90] It had become
the "God-protected city" under the special patronage of the Theotokos and,
as the "navel of the Universe and heart of the Earth," was destined to play a
central role in the apocalyptic drama of the Second Coming and the end of the
world.[91] By the beginning of the eighth century, the idea had developed that
the Christian world had shrunk to Constantinople and its hinterland west to
Thessalonika and east to Asia Minor.[92] Heaven was synonymous with the imperial court, and the citizens of the capital were blessed above all others in the
empire.[93] To repudiate "the queen of cities surpassing all others in the world"[94]
for a moribund agglomeration of decaying buildings on the Tiber would have

been an act of political folly and, in the eyes of the inhabitants of Constantinople, no less than blasphemy. Constans II was no fool, nor Theophanes Confessor imperceptive.[95]

Constans II never intended to abandon Constantinople as the seat of the empire or to transfer the capital to Rome. The claim that he planned to do so reflects no more than a determination on the part of Theophanes and those orthodox historians whose narratives depend upon him to calumniate an emperor whom they regarded as a heretic and a persecutor.[96] Constans could not possibly have been ignorant of the immense symbolic importance that Constantinople played in the ethos of the empire, nor of the belief, expressed by George of Pisidia, that God himself had entrusted its care and safety to the emperor, who alone would bear ultimate responsibility for its fate.[97] Nor could he have been unaware of the fact that possession of Constantinople, as Justinian I had learned during the Nika riots and as Heraclius had been admonished by the patrician Krispos, literally made the emperor, and that in order for one effectively to claim the purple he had to be firmly in control of the city and its massive walls, which were themselves a symbol of the empire's solidity.[98] Apart from these considerations, it would have made no sense to move the seat of government from the geographic position of near impregnability that Constantinople enjoyed to either Rome, Ravenna, or Sicily, none of which offered anything comparable in defensibility.

When Constans II left the capital bound westward sometime in the summer of 661, he did not do so with the intention of transferring the seat of government to Rome or any other place in Italy. Nor did he depart for any of the reasons that the Eastern sources posit or, as Paul the Deacon says, "to pluck Italy from the hand of the Lombards."[99] Constans did not leave until he had reasonably assured himself that those forces responsible for securing the empire's borders in Asia Minor, as well as the approaches to the capital from across the Sea of Marmara, had been sufficiently strengthened against the Arab menace.[100] His expedition was therefore neither a hasty and precipitous flight from disgrace nor a fanciful attempt to rekindle the extinguishing flame of empire and restore the *oikoumene* to its farthest boundaries and antique grandeur on the scale of imperial Rome.[101] Constans was no political romantic bent on a useless expenditure of the empire's energies in recapturing a lost splendor or searching for adventure.[102] The emperor was seeking neither gain nor glory, but simply survival. His goal was not to embark upon another Justinianic *reconquista*, but rather to secure and defend what little remained of the empire in Greece and Italy against the threat posed by the Slavs, the Lombards, and, most of all, the Arabs.[103] While his expedition confirms that Constans believed the West was a fundamental and important part of the empire whose safety had to be ensured and whose unity with the East was worth the struggle to preserve,[104] his ultimate concern, like that of every emperor before him, was to safeguard Constantinople, which for him, as for his predecessors, was and always would be "the center of the four corners of the earth."[105]

◦ᔓ

Constans II had reigned for twenty years when, in the summer of 661, he sailed from Constantinople along with an army consisting of troops drawn from the Anatolikon, Armeniakon, Thrakesion, and Opsikion themes, disembarking first at Thessalonika, where he obtained the submission of certain Slavic tribes that had been creating problems for the local imperial administration, and thereafter proceeding along the coast to Athens.[106] As the first step in a strategic and thoughtfully articulated policy of "defensive imperialism," by which the emperor set out to secure the territory that had been left to Byzantium following the loss of large areas to invaders over the course of the preceding hundred years, Constans had come to the Balkans with the specific intention of containing Slavic advances into imperial holdings in Greece and fortifying the defenses on her eastern and southern coasts against the possible reappearance of the Arab fleet whose danger to the empire had been unquestionably established six years earlier at Phoenix.[107] It was probably during his sojourn in Athens that the emperor established the Helladic theme and visited nearby Corinth, where, consistent with his general plan, he expelled the Onogur Bulgars and earned the praise of the local population that erected a statue in his honor.[108] Satisfied that he had sufficiently organized the defense of Greece against the Slavs from the north and the Arabs from the south and east, Constans turned his attention to Italy, for which he set sail, possibly from Corinth, arriving at Tarentum (Taranto) in the Byzantine-controlled region of Apulia (Puglia) sometime in the early spring of 663.[109]

In the late summer of 662, Grimuald, duke of Beneventum, had usurped the Lombard throne by eliminating Godipert and Perctarit, the sons and legitimate heirs of the deceased king Aripert I.[110] He had accomplished this by murdering Godipert and marrying his sister, while terrifying Perctarit into seeking refuge first with the Avars and later with the Franks. Thereafter, Grimuald installed his son Romuald as his successor in the duchy of Beneventum while he himself settled in Pavia in the north of Italy, where he continued to harbor a fierce hostility toward the empire both because of his own Arian religious sympathies and, more likely, because his older brothers Taso and Cacco had been treacherously murdered by the exarch Isaac in Oderzo nearly forty years earlier.[111] During the course of his adventurous life, Grimuald had witnessed the Lombards expand southward through the center of Byzantine Italy establishing their dominion over large portions of what had been imperial territory.[112] These intrusions had produced a virtual Lombardy Minor whose heart, the duchy of Beneventum, created a chasm between the eastern and western parts of the exarchate.[113] The Byzantines were pushed to the margins of the peninsula so that by the time of Grimuald's accession in 662 their holdings in southern Italy, including the duchy of Rome, faced the imminent menace of collapse before the efforts of a reinvigorated Lombard monarchy to establish total supremacy in Italy.[114] The empire's only hope of retaining its possessions in southern Italy was to arrest the Lombards by launching a campaign that had the specific goal of containing their advances into imperial territory. Constans hoped to achieve this by engaging in a rapid and concentrated offensive aimed at taking specific cities and towns in the Beneventine duchy and then turning toward the city of Beneventum itself.[115] The fact that Grimuald's forces were massed along the River Po in the north and the speed with which the emperor accomplished his initial objectives in the south strongly suggest that the Lombards were caught by surprise, apparently anticipating his arrival at Ravenna rather than at Taranto, and accordingly misjudging the limited strategic goals he had in mind.[116]

Constans appears to have set out from Taranto along the Via Appia and the Via Traiana, crossing the River Ofanto into Lombard-occupied territory and taking a number of towns including Ecana and Ortona as well as the wealthy city of Lucera, which he razed to the ground, although the highly fortified town of Acerenza, situated on one of the buttresses of Mt. Vulture, proved impregnable.[117] Arriving at last before the walls of Beneventum, the emperor found the city defended by a small army under the command of Grimuald's son duke Romuald, who, learning of Constans's impending arrival, had sent word to his father to send troops to assist him. When the emperor's efforts to take Beneventum ultimately proved fruitless and he learned of Grimuald's imminent arrival with reinforcements, Constans decided to lift the siege and attempt to arrive at an accommodation with the Lombards. In exchange for obtaining Romuald's sister Gisa as a hostage to ensure the fulfillment of an agreement whose terms have not survived, the emperor raised the siege and departed for Naples. It was only after he had handed Gisa over to the Byzantines that Romuald learned that Grimuald and his army were only about fifty miles from Beneventum.[118]

Although Paul the Deacon records that Mitola, the Lombard count of Capua, later routed the imperial army near the River Calore, which flows a little east of Beneventum, and that thereafter duke Romuald, with only a small part of Grimuald's reinforcements, defeated a force of twenty thousand imperial troops at Forino some twenty-five miles east of Naples, his account of what transpired following Constans's withdrawl from Beneventum is a gross exaggeration of what was probably some rearguard action as the Byzantines moved on toward Naples and indeed reflects a blatant violation of the armistice on the part of the Lombards.[119]

Constans II's limited and carefully organized campaign against the Lombards appears to have fully achieved its purposes. Far from being either a failure or an "inglorious adventure" that ended in a shameful retreat to the safety of southern Campania, Constans's expedition succeeded in containing Lombard aggression and blocking any further incursions by them into imperial territory in southern Italy.[120] Lombard lands in the duchy of Beneventum were widely traversed by imperial troops, many of their principal cities and towns were attacked or destroyed, and the Lombards were at last put on the defensive.[121] At the same time, the emperor succeeded in opening a line of communication between the empire's possessions on Italy's southeastern coast and its territories in the southwest, including Naples and the approaches to Rome.[122] These achievements were not the "anachronistic dreams of an inept tyrant,"[123] but rather the accomplishments of a practical tactician whose vision of the empire took serious account of the realities of Italian politics in the late seventh century and, as such, recognized that the presence of the Lombards on the peninsula was an irreversible fait accompli.[124] Constans effectively restored Italy's political equilibrium by curtailing Lombardic territorial designs against imperial holdings and establishing a bright line of demarcation that defined the extent to which the empire would tolerate any further barbarian intrusions. With the Lombards in check, the emperor could now turn his attention to the second phase of his expedition as he prepared to reestablish the religious equilibrium between East and West that had been disturbed as a result of the Monothelite controversy. Constans would crown the years of rapprochement that had drawn Constantinople closer to the Papacy since the unfortunate affair of Pope Martin by going in person to Rome. He would be the first and the last Byzantine emperor to do so.

The month of June was drawing to a close when in the summer of 663 Constans II and a large detachment of troops set out along the coastal road bordering the Gulf of Gaeta toward Formia and on to the strongly fortified town of Terracina, which, located at the southernmost frontier of the duchy of Rome, served as an important assembly point for imperial troops in Campania.[125] The emperor appears to have arranged his journey so that he would be in Terracina on June 29 in order to observe the feast day of SS. Peter and Paul, with whom the ecclesiastical history of the city was closely tied.[126] Terracina's forum had recently been renovated and embellished by Georgios, duke of Rome, in anticipation of the emperor's arrival. As a symbol of his successes against the Lombards, a column had been erected bearing an inscription in Greek, which, judiciously dissimulating on the Monothelite issue, acclaimed Constans and his sons and coemperors Constantine, Heraclius, and Tiberius as "Ὀρθοδόξων καί νηκητῶν βασιλέων," or "orthodox and victorious emperors," and, after the fashion of the Byzantine court and army, wished them a reign of many years.[127] Duke Georgios's contribution in refurbishing the forum was commemorated lower on the column in Latin.[128] The bilingual inscriptions on the column at Terracina were an indicator of a broader and harmonious symbiosis of a variety of Eastern and Western cultural elements in the Duchy of Rome in the late seventh century, and they reflected both its bonds with the Greek-speaking East and a simultaneous determination to preserve its native Latinity. From Terracina, the imperial entourage took the Via Appia that led directly to Rome and where, after a journey of less than a week, the emperor and his army arrived on Wednesday, July 5, 663.[129]

The approach to Rome along the Appian Way from the south overflowed with reminders of the ancient capital's glorious and bloodstained Christian past.

As he made his way to the city, the emperor saw the tomb of the great third-century martyr St. Sebastian,[130] next to whom was the place where for forty years the bodies of the holy apostles Peter and Paul had been interred. Farther along was the church where St. Quirinus, martyred in Pannonia in 308, had been buried. On the right stretched the cemetery of Praetextatus where the martyrs Valerianus and Maximus lay buried, and the "great cave" where St. Tiburtius had laid Pope Urban I to rest.[131] There also were the graves of Pope Xystus II's three deacons Felicissimus, Agapitus, and Januarius, all of whom had been beheaded in the time of Valerian and Decius for refusing to sacrifice to demons. The cemetery of Praetextatus also contained the tomb of the martyr Quirinus, father of St. Balbina,[132] as well as the grave of a pious Christian known only as Zeno. On his left the emperor passed the cemetery that Pope Callistus had built in the third century and where St. Cecilia[133] lay buried alongside "an innumerable multitude of martyrs," which included St. Soteris the virgin, ancestor of Ambrose of Milan, as well as fourteen Roman pontiffs from Zephyrinus (198/9–217) to Miltiades (310–314).[134]

At the sixth milestone from the city, Constans was met by Pope Vitalian, who, together with the Roman clergy and people, had come out to welcome the imperial entourage while it was still well beyond the walls of Rome.[135] The emperor's arrival in the ancient capital of the empire was thus transformed into an "imperial epiphany" assuming all the attributes of an *adventus* in the ancient style.[136] No doubt orchestrated by the Byzantine administration of the city with the active participation of the pope and Roman church, the emperor's reception in the antique manner was deliberately calculated to resurrect a ceremony that had always played an important role in imperial politics.[137] The concept of a personal encounter between ruler and subject had, since pagan times, served as an important means of expressing the interdependence that existed between the Romans and their emperor.[138] That notion still retained its vitality in the seventh century. On Constans's part, his *adventus* was both a celebration of his triumph against the Lombards and his claim to the city of Rome, which, although now devoid of any political importance, still preserved its immense moral prestige as the spiritual center of the empire.[139] For the pope and the people of Rome, the act of going out to meet him was an affirmative statement of their acceptance of him as emperor and a ratification of the proposition that he who carried the title of emperor was in fact and indeed their sovereign.[140] The imperial *adventus* and accompanying *receptio* were thus affirmations on both sides of the emperor's right to enter Rome as *basileus*. For Constans particularly, the encounter had to have been a reassuring sign that, although decades of bitter religious warfare had stretched thin the filament that bound Rome to Constantinople, the ties between East and West were still as strong as ever.

The imperial suite, which now included both emperor and pope, continued its procession along the Appian Way toward the Porta Appia, through which Constans would pass as he entered the city. The Porta Appia had originally consisted of a double-arched entrance flanked by semi-circular tile-faced towers, each of which was crowned with crenellations behind which sprawled large inner courtyards. During the reigns of Honorius and Valentinian III, the towers had been heightened and strengthened with quadrangular marble and brick bastions matched by a curtain of similar material. Eventually, the double arches were modified into a single arch, but the keystone, which had occupied the juncture between the two original arches, had been preserved.[141] As the emperor passed through the gate, he could look up and see that the stone over the Porta Appia bore the symbol of an incised cross in the same way that city gates in Constantinople had been embellished with crosses since the beginning of the fifth century.[142] At the top of the cross was an inscription which read "ΘΕΩ ΚΑΡΙΣ" or "Thanks be to God," while at the bottom were the words "ΑΓΙΕ ΚΩΝΟΝ"[143] ("Saint Conon") and "ΑΓΙΕ ΓΕΩΡΓΙ"[144] ("Saint George").[145] The familiar cross over the Porta Appia and the Greek inscription invoking two saints of Eastern provenance, especially Saint George, whose patronage would have been particularly important to this warrior emperor and his largely Eastern troops, must have further comforted Constans, whose relations with Rome over most of the past two decades had been marked largely by rancor and hostility.

The emperor then made his way past the massive Baths of Caracalla that stood at the southern slope of the Aventine toward the Circus Maximus, then along the *Porticus usque ad Elephantum*, passing the Theatre of Marcellus on the left and the Theatre of Pompey on the right, through the *Porta Sancti Petri* where, crossing the bridge that spanned the Tiber, the imposing Mausoleum of Hadrian lay directly before him. Turning sharply to the left, the imperial party followed the portico that led to the Vatican and St. Peter's basilica where, on the first day he arrived in Rome, Constans went to pray and present a gift to the prince of the Apostles.[146] Retracing his route, the emperor returned to the heart of imperial Rome where he took up residence in the impressive imperial palaces, which for half a millennium had spread with increasing splendor over the crest of the Palatine Hill.[147]

Two days later, on Saturday, July 8, the emperor went to the church of St. Mary *ad praesepe*, a sanctuary that had been the site of many of the tumultuous events that accounted for much of the animosity that had existed between Constans and the Romans.[148] It was in this church, where two decades earlier Pope Theodore had placed Christ's manger, that the *chartularios* Maurikios had taken refuge following his unsuccessful rebellion against the emperor, and from here that he was dragged by a halter placed around his neck and later beheaded outside Ravenna.[149] It was also in this church where the imperial *spatharios*, who had been dispatched by the exarch Olympios to murder Pope Martin, was instantly blinded and thus prevented from shedding the pontiff's blood.[150] And it was in St. Mary's where, in order to quell the unseemly roar of the crowd and finish saying the mass, Pope Eugenius I was compelled to renounce the patriarch of Constantinople's pro-Monothelite synodic letter.[151] As if to make amends for these occurrences, the emperor offered a gift to the Mother of God, whose pardon he might thus obtain for any part he had had in causing the stains that had sullied her sanctuary.[152] On Sunday, July 9, the emperor descended from the Palatine and, along with his troops, each of whom carried a wax candle, returned in solemn procession to St. Peter's. To complement the gift of golden gospels he had sent Pope Vitalian several years earlier, Constans now laid a pallium embroidered in gold upon the altar and, taking the first in a series of steps that would at last close the chasm that had separated Byzantium and Rome, the emperor attended the celebration of mass by the pope, from whom he doubtless received the sacrament of Holy Communion.[153]

Thereafter, the ceremonies were suspended for five days, from Monday, July 10, through Friday, July 14, during which time the emperor appears to have occupied himself in directing the dismantling of as much metal from the city's public buildings as he could amass. This seems to have consisted of large quantities of copper as well as bronze, including, to the great indignation of the two principal Western sources, the bronze tiles from the roof of the Pantheon, which, during the pontificate of Boniface IV, had by leave of the emperor Phocas been converted to a Christian church and dedicated to St. Mary and all the martyrs.[154] Although his detractors claimed that the emperor shipped the metal as booty to Constantinople, it is far more likely that it was converted to coin and used to defray the expenses of the Italian expedition and, in particular, to pay the troops.[155]

On Saturday, July 15, the emperor left the imperial palace on the Palatine and, going past the Colosseum to the other side of the Caelian Hill, arrived at the papal residence in the Lateran *patriarchium*. Constans was formally received by the Pope Vitalian in the basilica of Julius, which seems to have served as the scene for official receptions since the beginning of the century when the portraits of the emperor Phocas and his consort Leontia were unveiled and acclaimed there by the Roman clergy and people.[156] Before dining with the pontiff in the Julian basilica, the emperor is recorded to have bathed, probably in the octagonal baptistery of *San Giovanni in Fonte* located in the Constantinian basilica and in whose porphyry basin legend maintained that Pope Sylvester I had baptized Constantine the Great.[157] On Sunday, July 16, his last day in Rome, the emperor participated in a stational mass where liturgical processions from Rome's major basilicas and titular churches, in imitation of a practice reflecting the strong influence of Byzantium and the East, filed solemnly through the city's streets converging at last at St. Peter's.[158] There Pope Vitalian offered the Eucharist, Constans again received communion, and in the midst of the blistering heat of midsummer, departed for Naples never to see either Rome or the pontiff again.[159]

As with all other aspects of his Italian expedition, Constans II's visit to the city of Rome had been deliberately planned and carefully calculated to achieve specific purposes.[160] On the political level, it represented an affirmative assertion by a victorious emperor that Byzantium was determined to exercise dominion over the former capital of the empire and all of its territories in Italy, and to defend them vigorously against the inimical designs of any potential aggressor. The emperor's triumphant *adventus* and the antique-style reception, which he was accorded by Pope Vitalian and the clergy and the people of Rome who received him as "heir of the Caesars," must have given Constans a gratifying sense of reassurance that his often unruly Western subjects were prepared to concede to him the very sovereignty which he had come to reassert.[161] By taking up residence in the ancient imperial palaces on the Palatine Hill, Constans gave the Romans a visible sign of that sovereignty, which he later asserted even more explicitly by exercising his imperial prerogative to deal with Rome's public buildings as he saw fit. The censure later expressed by Western sources for what they considered to be his unpardonable exploitation of Rome's buildings and monuments has led to the belief that the Romans saw Constans more as a conqueror than a benevolent protector, and that the joy with which they received him was exceeded only by the joy with which they saw him leave.[162] Such conclusions fail to take into account the fact that even in the seventh century Rome's public buildings were deemed a "protected imperial preserve."[163] When Pope Boniface IV wished to convert the Pantheon into a Christian church, he had to obtain permission to do so from the emperor Phocas.[164] Later, when Pope Honorius I wanted to cover the roof of St. Peter's with bronze tiles, he did so only "by concession of the most pious emperor Heraclius."[165] Constans's removal of the bronze tiles from the roof of St. Mary *ad martyres* was calculated neither to "gratify his avarice" nor to affront the Romans, whom he had come to embrace and certainly not to offend.[166] Nor was it unprecedented. As recently as 622, when Heraclius departed on his campaign against the Persians, he had unilaterally appropriated "the candelabra and other vessels of the holy ministry from the Great Church [of Haghia Sophia], which he minted into a great quantity of gold and silver coin," intending thereby to pay for the costs of his war against Persia in the same way that Constans expected to pay for the costs of his expedition to Italy.[167] We may well wonder whether Paul the Deacon or the author of the *Liber Pontificalis* would have protested so vocally if Rome's precious monuments had been despoiled by an emperor whom they did not consider to be both a heretic and a persecutor.

In addition to its political agenda, Constans's Roman sojourn had a significant and specific religious goal. Replete with processions, ceremonies, and rituals centered around some of the city's most important religious sites, the emperor's stay in Rome was designed to reaffirm that the empire's ecclesiastical unity, sundered by decades of strife over Monothelitism, had been reformed under an orthodox sovereign, and was as strong as the political bonds that welded East and West. The fact that the emperor went to St. Peter's basilica on three separate occasions during his twelve-day stay in Rome, including a visit on the very day he arrived, indicates rather strongly his intent to reconcile Byzantium's rift with the Roman church on terms which paid the Apostolic See the highest deference. Constans reinforced that intention by personally presenting St. Peter's with lavish gifts and by descending from the Palatine to dine with the pope at his residence in the Lateran *patriarchium* rather than summoning the pontiff to dine with him in the imperial palace.[168] The culmination of the years of rapprochement between Rome and Constantinople following the episode of Pope Martin occurred when the emperor received the Holy Eucharist from Pope Vitalian's hands, thereby symbolically reforming the fractured communion between the two churches and expressing as no other act could the end of the years of religious discord and the return of unity to the Christian and orthodox empire.[169]

The inclination to see Constans's visit to Rome as a personal pilgrimage of expiation for his mistreatment of Martin and Maximos, the murder of his brother Theodosios, and his promulgation of the *Typos* appears to be based on the erroneous assumption that the emperor recognized wrongdoing in these actions and wanted desperately to repent for them.[170] It has even been claimed that by bathing in the Lateran baptistery where Pope Sylvester was said to have baptized Constantine the Great, Constans II was both ritually cleansing himself of his sins and, arising thereafter like some *novus Constantinus*, announcing his intention to return the Roman Empire to its ancient grandeur.[171] Such notions are, however, more fanciful than real and represent little more than an uncritical acceptance of chroniclers such as Theophanes whose histories intentionally set out to demonize him. By engaging in such romantic speculation, they likewise fail entirely to take into account the specific and limited goals Constans had in mind when he left Constantinople for the West in 661.[172]

Constans II left Rome secure in the belief that he had reestablished the religious unity of the empire, stabilized political conditions with respect to the empire's possessions in Italy, and reaffirmed the Papacy's loyalty toward Constantinople so that he could now without distraction concentrate his efforts entirely in organizing Byzantium's defenses against the Arabs. From the papal point of view, the peace that had been achieved between Vitalian and Constans was equally advantageous. The emperor's presence in Italy provided ample assurance of Byzantium's commitment to halt the advance of the Arabs and the threat that they posed to Christianity in the West. Moreover, the enormous esteem that Constans had shown toward the Apostolic See strongly suggests that the Papacy had secured a champion who would protect it against both the Lombards and the persistent pretensions of Milan and Ravenna for autocephaly.[173] Political exigency, triumphant over decades of religious warfare between Rome and Constantinople, had succeeded in relegating the acrimonious debate over whether Christ had one or two wills to the periphery of their concerns. Emperor and pope had set aside their differences before the great menace that loomed on the horizon toward Africa. Constans might despoil Rome's buildings for their metal with impunity; the pope would not protest. The emperor was orthodox and the *Typos* long forgotten. Where survival was at stake Christology became a trifling matter. The Papacy was now securely back within the imperial embrace. Pope Vitalian was and would forever remain its loyal subject. Passing through either the Porta Portuensis or the nearby Porta Ostiensis, Constans bade his final farewell to Rome, returning by the sea route first to Naples, and then by land along the coastal road to Rhegium (Reggio di Calabria) and across the straits to Sicily, an island that over the next two decades would give the Roman church four popes.[174]

⌘

Constans's arrival in Syracuse toward the end of the summer of 663 signaled the beginning of the final phase of his Italian expedition. Having contained the Lombards against further incursions into imperial territories in peninsular Italy and secured the political stability of the duchy of Rome through a renewed religious solidarity with the Papacy, the emperor could now focus on establishing a base against the Arabs and thereby fulfilling what had been from the start the principal objective of his campaign in the West.[175] The island of Sicily was in all respects ideally suited both as the place upon which to locate the imperial court and residence and to marshal and mobilize Byzantine forces. Constans recognized, as Belisarius had at the beginning of the Gothic campaign in 535, that Sicily's geographic position at the juncture of the principal sea routes in the Mediterranean basin, and in relation to Egypt and north Africa, made it a perfect base from which to launch a military offensive or establish a primary zone of defense.[176] Sicily, moreover, was considered private imperial property, independent of the exarchate of Italy, and governed by a *strategos* or *patricius* sent from Constantinople and answerable directly to the emperor.[177] In addition, it was without doubt Italy's richest province. Unaffected by the wars that had plagued the neighboring peninsula, it enjoyed considerable economic prosperity throughout the seventh century, continuing to provide Rome and Italy, as it had since ancient times, with their principal source of grain.[178] Furthermore, taxes paid on the abundant productivity of the Sicilian latifundia had always been an important source of revenue for the imperial treasury.[179] Constans would increase that already sizable burden by imposing an extraordinary and highly unpopular tax intended to finance the costs of his Arab campaign.[180] Finally, since Sicily was, and since antiquity had always been, the most heavily Hellenized imperial possession in the West, it had to have appeared particularly inviting to an emperor who was ethnically a Greek.[181]

The overwhelming number of Greek as opposed to Latin funerary inscriptions from the fourth and fifth centuries, especially in the eastern part of Sicily around Messina, Catania, and Syracuse, attests to the fact that the majority of the population in those areas was at that time ethnically Greek.[182] The Justinianic reconquest of the mid-sixth century added to Sicily's already substantial oriental population with fresh arrivals of Syrians, Armenians, and Greeks.[183] The letters of Gregory the Great, more than two hundred of which refer to Sicily, betray the fact that by the time of his pontificate the majority of the island's inhabitants, especially on its southern and eastern coasts, spoke only Greek.[184] The Persian and Arab invasions of the eastern part of the empire during the early seventh century drove even more immigrants westward, bringing Sicily yet another infusion of Easterners to add to the substantial numbers already present.[185] Sicily was ideally suited to receive the new refugees not only because its geographic position made it the first natural landfall, but perhaps even more importantly because its predominantly Greek population and cultural traditions were especially welcoming to these Levantine exiles, many of whom settled permanently on the island or at least stayed there temporarily before moving onto the continent.[186] By the middle of the seventh century, the Greek element in Sicily was by far predominant over its Latin counterpart, extending its influence into all aspects of Sicilian society and culture from staffing the civil administration to creating exquisite works of art.[187]

The Sicilian church, although under papal jurisdiction until the eighth century, was also heavily influenced by Easterners. During the course of the seventh century, they came to comprise most of the island's clergy and to occupy most of its episcopal sees, all of which were subject to the immediate authority of the metropolitan of Syracuse.[188] In the late sixth century, the see of Agrigentum (Agrigento) in southern Sicily was held by a certain Gregory, who, according to his biography by Leontios, abbot of the Roman monastery of St. Sabas, had left Sicily for Syria, where he had gone to pursue the monastic life, returning thereafter to Rome where Gregory the Great ordained him bishop of his native Agrigentum.[189] Although by the time of the Lateran Council of 649 a Latin named Felix had succeeded to the see of Agrigentum, the subscriptions to the acts of that synod reflect that Easterners occupied the majority of Sicily's bishoprics including those at Catania, Palermo, Carina, Lilibeo, and Tyndari.[190] Zosimus, Greek abbot of the monastery of St. Lucia, was appointed metropolitan of Syracuse by his Eastern compatriot Pope Theodore (642–649) after a disputed election.[191] When Zosimus died at the age of ninety, he was succeeded by Elias, another Easterner, who was in turn succeeded by yet another Greek named Theodoros.[192]

The Sicilian monastic community was similarly dominated by Easterners, whose learning and erudition was a product of their rich oriental heritage. John of Damascus, for example, had been extremely well educated in his youth by a Sicilian monk named Cosmas, for whose skill in science and theology John's father paid handsomely.[193] Cosmas was part of the burgeoning Eastern monastic population on the island to whom Maximos Confessor wrote a lengthy letter in Greek on the Monothelite question sometime in 646.[194] It appears, moreover, that during the course of the first half of the seventh century the leadership of Sicily's major monasteries had passed from Latin to Greek hands. The monastery of St. Lucia, ruled by the Latin abbot Faustus during the time of Gregory I, was led by the Greek abbot Zosimus, future metropolitan of Syracuse, thirty years later. Similarly, the monastery of St. Peter *ad Baias*, whose Latin abbot Caesarius received a letter from Pope Gregory in 597, was in 678 being led by the Syrian hegumen Theophanes. After serving as one of Pope Agatho's delegates to the Sixth Ecumenical Council in 680/681, Theophanes left Sicily to become patriarch of Antioch.[195] In view of the extensive easternization of Sicily's ecclesiastical establishment, especially by way of Syria, Palestine, and Egypt, it comes as no surprise that the island's liturgical practices, both within the regular church and the monastic community, mirrored more the rites of Antioch and Alexandria rather than those of Constantinople.[196]

The arrival of the emperor, members of the imperial court and civil administration, and contingents of the Byzantine army in Syracuse toward the end of 663 did not account for the Hellenization of Sicily that, as we have seen, had been taking place since antiquity.[197] It did, however, represent the introduction onto the island of large numbers of laypersons, including civil officials and soldiers, distinct from the principally ecclesiastical and hence mainly celibate population that had arrived in Sicily from the East as a result of the barbarian invasions earlier in the century. One consequence of this new infusion of Easterners was the rise of a military elite.[198] Another was an increase in the number of administrative personnel required to handle official imperial business.[199] Yet another was a strengthening of the political and cultural bonds between Byzantium and the West that followed as a natural consequence of the emperor's five-year stay in Sicily.[200] Byzantine influence on the island, building upon an already firm and vigorous oriental substratum, accelerated and intensified.[201] Constans II, for example, now personally intervened to appoint a talented Greek hymnographer named Georgios as metropolitan of Syracuse.[202] A Sicilian theme, embracing Calabria in southern Italy, was organized along the lines of similar military organizations that had been created in Asia Minor some two decades earlier, and an imperial mint was established at Syracuse.[203] Perhaps most importantly, Sicily now received an infusion of Easterners who married and reproduced and who, unlike the mainly monastic refugees who had preceded them, were not, in Pierre Batiffol's most apposite expression, "an eternal race into which no one is born."[204] Before the seventh century was over, this fecundity would result in the accession of four Sicilians of Eastern provenance to the Papacy.[205]

⋅⋄⋅

Constans II had been in Sicily for nearly five years when, on July 15, 668, he was fatally struck on the head with a pail by his attendant Andreas, son of the patrician Troilos, while bathing at a place called Daphne. Eastern sources, led by Theophanes, attribute the emperor's assassination to an allegedly universal hatred of him resulting from a combination of misdeeds including the murder of his brother Theodosios, the persecution of Martin, Maximos, and their disciples, and his intention to move the capital from Constantinople to Rome. The event immediately precipitating his murder seems to have been a directive that the empress and their three sons join him permanently in Syracuse.[206] Western sources record only his murder, strongly intimating, however, that the emperor's death was the consequence of a widespread hatred generated by his imposition of onerous taxes and other burdensome fiscal exactions as well as the plunder of "the sacred vessels and treasures of God's holy churches."[207] Since the Roman church was among the largest landholders in Sicily, the weight of Constans's financial exactions must have been particularly oppressive on the papal patrimony there.[208] Yet there is no evidence to support the hypothesis that the church of Rome was involved in a conspiracy to kill Constans because of the heavy tax burden he had imposed on its Sicilian possessions.[209] Nor is there any support for the contention that the Roman church joined in a surreptitious plot to assassinate the emperor because he had granted autocephaly to its fractious suffragan Ravenna two years earlier.[210] Despite the tax burden on the Papacy's Sicilian patrimony and the indignity of having Ravenna declared an autocephalous church, Pope Vitalian remained steadfast in the pledge of loyalty he had made to the emperor, providing tangible proof of his commitment to the empire's legitimate ruling house in the matter of the attempted usurpation by Mezezius.

The most likely participants in the decision to murder the emperor were the transplanted Easterners, who comprised the court circle in Syracuse, and the army, who, tiring of Constans's protracted stay in the West, anxious to return to their homes in the East, and probably believing that his tactical policy against the Arabs was becoming increasingly questionable, saw no alternative to ending their seemingly endless stay in Sicily than by physically removing him.[211] Immediately after his death, a certain Armenian named Mezezius, who was *comes* of the Opsikion theme and who may have held the rank of *patrikios*, or patrician, was proclaimed emperor by the Syracusans. Eastern sources intimate that his election was by universal approbation of the imperial court in Syracuse and that Mezezius was, moreover, persuaded to accept the office only by constraint.[212] Western accounts relate that he seized the imperial office by rebellion and usurpation.[213] In either case, imperial forces were quickly mobilized to oppose him. With the active support of Pope Vitalian, who appears to have collaborated unreservedly with the exarch, contingents of the imperial army in Italy converged on Sicily from places as far apart as Istria, Campania, Sardinia, and Africa.[214]

Constans's eldest son set sail at once from Byzantium with a large fleet and arrived in Sicily, where he captured and beheaded Mezezius and those who had participated in the assassination of his father, returning thereafter to Constantinople where he reigned jointly with his brothers Tiberios and Heraklios until deposing them in the latter part of 681 and becoming sole emperor as Constantine IV.[215] The young emperor would never forget Pope Vitalian's support in suppressing the attempted usurpation by Mezezius, steadfastly resisting subsequent pressure by both the patriarchs of Constantinople and Antioch to have Vitalian's name stricken from the diptychs of the Byzantine church.[216]

Pope Vitalian's support for Constantine IV was prompted both by a genuine commitment to the legitimate ruling house in Byzantium, which even before

Constans II's visit to Rome had shown itself favorably disposed toward the Papacy, as well as by a firm desire to maintain and indeed strengthen the recently renewed bonds between Rome and Constantinople.[217] Persistent efforts to interpret Vitalian's opposition to Mezezius as an effort to advance papal pretensions to sovereignty in Italy by eliminating the prospect of an imperial rival on Italian soil find no more support than the notion that the popes of the late seventh century intentionally set out to sow the seeds of a so-called Republic of St. Peter free and independent of Byzantium.[218]

When Constantine IV wrote Pope Donus in 678 of the great affection he had for Vitalian as a result of the efforts he had set in motion against the "tyrant," whom he never deigned to mention by name, he was referring not only to the pope himself but to the institution he personified and the fact that Rome and the Papacy had stood solidly with Byzantium.[219] Only a year before, the emperor had given perhaps the most conclusive proof of his great reverence for the Apostolic See by reversing his father's grant of autocephaly to Ravenna and returning it to the jurisdiction of Rome, thus stripping from the capital of his own exarchate the distinction and privilege of being able to elect and consecrate its own archbishop.[220] The ties that bound East and West would only grow stronger as the Papacy, now firmly within the imperial embrace, stood on the brink of a Greek intermezzo that would last for the next three quarters of a century.

Notes

1. "Constans moved to Sicily intending to transfer the seat of the empire to Rome." Georgios Monachos, *Chronicon*, p. 717; cf., Theophanes, *Chronographia*, p. 486. ("The emperor abandoned Constantinople and moved to Syracuse in Sicily, intending to transfer the imperial capital to Rome.")

2. Theophanes, *Chronographia*, pp. 485, 491; *LP* I, p. 338.

3. *PL* 87: 201; *Mansi* X, 861; Jaffé, id., No. 2080, p. 233. Martin probably wrote this letter in June, 655, a month after his arrival. Jaffé incorrectly dates it to June, 654 while the pope was still on the island of Naxos awaiting trial in Constantinople. Cherson or the Chersonese had been used as a place of exile for both religious and political dissidents in the eastern part of the empire since the middle of the fifth century when the emperor Leo I banished the Alexandrian patriarch Timothy III ("The Cat") there in 459/460. Theophanes, *Chronographia*, pp. 172–73. Justinian II was exiled to Cherson after his initial deposition in 695, and in 775/776 the emperor Leo IV banished his brother Nikephoros, along with various imperial officials whom he suspected of plotting against him, to this remote region in the Crimea. Id., pp. 520–21, 621.

4. *PL* 87: 203; *Mansi* X, 862; Jaffé, id., No. 2081, p. 233.

5. Ottorino Bertolini, *Roma di Fronte a Bisanzio e ai Longobardi* (Bologna, 1941), p. 350. Bertolini's belief that Pope Martin also served as a rallying point for Italian political separatism, which he describes as *nazionale* or "nationalistic," is mistaken. *Id.* None of the attempted usurpations in Italy and Sicily prior to 751 "aimed at the creation of an

independent Italian kingdom" nor did they "spring from hostility to the imperial ideal." T. S. Brown, *Gentlemen and Officers*, id., p. 159.

6. Judith Herrin, *The Formation of Christendom* (London, 1987), p. 257.

7. Theophanes, *Chronographia*, p. 478; *Chronicle of Michael the Syrian*, id., pp. 440–41; Stratos, id., Vol. 3, pp. 70–72.

8. Theophanes, *Chronographia*, pp. 478, 481. According to Theophanes, the raid on Rhodes in 653 resulted in the destruction of the famous Colossus, whose vast quantity of bronze, which required 900 camels to transport, the Arabs sold to a Jewish merchant from Edessa. Id.; *Chronicle of Michael the Syrian*, id., pp. 441–43.

9. Theophanes, *Chronographia*, p. 482; Georgios Monachos, *Chronicon*, p. 716; Leo Grammatikos, *Chronographia*, p. 158; Andreas N. Stratos, "The Naval Engagement at Phoenix," in *Studies in 7th-Century Byzantine Political History* (London, 1983), XII 229–44.

10. The first of such marauding expeditions against Sicily, erroneously placed by Theophanes in 662/663, may have occurred as early as 652 according to Amari. Theophanes, *Chronographia*, p. 487; see Michele Amari, *Storia dei Musumlani di Sicilia*, ed. C. A. Nallino (Catania, 1933–1939), Vol. I, 205 f.; 216 f. Stratos disputes Amari's chronology, contending that "in 652 peace existed between Arab and Byzantine and nowhere is there any record of its violation." Stratos, id., Vol. 3, p. 226.

11. T. C. Lounghis, *Les Ambassades Byzantines en Occident* (Athens, 1980), p. 119; Bertolini, id., p. 356.

12. Brown incorrectly describes Luni, an important Roman center that had suffered a major decline in the fifth century, as lying north rather than south of Sarzana. T. S. Brown, *Gentlemen and Officers*, id., p. 15.

13. Paul the Deacon, *Historia Langobardorum*, Lib. IV, 42–45, in MGH *Scriptores Rerum Germanicarum* (Hanover, 1987), pp. 169–71.

14. Bertolini, id., pp. 356–57.

15. See Judith Herrin, "Constantinople, Rome and the Franks in the seventh and eighth centuries," in Jonathan Shepard and Simon Franklin, eds., *Byzantine Diplomacy* (Aldershot, 1992), p. 97.

16. *PL* 89: 511. (Letter of Pope Gregory II to emperor Leo III.)

17. Jeffrey Richards, *The Popes and the Papacy in the Early Middle Ages 476–752* (London, 1979), pp. 230–32. Throughout the seventh century, no Roman pope ever "doubted the reality of imperial power and authority. In communication with Constantinople, popes addressed their secular overlords as *piisimi imperatores* and looked to them for protection and support." Herrin, "Constantinople, Rome and the Franks in the seventh and eighth centuries," id., p. 91.

18. Although Pope Martin had expressed the wish that in his absence the functions of the Papacy would be performed, as was traditional, by the archpriest, the archdeacon, and the *primicerius notariorum* of the Roman church (*PL* 87: 201), by 655 he was clearly aware that a new pope had been elected, although he does not appear to have known his identity, referring to him only as "*qui eis nunc praeesse monstratur*" or "he who now is ordained to preside over them." *PL* 87: 204.

19. *LP* I, 338; *Mansi* X, 849, 851; cf., *Liber Diurnus*, id., No. LX, pp. 50–54.

20. *LP* I, 341; Herrin, "Constantinople, Rome and the Franks in the seventh and

eighth centuries," id., p. 93. These were very difficult times for Constantinople since no source of grain had yet appeared to replace the permanently lost stores of Egypt.

21. LP I, 341; Herrin, The Formation of Christendom, p. 259; Bertolini, id., 352.

22. LP I, 341–42n3.

23. LP I, 341; L. Bréhier, "Les Colonies d'Orientaux en Occident au commencement du moyen-âge," Byzantinische Zeitschrift 12 (1903): 1, 4.

24. Pyrrhus I, who had been reinstated as patriarch of Constantinople on January 9, 654, died six months later. Peter was ordained patriarch on June 8 or 15, 654. Theophanes, Chronographia, p. 481n1.

25. Jaffé, Regesta Pontificum Romanorum, id. Nos. 2054, 2056, pp. 229–30.

26. PL 129: 613.

27. LP I, 341; Haldon, Byzantium in the Seventh Century, p. 311. Patriarch Peter's condemnation as a Monothelite in the Sermo Prosphoneticus of the Sixth Ecumenical Council was confirmed by edict of the emperor Constantine IV. Riedinger, Concilium Universale Constantinopolitanum Tertium, id., pp. 814–15, 834–35.

28. Bertolini, id., p. 355. Duchesne's misreading of the Greek text of Maximos's trial led him to conclude that Maximos's imperial captors said they would have treated Pope Eugenius in the same way they had treated Martin because of Eugenius's rejection of patriarch Peter's synodikon if "the political circumstances had been more favorable." LP I, p. 342. It was in fact Maximos, not Eugenius, whom they threatened with the same treatment Martin had suffered. PL 129: 653–54.

29. Mansi X, 1029–32; Dölger, Regesten der Kaiserurkunden des Oströmischen Reiches, Vol. I, No. 225, p. 26.

30. PL 89: 511. Some scholars have concluded that Gregory II's letter to Leo III is an apocryphal late Byzantine production. See, namely, Stephen Gero, Byzantine Iconoclasm During the Reign of Leo III (Louvain, 1973), p. 110. For the Hellenization of Campania, see Bernhard Bischoff and Michael Lapidge, eds., Biblical Commentaries from the Canterbury School of Theodore and Hadrian (Cambridge, 1994), p. 93; E. Ciaceri, Storia della Magna Grecia, 2nd ed., 3 vols. (Milan, Genoa, Rome, and Naples, 1928–1932), I, 296–382; III, 229–37; T. J. Dunbabin, The Western Greeks (Oxford, 1948), pp. 355–75; Agostino Pertusi, "Bisanzio e l'irradiazione della sua civiltà in Occidente nell'alto medioevo," in Centri e Vie di Irradiazione della Civiltà nell'Alto Medioevo, Settimane di Studio del Centro Italiano di Studi sull'Alto Medioevo (Spoleto, 1964), pp. 110–13; see also M. Frederiksen, Campania, ed. N. Purcell (London, 1984).

31. Bischoff and Lapidge, id., pp. 108–9; cf., Bernard Bavant, "Le Duché Byzantin de Rome. Origine, durée et extension géographique," Melanges de l'École française de Rome. Moyen Age-Temps Moderne 91 (1979), Fig. 1, p. 43.

32. LP I, p. 343; Ferdinand Gregorovius, History of the City of Rome in the Middle Ages, Vol. II, trans. Mrs. Gustavus W. Hamilton (London, 1902), p. 150; Filippo Burgarella, "Bisanzio in Sicilia e nell'Italia Meridionale: I Riflessi Politici," in Il Mezzogiorno dai Bizantini a Federico II (Turin, 1983), p. 176.

33. The name "Vitalian" or Vitalianus was common among both civil and military officials in Italy from the beginning of the Byzantine administration in the sixth century, throughout the seventh, and even after the fall of the exarchate in the mid-eighth century. See, T. S. Brown, "Prosopographical Index," in Gentlemen and Officers, id., pp. 280–81.

34. *LP* I, p. 343; Jaffé, id., No. 2085, p. 235. The *Liber Pontificalis* refers only to the letter, described as the *synodicam*, which Vitalian sent to the emperor and his sons (*piisimos principes*) Constantine (IV), who was made coemperor in 654, and Heraclius and Tiberius, who achieved that status in 659. See Ostrogorsky, *History of the Byzantine State*, rev. ed., trans. Joan M. Hussey (New Brunswick, NJ, 1969), p. 121. It omits any reference to the *synodikon*, or profession of the faith customarily exchanged among the five patriarchates, which Vitalian sent to patriarch Peter II of Constantinople. See, infra, n37.

35. *LP* I, p. 334; Ado of Vienne. *Chronicon, PL* 123: 114. For Byzantium's use of luxury books as diplomatic gifts, see John Lowden, "The luxury book as diplomatic gift," in Jonathan Shepard and Simon Franklin, eds., *Byzantine Diplomacy* (Alderhsot, 1992), pp. 249–60.

36. *Mansi* XI, 572; Jaffé, id., No. 2086; Riedinger, *Concilium Universale Constantinopolitanum Tertium*, id., p. 587.

37. Riedinger, *Concilium Universale Constantinopolitanum Tertium*, id., pp. 610–11, 852–53.

38. The letter from your holy and same-souled (ομοψύχου) fraternity caused us spiritual delight. Id.

39. Caspar, *Geschichte des Papsttums*, Vol. 2, p. 587.

40. Riedinger, *Concilium Universale Constantinopolitanum Tertium*, id., pp. 9, 211; *Mansi* XI, 200; *LP* I, p. 344n1. The diptychs were two tablets, one containing the names of the living and the other those of the dead, who were to be officially prayed for and commemorated in the prayers of the church. Gregory Dix, *The Shape of the Liturgy* (San Francisco, 1982), p. 502. See also Robert F. Taft, *The Diptychs*, Orientalia Christiana Analecta, Vol. 238 (Rome, 1991), pp. 7, 58.

41. The diptychs came into prominence at the beginning of the fifth century in connection with the dispute as to whether the name of St. John Chrysostom, who had been deposed from the see of Constantinople and had died in exile in 407, should be included or omitted. Dix, id., p. 502; see also Taft, id., p. 97ff., 100, 124. Maximos Confessor refused communion with the church of Constantinople as long as the names of patriarchs Sergius, Pyrrhus, and Paul were named in the diptychs of the dead. *PG* 90: 153CD. There was nothing comparable to the Greek diptychs in the Roman church. Id., pp. 506–7. The *Liber Pontificalis*'s assertion that Pope Vitalian "maintained in all ways, as was the custom, ecclesiastical discipline and authority" appears to reflect a desire by this decidedly pro-Western source to express a note of reassurance on behalf of a pontiff who, consistent with the program of his imperial masters and benefactors, appeared willing to be more pliable than doctrinaire in matters of the faith. *LP* I, p. 343.

42. Bede, *Historia Ecclesiastica*, IV, 1.

43. Id.; Bischoff and Lapidge, id., pp. 92, 120–23.

44. G. P. Bognetti, *L'età longobarda*, Vol. II (Milan, 1966–1968), pp. 335–40.

45. Bede, id., IV, 1, 2; Bischoff and Lapidge, id., pp. 84ff., 92.

46. Bede, id., IV, 1; Bischoff and Lapidge, id., p. 122.

47. *AA.SS.*, Aug. V, pp. 215–19; Bischoff and Lapidge, id., pp. 122–23.

48. Bede, id., IV, 1.

49. The manuscript *Würzburg Universitätsbibliothek, M. p. th. f. 38, 123v–124r* confirms Theodore's presence in Constantinople. A gloss at the end of the manuscript records

that "Theodore affirms that in Constantinople he saw the Twelve Baskets woven from palm branches and preserved as relics, which had been brought there by the empress Helena." The Twelve Baskets, or δωδεκάθρονον, to which reference is made in the gloss, were the baskets that Helena had discovered in Palestine and brought to the capital around 326 and which had contained the surplus bread collected following Christ's miracle of the loaves and fishes. Bischoff and Lapidge, id., pp. 42, 47, 549–52.

50. Bede, id., IV, 1, 2; Bischoff and Lapidge, id., pp. 63–64.

51. Guy Ferrari, *Early Roman Monasteries* (Rome, 1957), pp. 39–41. The Greek monastery of St. Anastasios at Aquas Salvias appears to have been established toward the end of the pontificate of Honorius I (625–638) at the place where St. Paul was beheaded. V. Capocci, "Sulla tradizione del martirio di S. Paolo alle Acque Salvie," Atti dello VIII Congresso Internazionale di Studi Bizantini, II, 3–10 April 1951, Palermo in *Studi Bizantini e Neoellenici*, Vol. 8 (Rome, 1953), pp. 11–19; R. Valentini and G. Zucchetti, eds., "De Locis Sanctis Martyrum Quae Sunt Foris Civitatis Romae," in *Codice Topographico della Città di Roma*, Vol. II (Rome, 1942), p. 109. It was most likely during his stay at Acquas Salvias that Theodore learned Latin. Cyril Mango, "La Culture Grecque et l'Occident au VIIIe siècle," in *I Problemi dell'Occidente nel secolo VIII*, Vol. 2, Settimane di Studio Del Centro Italiano di Studi sull'Alto Medioevo, 6–12 April 1972 (Spoleto, 1973), p. 686.

52. J. M. Hussey, *The Orthodox Church in the Byzantine Empire* (Oxford, 1986), p. 19. While two persons subscribed to the monastic tract as "Theodoros monachos," Riedinger, *Concilium*, p. 57, the most persuasive proof that one of these was Theodore of Tarsus is the fact that at a synod held at Hatfield in 680 over which he presided as archbishop of Canterbury, Theodore announced his adherence to the five ecumenical councils, adding, "[We] also accept the decisions of the council held in Rome under the blessed Pope Martin in the eighth indiction and ninth year of the reign of the most pious Emperor Constantine." Bede, *Historia Ecclesiastica*, IV, 17. It is highly unlikely that Theodore, like Maximos Confessor, would have equated the Lateran Council of 649 with the five general councils of the church that had preceded it if he had not himself participated in it.

53. Bischoff and Lapidge, id., p. 81.

54. *Baedae Opera Historica*, Vol. 2, trans., J. E. King (London, 1963), p. 6. *ne quid ille contrarium veritati fidei, Graecorum more, in ecclesiam cui praeesset, introduceret.*

55. Hadrian's two previous missions on behalf of the emperor caused sufficient concern on the part of Ebroin, the Frankish mayor of the palace, that while on their journey through Francia to Britain he allowed Theodore to proceed but detained Hadrian at Étaples long enough to assure himself that he was not carrying a message to the English kings that might be to the detriment of the Franks. Bede, *Historia Ecclesiastica*, IV, 1.

56. Bede, *Historia Ecclesiastica*, IV, 1.

57. Cyril Mango's contentions that Theodore's appointment to the see of Canterbury was "entirely fortuitous" and that Pope Vitalian "was not very sure of Theodore" should be seriously reconsidered, as should his claim that the subsequent spread of Greek culture to northern Europe as a result of the contributions of Theodore and Hadrian in Britain "is only an accident." Cyril Mango, "La Culture Grecque et l'Occident au VIIIe siècle," in *I Problemi dell'Occidente nel secolo VIII*, Vol. 2, Settimane di Studio Del Centro Italiano di Studi sull'Alto Medioevo, 6–12 April 1972 (Spoleto, 1973), p. 686.

58. Bede, *Historia Ecclesiastica*, IV, 2; AA.SS. April I (1675), 582.

59. Dix, id., pp. 572–73; Herman A. J. Wegman, *Christian Worship in East and West*, trans. Gordon W. Lathrop (New York, 1985), p. 152.

60. S. J. P. Van Dijk, "The Urban and Papal Rites in Seventh and Eighth Century Rome," *Sacris Erudiri* 12 (1961) 435, 467; S. J. P. Van Dijk, "Gregory the Great, founder of the urban 'schola cantorum,'" *Ephemerides Liturgicae* 77 (1963): 335–36. The earliest form of the papal rite is contained in the *Ordo Romanus I*, whose compilation both Duchesne and Andrieu place toward the later part of the seventh or at the beginning of the eighth century, but in no event prior to 600. L. Duchesne, *Christian Worship: Its Origin and Evolution*, 4th ed., trans. M. L. McClure (New York, 1912), p. 150; Michel Andrieu, *Les Ordines Romani du Haut Moyen Age II*, Les Textes (Ordines I–XIII) (Louvain, 1971), p. 39; see also John F. Baldovin, *The Urban Character of Christian Worship* (Rome, 1987), p. 131n114. For an English translation of the *Ordo Romanus I*, see E. G. Cuthbert F. Atchley, *Ordo Romanus Primus* (London, 1905), pp. 116ff. The striking similarities between the papal rite described in the *Ordo Romanus I* and Byzantine court ceremonial can be observed by comparing the pope's procession from the Lateran palace to one of the patriarchal basilicas for celebration of a stational mass as prescribed in the *Ordo* with the description of the procession of the imperial entourage from the palace to the Great Church of St. Sophia on major feast days contained in Constantine VII Porphyrogenitos's *De Ceremoniis*. See Constantin VII Porphyrogénète, *Le Livre des Cérémonies*, Vol. I, trans. Albert Vogt (Paris, 1967), p. 3ff.; see also Wegman, id., p. 184ff.

61. As late as the twelfth century, Vitalian's contribution to the creation of a new form of chant modeled on the liturgical music of Byzantium continued to be recognized. Romuald II Guarna, archbishop of Salerno, *Chronicon*, in L. Muratori, *Rerum Italicarum Scriptores*, Vol. 7, Pt. 1 (Milan, 1725), p. 127 ("He [Vitalian] composed the chant which the Romans today use."); Van Dijk, "Gregory the Great," id., pp. 340, 344.

62. Van Dijk, "The Urban and Papal Rites," id., p. 445. The reference to *Vitaliani* appears in the life of Notker the Stammerer by Ekkehard, Dean of St. Gall, where the hagiographer identifies Pope Vitalian as the pontiff "whose chant those called *Vitaliani* still perform in the pope's presence when the Apostolicus celebrates [the mass]." *AA.SS.* April I (1675), 582.

63. The patriarchal basilicas consisted of St. John Lateran, Sta. Maria Maggiore (*ad prasepe*), S. Croce in Gerusalemme, St. Peter's in the Vatican, St. Paul's outside the walls (*fuori le mura*), St. Lawrence, and St. Sebastian at the catacombs (*ad catacumbas*). Van Dijk, "The Urban and Papal Rites," id., pp. 431–32.

64. Amédéé Gastoué, *Les Origines du Chant Romain* (Paris, 1907), p. 106ff.; Van Dijk, "Gregory the Great," id., pp. 347, 349.

65. Van Dijk, "The Urban and Papal Rites," id., pp. 449–51; Egon Wellesz, "Supplemetary Note: Greek Hymns during Paschal Week in the First Roman *Ordo*," in *Eastern Elements in Western Chant* (Copenhagen, 1947), pp. 64–67. The text for the service of the Paschal vespers contains a number of liturgical prescriptions reflecting the influence of the East. For example, it directs that the *schola cantorum*, along with the entire clergy, convene in the "great church," an expression that is borrowed directly from the Greek phrase "η μεγάλη εκκλησία," which was used for describing a cathedral only in the Greek-speaking East. Thereafter, the text prescribes that at the conclusion of Psalm 112, which, according to the *Ordo Romanus I* is to be sung in Greek during the whole of the Octave

of Pascha, the choir is to intone the *Alleluia* followed by the prokeimenon Ό Κύριος εβασίλευσεν (The Lord is King) and the second verse Καί γάρ ἐστερέωσε (For He has established . . .), which are also to be sung in Greek. Later, the *primicerius* of the *schola cantorum* rises and, in the presence of the pontiff, sings the Paschal *stichera* or *troparia* which begin Πάσχα ἱερον ημιν σήμερον ἀναδέδεικται (A sacred Pascha has today been shown forth us to). Gastoué, id., Appendix V, pp. 286–99; H. W. Codrington, *The Liturgy of St. Peter* (Münster, 1936), p. 2; see also J. Mabillon, *Musaeum Italicum*, Vol. II (Paris, 1689), pp. 35, 104; P. Rodota, *Dell'origine progresso e stato del rito greco in Italia*, Lib. III (Rome, 1743), p. 245.

66. Amalar of Metz, "De ordine antiphonarii," in J. M. Hanssens, ed., *Amalarii episcopi opera omnia III*, Studi e Testi, Vol. 140 (Vatican City, 1950), p. 84; *LP* I, p. 343. On the title of *Apostolicus* given to Pope Vitalian in the *Liber Pontificalis* by his biographer, see P. Conte, *Chiesa e primato nelle lettere dei papi del secolo VII* (Milan, 1971), p. 147n86.

67. Michel Andrieu, "Ordo XV," in *Les Ordines Romani du Haut Moyen Age*, Vol. III, Les Textes (*Ordines XIV–XXXIV*) (Louvain, 1974), pp. 110ff.

68. Van Dijk, "The Urban and Papal Rites," id., pp. 455–58.

69. Herrin, *The Formation of Christendom*, id., p. 265; Taft, id., p. 193.

70. Van Dijk, "The Urban and Papal Rites," id., pp. 449–51.

71. G. Löw, "Il più antico sermonario di San Pietro in Vaticano," *Rivista di archeologia cristiana* XIX (1942) 249, 252.

72. Taft, id., p. 193.

73. Van Dijk, "The Urban and Papal Rites," id., p. 467.

74. Michael McCormick, "Clovis at Tours, Byzantine public ritual and the origins of medieval ruler symbolism," in *Das Reich und die Barbaren* (Vienna, 1989), p. 173n38; Evangelos Chrysos, "Byzantine Diplomacy, A.D. 300–800: means and ends," in Jonathan Shepard and Simon Franklin, eds., *Byzantine Diplomacy* (Aldershot, 1992), p. 35.

75. André Guillou, *Studies on Byzantine Italy* (London, 1970) II, 305. *la grande epoca della dominazione greca.*

76. Dölger, id., No. 226, pp. 26–27; Theophanes, *Chronographia*, p. 479 (records that the peace treaty was of two years' duration); Andreas N. Stratos, "The Naval Engagement at Phoenix," in *Studies in 7th-Century Byzantine Political History* (London, 1983), XII, 233; cf., Constantine VII Porphyrogenitos. *De Administrando Imperio*, ed. and trans. Gy. Moravcsik and R. J. H. Jenkins, Corpus Fontium Historiae Byzantinae, Vol. I. (Washington, D.C., 1967), pp. 85, 89.

77. Whittow, id., p. 87; cf., F. Donner, *The Early Islamic Conquests* (Princeton, 1981), pp. 111–55; R.-J. Lilie, *Die byzantinische Reaktion auf die Ausbreitung der Araber* (Munich, 1976), pp. 40–68.

78. Stratos, "The Naval Engagement at Phoenix," id., p. XII, 233.

79. Theophanes, *Chronographia*, p. 482; Georgios Monachos, *Chronicon*, p. 716; Leo Grammatikos, *Chronographia*, p. 158; *Chronicle of Michael the Syrian*, id., p. 445.

80. Theophanes, *Chronographia*, p. 482; Ioannes Zonaras, *Epitome Historiarum*, Vol. III, ed., L. Dindorf (Leipzig, 1870), p. 314; Michael Glykas, *Annalium Pars IV*, PG 158: 519–20.

81. Georgios Monachos, *Chronicon*, p. 716.

82. Theophanes, *Chronographia*, p. 482; *Chronicle of Michael the Syrian*, id., p. 446.

83. Theophanes, *Chronographia*, p. 485; *Chronicle of Michael the Syrian*, id., p. 446; Ioannes Kaestner, *De Imperio Constantini III (641–668)* (Leipzig, 1907), pp. 73–74; Stratos, id., Vol. III, p. 195.

84. Georgios Cedrenos, *Historiarum Compendium*, p. 762; Leo Grammatikos, *Chronographia*, p. 158.

85. Theophanes, *Chronographia*, pp. 462, 484–85; Georgios Cedrenos, *Historiarum Compendium*, pp. 761–62; Leo Grammatikos, *Chronographia*, p. 158; Georgios Monachos, *Chronicon*, p. 717.

86. Theophanes, *Chronographia*, pp. 484–85; see also Peter Schreiner, ed., *Die Byzantinischen Kleinchroniken, Corpus Fontium Historiae Byzantinae*, Vol XII/1 (Vienna, 1995) where, referring respectively to his Monothelitism and the alleged murder of his brother Theodosios, Constans II is described as ο δυσσεβής καί μιαιφόνος or "the impious and vile murderer." Id., p. 134.

87. Theophanes, *Chronographia*, p. 486; Ioannes Zonaras, *Epitome Historiarum*, Vol. III, p. 316; Georgios Cedrenos, *Historiarum Compendium*, p. 763; Georgios Monachos, *Chronikon*, p. 717; Michael Glykas, *Annalium Pars IV, PG* 158: 519–20; Leo Grammatikos, *Chronographia*, p. 159 (says only that Constans left Constantinople and came to Syracuse).

88. F. Dölger, "Rom in der Gedankenwelt der Byzantiner," *Zeitschrift für Kirchengeschichte* 56 (1937) 24; see also E. Gren, "Zu den Legenden von der Gründung Konstantinopels," *Eranos* 55 (1947) p. 153ff.; Alain Ducellier, *Le Drame de Byzance* (Paris, 1976), p. 141.

89. Excavations in Constantinople during the 1960s uncovered the church of St. Polyeuktos, an enormous and splendid palace-church built by Anicia Juliana in an effort to recreate the temple of Solomon. The church of the Anastasis, as well a garden of Gethsemane at Blachernae and a Mount of Olives above Galata, reflect similar attempts to replicate sites in and around Jerusalem. Cyril Mango, "Constantinople, ville sainte," *Critique* 48 (1992): 625–33.

90. Erwin Fenster, *Laudes Constantinopolitanae* (Munich, 1968), pp. 20ff., 55ff., 97ff., 132ff., 185ff., 219, 221, 241, 245–46, 250, 253, 258.

91. S. Yerasimos, "Apocalypses constantinopolitaines," *Critique* 48 (1992): 609–24; Gilbert Dagron, *Constantinople imaginaire* (Paris, 1984), pp. 315–30.

92. Whittow, id., p. 127.

93. See Lennart Rydén, "The Andreas Salos Apocalpyse, Greek Text, Translation, and Commentary," *Dumbarton Oaks Papers* 27 (1974): 219.

94. Constantine VII Porphyrogenitos, *De Thematibus*, ed., A. Pertusi (Vatican City, 1952), p. 84.

95. See Michel Kaplan, "La Ville Lumière," in *Tout l'or de Byzance* (Paris, 1991), pp. 55– 69.

96. Stratos persuasively and correctly contends that the "suggestion put forth by Theophanes and other Byzantine chroniclers of a transference of the capital to Rome is completely devoid of reason." Stratos, *Byzantium in the Seventh Century*, Vol. III, p. 202. The contrary views expressed by historians earlier this century must now be taken as superseded. See, namely, Ioannes Kaestner, *De Imperio Constantini III (641–668)* (Leipzig, 1907), pp. 73–74; Michele Amari, *Storia dei Musulmani di Sicilia*, Vol. I (Catania, 1933),

p. 213. Similarly, Bertolini's contention, based on Paul the Deacon, that Constans II intended to transfer the capital from Constantinople to Rome because he harbored some illusion of recapturing the ancient spirit and traditions of the Roman Empire finds no credible support. O. Bertolini, *Roma di Fronte a Bisanzio e ai Longobardi* (Bologna, 1941), p. 357ff; see Paul the Deacon, *Historia Langobardorum*, *MGH Scriptores Rerum Germanicarum* (Hanover, 1987), p. 186.

97. George of Pisidia, *Heraclius II*, *ll.* 210ff., and *Expeditio Persica III*, ll. 314ff., in *Poemi*, *I*. *Panegirici Epici*, trans. A. Pertusi (Ettal, 1960), pp. 250ff.; see also Περί των αθέων Ἀβάρων καί Πέρσων κατὰ τής θεοφύλακτον πόλεως μανιώδους κινήσεως, ed. A. Mai, *Patrum nova collectio*, Vol. 6 (Rome, 1883), p. 427.

98. André Guillou, *Régionalisme et Indépendence dans l'empire byzantin au VIIe siècle* (Rome, 1969), p. 249; cf., Nikephoros, *Short History*, id., p. 39; for the Nika riots of 532, see A. A. Vasiliev, *History of the Byzantine Empire, 324–1453*, Vol. I (Madison, 1970), p. 156ff.

99. Paul the Deacon, *Historia Langobardorum*, id., p. 186.

100. Stratos, *Byzantium in the Seventh Century*, Vol. III, id., p. 200; Whittow, id., pp. 120–21; Haldon, id., pp. 208–20; but see Walter E. Kaegi's review of Whittow's *The Making of Byzantium, 600–1025* in *Speculum* 74 (1999): 536, 538, criticizing Whittow for reviving "without explanation or discussion, a long-refuted theory of the etymology of the Byzantine themes (Byzantine army corps and their military districts)."

101. J. Vogt, "Orbis Romanus. Zür Terminologie des römischen Imperialismus," *Philosophie und Geschichte* 22 (1922): 23ff.

102. Pasquale Corsi, "Costante II in Italia," *Quaderni medievali* 5 (1978) 57–108; cf., E. Chrysos, "Byzantine Diplomacy, A.D. 300–800," in Jonathan Shepard and Simon Franklin, eds., *Byzantine Diplomacy*, id., p. 28, who maintains that Constans II "personally brought the Byzantine army to Italy again for a new *reconquista*," and that it was not until the accession of his son Constantine IV Pogonatos that Byzantium "made a clean break with the empire's traditional claims of universal uniqueness and perennial rule over the Mediterranean world." See also O. Bertolini, *Roma di Fronte a Bisanzio e ai Longobardi*, id., p. 358, where Constans II's expedition to the West is dismissed as "an inglorious adventure."

103. Alexander Kazhdan, "The notion of Byzantine diplomacy," in Jonathan Shepard and Simon Franklin, eds., *Byzantine Diplomacy*, id., pp. 7, 10.

104. J. B. Bury, *A History of the Later Roman Empire*, Vol. II (London, 1889), pp. 84–85, 292, 297–306; Pasquale Corsi, *La Spedizione Italiana di Costante II* (Bologna, 1983), p. 85; Haldon, id., pp. 59–60.

105. Fenster, *Laudes Constantinopolitanae*, id., pp. 273–74.

106. Riccardo Maisano, "La Spedizione Italiana dell'Imperatore Costane II," *Siculorum Gymnasium* XXVIII/1 (1975) 141; Andreas N. Stratos, "Expédition de l'empereur Constantin III surnommé Constant en Italie," in *Bisanzio e l'Italia. Raccolta di studi in memoria di Agostino Pertusi* (Milan, 1982), 348, 350–51; *LP* I, 343. A find of 817 coins in the Athenian agora bearing the image of Constans II has been held to constitute positive proof of his stay in the city during this time. M. Thompson, *The Athenian Agora, II: Coins from the Roman through Venetian Period* (Princeton, 1954), pp. 69–71. Corsi contends that Constans left Constantinople for the West in the summer of 662 rather than the summer

of 661. Pasquale Corsi, *La Spedizione Italiana di Costante II*, id., p. 108. The Armenian nobleman Mezezius, who attempted to usurp the throne following Constans's death in Sicily, was a count of the Opsikion theme. *LP* I, 346; Haldon, id., p. 214. The assertion by Bréhier and Aigrain that Constans's army was "composed in large part of Armenians" may be the result of their mistaken identification of Mezezius with the Armeniakon theme, while, as Haldon has shown, although he was an Armenian, Mezezius was connected not with the Armeniakon but with the Opsikion theme. Louis Bréhier and René Aigrain, *Histoire de l'Église*, Vol. 5 (Paris, 1947), p. 179. The father of Pope Conon (686–687) had been in the Thrakesion theme and would remain in Sicily following the emperor's death where he would raise his son and future pontiff. *LP* I, 368.

107. Dimitri Obolensky, "The Principles and Methods of Byzantine Diplomacy," in *Actes du XII Congrès International des Études Byzantines* I (Belgrade, 1963) p. 52; Stratos, "Expédition de l'empereur Constantin III," id., p. 350; E. Chrysos, "Byzantine Diplomacy A.D. 300–800," id., p. 28; A. Kazhdan, "The Notion of Byzantine Diplomacy," id., pp. 7, 10.

108. Stratos, "Expédition de l'empereur Constantin III," id., p. 351. Kent concluded that the inscription on the base of the statue, which reads Νικηφόρον Σεβαστόν Φλάβιον Κώνσταν η Κορινθίων πόλις (Victorious Reverence Flavius Constans the Corinthian city), dates from the seventh century and was dedicated to Constans II by the citizens of the city in gratitude for their deliverance from the Onogur Bulgars, who, he claims, inhabited Corinth from 642 until their expulsion by the emperor. John H. Kent, "A Byzantine Statue Base at Corinth," *Speculum* 25 (1950): 544–46; see also Kenneth M. Setton, "The Bulgars in the Balkans and the Occupation of Corinth in the Seventh Century," *Speculum* 25 (1950): 502–43. Peter Charanis challenged Kent's conclusion, maintaining that the "Onogurs, of course, did not take Corinth shortly after 641 and the Byzantines did not recapture it in 657–58." Peter Charanis, "On the Capture of Corinth by the Onogurs and Its Recapture by the Byzantines," *Speculum* 27 (1952): 343–50.

109. Paul the Deacon, *Historia Langobardorum*, id., p. 186; *LP* I, p. 343; Stratos, "Expédition de l'empereur Constantin III," id., p. 352; Corsi, id., p. 115, 117.

110. Paul the Deacon, *Historia Langobardorum*, id., pp. 174–76.

111. Id., pp. 179–85, 187–88; Paolo Delogu, "Il Regno Longobardo," in Paolo Delogu, André Guillou, and Gherardo Ortalli, eds., *Longobardi e Bizantini* (Turin, 1980), pp. 90–92; Corsi, id., p. 59–60 (incorrectly identifies the exarch who executed Grimuald's brothers as Gregory); Paul the Deacon, *History of the Lombards*, trans. William Dudley Foulke (Philadelphia, 1974), p. 209n1.

112. Corsi, id., p. 60.

113. N. Cilento, *Italia meridionale longobarda* (Milan, Naples, 1966), pp. 1–10; Filippo Burgarella, "Bisanzio in Sicilia e nell'Italia Meridionale: I Riflessi Politici," in André Guillou and Filippo Burgarella, eds., *L'Italia Bizantina* (Turin, 1988), p. 299.

114. Corsi, id., p. 60.

115. Filippo Burgarella, "Bisanzio in Sicilia e nell'Italia meridionale: i riflessi politici," in *Il Mezzogiorno dai Bizantini a Federico II*, Storia d'Italia, Vol. III (Turin, 1983), p. 177.

116. Paul the Deacon, *Historia Langobardorum*, p. 188; Kaestner, id., p. 80n4; Stratos, id., Vol. III, p. 210 Corsi, id., p. 61.

117. Paul the Deacon, *Historia Langobardorum*, p. 187; Romuald II Guarna, archbishop of Salerno, *Chronicon*, in L. Muratori, *Rerum Italicarum Scriptores*, Vol. 7, Pt. 1 (Milan,

1725), p. 129; Bulgarella, "Bisanzio in Sicilia e nell'Italia Meridionale: I Rifelssi Politici," id., p. 299; Stratos, id. Vol. III, p. 210; Corsi, id., p. 61ff. The Via Traiana began in Otranto and led to Brindisi, Bari, and Beneventum before ending in Capua. The Via Appia, which began at Brindisi, led to Taranto, Matera, Venosa, Beneventum, Naples, Capua, and Terracina, thereafter leading to the Porta Appia in Rome where it ended. Agostino Pertusi, "Bisanzio e l'irradiazzione della sua civiltà in Occidente nell'alto medioevo," id., p. 91.

118. Paul the Deacon, *Historia Langobardorum*, p. 188–89; Stratos, id., Vol. III, p. 211; Maisano, "La Spedizione Italiana dell'Imperatore Costante II," id., p. 142.

119. Paul the Deacon, *Historia Langobardorum*, pp. 189–190; Corsi, "Costante II in Italia," id, p. 79; Stratos, id., Vol. III, p. 212.

120. Kaestner, id., p. 82; Amari, id., p. 213; Bertolini, id., p. 358.

121. Corsi, *La Spedizione Italiana di Costante II*, id., p. 143; Corsi, "Costante II in Italia," id., p. 84.

122. Delogu, id., p. 299.

123. Corsi, "Costante II in Italia," id., p. 85.

124. Noble ignores entirely the contribution made by Constans II both in containing Lombard advances into imperial territory in Italy and in Constantinople's admission *as early as* 663 that the Lombard presence on the peninsula was permanent and irreversible. Based upon the seriously outdated works of Hartmann (1897–1911), Caspar (1933), and Bertolini (1941), he argues that it was not until 680 or 681 that Byzantium "recognized the ineradicable reality of a Lombard kingdom in northern Italy." Thomas F. X. Noble, *The Republic of St. Peter* (Philadelphia, 1984), p. 1, 1n1.

125. Stratos, Vol. III, id., p. 213; Stratos, "Expédition de l'empereur Constantin III surnommé Consatnt en Italie," id., p. XI 354; André Guillou, "Inscriptions du Duché de Rome," in *Culture et Société en Italie Byzantine (VIe–XIe siècles)* (London, 1978) III, 156–58.

126. F. Lanzoni, *Le diocesi d'Italia dalle origini al principio del secolo VII*, Studi e testi 35 (Faenza, 1927), p. 151.

127. The acclamation πολλά τά ετη, known as a *polychronion*, was made by the army to the reigning sovereign on the occasion of a military triumph, which was often accompanied by a distribution of largesse and preceded by a λιτή, or solemn procession. Guillou, "Inscriptions du Duché de Rome," id., III 150–54; see also Constantine VII Porphyrogenitos, *Le Livre des Cérémonies*, Vol. I, trans. Albert Vogt (Paris, 1967), p. 29ff., for use of the same acclamation in Constantinople on major religious feast days such as Christmas.

128. Guillou, "Inscriptions du Duché de Rome," id., III 155. *Mundificatus est forus iste tempore domini Georgii consul et dux.*

129. *LP* I, p. 343; Paul the Deacon, *Historia Langobardorum*, p. 190.

130. AA.SS. Ian. II (1643) 257–96.

131. H. Delehaye, *Étude sur le légendaire romain* (Brussels, 1936), pp. 73–95.

132. AA.SS. Maii I (1643) p. 378; Jacobus de Voragine, *The Golden Legend*, Vol. II, trans. William Granger Ryan (Princeton, 1993), pp. 35–36.

133. Delehaye, id., pp. 77–96.

134. Roberto Valentini and Giuseppe Zucchetti, eds., *Codice Topografico della Città di Roma*, Vol. 2 (Rome, 1942), pp. 85–88; *LP* I, pp. 139 (Zephyrinus), 141 (Callistus), 145 (Pontian), 147 (Anteros), 148 (Fabian), 151 (Cornelius), 153 (Lucius), 154 (Stephen I),

155 (Xystus II), 157 (Dionysius), 159 (Eutychianus), 161 (Gaius), 167 (Eusebius), 168 (Miltiades). For an extensive bibliography of sources on Roman cemeteries along the Appian Way, including the cemeteries of Callistus and Praetextatus, see L. Duchesne, *Le Liber Pontificalis*, Vol. III (Paris, 1957), pp. 37–38.

135. *LP* I, p. 343; Paul the Deacon, *Historia Langobardorum*, v, 11, id., p. 190.

136. Sabina G. MacCormack, *Art and Ceremony in Late Antiquity* (Berkeley, 1981), p. 25.

137. Sabina G. MacCormack, "Change and continuity in late antiquity: the ceremony of *adventus*," *Historia* 21 (1972), 721–52.

138. Id., pp. 54, 274.

139. François Paschoud, *Roma Aeterna* (Neuchâtel, 1967), p. 11.

140. MacCormack, id., p. 48.

141. Ian A. Richmond, *The City Wall of Imperial Rome* (Repr. College Park, MD, 1971), pp. 108, 121–42, 251–63.

142. Id., p. 107–8.

143. Conon, who came from a Greek Christian family of Nazareth, suffered martyrdom in Phrygia or Pisidia in the year 250 during the time of Decius for refusing to sacrifice to the pagan gods. He died as a result of having spikes driven into his feet and made to run ahead of his own chariot. H. Musurillo, *The Acts of the Christian Martyrs* (Oxford, 1972), pp. xxxii–xxxiii, 186–93; Ωρολόγιον τό Μέγα (Athens, 1973), p. 264.

144. George, who was born of a Cappadocian father and a Palestinian mother, was beheaded in 296 during the persecutions of Diocletian for having professed the Christian faith. His successes in battle made him the most popular warrior saint of the Church, and gave rise to a widespread cult, especially among members of the military, with feast days celebrated both in the East, where he came to be known as μεγαλομάρτυρος καί τροπαιοφόρος, or "great martyr and trophy-bearer," and in the West, where he is commemorated in both Jerome's Martyrology and the Gregorian Sacramentary. *AA.SS.* Apr. III (1675) 100–63; H. Delehaye, *Les Légendes grecques des saints militaires* (Paris, 1909), pp. 45–76; Ωρολόγιον τό Μέγα (Athens, 1973), p. 273.

145. Richmond dates both the incised cross and the Greek inscriptions on the Porta Appia sometime prior to the beginning of Belisarius's Italian campaign in 536. Id., p. 108.

146. *LP* I, p. 343.

147. Richard Krautheimer, *Rome: Profile of a City, 312–1308* (Princeton, 1980), p. 10.

148. *LP* I, p. 343.

149. *LP* I, p. 331–32, 333n3.

150. *LP* I, p. 338.

151. *LP* I, p. 341.

152. Id., p. 343.

153. Id.; Paul the Deacon, *Historia Langobardorum*, v, 11, id., pp. 190–91; Ado, bishop of Vienne, *Chronicon*, PL 123:114.

154. *LP* I, p. 317, 343; Paul the Deacon, id., p. 191.

155. See Whittow, id., pp. 59–60, 113, 117–19; see also Philip Grierson, *Byzantine Coins* (London, 1982), p. 71ff.; Hugh Goodacre, *A Handbook of Coinage of the Byzantine*

Empire (London, 1957), pp. 87, 97; Alfred R. Bellinger and Philip Grierson, eds., *Catalogue of the Byzantine Coins in the Dumbarton Oaks Collection and in the Whittemore Collection*, Vol. I (Washington, D.C., 1966), pp. 201-2, 258-59, 288, 368.

156. *Reg.*, Appendix VIII, p. 1101. The manuscripts of the *Liber Pontificalis* identified by Duchesne as type E, which are copies of *Vaticanus* 3764, refer to the building as the basilica of *Julius* or *Juili*, while the others refer to the structure as the basilica of *Vigilius* or *Vigilii*. See *LP* I, pp. cxcv, 343. The reference to the basilica of Julius appears to represent the correct tradition. It was in the basilica of Julius that, according to all manuscript traditions of the *Liber Pontificalis*, popes Boniface I (418–422) and Boniface II (530–532) were ordained, while their respective rivals, Eulalius and Dioscorus, were ordained in the nearby and better known basilica of Constantine. See *LP* I, pp. 227, 281. In the battle for succession to the Papacy following the death of Pope Conon in 687, those who supported the archdeacon Paschal are said to have occupied the basilica of Julius. *LP* I, p. 371. Except for the reference to a basilica of Vigilius contained in the *Liber Pontificalis's* life of Vitalian, there is no evidence that this church on the Lateran was ever known other than as the basilica of Julius.

157. *LP* I, p. 343; Corsi, *La Spedizione Italiana di Costante II*, id., p. 164. The ornate baptistery had been built in the late fifth century by Pope Hilarus, who had embellished its font with a gold lantern containing ten wicks, a golden dove, a sixty-pound silver tower adorned with dolphins, and the figures of three silver stags pouring water, each of which weighed thirty pounds. *LP* I, p. 243; Paul F. Kehr, *Italia Pontificia*, Vol. I, Roma (Berlin, 1961), p. 31. The emperor Constantine in fact received baptism not in Rome but at Ancyrona near Nicomedia on the eve of his impending death around the feast of Pentecost in 337. Eusebius of Caesarea, *Life of Constantine*, in Philip Schaff and Henry Wace, eds., *A Select Library of the Christian Church: Nicene and Post-Nicene Fathers*, 2nd series, Vol. I (Repr. Peabody, MA, 1995), pp. 555–57.

158. John F. Baldovin, *The Urban Character of Christian Worship*, Orientalia Christiana Analecta 228 (Rome, 1987), pp. 143–66.

159. *LP* I, p. 344; Paul the Deacon, id., p. 191.

160. For the claim that Constans II embarked upon his Italian expedition without having first established a clear plan of action and without adequate military preparation, see Vincenzo Monachino, "I tempi e la figura del Papa Vitaliano," id., p. 582.

161. Burgarella, id., p. 178.

162. Bertolini, id., pp. 359–60.

163. Bryan Ward-Perkins, *From Classical Antiquity to the Middle Ages: Urban Public Building in Northern and Central Italy* A.D. *300–850* (Oxford, 1984), pp. 204–5.

164. *LP* I, p. 317.

165. Id., p. 323.

166. See Ferdinand Gregorovius, *History of the City of Rome in the Middle Ages*, Vol. II, trans. Mrs. Gustavus W. Hamilton (London, 1902), p. 160.

167. Theophanes, *Chronographia*, p. 435.

168. See G. Rohault de Fleury, *Le Latran au Moyen Age* (Paris, 1877), pp. 24–25, 54–55, 65.

169. Corsi, *La Spedizione Italiana di Costante II*, id., p. 156.

170. Corsi, id., p. 156; Corsi, "Costante II in Italia," id., p. 99 (characterizing Constans's journey to Rome as "an anguished search for personal penance"); Bertolini, id., p.

360 (suggesting that the emperor was forced to engage in various ceremonies and rituals in order to cleanse himself of guilt for what he had done to Pope Martin and the other victims of his program of religious persecution).

171. Corsi, *La Spedizione Italiana di Costante II*, id., p. 164; Corsi, "Costante II in Italia," id., p. 105; F. X. Seppelt, *Storia della Chiesa*, I, *L'antichità cristiana* (Brescia, 1957), p. 104; Thomas Hodgkin, *Italy and Her Invaders*, Vol. VI (Oxford, 1895–1899), pp. 277–78. On the use and significance of the epithet *novus Constantinus*, see H. I. Bell, "A dating clause under Heraclius," *Byzantinische Zeitschrift* 22 (1913): 395–405, and H. Grégoire, "Sur les titres imperiaux," *Byzantion* 10 (1935): 763–75.

172. See, namely, Evangelos Chrysos, "Byzantine diplomacy, A.D. 300–800: means and ends," id., p. 27.

173. Corsi, "Costante II in Italia," id., pp. 101–2. Papal hopes that Constans would reject Ravenna's overtures for autocephaly would soon be disappointed. On March 1, 666, the emperor, exercising an imperial prerogative granted him by the seventeenth canon of the Council of Chalcedon, *Mansi* VII, 365, issued an edict from Syracuse declaring Ravenna an autocephalus church and sending archbishop Maurus a pallium as a symbol of his see's new privilege. *LP* I, p. 360; *Agnellus qui et Andreas Liber Pontificalis Ecclesiae Ravennatis*, ed., O. Holder-Egger, in *MGH Scriptores rerum Langobardicarum et Italicarum saeculum VI–IX* (Hanover, 1878), pp. 349ff.; Dölger, Nos. 232, 233, id., p. 27.

174. *LP* I, p. 344; Paul the Deacon, *Historia Langobardorum*, id., p. 191; *Chronicle of Michael the Syrian*, id., p. 446. Both Pertusi and Burgarella contend that Constans traveled to Naples by sea, although the primary sources are silent on the point, recording only that he went to Rhegium by land. See Filippo Burgarella, "Bisanzio in Sicilia e nell'Italia Meridionale: I Riflessi Politici," in *Il Mezzogiorno dai Bizantini a Federico II, Storia d'Italia*, Vol. III (Turin, 1983), p. 178 and A. Pertusi, "Bisanzio e l'irradiazione della sua civiltà in Occidente nell'Alto Medioevo," in *Centri e vie di irradiazione della civiltà nell'Alto Medioevo*, Settimane di studio del Centro italiano di studi sull'Alto Medioevo, XI (Spoleto, 1964), p. 85.

175. Corsi, *La Spedizione Italiana di Costante II*, p. 168; Bréhier and Aigran, *Histoire de l'Église*, Vol. 5, id., p. 179; Stratos, *Byzantium in the Seventh Century*, Vol. III, pp. 219ff.

176. Corsi, *La Spedizione Italiana di Costante II*, p. 170; Vera von Falkenhausen, "I Bizantini in Italia," in *I Bizantini in Italia*, 2nd ed. (Milan, 1986), p. 30; F. Gabrieli, "Greeks and Arabs in the Central Mediterranean Area," *Dumbarton Oaks Papers* 18 (1964): 57–65; G. Pardi, "La popolazione della Sicilia attraverso i secoli," *Archivio storico siciliano* 59 (1928), p. 146; M. I. Finley, *A History of Sicily* (London, 1968), pp. 117, 179; cf., Kaestner, id., p. 85 (hypothesizing that Constans intended to use Sicily as a launching point from which to retake Egypt).

177. Andreas N. Stratos, *Studies in 7th Century Byzantine Political History* (London, 1983) I, 422; von Falkenhausen, id., p. 6.

178. *Reg.* I, 2.

179. von Falkenhausen, id., p. 29; Finley, id., p. 153.

180. *LP* I, p. 344; Paul the Deacon, *Historia Langobardorum*, p. 191; Ado of Vienne, *Chronicon*, *PL* 123:114; Haldon, id., p. 61.

181. Agostino Pertusi, "Bisanzio e l'irradiazione della sua civiltà in Occidente nell'alto medioevo," id., pp. 96–101; Gerhard Rohlfs, *Scavi linguistici nella Magna Grecia*

(Rome, 1933), pp. 129–31; Jeffrey Richards, *Consul of God: The Life and Times of Gregory the Great* (London, 1980), p. 160; Corsi, *La Spedizione Italiana di Costante II*, id., p.168.

182. André Guillou, *Studies on Byzantine Italy* (London, 1970), XII, 81; Mario Scaduto, *Il Monachesimo Basiliano nella Sicilia Medievale* (Rome, 1982), p. xvii; Lynn White, "The Byzantinization of Sicily," *American Historical Review* XLII (1936–1937), pp. 1, 2 (in the Syracusan catacombs, Greek inscriptions outnumber Latin inscriptions 10 to 1); Gerhard Rohlfs, *Das Fortleben des antiken Griechentums in Unteritalien* (Cologne, 1933), p. 14 (of a total of eighty-seven funerary inscriptions found on the Liparian islands off the northeastern coast of Sicily, seventy-eight are in Greek and only nine in Latin); V. Strazzulla, *Museum epigraphicum* (Palermo, 1897), pp. 243–50; cf.; A. Ferrua, "L'epigrafia cristiana di Sicilia," *Epigraphica* V–VI (Milan, 1943–1944) 104–8.

183. Andreas Stratos, *Studies in 7th Century Byzantine Political History* (London, 1983), I, 422; Paolo Orsi, "Bizantinae Siciliae," *Byzantinische Zeitschrift* 19 (1910): 475. Procopius records that when he disembarked at Syracuse he found a childhood friend of his conducting business in the Sicilian city. Procopius, *De bello vandalico*, I, 14, ed., G. Dindorf (Bonn, 1833), p. 371; Guillou, id., XII, 81n3.

184. See, namely, *Reg.* IV, 26; VI, 49; IX, 26; X, 10; XII, 16; White, id., pp. 1–2; Stratos, id., p. I, 422.

185. See chapter 2.

186. White, id., p. 7; Scaduto, *id.*, p. xxi; Pierre Batiffol, *L'abbaye de Rossano* (Repr. London, 1971), p. vi.

187. Ernesto Sestan, "La Composizione Etnica della Società in Rapporto allo Svolgimento della Civiltà in Italia nel secolo VII," in *Caratteri del Secolo VII in Occidente*, Vol. 2, Settimane di Studio del Centro Italiano di Studi sull'Alto Medioevo, 23–29 April 1957 (Spoleto, 1958): 649–77; Gertrude Robinson, "Notes historiques sur le rit grec en Italie méridionale," *Irénikon* 7 (1930): 519; Paolo Orsi, "Giojelli Bizantini Della Sicilia," in *Mélanges offerts à M. Gustave Schlumberger*, Vol. I (Paris, 1924) pp. 391–95, especially pp. 393–94 for a seventh-century ring found near Syracuse bearing the inscription *K(ύριε) βοήθει Λέωντος νοταρίου* ["Lord help Leontios the notary"].

188. Jean Darrouzès, *Notitiae Episcopatum Ecclesiae Constantinopolitanae*, Vol. I (Paris, 1981), pp. 315–16; Jules Gay, "Notes sur l'hellénisme sicilien," *Byzantion* 1 (1924): 215.

189. PG 98: 742–1181. Gregory of Agrigentum was denounced to Pope Gregory, who summoned him to Rome to stand trial. After he was acquitted, he returned to his see and lived to an advanced age. cf., *Reg.* I, 70; III, 12; XIII, 20.

190. Riedinger, *Concilium Lateranense a. 649 celebratum*, Vol. I (Berlin, 1984), p. 393; P. B. Gams, *Series Episcoporum Ecclesiae Catholicae* (Repr. Graz, 1957), pp. 943–56. For a detailed account of the "byzantinization" of a particular Sicilian city, see Giuseppe Agnello, *Palermo Bizantina* (Amsterdam, 1969).

191. AA.SS. March III (1668) 837–43.

192. Gams, id., p. 943ff.

193. M. Jugie, "La vie de S. Jean Damascène," *Echos d'Orient* 23 (1924) 137–61; Guillou, id., XII, 81.

194. PG 91: 112–32.

195. LP I, p. 354; *Mansi* XI, 200; *Reg.* VII, 36; Scaduto, id., p. xxii (also noting that the monks of the monasteries of St. Nicholas and the Capitulana were Greek).

196. The most ancient manuscript reflecting this influence is the *Rotulus messanensis*, which is preserved at the monastery of S. Salvatore. Scaduto, id., p. xxii; see also C. Swainson, *The Greek Liturgies* (Cambridge, 1884) xviii, 226–34, 248–328; F. E. Brightmann, *Liturgies Eastern and Western* (Oxford, 1896), p. xlix; A. Messina, "I Siciliani di rito greco e il patriarcato di Antiochia," *Rivista di Storia della Chiesa in Italia* 32 (1978), 415–21.

197. Richards, *id.*, p. 160; White, id., p. 15; cf., T. S. Brown, *Gentlemen and Officers*, id., p. 147.

198. Batiffol, *L'abbaye de Rossano*, id., p. vii; Brown, id., pp. 101–8.

199. See, namely, Rudolf Schieffer, "Kreta, Rom und Laon: Vier Briefe des Papstes Vitalian vom Jahre 668," in Hubert Mordek, ed., *Papsttum, Kirche und Recht im Mittelalter. Festschrift für Horst Furhmann zum 65. Geburtstag* (Tübingen, 1991), p. 28 for the letter sent by Pope Vitalian to Vaano, cubicularius and imperial chartularios in Sicily, requesting his assitance in restoring the pope's suffragan, John, bishop of Lappa in Crete, to his see and episcopal possessions.

200. Carlo Battisti, "Appunti sulla storia e sulla diffusione dell'Ellenismo nell'Italia meridionale," *Revue de linguistique romane* 3 (1927): 85; Burgarella, "Bisanzio in Sicilia e nell'Italia Meridionale: I Rifelssi Politici," in *Il Mezzogiorno dai Bizantini a Federico II* (Turin, 1983), p. 185.

201. Stratos, "Expédition de l'empereur Constantin III surnommé Constant en Italie," id., p. 356; White, id., p. 16.

202. Pope Vitalian also wrote a letter to metropolitan Georgios in 668 requesting his assistance in restoring bishop John of Lappa in Crete to his bishopric. *Mansi* X, 19; *PL* 87: 1003–4. For a discussion and analysis of this letter, see Schieffer, id., pp. 29–30.

203. Constantine VII Porphyrogenitos. *De Administrando Imperio*, ed. and trans. Gy. Moravcsik and R. J. H. Jenkins (Washington, D.C., 1957), p. 236–37; Stratos, "Expédition de l'empereur Constantin III surnommé Constant en Italie," id., p. 356; Whittow, id., pp. 120–21.

204. Batiffol, id., p. v. *gens aeterna in qua nemo nascitur*.

205. *LP* I, pp. 350 (Agatho); 359 (Leo II); 368 (Conon); 371 (Sergius I).

206. Theophanes, *Chronographia*, p. 491 (recording additionally that the plot to abduct the imperial family to the West was thwarted by the *cubicularius* Andreas and Theodoros of Koloneia); Georgios Monachos, *Chronicon*, pp. 717–18; Georgios Cedrenos, *Historiarum Compendium*, p. 763; Leo Grammatikos, *Chronographia*, p. 159; Nikephoros, Patriarch of Constantinople, *Short History*, p. 85; Ioannes Zonaras, *Epitome Historiarum*, p. 316; Michael Glykas, *Annalium Pars IV*, PG 158: 519–520. Michael the Syrian considerably embellishes the events surrounding the emperor's assassination, recording that Andreas lathered Constans's head with a double dosage of soap so that he could not open his eyes, and that the fatal blow, administered with a bucket made of silver, resulted in the emperor's instantaneous death. *Chronicle of Michael the Syrian*, id., pp. 450–51. An anonymous thirteenth-century Syrian source contains the observation, found nowhere else, that Constans did not die at once, but rather two days later. *Chronicle of AD 1234* in *The Seventh Century in the West-Syrian Chronicles*, ed. and trans. Andrew Palmer (Liverpool, 1993), p. 193. The Monophysite Egyptian chronicler Severus of Asmounein, who refers to Constans as Augustus and incorrectly identifies him as having succeeded Tiberios (698–705), correctly places his death in Sicily where he says the emperor was "killed like

a slaughtered victim by one of his two attendants." Severus of Asmounein, *History of the Patriarchs of the Coptic Church of Alexandria*, III, ed. B. Evetts, Patrologia Orientalis Vol. V, Fasc. 1 (Paris, 1904), p. 11.

207. *LP* I, 344; Ado of Vienne, *Chronicon*, PL 123: 114; Bede, *Chronicon* in Joseph Stevenson, ed., *Venerabilis Bedae Opera Historica Minora* (London, 1841), p. 197; Paul the Deacon, *Historia Langobardorum*, p. 191 (characteristically adding *Grecorum avaricia* or "the avarice of the Greeks" as another factor motivating Constans's exactions and depradations).

208. Corsi, *La Spedizione Italiana di Costante II*, id., p. 202.

209. Cf., id., p. 202.

210. Dölger, id., No. 233, p. 27. The emperor's grant of autocephaly to the church of Ravenna was probably the result both of a desire to recognize its status as capital of the ex-archate and to reward it for the substantial financial assistance it had provided him from its extensive Sicilian patrimonies. See Agnellus, *Liber Pontificalis Ecclesiae Ravennatis*, id., p. 349ff.; Corsi, *La Spedizione Italiana di Costante II*, id., pp. 187–88, 188 n2; L. A. Ferrai, *I patrimoni delle chiese di Ravenna e di Milano in Sicilia* (Messina, 1895).

211. Corsi, *La Spedizione Italiana di Costante II*, id., pp. 205–6; Kaestner, id., p. 87.

212. Theophanes, *Chronographia*, p. 491; Georgios Monachos, *Chronicon*, p. 718; Georgios Cedrenos, *Historiarum Compendium*, p. 763; Leo Grammatikos, *Chronographia*, p. 159; *Chronicle of AD 1234*, id., p. 193. Michael the Syrian adds that, in addition to his physical comeliness (remarked upon by almost all the Eastern sources), Mezezius was morally upright. *Chronicle of Michael the Syrian*, id., p. 451. On Mezezius's position in the Opsikion theme, see Haldon, id., p. 214.

213. *LP* I, p. 346; Paul the Deacon, *Historia Langobardorum*, p. 191.

214. *LP* I, p. 346; Paul the Deacon, *Historia Langobardorum*, p. 191; Burgarella, "Bisanzio in Sicilia e nell'Italia Meridionale: I Riflessi Politici," id., p. 185.

215. Theophanes, *Chronographia*, pp. 491–92n2; Georgios Monachos, *Chronicon*, p. 718; Georgios Cedrenos, *Historiarum Compendium*, pp. 763–64 (adds that Constantine returned to the capital bearing the body of Constans II, which was interred in the church of the Holy Apostles); Ioannes Zonaras, *Epitome Historiarum*, p. 316; Leo Grammatikos, *Chronographia*, p. 159 (adds that Constantine IV acquired the surname "Pogonatos" or "Bearded" because he left Constantinople for Sicily beardless and returned with a beard); see *Chronicle of Michael the Syrian*, id., pp. 455–56, for details on Constantine IV's deposition of his brothers Tiberios and Heraklios. Western sources, which say nothing about Constantine IV's expedition against Mezezius, attribute his overthrow solely to the efforts of imperial forces in Italy. Cf., *LP* I, p. 346; Paul the Deacon, *Historia Langobardorum*, p. 191. E. W. Brooks, "The Sicilian expedition of Constantine IV," *Byzantinische Zeitschrift* 17 (1908): 455–59 rejects the historicity of Constantine IV's expedition to Sicily as "exceedingly improbable."

216. Rudolf Riedinger, ed., *Concilium Universale Constantinopolitanum Tertium* (Berlin, 1990), pp. 8–9.

217. Corsi, *La Spedizione Italiana di Costante II*, id., pp. 205–6; P. Corsi, "La Politica Italiana di Costante II," in *Bisanzio, Roma e l'Italia nell'Alto Medioevo*, Vol. II, Settimane di Studio del Centro Italiano di Studi sull'Alto Medioevo, 3–9 April 1986 (Spoleto, 1988), p. 784.

218. Thomas F. X. Noble, *The Republic of St. Peter: The Birth of the Papal State, 680–825* (Philadelphia, 1984).

219. *Mansi* XI, 195–201; Riedinger, id., pp. 8–9. The Greek word used is αγάπην; the Latin word is *caritatem*.

220. *LP* I, 348; Dölger, id., No. 238, p. 28.

CHAPTER VI

Et Dicit Acolitus Symbolum Graece Decantando in His Verbis: Πιστεύω Εις Ενα Θεόν[1]

Rome and the Papacy from Agatho to Sergius I, 678–701

It was midsummer when the papal delegation to the Sixth Ecumenical Council returned to Rome in 682 after an absence of nearly two years in Constantinople.[2] Agatho, a Greco-Sicilian monk whose elevation to the Papacy in 678 would inaugurate a nearly unbroken succession of Eastern pontiffs spanning the next three-quarters of a century, had been dead for over a year and a half.[3] During that time, the Papacy had remained vacant awaiting the arrival of the legates who, when they disembarked at last at Ostia for the short journey up the Tiber to Rome, were carrying a mass of documents, which included the imperial *iussio* authorizing the consecration of Agatho's successor, the text of the synodal acts and the imperial edict confirming them, as well as a letter from the emperor to the Roman synod, and a personal missive from Constantine IV to the pope-elect.[4] But it was not only documents that the papal envoys were bringing back with them from Constantinople. The spirit of solidarity accompanied them as well. A new era in relations between the eastern and western parts of the empire was about to unfold as Byzantium and Rome prepared to embrace one another with rekindled enthusiasm. The two halves of the *imperium Romanum Christianum* had emerged from the Sixth Ecumenical Council more united than ever before.

Although 165 bishops and episcopal representatives had joined in condemning the Monothelite heresy, thereby putting an end to the last Christological battle that the Church would face, only the exiled patriarch Makarios of Antioch and a handful of his supporters had stubbornly refused to relinquish their adherence to the discredited doctrine that had ruptured relations between Rome and Constantinople for most of the seventh century. Makarios had been deposed as patriarch of Antioch and replaced by Theophanes, Syrian abbot of the Sicilian monastery of St. Peter *ad Baias*; all were stripped of their clerical status.

Although they had escaped the censure of anathema, the synod had requested and the emperor had agreed to send the entire group to Rome and commit their fate to the unfettered judgment of the pope.[5] Constantine's letter to the new pontiff, who would be enthroned as Leo II, served as a formal transmittal of the recalcitrant former clerics into papal custody. Significantly, both emperor and synod were convinced that it was only in Rome, where correct doctrine had always been preserved pure and inviolate, that the stiff-necked heretics would be cured of their doctrinal malady.[6] With effusive expressions of admiration, the emperor declared that the Apostolic See had enlightened the synod, rekindled orthodox belief, and illumined the souls of those who love Christ. His rapturous declarations reflected a deference toward the Papacy, whose incumbent the emperor now addressed as "universal pope," that appeared to crown the unity and unequivocally seal the breach that had for so long separated East and West.[7]

The expressions of esteem were mutual.[8] Pope Leo II could hardly contain his exuberance when in the early fall of 682, only about a month after his elevation to the Papacy,[9] he hastened to write the emperor acknowledging receipt of the synodal acts.[10] The erudite Sicilian pontiff of Eastern ancestry was distinguished for his eloquence, scriptural learning, and proficiency in both Greek and Latin, as well as his mastery of liturgical chanting and psalmody, which he was reputed to be able to perform with the greatest subtlety and refinement.[11] Indeed, his splendid if fulsome letter to the emperor is nothing less than a monument to Leo's impressive education, linguistic versatility, and predilection for the lofty style.[12] After the pope had warmly commended Constantine for his heroic defense of the orthodox faith, he confessed his own adherence to the five ecumenical councils, approved with alacrity the recent decisions of the sixth synod, and pronounced the usual anathemas on what had by now become a well known list of heretics beginning with Arius, but which for the first time included his own predecessor Honorius I.[13] Leo then suddenly exploded into a "veritable dithyramb" on the emperor replete with all the conventions of late antique encomiastic verse.[14] Beginning with a metaphor that exhorted the church to shed her garment of gloom and vest herself in festive attire, there is hardly a single literary device that the pope failed to press into service as he launched into his panegyric on Constantine, whom he repeatedly glorified as the new David.[15] Although Leo's exalted style and prolix rhetoric may in its pretensions toward elegance have appeared sycophantic, the papal letter was far from an empty exercise in mimicking ancient *topoi* or simply attempting to flatter the emperor. It was, instead, an important indicator of the genuine and continuing reconciliation between the Papacy and the imperial government to which the emperor's earlier letter to Leo had also attested.[16] As we have seen, the foundations for a rapprochement between Rome and Constantinople had been laid some two and a half decades earlier by Constans II and Pope Vitalian. The culmination of that rapprochement, despite some notable clashes, would be achieved between the last emperors of the Heraclian dynasty, Constantine IV and Justinian II, and the long succession of oriental pontiffs who came to occupy the Apostolic See beginning in the last quarter of the seventh century.

✌

By the summer of 678 the Greek chroniclers recorded with unqualified assurance that peace and tranquility prevailed in both East and West.[17] Constantine IV had concluded a thirty-year truce with the Arabs, thereby putting an end to the series of naval engagements that between 674 and 678 had threatened Constantinople itself.[18] He had, at about the same time, achieved peace with the Avars and the Bulgars and, farther west, with the Lombards in Italy.[19] With the threat of external aggression thus contained, the emperor turned his attention to establishing peace in the Church that, through an apparent resurgence of Monothelitism, was about to be disturbed.[20] His solution was to convene what would become the Sixth Ecumenical Council.

Although the debate over Monothelitism appears to have lain dormant for over twenty-five years, the combined machinations of patriarchs Theodoros of Constantinople and Makarios of Antioch to resurrect the conflict by finding fault with the Papacy convinced the emperor that the Christological issue had to be settled once and for all.[21] Shortly after his elevation to the see of Constantinople in late 677, patriarch Theodoros, joined by the exiled Antiochian patriarch Makarios, began pressuring Constantine to remove Pope Vitalian's name from the diptychs of the church of Constantinople.[22] When the emperor refused to accede to their demand, both because he considered Vitalian to have been orthodox in his beliefs and because the pope had supported him in suppressing the revolt of Mezezius following the assassination of Constans II,[23] Theodoros took another approach. He strongly intimated that he had hesitated to send the customary synodical letter to Pope Donos (676–678), opting instead to send a less formal document, which he described as a "hortatory epistle," on the grounds that he did not want the church of Constantinople to suffer yet another affront to its dignity from Rome by having Donos reject his synodikon as previous pontiffs, meaning specfically Vitalian, Eugenius I, and Adeodatus (672–676), had rejected the synodika of his predecessors, patriarchs Peter II (654–666), Thomas II (667–669), John V (669–675), and Constantine I (675–677).[24] It soon became clear to the emperor that the stirrings of Theodoros and Makarios threatened to burst into a full-blown conflagration, which, unless promptly arrested, was sure to reverse the process that had steadily drawn Rome and Constantinople closer over the course of the last two decades.[25] Moreover, the highly pragmatic emperor cannot have failed to appreciate that Byzantium's lengthy truce with the Arabs effectively ended further imperial hopes of regaining Egypt, Syria, Palestine, and Armenia with their large Monophysite populations, thereby making moot the political purpose that had prompted Monothelitism in the first place.[26] The persistence of a doctrinal breach between Byzantium and Rome made no sense from any perspective.

On August 12, 678, Constantine IV directed Pope Donos to select and send a delegation of emissaries to the capital to consult with patriarchs Theodoros and Makarios in an effort to arrive at a correct statement of the faith and thereby to achieve "the unity of all Christians."[27] Although labeled a formal summons and mandate, the imperial letter was in all respects both personally deferential to the pope and highly conciliatory in tone. It requested the pontiff to choose men for the mission who were moderate and restrained in their demeanor and who, though clement and forbearing, were nonetheless both knowledgeable and God-inspired in asserting the "blameless doctrine of your Apostolic See and council." While he urged the papal legates to bring such books and texts as would enlighten the discussions, the emperor consistently returned to the refrain that their zeal be tempered with mildness. He assured the pope that he himself was perfectly neutral with regard to the issues that would be discussed, and that he would exercise no compulsion on the legates to arrive at a particular result. Indeed, the emperor went so far as to say that even if it were determined that his father Constans II had "strayed from the pure and unblemished faith, I will be the first to anathematize him."[28] While he hoped that an accord would be reached, Constantine insisted that if the conference ended in failure, he would allow the delegation safely to return to Rome. As final proof of his good faith, the emperor advised the pope that he had ordered Theodoros Kalliopas, the exarch of Italy, to supply the emissaries with whatever they required in order to make the journey to Constantinople, including, if they felt the need, the use of armed ships so that they might travel without fear of harm.[29]

The emperor specified with particularity the number of emissaries he desired the pope to send as well as the ranks from which they were to be drawn. Although tactfully phrased, it was plain that Constantine wanted no more than three representatives from the Roman church itself plus no more than twelve bishops from the episcopal synod under Rome's jurisdiction in the West. In addition, Pope Donos was to send "four monks from each of the four Byzantine monasteries" in the city.[30] Thus, sixteen, or in excess of half the total number of thirty-one papal emissaries, were to consist of Greek monks residing in Rome's Eastern monastic establishments. Since the emperor was no doubt aware of the fact that Rome's oriental monastic community had been the moving force behind the Lateran Council of 649, his decision to include such a large number of monks as part of the Roman delegation was most likely prompted by a desire to ensure that the majority of the papal envoys equaled their Eastern brethren in theological learning and erudition. But whether they would meet the emperor's criteria that they be moderate and restrained in their discussions was another matter. If the Lateran synod was any indicator of monastic demeanor when it came to matters of the faith, the conference that the emperor was planning to convene might be far livelier than he wanted.

Constantine waited over a year and a half for an answer to his summons to Pope Donos. When the reply at last arrived sometime after March, 680, it was from Agatho, Donos's successor. The pope apologized profusely both for the delay in responding, which he ascribed to his own debilitating infirmities and to the time it had taken to convene a synod of Western bishops in order to select their representatives to the conference, as well as for the paucity of learning among those whom he would be sending to Constantinople.[31] Agatho's apology for the poor quality of education of Rome's emissaries, despite his high praise for their personal piety, was probably less a *confessio humilitatis* than an accurate commentary on the comparatively low level of learning that continued to persist in Rome as compared with the East.[32] It doubtless also accounts for the fact that the delegation that was ultimately sent to Constantinople was less than half the size that the emperor had prescribed. After what appears to have been a laborious process of selection, the Western envoys who arrived in the capital in September, 680 included bishops Abundantius of Tempsa, John of Rhegium in Calabria, and John of Portus, who collectively represented the synod of Western bishops. The legates of the Roman church consisted of the priests Theodoros, Georgios, and Theodoros of Ravenna, the deacon John, and the subdeacon Constantine.[33] Those whom Agatho described as "the religious servants of God the monks" included Theophanes, abbot of the monastery at St. Peter *ad Baias* in Sicily, and only four monks chosen from three Eastern monasteries in Rome: Georgios from the monastery of Renati, Conon and Stephanos from Domus Arsicia, and Leontios from St. Sabas or Cella Nova.[34] Thus, of the West's thirteen delegates to what would become the Sixth Ecumenical Council, twelve were of Eastern provenance while only one was a Latin. Two who were Syrians would soon become Roman pontiffs.[35] The monks were all Greeks. Although now living in Rome, the roots of these monastics lay in the caves and caverns and sprawling desert expanses of the remote regions of the East.

Cascading down the side of a cliff overlooking the west bank of the Cedron valley along the road to Jerusalem, the Great Lavra built by St. Sabas late in the fifth century, with its sprawling agglomeration of "domes and cupolas, balconies and cave cells, staircases and platforms, all propped up on narrow artificial ledges by great ranks of heavy, stepped buttresses,"[36] appears like a phantom against the stark Judean wilderness that surrounds it.[37] Although plagued by internal disputes, which caused St. Sabas to depart and found the New Lavra in 507, and later caught up in the highly divisive Origenist controversy, the Great Lavra appears nonetheless to have been flourishing early in the seventh century according to the testimony of John Moschos.[38] But soon the threat posed by the Persians and a devastating attack by Saracen marauders in 614, which resulted in the slaughter of forty-four monks, caused most of the monastic community, then under the leadership of the hegumen Nicodemos, to flee for protection into the Arabian desert.[39] While some of the monks under Nicodemos's successor

Thomas appear to have returned to the Great Lavra around 617, their solitude was relatively short lived. By the mid to late 630s, the Arabs had taken all the major cities of Palestine and Syria and a large body of Sabaite monks was again forced to flee.[40] This time they made their way westward following the Mediterranean littoral across Egypt into the province of Byzantine Africa, where they appear to have joined a Sabaite monastic community that had been established as a filiation of the Great Lavra by monks who had earlier fled from Palestine in the wake of the Persian invasions.[41] But they were to find only brief respite in Carthage. By late 646 the Arabs had begun raiding parts of Africa.[42] The exarch was defeated and ignominiously forced to flee to Constantinople.[43] Both the Sabaite monks who had been in Africa since the Persian invasions as well as those recently arrived from the East were similarly compelled to seek refuge. Unlike the exarch, however, these fiercely Chalcedonian monks set sail for Rome, arriving in the city late in 646 or in early 647.[44]

The Sabaite monks quickly established a monastery in Rome on the *piccolo Aventino*, or little Aventine, in the Greco-oriental quarter of the city just behind the walls of Servius Tullius and near the Porta Ostiensis or Sancti Pauli.[45] Pope Theodore, who was himself a Palestinian,[46] was doubtless their patron and probably responsible for arranging their new quarters on the Aventine.[47] Maximos Confessor occupied a cell at St. Sabas after his arrival in Rome from Africa, and Leontios, a late-seventh-century hegumen of the monastery, recorded that, before becoming bishop of his hometown in Sicily, Gregory of Agrigentum had also resided at St. Sabas.[48] When in 678 Constantine IV requested that the pope include among his delegates to Constantinople four monks from each of Rome's four Byzantine monasteries, the community of St. Sabas, although probably not the oldest in the city, was certainly known to the emperor and surely among those to which he was referring.[49]

Rome's monastic delegates to the Sixth Ecumenical Council also included the priest/monks Conon and Stephanos from the Greek monastery known by the Latin name of Domus Arsicia.[50] Although he designated no monastic community by name, Constantine IV was certainly aware of the existence of Domus Arsicia and intended that it be included among those from which the pope was to select his monastic emissaries. The fact that Pope Agatho designated more monks from Domus Arsicia than from any other Byzantine monastery in Rome to serve as monastic legates to Constantinople, and that it was Stephanos upon whom the emperor called at the council's seventh session to present the extensive papal *florilegium* demonstrating the errors of the Monothelite position, strongly suggests that the Greek community of Domus Arsicia was the most educated of Rome's Byzantine monastic establishments and probably responsible for compiling the text that set forth the orthodox case.[51] Ironically, apart from the references to Domus Arsicia contained in the proceedings of the Sixth Ecumenical Council, nothing whatsoever, including its location, is known about this community, which, although clearly prominent among Rome's Greek monasteries in the late seventh century, seems to have disappeared altogether by the beginning of the ninth century.[52]

Pope Agatho also included the priest/monk Georgios from the Byzantine monastery of Renati among his monastic delegates to the council that was to take place in the capital.[53] As with St. Sabas and Domus Arsicia, Constantine IV was almost certainly aware of the existence of Renati and intended that the pope include monks from this community as part of the papal embassy to Constantinople. The monastery of Renati which appears to have been situated on the southeast corner of the Esquiline in the vicinity of the trophies of Marius and not far from the Porta Labicana, was in existence by the end of the sixth century since Gregory the Great refers to its abbot Probus both in his *Dialogues* and in a letter dated October 5, 600, in which he and a synod of five bishops assent to Probus's petition to make a will disposing of his possessions.[54] At the time of Probus's tenure, Renati appears to have also been known as SS. Andreas and Lucia and to have housed Latin monks.[55] But, as a result of the arrival of oriental monks in Rome in the face of the Persian and Arab invasions of the East, the ethnic composition of Renati underwent a change over the course of the first half of the seventh century. By the time of the Lateran Council of 649, the monastery housed Greek-speaking Armenian monks, its hegumen bore the unmistakably eastern name of Thalassios, and, although still dedicated to Saint Andreas, the Theotokos had replaced Saint Lucia as the monastery's female patron.[56]

In mid-seventh-century Rome, a pilgrim seeking to venerate the places where the saints and martyrs had met their death would have followed an itinerary that led through the Porta Ostiensis to the place where Timothy of Antioch, preaching in Rome during the time of Diocletian, had been decapitated. Thereafter, he would have come upon the basilica of St. Stephen, where, placed upon the altar, lay the stone which had bludgeoned the first Christian martyr. Not far to the south along the Via Laurentina, the pilgrim would have arrived at the monastery of Aquas Salvias where sometime between 634 and 649 Palestinian monks fleeing the Arabs had arrived in Rome and deposited the head of St. Anastasios the Persian and where, centuries earlier, the Apostle Paul had been beheaded under a stone-pine tree.[57]

Writing sometime between 972 and 1000, the monastic chronicler Benedict of Soracte recorded that the patrician Narses had constructed both a church and a monastery dedicated to St. Paul at Aquas Salvias, thereby placing the foundation of a monastic community there in the second half of the sixth century.[58] There is, however, no certainty regarding the year in which the monastery was founded. While a monastic community may have been established at Aquas Salvias by Pope Honorius I around the year 625 on a tract of land that Gregory the Great had bestowed upon the basilica of St. Paul on the Via Ostiensis in 604,[59] nothing more certain can be said except that a monastery was founded at Aquas Salvias sometime during the first half of the seventh century on the site where tradition held that St. Paul had been decapitated.[60]

The monastery at Aquas Salvias was from its beginnings a community of Eastern monastics originally from Cilicia in southeastern Asia Minor who, fleeing either the Persians or Arabs, established themselves quite naturally at the place where their illustrious compatriot Paul of Tarsus had achieved the palm of martyrdom.[61] The Cilician monastic community at Aquas Salvias was already well established when the head of St. Anastasios the Persian, who had been strangled and decapitated in Caesarea in 628, was at last brought to Rome after briefly reposing in a monastery in Jerusalem. Upon its arrival in the city, the treasured relic was deposited in the monastery at Aquas Salvias that, as a result, had by the late eighth century come to be known as the monastery of St. Anastasios.[62] While Constantine IV surely intended to include Aquas Salvias among the four Byzantine monasteries from which the pope was to draw his monastic emissaries, no monk from this community was sent by Agatho to Constantinople. Given the prominent role that its fiercely Chalcedonian hegumen and monks played at the Lateran Council of 649, as well as its reputation and prominence among Rome's Greek monastic establishments in the late seventh century, the absence of any representatives from Aquas Salvias at the Sixth Ecumenical Council is truly mystifying.

Although Constantine IV alluded to only four Byzantine monasteries in his letter to Pope Donos, there were at least two, and probably several more, Eastern monastic communities that existed in late-seventh-century Rome. Donos himself discovered that a community of Syrian monks, who had taken up residence in a monastery known as the Boetiana,[63] continued to adhere to the teaching of Nestorius, the fifth-century patriarch of Constantinople whose Antiochene Christology, obviously still attractive to the Syrian monks of this monastery as late as 677, had nonetheless been condemned at the Third Ecumenical Council in Ephesus in 431.[64] In an effort to suppress their heresy, the pontiff dispersed them among various monasteries in the city and repopulated the Boetiana with Roman monks of indubitable Christological orthodoxy.[65]

The other unquestionably Eastern coenobitic community in late-seventh-century Rome was the monastery of St. Erasmus, which was situated on the Caelian Hill on the left side of the road leading from the Septizonium past the churches of San Giovanni e Paolo and San Stefano Rotondo toward the Porta Metrovia.[66] Erasmus, its patron saint, had been born in Antioch where he became a bishop. Fleeing the persecutions of Diocletian and Maximian, he sought refuge on Mount Lebanon in the Syrian desert, where he spent seven years as a hermit nurtured by crows, performing miracles, and conversing with the angels. Eventually, he was seized by the authorities, rolled in pitch, set on fire, imprisoned, and then released by the Archangel Michael, who took him first to Illyricum, where he converted forty thousand persons to Christianity, and thereafter to Formiae in the Campagna, where he ended his life as its bishop.[67] By the beginning of the seventh century, Erasmus's name had entered the popular calendar of the Roman church, and two monasteries, one at Mount Soracte and the other on the Caelian Hill in Rome, had been placed under the protection of this Eastern saint.[68] Some sort of monastic *koinonia* was probably in existence at the site of St. Erasmus from about the fourth decade of the seventh century if, as the *Liber Pontificalis* relates, Pope Adeodatus (672–676) seems to have grown up there in the care of its monks.[69] The most compelling evidence that St. Erasmus was a Greek monastery, if not from inception then certainly by the fourth quarter of the seventh century, is an inscription in Greek placed upon a marble slab, which was conspicuously exposed to public view probably near the monastery's entrance. Discovered in the nineteenth century in a vineyard near the Porta Pinciana, the inscription enumerates in detail the names of the various ωνιακά προάστεια or revenue-producing villas that Pope Adeodatus bestowed upon St. Erasmus.[70] The pope's generous endowment probably coincided with his construction of "many new buildings" at the monastery, and with his formalization of what seems to have been a loose, perhaps idiorhythmic, community into a more tightly organized cenobium under the supervision of an abbot.[71]

The monasteries of seventh century Rome thus cloistered a sizable population of Greek monks the majority of whom had, as we have seen, arrived in the city during the early decades of the century seeking refuge from persecution both by their Monothelite coreligionists and from the Persian and Arab invaders. One of these monks was a certain Pamphilos, who arrived in Rome sometime after 620 and while there composed an encomium in Greek on the life of St. Soteris, a virgin of noble lineage who was martyred at the same time as St. Pancratios, bishop of Taormina in Sicily.[72] After composing the panegyric, Pamphilos returned to the East where he then received ordination and served at the church of the Anastasis until he died.[73] But it is equally possible, and indeed more likely, that Pamphilos was already a priest/monk when he arrived in Rome and that he continued to identify himself with his former position in Jerusalem, although he was never again to return to the East. If so, the example of Pamphilos reflects the fact that most of the Eastern monks who came to Rome in the seventh century held fast to their oriental identities and roots, especially to the Greek language, and that while they became a permanent and influential part of the Roman ecclesiastical establishment, they never ceased to regard themselves as Easterners nor forsake the customs, traditions, and institutions of the Orient, many of which they transferred faithfully and in whole cloth to their new homeland in the West.

✧

Late-seventh-century Rome also witnessed the rise of charitable institutions known as *monasteria diaconia*, or monastic diaconies.[74] Previously unknown in Rome, these eleemosynary institutions were imported to the city from the East by monks fleeing the calamities that plagued the eastern part of the empire during the first half of the seventh century. By the eighth century, these quintessentially oriental institutions would come to play an indispensable role in providing for the needy among Rome's population as they undertook to serve the poor, the aged, and the ill.[75] The concept of Christian charity, which underlay the work of Rome's diaconies in providing for the ailing and impoverished, and in particular distributing grain to the city's indigent, was grounded upon an ethos that stretched beyond the traditions familiar to the many Greek, Syrian, and Palestinian monastics inhabiting seventh-century Rome to find its source deep in the spirit of love demonstrated by the monks of the Egyptian desert.[76]

The commandment to love, which was the bedrock of desert monasticism, was not limited to the practice of heroic gestures, but embraced and encouraged simple acts of charity and kindness toward human beings in need or in distress.[77] As early as the fourth century, Pambo of Nitria began a custom whereby each year the monks where he lived would give a measure of grain "to those in need, distributing them to the hospices for lepers and to the widows and orphans."[78] By the end of the fourth and the beginning of the fifth century, centers known as διακονίαι, or diaconies,[79] which were devoted to providing necessities to the poor, began to appear with increasing frequency in Lower Egypt.[80] The earliest diaconies seem to have been under the stewardship of monks, as in the case of John the Persian and Elias, and to have been endowed by gifts from pious lay benefactors such as a certain Theonas of Dioclos, who, according to John Cassian, eventually became head of the diaconie he had patronized as a layman.[81] By the sixth century, a number of Egyptian monasteries, including the communities of Pharaous, Aphrodito, Metanoia, Psinabla, Oasites, and Apollos, had institutionalized the injunction to practice charity by establishing separate and distinct diaconies under the administration of a monk, known as the διακονητής, or diaconites, whose function was to serve as places for the collection, organization, and distribution of alms, particularly grain, to the poor and needy.[82] Since these diaconies were, in a sense, dependencies of the monastic communities that sponsored their activities, they soon came to be called μοναστήρια διακονία, or monastic diaconies, although papyri clearly indicate that they possessed a certain degree of autonomy and juridical independence from the monasteries, which were their patrons.[83]

Inspired to imitate as much as possible the virtues of the desert fathers of Egypt,[84] the monks of Palestine had by the middle of the sixth century established diaconies in Judaea and Transjordan on the Egyptian model.[85] One such diaconie was founded at Gerasa (Jerash) in the month of May, 565.[86] As with diaconies that would later appear in Pesaro, Naples, Ravenna, and finally in Rome, the diaconie at Gerasa was located in a former pagan temple in the center of the city and on a principal route, thereby facilitating both the accumulation and distribution of grain and other necessities to the needy. The essential design of the diaconie at Gerasa, which included an atrium for receiving the indigent, encircling storage facilities for keeping grain and other supplies, and a small chapel or oratory, would also be reproduced in Italy.[87] As with so much else we have seen, the concept of the monastic diaconie, including its location as well as its design, was brought westward by monastics. Indeed, a version of the *Typikon* of St. Sabas refers specifically to "diaconites who perform their functions in diaconies," thus indicating that the institution was familiar to the Sabaite monks of Palestine who made their way to Rome in the seventh century where they, as well as other Eastern monastics, founded monasteries and, in imitation of a tradition they had inherited from the monks of Egypt, also transmitted the idea of the diaconie as a part of the ministry of those communities.[88]

Although charitable foundations, such as the *nosocomium*, or hospital, established by Fabiola in the fourth century and the *xenodochium*, or travelers' hostel, built by Belisarius in the first half of the sixth century near what is now S. Maria di Trevi, existed in Rome prior to the seventh century, the term "monastic diaconie," whose essential function was to distribute food to the city's poor, does not appear in any text earlier than the time of Pope Benedict II (684–685).[89] While recent archaeological evidence suggests the existence of welfare centers in Rome dating from around the year 600 or earlier, diaconies on an Eastern model do not appear until the middle of the seventh century at about the time that the imperial *annona*, or grain distribution, ceases.[90] Prompted by the failure of the civil administration to provide bread for the city's indigent, Rome's Eastern monastic communities as well as a substantial number of its churches, supported by the generous donations of pious lay benefactors, drew upon their oriental traditions and created diaconies to serve this purpose.[91]

The association of Rome's seventh century diaconies with Eastern elements in the city belies their oriental origins, while the many striking similarities between them and their Eastern paradigms is unmistakable. As with their Eastern counterparts, Rome's diaconies were located predominantly in the center of the city.[92] Eight of a total of eighteen occupied the area between the quays along the Tiber at the foot of the Aventine in the Greek quarter of the city, where grain arrived from Ostia, and the imperial forum at the foot of the Palatine, while the remainder were situated along the city's principal routes, such as the Via Lata, in order to be able more efficiently to assemble and dole out grain to the poor.[93] While many of Rome's diaconies were established in abandoned public buildings such as the Horrea Agrippiniana and the Forum Boarium, both of which had previously served as imperial *statio annonae*, many, such as the diaconies of S. Maria Antiqua, S. Maria in Aquiro, and S. Maria in Cosmedin, were founded on the sites of or alongside former pagan temples.[94] Rome's diaconies, like those in Egypt and Palestine, depended heavily upon the patronage of wealthy laymen.[95] Known variously as *patres diaconiae* and *dispensatores*, the identities of the most illustrious patrons of Rome's diaconies reflect their Eastern provenance.[96] A certain duke Eustathios, who served as Pope Stephen II's emissary to Ravenna in the eighth century, is recorded as the *dispensator* or donor of lands to the diaconie of S. Maria in Cosmedin.[97] The same inscription memorializing Eustathios's gift records a donation to the diaconie by a certain "Georgios, gloriosissimus" and his brother David.[98] Theodotos, a consul and duke, who was also the uncle of Pope Hadrian I, was a benefactor of both the diaconies of S. Paul and of Sant'Angelo in Foro Piscium.[99]

Nearly all Roman diaconies that came into existence from the late seventh-century forward were founded at or near churches whose patron saints or congregations were of Eastern provenance.[100] Thus, for example, a diaconie was established at the church of S. Theodoros at the west foot of the Palatine in the seventh century, while at about the same time a diaconie was founded at SS. Boniface and Alexios on the Aventine at a place known as Blachernae, after the district of the same name in northwestern Constantinople.[101] In the eighth century, Pope Hadrian I founded a diaconie at the church of the SS. Cosmas and Damian, which had been substantially restored and embellished in the late seventh century by the Syrian Pope Sergius I, while earlier in the century a diaconie had been established at the church of SS. Sergius and Bacchus, which stood near the arch of Septimius Severus.[102] The churches of S. Maria in Cosmedin, located in the area at the foot of the Aventine long known as the *schola Graeca*, and the church of S. Maria Antiqua, lavishly decorated with Byzantine-style frescoes by the Greek Pope John VII in the early eighth century, both had diaconies, as did the church of St. George in Velabro.[103] Located at the Forum Boarium opposite the square of Janus Quadrifons, the church of St. George, dedicated to the most popular military saint of the East,[104] was, if not actually built by the Greco-Sicilian Pope Leo II in the second half of the seventh century,[105] certainly in existence by the middle of the eighth century when the Greek Pope Zacharias, having discovered the head of St. George enclosed in a casket in the Lateran *patriarchium*, conveyed it in solemn procession accompanied by hymns and chants to the diaconie "which is dedicated to him [St. George] in this city of Rome in the second region at Velabrum."[106] A group of four badly fragmented Greek inscriptions reflect that the congregation of the church of St. George consisted of members of Rome's Greek colony, many of whom appear to have been highly educated, and whose clerics, chosen from among them, were equally erudite and cultured.[107] For St. George in Velabro's ministry to have included a diaconie to serve the poor in a manner consistent with the traditions that its congregation had inherited from the East was hardly unexpected.

Nor is it at all surprising that Pope Benedict II's munificence toward Rome's diaconies would be continued by his three immediate successors, all of whom were of Eastern provenance. Pope John V, a Syrian from the province of Antioch, distributed a gift of nineteen hundred *solidi* to "all the clergy, the monastic diaconies, and the *mansionarii*," while a benefaction of an unspecified sum of gold was made to the same three causes by Pope Conon, who was raised in Sicily and whose father had served in the Thrakesion theme that had accompanied the emperor Constans II there in the mid-660s.[108] Before the end of the century, the Syrian Pope Sergius I had founded a diaconie at the church of S. Maria in Via Lata located along the Corso leading from the Porta Flaminia to the foot of the Capitoline Hill in an area which, by the eighth century, had become a socially prominent quarter of the city.[109] In fact, papal patronage of Rome's diaconies appears to have become so widespread that the late-seventh-century pontifical formulary known as the *Liber Diurnus* contains four formulas relating to them.[110] One sets forth the form to be used by the pope in bestowing lands and tenements upon *monasteria diaconia*, while a second provides the text for use in granting lands to a monastic community where the property conveyed includes an existing diaconie.[111] A third formula contains the language to be used where the pope has determined to place a diaconie under perpetual papal protection, while the final formula sets down the text to be used for providing notice of the papal foundation of a diaconie.[112] The growth and expansion of papal patronage of Rome's diaconies beginning at a time when the Papacy came to be occupied by a series of pontiffs of Eastern origin was thus not simply fortuitous, but rather yet another indicator that both Easterners and the oriental institutions and practices familiar to them were becoming increasingly a part of daily life in late-seventh-century Rome.[113]

Orbetello sits upon a narrow strip of land jutting out into the Tyrrhenian Sea to the east of the Via Aurelia at a strategically important location guarding coastal access from the north to the Byzantine duchy of Rome. The remnants of a church wall, discovered there in 1759, contain a funerary inscription in Greek memorializing the entombed remains of a Syro-Palestinian or Egyptian family which had probably emigrated to Rome in the second half of the seventh century and whose members would rapidly rise to occupy important positions within the Roman civil and military administrations.[114] The *paterfamilias* was a certain Sergius, whose title κονσιλιάριος, or *consiliarius*, indicates that he was a leading military official of the exarchate.[115] Sergius and his wife Marousa had a son named Anastasios who, as a σκρινιάριος, or *scriniarius*, was a secretary in the imperial administration of the Roman duchy.[116] He and his wife Agatha produced a son by the name of Mamalos who, like his father, was also an imperial *scriniarius* and, like both his father and grandfather, married a woman of Eastern origin by the name of Moschousa.[117] The family tomb also contained the body of a certain Moschos, possibly Moschousa's brother, who, according to the inscription, had achieved the exceptionally high position of "archdeacon of the most holy Church."[118] A late-seventh-century funerary inscription located at S. Maria *ad praesepe* in Rome confirms a gift to the church of a parcel of land in the territory around Nepi due north of the city by the *vestiarius* Theophylaktos and his wife the *vestiarissa* Theodora in memory of their children Sergia and Bonifatios, "who lived [respectively] seven months and one year."[119] Although occupying positions of relatively modest rank within the imperial wardrobe, this obviously oriental couple had nonetheless accumulated enough wealth to be able to make a generous donation of realty to a church where, according to tradition, their fellow Easterner Pope Theodore I had placed Christ's manger, which he had carried with him as he fled Jerusalem in advance of the Arab invasions of the Holy Land.[120]

The examples of these two Eastern families highlight the fact that, although monastics exercised a profound influence upon the church of Rome and Roman society in the late seventh century, it was not monks alone who brought the impact of the East to bear upon Byzantine Italy. Indeed, both because monks were bound by a vow of celibacy and because their vocation necessarily precluded them from holding positions in the civil and military administrations, lay persons, such as the families of Sergius and Marousa and Theophylaktos and Theodora, probably exercised a greater impact upon a broader segment of Roman society than did the monks. Unlike monastics, for instance, lay people married and procreated and, in this regard, Easterners living in Rome appear to have been as prolific as Westerners.[121] The order for the sacrament of baptism set forth in the *Ordo Romanus XI*, composed in Rome in the seventh century for use by the priests who served the titular churches and basilicas, is particularly revealing in this regard. After the priest asks those who are about to receive the sacrament to profess their faith in Christ, the acolyte is directed to take up an infant from among the male children, whereupon the priest asks him to declare "in which language our Lord Jesus Christ is to be confessed." When the acolyte replies that the confession is to be made in Greek, the priest tells him to "proclaim the faith of those in the manner in which they believe." The acolyte then recites the Creed in Greek beginning with the words Πιστεύω εις ενα Θεόν ("I believe in one God"). Only after the Creed had been said in Greek does the acolyte take up a child "from among the Latin infants" and, following the same rubric as before, recites the Creed in Latin beginning with the words *Credo in unum Deum*.[122] The recitation of the Nicene-Constantinopolitan Creed in Greek for those children whose parents and families were Greek-speaking thus clearly indicates the presence among the population of late-seventh-century Rome of a substantial number of Easterners who, as we have seen, had by then become an integral part of the fabric of Roman society.[123] Although a late-seventh-century couplet reminiscent of Juvenal reflected a persistent undercurrent of resentment still harbored by many Latins against those from the East, it was abundantly clear that those voices were becoming part of an increasingly distinct minority.[124]

Nowhere was the proliferation of Easterners into Roman institutions more apparent than in the clergy of the church of Rome. Over half of the fifteen bishops who attended a synod convened in the Constantinian basilica adjacent to the Lateran patriarchium by the Greco-Sicilian Pope Agatho in 679 were Easterners, while the same was true of two-thirds of the priests in attendance.[125] The appearance of a proportionately greater number of Greek in relation to Latin names among the ranks of the Roman clergy, as revealed by the identities of those who attended the synod of 679, indicates in a very tangible way the onset of the period during which the church of Rome would begin to encounter most profoundly the impact of the East.[126] Indeed, the choice of certain names particularly identifiable with the East reflects an intention on the part of Eastern clerics not only to retain, but indeed to emphasize, both their oriental identities as well as their unique heritage and traditions. Several such names, including Sissinius, Georgios, Thalassios (or its Latin equivalent Marinos), Conon, and Sergius appear to have enjoyed "remarkable popularity" among Easterners in Rome beginning in the late seventh century.[127]

The name Sissinius, whose cognate Sisinnes, which stretches back to the time of Alexander the Great and in the first century B.C. was the sobriquet of one Archelaus of Cappadocia, was carried by more Eastern priests who attended the Roman synod of 679 than any other name.[128] The *Hagiologion* of the Greek church identifies a Sissinius among the forty martyrs killed at Sebasteia during the time of Licinius, a Sissinius known as the Wonderworker, as well as two other martyrs and one confessor by that name.[129] Patriarch Sissinius I occupied the see of Constantinople from 426 to 427.[130] Early Jacobite menologies from Syria commemorate a martyr named Sissinius on November 23.[131] From the mid-seventh century forward, over seventy percent of the episcopal sees in southern and southwestern Anatolia and the Aegean islands, including Cilicia, Isauria, Pisidia, Caria, Lycia, Pamphylia, and the Cyclades, were occupied by bishops named Sissinius.[132] The name Sissinius continued to experience widespread popularity both in the East as well as in Rome for the remainder of the seventh and well into the late eighth century.[133]

The name Georgios also enjoyed great popularity in late-seventh-century Rome. Probably the most famous military saint of the East, the cult of St. Georgios was imported to Byzantine Italy by troops of the Anatolikon theme, contigents of which had accompanied the emperor Constans II on his Italian expedition in 661.[134] Already immensely popular in the East, where before the end of the seventh century over twenty-five bishops in dioceses located in southwestern Anatolia and along the Aegean seacoast had taken the name of the illustrious soldier/martyr, Georgios quickly became a favorite in the West as well.[135] Among the thirty-two occurrences of the name Georgios in the clergy of the church of Rome, none predates the year 651, thereby indicating a connection between the wide prevalence which the name enjoyed among Roman ecclesiastics and the period during which Byzantine influence began its rapid ascendancy after mid-century.[136] Three priests named Georgios participated in the Roman synod of 679, and a priest by that name was part of the delegation sent by Pope Agatho to the Sixth Ecumenical Council in 680.[137] The Greco-Sicilian Pope Leo II may well have founded the church of St. Georgios *ad Velabro*, dedicated to the renowned Eastern saint, sometime between 682 and 683.[138] When Pope Constantine I departed for the imperial city in 710, the papal retinue included a bishop, a priest, and an official of the papal household known as a *secundicarius*, all of whom were named Georgios.[139] As with the name Sissinius, Georgios's popularity among Roman clerics extended throughout the eighth century.[140]

The Greek name Thalassios, which was Latinized to Marinos, also enjoyed wide currency among clerics of the church of Rome possibly as a result of the fact that a substantial number of men from the naval theme of the *Karabisianoi*, which was based on the south Anatolian coast and whose contingents had accompanied Constans II on his Italian expedition, had remained in Sicily and southern Italy where they married and raised families after the emperor's assassination in 668.[141] Conon, an ancient Attic name widely used in the East but rarely seen in the Latin West, had also acquired a measure of popularity among the Roman clergy by the late seventh century.[142] While the name seems to have enjoyed some currency in Syria, it appears most frequently in eastern Asia Minor, including Lycaonia, Phrygia, Lydia, Caria, Pisidia, and Cilicia, where parents bestowed it liberally on their children hoping thereby to secure the patronage and protection of various local saints and martyrs whose name was Conon.[143] The monks of the monastery of St. Conon in Constantinople appear to have taken an active part in the Nika riots early in the reign of Justinian I.[144] Indeed, the name Conon seems to have been a favorite among Eastern monastics. Maximos Confessor corresponded with a priest-abbot named Conon sometime in the seventh century, while John Moschos identified an ιερομόναχος or priest-monk by that name living at the monastery of Penthucla in Palestine in the sixth century. A Lycian named Conon, "celebrated for monastic attainments and orthodox doctrines," was elected by his brothers to be hegumen of the Great Lavra of St. Sabas, while, in the life of St. Eustratios, a certain Bithynian monk named Conon occupied a cloister on Mount Olympus.[145] Surely the most celebrated person to have been known by the name of Conon was the emperor Leo III, who, possibly to minimize his Syrian ancestry and choose a name that emphasized his adherence to Chalcedonian orthodoxy, changed his baptismal name to one quite popular among Byzantines when he acceded to the throne in 717.[146]

Finally, the name Sergius achieved exceptionally wide popularity with Roman ecclesiastics, especially among those of Syrian extraction, from the late seventh century forward.[147] There had been any number of saints, martyrs, bishops, and holy men with the name of Sergius in the East, including Syria, Palestine, Armenia, Mesopotamia, and Constantinople.[148] A Sergius, along with his compatriot Bacchus, had suffered martyrdom in the time of Diocletian and Maximian, while another martyr named Sergius had been slain during the Great Persecutions in Palestinian Caesarea.[149] A disciple of St. Symeon the Stylite by the name of Sergius came to Constantinople to announce the holy man's death, bearing his cloak to the emperor Leo I as proof of the saint's passing.[150] An Armenian text recites the passion of the megalomartyr Saint Sergius Stratelatos.[151] A bishop Sergius of Urd was among the Syrian Monophysite prelates who accompanied Athanasios Camelarios to a meeting of the Syrian episcopate with the emperor Heraclius around 630.[152] Theophanes described the early-seventh-century patriarch Sergius of Constantinople as "being himself of Syrian origin," doubtless in order to prove his Monophysite proclivities.[153] In Iraq, a monastery built in the sixth century was dedicated to a certain Mar Sergius, while another monastery, built between 559 and 575 and dedicated to a different Mar Sergius, became embroiled in the Nestorian and Jacobite conflicts that arose at the end of the sixth and the beginning of the seventh centuries.[154] Yet another monastery, which appears to have been responsible for saving many people from exposure and starvation and which was dedicated to a Mar Sergius, was built in the desert near Tikrit in Mesopotamia between 629 and 645.[155] Beginning in the seventh century, Nestorians dedicated a variety of religious sites to saints named Sergius, including the church of the convent of Saint Sergius at Mabrakta near Seleucia-Ctesiphon, and a monastery near Hira, which is probably identifiable with the monastic community of Dair Sargis of Sabusti.[156] By far the most renowned person to bear the name of Sergius was the Syrian saint buried in the desert at Resapha about twenty-five kilometers south of Sura on the right bank of the Euphrates where he was martyred. The bishop of nearby Hierapolis (Mabboug) built a shrine at the place where Sergius of Resapha had been slain, and it soon formed the hub of a small desert city where Bedouins, Persians, and Arabs joined Christians in making pilgrimages to the saint's tomb in search of his patronage.[157]

The gradual disappearance of names such as Probus, Faustus, Venantius, and Importunus among ecclesiastics and the laity in Rome during the later decades of the seventh century and the concomitant appearance of substantial numbers of clerics and lay persons with names such as those described above, as well as others such as Gregorios, Ioannes, Paschalis, Stephanos, and Theodoros, represented a radical transformation in the ethnic composition of the city.[158] By the beginning of the 680s, orientals had actually come to comprise a substantial portion, if not the majority, of the Roman clergy and, as we have seen, of the influential laity as well.[159]

The emperor Constantine IV took notice of this sea change in the ethnicity of Rome's ecclesiastical and lay populations. During the pontificate of Benedict II (684–685), he removed the requirement of imperial approval as a precondition to the consecration of a pope, directing that "the one elected to the Apostolic See may be ordained pontiff from that moment and without delay."[160] Thereafter, in a return to "ancient practice," which had doubtless first received imperial endorsement, Benedict II's successor, the Syrian Pope John V, was elected "by the general population."[161] The emperor's decision to allow these two significant changes in the means by which Roman pontiffs were elected and consecrated was likely the result of what he perceived to be Rome's proven political loyalty to and doctrinal sympathy with Byzantium. But it may also have been prompted by the confidence he felt that the metamorphosis in the ethnic content of the clergy of the Roman church and the city's lay population would assuredly result in the election of popes of Eastern provenance, and thus of pontiffs more closely attached to the ways of the East and hopefully to the imperial court at Constantinople. The succession of ten popes of Eastern descent following the death of the Greco-Sicilian Pope Agatho in 681 is ample proof that Constantine IV's concessions had the results he had foreseen and likely intended.[162]

It was perhaps predictable that broadening the electorate to embrace the general population would result in potentially acrimonious battles over papal succession. But given Rome's ethnic composition in the late seventh century, it is hardly surprising that the contestants appear consistently to have been of Eastern provenance and that the victors, while not necessarily one of the contestants, turned out always to be of oriental extraction. The death of Pope John V in August, 686, for example, resulted in a heated debate over his successor. The clergy favored the election of the archpriest Petros, while the army supported a priest named Theodoros. As the clerical faction gathered outside the Constantinian basilica and the military occupied the church of St. Stephen, negotiators shuttled between the two groups in a futile effort to come to an accord. At last, the ecclesiastical faction entered the papal residence on the Lateran where, forsaking Theodoros, they elected the Greco-Sicilian Conon as John V's successor. Conon's "angelic appearance, venerable grey hair, truthfulness of speech, simplicity of soul [and] peaceful habits," together with the fact that he had led a religious life and had never engaged in worldly affairs, won the approval of the civil and military faction, which, in a few days, abandoned Petros and gave their assent to Conon's consecration.[163]

Pope Conon's death a mere eleven months later resulted in a far uglier confrontation. Once again, however, the contestants, as well as the one who ultimately prevailed, were Easterners. Separating into two factions, a portion of the city's population again proposed the election of the archpriest Theodoros, while another group supported the candidacy of the archdeacon Paschalios. Theodoros's adherents managed to occupy the Lateran patriarchium as Paschalios's group took over an adjacent oratory and basilica. The ensuing combat, during which each side tried to dislodge the other from the places they had occupied, eventually ended when a group of judges together with members of the army, the clergy, and a large number of citizens proposed the candidacy of a Syrian priest named Sergius, whom they first brought to the imperial palace on the Palatine and thereafter led to the papal residence on the Lateran. Forcing their way into the patriarchium, they succeeded by virtue of sheer numerical superiority in causing Theodoros to admit defeat and acknowledge Sergius as pope. Paschalios, however, was not so easily convinced. Although he made a pretense of accepting Sergius's election, he secretly sent messengers to Ravenna where, with the promise of a hundred pounds of gold, the envoys persuaded the exarch John Platyn to come to Rome and support Paschalios's candidacy. But when he arrived in the city, the exarch quickly realized that Paschalios's cause was hopeless. His cupidity, however, would not permit him to depart without exacting the gold Paschalios had promised. Thus, while Sergius was finally consecrated pope, the exarch left for Ravenna with a large quantity of ornaments looted from St. Peter's, and Paschalios, eventually deprived of his ecclesiastical position for practicing witchcraft, was confined to a monastery.[164]

With Sergius's consecration, the battles for succession to the Papacy came to an end for as long as Byzantine authority prevailed in Italy. For the next half-century, popes would be elected without incident. The imperial decision to return to "ancient practice" had had the consequences Constantine IV had envisioned. Until the middle of the eighth century, every Roman pontiff but Gregory II was to be of Eastern provenance.

⌁

It may not have been altogether fortuitous that the bounty of imperial favor fell richly upon the Papacy during the period of the Greek popes. Agatho's emissaries to the Sixth Ecumenical Council were installed in the Placidia Palace where the emperor provided them with every conceivable comfort, including a string of saddled horses and an escort to convey them from their residence to the church of the Theotokos at Blachernae where they took part in a procession on the first Sunday after their arrival.[165] On the legates' last Sunday in Constantinople, bishop John of Portus celebrated mass in Latin in the presence of the emperor before the altar of the Great Church of St. Sophia.[166] When he returned to Rome, the bishop of Portus was carrying an imperial decree in which Constantine IV had, at Pope Agatho's request, abolished the fee customarily paid as a precondition to the consecration of a newly-elected pope.[167] During the pontificate of Agatho's successor, the Greco-Sicilian Leo II, Constantine IV reversed the sixteen-year-old edict of his father Constans II and restored the church of Ravenna to the jurisdiction of the Roman church. In what was simultaneously a resounding victory for the Apostolic See and a bitter blow to the Ravennates, the emperor decreed that the newly-elected archbishops of Ravenna had to travel to Rome to be ordained, and that the annual requiem mass for archbishop Maurus, who had obtained the decree of autocephaly for Ravenna from Constans II, was no longer to be observed.[168] In addition to making the momentous concession allowing a newly-elected pope to be consecrated without first obtaining the imperial *iussio*, Constantine IV honored Pope Benedict II, as well as the Roman clergy and army, by sending them locks of the hair of his sons Justinian and Heraclius, thereby symbolically placing the young princes under the protection of both the Papacy and the people of Rome through a gesture which, in both East and West, was comparable to creating a bond as strong and inviolable as baptismal sponsorship, adoption, and marriage.[169] During the pontificate of the Syrian Pope John V (684–685), the emperor abolished a substantial portion of the taxes due from the papal patrimonies in Sicily and Calabria, in addition to eliminating various other imposts, including a surtax on the sale of grain, which the Roman church was having difficulty paying each year.[170] In the brief time that the Greco-Sicilian Pope Conon (686–687) occupied the Papacy, the emperor Justinian II, continuing the precedent established by his recently deceased father, issued decrees abolishing a significant measure of the tax burden imposed

on the papal patrimonies of Bruttium and Lucania, while at the same time ordering that persons being held by the army as security for the payment of imperial
taxes due from those regions, as well as from the papal patrimonies in Sicily, be
released to return to their families.[171]

While the popes had to have been deeply gratified by the fecundity of imperial
favor, their political loyalty to Byzantium was never conditioned upon receiving
concessions or largesse from Constantinople or upon imperial adherence to doctrinal orthodoxy. Although badly mistreated by Constans II, Pope Martin never
wavered in his conviction that the "most clement emperor" had been deceived by
evil counselors into issuing the *Typos*.[172] Promptly upon his ordination, Pope Vitalian dispatched his *apokrisiarii* to the "most pious emperors in the imperial city"
notifying them of his consecration as pontiff and receiving in return from "their
clemencies" a gift of golden gospels.[173] When Pope Adeodatus granted certain
privileges to the monks of the monastery of SS. Peter and Paul in Canterbury, he
dated his letter by reference to the regnal year of the emperor Constantine IV and
his brothers Heraclius and Tiberius.[174] Pope Agatho's letter to the emperor Constantine IV and his brothers, read at the fourth session of the Sixth Ecumencial
Council on November15, 680, addressed them as "the most pious, victorious, and
triumphant lords."[175] The papal letter recognized imperial sovereignty over the
city of Rome, acknowledged the universal authority of the Christian emperor in
Constantinople, whom, the pontiff confessed, he was forever bound to serve and
obey, and prayed that all nations "may lay down most humbly their necks beneath
the scepter of your most powerful rule, that the power of your most pious kingdom may continue until the ceaseless joy of the eternal kingdom succeeds to this
temporal reign." Agatho's epistle concluded with a prayer that the Lord preserve
the empire "untouched and exalted" and, following the subscription, contained a
benediction that "the grace from above keep your empire, most pious lords, and
place beneath its feet the neck of all nations."[176] For Pope Leo II, the emperor in
Byzantium was and would forever remain his lord and sovereign, the "most Christian prince and champion . . . benefactor . . . bestower of the greatest riches."[177]
When Pope Benedict II received locks of the hair of the princes Justinian and
Heraclius, he accepted them with full knowledge that the imperial children were
now under special papal protection, as much his spiritual children as his future
sovereigns.[178] For the Roman pontiffs, the barbarian kings were simply their sons;
but as long as Byzantium wielded power on the Italian peninsula, the emperors
in Constantinople were their lords.[179] Byzantine lordship, however, did not mean
blind obedience to the emperor on matters of the faith. Although an unbroken
line of politically loyal pontiffs occupied the Apostolic See until the death of
Pope Zacharias in 752, that loyalty did not always extend to questions of religion. Where East and West diverged on religious issues, Constantinople quickly
learned that the oriental popes were irritatingly intractable. For whether ethnically Sicilian, Syrian, or Greek, on matters of religion the Eastern pontiffs never
faltered from allegiance to the practices and doctrines of the church of Rome.

❧

There was nothing to suggest that the rapprochement between Rome and Constantinople, which had been initiated by Constans II and studiously cultivated by Constantine IV, would not continue when the sixteen-year-old Justinian II succeeded his father, dead of dysentery at the age of thirty-three, as emperor in the fall of 685.[180] Indeed, two occurrences early in his reign should have given the Papacy great confidence that the new emperor, like his father, held the Roman church in the highest regard and was a fervent defender of the orthodox faith.[181]

Shortly after his accession, Justinian II discovered that the acts of the Sixth Ecumenical Council had been returned to "certain of our judges," who appear to have permitted them to leave the imperial archive without the emperor's knowledge or consent. Fearing that while on loan they may have been falsified, Justinian wrote to assure Pope John V that he had convened a synod of high-ranking civil and ecclesiastical officials, including the papal *apokrisiarios* and members of the empire's military forces, and had caused the text of the council held during the reign of his father to be read in their presence and thereafter to be sealed and acknowledged by all as containing a true and accurate profession of the faith. Since God had ordained him to preserve the Christian religion immaculate, Justinian wished the pope to know that henceforth the acts of the ecumenical synod would be maintained "unimpaired and unchanged."[182]

Justinian II's continued attack upon the Paulicians was yet another indicator of the new emperor's commitment to preserve the orthodox faith inviolate.[183] The Paulicians, who are first mentioned in a Greek chronicle by Theophanes in the middle of the eighth century, were a sect of heretical Christians who subscribed to the doctrine of adoptionism with an emphasis on the importance of baptism and a firm opposition to icons.[184] A certain Constantine-Silvanus appears to have been introduced to the sect in Syria and thereafter to have imported it to his native Armenia from where it began to spread westward beginning in the middle of the seventh century. After leading the Paulicians for twenty-seven years, Constantine-Silvanus was killed at Koloneia in the province of Armenia II sometime around 681 during a persecution initiated by Constantine IV. But the death of Constantine-Silvanus was not enough to extirpate the sect. By about 690, some five years into the reign of Justinian II, the Paulicians under their new leader Symeon-Titus appear to have become enough of a threat to alarm the bishop of Koloneia, who informed the emperor that the sect was on the rise. Justinian II responded to the bishop's apprehension by launching another attack on the Paulicians, which resulted in the death of Symeon-Titus as well as most of his followers. The Paulician heresy would not pose a threat to orthodoxy for another fifty years.[185]

Justinian II's decision to convene a church council for the express purpose of enacting disciplinary canons intended to establish standards of conduct for both clerics and lay persons consistent with the doctrinal pronouncements of the ecumenical synods that had been held under Justinian I in 553 and Constantine IV in 680/681 was yet another example of the emperor's commitment to preserving the Christian faith inviolate and proving that he was as orthodox as his father Constantine IV had been.[186] Known both as the Quinisext Council, because it was intended to complete the unfinished work of the previous two ecumenical councils by issuing canonical legislation where they had not done so, and as the Council *in Trullo*, since it was held in the Trullanum or great domed hall of the imperial palace, the synod took place sometime between September 691 and August 692 and drew episcopal representatives from over two hundred dioceses, including the patriarchates of Constantinople, Alexandria, Antioch, and Jerusalem. Although the Syrian-born Pope Sergius I did not himself attend the Quinisext Council, his legates, consisting probably of the papal *apokrisiarii* at the imperial court, were present along with the pope's suffragan Basil, bishop of Gortyna in Crete, who subscribed to the canons of the council as "holding the place of the entire synod of the Holy Roman Church."[187] The text of its canons makes it plain that both its participants and the emperor intended the Quinisext Council to be an ecumenical synod insofar as its canonical decrees were to be a continuation of the work of the Sixth Ecumenical Council and as such to apply to the whole church.[188] Despite their universal applicability, however, the canons of the Trullan council were directed primarily at correcting erroneous practices and irregularities prevailing among clerics and the laity in the East rather than the West.[189]

The exceptionally broad spectrum of activities and practices on which the Quinisext Council legislated reflects in large measure Justinian's view of himself as God's specially appointed protector of the Christian faith. The actions of ecclesiastics drew particular attention. Clerics were forbidden from all kinds of improper and illicit relations with women.[190] Simony was prohibited, as was the practice of charging a fee for administering the Eucharist.[191] Those in holy orders were enjoined from entering public houses, engaging in usurious practices, attending horse races at the Hippodrome, wearing unsuitable clothes, and celebrating the liturgy in private homes without the consent of their bishop.[192] Both clerics and laypersons were prohibited from gambling at dice, attending theatrical performances, or consulting soothsayers.[193] No one was to continue to observe the pagan festivals of Bota, the Kalends, or the Brumalia, maintain a house of prostitution, induce abortions, arrange hair in ornate plaits, or promote pornography, and law students at the University of Constantinople were to stop engaging in transvestism.[194]

The canons of the Quinisext Council also addressed a host of liturgical practices. Wine and water were to be mixed when administering Holy Communion, and neither grapes, milk, nor honey were to be offered at the altar.[195] Whoever came to receive the Eucharist was to hold his hands in the form of a cross, and the sacrament was not to be given to dead bodies.[196] During the liturgy, the

psalms were to be chanted in modest and dulcet tones, the phrase "Who was cru-
cified for us" was not to be added to the Trisagion, and on Sundays in particular
prelates were to preach the Gospel as expounded by the fathers.[197] Priests were
given special instructions on how to deal with those who could not prove they
had been baptized, as well as the rubrics to be followed when admitting heretics
to the true faith.[198] Armenians were prohibited from ordaining as clerics only
those of priestly descent and from eating eggs and cheese on the Saturdays and
Sundays of Great Lent as they had traditionally done.[199]

The purpose of the Trullan canons was to establish uniformity in ecclesiastical discipline and practice that would be binding upon the imperial Church as a
whole. Not surprisingly perhaps, the basis for such uniformity was founded not
just on Eastern traditions but on the specifically Greek-based traditions of the
church of Constantinople and its dependencies since, as we have seen, even
Armenian practices were rejected. The council's predilection for Byzantine traditions over all others reflected the shift in the empire's center of gravity toward
the Greek East that had been taking place throughout the seventh century. But
while that proclivity may well have expressed the emperor's insistence that the
unity of the imperial Church in terms of its customs and liturgical practices was
to rest upon a Greco-Byzantine foundation, the council's canonical legislation
was in no way aggressively inimical toward what in many instances were the very
different traditions of the church of Rome.[200] Where the council adopted a disciplinary position that followed Greek instead of Roman tradition, as in the matter
of the second marriage of clergy, it expressed its choice with great deference to
the practice of the church of Rome, painstakingly seeking to reconcile the "rule
of strict observance" followed in the Roman church with the "rule of clemency
and compassion" observed in Constantinople, combining "both into one in a
manner at once in keeping with the fathers and pleasing to God, admitting neither unrestrained mildness nor harsh severity."[201] But despite a determined effort
to mollify Roman sensibilities, it quickly became apparent that the church of
Rome was not prepared to comply obediently with any legislation that conflicted
with its own practices.

Whether or not a pope's personal assent was as a matter of canon law an indispensable prerequisite in order for the acts of a church council to have ecumenical
effect, Justinian II believed that to be the case. For the emperor, the Quinisext
Council could not lay claim to ecumenicity or assert that its acts were valid and
legitimate for the entire church without the imprimatur of the Apostolic See.
While only the emperor could convene a council purporting to be ecumenical,
his initiative alone was insufficient to invest its decisions with the force of law
throughout the imperial *oikoumene*. For this to occur, the conciliar acts had to
be approved by the bishop of Rome without whose confirmation the unity of the
faith and the assurance of its freedom from doctrinal error could not be guaran-
teed. Therefore, having written his name in brilliant scarlet on each of the six
sets of the Trullan canons, Justinian dispatched them to Rome so that the space

directly beneath that of the emperor could be signed by the "most holy pope of Rome," thereby assuring their doctrinal soundness.[202] But the recalcitrant pontiff was never to sign. Ironically, Justinian's antagonist was not himself a Roman, but a Sicilian of Syrian ancestry whose sympathies with the ways of the East the emperor had woefully misjudged.[203]

Rome's opposition to those canons that varied from its own traditions was expressed with unexpected obstinacy.[204] For although he was and always would be Byzantium's loyal subject, as Roman pontiff Sergius I was not about to be its captive in matters of religion. We do not know exactly which of the Trullan canons Pope Sergius condemned as being "outside of ecclesiastical usage" and "invalid," preferring, as he exclaimed, "to die rather than consent to erroneous novelties."[205] It is unlikely that Sergius objected to that portion of Canon 1, which repeated the anathema on his predecessor Pope Honorius I first expressed by the Sixth Ecumenical Council in 680/681, since the *Liber Diurnus* or papal formulary then in use in Rome contained the same anathema in a least two separate formulas.[206] Nor is it probable that the pontiff objected to Canon 36, which declared that the church of Constantinople enjoyed equal privileges with that of Rome, but that it ranked second to Rome in place of honor, since this was hardly a novelty but merely a restatement of Canon 3 of the Second Ecumenical Council held in Constantinople in 381 and of Canon 28 of the Fourth Ecumenical Council convened in Chalcedon in 451.[207] It is far more likely that Rome took offense at the Quinisext Council's approval of the entire eighty-five Apostolic Canons, since the Roman church recognized only the first fifty.[208] In addition, papal resistance and anger must have been aroused against those canons which effectively censured a variety of Roman customs and traditions that were at variance with the practices of the church of Constantinople and the other churches of the East. Specifically rejecting the Roman church's prohibition against deacons and priests cohabiting with their wives after they had been ordained, Canon 13, in what was termed "compliance with ancient practice and apostolic accuracy and order," decreed that after ordination deacons and priests need not dissolve their marriages nor abstain from marital relations.[209] Canon 55, in another denunciation of a Roman practice that it described as "against traditional ecclesiastical observance," prohibited fasting on the Saturdays of Great Lent upon pain of deposition for clerics and excommunication for laypersons.[210] Canon 3, as we have seen, departed from the Roman practice of prohibiting anyone who married twice from remaining a cleric by giving priests who married a second time the opportunity to retain their clerical status by repenting and putting aside their second wives.[211] In yet another censure of a Roman practice that, in reliance upon the writings of no less a figure than Augustine allowed human consumption of the blood of birds and beasts, Canon 67 of the Quinisext Council prohibited both clerics and lay persons from eating blood and the meat of strangled animals.[212] Finally, Canon 82 prohibited the visual depiction of Christ as a lamb decreeing that, in χρωματουργίας, or colored expressions,

Jesus was always to be represented in human form.²¹³ The insistence that the Lamb of God not be represented in animal form seems to have been of particular concern to Justinian II, whose coinage, which for the first time in the history of the empire bears the image of Christ, may reflect the emperor's determination to extirpate the visual association of the second person of the Trinity with the image of a lamb.²¹⁴

Although ethnically a Syrian whose father had come from the region of Antioch, Sergius's loyalty in matters of religion lay solidly with the customs, practices, and traditions of the Roman church. Arriving in Rome from his native Sicily sometime during the pontificate of Adeodatus, Sergius was between nineteen and twenty-three when he became an acolyte, thereafter passing through the ranks of the Roman clergy until ordained as a presbyter by his Sicilian compatriot Pope Leo II, who assigned him to serve the titular basilica of St. Susanna, where Sergius remained as a parish priest for about seven years until he was elected pope in 687.²¹⁵ It should therefore have come as no surprise that when confronted with the emperor's demand that he confirm the canons of the Quinisext Council, including those which departed from and in some instances affirmatively rejected various Roman practices, Sergius protested that he would sooner die than denounce the customs and traditions of the church that had nurtured him since adolescence.²¹⁶ Indeed, in a brazen display of disregard for a matter that was especially important to the emperor, Pope Sergius declared that at the fraction of the Host during Mass both the clergy and the people were to chant the hymn "Lamb of God, who takest away the sins of the world, have mercy on us."²¹⁷ As if this were not enough, he also took particular care to restore the partially destroyed façade mosaic on the front of the atrium of St. Peter's that included the scene of the Worship of the Lamb.²¹⁸

Justinian's anger was uncontainable. In a display of outrage at the pontiff's conduct indicative of the reputation which the emperor would earn as a man of unrestrained impulses and irrational actions,²¹⁹ he dispatched an imperial *magistrianus*, whose name coincidentally was Sergius, to Rome with instructions to arrest bishop John of Portus, who had served as chief papal legate to the Sixth Ecumenical Council, as well as the papal counselor Boniface, and to bring them to Constantinople.²²⁰ The emperor may have intended these arrests to serve as a warning to the recalcitrant pope as to what might be in store for him if he persisted in his resistance, or as a possible effort to gain the support of two high-ranking and Greek-speaking ecclesiastics who might in turn persuade Pope Sergius to capitulate.²²¹ The pontiff, however, remained unmoved. Repeating what his grandfather Constans II had done to Pope Martin some forty years earlier,²²² Justinian II sent his *protospatharios* Zacharias, the notoriously ferocious chief of the imperial bodyguard, to Rome with orders to arrest the pope and bring him to Constantinople.²²³ But the imperial emissary was not to abduct Pope Sergius as effortlessly as the exarch along with the emperor's chamberlain had seized Pope Martin in 653. Confronted with military opposition from a combination of troops drawn from Ravenna and the duchy of Pentapolis, Zacharias ordered the city gates to be shut and the pope held prisoner in the Lateran *episcopium* where, fearful that he might lose his own life, Zacharias also took refuge. The soldiers, however, soon succeeded in entering the city from the northwest through St. Peter's Gate and making their way to the papal residence where, in response to the rumor that Sergius had been smuggled out and put on a ship bound for the East, they threatened to raze the papal palace if they were not immediately admitted. Terrified that he would be killed by the mob, Zacharias hid under the pontiff's bed while the pope, assuring the mortified *protospatharios* that he would be perfectly safe, defused the crisis with soothing words delivered from a seat which he fittingly assumed just below the portraits of SS. Peter and Paul in the nearby basilica named for Pope Theodore.[224] The angry populace was not, however, fully satisfied until it had expelled Zacharias from Rome with reproaches and insults for the injury he had tried to inflict on the Roman church and its pope.[225]

While the solidarity shown by certain segments of the exarchate's military forces with Pope Sergius and their support for his resistance to those canons of the Quinisext Council that were contrary to Roman *religious* practices and traditions reflect that under certain circumstances Italian loyalties "could be shifted from the imperial to the papal banner," we must not overstate the *political* implications of this incident or conclude that the issues that it raised transcended "exclusively spiritual ones."[226] Efforts to interpret the confrontation between Pope Sergius and Justinian II's *protospatharios* as evidence that the early Eastern popes "began the emancipation of central Italy from the Byzantines" and thereby sowed the first seeds of what would later become a politically independent papal republic fail entirely to account for how the pope handled the incident.[227] For rather than taking advantage of a perfect opportunity to promote papal political independence from Byzantium by exacerbating Roman outrage, Sergius calmed the acrimony, mollified the passions, and "with a suitable and gentle response" to the populace's wrath, allowed Justinian's envoy to depart with his dignity considerably diminished but his life intact.[228] A pontiff with a separatist political agenda would have acted otherwise.

Nor would it be correct to see the first traces of papal political independence from Byzantium in Sergius's refusal to confirm the canons of the Quinisext Council.[229] As the decidedly pro-Western *Liber Pontificalis* explicitly records, the pope rejected the Trullan decrees only because certain unspecified canons (*quaedam capitula*) were contrary to the ecclesiastical practices of the Roman church.[230] There is nothing to suggest that Sergius had any opposition to those canons that were consistent with Roman practices or clearly inapplicable to Rome. Nor can it be claimed that Sergius was hostile to the religious customs of the East and that he and the other "Greek popes" were determined to immunize the Roman church from eastern religious practices.[231] Indeed, as we shall see, it was Sergius himself who introduced the observance of four feast days of indubitably Eastern provenance into the liturgical calendar of the Roman church.[232]

As with the Eastern pontiffs who preceded and would follow him, it is certainly true that Sergius would not suffer the church of Rome to be infected with the East's propensity to lapse into theological speculation and hence depart from the "undefiled badges of the Fathers."[233] Neither, however, was he prepared to reject those Eastern customs and practices that were part of his oriental heritage and that did not clash with Rome but instead enriched it spiritually. Justinian II, Leontios, and Tiberios II Apsimaros would remain his lords and sovereigns to the end, but Peter, Paul, and Leo had sole claim upon him in matters of the faith.[234]

Notes

1. *Ordo XI* in Michel Andrieu, *Les Ordines Romani du Haut Moyen Age*, Vol. II. Les Textes (*Ordines I–XIII*) (Louvain, 1971), p. 434 ("And the acolyte says the creed in Greek chanting in these words: 'I believe in one God.'").

2. Franz Dölger, *Regesten der Kaiserurkunden des Oströmischen Reiches von 565–1453*, Vol. I (Repr. Hildesheim, 1976), No. 247, p. 30. The papal legates had left Rome for Constantinople sometime during the summer of 680. Luigi Magi, *La Sede Romana nella Corrispondenza degli Imperatori e Patriarchi Bizantini (VI–VII sec.)* (Louvain, 1972), p. 239.

3. *LP I*, pp. 350–55.

4. Dölger, id., Nos. 247, 248, and 249, p. 30. Constantine IV appears to have withdrawn the exarch's right to confirm the consecration of a pope and returned to the earlier custom of reserving that privilege to the emperor alone. *LP I*, p. 354–55. The text of the synodal acts that the legates brought back from Constantinople was in Greek. *LP I*, p. 359; Paul the Deacon, *Historia Langobardorum*, in *Monumenta Germaniae Historica, Scriptores Rerum Germanicarum* (Hannover, 1987), p. 213; Rudolf Riedinger, ed., *Concilium Universale Constantinopolitanum Tertium* (Berlin, 1992), pp. 832–67, 894–97.

5. Makarios, Stephen, and Polychronios were confined in various monasteries for as long as they insisted on adhering to their doctrinal error. Anastasios the priest and Leontios the deacon appear to have recanted, since the pope allowed them to receive communion on Epiphany. There is no record of what happened to the monks Anastasios and Epiphanios. *LP I*, 354, 359; Riedinger, id., p. 896. The eleventh-century *Chronicle* of the Monophysite bishop Michael the Syrian, which confirms that Makarios was sent to Rome "where he remained imprisoned until the end of his life," praises the Antiochian patriarch for having persisted in his efforts to convince the council that, based upon the writings of Cyril of Alexandria, "it is a heresy to confess two wills or operations in Christ." According to Michael the Syrian, the delegates from Rome led the battle to smear Makarios by portraying him as a partisan of the Monophysite Severus of Antioch. Id., p. 452.

6. Riedinger, id., pp. 896–97.

7. Riedinger, id., p. 897; Magi, id., p. 250; Jaroslav Pelikan, *The Spirit of Eastern Christendom (600–1700)* (Chicago, 1974), p. 154.

8. Magi, id., p. 247.

9. Although Leo II notified Constantine IV of his election to the Papacy sometime prior to December, 681, the papal legates carrying the imperial *iussio* authorizing his con-

secration did not reach Rome until July, 682. Jaffé, *Regesta Pontificum Romanorum*, Vol. I (Graz, 1956), No. 2116, p. 240. Leo was not enthroned as pope until August 17, 682, over a year and seven months following the death of his predecessor Pope Agatho on January 10, 681. *LP I*, pp. 355, 360.

10. Riedinger, id., pp. 866–85; *Mansi* XI, 725; *PL* 96: 399; Jaffé, id., No. 2118, p. 240 (places the date of Leo II's letter to Constantine IV sometime between September and December 682; Erich Caspar, *Geschichte des Papsttums*, Vol. 2 (Tübingen, 1933), pp. 612–13 (places the date of the letter in August, 682). The first session of the Sixth Ecumenical Council was convened by the emperor Constantine IV in the *Trullum*, or domed hall of the imperial palace, on November 7, 680 and the eighteenth and last session was held nearly a year later on September 16, 681. Karl Hefele, *A History of the Councils of the Church*, Vol. V, trans. William R. Clark (Edinburgh, 1896), pp. 149–50.

11. *LP I*, p. 359.

12. It has been suggested that Pope Leo II composed the homily to be delivered by a newly consecrated pope that is contained in the late-seventh-century papal formulary known as the *Liber Diurnus*. Theodor E. Von Sickel, ed., *Liber Diurnus Romanorum Pontificum*, LXXXV (Darmstadt, 1966), pp. 103–10; *LP I*, p. 361n1. This contention is based principally upon the homily's call for an end to dissension and discord (*finiantur, quaeso, simultates et discordiae*), which was erroneously believed to be the reason for the year-and-seven-month vacancy in the Papacy between Pope Agatho's death and Leo II's election. But the *Liber Pontificalis* makes no reference to a contested election following Pope Agatho's death in 681. Although contested elections preceded the enthronements of both popes Conon (686–687) and Sergius I (687–701), thereby making either of them the potential author of the homily, they too must be excluded, since Constantine IV, who convened the Sixth Ecumenical Council and who died in September, 685, before both of their pontificates, is referred to in the homily in terms indicating that he was still alive when it was written. Duchesne's hypothesis that Pope Benedict II (684–685) wrote the homily appears to be the most viable. *LP I*, p. 361n1. Unlike what might have been expected from Leo II, the homily's style is plain, unaffected, and almost prosaic, and therefore consistent with the *Liber Pontificalis's* description of Benedict II as "humble, mild, and compassionate to all." *LP I*, p. 363.

13. Leo's unprecedented and blistering excoriation of the former pontiff charged Honorius with having failed to "bring the apostolic doctrine of this apostolic church to light, [and] by his impious betrayal allowed the immaculate faith to be falsified and all those who have since died to be led into his error. Riedinger, *Concilium Universale Constantinopolitanum Tertium*, pp. 878–79; Hefele, id., pp. 184–85.

14. Riedinger, *Concilium*, pp. 866–81; Charles Diehl, *Études sur l'Administration Byzantine dans l'Exarchat de Ravenne (568–751)* (Repr. New York, 1959), p. 374.

15. Riedinger, id., pp. 882–85.

16. Bertolini's argument that Leo II's letter to Constantine IV, although admittedly a "ringing hymn of triumph to the emperor," nevertheless concealed a political ideology that reflected a developing separation from the East as well as a desire for autonomy on the part of the Papacy finds no more support in the plain words of the papal letter than does his contention that the pope praised Constantine's achievement only because he employed the imperial power to assert the authority of the Roman church over all of

Christendom, thereby recognizing that submission to the "supreme ministry of the pope" was a precondition to the attainment of "eternal bliss." Ottorino Bertolini, *Roma di Fronte a Bisanzio e ai Longobardi* (Bologna, 1941), pp. 390–91.

17. Theophanes, *Chronographia*, p. 496; Nikephoros, *Short History*, p. 87.

18. Theophanes, *Chronographia*, p. 496; Georgios Cedrenos, *Historiarum Compendium*, p. 766; Nikephoros, *Short History*, p. 87; Dölger, id., No. 239, p. 28.

19. Theophanes, *Chronographia*, p. 496; Georgios Cedrenos, *Historiarum Compendium*, pp. 766, 770; Georgios Monachos, *Chronicon*, pp. 728–29; Nikephoros, *Short History*, p. 87; Dölger, id., Nos. 240 and 241, p. 28.

20. Nikephoros, *Short History*, pp. 91–92; Georgios Cedrenos, *Historiarum Compendium*, p. 770; Leo Grammatikos, *Chronographia*, p. 162.

21. Judith Herrin, *The Formation of Christendom* (London, 1987), p. 275.

22. Herrin argues that patriarch Theodoros's efforts were prompted by his belief that Pope Vitalian had been what she describes as "insufficiently Monothelete." Id., p. 276

23. Riedinger, id., p. 9.

24. Riedinger, id., pp. 4–5. προτρεπτική ἐπιστολή; Hefele, Vol. 5, id., pp. 138–39; Erich Caspar, *Geschichte des Papsttums*, Vol. 2 (Tübingen, 1933), pp. 587–89; J. N. D. Kelly, *The Oxford Dictionary of Popes* (Oxford, 1986), p. 76. In order to achieve his purpose of fomenting discord, Theodoros appears to have intentionally misrepresented the reception accorded by Pope Vitalian to the synodikon of patriarch Thomas II, with whose doctrinal profession the pope appears to have concurred. *Mansi* XI, 576C. Eugenius I seems to have rejected patriarch Peter II's synodikon more from a desire to quell the disturbance that it caused in the church where he was celebrating Mass than from any doctrinal disagreement with it. *LP* I, p. 341.

25. Andreas N. Stratos, *Byzantium in the Seventh Century*, trans. Harry T. Hionides, Vol. IV (668–685) (Amsterdam, 1978), p. 117.

26. Magi, id., p.228.

27. Riedinger, id., pp. 6–7; *PG* 87: 1145. It is curious that the emperor would have addressed his letter to Pope Donos, who by August, 678, had already been dead for four months, instead of Pope Agatho, who was enthroned in either June or July, 678, and of whose consecration the exarch had surely notified the emperor by August. Stratos ascribes the anomaly to a scribal error. Id., p. 120.

28. *Mansi* XII, 967–68; Friedhelm Winkelmann, "Die Quellen zur Erforschung des monoenergetisch-monotheletischen Streites," *Klio* 69 (1987), No. 160: 548; Magi, id., p. 239.

29. Riedinger, id., pp. 3–11.

30. Riedinger, id., pp. 6–7. ἐκ δε τῶν τεσσάρων Βυζαντίων μοναστηρίων ἐξ ἑκάστου μοναστηρίου αββάδας τέσσαρας.

31. *PL* 87: 1161; *Mansi* XI, 234; Jaffé, id., No. 2109, p. 239. The Roman synod of 680, which Pope Agatho convened at the emperor's request in order that the churches in the West "might send fully instructed deputies to Constantinople," was held between March 25 and 27, 680, and attended by 125 bishops. Hefele, id., Vol. V, p. 141; *Mansi* XI, 286–315; *PL* 87: 1215–48; Jaffé, id., No. 2108, p. 238; Magi, id., p. 239. The *Synodicon Vetus* erroneously records that this synod "anathematized Sergius, Cyrus, Peter, Paul, and Pyrrhus" and that it sent its decree to that effect to the "Emperor Leo [an error for Con-

stantine IV], the son of Constantine Pogonatos and the father of Justinian Rhinotmetos." *The Synodicon Vetus*, trans. John Duffy and John Parker, *Corpus Fontium Historiae Byzantinae*, Vol. XV (Washington, D.C., 1979), No. 140, p. 117.

32. André Guillou, "L'École dans l'Italie Byzantine," in *Culture et Société en Italie Byzantine (VIe–IXe siècles)* (London, 1978), VI, 293.

33. Ado of Vienne, *Chronicon, PL* 123:114.

34. *Mansi* XI, 329; Guillou, id., VI, 292–93. The Sicilian abbot Theophanes attended and subscribed to all but the last four sessions of the council. Leontios of the monastery of St. Sabas attended and subscribed to only the final two sessions, while Georgios of the monastery of Renati and Conon and Stephanos from Domus Arsicia attended and subscribed to all eighteen sessions. Riedinger, id., pp. 18–19, 30–31, 38–39, 50–51, 164–65, 174–75, 184–85, 194–95, 266–67, 282–83, 408–9, 520–21, 576–77, 636–37, 672–73, 694–95, 710–11, 764–65.

35. John and Constantine, both Syrians, would later become respectively Pope John V (685–686) and Pope Constantine I (708–715). *LP* I, pp. 366, 389; Ado of Vienne, *Chronicon, PL* 123: 114.

36. William Dalrymple, *From the Holy Mountain* (London, 1998), p. 288.

37. Cyril of Scythopolis. *Life of Sabas* in *The Lives of the Monks of Palestine*, trans. R. M. Price (Kalamazoo, 1991), pp. 110–11; Joseph Patrich, *Sabas, Leader of Palestinian Monasticism* (Washington, D.C., 1995), pp. 61–63; Yizhar Hirschfeld, *The Judean Desert Monasteries in the Byzantine Period* (New Haven, 1992), pp. 24–25.

38. Derwas J. Chitty, *The Desert a City* (Crestwood, NY, 1995), pp. 111–12; 123ff.; PG 37/3: 2992, 3000.

39. Bernard Flusin, *Saint Anastase le Perse et l'histoire de la Palestine au début du VIIe siècle*, Vol. II, *Commentaire: Les Moines de Jérusalem et l'invasion Perse* (Paris, 1992), p. 187; PG 89: 1414ff.

40. Ferdinando Antonelli, "I Primi Monasteri di Monaci Orientali in Roma," *Rivista di Archeologia Cristiana* 5 (1928) 117; Whittow, id., p. 86.

41. Jean-Marie Sansterre, *Les moines grecs et orientaux à Rome aux époques byzantine et carolingienne (milieu du VIe s.–fin du IXe s.)*, I. Texte (Brussels, 1980), p. 29.

42. Stratos, id., Vol. III, p. 67ff.

43. Theophanes, *Chronographia*, p. 478.

44. Sansterre, id., p. 28; Italiani B. M. Margarucci, "Omaggio a San Saba," *Strenna dei Romanisti* 30 (1969), p. 286ff.

45. Sansterre, id., p. 22; Antonelli, id., p. 114; Guy Ferrari, *Early Roman Monasteries* (Vatican City, 1957) p. 283. Ferrari suggests that the monastery of St. Sabas may have been originally founded by Greek monks early in the seventh century, while Grégoire contends that it was established toward the end of the sixth century by acoemete, or "sleepless" monks, who perhaps came to Rome from Constantinople. Ferrari, id., p. 290; Réginald Grégoire, "Monaci e Monasteri in Roma nei secoli VI–VII," *Archivio della Società romana di storia patria* 104 (1981), p. 22. Arguments that the original inhabitants of St. Sabas were Latin monks, based primarily on John the Deacon's *Life* of Gregory the Great and a twelfth-century bull of Pope Lucius II giving the monastery to Cluny, have been persuasively discredited. Ferrari, id., p. 283ff; cf., Paul Kehr, *Regesta Pontificum Romanorum, Italia Pontificia*, Vol. I (Berlin, 1961), p. 118.

46. *LP* I, p. 331.

47. Sebastian Brock, "An Early Syriac Life of Maximus the Confessor," *Analecta Bollandiana* 91 (1973), 318–19. Since the Sabaites arrived in Rome in late 646 or early 647, some two years before Martin became pope, it is more likely that Theodore arranged for their accommodations. In an obvious effort to portray Maximos and his companions as abject heretics, this virulently pro-Monophysite text identifies him and his followers as Nestorians. Id. It also erroneously translates *cella novae* as "nine cells" rather than "new cells" or "new lavrae," which the new Sabaite monastery on the Aventine, in imitation of the practice followed in naming daughter houses in the East, eventually came to be called. *LP* I, pp. 471–72, 511.

48. *PG* 90:114; J. M. Garrigues, "Le martyre de saint Maxime le confesseur," *Revue Thomiste* 76 (1976): 411; *PG* 98: 616; Antonelli, id., p. 114; Ferrari, id., p. 287.

49. By the beginning of the ninth century, the monastery of St. Sabas was pre-eminent among the oriental monastic communities then flourishing in Rome. Alessandro Calandro, "I monasteri orientali piu antichi di Roma," *Lazio, ieri e oggi* 15 (1979), p. 237.

50. Riedinger, id., pp. 18–19. Conone et Stephano presbiteris et monachis monasterii quod cognominatur Domus Arsicia, positi similiter in antiqua Roma.

51. Riedinger, id., pp. 186–87 (the authorship of the *florilegium* was officially attributed to Pope Agatho himself); Caspar, id., p. 600n3; Sansterre, id., p. 120.

52. Sansterre, id., pp. 38–49; Ferrari, id., p. 117; Grégoire, id., p. 20. A bull issued by Pope Gregory VII on March 14, 1081, which confirmed ownership of a tract of land along the Via Collatina between the Via Praenestina and the Via Tiburtina described as the *Casale quod vocatur Casa Arsicia* in the monastery of St. Paul *fuori le mura*, raised the possibility among some scholars that the seventh-century Roman monastery of Domus Arsicia was somehow related to an eleventh-century foundation known as Casa Arsicia in the Campagna Romana near Tivoli. However, both Antonelli and Ferrari have concluded that this is a tenuous hypothesis. Antonelli, id., p. 119n1; Ferrari, id., p. 117. Kehr makes no reference to Domus Arsicia even among monasteries whose location he classifies as uncertain. Id., p. x.

53. Riedinger, id., pp. 18–19. Georgio presbitero et monacho monasterii Renati positi in antiqua Roma.

54. Antonelli, id., p. 107, 107nn1–2, 4; Sansterre, id., p. 12; Gregory the Great, *Dialogues*, IV, c. 12–13; *Reg.* XI, 15.

55. Antonelli, id., p. 107; Ferrari, id., pp. 277–78.

56. Riedinger, id., pp. 50–51; Antonelli, id., pp. 107–8; Ferrari, id., p. 278; Sansterre, id., p. 13; Kehr, id., p. 89; Grégoire, id., p. 19. By the tenth century, the monastery of Renati seems to have returned to the Latin rite and, although still known as Renati, had since the eighth century regained its dedication to Saint Lucia. *LP*, II, pp. 11, 24, 79; Ferrari, id., pp. 277, 279–80.

57. "De Locis Sanctis Martyrum Quae Sunt Foris Civitatis Romae," in Roberto Valentini and Giuseppe Zucchetti, eds., *Codice Topografico della Città di Roma*, Vol. II (Rome, 1942), p. 108–9; William of Malmesbury, *Gesta regum Anglorum* in Valentini and Zucchetti, id., p. 150; David Hugh Farmer, *The Oxford Dictionary of Saints*, 2d ed. (Oxford, 1987), p. 414; Bernard Flusin, "Commentaire: Les Moines de Jérusalem et l'invasion Perse," Vol. II, *Saint Anastase le Perse et l'histoire de la Palestine au début du VIIe siècle*

(Paris, 1992), p. 370; R. A. Lipsius, ed., *Acta Apostolorum Apocrypha*, Vol. I, "Acta Petri et Pauli," (Darmstadt, 1959), p. 214. απεκεφάλισαν δέ αυτον εις μάσσαν καλουμένην Άκουαι Σαλβίας πλησίον του δένδρου του στροβίλου.

58. Scholarly opinion has tended to contest Benedict's statement suggesting instead that while Narses may well have built a chapel dedicated to St. Paul at Aquas Salvias around the middle of the sixth century, the foundation of a monastery there did not occur until the seventh century. Giuseppe Zucchetti, ed., *Il Chronicon di Benedetto monaco di S. Andrea del Soratte*, Fonti per la Storia d'Italia (Rome, 1920), p. 32. Narses vero patricius fecit ecclesia cum monasterium Beati Pauli apostoli, qui dicitur ad aquas Salvias.

59. Antonelli, id., pp. 113–14; Kehr, id., p. 171, *Reg.* XIV, 14.

60. Sansterre, id., p. 17; Ferrari, id., p. 46.

61. Kehr, id., p. 171; Riedinger, ed., *Concilium Lateranense a. 649 celebratum*, id., pp. 50–51.

62. Bede, *Chronicon*, in Theodor Mommsen, ed., *MGH Auctores Antiquissimi*, Vol. XIII (Berlin, 1898), p. 311. For the life of St. Anastasios the Persian, see, *AA.SS.* Ian. III (1794) 35–54; Flusin, id., pp. 185–263. Eastern monks continued to reside at St. Anastasios even after it became a Cistercian community in 1140. As late as 1305, Armenian monks were in charge of the church of St. Paul. Alessandro Calandro, "I monasteri orientali piu antichi di Roma," *Lazio, ieri e oggi* 15 (1979), 236.

63. Nothing is known either of the foundation or the location of this monastery. Its name, however, suggests some early connection with the Roman family Boetii and possibly even with Boethius himself. Anton Michel, "Die griechischen Klostersiedlungen zu Rom bis zur Mitte des 11. Jahrhunderts," *Östkirchliche Studien* 1 (1952), 41; Ferrari, id., p. 49; Kehr, id., p. 155; Grégoire, id., p. 19.

64. *LP* I, 348; Philip Schaff and Henry Wace, eds., *A Select Library of the Christian Church. Nicene and Post-Nicene Fathers*, Vol. 14, "The Seven Ecumencial Councils," Second Series (Peabody, Mass., 1995), pp. 189–242; J. N. D. Kelly, *Early Christian Doctrines*, rev. ed. (San Francisco, 1978), pp. 310–17.

65. *LP* I, 348.

66. Valentini and Zucchetti, id., pp. 197–98; Ferrari, id., pp. 130–31.

67. *AA.SS.* Iun. I (1695) 211–19; *BHL* 2578–86; Albert Du Fourcq, *Étude sur les Gesta Martyrum Romains*, Vol. I (Repr. Paris, 1988), pp. 373–375; Sophronios Eustratiades, Άγιολόγιον της Όρθοδόξου Έκκλησίας (Athens, 1995), p. 135; see *Reg.* VII, 16, in which Pope Gregory the Great remarks on the decay and disrepair of the church at Formiae to bishop Agnellus of Terracina.

68. *PL* 123: 159–60. In Campania, Erasmi episcopi et martyris; Camobreco, "Il monastero di S. Erasmo sul Celio," *Archivio della R. Società di Patria* 28 (1905), 265.

69. *LP* I, 346. The expression *in quo concrevisse visus est sanctissimus vir [Adeodatus]* suggests that the pope's biographer was somewhat unsure of the information regarding the place where Adeodatus had been raised and qualified it by using the words "visus est" or "it seems." See Ferrari, id., p. 124.

70. For the text of the inscription, see *Scriptorum Veterum. Nova Collectio e Vaticanis Codicibus Edita*, ed. Angelo Mai (Rome, 1831), p. 236, and *LP* I, p. 347n6.

71. *LP* I, p. 346. By far the most striking aspect of the inscription at St. Erasmus is the recitation that the names of the benefices bestowed upon the monastery were inscribed

"under Theodosios the least of presbyters." Mai, id., p. 236. Ὑπό Θεοδοσίου ἐλάχιστου πρεσβυτέρου. Since the inscription conforms precisely with the *Liber Pontificalis's* recitation that Adeodatus sought out and assembled farmsteads for St. Erasmus, the Theodosios of the inscription is almost certainly Pope Adeodatus, who, when he was a presbyter or priest at some point before becoming pope, had arranged for the benefactions. *LP* I, p. 346. The fact that he is referred to in the inscription by the name Theodosios, which is the precise Greek equivalent of the Latin name Adeodatus ("having been given by God") is further proof not only that the presbyter and pope were one and the same person, but that St. Erasmus was indeed a Greek community and that Adeodatus, although ethnically a Roman, was closely attached to a Greek monastic *koinonia*, fluent in Greek, and had at one time been known by the Greek form of the Latin name he adopted as pope. Thus, although the succession of Eastern pontiffs who came to occupy the Apostolic See is generally held to have begun in 678 with the Greco-Sicilian Agatho, the pontificates both of Adeodatus and his immediate predecessor Vitalian show that, while both were ethnically Italians, they bore the unmistakable imprint of the Greek East.

72. AA.SS. Mai III (1695) 21.

73. J. H. Declerck, ed., *Diversorum Postchalcedonensium Auctorem Collectanea I*, Corpus Christianorum Series Graece, No. 19 (Turnhout, 1989), p. 278.

74. Around the time of his death shortly after Easter Sunday in 685, Pope Benedict II made a handsome distribution of thirty pounds of gold for various causes including Rome's *monasteria diaconia* or monastic diaconies. *LP* I, p. 364.

75. Ottorino Bertolini, "Per la storia delle diaconie romane nell'alto medio evo sino all fine del secolo VIII," *Archivio della Società romana di Storia patria* 70 (1947), pp. 1–145; Bryan Ward-Perkins, *From Classical Antiquity to the Middle Ages. Urban Public Building in Northern and Central Italy*, A.D. *300–850* (Oxford, 1984), pp. 57, 64, 138–39, 222, 238, 240, 253.

76. Douglas Burton-Christie, *The Word in the Desert* (Oxford, 1993), pp. 282–91; Bertolini, id., pp. 10–12, 91–95.

77. Benedicta Ward, trans., *The Sayings of the Desert Fathers* (Kalamazoo, 1975), pp. 12 (Abba Arsenius); 24 (Abba Ammonas); 107–8 (Abba John the Persian); 149 (Abba Motius); 170; 177 (Abba Poemen); Burton-Christie, id., pp. 287–90.

78. Tim Vivian, trans., "Life of Pambo," *Coptic Church Review* 20, No. 3 (1999): 94.

79. The word "diaconie" is derived from the Greek verb διακονέω, meaning "to serve" and the noun διακονία, meaning "service." See Basil the Great, *Logos Asketikos*, 9; PG 31:645A; Bertolini, id., pp. 9; 22–23.

80. H. Marrou, "L'origine orientale des diaconies romaines," *Mélanges d'archeologie et d'histoire* 57 (1940), 134.

81. PG 65: 184; 237; John Cassian, *Conlationes XXI*, 1,2; 1,3; 2,1; 8,1; 9,7, in Michael Petschenig, ed., *Iohannis Cassiani Conlationes XXIIII, Corpus Scriptorum Ecclesiasticorum Latinorum*, Vol. 13 (Vienna, 1886) pp. 574, 581, 584.

82. Marrou, id., 120ff. A papyrus from ca. 525–530 records that the famous Alexandrian monastery of the Metanoia shipped a quantity of wheat, under the care of two monks known as the "diaconites of the annona," to a diaconie that it had established at Antaiopolitae in the Thebaid. Id., pp. 129–31.

83. Marrou, id., pp. 126–27.

84. Robert C. Gregg, trans., *Athanasius, The Life of Antony and the Letter to Marcellinus* (New York, 1980), p. 29.

85. Marrou, id., p. 111.

86. J. W. Crowfoot, *Churches at Jerash. A preliminary report of the joint Yale-British School expedition to Jerash, 1928–1930*, British School of Archaelogy in Jerusalem, Supplementary Papers, 3 (London, 1931), pp. 13–16; Marrou, id., pp. 112–13. ευδοκία θεου συνέστη η διακονία εν μη[ν(ί) Ἀρτε]μισ(ίω) ινδ(ικτιωνος) ιγ' ετους χκζ.

87. Marrou, id., pp. 114–15.

88. Marrou, id., p. 111. διακονηταί σχολάζουσιν εν ταις διακονίαις. Diaconies also existed in late-sixth-century Constantinople. John of Ephesus refers to two such institutions that were operated in the capital by Monophysites and which, known as λούσματα or bathhouses, were devoted to washing the poor and infirm. It appears that the Chalcedonians succeeded in obtaining imperial permission to close one of the λούσματα and rout the Monophysites who were in charge of it to an island where, persisting in their mission, they continued to minister to the poor by washing them. John of Ephesus, *Third Part of the Ecclesiastical History* in E. W. Brooks, trans., *Corpus Scriptorum Christianorum Orientalium, Scriptores Syri*, Ser. 3a, Vol. III, chapters XV and XVI (Louvain, 1936), pp. 55ff; see also *Chronicle of Michael the Syrian*, id., p. 306. For additional details on the λούσμα, see Marrou, id., pp. 116–20.

89. Ward-Perkins, id., App. 2, pp. 239–40; *LP* I, p. 364; Bertolini, id., pp. 20, 63; Eugen Ewig, "The Papacy's Alienation from Byzantium and Rapprochement with the Franks," in Hubert Jedin and John Dolan, eds., *Handbook of Church History*, Vol. III (London, 1969), p. 4. For textual references in the *Liber Pontificalis* to almshouses and homes for the poor in Rome prior to the seventh century, see Kehr, id., pp. 155–56.

90. Richard Krautheimer, *Rome: Profile of a City, 312–1308* (Princeton, 1980), p. 77; J. Lestocquoy, "Administration de Rome et Diaconies du VIIe au IXe siècle," *Rivista di archeologia cristiana* 7 (1930), 270.

91. Bertolini, id., pp. 50, 90; Lestocquoy, id., p. 271; Marrou, id., p. 96. Rome's seventh-century monastic diaconies have no relationship with Pope Fabian's (236–250) division of the city into seven diaconal regions for purposes of ecclesiastical administration in the third century. *LP* I, p. 148; L. Duchesne, "Les titres presbyteraux et les diaconies," *Mélanges d'archaeologie et d'histoire* 7 (1887), pp. 218, 237. Without challenging the proposition that diaconies originated as an outreach of Eastern monastic communities, Sjöquist has contended that from about the time of Pope Gregory III (731–741) the term *monasterium diaconiae* or monastic diaconie fell into disuse in Rome and was replaced by the simple word *diaconia* or diaconie. K. Sjöquist, "Studi archeologici e topografici intorno alla Piazza del Collegio Romano, con un capitolo sulle pitture murali nei sotterranei della Chiesa di S. Maria in Via Lata," in *Skrifter utgivna av Svenska Institutet in Rom XII, Opuscula archaeologica* IV (Lund, 1946), p. 132. Bertolini challenged Sjöquist's contention, pointing out that the term *monasterium diaconiae* continued to be used during the time of Pope Stephen II (752–757) and in the second half of the eighth century. Id., p. 141n1.

92. Bertolini, id., p. 64.

93. Marrou, id., pp. 97–98; Duchesne, id., pp. 239–40.

94. Marrou, id., pp. 98–99; Duchesne, id., pp. 240, 242–43; Lestocquoy, id., p. 272, 294–95; A. Bartoli, "Gli horrea Agrippiniana e la diaconia di S. Teodoro," *Monumenti*

Antichi pubbl. per cura della R. Accad. Naz. dei Lincei 27 (1921), cols. 373–402.

95. Lestocquoy argues unconvincingly that Rome's diaconies were not originally ecclesiastical foundations and that monastics played only a minor role in their administration. Id., pp. 283–84. As Marrou points out, however, his efforts to prove that these institutions were not the outgrowth of monastic efforts to provide for the poor, but were instead the foundations and instruments of rich and pious laymen who directed their operations, "have not been crowned with success." Marrou, id., p. 99n3. Bertolini is similarly unconvinced by Lestocquoy's thesis. Id., pp. 9, 12, 127ff.

96. Bertolini, id., pp. 24–38. A *pater diaconiae* was deemed to be of such high rank that he was among those who, according to the *Ordo Romanus I*, received the pope upon his arrival at stational churches, which sponsored diaconies to celebrate mass on great feast days. *PL* 78:939; E. G. Cuthbert F. Atchley, *Ordo Romanus Primus* (London, 1905), p. 123 ("When the pontiff draws near to the church, the acolytes and defensors of that region whose duty it is that day, stand humbly awaiting him at the appointed spot . . . in like manner the patron of the diaconie (should that church happen to have one) . . . and they all bow their heads when he arrives.").

97. Bertolini, id., pp. 28, 57; Lestocquoy, id., pp. 277–80; T. S. Brown, *Gentlemen and Officers*, pp. 172–73; G. B. Giovenale, *La basilica di S. Maria in Cosmedin* (Rome, 1927).

98. Bertolini, id., pp. 39, 143. Haec tibi praeclara virgo caelestis regina sancta superexaltata et gloriosa domina mea Dei genetrix Maria de tua tibi offero dona ego humillimus servulus tuus Eustathius inmeritus dux . . . item et ego Georgius gloriosissimus offero . . . una cum germano mio Davit; Brown, id., p. 173.

99. Bertolini, id., pp. 41–42; Brown, id., p. 172; Lestocquoy, id., pp. 281–82.

100. Bertolini, id., p. 90.

101. Bertolini, id., pp. 62, 90; Kehr, id., pp. 115–16; Duchesne, id., p. 238–39; Chr. Huelsen, *Le chiese di Roma nel Medio Evo* (Florence, 1927) pp. 171–72. For the life of S. Theodoros, one of the most famous soldier-martyrs of the East and whose cult was based in Pontus, see, AA.SS. Feb. II (1658) 28–37 and Nov. IV (1925) 11–89. The St. Boniface, for whom this monastery and diaconie are named, was not a native Roman but rather an Easterner martyred at Tarsus whose body appears to have been brought to Rome for burial. Raymond Davis, trans., "The Life of Pope Leo III," in *The Lives of the Eighth-Century Popes* (Liverpool, 1992), p. 194n73; Enrica Follieri, "Santi Occidentali nell'Innografia Bizantina," in *Atti del Convegno Internazionale sul Tema: L'Oriente Cristiano nella Storia della Civiltà*, Accademia Nazionale dei Lincei (Rome, 1964), pp. 252–53; P. Franchi de'Cavalieri, "Dove fu scritta la leggenda di S. Bonifazio?," *Nuovo bulletino di Archeologia Cristiana* 6 (1900), pp. 205–34; L. Duchesne, "Notes sur la topographie de Rome au moyen-âge VII: les légendes chrétiennes de l'Aventin," *Mélanges de l'école française de Rome* 10 (1890), pp. 225–50; For the life of St. Alexios, see AA.SS. Iul. IV (1725) 238–70; see also A. Amiaud, *La Légende syriaque de S. Alexis l'Homme de Dieu* (Paris, 1889); F. M. Esteves Pereira, "Légende grecque d'Homme de Dieu Saint Alexis," *Analecta Bollandiana* 19 (1900), 241–53.

102. Bertolini, id., p. 90; For the lives of SS. Cosmas and Damian, martyred at Cyrrhus in Syria, see AA.SS. Sept. VII (1760), 430–77; *LP* I, p. 375 (for details on the restoration and embellishment of the church of SS. Cosmas and Damian by Pope Sergius I). SS. Sergius and Bacchus were martyred at Augustopolis near the river Euphrates upon the orders

of a certain duke Antiochus when, during the reign of the emperor Maximian (286–305), they refused to renounce Christianity. Ευστρατιάδου, id., p. 422.

103. Kehr, id., pp. 113–14; Duchesne, id., pp. 238–39; LP I, p. 385; Pietro Romanelli and Per Jonas Nordhagen, S. Maria Antiqua (Rome, 1964); Per Jonas Nordhagen, The Frescoes of John VII (A.D. 705–707) in S. Maria Antiqua in Rome (Rome, 1968); W. De Grueneisen et al., eds., Sainte Marie Antique (Rome, 1911); E. Tea, La basilica di S. Maria Antiqua (Milan, 1937).

104. For the life of St. George, see AA.SS. Apr. III (1675) 100–63; see also H. Delehaye, Les Légendes grecques des saints militaires (Brussels, 1909), pp. 45–76.

105. LP I, p. 362n13.

106. LP I, p. 434.

107. Federico di San Pietro, Memorie istoriche del sacro tempio o sia diaconia di San Giorgio in Velabro (Rome, 1791); Pierre Battifol, "Inscriptions Byzantines de Saint-Georges au Vélabre," Mélanges d'archaeologie et d'histoire 7 (1887), pp. 419–31.

108. LP I, pp. 367, 369, 369n1; Bertolini, id., p. 89; Lestocquoy, id., p. 272. The Thrakesion theme appears to have derived its name from the Thracian region of Asia Minor where Byzantine troops were deployed in order to colonize territories whose population had been depleted by the Persian invasions early in the seventh century. Pertusi contends that Pope Conon's father was actually named Thrakesios and that he took his name from the theme of which he was a member. Constantine VII Porphyrogenitos, De Thematibus, ed., Agostino Pertusi, Studi e Testi, No. 160 (Vatican City, 1952), pp. 67–68, 124.

109. Kehr, id., p. 78; Lestocquoy, id., p. 274.

110. Duchesne describes the Liber Diurnus as the "manuel quotidien" or daily manual of the papal chancery, and dates it between 685 and 754. L. Duchesne, "Liber Diurnus," in Dictionnaire d'Archéologie Chrétienne et de Liturgie, Vol. IX, Pt. 1 (Paris, 1930), pp. 243ff.

111. Theodor E. Von Sickel, ed., Liber Diurnus Romanorum Pontificum (Darmstadt, 1966), LXXI, p. 68; LXXXVIII, p. 116.

112. Id., XCV, pp. 123–25; XCVIII, pp. 129–31. The formula contained in the Privilegium Confirmations Loci, XCVIII, recites that the diaconie is founded "in honor of the holy Mother of God and ever-Virgin Mary," reflecting what we shall see to be a growing devotion to the cult of the Theotokos in Rome promoted by the eastern popes beginning in the latter part of the seventh century. See, infra, pp. 248, 256ff.

113. Bertolini, id., pp. 89–91, 140.

114. A. Kirchhoff, ed., Corpus inscriptionum Graecarum, IV, inscriptiones Christianae (Berlin, 1854), No. 9853; Salvatore Cosentino, Prosopografia dell'Italia Bizantina (493–804), Vol. I, Appendice III (Bologna, 1996), p. 507.

115. T. S. Brown, id., p. 141.

116. The Chronicle of Theophanes Confesssor, trans., Cyril Mango and Roger Scott (Oxford, 1997), p. 693.

117. In May 781, a primicerius named Mamalos formed part of an embassy dispatched by the empress Irene to Charlemagne with the intention of betrothing his daughter Erythro to the future emperor Constantine VI. The Chronicle of Theophanes Confessor, id., p. 628.

118. Cosentino, id., pp. 508–9.

119. Angelo Mai, Scriptores veterum nova collectio e vaticanis codicibus, Vol. V (Rome, 1825–1838), p. 215.

120. *LP* I, p. 333n3.

121. Pierre Batiffol, *L'abbaye de Rossano* (Paris, 1891), p. v.

122. Michel Andrieu, "Ordo XI," in *Les Ordines Romani du Haut Moyen Age*, Vol. II, Les Textes, (Ordines I–XIII) (Louvain, 1971), pp. 413, 433–35.

123. Andrieu, id., p. 394; Cosentino, id., p. 516. The *Codex Laudianus*, Oxfr. Bod. Gr. 35, may provide further evidence for the existence of a substantial Greek-speaking community in late-seventh-century Rome. Batiffol contends that the presence of what appear to be the opening lines of an edict by a certain Flavius Pancratius, *dux* of Sardinia Φλαυιος Πανκρατιος συν Θεο απο επαρχιον δουξ Σαρδινιας proves only that at some point in the seventh century the manuscript was in Sardinia and not necessarily that it was composed there. He goes on to show that it is more likely that the *Codex Laudianus* was composed in Rome and brought to England, perhaps by Theodore and Hadrian, where it is undisputed that Bede had access to it in the early 730s when he revised his commentary on the Book of Acts. If so, the manuscript's reference to "the servant [of God] Gregory the deacon, the servant [of God] Eupraxia the deaconess . . . [and] the servant [of God] John who is called Karamallas" (του δουλου σου Γρηγωριου διακονου . . . της δουλης σου Ευπραξιας διακονισις . . . του δουλου σου Ιωαννου το επικλιν Καραμαλλας) is proof of yet another family of Greek provenance living in late-seventh-century Rome, two of whose members, in this case, held positions in the church. Pierre Batiffol, "Libraires Byzantines à Rome," *Mélanges d'archeologie et d'histoire* 8 (1888), pp. 297–308. For a different interpretation, see Bernhard Bischoff and Michael Lapidge, eds., *Biblical Commentaries from the Canterbury School of Theodore and Hadrian* (Cambridge, 1994), p. 170n156.

124. L. Muratori, *Antiquitates italicae medii aevii* (Milan, 1738), II, 147 ("The masses stripped from the farthest parts of the world; the servants of servants are now your masters.").

125. *Mansi* XI, 179. The bishops of Eastern provenance included Phoberias Andreas of Ostia, Maurikios, Ioannes, Theodotios (or Theodsios) of Syracuse, Paulus Ioannes, Theodatos, and Georgios of Agrigento and Georgios of Catania, both Greco-Sicilians. The priests of Eastern origin consisted of four named Sissinios, three each by the names of Georgios, Petros, Theodoros, and Ioannes, and one each by the names of Theodosios, Paulos, Epiphanios, Theopistos, and Eutychios. Although deacons were in attendance, their individual names do not appear in the list of subscribers. Significantly, the synod is dated by reference to the regnal year of the emperor Constantine IV, thereby emphasizing the Papacy's indisputable identification with and acknowledgement of the authority of the government in Constantinople. Id.

126. P. A. B. Llewellyn, "The Names of the Roman Clergy, 401–1046," *Rivista di Storia della Chiesa in Italia* 35 (1981), p. 360.

127. Llewellyn, "The Names of the Roman Clergy, 401–1046," id., p. 357, 360–61.

128. *Mansi* XI, 179; P. A. B. Llewellyn, "Constans II and the Roman Church: A Possible Instance of Imperial Pressure," *Byzantion* 46 (1976): 121n7.

129. F. Halkin, ed., *Bibliotheca Hagiographica Graeca*, Vol. 2 (Brussels, 1957), p. 242; Eustratiades, id., pp. 426–27; Ωρολόγιον τό Μέγα, id., p. 265.

130. Theophanes, *Chronographia*, pp. 136–37; *Synodicon Vetus*, id., pp. 73–75. A patriarch Sissinios II also occupied the see of Constantinople between 996 and 998. George Ostrogorsky, *History of the Byzantine State*, rev. ed. (New Brunswick, NJ, 1969) p. 585.

131. F. Nau, trans. and ed., *Un Martyrologe et Douze Ménologes Syriaques*, *Patrologia Orientalis*, Vol. X, Fasc. 1 (Paris, 1912), pp. 66, 115.

132. Llewellyn, "Constans II and the Roman Church," id., p. 121; Llewellyn, "The Names of the Roman Clergy, 401–1046," id., p. 360.

133. In the East, both Georgios Cedrenos and Leo Grammatikos refer to a *dux* and patrician named Sissinius, who was elevated to the rank of *spatharios* under Justinian II. Georgios Cedrenos, *Historiarum Compendium*, p. 789; Leo Grammatikos, *Chronographia*, p. 175. Sissinius Pastillas of Perge in Pamphylia was among those who presided over the iconoclastic Council of Hieria in 753, Theophanes, *Chronographia*, p. 591; *Mansi* XIII, 400A; 416C, while nine bishops and two abbots (hegumens) named Sissinius attended the Seventh Ecumencial Council (Nicaea II), which restored the veneration of icons in 787. *Mansi* XIII, 151, 155, 723–25, 727. A patrician named Sissinius served as *strategos* of the Thrakesion theme under the emperor Constantine V. Theophanes, *Chronographia*, p. 575; Nikephoros, *Short History*, pp. 135, 137. The patrician Sissinius Rendakis was *strategos* of the Anatolikon theme during the reign of the emperor Leo III and may be identifiable with the Sissinius who, according to the Miracles of St. Demetrios, commanded the imperial fleet that delivered Thessalonika from the barbarians. Theophanes, *Chronographia*, p. 552–553n10; Nikephoros, *Short History*, p. 127; Paul Lemerle, ed., *Les Plus Anciens Recueils des Miracles de Saint Démétrius*, Vol. I, Le Texte, (Paris, 1979), pp. 225–27; id., Vol. II, Commentaire, p. 154ff.; Th. L. F. Tafel, *Historia Thessalonicae* (Tübingen, 1835), pp. 68–69. A Sissinius Triphyllos is identified as strategos of Thrace late in the eighth century under the empress Irene. Theophanes, *Chronographia*, p. 651. In Rome, the Syrian Pope Sissinius occupied the Papacy for only twenty days between January 15 and February 4, 708. *LP* I, p. 388. A nomenclator named Sissinius accompanied another Syrian pontiff, Constantine I (708–715), on his voyage to Constantinople, *LP* I, p. 389. Two priests named Sissinius attended a Roman synod held in 721 during the pontificate of Gregory II, *Mansi* XII, 265, and two bishops and a priest by that name subscribed to a Roman council held by yet another Syrian pope, Gregory III, in 732. *LP* I, p. 423n13. An undated funerary inscription of a Sissinius described only as *sacerdos* has been identified by De Rossi. G. B. de Rossi, *Inscriptiones Christianae Urbis Romae* II, id., p. 65n14.

134. Llewellyn, "Constans II and the Roman Church," id., p. 123. The Anatolikon theme consisted of the armies of the former *magister militum per orientem*, which had been based in Mesopotamia and Syria and where the cult of St. Georgios arose. Whittow, id., p. 120; *AA.SS.* Apr. III (1675) 100–63; H. Delehaye, *Les Légendes grecques des saints militaires* (Brussels, 1909), pp. 45–76; K. Krumbacher, "Der heilige Georg," *Abhandhungen der Kaiserlich bayerischen Akademie* xxv (no. 3) (1911); F. Cumont, "La plus ancienne Légende de saint George," *Revue d'Histoire des Religions* 114 (1936): 5–51.

135. Llewellyn, "Constans II and the Roman Church," id., pp. 121–22.

136. Llewellyn, "The Names of the Roman Clergy, 401–1046," id., pp. 366–67.

137. *Mansi* XI, 179; *LP* I, p. 350.

138. *LP* I, p. 362n13; Emil Donckel, *Außerrömische Heilige in Rom* (Luxembourg, 1938), pp. 49–51.

139. *LP* I, p. 389.

140. See, namely, *Mansi* XII, 265, for the subscriptions to the Roman synod of 721 convened by Pope Gregory II in which two bishops named Georgios participated; see also

P. B. Gams, *Series Episcoporum Ecclesiae Catholicae* (Repr. Graz, 1957) pp. 659ff, 943–56, for appearances of the name Georgios among Italian bishops in the seventh and eighth centuries.

141. Llewellyn, "The Names of the Roman Clergy, 401–1046," id., pp. 360–61, 367; Hélène Ahrweiler, *Byzance et la mer* (Paris, 1966), pp. 19–26; Whittow, id., pp. 125–26; cf. *LP* I, p. 368.

142. Llewellyn, id., p. 361. For appearances of the name Conon in classical Greece, see R. Pauly and G. Wissowa, *Realenzyklopädie der classischen Altertumswissenschaft*, XI (Stuttgart, 1894–1963), cols. 1318–41, and J. Kircher, *Prosopographia Attica*, Vol. I (Berlin, 1901), pp. 583–87. For classical Latin literary references to Conon, see Stephen Gero, *Byzantine Iconoclasm during the Reign of Leo III, Corpus Scriptorum Christianorum Orientalium*, Vol. 346 (Louvain, 1973), p. 17n15.

143. A bishop Conon of Apamea in Syria abandoned his episcopacy and, returning to what may have been a previous military career, led an insurrection in Isauria during the second year of the reign of the emperor Anastasios I. Theophanes, *Chronographia*, pp. 211, 212n8; J. Bidez and L. Parmentier, eds., *The Ecclesiastical History of Evagrius* (London, 1898), pp. 134–35; John Malalas, *Chronographia*, PG 97: 381; Gero, id., pp. 20–22. Two Conons, father and son, were martyred at Iconium during the reign of Aurelian. BHG, 360, Vol. I. A Conon *hortulanus* or gardener was martyred in Pamphylia during the persecutions under Decius, BHG 361, Vol. I, and the healer-saint Conon of Bidana enjoyed great popularity in Isauria where, after his death, his house was converted into a church and became a place of pilgrimage. BHG 2077, 2078, 2079, Vol. II; PG 117: 340BC; Gero, id., pp. 18, 19n31.

144. Theophanes, *Chronographia*, p. 279.

145. PG 91: 613; PG 87: 2853–54; BHG 2080 and 2080a, Vol. III; Cyril of Scythopolis, *The Lives of the Monks of Palestine*, trans. R. M. Price (Kalamazoo, 1991), pp. 205–6; A. Papadopoulos-Kerameus, Ἀνάλεκτα Ἱεροσολυμιτικῆς Σταχυλογίας IV (St. Petersburg, 1891–1898), 380.

146. Theophanes, *Chronographia*, p. 564. το βαπτιστικόν μου όνομα εν αληθεία Κόνον εστίν; Georgios Cedrenos, *Historiarum Compendium*, p. 788; Georgios Monachos, *Chronicon*, p. 735; Ioannes Zonaras, *Epitome Historiarum*, p. 339; Gero, id., p. 24.

147. Llewellyn, "The Names of the Roman Clergy, 401–1046," id., p. 367.

148. For evidence of the extensive use of the name Sergius in the East, see J.-B. Chabot, ed., *Synodicon orientale* in *Notices et extraits des manuscrits de la Bibliothèque Nationale* 37 (Paris, 1902), p. 662.

149. BHL 7598; 7599–7607, Vol. 2, ed., Society of Bollandists (Brussels, 1900–1901); Andrew Palmer, trans., "A Chronicle Composed in AD 640," in *The Seventh Century in the West-Syrian Chronicles* (Liverpool, 1993), p. 20.

150. H. Delehaye, *Les saints stylites* (Brussels, 1923), pp. 23–24.

151. Paul Peeters, "La passion arménienne de S. Serge le Stratélate," *Recherches d'histoire et de philologie orientales*, Vol. I, Subsidia hagiographica 27 (Brussels, 1951), pp. 25–36.

152. Palmer, "History of Dionysios of Tel-Mahre," id., p. 142n332.

153. Theophanes, *Chronographia*, p. 461.

154. J.-M. Fiey, "Les saints Serge de l'Iraq," *Analecta Bollandiana* 79 (1961), pp. 104–6.

155. Id., p. 109.

156. Id., p. 110. The Nestorians appear to have become disaffected with the name Sergius probably because the Jacobites started using Saints Sergius and Bacchus as the subjects of great encomia. Both Jacob of Saroug and Severus of Antioch wrote such eulogies. See BHO 1054 and 1055, ed. Society of Bollandists (Brussels, 1910).

157. Paul Peeters, Les Tréfonds Oriental de l'Hagiographie Byzantine (Brussels, 1950), pp. 68–69; cf., J. Sauvaget, "Les Ghassanides et Sergiopolis," Byzantion 14 (1939): 126–30; Llewellyn, "The Names of the Roman Clergy, 401–1046," id., p.361.

158. Names, however, are not always a true indicator of ethnicity. Patrick Amory, People and Identity in Ostrogothic Italy, 489–554 (Cambridge, 1997) pp. 32, 88, 90, 119–20. A certain Bonifatius, who was counselor to Pope Benedict II (684–685) and who translated an encomium on SS. Cyrus and John written by Sophronios of Jerusalem from Greek to Latin, may have been of Eastern provenance. PG 87: 3379–3422, 3423–3675. But it is equally possible that he was a Latin who knew Greek exceptionally well.

159. Charles Diehl, Études sur l'Administration Byzantine dans l'Exarchat de Ravenne (568–751) (Repr. New York, 1959), p. 278; Lynn T. White, Latin Monasticism in Norman Sicily (Cambridge, MA, 1938), p. 22; Jean-Marie Sansterre, Les moines grecs et orientaux à Rome aux époques byzantine et carolingienne, I. Texte (Brussels, 1980), p. 20; cf., Jules Gay, "Quelques Remarques sur les Papes Grecs et Syriens Avant la Querelle des Iconoclastes (678–715)," in Mélanges offerts à M. Gustave Schlumberger (Paris, 1924), pp. 53–54.

160. LP I, p. 363; Dölger, No. 252, id., p. 30.

161. LP I, p. 366.

162. Llewellyn's argument that the succession of Eastern pontiffs following the death of Pope Donus in 678 was the result of a process of "accelerated promotion" through the ecclesiastical grades instigated by pressure from the emperor Constans II is without any support in the sources. There is no evidence that Constans II had any contacts with Rome after his departure from the city for Sicily in 663, and certainly nothing to show that, during the five years he resided in Syracuse, the emperor pressured the Roman church to admit Easterners into the ranks of its clergy and thereafter insist that they be placed on a promotional "fast track." Indeed, the great respect and deference that the emperor displayed toward the church of Rome and its clergy during his sojourn in the city, see LP I, p. 343, makes Llewellyn's assertion that "Constans II dealt with the Roman Church as brusquely as he dealt with Roman buildings" particularly unpersuasive. P. A. B. Llewellyn, "Constans II and the Roman Church: A Possible Instance of Imperial Pressure," Byzantion 46 (1976): 120–26.

163. LP I, p. 368.

164. LP I, pp. 371–72.

165. LP I, p. 351.

166. LP I, p. 354.

167. LP I, p. 354; Dölger, No. 249, id., p. 30.

168. LP I, p. 360; Dölger, No. 251, id., p. 30. For archbishop Maurus's role in the extensive and acrimonious struggles of the church of Ravenna to obtain autocephaly, see Agnellus (qui et Andreas), Liber pontificalis ecclesiae Ravennatis, ed. O. Holder-Egger, MGH SSrL (Hanover, 1878) p. 349ff. Agnellus's high praise for archbishop Maurus contrasts sharply with the enmity he shows toward his successor, archbishop Theodore

(677–691), whom he accuses of secretly conspiring with both popes Agatho and Leo II to return the church of Ravenna to "the yoke of Roman servitude." Id.

169. *LP* I, p. 363; Dölger, No. 252, id., pp. 30–31; cf., Paul the Deacon, *Historia Langobardorum*, VI, 53, id., p. 237; Luigi Magi, *La Sede Romana nella Corrispondenza degli Imperatori e Patriarchi Bizantini (VI–VII sec.)*, Bibliothèque de la Revue d'Histoire Ecclésiastique, Fasc. 57 (Louvain, 1972), p. 258; see Ruth Macrides, "Dynastic marriages and political kinship," in Jonathan Shepard and Simon Franklin, eds., *Byzantine Diplomacy* (Aldershot, 1992), pp. 263–80.

170. *LP* I, p. 366; Dölger, No. 250, id., p. 30.

171. *LP* I, p. 369; Dölger, Nos. 255, 256, id., p. 31.

172. *LP* I, p. 336.

173. *LP* I, p. 343.

174. *PL* 87: 1146; Jaffé, No. 2104, id., p. 237.

175. Riedinger, *Concilium Universale Constantinopolitanum Tertium*, id., p. 53; see *Liber Diurnus I*, "Indiculus Epistolae Faciendae," id., p. 1.

176. Schaff and Wace, eds., "The Seven Ecumenical Councils," Volume 14, id., pp. 328–39; Riedinger, id., pp. 55–123; see also *Liber Diurnus LXXV*, id., pp. 103–10.

177. Riedinger, id., p. 883.

178. *LP* I, p. 363; Constance Head, *Justinian II of Byzantium* (Madison, 1972), p. 27.

179. *Mansi* XI, p. 22, *PL* 87: 1007; Jaffe, No. 2101, id., p. 237; *Liber Diurnus I*, id., p. 1. Domino piissimo et serenissimo victori ac triumphatori, filio, amatori dei et domini Iesu Christi.

180. Theophanes, *Chronographia*, pp. 504, 507; Georgios Monachos, *Chronicon*, p. 729; Leo Grammatikos, *Chronographia*, p. 162; Constance Head, *Justinian II of Byzantium* (Madison, 1972), p. 27; Franz Görres, "Justinian II und das römische Papsttum," *Byzantinische Zeitschrift* 17 (1908): 434. For a bibliography on the dispute over the exact date of Constantine IV's death, see Cyril Mango, trans., *Nikephoros, Patriarch of Constantinople, Short History* (Washington, D.C., 1990), pp. 196–97n37 and Cyril Mango and Roger Scott, trans., *The Chronicle of Theophanes Confessor* (Oxford, 1997), p. 505n1.

181. Magi, id., p. 261; Görres, id., p. 440.

182. *Mansi* XI, 737–38; *PL* 96: 425–28; Riedinger, *Concilium Universale Constantinopolitanum Tertium*, id., pp. 886–87; Hefele, *A History of the Councils of the Church*, Vol. V, pp. 219–21; Dölger, No. 254, id., p. 31; Caspar, *Geschichte des Papsttums*, Vol. 2, id., p. 632; Judith Herrin, *The Formation of Christendom* (London, 1987), pp. 281–82. Although the emperor's letter is addressed to "John pope of the city of Rome," the *Liber Pontificalis* records that it was received by Pope Conon. *LP* I, p. 368. Hic suscepit divalem iussionem domni Iustiniani principis. Since John V died on August 2, 686, and Conon was enthroned on October 21, 686, the imperial letter had probably been sent at a time when the emperor thought John V was still alive, but not received in Rome until Conon's accession.

183. Head, id., p. 63.

184. Theophanes attributes the spread of the Paulician heresy beginning in the middle of the eighth century to the fact that the emperor Constantine V had transferred a number of Syrians and Armenians, whom he had brought from Theodosioupolis and Melitene, westward to Thrace. Theophanes, *Chronographia*, p. 593. Georgios Monachos,

with undisguised hatred of the iconoclastic Constantine V, says that the emperor "was not a Christian, heaven forbid, but a Paulician." Georgios Moanchos, *Chronicon*, p. 751. Adoptionism, whose principal exponent, Paul of Samosata, was condemned at a synod held in Antioch in 268, maintained that "Christ was a 'mere man' (ψιλός ἄνθρωπος: hence 'psilanthropism') upon whom God's Spirit had descended." J. N. D. Kelly, *Early Christian Doctrines*, rev. ed. (San Francisco, 1978), pp. 115–19.

185. Petros Sikeliotes, *Historia Manichaeorum*, PG 104:1279–82; Nina G. Garsoïan, *The Paulician Heresy* (The Hague, 1967), pp. 231–33; Andreas N. Stratos, *Byzantium in the Seventh Century*, Vol. IV, id., pp. 131–34; Paul Lemerle, "L'Histoire des Pauliciens d'Asie Mineure," *Travaux et Mémoires* 5 (1973): 1–135; Head, id., pp. 63–64.

186. The *Synodicon Vetus* records that "Justinian, then, having taken over the Empire from his father, brought together a divine and sacred synod of two hundred and forty God-bearing bishops in Constantinople, which issued the canons left out by the holy Fifth and Sixth Councils and purged the Churches of all Greek, Jewish, and heretical teaching." Id., p. 121; Magi, id., p. 261; Head, id., p. 65; Herrin, id., p. 285; Görres, id., p. 440; V. Laurent, "L'oeuvre canonique du concile in Trullo (691–692), source primaire du droit de l'Église orientale," *Revue des études byzantines* 23 (1965): 7–41. Theophanes refers to the canons of the Quinisext Council as the "Summary Definitions of the Sixth [Ecumenical] Council." Theophanes, *Chronographia*, p. 504.

187. *LP* I, p. 372; *Mansi* XI, 989–90; Heinz Ohme, *Das Concilium Quinisextum und seine Bischofsliste* (Berlin, 1990), pp. 235–51. Bishop Basil of Gortyna had also attended the Sixth Ecumenical Council in 680/681 subscribing to its acts as "legate of the holy council of the Apostolic See of Old Rome." Riedinger, *Concilium Universale Constantinopolitanum Tertium*, p. 781.

188. Nicolae Dura, "The Ecumenicity of the Council in Trullo: Witnesses of the Canonical Tradition in East and West," in George Nedungatt and Michael Featherstone, eds., *The Council in Trullo Revisited* (Rome, 1995), pp. 229–62.

189. Nedungatt and Featherstone, id., Canons 33, 56, 24, and 62, pp. 110–11, 137–38, 99, 142–44.

190. See, namely, Canons 4, 5, 6, 12, 26, and 92 in Nedungatt and Featherstone, id., pp. 74–76, 82–83, 100–1, 171–72.

191. Id., Canons 22 and 23, pp. 97–98.

192. Id., Canons 9, 10, 24, 27, and 31, pp. 80–81, 99, 102, 106.

193. Id., Canons 50, 51, and 61, pp. 132–33, 140–42.

194. Id., Canons 62, 86, 91, 96, and 100, pp. 142–44, 166, 171, 177–78, 180–81.

195. Id., Canons 28, 32, and 57, pp. 102–3, 106–10, 138.

196. Id., Canons 83, 101, pp. 164, 181–83.

197. Id., Canons 19, 75, and 81, pp. 94–96, 156–57, 161–62.

198. Id., Canons 84 and 95, pp. 164–65, 174–77. The rubrics for admitting heretics may reflect Justinian II's particular disdain for the Paulicians, whom he had persecuted early in his reign. While heretics such as Arians, Macedonians, Novatians, and Apollinarians need only be chrismated upon producing their baptismal certificates, Paulicians had to be rebaptized. Id., p. 175.

199. Id., Canons 33 and 56.

200. Heinz Ohme, "Die sogennanten 'antirömischen Kanones' des Concilium Quini-

sextum (692)–Vereinheitlichung als Gefar für die Einheit der Kirche," in Nedungatt and Featherstone, id., pp. 307–21.

201. Canon 3, Nedungatt and Featherstone, id., p. 70.

202. Périclès-Pierre Joannou, *Pape, Concile et Patriarches dans la tradition canonique de l'église orientale jusqu'au IXe siècle*, Badia Greca di Grottaferrata, (Rome, 1962); *Mansi* XI, 987–88; *LP* I, p. 373; Hefele, Vol. V, id., p. 237. The text recites that the emperor signed his name "Flavius Justinianus" *per cinnabarium* (διὰ κινναβάρεως) or with the red ink traditionally used by Byzantine emperors to execute documents. Spaces were similarly left for the signatures of the bishops of Thessalonika, Heracleia in Sicily, Sardinia, Ravenna, and Corinth, all of whom were under Rome's ecclesiastical jurisdiction. *Mansi* XI, 989–90.

203. *LP* I, p. 371.

204. *LP* I, pp. 372–74.

205. The *Liber Pontificalis* records only that Pope Sergius rejected *quaedam capitula* or "certain chapters" of the Quinisext Council. *LP* I, p. 373.

206. Nedungatt and Featherstone, eds., id., Canon 1, pp. 55–64; *Liber Diurnus* LXXXIII and LXXXV, id., pp. 90–93, 103–10. The date of the *Liber Diurnus* has been placed somewhere between the death of Constantine IV in September, 685, and July, 754, when Pepin became patrician of Rome. See "Liber Diurnus" in *Dictionnaire d'Archéologie Chrétienne et de Liturgie*, Vol. IX, Pt. 1 (Paris, 1930), p. 249.

207. Nedungatt and Featherstone, id., p. 114; Head, id., pp. 75–76; Herrin, id., p. 286.

208. Nedungatt and Featherstone, id., Canon 2, pp. 64–69; Herrin, id., p. 286. For the Greek text of the Apostolic Canons, see Lauchert, id., pp. 1–13. The eighty-five Apostolic Canons approved by the Quinisext Council are found in the eighth book of the *Apostolic Constitutions*, a collection of eight books containing ecclesiastical directives alleged to have been composed by the Twelve Apostles and transmitted by them to Pope Clement I. In fact, the *Apostolic Constitutions* dates from between 375 and 400 and is believed to have been composed by an Arian. The first six books of the *Apostolic Constitutions* are based on a third-century Syrian work known as the *Didascalia Apostolorum*, while the seventh book contains material based on the *Didache*, a text written in the second century in either Syria or Egypt. The principal source of the eighth book, which contains the Apostolic Canons, is the *Apostolic Tradition*, a work produced sometime around the beginning of the third century by Hippolytus of Rome. R. Hugh Connolly, *Didascalia Apostolorum* (Oxford, 1929), p. xx; David A. Fiensy, *Prayers Alleged to be Jewish: An Examination of the Constitutiones Apostolorum* (Chico, CA, 1985), pp. 19–25; Adolf Harnack, *Sources of the Apostolic Canons*, trans. Leonard A. Wheatley (London, 1895). Since the Quinisext Council concluded that only the eighty-five canons contained in the eighth book of the *Apostolic Constitutions* had survived in uncorrupted form; they alone were incorporated into the corpus of canon law. Alivisatos, id., pp. 581–585.

209. Lauchert, id., pp. 107–8. τῷ ἀρχαίῳ εξακολουθούντες κανόνι τῆς ἀποστολικῆς ἀκριβείας καί τάξεως; Hefele, Vol. V, id., p. 226.

210. Id., p. 124. παρὰ παραδοθείσαν ἐκκλησιαστικήν ἀκολουθίαν; Hefele, Vol. V., id., p. 231.

211. Id., pp. 102–3; Hefele, Vol. V, id., pp. 224–25.

212. Id., p. 128; Hefele, Vol. V, id., p. 232; see Schaff and Wace, eds., *"Reply to Faustus the Manichaean,"* Book XXXII, Chapter 13, in Volume 4, *"Augustine: The Writings Against the Manichaeans and Against the Donatists,* id., p. 336.

213. Lauchert, id., p. 132; Hefele, Vol. V, id., p. 234n2.

214. James D. Breckenridge, *The Numismatic Iconography of Justinian II* (New York, 1959), pp. 83–86.

215. *LP* I, p. 371; Kehr, id., pp. 61–62.

216. *LP* I, pp. 372–73.

217. Id., pp. 376, 381n42; Palachkovsky, id., pp. 38–39.

218. *LP* I, p. 375; H. Grisar, "Die alte Peterskirche zu Rom und ihre frühesten Ansichten," *Römische Quartalschrift* 9 (1895): 264ff.

219. A Byzantine chronicle describes Justinian II as "most savage in temperament and manners" and "of uncontainable rage." Peter Schreiner, ed., "Chronik 14," in *Die Byzantinischen Kleinchroniken* (Vienna, 1975), p. 135. Georgios Cedrenos calls him "a man of unrestrained impulses and rash thoughtlessness in all things." *Historiarum Compendium,* p. 771. The Monophysite chronicler Michael the Syrian claims that Justinian II bore the eponym "the Arrogant." *Chronicle of Michael the Syrian,* id., p. 473.

220. *LP* I, p. 373. A high-ranking papal official with an impeccable command of both Greek and Latin, as appears from his superb translation of Sophronios of Jerusalem's *Miracula SS. Cyri et Johanni,* Boniface's long and distinguished career as archdeacon of the Roman church and papal counselor began around 654 and spanned the pontificates of thirteen popes from Martin I to Constantine I. Walter Berschin, "Bonifatius Consiliarius. Ein römischer Übersetzer in der byzantinischen Epoche des Papsttums," in Albert Lehner and Walter Berschin, eds., *Lateinische Kultur im VIII. Jahrhundert* (St. Ottilien, 1989), pp. 25–40. On instructions from Pope Benedict II, Boniface debated for forty consecutive days with Makarios, the former patriarch of Antioch who had been exiled to Rome by the Sixth Ecumenical Council, in a futile attempt to convince the recalcitrant Antiochene of the errors of Monothelitism. *PL* 129: 227. His piety and erudition impressed Bishop Wilfrid, who first met him while visiting Rome in 654, and from whom, according to Bede, the English prelate "learned each of the Gospels in turn and the correct method of calculating Easter, while through this tutor he came to understand many other things relating to church order about which he had known nothing in his own country." Bede, *A History of the English Church and People,* trans. Leo Sherley-Price (Baltimore, 1965), p. 302.

221. Herrin, id., p. 287.

222. *LP* I, p. 338.

223. *LP* I, p. 373; Ado of Vienne, *Chronicon, PL* 123:116; Bede, *De Sex Huius Seculi Aetatibus,* id., p. 200; Paul the Deacon, *Historia Langobardorum,* id., p. 216; Dölger, No. 259, id., p. 32.

224. *LP* I, pp. 373–74; Görres, id., p. 450.

225. *LP* I, p. 374; Bede, *De Sex Huius Seculi Aetatibus,* id., p. 200; Paul the Deacon, *Historia Langobardorum,* id., p. 216; Hefele, Vol. V, id., p. 239; Head, id., pp. 77–79; Herrin, id., p. 287.

226. See Thomas F. X. Noble, *The Republic of St. Peter* (Philadelphia, 1984), pp. 17–18.

227. Id., p. 188.

228. *LP* I, p. 374.

229. Noble, id., p. 188.

230. *LP* I, p. 373, 385. *in quibus diversa capitula Romanae ecclesiae contraria scripta inerant.*

231. Noble, id., pp. 187–88.

232. *LP* I, p. 376; see, infra, pp. 256; 261ff.

233. The inscription on the tomb of Pope Agatho praises "the highest priest Agatho [who] holds firm the covenants of the Apostolic See. There is piety! There is the ancient Faith! The undefiled badges of the Fathers remain, nourisher, through your efforts." G. B. de Rossi, *Inscriptiones Christianae Urbis Romae Septimo Seculo Antiquiores*, Vol. 2, Pt. 1 (Rome, 1888), pp. 52–53; *LP* I, p. 358. The inscription on the tomb of Pope John V similarly extols his efforts against Monothelitism at the Sixth Ecumenical Council: "With the titles of the faith, keeping such vigilance, you united the minds so that the inimical wolf mixing in might not seize the sheep, or the more powerful crush those below." De Rossi, id., pp. 129–130, 207.

234. *LP* I, pp. 374–75. Pope Sergius I died in 701. *LP* I, p. 376. Justinian II was deposed and exiled to the Chersonese in 695. He was succeeded by Leontios, who reigned until 698. Tiberios II, also known as Apsimaros, then became emperor and reigned until 705 when Justinian II returned to the throne. Theophanes, *Chronographia*, pp. 515–23; Georgios Cedrenos, *Historiarum Compendium*, pp. 776–80; Georgios Monachos, *Chronicon*, pp. 731–33; Leo Grammatikos, *Chronographia*, pp. 165–68.

CHAPTER VII

~

Ο Αμνός Του Θεού, Ο Αίρων Τήν Αμαρτίαν Του Κόσμου, Ελέησον Ημάς[1]

Eastern Influences on Rome and the Papacy from Sergius I to Zacharias, 701–752

When Wilfrid of York first visited Rome as a young and impressionable monk in 654, he formed a fast friendship with an influential and erudite Greek cleric named Boniface, who was both archdeacon of the church of Rome, and thus one of the three ecclesiastical officials who directed the affairs of the Apostolic See during a vacancy in the Papacy, as well as a counselor and confidante of the venerable Eugenius I, who had just been elected pontiff in place of the deposed and exiled Pope Martin.[2] Wilfrid immediately fell under the spell of this brilliant Easterner under whose tutelage the twenty-year-old English monastic "learned each of the Gospels in turn and the correct method of calculating Easter, while through this tutor he came to understand many other things relating to church order about which he had known nothing in his own country."[3] As a distinguished theologian, skilled diplomat, and accomplished translator, Boniface was typical of the growing number of Easterners who, from the middle of the seventh century onward, entered the ranks of the Roman church and rose to positions of power and authority in the papal service.[4] In the meantime, while Boniface and other Easterners like him were making their ecclesiastical careers in the church of Rome, Wilfrid had returned to England, been ordained a priest, and eventually consecrated bishop of Northumbria. Expelled from his see during the reign of King Egfrid, Wilfrid, now forty-four years old, returned to Rome in 678 to appeal his expulsion as bishop of York.[5] Upon his arrival, he discovered that one of those many upwardly mobile Easterners who, like his mentor Boniface had risen in the echelons of the Roman church, was now the pope. On June 27, 678, a former Greco-Sicilian monk named Agatho had been elected pontiff, inaugurating what would be a nearly unbroken succession of popes of Eastern provenance for the next three-quarters of a century.[6] Pope Agatho and a synod of bishops unanimously acquitted Wilfrid of all charges that had been brought against him, whereupon he was declared "worthy of his bishopric" and restored to the church of York.[7]

But Wilfrid's restoration was not permanent. In 704, now seventy years old, he found himself again expelled from his see and once more on his way to Rome to lay his case "before the apostolic Pope John [VI]," a Greek who had been consecrated pontiff some three years earlier.[8] The papal court before which Wilfrid was to plead his cause had undergone a marked transformation from that which he had encountered as a youth in 654 and even as a bishop some twenty-five years earlier. The extent of that transformation was made abundantly clear when at one point during the synod convened to consider Wilfrid's case, John VI and the assembled bishops began to chatter animatedly among themselves in Greek, exchanging furtive smiles, and giving the bewildered Englishman and his entourage the distinct impression that they had lapsed into a foreign language so that they might conceal what they were saying.[9] But bishop Wilfrid need not have been alarmed. Exonerated once again, he was eventually restored to his see, which he held in peace until his death in 709.[10] As for Pope John VI and his episcopal colleagues, the ease with which they lapsed into their native tongue was perhaps more an indication of the extent to which Easterners had risen in the ranks of the church of Rome by the beginning of the eighth century rather than a conscious effort by the pope and his confidantes to mask their thoughts from those who spoke no Greek. For as the new century dawned, Eastern clerics like the papal counselor Boniface, who although advanced in years still appeared as a witness on Wilfrid's behalf in 704, continued to fill prominent positions in the Roman church and throughout Italy in ever increasing numbers.[11]

Between 701 and 750 ethnic Greeks in the ranks of the Roman clergy outnumbered Latins by nearly three and a half to one.[12] Eleven of the thirteen clerics who accompanied the Syrian Pope Constantine I on his journey to Constantinople in 710 were Easterners. Only a deacon, the future Pope Gregory II, and a subdeacon named Julian were Latins, while the two bishops, three priests, and all the high-ranking officials of the papal chancery and household were either Greeks or Syrians.[13] In 721, Pope Gregory II convened a synod of the Roman church to deal with the issue of illicit conjugal relations. Ten of the twenty-two subscribing bishops, all fourteen of the priests, and three of the four deacons, including the archdeacon, were Easterners, thereby reflecting that fully two-thirds of those in attendance were from families of oriental provenance.[14] A fragment of an inscription discovered in the Vatican crypt contains a portion of a statement made by the Syrian Pope Gregory III in the presence of a group of clerics in 731 during an anti-iconoclastic synod that the pope had convened in Rome shortly after he was consecrated on March 18, 731. The nine ecclesiastics whose names appear after the pope's expression of unworthiness and gratitude for his many blessings, including elevation to the Papacy, and who we would probably be safe in concluding consisted of those within his inner circle, are all of Eastern provenance.[15]

At a synod of the Roman church held on April 12, 732, Pope Gregory III erected three stone tablets in an oratory that he had built within St. Peter's upon which he inscribed the acts of the council as well as the *typika*, or rubrics, which he prescribed were to be followed on the feast days of the various apostles, martyrs, confessors, and other holy persons whose relics he enclosed within the chapel.[16] Two of the tablets contain the names of the thirty-one subscribing clerics who attended the council. In addition to the Syrian pope, all but one of the seven bishops were of Eastern origin. Similarly, eighteen of the nineteen priests had names reflecting an oriental provenance. All five deacons, including the future Pope Zacharias, were unquestionably Syrians or Greeks.[17] Thus, more than ninety percent of the clerics who attended Pope Gregory III's Roman synod at the beginning of the third decade of the eighth century were ethnic Easterners.

Easterners continued to flood into the highest echelons of the church of Rome as the eighth century progressed. Although the percentage of oriental ecclesiastics attending Pope Zacharias's Roman council in 743, convened to legislate on matters of clerical conduct and issues related to marriage, was lower than the ninety percent who had participated in Gregory III's synod in 732, still almost half of the attending clergy were undoubtedly of Eastern origin.[18] When Zacharias convened a second Roman synod in October, 745, to inquire into the activities of the heretics Adalbert and Clement, over ninety-five percent of those who attended were ethnic Easterners.[19] The subscription lists from Roman synods held during the first four decades of the eighth century reflect that Easterners continued to enter the highest levels of the Roman church in ever burgeoning numbers during this period, thereby continuing a trend that had been going on since the middle of the seventh century.

Nowhere is the effect of this persistently expanding influx of orientals into Roman society more evident than in the continued elevation of Easterners to the papal throne. Following the death of the Syrian Pope Sergius I in 701, the Greek John VI was elected pontiff after a vacancy in the Papacy of less than seven weeks.[20] When John VI died in 705, he was succeeded in less than two months by Pope John VII, who was also of Greek ancestry.[21] After a pontificate of slightly over two and a half years, the Papacy remained vacant for only three months until John VII was succeeded by a grievously ill and crippled Syrian named Sissinius, who occupied the Apostolic See for a mere twenty days.[22] Again, in less than two months, Sissinius was succeeded without incident by another Syrian, Constantine I, who ascended the papal throne in March, 708, and died seven years later in April, 715.[23] Only forty days elapsed from the day Pope Constantine died until the Roman electors chose Gregory II to succeed him, thereby elevating to the Papacy the first non-Eastern pontiff since Pope Agatho had been elected nearly forty years earlier.[24] But when Gregory II died after a long pontificate of over fifteen years, he was succeeded in slightly over a month by the Syrian Gregory III, whose ten-year reign was followed, after an interval of only eight days, by the election of the Greek Pope Zacharias, who occupied the Apostolic See for over a decade until his death in 752.[25]

The virtually uninterrupted succession of Eastern pontiffs beginning with Pope Agatho in 678 and ending with Pope Zacharias in 752 can only be explained by the concomitant and continuously increasing influx of orientals into both the church of Rome and Roman lay society that we have seen. It is no mere coincidence that the emperor Constantine IV's decision to revert to the "ancient custom" of allowing the Roman pope to be elected by the general population of the city immediately resulted in the election of the Syrian Pope John V in July, 685, to succeed the Roman-born Benedict II after a vacancy in the Papacy of only six weeks.[26] Nor was it unexpected that for the same reason John V was succeeded by the Greco-Sicilian Pope Conon in October, 686, and he, in turn, by the Syrian-born Sergius I in December, 687.[27] From 678 until 752, men of Greco-Sicilian, Syrian, and Greek heritage succeeded to the Papacy not because the native Latin population of Rome condescended to engage in "exemplary self-abnegation in the interest of an alien minority,"[28] but instead because Easterners were in the lay and clerical majority and the return to the "ancient custom" of electing the Roman pontiff naturally tended to favor candidates chosen from their ranks.[29]

Nor were Latin sensibilities entirely unoffended by the succession of pontiffs from the East. Pope Agatho's Roman biographer chafed at the pontiff's departure from custom when, assuming the position of *arcarius* or treasurer of the Roman church, he personally dealt with the ecclesiastical coffers, "issuing receipts by his own hand through a nomenclator."[30] Pope Conon was also criticized for acting against custom and without clerical consent when, "incited by malicious men and in repugnance to men of the church," he appointed a certain Constantine, doubtless an Easterner, to be rector of the papal patrimony in Sicily.[31] When Pope John VII simply sent the canons of the Quinisext Council back to Constantinople "without any emendations at all," it was intimated that his death shortly thereafter was an appropriate reproof for the unpardonable "human weakness" he had shown in failing to reject them outright.[32]

But the few instances of Latin umbrage toward the pontiffs from the East was far outweighed by praise for their devotion to the Roman church and people. Sergius was celebrated for boldly asserting that he would sooner die than assent to the anti-Roman practices prescribed by certain of the Trullan canons.[33] The "whole assembly of the Roman city" united behind their pontiff when in 712 Pope Constantine courageously rejected the emperor Philippikos's mandate reviving Monothelitism, refusing to receive the imperial portrait as well as gold coins with his image or to commemorate him in the mass.[34] As a result, Philippikos was brutally reviled in Rome where opposition to him became particularly acrimonious. In the miracles of St. Anastasios the Persian, which were written in Rome sometime between the fall of 713 and the late summer of 714, for example, a demon, who has taken possession of the young daughter of a Syrian bishop, boasts that it was through him that Philippikos received the imperial chrism, "because he was my friend."[35] Twenty years later the *Liber Pontificalis* once more extolled an Eastern pontiff's determination to uphold "the ancient custom of the apostolic church" when it praised Pope Gregory III for convening a synod that condemned with undiluted vigor the edict against icons that had been issued by the emperor Leo III in 726, and declared those who would destroy sacred images to be severed "from the body and blood of our Lord Jesus Christ and from the unity and fabric of the entire church."[36] Continuing a vigilance for the safety of Rome and its inhabitants that dated from the time of Gregory the Great, Pope John VI was lauded for single-handedly convincing the Lombard duke Gisulf of Benevento, who had devastated the neighboring Campanian countryside and constructed an encampment within sight of the city walls of Rome, to withdraw his forces and return home.[37] Nor did John VII's success with the Lombards remain unnoticed, for during his pontificate King Aripert was convinced to return the Cottian Alps to their rightful place among the patrimonies of the Apostolic See.[38] Even Pope Sissinius, though he occupied the Papacy a mere three weeks, showed concern for the protection of the city by ordering that lime be burned in order to restore portions of its walls.[39] As for Pope Zacharias, whose spectacular achievements against the Lombards had held them largely at bay and permitted the citizens of Rome to live their lives "in great security and joy," his papal biographer rhapsodized that for the safety of the Roman people the pontiff would doubtless have laid down his own life.[40]

The same solicitude which the Eastern popes displayed for the doctrines and customs of the Roman church and for the protection of the city's population from external danger extended to the restoration and embellishment of Rome's sacred buildings. Pope Sergius built an ambon (pulpit) and a canopy, while at the same time casting sheets of lead to strengthen the cupola of the basilica of Saints Cosmas and Damian, which had been originally built in the early sixth century along the Via Sacra by Pope Felix IV and dedicated to the famous pair of Eastern saints celebrated for practicing the art of healing without accepting fees.[41] He similarly restored the roofs of the basilicas dedicated to Saints Euphemia, Aurea, and Susanna (where he had served as a priest), while completely reconstructing the church of St. Paul, which had fallen into an abysmal state of disrepair.[42] John VI constructed a new ambon in the basilica of St. Andrew the Apostle, provided a new altar cloth for St. Mark's, and suspended diaphanous white veils between the columns on either side of the altar in St. Paul's.[43] John VII restored portions of the deteriorating basilica of St. Eugenia, while lavishly decorating the presbytery and adjacent areas of St. Maria Antiqua with frescoes whose style was borrowed directly from Constantinople and which reflected his passion for the cult of the Theotokos then flourishing in Rome.[44] Continuing John VII's devotion to the Mother of God, Gregory III adorned the oratory of

St. Maria *ad praesepe* with a golden image of the Theotokos embracing Christ, restored the decaying roof of the Pantheon, which in the time of Pope Boniface IV had been converted from a pagan temple and dedicated to the Virgin Mary and all the martyrs, and substantially expanded a small oratory within the basilica of St. Maria in Aquiro.[45] Churches dedicated to lesser-known saints received equal consideration. A glistening silver canopy was installed at St. Chrysogonus to complement an array of crowns, chandeliers, patens, chalices, veils, and altar cloths, which the Syrian pontiff bestowed on this church dedicated to a fourth-century martyr beheaded at Aquileia.[46] A silver crown with six gamboling dolphins was suspended over a new altar, which the pope built within the church of St. Genesius of Arles on the Via Tiburtina, while the roofs of the basilica of the early Roman martyrs Processus and Martinian on the Via Aurelia and the church of the pope and martyr Callistus were freshly reconstructed.[47]

Not unexpectedly, St. Peter's basilica received particular attention from the Eastern popes. Pope Sergius ornamented it with three gold images of Peter, a ponderous censer ceaselessly emitting clouds of fragrant incense, a silver canopy with silver lights, a golden paten cinctured with pearls and inlaid with a cross of hyacinthine blue, while the altar was encircled with pellucid veils of white and scarlet cloth.[48] John VII embellished the basilica with an oratory dedicated to the Theotokos whose walls he decorated with mosaics, adorning it with gold and silver and setting up images of the fathers of the church along both sides.[49] Gregory III also built an oratory within St. Peter's endowing it with relics of various apostles, saints, martyrs, and confessors, and richly decorating it with golden bowls and canisters, hanging crosses, gilded vessels, crowns bedizened with precious stones, patens, chalices, and silver basins, and, on the icon of the Theotokos, a gold jewelled diadem and matching necklace.[50] Pope Zacharias enriched it with a gold-wrought altar cloth depicting the Nativity of Christ as well as with four veils of purple silk and a silver crown with sculpted dolphins weighing over one hundred pounds.[51]

The riches that the oriental pontiffs lavished on Rome's churches coincided with the continued development of a similarly opulent ecclesiastical ceremonial. Beginning with the pontificate of Leo II (682–683) and extending without interruption through the time of Zacharias (741–752), the Roman church experienced a liturgical byzantinization led by the Papacy which suffused the church of Rome, hitherto reluctant to embellish its rites with innovations and "purely decorative additions,"[52] with a splendor and an aura reminiscent of the Orient and redolent of the spectacles of the imperial court in Constantinople. The Greek antiphons that Pope Sergius would intone in 695 were worlds apart from the Latin chants familiar to Pope Gregory exactly a hundred years before.[53] With the advent of the pontiffs from the East, the drama of oriental ritual and rite would add a quality to Rome's staid ceremonial that it had never known and never would forget.

∽

Between 360 and 382 Latin gradually replaced Greek as the official liturgical language of the Roman church signaling, at the same time, the end of nearly three centuries during which ethnic Easterners, particularly Greeks, had occupied the Apostolic See.[54] With the election of the Greco-Sicilian Pope Agatho in 678, the use of Greek began to reappear with increasing frequency in the liturgical rites of the church of Rome as Easterners continued their influx into both Roman lay society as well as high and influential positions within the Roman church. It should come as no surprise that the rebirth of Greek as a liturgical language in Rome coincided with a period during which four Sicilians in close succession occupied the Papacy, since, lying at the crossroads of the Mediterranean basin, Sicily had for centuries served as the conduit through which the culture of the East had been transmitted to the West and where the practices and traditions of Greeks and Latins had converged and coalesced.[55] Thus, the first appearance of a Greek translation of what was originally an early-sixth-century Latin text of the laudatory hymn *Te Deum* (*Σέ Θεόν αινούμεν*) occurred in Rome during the pontificate of Sicilian Pope Leo II, who, proficient in both Greek and Latin and distinguished for his chanting and psalmody, must have introduced it late in the seventh century to accommodate the large numbers of Greek speakers in Rome who had begun to join the city's native Latin population in attending liturgical events.[56] Similarly, Pope Sergius I, who was also renowned for his competence in hymnology, prescribed that at the fraction of the Host during celebration of the Mass both the clergy and people were to sing the *Agnus Dei*, which was no doubt chanted in both Greek and Latin depending upon the ethnicity of the believer.[57]

By the beginning of the eighth century, and perhaps even earlier, such bilingual chanting and recitation during liturgical services appears to have become standard practice in the Roman church with Greek consistently taking precedence over Latin.[58] During the Mass, it became customary to read the epistle and gospel pericope proper to the day, as well as to sing the *Gloria* and to recite the Creed, first in Greek and then in Latin.[59] At baptisms administered by the priests of the city's titular basilicas during the third week of Lent, the Creed was recited first in Greek and then in Latin.[60] Where the pope officiated at baptisms, which customarily took place on Holy Saturday in the Constantinian basilica of the Savior on the Lateran, the prescribed lessons and canticles were read by the regionary subdeacon first in Greek and thereafter in Latin.[61] During the office of the Ninth Hour on Holy Saturday, the reading from the Book of Genesis was intoned from the ambon initially in Greek and immediately thereafter in Latin, as were the subsequent lessons *Factum est in vigilia matutina*, with its accompanying canticle *Cantemus Domino*, *Apprehendent septem mulieres* and its canticle *Vinea*, as well as the lesson *Scripsit Moyses canticum* and the concluding psalm *Sicut cervus*.[62]

Bilingual liturgical chanting in late-seventh- and early-eighth-century Rome reached its high point at Easter where, beginning with the vespers sung on Easter Sunday and continuing each evening (with the notable and unexplained exception of Wednesday and Thursday) through the first Sunday after Easter, the prescribed verses from the Book of Psalms, interpolated with the singing of *Alleleuia*, were chanted alternately in Greek and Latin.[63] Thus, the *Alleleuia* chanted at vespers on Easter Sunday was followed by the psalmic verse *Ὁ Κύριος εβασίλευσεν* and then by *Dominus regnavit*, after which the verse *Καί γάρ Εστερέωσε* was sung, followed by *Etenim firmavit*.[64] Indeed, the rhythmic patterns not only confirm that these Paschal *Alleleuias* were compiled during the late seventh and early eighth centuries, but that they were originally written to be chanted in Greek, with the Latin text being a translation of the original Greek and hence at various places not entirely compatible with the musical meter.[65]

Elements of Eastern hymnology and liturgical practice penetrated and influenced nearly every major feast day observed in the annual calendar of the late-seventh- and early-eighth-century Roman church. At Pentecost, as was the case during Easter time, the vigil lessons from the prophets were read in both Greek and Latin.[66] The communion anthem *Gustate et videte*, which was sung on the eighth Sunday after Pentecost, is identical to the communion hymn *Γεύσασθε καί ἴδετε* contained in the Byzantine Liturgy of the Presanctified Gifts.[67] Similarly, the gradual *Dirigatur Domine*, which was chanted on the nineteenth Sunday after Pentecost (as well as on the First Sunday in Lent) is the same as the hymn *Κατευθυνθήτω ή προσευχή μου*, which also appears in the Presanctified Liturgy.[68] The antiphon of the second vesperal magnificat *Nativitas tua*, sung during the celebration of the Birth of the Virgin Mary on September 8, is identical to the apolytikion or dismissal hymn *Ἡ γέννησίς σου Θεοτόκε* chanted during Great Vespers of the same feast day in the East.[69] Similarly, the antiphon *Crucem tuam adoramus*, sung during the feast of the Elevation of the Cross on September 14 (as well as on the Third Sunday of Lent), is identical to the hymn *Τόν Σταυρόν σου* chanted during matins of the same feast in the eastern tradition.[70]

A variety of chants in both the Roman and monastic offices for the period from the forefeast of Christmas on December 24 through the Circumcision on January 1 have a pronounced Byzantine flavor directly traceable to Eastern hymnological antecedents, which made their first appearance in the church of Rome during the seventh and eighth centuries. The second response of Christmas, which begins with the words *Hodie nobis de caelo*, for example, is illustrative of a *Hodie-Σήμερον* ("Today") motif of oriental provenance that appears repeatedly, for instance, in the ninth ode of the second canon sung during matins on Christmas day in the Byzantine East.[71] Similarly, the fourth monastic response for Christmas, *Descendit de caelis missus*, as well as the antiphon *Magnum hereditatis mysterium*, sung during the second vespers of the Circumcision on January 1, are of unquestionably oriental origin, as is the antiphon *Mirabile mysterium* (*Παράδοξον μυστήριον*), which is sung at the *Benedictus* of the Circumcision and

whose Eastern antecedents can be found in the kontakia of Romanus the Melodist as well as the sticherous hymns of Patriarch Germanos of Constantinople
and the irmoi of Cosmas Hagiopolites.[72]

Various chants and hymns sung during feast days between Advent and Lent
also reflect the impact of the East. The series of antiphonal praises *Veterem
hominem renovans*, chanted during the Octave of Epiphany, are identical to the
Greek antiphons sung on the same day.[73] The greater part of the text for a service
entitled *Benedictio aquarum theophaniarum secundum ordinem orientalium eccle-
siarum*, or "Blessing of the waters of Theophany according to the rite of the oriental churches," was taken from the service of the Great Blessing of the Waters
(Ἀκολουθία τοῦ Μεγάλου Ἁγιασμοῦ contained in the Byzantine euchologion.[74]
Similarly, the first responsory hymn *Adorna thalamum*, sung on February 2 during
the feast of the Presentation of the Lord in the Temple, known in the East as the
Ypapante,[75] is the same as the first apostichon Κατακόσμησον τόν νυμφῶνά σου,
or "Adorn Thy Bridalchamber," sung according to the Byzantine tradition during the Great Vespers of this feast.[76] Likewise, the processional hymn *Ave Maria*,
also sung during the feast of the Presentation, is a direct translation of the Greek
apolytikion Χαῖρε κεχαριτωμένη Μαρία or "Hail Mary full of grace."[77]

The influence of the East also penetrated Roman liturgical practices in the
period of Great Lent and especially during Holy Week. The antiphons that begin
with the word *Hodie* in the office of Palm Sunday and in the responsories of the
last three days of Holy Week, such as the response *Ingrediente domino* (Ἐρχόμενος
ὁ Κύριος), contain words so strikingly similar to Greek practice that they were
undoubtedly borrowed from the East.[78] Similarly, the reproaches known as the
Improperia, as well as the chanting of the Trisagion hymn "Holy God, Holy
Mighty, Holy Immortal," both of which occurred on Good Friday, are of unmistakably Eastern origin.[79] Indeed, sometime during the second half of the seventh
century, the church of Rome, historically averse to adopting the liturgical usages
of other regions, began the practice of conducting a procession of palms on the
evening of Palm Sunday in imitation of a similar practice that had existed in
Jerusalem since at least the fourth century.[80] By the middle of the eighth century,
the procession had become so integral a part of the Roman rite for Palm Sunday
evening (*Dominica in Palmis*) that a special benediction, absent from any Roman
formulary before the mid-seventh century, was pronounced by Pope Zacharias
over the palms before they were distributed to the people.[81]

The events of Holy Week culminated with Easter Sunday vespers, which, by
the middle of the eighth century, customarily took place in the Constantinian
basilica on the Lateran in the presence of the pope and the suburbicarian bishops along with the priests of Rome's titular basilicas. During the time of Pope
Zacharias, the participating clergy would, at the conclusion of the service, be
invited by the notarial *vice dominus* to the papal residence, where the pontiff had
constructed a new *triclinium*, or ceremonial banqueting hall, splendidly adorned
with various kinds of "marble, glass, metal, mosaics, and paintings," doubtless

in imitation of the dazzling Triklinos of Nineteen Couches located in the wing of the imperial palace in Constantinople near the Hippodrome.[82] There, while the *primicerius* and chorus of the papal school of chant regaled them with the glorious Paschal stichera that begin with the hymn *Πάσχα ιερόν υμίν σήμερον Αναδέδεικται* ("A sacred Pascha has today shown forth to us"), the assembled clerics joined the pontiff in drinking a cup of wine containing samplings from three vintages and signifying the accord and harmony between them, exactly as on Easter Sunday in Byzantium when the emperor, following the kiss of peace and Holy Communion, shared a similar admixture with the imperial dignitaries in a *triclinium* of the Great Palace.[83]

The oriental popes also absorbed Constantinople's fascination with great liturgical ceremonies and spectacles into the religious rites and practices of the Roman church.[84] Nowhere was this attraction to Eastern ceremonial more evident than in the elaborate papal processions that took place on great feast days. In a manner nearly identical to that of the emperor processing with great pomp from the imperial palace to the Great Church of St. Sophia to attend the Divine Liturgy on major ecclesiastical holidays in Constantinople, the pontiff would depart from the Lateran *patriarchium* and proceed through the city to one of Rome's titular basilicas to preside at mass.[85] The late-seventh or early-eighth-century *Ordo Romanus I*, which prescribes the order for such pontifical processions on solemn feast days, is laden with a variety of Greek words rendered in their Latin equivalents, thus unmistakably betraying the *ordo*'s Byzantine model and inspiration.[86] Attended by *stauroforoi (σταυροφόροι)*, or cross-bearers, the pope emerged from his residence flanked by two *stratores laici (στρατόρος λαϊκός)*, or lay groomsmen, who assisted him in mounting his horse. Among those who marched in the procession were various officials of the papal household, which included the *sakellarios (σακελλάριος)*; who was responsible for managing the pope's finances; a subdeacon, who carried the *apostolos (απόστολος)*, or epistle book; the archdeacon, who carried the *evangelium (εὐαγγέλιον)* or gospel; and a host of *acolyti (ακόλουθοι)*, or acolytes, bearing *chrisma (χρίσμα)*, or chrism, *sindones (σινδώνια)*, or linen cloths, *sciffos (σκύφοι)*, or communion cups, *cereostata (κηριόστατα)*, or candlesticks, and additional *evangelia (εὐαγγέλια)*, or texts of the gospel books.[87] Upon arrival at the stational church, the pope entered the sacristy and took his seat upon a *sella (σέλλα)*, or sedan chair, brought specially from the Lateran, placed his feet on a *scamni (σκαμνή)*, or footstool, and, while the sacristan kindled a *tymiamaterium (θημιαμητίριον)*, or censer, in his honor, the pontiff received obeisances from the assembled clergy, changed into his liturgical vestments, which included the *anabolaium (αναβόλαιον)*, or amice, whereupon he was saluted by a deacon with the words *Iube domne, benedicere* ("Give a blessing, my Lord") and the Mass began.[88] By the year 700, the prayer that begins with the words *Hic est enim calix sanguinis mei* ("For this is the cup of my blood"), recited by the celebrant over the chalice at the consecration of the elements during that Mass, would have included the words *mysterium fidei* or " the mystery of the faith." Absent from the original Roman rite, these words had been borrowed from various oriental liturgies, including possibly a Syrian consecration formula, and may have been inserted into the liturgical prayers of the church of Rome by any of a number of Eastern pontiffs from Leo II to Sergius I.[89]

Roman hagiological observances also experienced the impact of the East as the church's calendar expanded over the course of the seventh century to include a variety of feast days imported from the orient and previously unknown in Rome.[90] Pope Boniface IV's conversion of the Pantheon from a pagan temple to a Christian church in 609 or 610 resulted in the institution of an annual feast on May 13 honoring all the martyrs as well as the celebration there of a stational liturgy *ad martyres* or "for the martyrs" on the first Thursday after Easter.[91] It is no coincidence that a feast in honor of all the holy martyrs had been observed on May 13 in Edessa since 359, or that from 411 the Syrians had celebrated a liturgy in recognition of all the church's martyrs on the first Thursday after Easter as well.[92] Similarly, the institution of a feast on the first Sunday after Pentecost, identified in the seventh-century Roman Lectionary of Würzburg as the "Sunday of the birth of the saints,"was doubtless borrowed from a feast called $\tau\widetilde{\omega}v$ $\dot{\alpha}\gamma\dot{\iota}\omega v$ $\pi\dot{\alpha}v\tau\omega v$, or "all saints," which had been observed on the same day in the East and known in Antioch since the time of Ephrem the Syrian and St. John Chrysostom.[93] Indeed, around 690, Pope Sergius I either commissioned or composed a seventeen-verse litany entirely in Greek to be recited in Rome's churches on the feast of all saints.[94]

Pope Honorius added St. Hadrian, martyred at Nicomedia under Maximian and later translated to Constantinople, to the Roman calendar (September 8), in addition to converting the Senate House on the Forum Romanum into a church in honor of this Eastern saint.[95] The Dalmatian Pope John IV was almost certainly responsible for including his countryman St.Venantius of Salona in the calendar (May 18), while at the same time constructing a church on the Lateran to house both Venantius's relics as well as those of his companions Anastasios the Fuller and Maurus as well as various other Illyrian martyrs.[96] St. Anastasios the Persian, whose head was brought to Rome sometime between 634 and 649 by Palestinian monks fleeing the Arab invasions and installed in the monastery of Aquas Salvias, entered the Roman calendar (January 22) most likely during the time of the Greco-Palestinian Pope Theodore I, who was also doubtless responsible for introducing the feasts of the martyred Sicilian deacon Euplus of Catania (August 12) and the Eastern soldier/martyr St. Theodore Stratelates (November 9), as well as the quintessentially Palestinian observances of the beheading of St. John the Baptist and the repose of the prophet Elisha, both of which were celebrated on August 30.[97] St. Boniface of Tarsus, who met his death in Cilicia where he had been sent by his erstwhile paramour Aglaea to collect the relics of various martyrs, probably entered the Roman calendar (May 14) around 650 during the pontificate of Martin I, although his cult appears to have taken root in Rome during the time of Pope Boniface IV, who constructed a church on the

Aventine to house the relics of his martyred namesake.[98] It was also during Pope Martin's time that the Alexandrian-born St. Isidore of Chios, martyred during the Decian persecutions, entered the calendar of the church of Rome (observed along with St. Boniface on May 14),[99] as did the feast of the forty soldier/martyrs of the "thundering Legion," who died at Sebasteia in Cappadocia during the persecutions of Licinius in 320 and whose cult was celebrated in the sermons of Basil the Great, Gregory of Nyssa, and John Chrysostom.[100] Having become a part of the calendar of the church of Constantinople in the fifth century, the story of their mass martyrdom had probably made such an impression on Martin during his days as papal *apokrisiarios* in Constantinople that he decided to incorporate the feast into the Roman calendar (March 10) when he became pope.[101]

The East also influenced the development of liturgical observances within the Roman church related to the veneration of the Holy Cross. Known initially as the Discovery or Invention of the Cross, the celebration that would eventually become the feast of the Elevation or Exaltation of the Holy Cross first took place on September 14, 335, in Jerusalem when, during the consecration of the basilica that Constantine the Great had built on the site of the Holy Sepulchre, the presiding bishop raised the True Cross of Christ above the assembled multitude, who, upon seeing it for the first time, spontaneously burst forth into a litany of *Kyrie Eleisons*.[102] The practice of elevating the Holy Cross at the Constantinian basilica thereafter became an annual event whose festivities consumed an entire week, attracting between forty and fifty bishops along with great throngs of people of all nationalities, and resulting in the composition of sermons and encomia on the meaning and significance of the feast by such renowned figures as Sophronios of Jerusalem and later St. Andrew of Crete.[103] From Jerusalem, a feast in honor of the Holy Cross appears to have spread to Egypt where the Monophysite bishop John of Nikiu recorded that the church of Alexandria observed such a festival on the seventeenth day of Maskaram, which is the equivalent of September 14.[104] Special veneration of the True Cross also made its way to Syria, where Evagrius records that bishop Thomas of Apamea led a procession around the city's cathedral while holding a piece of the Cross in an effort to repel an imminent attack by the Persians, who had just ravaged and burned Antioch.[105]

From Palestine, Egypt, and Syria, the feast of the Exaltation of the Cross eventually made its way to Constantinople, where it appears to have been observed around the end of the fourth century, since the historian George of Alexandria records that St. John Chrysostom, in a characteristic fit of pique against his renowned adversary, refused the empress Eudoxia leave to enter Haghia Sophia to attend the "feast of the Exaltation."[106] By the middle of the sixth century, the feast had definitely become part of the calendar of the church of Constantinople, where, according to Alexander Monachos, it was known as the Ὕψωσις τοῦ Τιμίου Σταυροῦ or Exaltation of the Holy Cross and was observed annually on September 14.[107] Indeed, the significance that this feast achieved in the capital from the middle of the sixth century forward reflected the importance that came to be attached to the Cross as a victory-bearing talisman vital to the survival of an empire whose enemies were threatening it from all sides.[108] When he departed on his Thracian expedition in 593, the emperor Maurice carried a fragment of wood from the Cross fixed on a lance, while on his first campaign against the Persians, which began in the autumn of 622, the emperor Heraclius did precisely the same. By the tenth century, Constantine VII Porphyrogenitos asserted that the practice of carrying a fragment of the True Cross into battle was de rigeur for all Byzantine emperors.[109]

The emperor Heraclius's recovery of the True Cross from the Persians, who had seized it when they took Jerusalem in 614, and its triumphal restoration to the Holy City in March, 630, resulted in an immense outpouring of emotion, including a 116-line panegyric in dactyls by the court poet George of Pisidia, which added lustre to what had already become one of the most important ecclesiastical feast days in the East and reinforced the symbol of the Cross and its veneration as instruments for promoting imperial unity.[110] The observations of the Gallican bishop Arculf, who witnessed the great procession that took place in Jerusalem on the feast day of the Exaltation of the Cross and who was permitted to examine a fragment of the Cross, when he visited the Great Church of Haghia Sophia in Constantinople in 670, attest to the enormous reverence which the Cross continued to generate during the course of the seventh century in the eastern part of the empire.[111] Indeed, the Quinisext Council went so far as to enact a canon providing that symbols of the Cross placed upon the pavement were to be removed forthwith "so that our trophy of victory might not be dishonored by being stepped upon."[112]

Nothing even remotely comparable to the elaborate observances that developed in the East in connection with the veneration of the Holy Cross occurred in the church of Rome until the latter part of the seventh century. Although Pope Symmachus (498–514) built an oratory of the Holy Cross within St. Peter's in which he "enclosed the Lord's wood," the only liturgical observance that seems to have developed around this relic is identified in the sixth century Gregorian Sacramentary as *ad crucem salutandam in sancto Petro*, or the "salutation of the Cross in St. Peter's," during which the fragment of wood was simply exhibited and adored.[113] No Roman formulary or sacramentary prior to the seventh century refers to the invention, exaltation, or elevation of the Holy Cross on September 14, and no Mass or service related to the Cross is prescribed for that day in any such document.[114] Between 650 and 680, however, the church of Rome seems to have expanded the relatively restrained observances related to the Holy Cross contained in the Gregorian Sacramentary to the point where a Mass was celebrated on September 14 in those churches that possessed a fragment of the precious wood.[115] Thereafter, and doubtless as a result of the influx of Easterners into the Roman church, the liturgical observances related to September 14 assumed an increasingly Eastern flavor. Even before the pontificate of Sergius I, the church of Rome was celebrating the feast of the Exaltation of the Cross on an oriental model complete with a Mass, a gospel reading, special prayers proper to the day, and at least one hymn, which, although written in Latin, contained a variety of literary forms and usages indicating that it had been borrowed from a Syrian archetype and was thus unquestionably of oriental provenance.[116] When Pope Sergius I discovered a large fragment of wood from the True Cross, which had lain forgotten in a tarnished silver reliquary in the dark recesses of St. Peter's, and ordained that henceforth it would be venerated on the feast day of the Exaltation of the Cross in the basilica built by the emperor Constantine on the Lateran, the pontiff was fully aware that it was in a similar basilica built by the same emperor at the site of the Holy Sepulcher in Jerusalem where nearly four centuries earlier the same Cross had been exalted and worshiped for the first time.[117] Yet again the opulent and dramatic religious traditions of the East had radiated westward to enrich the liturgical rites of the church of Rome.[118]

※

By far the most important contribution made by the East to the liturgical worship and religious devotion of the Roman church during the period of Byzantine pre-eminence in Italy related to the Theotokos or Mother of God whose cult, in terms of liturgy, hymnography, homiletics, poetry, and iconography, achieved its peak in the Orient from where it too made its way to Rome during the course of the seventh and early eighth centuries.[119] Although the Virgin Mary certainly attracted the attention of the Latin fathers of the early Church, including Irenaeus of Lyons, Tertullian, Hippolytus of Rome, Ambrose of Milan, and St. Augustine, it was primarily in the East where she was extensively celebrated in such works as the *Stromata* of Clement of Alexandria, the biblical commentaries of Origen, the polemical writings of Athanasius the Great, the tender Nativity poems of Ephrem the Syrian, the *Catecheses* of Cyril of Jerusalem, the letters and homilies of the Cappadocian fathers Basil of Caesarea, Gregory of Nyssa, and Gregory Nazianzen, and the powerful discourses of St. John Chrysostom.[120] The Christological controversies that consumed the attention of the early church, and in particular the proclamation by the Council of Ephesus (431) that "the Holy Virgin is the Mother of God (Θεοτόκος)," gave added impetus to her already burgeoning cult in the East and the doctrinal and devotional literature associated with it.[121] But it was in Constantinople during the first half of the sixth century, starting around the time of the Nika riots, which nearly resulted in the deposition of the emperor Justinian I, that the cult of the Theotokos began to develop with what has been justifiably described as "an astonishing rapidity."[122] Threatened not only internally, but beginning in the early 560s with steadily increasing severity from outside its borders, Justinian's successors began to promote an imperial ideology that invoked the patronage of the Virgin Mary as the special protector and guardian of the empire generally and of the city of Constantinople in particular.[123] Realizing that it was no longer safe or prudent to rely exclusively on their own abilities to repel the barbarian menace, the emperors Justin II, Tiberius, and Maurice turned to the Theotokos not only as a new and far less fallible symbol around which to rally a dispirited realm, but more importantly as the single most powerful intercessor available to plead the empire's desperate cause before God.[124]

The importance of the Virgin Mary as Constantinople's special protector manifested itself in a variety of ways. As an indicator of her increasing significance as the capital's guardian and as a talisman of success against the empire's enemies, the Virgin Mary began to appear on bronze weights cast during the reign of Justin II with the inscription Ἁγία Μαρία βοήθεισον, or "Holy Mary Help," while on Maurice's seals traditional pagan symbols of triumph were replaced with the image of the Theotokos and child as emblems of victory.[125] When Heraclius departed from Africa in 609 bound for Constantinople to relieve the empire of the tyranny of Phocas, the masts of his ships displayed "reliquaries and icons of the Mother of God."[126] The diadem with which he was subsequently crowned may well have been taken from the church of the Theotokos at Artake (Erdek) in recognition of her assistance in his success.[127] But this was only the beginning.

The part played by the Virgin Mary in delivering Constantinople from the Avar siege of 626 positively sealed her role as the capital's principal defender.[128] Comparing her in prowess to the hunter-goddess Artemis, George of Pisidia grandiloquently declaimed that no painter could truthfully depict an image of Byzantium's triumph against the Slavic foe without including a portrait of the Theotokos.[129] Indeed, the homily delivered in the Great Church on the day of victory by Theodore Synkellos, a priest of Haghia Sophia, describes her valiant role in the same rhapsodic terms, thus confirming what might otherwise be ascribed to the court poet's characteristic proclivity to lapse into hyperbole.[130] Patriarch Sergius had placed icons of the Virgin all along the city's western gates as phylacteries against the Avars.[131] The emperor's children had prayed for her assistance in the chapels of the palace consecrated in her honor, while the populace had sent up its unremitting supplications.[132] On August 7 the city's prayers were answered as the Virgin Mary, in a spectacular affirmation of her solicitude for Constantinople, sank the Avar flotilla, turning the sea red with barbarian blood.[133] The Avar Chagan, seeing the Theotokos in the guise of "a woman in stately dress rushing about on the wall all alone," retreated westward, while the population of the city, led by the emperor's young son and the patriarch, proceeded to the church of the Theotokos at Blachernae "to offer unto God their prayers of thanksgiving."[134] Constantinople had incontestably become the city of the Theotokos.[135]

The Mother of God would forever after remain Byzantium's special patron, reappearing between 674 and 678 to help Heraclius's great grandson Constantine IV fend off the Arabs in a series of naval engagements that took place along the coast of Constantinople.[136] The spectacular victories of the Isaurian emperor Leo III against the Arabs between 717 and 718 were similarly attributed to the "intercession of the all-pure Theotokos."[137] By the twelfth century, the Virgin Mary had come to be regarded as the indispensable battle companion of every Byzantine emperor.[138]

Enthusiasm for the Mother of God also gave rise to voluminous literary pro-ductivity, which included the Syrian poet Jacob of Saroug's (d. 538) lengthy *Ode on the Blessed Virgin Mary* as well as rapturous and lyrical poetry by Severus of An-tioch (ca. 465–538).[139] By the middle of the sixth century, Constantinopolitans such as the hymnologist Romanos the Melodist (ca. 490–560) were producing literary works of deep intensity and pathos in praise of the Theotokos. Drawing upon his Syrian heritage, and in particular on the sensuous early-fourth-century Syriac poems to the Virgin Mary written by St. Ephrem, many of Romanos's *kontakia* attest to the fact that the cult of the Theotokos was increasing with astonishing rapidity during the sixth century not only in the capital but in the eastern part of the empire generally.[140] The *Akathist* hymn, which was probably composed by Romanos, was reworked by adding the new *proeimion*, or preface, Τῇ ὑπερμάχῳ ("To You Invincible Champion"), which is generally believed to have been composed by patriarch Sergius as a special hymn of thanksgiving to the Theotokos for her delivery of the capital from the Avars.[141] A host of others joined Sergius in conspicuous expressions of piety and ardor toward the Virgin Mary.[142] By the end of the seventh and the beginning of the eighth century, patriarch Germanos of Constantinople, St. John of Damascus, Cosmas of Jerusa-lem, and archbishop Andrew of Crete, had added their voices to the seemingly endless stream of works being composed in the East in praise and honor of the Mother of God.[143]

The Marian writings of St. Andrew of Crete are worthy of particular attention since they may well have had a role in promoting the cult of the Theotokos in Rome. Born in Syria around 660, Andrew left his native Damascus for Jerusalem, where in 678 he received the monastic tonsure from patriarch Theodore, there-after spending a number of years attached to the church of the Holy Sepulcher. By the autumn of 685, he was in Constantinople, where he continued to lead the monastic life until he was ordained a deacon of St. Sophia and placed in charge of an orphanage and old-age home in the Eugeniou quarter of the capital. Consecrated archbishop of Gortyna and primate of Crete sometime after 692, Andrew occupied his see with distinction, apart from what appears to have been a brief lapse into Monothelitism in 711/712 during the reign of Philippikos, until his death in 740.[144] Perhaps the most influential preacher and poet of his day, St. Andrew's years both in Jerusalem and especially in Constantinople doubtless contributed to the fervor with which he embraced the cult of the Virgin Mary.[145] The Theotokion of the Ninth Ode of his renowned Great Canon epitomizes as well as any liturgical composition the Mother of God's role as mistress of Byzantium.[146] In addition to this *magnum opus*, St. Andrew wrote a plethora of pieces extolling the Virgin Mary, including four lengthy sermons and a canon of nine odes for the feast of her Nativity, a homily and an ode on the occasion of her Annunciation, three sermons for her Dormition or Koimesis, and a three-ode *idiomelon*, or short song, for the feast of the Ypapante or Presentation of the Lord in the Temple.[147] Since during his tenure as archbishop of Gortyna the island of Crete was under Rome's ecclesiastical jurisdiction, it is almost certain that as a major suffragan of the Papacy from sometime after 692 until his death in 740, St. Andrew had contact if not in person or by emissaries then certainly through correspondence with all the popes from Sergius I through Gregory III. As such, it is reasonable to suppose that these pontiffs would have been familiar with their famous subordinate's devotion to the Virgin Mary as well as with the extensive compositions he had written in her honor. Thus, it is quite likely that St. Andrew's ardor for the Theotokos contributed, along with other factors, to what we shall see was the development and spread of the cult of the Virgin Mary in Rome from the late seventh century onward.

The liturgical calendar of the church reflected the impact of the blossoming cult of the Mother of God in the eastern part of the empire. By the end of the sixth century, the Constantinopolitan church had adopted the full Marian festal cycle, including the observance of her Nativity on September 8, the Ypapante, which celebrated the Virgin's presentation of Christ in the Temple on February 2, her Annunciation by the archangel Gabriel on March 25, and finally her Koimesis or Dormition on August 15.[148] Each feast produced an inexhaustible wealth of appropriate *theotokia*, *stavrotheotokia*, *troparia*, *stichera*, *kathismata*, *idiomela*, *prosomia*, canons, *eirmoi*, and similar hymns and prayers that filled the pages of the Eastern churches' numerous liturgical books.[149] A λιτανεία ("litany" or "procession"), which lay at the heart of Byzantium's indisseverable attachment to the concept of τάξις ("ceremony" or "order"), was prescribed for each principal ecclesiastical holiday by every euchologion or liturgical service book used by the churches in the East, and thus constituted an indispensable part of every major feast day of the church's calendar, including the main feasts in honor of the Virgin Mary.[150] Among the sixty-eight processions prescribed by the *Typikon* of the Great Church of St. Sophia, for instance, eleven took place on either the four principal Marian feasts or on the anniversary of the consecration of churches dedicated to the Virgin in Constantinople, including the famous churches of the Theotokos at Blachernae, which housed her robe, and at Chalkoprateia, which contained her belt.[151] Well before the seventh century ended, the Theotokos had achieved a peerless pre-eminence over all religious figures in the East, where she was celebrated far and wide with epithets of boundless adoration.[152]

When in an effort to abate the plague that struck Rome in 590, Pope Gregory the Great ordered the city's population to celebrate the "septiform litanies" by processing through the streets while chanting *Kyrie Eleison* and converging at the basilica of the "Holy Mother of the Lord" to implore God for Rome's deliverance, the pontiff was revealing both the influence upon him of the many years he had spent as papal *apokrisiarios* in Constantinople as well as the enormous importance which the Virgin Mary had achieved in the eastern part of he empire as a champion and an intercessor.[153] But Pope Gregory's prescription was in many ways an innovation both for Rome and for the West in general where nothing approaching the East's intense enthusiasm for the cult of the Theotokos existed prior to the end of the sixth century. Although both Gregory of Tours and Venantius Fortunatus composed works on the Virgin Mary, their writings are more reflective of the close contacts each had with Byzantium rather than of any contemporaneous Western equivalent to the East's widespread devotion to the Theotokos.[154] Indeed, except for the short-lived practice of celebrating a Mass in honor of the Virgin Mary on January 1, the church of Rome observed no feast day in honor of the Virgin Mary prior to the seventh century when, as a consequence of the impact exerted by the increasing numbers of Easterners who came to Rome from the early 600s onward, it adopted each of the four major Marian festivals long celebrated by the churches of the East.[155] The Orient's deep devotion to the Mother of God would rapidly expand westward through the Mediterranean basin to inspire identical liturgical observances by the Roman church.

Although a feast in honor of the Nativity of the Virgin Mary had become part of the ecclesiastical calendar of the church of Constantinople well before the sixth century ended, the earliest mention of any Roman observation of the Virgin's birth occurs sometime around 590 when some of the city's titular churches, including probably St. Mary Major, appear to have begun saying a mass *in natale sanctae Mariae* ("on the birth of St. Mary").[156] The Mass, however, was celebrated on the day of Christ's Circumcision or January 1 rather than on September 8 as in the East, and thus appears to have focused less upon the Theotokos and more upon her son.[157] But by around 670, the titular churches where this Mass was said had moved its observance to September 8 both in conformity with Eastern practice and as an indicator that the Virgin Mary had come to be honored in her own right.[158] By the time of the pontificates of the Greco-Sicilian popes Agatho and Leo II, the festival of the Theotokos's Nativity had become an established part of the papal liturgy.[159] Thus, when Pope Sergius I directed, sometime between 687 and 701, that on the day of the celebration of the Virgin's birth a litany should go forth from the church of St. Adrian and proceed to St. Mary Major, the Syrian pontiff was embellishing with typical Byzantine splendor the festivities related to a holiday which Eastern pontiffs has already absorbed into the annual papal ritual.[160]

Probably the earliest of the four principal Marian holidays, the feast of the Ypapante (Ὑπαπαντή), or Presentation of Christ in the Temple, appears to have originated in Jerusalem, where, around the end of the fourth century, the Roman noblewoman Egeria recorded that it was observed in the church of the Anastasis "with special magnificence" on the fortieth day after Epiphany.[161] From there, observation of the Ypapante seems to have spread to Asia Minor where toward the end of the fourth century Amphilochius of Iconium preached a homily on the subject.[162] Although St. John Chrysostom also delivered a sermon on the Ypapante in Constantinople at about the same time, the feast did not officially become part of the calendar of the Constantinopolitan church until 542 during the reign of Justinian I.[163] Curiously, the church of Antioch did not adopt the Ypapante until the latter part of the sixth century after both Jerusalem and Constantinople had made it a part of their ecclesiastical calendars.[164] A series of Greek verses dating from around the year 600 discovered at a Coptic convent probably identifiable with the monastery of St. Phoebammon suggests that the feast was also late in arriving in Egypt.[165] Absent from any Roman sacramentary prior to the seventh century, the feast of the Presentation of Christ in the Temple was added to the papal liturgy by the Greco-Palestinian Pope Theodore I, both because of his familiarity with the feast from his days in Jerusalem and partly perhaps as a result of the influence of Maximos Confessor, with whom the pope had extensive contacts and whose Mariological writings contained references to the subject.[166] By the time of Pope Vitalian, the Presentation had entered the sacramentaries of the city's titular churches.[167] As he had ordained for the feast of the Virgin's nativity, Pope Sergius I decreed that on the day of St. Simeon, "which the Greeks call Ypapante," a procession was also to take place from the church of St. Adrian to St. Mary Major.[168] In addition, the pontiff appears to have composed special antiphons to be sung during this procession. Both their Byzantine musical style as well as the fact that they were to be chanted alternately in Greek and Latin indicates yet again the impact of the East on late-seventh-century Roman liturgical practices.[169]

As with the Ypapante, the feast of the Annunciation of the Theotokos also appears to have originated in Jerusalem where it was observed annually on March 25 beginning sometime between 425 and 430.[170] The earliest extant homily on the Virgin's Annunciation seems to have been delivered in the Holy City around the early to middle years of the fifth century by a certain Hesychius, whom Cyril of Scythopolis describes in his *Life of St. Euthymius* as an "inspired priest and teacher of the church."[171] From Palestine, the feast seems to have spread rapidly to Constantinople where on March 25, 431, in the presence of patriarch Nestorius, bishop Proclus of Kyzikos preached a sermon on the Annunciation, which, beginning with the words "Today is the Virgin's festival, brothers" and referring to Mary as the Mother of God, resulted, according to Theophanes, in the universal hatred of Nestorius "for his vanity and heresy."[172] It is perhaps indicative of the importance which the Annunciation had achieved in Constantinople by the middle of the sixth century that the hymnographer Romanos the Melodist composed some of his most poignant poetry in honor of this feast.[173] The growth of the cult of the Theotokos and her role as Constantinople's protector appears thereafter to have given March 25 an almost superstitious significance. The emperor Heraclius, for example, seems to have been particularly keen on departing from the capital for the East in 624 "on the day of the Annunciation of Our Lady the Mother of God."[174] The Roman church did not incorporate the feast of the Annunciation into its calendar until around 650 when Pope Martin, who, like Gregory the Great had been deeply influenced by his years as papal *apokrisiarios* in Constantinople, probably introduced its observance into the papal liturgy. It seems, however, that Rome's titular churches delayed in following the papal lead and did not absorb the Annunciation into their sacramentaries until shortly before the pontificate of Sergius I.[175] The Syrian pontiff for his part ascribed a great importance to the feast, prescribing that it also be enhanced with a procession accompanied by chants and hymns of unmistakably Eastern provenance.[176]

The earliest observation of a Marian feast day associated with the Virgin's *κοίμησης*, meaning dormition or repose, seems to have occurred on August 15 in Jerusalem, where, sometime in the middle of the fifth century, patriarch Juvenal instituted a festival known as the "remembrance of the Theotokos."[177] As with so many other feast days, the church of Jerusalem feted the Virgin's dormition with elaborate litanies and processions that, as we have seen, were later absorbed into the liturgical practices of the churches of both Constantinople and Rome.[178] Sometime between 550 and 650, but not later than the seventh century, bishop Theoteknos of Livias, a city under the jurisdiction of the church of Jerusalem located on the left bank of the Jordan River opposite Jericho, composed an encomium on the Virgin Mary that focused upon August 15 as the day of her *ανάλημψις*, meaning ascension or assumption.[179] Theoteknos's panegyric appears to have been absorbed into the *typikon* of the Palestinian monastery of St. Sabas, where it was read annually on August 15.[180]

The feast of the Dormition of the Theotokos was officially adopted into the calendar of the church of Constantinople and fixed at August 15 by decree of the emperor Maurice who, in 588, ordained that each year on that date a litany was to be held at the church of the Virgin Mary at Blachernae "in memory of the holy Mother of God, at which laudations of our Lady were to be delivered."[181] By the beginning of the seventh century, the East was experiencing a veritable explosion of literary works on the Virgin's dormition.[182] Early in the century, for instance, bishop John of Thessalonika (610–649) composed a homily on the repose of the Theotokos based on a Greek text dating from the fifth or sixth centuries, which in turn derived from a late-fifth-century Syriac fragment on the subject. Although John of Thessalonika's sermon was later criticized severely by such prominent figures as patriarch Germanos of Constantinople, St. Andrew of Crete, and St. John of Damascus, it nonetheless represents the earliest extant text establishing a Greek literary tradition of the Virgin's dormition.[183] It was also during the first half of the seventh century that Maximos Confessor formulated his own theology of the Virgin's repose, which he expressed in a work bearing the lengthy title of "A canticle and glorification, eulogy and act of praise of our all-holy Queen, the immaculate and ever-blessed Theotokos, Mary, the ever-virgin, and a notice about her stainless and blessed life from her birth to her passing-over, written by our blessed Father Maximos the philosopher and confessor."[184] Considering Maximos's influential role as an agent of religious and cultural transfer between East and West, it is virtually certain that his Mariology had an impact on the Roman church.

It was not, however, until the middle of the seventh century that the feast of the Virgin's dormition entered the rites of the Roman church, where it most likely became a part of the papal liturgy during the pontificate of Pope Theodore I.[185] Influenced by a combination of factors including Rome's Sabaite monastic community, which would have been familiar with the feast of the Virgin's dormition from Theoteknos of Livias's encomium, the writings of his friend and confidant Maximos Confessor, as well as by his own experiences as a child and adolescent in Jerusalem before his arrival in Rome, the feast that would come to be known in the West as the Assumption of the Virgin Mary almost assuredly made its initial appearance in the ecclesiastical calendar of the church of Rome during the time of this Greco-Palestinian pontiff.[186]

While introduced into the papal liturgy by a Greek pope from Palestine, the solemnities associated with the feast of the dormition of the Theotokos were enriched toward the end of the seventh century by another Eastern pontiff who likewise drew upon his oriental heritage to embellish the rites of the Roman church. For in addition to prescribing that an annual procession take place on the feast of the Virgin's dormition, the Syrian Pope Sergius I, renowned for his skill in liturgical music, appears to have adapted, if not virtually copied, the Greek *kontakion* for the feast into a Latin composition to be sung during the litany.[187] Sergius's hymn *Veneranda* ("Venerable") focuses in the same way and in almost identical language as the feast's Eastern *kontakion* Τήν εν πρεσβείαις ακοίμητον θεοτόκον ("Sleepless in her prayers the Theotokos") on the theme that neither the tomb nor death could contain the Mother of Life.[188] Significantly, that same theme had been expressed in a homily by St. Andrew of Crete, thus strengthening the probability that the works of the Papacy's illustrious suffragan were known in Rome at least by the time of Pope Sergius.[189] The strong similarities between the Greek *kontakion* for the feast of the Dormition, the homily of Andrew of Crete, and Pope Sergius's hymn *Veneranda* show yet again that in liturgics and hymnography as in so much else the iridescence of the Orient continued to suffuse the Roman church with splendor as the seventh century came to a close.

ᢍ

The convulsions that began to rock the empire beginning in the later years of the reign of Justinian I, and which continued to imperil its very existence throughout the remainder of the sixth century and on into the seventh, also affected religious art.[190] In addition to a vastly increased use of icons in worship and devotional practices, from about 550 onward imperial iconography underwent a significant sytlistic change intentionally designed to enlist the help of the heavenly host in Byzantium's struggle for survival. Religious figures began to be depicted as gaunt and disembodied abstractions whose angular clothing, elongated bodies, and geometric faces staring starkly into space conveyed an impression of authority and timelessness that reflected their eternal archetypes and thus were believed to act as a conduit for transmission of the divine assistance desperately needed by an empire under siege.[191] At the same time as it was producing such images of chill and barren isolation, however, Constantinople also turned to its classical Greek past in the hope that, by replicating forms from an age whose traditions it had faithfully guarded through the centuries, it might find reassurance, strength, and sustenance in its struggle to survive.[192] Floor mosaics in the palaces of the capital reflected pastoral tableaus of unmistakably Hellenistic provenance, while silverwork similarly displayed a wide range of classical imagery as gambolling maenads, sensuous Nereids, and plumpish Silenuses exhibited a free and natural style that contrasted sharply with the lugubrious countenances of saints and martyrs.[193] It was not long, however, before these vastly different styles fused to form a harmony of classical and religious motifs. In Heraclius's time, artists in the capital would produce an icon of the Virgin Mary whose grave, hypnotic gaze and apparitional demeanor was softened by a pair of angels "breathing with barely closed lips the spirit of the classical tradition."[194] Similarly, scenes of cupids battling sea monsters depicted in a style redolent of the free and delicate art of classical Greece would come to exist side by side with the glum and glacial images of the art of an empire that tolerated no departure from strict control in every sphere of life.[195]

It was not long before the abstraction and dematerialization characteristic of Constantinople's new iconographic piety reached Rome.[196] Even before the end of the sixth century, mosaics in churches such as San Lorenzo *fuori le mura* and San Teodoro were being embellished with figures whose rigid bodies and transcendental faces, highlighted by blots of darker tesserae, represented a marked departure from the shapely bodies and faces strongly molded in light and shade, indicative of local Roman craftsmanship, that had adorned such churches as Saints Cosmas and Damian during the first half of the century.[197] By the early years of the seventh century, the capital's artistic influence could be seen in the former Pantheon that, with imperial permission, had been converted by Pope Boniface IV in 609 or 610 from a pagan temple into a church and dedicated to the Virgin Mary.[198] On the occasion of its consecration, the pontiff had adorned the new sanctuary with an icon of the Theotokos as *Panagia Hodegetria* ("All Holy Directress"), thereby depicting her in a style that was both unmistakably Eastern in origin and particularly meaningful in Constantinople.[199] To further emphasize its oriental prototype, the Christ-child was painted with wide, staring eyes, an elongated nose, small pursed lips, a rounded chin, and a general rigidity directly traceable to the ateliers of Byzantium.[200] The apsidal mosaic decorations made by Pope Honorius I at the church of St. Agnes on the Via Nomentana represented a new height of eastern iconographic abstraction in Rome.[201] Rising like three vertical columns suspended in space against a flat gold background, St. Agnes, dressed in the ceremonial attire of a Byzantine empress, is flanked by popes Symmachus and Honorius I, each of whom is clothed in a pallium of imperial purple. The saint's grave, geometrically shaped eyes stare out of a pallid face, which is accented by yellowish-brown spots on the cheeks. Together with a rigid and elongated body, she conveys the impression of a dessicated phantom instead of a guileless child of thirteen who chose to die rather than abandon her vow of virginity.[202] Yet the composition mirrored an identical style of gaunt and lofty remoteness in iconography taking place in the East at the very same time.[203]

Shortly before the middle of the seventh century, the Greco-Palestinian Pope Theodore I commissioned an apse mosaic for the Lateran oratory of San Venanzio, a church that had been built by his immediate predecessor the Dalmatian Pope John IV to house the relics of various saints and martyrs from his native Illyricum.[204] Dominated by a bust of Christ flanked by angels, along with the Virgin Mary in prayer amidst saints and apostles, Pope Theodore's assertively vertical figures are stiff and elongated, with black-framed faces that exhude a severity almost identical to contemporary votive panels in the church of St. Demetrios in Thessalonika.[205] The same pontiff commissioned yet another apse mosaic for the church of St. Stefano Rotondo. Not surprisingly, the icon's jeweled Cross surmounted by a bust of Christ flanked by Saints Primus and Felician bears a striking similarity to patterns of Palestinian iconography related to the Crucifixion with which the pope would have been intimately familiar from his days in Jerusalem. Nor is it unexpected that the mosaic's blanched and colorless forms reflect styles already seen at St. Agnes and in San Venanzio.[206] Pope Theodore's successors continued to patronize the production of religous art in Rome that mirrored the style of contemporary Constantinople. The wall painting of St. Anne commissioned by Pope Martin I in 649 for St. Maria Antiqua, the fresco of the Maccabees in the same church, and the portrait of San Sebastian in the church of S. Peter *in vincoli* painted sometime during the pontificate of Pope Agatho, all bear witness not only to the gauntness and gravity that had become synonymous with Byzantium's new iconographic piety, but also to the subtle, undeniable hint of the "perennial Hellenism" that, preserved in Constantinople, found its way through the hands of Eastern masters to the churches of seventh-century Rome.[207]

By far the most outstanding patron of the Byzantine iconographic style was the Greek Pope John VII, during whose pontificate Rome witnessed a lavish program of artistic productivity that was fully within the mainstream of forms and styles then being fashioned in Constantinople.[208] The son of a Byzantine official who had been curator of the imperial palace on the Palatine, John VII commissioned an extensive number of works, which were created by traveling Greek craftsmen summoned from the capital, thereby reflecting Rome's continuing cultural links with Byzantium and the fact that as late as the beginning of the eighth century, Roman religious art had not yet begun to pursue a path of development independent from that of Constantinople.[209] Thus, the wide-open eyes of the weightless and elongated Theotokos, dressed as a Byzantine Augusta before whom John

VII kneels in supplication in the church of St. Maria in Trastevere, stare starkly into space from a face calculated to convey the full force of imperial power and splendor, while the gentle faces of the flanking angels temper her austerity with classical Hellenic calm.[210] But as an example of the finest fusion of monumental Byzantine iconographic severity with those elements of classical Hellenism that were kept alive in Heraclian Constantinople, nothing compares with Pope John VII's extensive redecoration of the chancel of the church of St. Maria Antiqua, which occurred in the years 705 through 707.[211] There, the same dark, staring eyes and commanding bodily presences with which religious art in post-Justinianic Constantinople sought to enlist the aid of heaven in the empire's struggle for survival are repeated in the faces of the apostles, whose busts in medallions embellish the side walls of the chancel.[212] Figures continue to appear stiff and dehydrated as they stand suspended on a "neutral ground of nonspace."[213] But there too, a curly-headed seraph with barely parted lips and slightly tilted head smiles sweetly from the triumphal arch in the church's presbytery, while a delicate Annunciation angel evokes the illusionism of first-century Pompeian painting.[214] And there as well, the power of Greek monastics, by then an influential segment of Rome's population, can be seen in the less classical aspects of the Eastern pontiff's frescoes, as their somber hands have moved to purge whatever traces there may be of free and tender classical embroidery.[215]

While the papal decorations at St. Maria Antiqua may well have proclaimed that Rome had succumbed to Byzantium in the important sphere of religous art, the very same iconography also conveyed the message that the Roman church was not so unreservedly willing to submit to Constantinople on matters of religious doctrine. In this arena, the pope was prepared to make concessions, but in no way to capitulate. Although Greek by family, he was unshakably Roman by faith. In the place of Pope Sergius's intransigence on the matter of Rome's acceptance of the canons of the Quinisext Council, for example, John VII's frescoes reflect a willingness to compromise with Constantinople, while at the same time insisting on the Papacy's role as the pre-eminent guardian of orthodox belief.[216] Thus, in a departure from traditional Roman iconographic practice, the pontiff placed a massive Cross surrounded by the blessed of all nations, instead of the figure of a lamb, at the top of the triumphal arch of the presbytery, thereby yielding both to the Quinisext Council's prohibition against the depiction of Christ as a lamb and its exaltation of the symbol of the Cross.[217] The figure of Christ suspended on this Cross also reflects the pope's identification with Byzantium and his desire to accommodate and mimic the new symbols of imperial authority. Like the image of Christ depicted on Justinian II's coinage issued after his return to power in 705, John VII's Jesus is youthful, curly-haired, and unbearded.[218] But the papal composition also contained a caveat, for in the wall space immediately below the adoration of the Cross, John VII arranged the figures of four popes, consisting of himself standing next to Pope Leo I on the left side, and on the right Pope Martin alongside what is probably Pope Agatho. His choice of Roman pontiffs could not have sent a clearer message to Byzantium. In Leo I, the pope had chosen to depict the champion of the Council of Chalcedon, whose famous *Tome* had routed the Monophysites and enunciated the doctrine of Christ's two natures.[219] With Martin, John VII had resurrected the specter of the pope who at the Lateran Council of 649 had dared to openly oppose Justinian II's grandfather Constans II and who had paid for his contempt of imperial authority by being arrested, deposed, and exiled.[220] In Agatho, the spiritual father of the Sixth Ecumenical Council, Pope John was setting up the image of the pontiff who had brought East and West together by healing at long last the festering wound of Monothelitism.[221]

John VII's embellishment of the triumphal arch of the presbytery in St. Maria Antiqua thus shows that he was far less pusillanimous and irresolute a pontiff than the *Liber Pontificalis* portrays him.[222] Indeed, its adroit fusion of images simultaneously proclaiming Rome's obedience to Byzantium while asserting that the Roman church would remain inflexibly orthodox in matters of the faith reveal him to have been unusually subtle and astute.[223] Ever devoted to an ideology in which the Papacy was the ultimate fount of doctrinal rectitude, the Rome of the pontiff whose father had been a Byzantine civil servant was entering the eighth century firmly within the imperial fold, as the voyage of Pope Constantine I to the imperial city would soon confirm.[224]

⁓

Justinian II was sixteen years old when he succeeded his father Constantine IV Pogonatos as emperor in 685.[225] Rather than cultivate the peace that his father had established between Byzantium and its enemies, the rash and headstrong young emperor broke the truce that Constantine IV had concluded with the Bulgarians, sent a force of cavalry into Thrace, and attacked the Slavonians. In the East, he moved against the Arabs, sending an expedition under Leontios into Armenia and launching offensives in both North Africa and Syria. Although at first successful against the Caliphate, the Byzantine army was disastrously defeated at Sebastopolis in 692.[226] In Constantinople, the emperor, described by a chronicle as "ferocious in his manner and of uncontainable anger,"[227] surrounded himself with public officials of equally savage temperament, including Stephen the Persian, a eunuch who as imperial *sakellarios* was pitiless in his cruelty (which even extended to whipping the emperor's mother Anastasia), as well as a former monk named Theodotos who, as imperial *logothete* or treasurer, pursued the collection of taxes and other financial exactions with uncommmon brutality.[228] When patriarch Kallinikos of Constantinople refused to accommodate Justinian's demand that he recite a prayer authorizing the demolition of the church of the Theotokos *ton metropolitou* in order to make way for a fountain and benches, which he wished to construct so that the Blue faction might come and receive him, the emperor became incensed at the patriarch's intransigence, and, although uncharacteristically restraining his fury for the moment, he harbored his hatred for the patriarch for over a decade before exacting his revenge.[229] By 695, Justinian II's reign was drawing rapidly to a close. A group of men led by the patrician Leontios, whom Justinian had recently released from prison, appointed *strategos* of Hellas, and ordered to depart forthwith from Constantinople, succeeded in entering the Praetorium where the cells were emptied of prisoners, mostly soldiers, some of whom Justinian had confined for as many as eight years. Eventually, a large crowd gathered in the atrium of Haghia Sophia where, inspired by patriarch Kallinikos, they hastened to the Hippodrome. There, Justinian was brought at daybreak, his nose was slit so that thus disfigured he might never rule again, and, because of Leontios's affection for Constantine IV, was spared his life and banished instead to the Chersonese where for the next ten years he plotted his return to power.[230]

By early 705, Justinian was on his way back to Constantinople prepared to regain his lost empire and to spare none of those who had participated in his ouster.[231] With the assistance of the Bulgarian chieftain Terbelis, Justinian approached the capital from the northwest and camped by the walls of Blachernae where his repeated demands that the citizens receive him back as emperor were dismissed with obscenities and ridicule. Making his way through the aqueduct of Valens, which enters the city near the Adrianople Gate, Justinian entered Constantinople and established his residence for a short time in the palace at Blachernae. By the spring of 705, his lacerated nose concealed behind a golden plate, he was back upon the throne.[232]

The revenge that Justinian visited upon those whom he believed had participated in his disfigurement and deposition appears to have exceeded the terrors of his first reign, causing the near contemporary *Parastaseis Syntomoi Chronikai* to label him the "tyrant of Constantinople."[233] Leontios, who had followed him as emperor, as well as Tiberius II Apsimaros, who had deposed Leontios and succeeded him in 698, were paraded through the city in chains and brought to the Hippodrome where Justinian trampled on their necks and then sent them off to be beheaded.[234] Patriarch Kallinikos was blinded and exiled to Rome where John VII was occupying the Papacy.[235] People were appointed to high civil and military positions only to be arrested and executed a few days later. Imperial dinner guests were slain at their table, while others were cast into the sea in sacks.[236] Nor did Justinian confine his vengeance to Constantinople. Suspecting that the citizens of Ravenna had participated in the plot against him, Justinian launched a virulent attack upon the capital of the Italian exarchate, capturing and slaughtering a large number of its nobility. Archbishop Felix, whom Pope Constantine I had ordained bishop of Ravenna sometime in 708 and whom Justinian also believed had been a party to his overthrow, was arrested by the patrician Theodoros and brought to the capital, where in 709 he was blinded with acid.[237] It was in this atmosphere of universal fear and cruelty that in the summer of 710 Justinian II issued an imperial mandate directing Pope Constantine to appear before him in Constantinople.[238]

Both Justinian II and his father Constantine IV had shown great deference toward the church of Rome. For their part, the Roman pontiffs had consistently shown themselves to be loyal imperial subjects. Constantine had revoked Ravenna's autocephaly and restored it to the jurisdiction of the Apostolic See declaring that henceforth the newly elected bishop of Ravenna was required to travel to Rome to be ordained by the pope.[239] He also decreed that a newly elected pope could be ordained immediately and need not await imperial or exarchal approval before being consecrated.[240] Finally, Constantine had abolished the burdensome imperial taxes on the papal patrimonies in Sicily and Calabria as well as other financial exactions that the church of Rome had experienced difficulty in paying each year.[241] Justinian II had also relieved the Roman church of a significant portion of its annual tax obligations on the papal patrimonies in Bruttium and Lucania and had ordered the release of papal dependents whom the imperial army was holding as security for taxes owed by the church.[242] Imperial relations with the Roman church were severely strained, when, in response to Pope Sergius I's refusal to accede to the canons of the Quinisext Council, Justinian dispatched his *protospatharios* to Rome with orders to arrest the pontiff and transport him to Constantinople. Although thwarted in his mission by the intervention of the army of Ravenna and in imminent fear of losing his life, the imperial agent was nonetheless protected by the pope, who calmed the crowd and restored order to the city.[243] Sergius' successor John VI similarly intervened several years later to prevent injury to the exarch Theophylaktos, who had come to Rome ostensibly to cause trouble for the pontiff.[244]

When he returned to power in 705, Justinian II once more addressed the delicate issue of Rome's adherence to the canons of the Quinisext Council. This time, however, he applied conciliation and compromise rather than brute force. Dispatching two metropolitan bishops to Pope John VII, the emperor requested that the pontiff confirm those canons that he approved while rejecting those he found offensive. The pope, however, took no action and returned the canons without any comment whatsoever.[245] When Pope Constantine was summoned to the capital in the summer of 710, it was obvious that the relentless emperor meant to settle once and for all the issue of Rome's acceptance of the Trullan decrees.[246] While many of his predecessors would have dreaded the command, Pope Constantine appears to have responded to it with alacrity.[247]

The pontiff's haste to obey the imperial summons was the result of many factors.[248] Constantine identified with Byzantium as perhaps no Roman pontiff before him ever had. Except for an antipope who lasted for only a year, Pope Constantine I is the only pope ever to have chosen to be called Constantine. In making that choice, he selected a name that was not simply Eastern, but quintessentially so. Paradoxically, too, he was identifying himself with the emperor whose foundation of a new and resplendent capital on the Bosphorus had eclipsed Old Rome, robbing it of its ancient imperial glory and creating an enmity for Constantine the Great that the abandoned former capital would harbor forever after.[249] Pope Constantine was also familiar with Constantinople. He had already visited the capital on two occasions, first as one of the Roman legates to the Sixth Ecumenical Council in 680/681 and again in 682 when he delivered Pope Leo II's fulsome letter to the emperor Constantine IV.[250] It is likely that he had met the prince Justinian on both of these occasions and perhaps had formed a bond with the young heir apparent that he probably thought he could advantageously employ on Rome's behalf. As a Syrian, moreover, Constantine was fluent in Greek, intimately familiar with the practices and traditions of the East, and thus fully at ease in the oriental milieu of the early-eighth-century Byzantine court.[251] The pope was careful to ensure that those who traveled with him to the capital were cut from similar cloth. For it is both an indicator of the ethnic composition of the papal court in 710 and a tribute to the pope's sagacity that of the sizeable retinue that accompanied him to Constantinople all but two of the thirteen identified by name were from families of Eastern provenance.[252] Moreover, the pontiff's confidence in the emperor's continued high regard for the Apostolic See, and thus for the ultimate success of his voyage to Byzantium, can only have been intensified by Justinian II's brutal treatment of the Ravennates. For in the eyes of the Roman church, the blinding of archbishop Felix was not so much a consequence of his participation in the plot to overthrow the emperor as the product of God's will, which, working through Justinian, had once again shown its favor for Rome, this time by punishing the disobedience of its perennially rebellious suffragan.[253] But more than anything else, Pope Constantine's speed to obey the imperial summons was dictated by the desire to forestall, if at all possible, a rupture between Rome and Byzantium. For the early-eighth-century pontiffs, whether Easterners like Constantine, Gregory III, and Zacharias or a Latin like Gregory II, were not prepared to countenance anything that might lead to a break with Constantinople, if it was in their power to prevent it.[254]

On October 5, 710, Pope Constantine and his entourage set sail from Portus bound for the imperial court. Stopping at Naples, they met the exarch John Rizokopos, who was on his way to Rome where, shortly thereafter, he executed four high-ranking papal officials by cutting their throats.[255] It is possible that Rizokopos, acting on the emperor's orders, had committed these murders so as to eliminate a small but influential coterie of church officials who opposed Pope Constantine's policy of rapprochement with Constantinople and, as a show of protest, had refused to join him.[256] The pontiff had to have been aware of the exarch's acts before he left Italy since from Naples the papal party went on to Sicily, then to Gallipoli, and finally to Otranto where they spent the winter.[257] But even so, Constantine was undeterred. Crossing the Ionian Sea to Greece and on to the island of Chios, where the *strategos* of the imperial fleet of the Karabisianoi received him "with the highest honor," the pope proceeded toward Constantinople.

The pontiff was lavishly received into the capital. Seated upon a horse caparisoned with gilded saddle cloths and golden bridles and bearing on his head the *kamelaukion*, or diadem, which the sovereign alone was authorized to wear and then only on "a great public festival of the Lord," Pope Constantine was greeted in the manner of an imperial *adventus* at the seventh milestone from the city by Justinian's son, the coemperor Tiberios, along with the patriarch Kyros, members of the senate, the city's leading nobles, as well as numerous clerics and a throng of citizens.[258] The emperor, who was in Nicaea when the pope arrived, urged the pontiff to meet him in Nicomedia where the *Liber Pontificalis* and other Western sources describe the grossly exaggerated and highly unlikely scene of Justinian, crown upon his head, prostrating himself before the pontiff, begging forgiveness for his sins, and kissing the pope's feet.[259] It is far more probable that the two men exchanged mutual salutations with equal dignity.[260] While Justinian II may indeed have held Pope Constantine in high esteem, he would hardly have gone so far as to compromise the higher regard in which he held himself and his imperial position by groveling before the bishop of Rome.

On Sunday, the pontiff celebrated Mass, and Justinian received communion from his hands, thereafter vaguely confirming all the Roman church's privileges. Those privileges may have included a reaffirmation of Rome's ecclesiastical primacy, its authority over the church of Ravenna, and its exemption from taxes on the papal patrimonies that Constantine IV and Justinian II had previously granted.[261] The matter of Rome's acceptance of the Trullan canons appears to have been diplomatically skirted. Notwithstanding the claim that the deacon Gregory's replies to the emperor's inquiries "about certain chapters . . . solved every disputed point," no definitive result seems to have been reached.[262] That may, however, have been precisely what the parties had determined was the best course to pursue. While probably making concessions on grounds of *economia* that were enough to avoid the emperor's notorious temper, the pope does not appear to have retreated from the Roman church's refusal to accept those canons that it found objectionable.[263] For his part, Justinian seems to have obtained enough of a papal imprimatur of the Trullan canons so that the council's comprehensive program of canonical reform could at least nominally be deemed to have been a success.[264]

The so-called Compromise of Nicomedia demonstrated that neither the pope nor the emperor was willing to see the unity of the empire fractured over a handful of customs in which Roman practice differed from those of Constantinople. While Justinian II's legendary temper had led him to force the issue of Rome's acceptance of all the Trullan canons with Sergius I and John VII, by the time Constantine I came East some two decades later both he and the pope had come to the realization that imperial unity was to be preferred over ecclesiastical uniformity. By ordering and obtaining the presence of the pope in Constantinople, Justinian had reasserted his authority over the Papacy proving that the imperial writ still ran in Rome with sufficient authority to compel the empire's leading subject in the West to come to the capital when the emperor commanded. But most of all, the dreaded possibility of a rupture between Byzantium and Rome had been averted. The *imperium Romanum Christianum* was, like the Trinity, still one and undivided.

Notes

1. The recitation of the prayer *Agnus Dei, qui tollis peccata mundi, miserere nobis* ("The Lamb of God, who removeth the sin of the world, have mercy on us.") in both Greek and Latin at the Fraction of the Host during the Mass was instituted by the Syrian Pope Sergius I sometime before 701. *LP* I, p. 376.

2. *Vita Sancti Wilfridi* in B. Krutsch and W. Levison, eds., *MGH Scriptores Rerum Merovingicarum* VI, c. 5 (Hanover, 1913); Bede. *A History of the English Church and People*, trans. Leo Sherley-Price (Baltimore, 1965), pp. 300–2; "LXIX. Nuntius ad Exarchum de Transitu," in *Liber Diurnus Romanorum Pontificum*, ed. Theodor E. Von Sickel (Darmstadt, 1966), p. 49; *LP* I, p. 341; Walter Berschin, "Bonifatius Consiliarius: Ein römischer Übersetzer der byzantinischen Epoche des Papsttums," in A. Lebner and W. Berschin, eds., *Lateinische Kultur im VIII Jahrhundert. Traube-Gedenkschrift* (St. Ottilien, 1989), pp. 25–40.

3. Bede, id., p. 302.

4. As counselor to Pope Sergius I and probably because he had advised the pontiff to reject the canons of the Quinisext Council, Boniface was arrested on orders of Justinian II and taken to Constantinople. *LP* I, p. 373. He returned to Rome sometime in the mid to late 690s where, at the request of a certain Theodoros, *primicerius defensorum* of the Roman church, he translated Sophronios of Jerusalem's hagiographical work the *Miracula SS. Cyri et Iohannis* from Greek to Latin. Berschin, id., pp. 31–40.

5. Bede, id., pp. 303–4.

6. *LP* I, p. 350.

7. Bede, id., p. 304; Philip Jaffé, *Regesta Pontificum Romanorum*, Vol. I (Graz, 1956), p. 238.

8. *LP* I, p. 383.

9. *Vita Sancti Wilfridi*, id., p. 247; Colgrave, *The Life of Bishop Wilfrid by Eddius Stephanus*, id., p. 113; Jaffé, id., p. 246.

10. Bede, id., p. 307.

11. Bede, id., p. 305; Berschin, id., p. 36.

12. P. A. B. Llewellyn, "The Names of the Roman Clergy, 401–1046," *Rivista di Storia della Chiesa in Italia* 35 (1981), Table IV, p. 369.

13. The Easterners included bishops Niketas of Silva Candida and Georgios of Portus, the priests Michael, Paulus, and Georgios, the *secundicerius notariorum* Georgios, the *primicerius defensorum* Ioannes, Cosmas the *sakellarios*, Sissinius the *nomenclator*, Sergius the *scriniarius*, and a subdeacon named Dorotheos. *LP* I, p. 389.

14. Easterners attending the Roman synod of 721 included the bishops Ioannes, Georgios, Gregorios, Andreas, Anastasios, Sergius, and Petros. Among the priests, four were named Ioannes, two each Sissinius, Gregorios, and Marinos, and the remaining presbyters consisted of Eustratios, Thalassios, Constantinos, and Epiphanios. The orientals among the diaconate included the archdeacon Petros, and the deacons Moschos and Gregorios. Among its acts, the synod anathematized an Eastern diaconissa named Epiphania. *Mansi* XII, 261–66.

15. Petros, Theophanes, Sergius, and Iordanes (or Ioannes) were probably bishops. The deacons included the archdeacon Moschos, Zacahrias, the future pope, Ioannes, The-

ophylaktos, and Gemmulos. *Mansi* XII, 299–300; Angelo Mai, *Scriptorers veterum Vaticana collectio*, Vol. V (Rome, 1825–1838), pp. 210–11.

16. *LP* I, 417.

17. The subscribing bishops who were Easterners consisted of Ioannes, Andreas, Epiphanius, Gregorios, and two named Sissinius. The oriental presbyters included three named Ioannes, including the archpriest of the church of Rome, four named Sergius, two named Gregorios, and two named Theodoros. The remaining priests consisted of Eustra-tios, Stephanos, Andreas, Sissinius, Petros, Theophanios, and Iordanes. The diaconate included the archdeacon Moschos and the deacons Zacharias, Ioannes, Theophylaktos, and Gemmulos. *LP* I, p. 423; G. B. de Rossi, *Inscriptiones Christianae Urbis Romae Septimo Saeculo Antiquiores*, Vol. 2, Pt. 1 (Rome, 1888), p. 414nn8–9.

18. Bishops of eastern provenance included seven named Ioannes, two each named Theophanes, Arkadios, Petros, Thomas, Andreas, Maurikios, Niketas, and Vitalianos, and one each named Theodoros and Gregorios. Greek presbyters consisted of two each named Gregorios, Anastasios, and Leo and one each named Ioannes, Theodoros, An-dreas, Petros, Iordanes, Theophylaktos, and Epiphanios. Among the diaconate, there were two each named Theodoros, Ioannes, and Gregorios, and one each named Stepha-nos and Paulos. *Mansi* XII, 384c–384d.

19. The bishops of Eastern origin included Epiphanios, Gregorios, Niketas, and Theodoros, while the Greek priests consisted of three named Stephanos, two each named Gregorios and Leo, and one each named Ioannes, Theodoros, Anastasios, Georgios, Sergius, Iordanes, Theophanios, Eustathios, and Procopios. Only a certain priest named Dominicus from the titular church of St. Prisca was Latin. There were no subscribing deacons. *Mansi* XII, 384r–384s.

20. *LP* I, pp. 376, 383.

21. Id., pp. 383, 385.

22. Id., pp. 386, 388.

23. Id., pp. 388–93.

24. Id., pp. 393, 396.

25. Id., pp. 410, 415–21, 426–35.

26. Id., pp. 364, 366–67.

27. Id., pp. 367–69, 371.

28. Lynn T. White, *Latin Monasticism in Norman Sicily* (Cambridge, MA, 1938), p. 22.

29. Charles Diehl, *Études sur l'Administration Byzantine dans l'Exarchat de Ravenne (568–751)* (New York, 1959), pp. 258, 278–79; Jules Gay, "Quelques remarques sur les papes grecs et syriens," *Melanges offerts à M. Gustave Schlumberger* (Paris, 1924), pp. 40–54.

30. *LP* I, p. 350.

31. Id., p. 369.

32. Id., p. 386.

33. Id., p. 373.

34. Id., pp. 391–92; Paul the Deacon, *Historia Langobardorum*, VI, 34, MGH *Scrip-tores Rerum Germanicarum* (Repr. Hanover, 1987), pp. 226–27; Franz Dölger, *Regesten der Kaiserurkunden des Oströmischen Reiches von 565–1453* (Hildesheim, 1976), No. 271,

p. 33; Jaffé, id., p. 248. Philippikos Bardanes, son of a certain Nikephoros of Pergamum, had been exiled to the Chersonese. In November, 711, he deposed and executed Justinian II, thereafter ordering that the slain emperor's severed head be sent westward as far as Rome. After being proclaimed emperor, Philippikos convened a synod that rejected the Sixth Ecumenical Council and officially restored Monothelitism. The names of Patriarch Sergius of Constantinople and Pope Honorius I were restored to the diptychs, while the acts of the Sixth Ecumenical Council were publicly burned and the picture of the synod removed from the imperial palace. Agathon, *Epilogos, Mansi* XII, pp. 189–96; Theophanes, *Chronographia*, pp. 527–30; Georgios Cedrenos, *Historiarum Compendium*, pp. 784–85; *The Synodicon Vetus*, trans. John Duffy and John Parker (Washington, D.C., 1979), p. 121; Nikephoros, Patriarch of Constantinople, *Short History*, trans. Cyril Mango (Washington, D.C., 1990), p. 113; see Dorothy deF. Abrahamse, "Religion, Heresy and Popular Prophecy in the Reign of Philippikos Bardanios (711–713)," *East European Quarterly* 13 (1979): 385–408.

35. BHG 89; Bernard Flusin, *Saint Anastase le Perse et l'histoire de la Palestine au début du VIIe siècle*, Vol. I, Les Textes (Paris, 1992), p. 176. Ἐγώ ἐποίσα ἵνα χρισθή ὁ Φιλιππικός εἰς βασιλέα, καθότι φίλος μου ἦν.

36. *LP* I, p. 416; Jaffé, id., p. 257. The clash between Rome and Constantinople over sacred images had been preceded by years of conflict between Pope Gregory II and the emperor Leo III over the issue of imperial taxes on the papal patrimonies in Italy. The flow of substantial sums of money from Rome to Byzantium had been severely draining the fiscal resources of the Papacy, and frustrating papal plans to utilize those revenues to provision the city and thus relieve Rome from dependence on long-distance grain supplies. Milton V. Anastos, "Leo III's Edict against the Images in the Year 726–727 and Italo-Byzantine Relations Between 726 and 730," *Byzantinische Forschungen* 3 (1968) 5–41; Federico Marazzi, "Il Conflitto fra Leone III Isaurico e il Papato fra il 725 e il 723, e il 'Definitivo' Inizio del Medioevo a Roma: Un' Ipotesi in Discussione," *Papers of the British School at Rome* 59 (1991): 231–57. Pope Gregory III's synodal initiative in 731 resulted in Leo III's confiscation of the papal patrimonies in Sicily, Calabria, and Illyricum, and the transfer of ecclesiatical jurisdiction over those regions from Rome to Constantinople. Dölger, id., Nos. 300 and 301, p. 36; Milton V. Anastos, "The Transfer of Illyricum, Calabria and Sicily to the jurisdiction of the Patriarch of Constantinople in 732–733," *Studi Bizantini e Neoellenici in Onore di S.G. Mercati* (Rome, 1957), pp. 14–31.

37. *LP* I, p. 383; Paul the Deacon, *Hisotria Langobardorum*, VI, 27, id., p. 224; Bede, *Anglo Saxonis Chronicon sive De Sex Huius Seculi Aetatibus* in *Opera Historica Minora*, ed. Joseph Stevenson (London, 1841), p. 201.

38. *LP* I, p. 385; Paul the Deacon, *Historia Langobardorum*, VI, 28, id., p. 225; Bede, *Anglo Saxonis Chronicon*, id., p. 201.

39. *LP* I, p. 388.

40. *LP* I, pp. 427, 435.

41. Id., pp. 279, 375; AA.SS. Sept. VII (1760), pp. 430–77; H. Delehaye, "Les recueils antiques de Miracles des Saints," *Analecta Bollandiana* 43 (1925): 8–18; Paul Kehr, *Italia Pontificia*, Vol. I (Berlin, 1961), pp. 68–69.

42. *LP* I, p. 375.

43. Id., p. 383.

44. Born in Rome during the time of Commodus, Eugenia accompanied her parents and siblings to Alexandria where her father had been appointed eparch and where she received a rigorous classical education. After reading the epistles of St. Paul, she became so impressed with Christianity that she decided to convert, secretly leaving her home and entering a nearby monastery disguised as a man. She eventually received the monastic schema, revealed her true identity, and returned to Rome where, after refusing to sacrifice to the pagan gods, she was beheaded. Sophronios Eustratiades, Ἁγιολόγιον τῆς Ὀρθοδόξου Ἐκκλησίας (Athens, 1995), p. 129; Per Jonas Nordhagen, *The Frescoes of John VII* (A.D. 705–707) *in S. Maria Antiqua in Rome* (Rome, 1968); Pietro Romanelli and Per Jonas Nordhagen, *S. Maria Antiqua* (Rome, 1964).

45. *LP* I, pp. 317, 418–19.

46. Id., p. 418; Kehr, id., p. 125; H. Delehaye, *Étude sur le légendier romain* (Brussels, 1936), pp. 151–71.

47. *LP* I, p. 419; *AA.SS.* Aug. V (1741), pp. 119–36 (Genesius of Arles); *LP* I, p. 419; H. Delehaye, *Commentarius Perpetuus in Martyrologium Hieronymianum*, *AA.SS.*, Vol. 65 (1931), pp. 347–48 (Processus and Martinian); *LP* I, p. 419; 141(Callistus).

48. *LP* I, pp. 374–75.

49. Id., p. 385.

50. Id., pp. 417–18; Kehr, id., p. 137.

51. *LP* I, p. 432; Kehr, id., pp. 137–38.

52. Gregory Dix, *The Shape of the Liturgy* (Repr. San Francisco, 1982), p. 457.

53. Amédée Gastoué, *Les Origines du Chant Romain* (Paris, 1907), p. 113.

54. Theodor Klauser, "Der Übergang der Römischen Kirche von der Griechischen zur Lateinischen Liturgiesprache," in *Miscellenea Giovanni Mercati*, Vol. I, Studi e Testi No. 121 (Vatican City, 1946), p. 496. During the first two centuries of the Roman church, ten of the fourteen popes were Greek. Seven of the fourteen popes during the third century were Greek. But, of the eleven pontiffs who occupied the Apostolic See in the fourth century, only one was Greek. Id., p. 469n9.

55. Popes Agatho (678–681), Leo II (682–683), Conon (684–685), and Sergius I (687–701) were all either born or raised in Sicily. *LP* I, pp. 350, 359, 368, 371; Jules Gay, *L'Italie méridionale et l'Empire Byzantin* (Paris, 1904), pp. 10–11. The confluence of Byzantine and Latin liturgical practices in Sicily was illustrated by the discovery there of three censers in the late nineteenth century. Each censer contains the identical Greek inscription from a liturgical text known as the Prayer of the Censer (Εὐχή τοῦ Θυμιάματος), which is found in the Byzantine liturgy and is based on the biblical text in the Gospel according to Luke where Zacharias, father of John the Baptist, recounts an angelic vision. The prayer appears to have been incorporated into the so-called Liturgy of St. Peter, a Latin Mass composed in the ninth century and translated into Greek in the tenth century, or possibly earlier, which contains a mixture of Byzantine and Roman elements and which appears to have been used by Greek-speaking priests who celebrated the liturgy according to the Latin rite. S. Petrides, "À propos d'encensoirs byzantins de Sicile," *Byzantinische Zeitschrift* 13 (1904): 480–81; Paolo Orsi, "Incensiere bizantino della Sicilia," *Byzantinische Zeitschrift* 5 (1896): 567–69; Paolo Orsi, "Nuovo incensiere bizantino della Sicilia," *Byzantinische Zeitschrift* 7 (1898): 29; H. W. Codrington, *The*

Liturgy of St. Peter (Munster, 1936). The Greek text of the Prayer of the Censer appears in *Vat. MS. Gr.* 1970 (Rossano) as follows: Ο Θεός ὁ ἅγιος ὡς προσδέξω τό θυμίαμα τοῦ Ζαχαρίου οὕτω καί ἔκ τῶν χειρῶν ἡμῶν τῶν ἁμαρτωλῶν πρόσδεξαι τό θυμίαμα τοῦτο εἰς ὀσμήν εὐωδίας. Id., p. 137.

56. *LP* I, p. 359; Paul Cagin, *Te Deum ou Illatio?* (Abbaye de Solesmes, 1906), pp. 155–57, 168; see also Anton Baumstark, "'Te Deum' und eine Gruppe Griechischer Abendhymnen," *Oriens Christianus*, Vol. 12, Ser. 3 (1937), pp. 1–26.

57. *LP* I, p. 371. Latin speakers were directed to sing *Agnus Dei, qui tollis peccata mundi, miserere nobis, LP* I, p. 376, while those who spoke Greek would have intoned the words *Ο ἀμνός τοῦ θεοῦ ὁ αἴρων τῆν ἁμαρτίαν τοῦ κόσμου Ελέησον ἡμᾶς*. Codrington, id., p. 144.

58. Van Dijk attributes Greek precedence over Latin as either a relic from the time when Greek was the liturgical *lingua franca* of the Roman church or as a mark of respect for the fact that the Greek text was in most cases the original. He specifically rejects the hypothesis that Greek preceded Latin because Greeks outnumberd the native Latin population. S. J. P. Van Dijk, "The Medieval Easter Vespers of the Roman Clergy," *Sacris Erudiri* 19 (1969–1970), p. 314. See Walter Berschin, *Greek Letters and the Latin Middle Ages*, trans. Jerold C. Frakes (Washington, D.C., 1988), pp. 89–90.

59. Antoine Chavasse, *Le Sacramentaire Gélasien (Vaticanus Reginensis 316)* (Paris, 1958), pp. 107–110; L. Duchesne, *Origines du culte chrétien* (Paris, 1889), pp. 158–59ff.; E. Martene, *De antiquis ecclesiae ritibus* (Antwerp, 1736), col. 279–80.

60. *Ordo Romanus XI* in Michel Andrieu, *Les Ordines Romani du Haut Moyen Age*, Vol. II. Les Textes. (Ordines I–XIII) (Louvain, 1971), pp. 412–13, 434.

61. *Ordines Romani XXIII and XXX B*, id., Vol. III, pp. 272, 471–72; J. Mabillon, *Museum Italicum*, Vol. II (Paris, 1689), p. 25n40.

62. *Ordo Romanus XXVIII*, id., p. 412; *PL* 78: 955ff.; L. Brou, "Les chants en langue grecque dans les liturgies latines," *Sacris Erudiri* 1 (1948), p. 171.

63. *PL* 78: 965–68; Van Dijk, "The Medieval Easter Vespers of the Roman Clergy," id., pp. 314–15.

64. Ugo Gaisser, "Brani greci nella liturgia latina," *Rassegna gregoriana per gli studi liturgici e per il canto sacro*, 8–9 (1902), p. 126. On Easter Monday, the alternating verses were *Ο ποιμαίνων τόν Ισραήλ* and *Qui regis Israel, Ο καθήμενος επί τῶν Χερουβίμ* and *Qui sedes super Cherubim*, and *Αμπελον ἐξ Αἰγύπτου* and *Vineam de Aegypto*. For Easter Tuesday, the verses were *Προσέχετε λαός μου* and *Attendite popule meus*, and *Ανοίξω ἕν παραβολαῖς* and *Aperiam in parabolis*. On Easter Friday, the verses consisted of *Επί σοί, Κύριε, ἤλπισα* and *In te, Domine, speravi*, and *Κλῖνον πρός μέ τό οὖς σου* and *Inclina ad me aurem tuam*. On Easter Saturday, the verses were *Οἱ οὐρανοί διηγοῦντα* and *Coeli enarrant*, and *Ημέρα τῇ ἡμέρα ἐρεύγεται* and *Dies diei eructat*. On the Octave of Easter, or the first Sunday after Easter, the three alternating verses were *Δεῦτε ἀγαλλασώμεθα* and *Venite exultemus*, *Προφθάσωμεν τό πρόσοπον αὐτοῦ* and *Praeveniamus faciem eius*, and *Ότι Θεός μέγας* and *Quoniam Deus magnus*. Id., p. 126; Brou, id., p. 172; Van Dijk, "The Medieval Easter Vespers of the Roman Clergy," id., p. 294ff.

65. Gaisser, "Brani greci nella liturgia latina," id., pp. 126–27.

66. Chavasse, *Le Sacramentaire Gélasien*, id., pp. 107–9; V. Gastoué, *Pâques à Rome au VIIe siécle* (Saint Gervais, 1901); Gaisser, id., p. 129.

67. Codrington, id., pp. 3, 9; Ἡ Θεία Λειτουργία τῶν Προηγιασμένων (Athens, 1987), p. 217; "The Divine Office of the Presanctified Gifts," in *The Orthodox Liturgy* (Oxford, 1982), p. 196.

68. Codrington, id., pp. 3; Ἡ Θεία Λειτουργία τῶν Προηγιασμένων in *Ιερατικόν*, id., p. 209; "The Divine Office of the Presanctified Gifts," in *The Orthodox Liturgy*, id., p. 181.

69. *The Festal Menaion*, trans. Mother Mary and Kallistos Ware (Repr. London, 1984), p. 107; Gaisser, id., p. 131; Brou, id., p. 172; Codrington, id., p. 3.

70. *The Festal Menaion*, id., p. 155; Codrington, id., p. 3. The prayer *Ecce enim propter lignum*, which was added to the antiphon *Crucem tuam adoramus* and recited by the deacon or priest during Sunday matins and every day of Great Lent, is the same as a part of the troparion Ἀνάστασιν Χριστοῦ θεασάμενοι, which is recited during the service of the Ὄρθρος in the Eastern tradition. *Ιερατικόν*, id., p. 57; Gaisser, id., p. 131.

71. Anton Baumstark, "Byzantinisches in den Weihnachtexten des Römishcen Antiphonarius Officii," *Oriens Christianus*, Vol. 11, Ser. 3 (1936), pp. 166–73. The *stichoi* of the second canon that contain this motif include "Today the Virgin bears the Master within the cave"; "Today the Master is born as a babe of a Virgin Mother"; "Today shepherds behold the Saviour wrapped in swaddling clothes and laid in a manger"; "Today the Master who cannot be touched is wrapped as a babe in swaddling rags"; and "Today all creation rejoices greatly and makes glad, for Christ is born of a Virgin Maid." Mother Mary and Ware, *The Festal Menaion*, id., p. 283. The most famous hymn reflecting the *Hodie-Σήμερον* motif is undoubtedly the *kontakion* "Today the Virgin gives birth to Him who is above all being," written by the sixth-century hymnographer Romanos the Melodist, who was born in the Syrian city of Emesa, served as a deacon in the church of the Resurrection in Beirut, and came to Constantinople during the reign of the emperor Anastasios where he was attached to the church of the Virgin Mary in the Hexi-Marmara suburb of the capital. Barry Baldwin, *An Anthology of Byzantine Poetry* (Amsterdam, 1985), pp. 112–13.

72. Baumstark, "Byzantinisches in den Weihnachtexten des Römishcen Antiphonarius Officii," id., p. 163ff.; Brou, id., p. 169; Gaisser, id., p. 130; Codrington, id., p. 3.

73. Gaisser, id., p. 130.

74. Placid De Meester, *Rituale-Benedizionale Bizantino* (Rome, 1930), p. 422; Placid De Meester, "Formulaire grec dans une traduction latine ancienne," *Revue Bénédictine* 29 (1912): 29–30. The *stichera* for the Byzantine service of the Great Blessing of the Waters have been attributed to Sophronios of Jerusalem. *The Festal Menaion*, id., p. 348.

75. *LP* I, p. 376.

76. Gaisser, id., p. 130; Codrington, id., p. 3. Brou refers to an eighth- or ninth-century bilingual manuscript known as the *Codex Blandiniensis*, which contains an *ordo* for the feast of the Presentation with the antiphons *Ave Maria* and *Adorna thalamum* set forth in Greek and Latin. Id., p. 170.

77. Gaisser, id., p. 130.

78. Anton Baumstark, "Die Hodieantiphonen des römischen Breviers und der Kreis ihrer griechischen Parallelen," *Die Kirchenmusik* 10 (1909), pp. 153–60; see also Anton Baumstark, Übersetzungen aus dem griechischen in den Responsoriem der Messen des Triduum Sacrum," *Der Katholik* 93, I (1913): 209–20; Anton Baumstark, "Orientalisches

in den Texten der abendländischen Palmenfier," *Jahrbuch für Liturgiewissenschaft* 7 (1927), p. 148.

79. Gaisser, id., p. 130; Brou, id., p. 171; Jean-Michel Hanssens, *Institutiones Liturgicae de ritibus orientalibus*, Vol. 3 (Rome, 1932), pp. 96–156.

80. Anton Baumstark, "Orientalisches in den Texten der abendländischen Palmenfier," id., p. 148; see generally, H. Quentin, *Les Martyrologes historiques du moyen-âge* (Paris, 1908). During her pilgrimage to the East sometime between 381 and 384, the Roman noblewoman Egeria visited Jerusalem, where she recorded that on Palm Sunday evening at "five o'clock the passage is read from the Gospel about the children who met the Lord with palm branches, saying, 'Blessed is he that cometh in the name of the Lord.' At this the bishop and all the people rise from their places, and start off on foot down from the summit of the Mount of Olives. All the people go before him with psalms and antiphons, all the time repeating, 'Blessed is he that cometh in the name of the Lord. . . . ' Everyone is carrying branches, either palm or olive, and they accompany the bishop in the very way the people did when once they went down with the Lord." *Egeria's Travels*, trans. John Wilkinson (London, 1971), p. 133.

81. C. Coebergh, "Le pape Zacharie et la bénédiction des rameaux," *Studia Patristica* X, Pt. 1, Papers presented to the Fifth International Conference on Patristic Studies, Oxford, 1967 (Berlin, 1970), pp. 328–32. For the text of the benediction, which appears in a letter from Pope Zacharias to St. Boniface, see G. Morin, "Notes liturgiques. Une Formule de la bénédiction des rameaux," *Revue Bénédictine* 27 (1910), pp. 401–2.

82. *Ordo XXVII* in Andrieu, id., pp. 362ff.; *LP* I, p. 432; Jan Kostenec, "Studies on the Great Palace in Constantinople. 1. The Palace of Constantine the Great," *Byzantinoslavica* 49, 2 (1998), p. 282. The northern end of the Triklinos of Nineteen Couches, which was raised and accessible by a stairway, was known as the Imperial or Great Akkoubiton. It was there that the emperor changed from his ceremonial clothes into less formal garments and, screened by columns and curtains so that he could not be observed, dined during imperial banquets. Id., p. 288; Constantine VII Porphyrogenitos. *Le Livre des Cérémonies*, trans. Albert Vogt, Commentaire (Paris, 1967), pp. 68–69; Liutprand, *Antapodosis*, ed., A. Bauer and R. Rau in *Quellen zur Geschichte der sächsischen Kaiserzeit* (Darmstadt, 1971), VI, 8; see also Cyril Mango, *The Brazen House* (Copenhagen, 1959). Pope Zacharias's admiration for the imperial palace was also reflected in his construction of a new portico and entrance tower for the Lateran *patriarchium* complete with with bronze doors and railings all of which was "almost certainly erected in imitation of the Chalke entrance to the imperial palace of Constantinople." Bryan Ward-Perkins, *From Classical Antiquity to the Middle Ages: Urban Public Building in Northern and Central Italy* A.D. *300–850* (Oxford, 1984), p. 175; Richard Krautheimer, *Rome: Profile of a City, 312–1308* (Princeton, 1980), p. 121.

83. For the Greek text of the *stichera* of Easter, see Πεντηκοστάριον (Φῶς Press: Athens, 1984), p. 5. The potion is referred to by Constantine VII Porphyrogenitos as κράματος, the genitive form of the noun κρᾶμα, meaning a "mixture," and probably related to the expression κεκραμένος οἶνος, or diluted wine. *Le Livre des Cérémonies*, trans. Albert Vogt, Texte (Paris, 1967), p. 20; E. A. Sophocles, *Greek Lexicon of the Roman and Byzantine Periods* (Repr., Hildesheim, 1975), p. 688. Andrieu renders the relevant text of the various manuscripts of *Ordo Romanus XXVII* dealing with the common drink at Easter as follows:

Deinde descendunt primates ecclesiae ad accubita invitante notario vicedomni et bibunt ter, de greco I, de pactisi I et unum de procoma. Ordo XXVII in Andrieu, id., p. 366. Van Dijk has interpreted this to mean that the pope and clergy shared a three-fold drink consisting "*de greco I, de pactisi I et unum de procoma,*" S. J. P. Van Dijk, "The Medieval Easter Vespers of the Roman Clergy," id., p. 349, although it seems that a more accurate interpretation of the text is that the celebrants, consistent with what was probably similar Constantinopolitan practice, partook of a single drink of wine containing elements from three vintages after the fashion described by Constantine VII Porphyrogenitos in *De Ceremoniis*.

84. Guglielmo Cavallo, ed., *The Byzantines* (Chicago, 1997), pp. 4, 248; V. V. Bykov, *L'estetica bizantina: Problemi teorici* (Galatina, 1983), pp. 148–52.

85. Constantine VII Porphyrogenitos. *Le Livre des Cérémonies, Vol. I,* id., p. 3ff.; Cavallo, id., pp. 248–52.

86. *Ordo Romanus Primus* in Andrieu, id., pp.67–108; E. G. Cuthbert F. Atchley, *Ordo Romanus Primus* (London, 1905), Appendix 1, pp. 116–49.

87. Andrieu, id., p. 73; H. Leclercq, "Ordines Romani," in *Dictionnaire d'Archéologie Chrétienne et de Liturgie,* Vol. XII, Pt. 2 (Paris, 1936), p. 2417. In these examples, the Latin version of the texts is followed in parentheses by the Greek original.

88. Andrieu, id., pp. 74–75, 79; Leclercq, id., p. 2418.

89. J. Brinktrine, "Mysterium Fidei," *Ephemerides Liturgicae* 44 (1930), pp. 493–500. The words *mysterium fidei* are the equivalent of the expression μυστήριον τῆς πίστεως, which is based on the text of I Timothy 3:9, and is recited during that part of the Byzantine liturgy when the priest takes heated water from the deacon, pours it onto the wine in the chalice, and says the words Ζέσις πίστεως πλήρης Πνεύματος Ἁγίου or "The heat of the faith filled with the Holy Spirit." Id., p. 499.

90. For the ecclesiastical calendar of saints and feast days recognized in the East in the late seventh century, see the *Menologion* of Basil II, which was compiled in the tenth century by Simeon Metaphrastes at the request of the emperor Basil II (976–1025) and reflected the hagiological observances of the oriental churches around the year 662. PG 117: 15–18, 19ff.; H. Delehaye, "Les Ménologes grecs," *Analecta Bollandiana* 16 (1897): 311–29; *Enciclopedia Cattolica,* Vol. 8 (Rome, 1952), pp. 689–90. See also Enrica Follieri, Santi Occidentali nell'Innografia Bizantina," in *Atti del Convegno Internazionale sul Tema: L'Oriente Cristiano nella Storia della Civiltà,* Rome, March 31–April 3, 1963 (Rome, 1964): 251–72.

91. *LP* I, p. 317; Jaffé, id., p. 220.

92. G. Morin, "Liturgie et Basilisques de Rome au milieu du VIIe siècle," *Revue Bénédictine* 28 (1911): 327–28.

93. PG 50: 705; Morin, id.; David Hugh Farmer, *The Oxford Dictionary of Saints,* 2nd ed. (Oxford, 1987), p. 13.

94. Pope Sergius's Greek litany, which appears on the last leaf of the so-called Athelstan Psalter (*Cotton MS. Galba A xviii*), is commonly known as the Galba manuscript. It originated in Rome and probably came to England through a copy made in the late seventh or early eighth century at Winchester. Edmund Bishop, *Liturgica Historica* (Oxford, 1918), pp. 141–51.

95. *LP* I, p. 324; Jacobus de Voragine. *The Gold Legend: Readings on the Saints,* Vol. II, trans. William Granger Ryan (Princeton, 1995), pp. 160–64; Krautheimer, id., p. 72;

Kehr, id., p. 69; Emil Donckel, *Außerrömische Heilige in Rom* (Luxembourg, 1938), pp. 54–55.

96. *AA.SS.* Sept. III (1729) 22–23; *LP* I, p. 330; Kehr, id., p. 31; Donckel, id., pp. 28–30. For St. Anastasios the Fuller of Salona, see H. Delehaye, "S. Anastase, martyr de Salone," *Analecta Bollandiana* 16 (1897): 488, Albert Du Fourcq, *Étude sur les Gesta Martyrum Romains*, Vol. III (Repr. Paris, 1988), pp. 24–25, and *PL* 123: 167–68.

97. *AA.SS.* Ian. III (1729) 35–54 (St. Anastasios the Persian); Bernard Flusin, *Saint Anastase le Perse et l'histoire de la Palestine au début du VIIe siècle, Commentaire*. Vol. II (Paris, 1992), p. 370; Donckel, id., pp. 13, 38–39; Morin, id., pp. 297, 314, 318; *LP* I, p. 333. The feast day of St. Euplus (or Euplius) appears in the Roman calendar for the first time in the seventh century under the rubric "*Catanae, Eupli diaconi et martyris.*" *PL* 123:165–66. St. Euplus's *gesta*, or deeds, exist in both a Greek and Latin version, thus reflecting the cross-cultural ambience prevalent in Italy following the Byzantine Reconquest. See *BHL* 2728–29; *PG* 115: 524–39. The Greek *gesta*, which were probably written in an Eastern monastic community in Rome, Calabria, or Sicily, are, however, far more developed than their Latin counterpart, thereby reflecting the highly detailed and ornamented hagiographic style typical of the East. Du Fourcq, id.,Vol. II, pp. 183. For St. Theodore Stratelates, whose cult was based on his shrine at Euchaita in Pontus and whose abilties as a wonder-worker were extolled by Gregory of Nyssa, see *AA.SS.* Feb. II (1658) 23–37 and *AA.SS.* Nov. IV (1925) 11–89. St. Theodore's cult in Rome seems to have been centered at a church built in his honor at the foot of the Palatine during the middle of the seventh century. *LP* II, p. 41n6; Morin, id., p. 316.

98. Donckel, id., pp. 16–17; Jacobus de Voragine, Vol. I, id., pp. 289–91; Du Fourcq, Vol. I, id., p. 168. The strength and prevalence of St. Boniface's cult in early-seventh-century Rome may well be reflected in the fact that three popes in close succession—Boniface III (607), Boniface IV (608–615), and Boniface V (619–625)—all took the name of this martyr. *LP* I, pp. 316–17, 321. The *Gesta Bonifacii*, which exist in both Greek and Latin versions, were probably written in Rome during the first half of the seventh century by Cilician monks living in the monastery of St. Anastasios at Aquas Salvias. Du Fourcq has convincingly shown how the *Gesta's* conflation of Greek and Latin legends and their curious combination of Greek and Latin terms such as, for example, rendering Latin words in Greek characters, reflects, as in the case of the *Gesta* of St. Euplus, the Greco-Latin milieu that was already taking shape in Rome early in the seventh century. Du Fourcq, Vol. V, id., pp. 336–342.

99. Donckel, id., p. 56; Sophronios Eustratiades, Ἁγιολόγιον τῆς Ὀρθοδόξου Ἐκκλησίας (Athens, 1995), p. 226; J. P. Kirsche, *Der stadtrömische christliche Festkalender* (Münster, 1924), p. 148.

100. *AA.SS.* Mar. II (1668) 12–29; H. Delehaye, *Les passions des martyrs et les genres littéraires* (Brussels, 1921), pp. 210–35; P. F. de Cavalieri, "I quaranta martiri di Sebastia," in *Note agiographice, Studi e Testi* 49 (1928), pp. 155–84.

101. Donckel, id., pp. 108–9.

102. *Chronicon Paschale 284–628* A.D., trans. Michael Whitby and Mary Whitby (Liverpool, 1989), p. 20; *Egeria: Diary of a Pilgrimage*, trans. George E. Gingras (New York, 1970), p. 255n488; *PG* 117: 48.

103. Sozomen, *Historia Ecclesiastica* II, 26, *PG* 67: 1008; H. Usener, ed., *Der heilige Theodosios, Schriften des Theodosios und Kyrillos* (Leipzig, 1890), p. 71 (St. Theodosios the

Cenobiarch); AA.SS. Jul. I (1643), p. 138 (Life of St. Symeon); *Égérie, Journal de Voyage (Itinéraire)*, ed. and trans. Pierre Maraval, Sources Chrétiennes No. 296 (Paris, 1982), pp. 316–19; Sophronios of Jerusalem, *In Exaltationem S. Crucis*, PG 87: 3305; Sophronios of Jerusalem, *Life of St. Mary of Egypt*, PG 87: 3733; St. Andrew of Crete, *On the Exaltation of the Holy Cross*, PG 97: 1017–36; 1035–46; PG 117: 1040; L. Duchesne, *Christian Worship: Its Origin and Evolution*, trans. M. L. McClure (London, 1912), p. 274.

104. John, Bishop of Nikiu. *The Chronicle*, trans. R. H. Charles (London, 1916), pp. 192, 200.

105. *PG* 86: 2745.

106. AA.SS. Sept. IV (1753) p. 544; Duchesne, id., p. 275.

107. Alexander Monachos, *De Inventione Sanctae Crucis*, PG 87: 4062; 4064; 4072. Its obervance by the church of Constantinople on September 14 is also attested to by St. Sylvia of Aquitaine, St. Theodosios the Cenobiarch, and St. Andrew of Crete. P. Bernardakis, "Le Culte de la Croix chez les Grecs," *Echos d'Orient* 5 (1901–02), p. 196. On the occasion of the celebration of the feast of the Exaltation of the Cross on September 14, 614, the Precious Sponge "was itself also exalted with it [the Cross] in the Great Church. . . . " *Chronicon Paschale 284–628 A.D.*, id., p. 157. For prayers specially composed on the occasion of the feast of the Exaltation of the Holy Cross, see Nikephoros Kallistos Xanthopoulos, *Ecclesiasticae Historiae*, PG 147: 585.

108. A. Frolow, "Le culte de la relique de la Vraie Croix à la fin du VIe et au début du VIIe siècles," *Byzantinoslavica* 22 (1961), p. 336.

109. *The History of Theophylact Simocatta*, V, 16, trans. Michael and Mary Whitby (Oxford, 1986), p. 156; *Expeditio Persica II* in Agostino Pertusi, trans., *Giorgio di Pisidia. Poemi. I. Panegirici Epici*, (Ettal, 1959), p. 109, ll. 252–55; Constantine VII Porphyrogenitos. *De ceremoniis aulae byzantinae libri duo*, ed. J. J. Reiske (Bonn, 1829), p. 485; Frolow, "Le culte de la relique de la Vraie Croix à la fin du VIe et au début du VIIe siècles," id., p. 336; see also Nicholas Oikonomides, "The Concept of 'Holy War' and Two Tenth-century Byzantine Ivories," in *Peace and War in Byzantium. Essays in Honor of George T. Dennis, S. J.* (Washington, D.C., 1995), pp. 62–86.

110. *Chronicon Paschale 284–628 A.D.*, id., p. 156; Nikephoros, Patriarch of Constantinople, *Short History*, id., pp. 55, 63, 65; Theophanes, *Chronographia*, pp. 431, 459; Sebeos, *Histoire d'Héraclius*, trans. F. Macler (Paris, 1904), p. 91; George of Pisidia, *In restitutionem S. Crucis*, in Pertusi, id., pp. 225–30; Frolow, "Le culte de la relique de la Vraie Croix à la fin du VIe et au début du VIIe siècles," id., p. 338–339; P. Bernardakis, "Le Culte de la Croix chez les Grecs," id., p. 199.

111. Adamnanus, *Arculfi relatio de locis sanctis*, III, 3 in P. Geyer, ed., *Itinera, Corpus Scriptorum Ecclesiasticorum Latinorum*, Vol. 39 (Repr., New York, 1962), pp. 225, 287–88.

112. Canon 73 of the Quinisext Council in Friedrich Lauchert, ed., *Die Kanones der Wichtigsten Altkirchlichen Concilien* (Frankfurt am Main, 1961), p. 130. ὡς ἂν μή τῶν βαδιζόντων καταπατήσει τό τῆς νίκης ἡμῖν τρόπαιον ἐξυβείζοιτο.

113. *LP* I, p. 261; Antoine Chavasse, *Le Sacramentaire Gélasien* (Tournai, 1958), p. 358.

114. Chavasse, id., pp. 358–59. The earliest hymns to the Holy Cross anywhere in the West appear to have been composed at Poitiers by Venantius Fortunatus (ca. 530–ca. 600)

in the middle of the sixth century. Perhaps inspired by his eulogies, Queen Radegund sent a delegation to Constantinople to request a fragment of the True Cross from the emperor Justin II. See Gregory of Tours, *History of the Franks*, IX, 40, trans. Lewis Thorpe (London, 1974), p. 530. When they returned to Gaul with the treasured relic in 569, the legates were greeted by a procession singing the three hymns that Fortunatus had composed. Joseph Szövérffy, "Venantius Fortunatus and the Earliest Hymns to the Holy Cross," *Classical Folia* 20 (1965–1966): 107–22.

115. Chavasse, id., p. 360.

116. Id., pp. 358–60; *LP* I, n. 29, pp. 378–79. Baumstark contends that this hymn was introduced in Rome during the pontificates of either the Syrian popes Constantine I (708–715) or Gregory III (731–741), by which time the feast of the Elevation of the Cross had indisputably become part of the papal liturgical calendar. Anton Baumstark, "Der Orient und die Gesänge der Adoratio crucis," *Jahrbuch für Liturgiewissenschaft* 2 (1922), p. 16.

117. *LP* I, p. 374; Agnellus qui et Andreas, *Liber Pontificalis Ecclesiae Ravennatis* in O. Holder-Egger, ed., *MGH Scriptores Rerum Langobardicarum et Italicarum saeculum VI–IX* (Hanover, 1878), pp. 420–21.

118. Although Byzantium's promotion of the cult of the Holy Cross was undoubtedly an instrument of imperial propaganda designed to foster a sense of solidarity between the empire's Eastern subjects and Constantinople in the face of the Persians and later the Arabs, it is highly unlikely, as Dom Labot argues, that Pope Sergius I instituted the feast of the Exaltation of the Cross in Rome in order to rally the empire's Italian subjects against the Arabs. C. Labot, "Les Litanies des Saints," *Revue liturgique et monastique* (1930), pp. 330–31. Except for the fall of Byzantine Africa in 698, the period of Sergius's pontificate from 687 to 701 was not a time when the Arabs posed any real danger to the empire. Whittow, id., p. 138.

119. Luigi Gambero, *Mary and the Fathers of the Church*, trans. Thomas Buffer (San Francisco, 1999), p. 323.

120. Hilda Graef, *Mary: A History of Doctrine and Devotion* (London, 1987), pp. 38–46, 48–55, 57–68, 77–89, 94–100; *PG* 7: 959–60, 1175–76 (Irenaeus of Lyons); *PL* 2: 828, 833–36 (Tertullian); *PG* 10: 732, 826–27 (Hippolytus of Rome); A. Pagnamenta, *La mariologia di S. Ambrogio* (Milan, 1932); Charles William Neumann, *The Virgin Mary in the Works of St. Ambrose* (Fribourg: University Press, 1962); J. Huhn, "Das Mariengeheimnis beim Kirchenvater Ambrosius," *Münchener Theologische Zeitschrift* 2 (1951), pp. 130–46; Michele Pellegrino, *S. Agostino: La Vergine Maria*, 2nd. ed. (Milan, 1987); D. Casagrande, *Enchiridion Marianum Biblicum Patristicum* (Rome, 1974), pp. 562–635; Luigi Gambero, "La Vergine Maria nella dottrina de Sant'Agostino," *Marianum* 48 (1986), pp. 557–99; *PG* 9: 349, 529–30 (Clement of Alexandria); *PG* 14: 316, 641–44, 784, 956–57, 1298; (Origen); Athanasius. *De virginitate*, trans. and ed. T. Lefort in *Le Muséon* 42 (1929), pp. 197–275; Ephrem the Syrian, *Hymns*, trans. Kathleen E. McVey (New York, 1989); *PG* 33: 465A, 465B–468A, 725A, 728B–C, 728C–729A andff.; Georg Söll, "Die Mariologie der Kappadozier im Lichte der Dogmengeschichte," *Theologische Quartalschrift* 131 (1951): 163–88, 288–391, 426–57; Luigi Gambero, "La Madonna negli scritti di San Basilio di Cesarea," *Marianum* 44 (1982), pp. 9–47; *PG* 45: 1136CD; *PG* 46: 1133D–1136B; 1137A–B; 1140C–1141A (Gregory of Nyssa); *PG* 35: 1177C– 1181A; *PG* 36: 325B (Gregory Nazienzen); *PG* 54: 446; *PG* 56: 166–67;

PG 57: 43, 45, 56, 58, 465; PG 59: 130, 100A–B, 1565D–1566A, 537A–538A (John Chrysostom); P. Dieu, "La Mariologie de saint Jean Chrysostôme," *Mémoires et rapports du Congrès Marial de Bruxelles*, Vol. I (Brussels, 1922), pp. 71–83.

121. Cyril of Alexandria, *Opera*, PG 77: 119; A. Eberle, *Die Mariologie des hl. Kyrillos von Alexandrien* (Freiburg im Breisgau, 1921); Proclus of Constantinople, *Homily 3 on the Incarnation*, PG 65: 703–708; *Homily 4 on the Nativity of the Lord*, PG 65: 713–16; R. Caro, "Proclo de Costantiopla, orador mariano del siglo V," *Marianum* 29 (1967), pp. 377–492; Theodotus of Ancyra, *Homily I on the Nativity of the Lord 1–2*, PG 77: 1349–52; *On the Mother of God and on the Nativity*, *Patrologia Orientalis* 19 (Paris, 1903), pp. 330–31.

122. M. Jugie, "Homélies Mariales Byzantines," *Patrologia Orientalis* 19, 3 (Paris, 1903), p. 308; A. Frolow, "La Dédicace de Constantinople," *Revue de l'histoire des Religions* 127 (1944), p. 93; Theophanes, *Chronographia*, pp. 276–80.

123. Averil Cameron, "Images of Authority: Elites and Icons in Late Sixth-Century Byzantium," *Past and Present* 84 (1979), pp. 3–5, 15.

124. Norman Baynes, "The Supernatural Defenders of Constantinople," *Analecta Bollandiana* 67 (1949), pp. 165–77; Averil Cameron, "The Theotokos in Sixth-Century Constantinople: A City Finds Its Symbol," *Journal of Theological Studies*, n.s. 29 (1978), pp. 101, 103–4; John F. Haldon, "Ideology and Social Changes in the Seventh Century," *Klio* 68 (1986), pp. 139–90. As the Mother of God, the Virgin Mary had both intercessory abilities (πρεσβεία) and the ability to communicate directly (παρρησία) with God. Averil Cameron, "The Virgin's Robe: An Episode in the History of Early Seventh-Century Constantinople," *Byzantion* 49 (1979): 566n58. Severe outbreaks of plague in the East, including the major population centers of Antioch and Constantinople, also contributed to the rise of the cult of the Theotokos. See D. Jacoby, "La population de Constantinople à l'époque byzantine: un problème de démographie urbaine," *Byzantion* 31 (1961): 81ff.

125. Cameron, "The Theotokos in Sixth-Century Constantinople: A City Finds Its Symbol." id., p. 97.

126. Theophanes, *Chronographia*, p. 427; George of Pisidia, *Heraclius II*, id., p. 252, l. 15; Frolow, id., pp. 104, 115. The Byzantine naval theme known as the *Karabisianoi* would later replicate Heraclius's example by displaying the image of the Theotokos on the standards of its ships. K. Saraphè-Pitzipios, Ἑλληνικός Αὐτοκρατορικός Στόλος (Athens, 1907), p. 103; Frolow, id., p. 110.

127. Theophanes, *Chronographia*, p. 428.

128. For a detailed account of the Avar siege of 626, see J. Howard-Johnston, "The siege of Constantinople in 626," in C. Mango and G. Dagron, eds., *Constantinople and Its Hinterland* (Aldershot, 1995), pp. 131–42 and F. Barisic, "Le siège de Constantinople," *Byzantion* 24 (1954): 371.

129. George of Pisidia, *Bellum Avaricum*, id., p. 176, ll. 1–3; p. 185, l. 208.

130. George of Pisidia had declared in two epigrams that the Avar defeat had been the result of the Virgin Mary supplicating Christ "to overturn the natural order of things." George of Pisidia, *Anthologie Palatine* I, 120 and 121, PG 92: 1736ff. For the homily of Theodore Synkellos see L. Sternbach, ed., *Analecta Avarica* (Cracow, 1900), pp. 73–121.

131. George of Pisidia, *Bellum Avaricum*, id., p. 193, ll. 370–73; pp. 220–21.

132. *De Obsidione Constantinopolitana sub Heraclio imperatore* in A. Mai, *Nova Patrum Bibliotheca*, VI, 2 (Rome, 1853), pp. 426–28.

133. *Chronicon Paschale*, id., pp. 178–79; see also Theophanes, *Chronographia*, p. 447; Georgios Monachos, *Chronicon*, pp. 670–71; Leo Grammatikos, *Chronographia*, p. 151.

134. *Chronicon Paschale*, id., p. 180; Nikephoros, *Short History*, id., p. 61.

135. The seemingly endless stream of military epithets lavished on the Theotokos in both the sacred and secular literature, including "mistress of war," "immutable general," "double-edged sword cutting down the phalanx of the adversary," "defender," "invincible," "shield," "helper," "shield-bearer," "armor," "strength," "victor," "weapon," "axe," "ally," "impregnable wall," and "champion," attest to her unassailable position as Constantinople's special protector. See, namely, George of Pisidia, *Bellum Avaricum*, id., p. 193, l. 366; p. 194, l. 405; Niketas Choniates, *Historia* (Bonn, 1835), pp. 26, 205, 497; see also Sophronios Eustratiades, Ἡ Θεοτόκος ἐν τῇ ὑμνογραφίᾳ (Paris-Chennevières-sur-Marne, 1930); Frolow, id., p. 98ff. According to the *Life of St. Andrew the Fool*, "so cherished was this City [Constantinople] by the Theotokos that no one could pluck it from her sacred hand." *PG* 111: 853.

136. *Chronicon Paschale*, id., pp. 183–84, 187; Andrea Dandolo, *Chronica*, in *Rerum Italicarum Scriptores*, Vol. 12, Pt. 1, ed. L. A. Muratori (Bologna, 1728), p. 92; Theophanes, *Chronographia*, id., pp. 447–49, 494; Frolow, id., p. 97.

137. Theophanes, *Chronographia*, pp. 545–46, 560–61.

138. In 1133, the emperor John II Komnenos (1118–1143) celebrated his triumphant return to Constantinople with a processsion whose centerpiece was a silverplated chariot adorned with semiprecious jewels in which the emperor had mounted an icon of the Mother of God, whom he exalted as his συστρατηγέτιδι or "fellow general," while he himself humbly preceded the quadriga with a cross in his hand. Niketas Choniates, *Historia*, ed. J. A. van Dieten (Berlin-New York, 1975), p. 19; *O City of Byzantium, Annals of Niketas Choniates*, trans. Harry J. Magoulias (Detroit, 1984), p. 12. The nearly identical scene was repeated by the emperor Manuel I Komnenos (1143–1180) in 1168. Niketas Choniates, *Historia*, id., p. 158; *O City of Byzantium, Annals of Niketas Choniates*, id., p. 90.

139. Jean-Baptiste Abbeloos, *De vita et scriptis Sancti Jacobi, Batnarum Sarugi in Mesopotamia* (Louvain, 1867); Paul Bedjan, ed., *Homiliae Selectae Mar-Jacobi Sarugensis* (Paris, 1905–1910); Gambero, id., pp. 310–19.

140. A *kontakion* is an abbreviated hymn or homily usually consisting of between eighteen to twenty-four metrically identical stanzas or *oikoi*. Stanzas, whose initial letters form an acrostic, range in length from four to eighteen lines. The *kontakion* was supposed to be chanted by the priest from the pulpit "with either choir or congregation joining in the refrain." Baldwin, id., p. 114; Averil Cameron, "The Theotokos in Sixth-Century Constantinople: A City Finds Its Symbol," id., p. 87; Robert Murray, *Symbols of Church and Kingdom* (Cambridge, 1975), p. 144ff.; see also A. Vööbus, *Literary, critical and historical studies in Ephrem the Syrian* (Stockholm, 1958) and E. Beck, "Die Mariologie der echten Schriften Ephräms," *Oriens Christianus* 40 (1956): 22ff.

141. For the Greek text of the *Akathist* hymn with an English translation, see George Papadeas, trans., *The Akathist Hymn* (Athens, Greece, 1972), pp. 27–42. For a more recent English translation of the *Akathist*, see Gambero, id., pp. 342–51. The authorship of the *Akathist* hymn has been intensely debated, with scholars ascribing it variously to George of Pisidia, patriarch Sergius of Constantinople, patriarch Photios of Constantinople, and Photios's disciple George of Sicily. See Gambero, id., p. 338; C. A.

Trypanis, *Fourteen Early Byzantine Cantica* (Vienna, 1968); A. Papadopoulos-Kerameus, Ὁ πατριάρχης Φώτιος καί ο ακάθιστος ὑμνος (Trieste, 1904). It now appears to be generally agreed that the *Akathist* itself was composed by Romanos the Melodist. Sophronios Eustratiades, Ὁ Ρωμανός ο Μελωδός καί ἡ Ἀκάθιστος (Thessalonika, 1917); P. F. Krypiakiewicz, "De hymni Acathisti auctore," *Byzantinische Zeitschrift* 18 (1909): 357–82. The *Akathist's* original proeimion or preface Τό προσταχθέν ("The command") was probably also written by Romanos before he arrived in Constantinople from Syria during the reign of the emperor Anastasios I (491–518). Krypiakiewicz, id., pp. 371, 380. The new proeimion Τη υπερμάχω ("To You Invincible Champion") was almost certainly composed by patriarch Sergius in gratitude to the Virgin for her delivery of Constantinople from the Avars in 626, E. Wellesz, "The Akathistos," *Dumbarton Oaks Papers* 9–10 (1955–1956): 143ff., although both Krypiakiewicz and Frolow contend that it was written by patriarch Photios in gratitude for her intervention in delivering the capital from the Rus raid of June, 860. Krypiakiewicz, id., pp. 360–61, 380; Frolow, id., p. 69; see also Jacqueline Lafontaine-Dosogne, "Nouvelles Remarques sur l'Illustration du *Prooimion* de l'Hymne Akathiste," *Byzantion* 61 (1991): 448–57.

142. Among Greek writers were bishop John of Thessalonika, patriarchs Modestos and Sophronios of Jerusalem, bishop Theoteknos of Livias in Palestine, Maximos Confessor, Theodore Synkellos, and George the Hymnographer, while those who composed in Syriac, Coptic, Arabic, and Ethiopian also produced a substantial number of works. See, namely, Martin Jugie, "Saint Jean, Archevêque de Thessalonique (mort vers 630), Discours sur la Dormition de la Sainte Vierge," *Patrologia Orientalis* 19 (1925): 375–405; F. Halkin, "Une légende byzantine de la Dormition: l'Épitomé du récit de Jean de Thessalonique," *Revue des Études Byzantines* 11 (1953): 156–64; A. Wenger, *L'Assomption de la T.S. Vierge dans la tradition byzantine du VIe au Xe siècle. Études et documents* (Paris, 1955), pp. 96–100, 271–91 (Theoteknos of Livias); PG 86/2: 3277–3312 (Modestos of Jerusalem); Maximos Confessor, *Vie de la Vierge*, trans. M.-J. Van Esbroeck, *Corpus Scriptorum Christianorum Orientalium 478 and 479, Scriptores Iberici 22* (Louvain, 1986); Gambero, id., p. 324. For a bibliography of both primary and secondary materials see Mimouni, id., pp. 682–95.

143. For the Mariology of patriarch Germanos of Constantinople, see I. Carli, *La dottrina sull'Assunzione di S. Germano di Costantinopoli* (Rome, 1944); E. Perniola, *La Mariologia di S. Germano* (Rome, 1954); T. Horvath, "Germanus of Constantinople and the Cult of the Virgin Mary, Mother of God, Mediatrix of All Men," *De cultu mariano saeculis VI–XI*, Vol. 4 (Rome, 1972), pp. 285–99. For the Marian doctrine of John of Damascus, see M. Schumpp, "Zur Mariologie des hl. Johannes Damascenus," *Divus Thomas* 2 (1924): 222–34; C. Chevalier, "La Mariologie de saint Jean Damascène," *Orientalia Christiana Analecta* 109 (Rome, 1936); Valentine A. Mitchel, *The Mariology of Saint John Damascene* (Turnhout, 1930); V. Grumel, "La Mariologie de saint Jean Damascène," *Echos d'Orient* 40 (1937): 318–46. For Cosmas of Jerusalem, see the review of the patriarchate of Jerusalem entitled *Nea Sion* 28 (1933), pp. 83– 99, 143–58, 192–218, 330–38, 400–16, 489–505, 530–44.

144. S. Vailhé, "Saint André de Crete," *Echos d'Orient* 5 (1901–1902): 378–87; G. Dagron, et al., eds., "Evêques, moines, et empereurs (610–1054)," in *Historie du Christianisme*, Vol. 4 (Paris, 1993), p. 293; Theophanes, *Chronographia*, p. 532.

145. H.-G. Beck, *Kirche und theologische Literatur im byzantinischen Reich* (Munich, 1959), p. 500ff.

146. "Save your city, all pure Mother of God: for through you she piously reigns, through you she is strong, and thanks to you, she victoriously overcomes her ordeals, despoils her enemies, and governs her subjects." Andrew of Crete, "Great Canon" in *Triodion* (Athens, 1989), p. 313 (translation by the author); see also W. Christ and M. Paranikas, eds., *Anthologia graeca carminum christianorum* (Leipzig, 1871), p. 157.

147. PG 97: 805–20, 820–44, 844–62, 862–82, 1315–30, 882–914, 1329–30, 1045–72, 1071–90, 1089–1110, 1435–36.

148. The feast of the Ypapante or Presentation of the Lord in the Temple was first observed in Byzantium on February 2, 542, during the fifteeenth year of the reign of Justinian I. Theophanes, *Chronographia*, p. 322; Nikephoros Kallistos Xanthopoulos, *Ecclesiasticae Historiae*, PG 147: 291–92. The Annunciation was already a well-established feast in Constantinople when Heraclius departed for the East on March 25, 624. *Chronicon Paschale*, id., p. 166. Although Nikephoros Kallistos Xanthopoulos claims that the emperor Maurice established the feast of the Dormition of the Theotokos on August 15, PG 147: 291–292, καί Μαυρίκιος ου πολλω ὕστερον τήν της πανάγνου καί θεομήτορος κοίμησιν κατά τήν πεντεκαιδεκάτην του Αυγούστου μηνός, the Koimesis of the Theotokos was probably already a part of the calendar of the church of Constantinople when in 587 or 588 "the emperor Maurice introduced a litany at Blachernae in memory of the holy Mother of God, at which laudations of our Lady were to be delivered." Theophanes, *Chronographia*, p. 387. The Nativity of the Virgin Mary seems to have been a part of the Constantinopolitan church's calendar before the end of the sixth century. Averil Cameron, "A Nativity Poem of the Sixth Century A.D.," *Classical Philology* 79 (1979): 222–32. See Frolow, id., p. 93.

149. Joseph Ledit, *Marie dans la Liturgie de Byzance* (Paris, 1976), p. 11ff.

150. Symeon of Thessalonika, Περι της θείας προσευχης, PG 155: 613–17; Placidio de Meester, *Rituale-Benedizionale Bizantino* (Rome, 1929), p. 513ff.; see, Michael McCormick, "Emperors," in Guglielmo Cavallo, ed., *The Byzantines*, trans., Thomas Dunlap, et al. (Chicago, 1997), p. 248ff.; Gastoué, id., p. 276.

151. John F. Baldovin, *The Urban Character of Christian Worship: The Origins, Development, and Meaning of Stational Liturgy* (Rome, 1987), pp. 196–97; R. Janin, "Les processions religieuses à Byzance," *Revue des Études Byzantins* 24 (1966): 68–88. The most important of the churches dedicated to the Virgin Mary in Constantinople, the church of the Theotokos at Blachernae, was begun by the empress Pulcheria, consort of the emperor Marcian, between 450 and 453 and completed by the emperor Leo I (457–474). R. Janin, *Le Siège de Constantinople et le Patriarcat Oecuménique: Les Églises et les Monastères* in *La Géographie Ecclésiastique de l'Empire Byzantin*, Vol. III, Pt. 1 (Paris, 1953), p. 169ff. The Virgin's robe, which had been sent from Jerusalem to Constantinople at the empress's request, was considered to be "a wonder-working relic guaranteeing the intimate connection between the Virgin herself and the city which possessed it." Averil Cameron, "The Virgin's Robe: An Episode in the History of Early Seventh-Century Constantinople," id., p. 44. The church of the Theotokos at Chalkoprateia was similarly begun by the empress Pulcheria and completed by Leo I. Janin, id., p. 246ff. The early sixth-century patriarch of Constantinople Timothy I (511–518) had directed that processions take place on Friday evenings at this church. Theodore Anagnostes, "Fragment 56–Epitome 494," in *Ecclesias-*

tical History, ed. G. C. Hansen (Berlin, 1971), p. 140, ll. 16–17. According to Nikephoros Kallistos Xanthopoulos, the church of the Theotokos at Chalkoprateia also contained the ζώνη or belt of the Virgin Mary. *PG* 146: 1061B, 1233AB. More churches and monasteries were dedicated to the Theotokos in Constantinople than to any other religious figure. According to Janin, 123 such edifices were consecrated in her honor. Id., pp. 164–255.

152. In the *Akathist* hymn, the Virgin Mary is referred to in an immeasurable variety of laudatory epithets including "star that bore the Sun," "Mother of the unsetting Star," "Splendor of the Mystic Day," "flower of incorruption," "mirror of the life of Angels," "Key of Christ's Kingdom," "gate to the sacred mystery," "harbor of this life's seafarers," "vessel of God's widsom," "fragrance of Christ's sweetness," "precious diadem of pious emperors," and the "Church's unassailable tower." Gambero, id., p. 342 passim.

153. Gregory of Tours, *History of the Franks*, trans. Lewis Thorpe (London, 1974), pp. 543–46; *Reg. App.* IX, id., p. 1102–4; *Mansi* X, p. 340; *PL* 76:1311. The basilica of the "Holy Mother of God" to which the pope referred was the church of Santa Maria Maggiore or St. Mary Major. Kehr, *Italia Pontificia*, id., p. 55.

154. Cameron, "The Theotokos in Sixth-Century Constantinople: A City Finds Its Symbol," id., p. 89ff.

155. Bernard Botte, "La première fête mariale dans la liturgie romaine," *Ephemerides Liturgicae* 47 (1933): 425–30; Chavasse, *Le Sacramentaire Gélasien*, id., p. 376. None of the four principal Marian feasts appears in the Leonine Sacramentary nor were they observed in Rome in the time of Gregory the Great. Duchesne, *Christian Worship: Its Origin and Evolution*, id., p. 270; R. Todd Ridder, *Musical and Theological Patterns Involved in the Transmission of Mass Chants for the Five Oldest Marian Feasts* (UMI Dissertation Services: Ann Arbor, Michigan, 1993), p. 39.

156. Ledit, id., p. 112; Botte, id., pp. 425–30.

157. See P. Jounel, *La Liturgie et le Temps*, Vol. 4 in *L'Église en Prière* (Paris, 1983), p. 132.

158. See *Ωρολόγιον τό Μέγα* (Athens, 1984), p. 168.

159. Ridder, id., p. 59.

160. *LP* I, p. 376; see Baldovin, id., pp. 167–26. Pope Sergius's prescription that a litany should begin at the church of St. Adrian and end at St. Mary Major on this as well as on the three other principal Marian feasts may well have been prompted by the fact that both the Virgin's birth and that of St. Adrian are observed on September 8. Donckel, id., p. 54. Sometime between 628 and 638, Pope Honorius I had transformed the former Senate House in the Forum Romanum into the church of St. Adrian in honor of the Easterner who had been martyred in Nicomedia and whose body had been translated to Rome sometime in the seventh century. *LP* I, p. 326n18; Kehr, id., p. 69; Krautheimer, id., pp. 72, 75–76, 87.

161. *Egeria's Travels*, id., p. 128; *Égérie, Journal de Voyage (Itinéraire)*, Pierre Maraval, ed. and trans. (Paris, 1982), pp. 254–57. For homilies on the Ypapante delivered by Hesychius, a priest of the church of Jerusalem, see M. Aubineau, *Les Homélies Festales d'Hésychius de Jérusalem*, Vol. I: *Les Homélies I–XV* (Brussels, 1978), pp. 1–75 and G. Garitte, "L'Homélie géorgienne d'Hésychius de Jérusalem sur l'Hypapante," *Le Muséon* 84 (1971): 353–72. For a homily on the Ypapante by Cyril of Jerusalem dated ca. 450, see *PG* 33: 1187–1204. The feast of the Ypapante celebrated the fulfillment of God's promise

to St. Simeon that he would not die until he had beheld the Messiah. After receiving the child from the Virgin Mary and pronouncing a blessing upon it, Simeon declared "Lord, now lettest thou thy servant depart in peace, according to thy word, for mine eyes have seen thy salvation, which thou has prepared before the face of all peoples: a light to lighten the Gentiles, and the glory of thy people Israel." *Luke* 2: 29–32. The Presentation of Christ in the Temple, observed on February 2, should not be confused with the feast of the Presentation of the Virign Mary in the Temple, which is celebrated in the East on November 21 and which did not enter the calendar of the churches of Jerusalem and Constantinople until the end of the seventh century at the earliest. S. Vailhé, "La Fête de la Présentation de Marie au Temple," *Echos d'Orient* 5 (1901–1902): 221–24.

162. E. Bickersteth, "John Chrysostom and the Early History of the Hypapante," in *Atti dello VIII Congresso Internazionale di Studi Bizantini* (Rome, 1953), p. 401.

163. Theophanes, *Chronographia*, p. 322. The feast, which appears formerly to have been observed on February 14, was officially established by the emperor on February 2. Georgios Monachos, *Chronicon*, PG 110:777. For a homily on the Ypapante attributed to Gregory of Nyssa, see PG 46: 1152–81.

164. The 125th sermon of Severus of Antioch appears to confirm that the churches of Jerusalem and Constantinople both observed the Ypapante prior to its adoption by the church of Antioch. Ignatius Ephraem II Rahmani, *Vetusta Documenta Liturgica, Studia Syriaca*, Fasc. III (Lebanon, 1908), p. 79; Bickersteth, id., p. 403.

165. The text of the verses reads as follows: Χαιρε κεχαριτωμένη Μαρία ο Κύριος μετά σου. Ευλογημένη σύ εν γυναιξί καί ευλογημένος ο καρπός της κοιλίας σου. οτι Χριστόν συνέλαβες τόν Υιόν του Θεου τόν λυτρώτην των ψυχων ημων. ("Hail Mary, imbued with grace; The Lord is with thee; blessed are you among women, and blessed is the fruit of thy womb, because you did conceive Christ, the son of God, the redeemer of our souls.") Duchesne posits that these verses, probably sung at the feast of the Ypapante before the Gospel and the Aspsamos or kiss of peace, are the precursors of the Western hymn *Ave Maria*. Duchesne, *Christian Worship: Its Origin and Evolution*, id., pp. 271–72, 546.

166. Aidan Nichols, ed., *Byzantine Gospel* (Edinburgh, 1993), p. 116.

167. H. Gaisser, "La Festa della Purificazione," *Rassegna gregoriana* 1, no. 2 (February 1902): 20–21.

168. *LP* I, p. 376.

169. Gastoué, id., pp. 113, 261n4.

170. S. Vailhé, "Origines de la Fête de l'Annonciation," *Echos d'Orient* 9 (1906): 143, 145.

171. PG 93: 1453–60; Cyril of Scythopolis, *The Lives of the Monks of Palestine*, trans. R. M. Price (Kalamazoo, Michigan, 1991), p. 22. Hesychius's homily on the Incarnation of the Word was echoed shortly thereafter by Chrysippus, another Jerusalemite priest who sometime between 453 and 479 preached another famous sermon on the subject. Vailhé, "Origines de la Fête de l'Annonciation," id., p. 143.

172. PG 65: 680 et seq.; Theophanes, *Chronographia*, pp. 137–38; P. J. Löw, "Ein stadtrömisches Lektionar des VIII. Jahrhunderts," *Römische Quartalschrift für christliche Altertumskunde und für Kirchengeschichte* 37 (1929): 31.

173. Vailhé, "Origines de la Fête de l'Annonciation," id., p. 140; M. Jugie, "La première fête mariale en Orient et en Occident," *Echos d'Orient* 22 (1923): 129–52.

174. *Chronicon Paschale*, id., p. 166.

175. Ridder, id., p. 59.

176. Gastoué, id., p. 114.

177. Bernard Capelle, "La fête de la Vierge à Jérusalem au Ve siècle, *Le Muséon* 56 (1943): 1–33. The late-seventh-century *typikon* of the church of Jerusalem refers to the feast day as the "koimeisis" or dormition of the Theotokos. S. Kékélidzé, *Le canonarium de Jérusalem au VIIe siècle* (Tiflis, 1912).

178. Michel van Esbroeck, "Le Culte de la Vierge de Jérusalem à Constantinople aux VIe–VIIe siècles," in *Aux origines de la Dormition de la Vierge* (Aldershot, 1995), X, p. 190; *LP* I, p. 376.

179. Sinait. gr. 491, f. 238r–246r. Theoteknos's encomium appears to have been based on earlier texts dealing with the Virgin's dormition composed by the Syrian Jacob of Saroug and by Theodosios I (535–567), a Monophysite patriarch of Alexandria praised as "a master of the literary style used in ecclesiastical writings." Antoine Wenger, *L'Assomption de la T.S. Vièrge dans la Tradition Byzantine du VIe au Xe siècle* (Paris, 1955), p. 99ff.; Severus of Asmounein, *History of the Patriarchs of the Coptic Church of Alexandria*, trans. B. Evetts, *Patrologia Orientalis*, Vol. I, Fasc. 2 (Paris, 1904), pp. 455–56.

180. Wenger, id., p. 109.

181. Theophanes, *Chronographia*, p. 387; Georgios Cedrenos, *Historiarum Compendium*, p. 694. The church of the Theotokos at Blachernae had been specially chosen as the venue for these processions because it was there that in the fifth century the empress Pulcheria had solemnly placed the robe of the Theotokos, which she had received from patriarch Juvenal of Jerusalem. The feast of the robe's deposition was thereafter observed by the church of Constantinople annually on July 2. Michel van Esbroeck, "Un Témoin Indirect de l'Histoire Euthymiaque dans une lecture Arabe pour l'Assomption," in van Esbroek, id., VII, p. 480; H. Delehaye, *Synaxarium Ecclesiae Constantinopolitanae* (Brussels, 1902), col. 794. The church of Constantinople paid special reverence to the Theotokos during the entire month of August. V. Grumel, "Le Mois de Marie des Byzantins," *Echos d'Orient* 30 (1931): 485–97. In 1297, the emperor Andronicus II (1282–1328) decreed that the month of August would henceforth be dedicated to the Virgin Mary. Ledit, id., p. 223n9.

182. See Michel van Esbroeck, "Étude Comparés des Notices Byzantines et Caucasiennes pour la fête de la Dormition," in van Esbroeck, id., VII, pp. 479–91.

183. Vatic. gr. 1982, f. 181–89v; Wenger, id., p. 65ff.

184. Maximos Confessor, *Life of the Virgin*, trans. Michel van Esbroeck, *Corpus Scriptorum Christianorum Orientalium* 479, *Scriptores Iberici* 22 (Louvain, 1986), p. 1ff.

185. M. Jugie, *La mort et l'assomption de la Sainte Vierge*, *Studi e Testi* 114 (Vatican City, 1944); Bernard Capelle, "L'Assunzione e la Liturgia," *Marianum* 15 (1953): 241–76.

186. Wenger, id., p. 140; Ridder, id., p. 57.

187. *LP* I, pp. 371, 376.

188. Bernard Capelle, "La tradition orientale de l'assomption d'après un ouvrage récent," *Revue Bénédictine* 68 (1958): 173–86. The text of the Latin hymn is: "Venerable to us, Lord, is this day of feasting in which the Holy Mother of God underwent an earthly death, yet still she should not be restrained by the bonds of death since from you she gave

birth to your incarnate Son our Lord." Bernard Capelle, "L'Oraison 'Veneranda' à la Messe de l'Assomption," *Ephemerides Theologicae Louvaniensis* 26 (1950): 354–64. The Greek *kontakion* for the feast is: "Neither the tomb nor death had power over the Theotokos, who is ever watchful in her prayers and in whose intercession lies unfailing hope. For as the Mother of Life she has been transported into life by Him who dwelt within her ever-virgin womb." *The Festal Menaion*, id. (London, 1984), p. 520; see also E. Mercenier and F. Paris, *La prière des Églises de rite byzantin*, II (Chevtogne, 1937–1938), p. 303.

189. PG 97: 1082.

190. Averil Cameron, "Images of Authority: Elites and Icons in Late Sixth-Century Byzantium," *Past and Present* 84 (1979): 3–35.

191. Averil Cameron, "The Language of Images: The Rise of Icons and Christian Representation," in Averil Cameron, *Changing Cultures in Early Byzantium* (Variorum: Aldershot, 1996), XII, p. 4; Ernst Kitzinger, *Byzantine Art in the Making* (Cambridge, MA, 1995), pp. 99–107.

192. Kitzinger, *Byzantine Art in the Making*, id., pp. 108–11.

193. John Beckwith, *Early Christian and Byzantine Art*, 2nd ed. (New Haven, 1979), p. 166.

194. Id., pp. 92, 101, 167.

195. Ernst Kitzinger, *Early Medieval Art*, rev. ed. (Bloomington, Indiana, 1990), pp. 34–36, 39.

196. Kitzinger, *Byzantine Art in the Making*, id., p. 114.

197. Richard Krautheimer, *Rome: Profile of a City, 312–1308* (Princeton, 1980), pp. 94–97; Pericle Ducati, *L'Arte in Roma dalle Origine al Sec. VII, Storia di Roma*, Vol. 26 (Bologna, 1938), pp. 389–407.

198. *LP* I, p. 317.

199. The icon of the *Panagia Hodegetria*, whose original was said to have been painted by St. Luke, derived its eponym from the fact that the Virgin Mary points or directs her hand toward the Christ-child as the way of truth and life. Beckwith, id., pp. 88–89. This depiction of the Theotokos was especially significant in Constantinople since emperors traditionally carried it with them as a talisman of victory on military expeditions. Michael Attaliates, *Historia*, ed., Vladimir Bruneto de Presle, *Corpus Fontium Historiae Byzantinae* (Bonn, 1853), p. 153; N. Kondakov, *Russkaja ikona*, Vol. II (Prague, 1933), p. 124ff. An icon of the *Panagia Hodegetria* dating from ca. 640 was originally housed in S. Maria Nova and is now located in the sacristy of S. Francesca Romana. Beckwith, id., p. 90.

200. Krautheimer, id., p. 97.

201. *LP* I, p. 323; Kitzinger, *Byzantine Art in the Making*, id., p. 103.

202. Beckwith, id., p.149; Krautheimer, id., p. 97; Kitzinger, *Byzantine Art in the Making*, id., pp. 103–4; *LP* I, p. 325n9; AA.SS. Ian. 11 (1643), pp. 350–63.

203. Krautheimer, id., p. 97.

204. *LP* I, p. 330.

205. Kitzinger, *Byzantine Art in the Making*, id., pp. 105–6; Krautheimer, id., pp. 97–98; Beckwith, id., p. 150.

206. Krautheimer, id., p. 97; Beckwith, id., p. 151. Saints Primus and Felician had been martyred at Nomentum, some twelve miles from Rome, during the time of Diocletian.

AA.SS. Iun. 2 (1698), pp. 149–54. Pope Theodore disinterred their relics and translated them to the church of St. Stefano Rotondo, which, in addition to embellishing with this apse mosaic, he adorned with gold bowls, silver arches, and a silver panel in front of the confessio. *LP* I, p. 332.

207. Kitzinger, *Byzantine Art in the Making,* id., pp. 113–19; Krautheimer, id., p. 99, 104; Beckwith, id., pp. 151, 153–54.

208. *LP* I, p. 385; Kitzinger, *Byzantine Art in the Making,* id., p. 119; Krautheimer, id., p. 100.

209. *LP* I, p. 386; De Rossi, *Inscriptiones Christianae Urbis Romae Septimo Saeculo Antiquiores,* Vol. 2, Pt. 1, id., p. 442; Krautheimer, id., p. 104; Per Jonas Nordhagen, "Italo- Byzantine Wall Painting of the Early Middle Ages: An Eighty-Year-Old Enigma in Scholarship," in *Studies in Byzantine and Early Medieval Painting* (London, 1990), p. 456, 457–58; J. D. Breckenridge, "Evidence for the Nature of Relations Between Pope John VII and the Byzantine Emperor Justinian II," *Byzantinische Zeitschrift* 65 (1972): 364.

210. Carlo Bertelli, *La Madonna di Santa Maria in Trastevere* (Rome, 1961); Beckwith, id., p. 96. Kitzinger describes the synthesis as a combination of "hieratic solemnity" with "a good deal of Hellenism." Kitzinger, *Byzantine Art in the Making,* id., p. 119. For Nordhagen, the fusion represents "Christian monumental art deply imbued with 'Hellenism.'" Nordhagen, "Italo-Byzantine Wall Painting of the Early Middle Ages," id., p. 450.

211. Kitzinger, *Byzantine Art in the Making,* id., p. 119; Pietro Romanelli and Per Jonas Nordhagen, *S. Maria Antiqua* (Rome, 1964); Per Jonas Nordhagen, "S. Maria Antiqua Revisited," in *Studies in Byzantine and Early Medieval Painting,* id., p. 309. St. Maria Antiqua became a church in the sixth century following the Byzantine reconquest when the former guardroom of the imperial palace on the Palatine was converted into a Christian sanctuary. Krautheimer, id., p. 97.

212. Per Jonas Nordhagen, *The Frescoes of John VII (A.D. 705–707) in S. Maria Antiqua in Rome* (Rome, 1968), pp. 106–7, 109, 112, 114; Kitzinger, *Byzantine Art in the Making,* id., p. 119.

213. Krautheimer, id., p. 104.

214. Romanelli and Nordhagen, id., Figure 5, opposite p. 34; Krautheimer, id., pp. 98–99.

215. Nordhagen, "S. Maria Antiqua Revisited," id., p. 310. Pope John VII's redecoration of St. Maria Antiqua also reflects what Nordhagen has described as the pontiff's "almost manic" preoccupation with the cult of the Theotokos, whose images in every conceivable size, style, and setting (and almost always accompanied by a portrait of himself bending down in fervent supplication) he caused to be placed not only in St. Maria Antiqua but in a number of churches in Rome. The pope also constructed an elaborate oratory to the Virgin Mary in St. Peter's that he adorned with mosaics and "a large amount of gold and silver." John VII's particular devotion to the Theotokos is further evidence of the intensity that her cult enjoyed in Rome at the turn of the seventh century. *LP* I, p. 385; Bede, *Anglo-Saxonis Chronicon sive De Sex Huius Seculi Aetatibus,* id., p. 201; Nordhagen, *The Frescoes of John VII (A.D. 705–707) in S. Maria Antiqua in Rome,* id., p. 88–91; André Grabar, "L'Église et les Images," in *L'Iconoclasme Byzantin: Dossier Archéologique* (Paris, 1957), p. 84.

216. *LP* I, p. 373; Jean-Marie Sansterre, "À propos de la Signification Politco-Religieuse de certaines Fresques de Jean VII à Sainte-Marie-Antique," *Byzantion* 57 (1987): 440; J. D. Breckenridge "Evidence for the Nature of Relations Between Pope John VII and the Byzantine Emperor Justinian II," id., p. 374.

217. See Canons 73 and 82 of the Quinisext Council in Lauchert, *Die Kanones der wichtigsten Altkirchlichen Concilien,* id., pp. 130, 132. Nordhagen, *The Frescoes of John VII (A.D. 705–707) in S. Maria Antiqua,* id., pp. 39–54, 95–98 and Plates XLI–LXX, CXXV, and CXXXV; Sansterre, "À propos de la Signification Politco-Religieuse de certaines Fresques de Jean VII à Sainte-Marie-Antique," id., pp. 435, 438–39; Breckenridge, "Evidence for the Nature of Relations Between Pope John VII and the Byzantine Emperor Justinian II," id., pp. 365–66; 368. For evidence of the traditional Roman practice of decorating triumphal arches with scenes of the worship of the Lamb, as, for example, in the sixth-century church of SS. Cosmas and Damian, see G. Matthiae, *Pittura romana del medioevo* (Rome, 1965), p. 95n4 and Plates 12–13.

218. Nordhagen, *The Frescoes of John VII (A.D. 705–707) in S. Maria Antiqua,* id., p. 53; Nordhagen, "Italo-Byzantine Wall Painting of the Early Middle Ages," id., p. 453; Sansterre, "À propos de la Signification Politco-Religieuse de certaines Fresques de Jean VII à Sainte-Marie-Antique," id., p. 435; Breckenridge, "Evidence for the Nature of Relations Between Pope John VII and the Byzantine Emperor Justinian II," id., pp. 368–69. The bust of Christ on coins issued by Justinian II between 692 and 695 contain the legend *rex regnantium* and show Him as long-haired and bearded. The reverse show the emperor standing to the right, wearing a loros, and holding a cross on steps in his right hand with the legend *servus Christi.* However, the bust of Christ on coins issued after Justinian II's return to power in 705 show Him as youthful, with curly hair and no beard. The reverse shows the emperor holding a cross in his right hand and an orb with the word *pax* surmounted by a patriarchal cross to his left. Compare Figures 25 and 26 with Figures 245 and 246 in P. D. Whiting, *Byzantine Coins* (New York, 1973).

219. *PL* 54: 756ff.

220. *LP* I, pp. 337–38.

221. *PL* 87: 1247ff.

222. *LP* I, pp. 385–86; Louis Bréhier and René Aigrain, *Histoire de l'Église,* Vol. 5 (Paris, 1947), p. 199; Caspar, *Geschichte des Papsttums,* Vol. 2, id., p. 637.

223. Nordhagen, *The Frescoes of John VII (A.D. 705–707) in S. Maria Antiqua,* id., p. 95; Ernst Kitzinger, "The Cult of Images before Iconoclasm," *Dumbarton Oaks Papers* 8 (1954): 128; E. Tea, *S. Maria Antiqua* (Milan, 1937), pp. 66–68; see also G. M. Rushforth, "The Church of S. Maria Antiqua," *Papers of the British School at Rome* I (1902): 1ff.

224. Jean-Marie Sansterre, "Jean VII (705–707): idéologie pontificale et réalisme politique," in Lydie Hadermann-Misguich and Georges Raepsaet, eds., *Rayonnement Grec: Hommages à Charels Delvoye* (Brussels, 1982), pp. 377–88. As was the case with his predecessors, Pope John VII dated all his papal documents by reference to the regnal years of the reigning emperors in Constantinople. Ignazio Giorgi and Ugo Balzani, eds., *Il Regesto di Farfa,* Vol. 2 (Rome, 1879), p. 25 (papal privileges granted to the monastery of Farfa by Pope John VII on 30 June 705 at the request of duke Faroald of Spoleto are dated by reference to the eighth year of the reign of the emperor Tiberios II Apsimaros).

225. Theophanes, *Chronographia*, p. 507; Nikephoros, *Short History*, p. 93.

226. Theophanes, *Chronographia*, p. 507ff.; Nikephoros, *Short History*, pp. 93–94; Georgios Cedrenos, *Historiarum Compendium*, p. 771ff.; Leo Grammatikos, *Chronographia*, p. 162ff.; Georgios Monachos, *Chronicon*, p. 729ff.; Head, id., pp. 28–51.

227. Peter Schreiner, *Die Byzantinischen Kleinchroniken*, id., p. 135.

228. Theophanes, *Chronographia*, p. 513; Nikephoros, *Short History*, p. 95.

229. Theophanes, *Chronographia*, p. 513.

230. Theophanes, *Chronographia*, pp. 514–15; Nikephoros, *Short History*, pp. 96–97; Leo Grammatikos, *Chronographia*, p. 165; Georgios Cedrenos, *Historiarum Compendium*, p. 775; Georgios Monachos, *Chronicon*, p. 731. Theophanes, Nikephoros, and Georgios Monachos record that both Justinian II's nose and tongue were severed. Leo Grammatikos and Georgios Cedrenos relate that only his nose was slit.

231. Caught up in a violent storm in the Karkinitic gulf on his voyage from the Chersonese to Constantinople, Theophanes records that Justinian rejected the pleas of a servant who, fearing that all would perish, begged him not to take revenge on his enemies if he succeeded in regaining his throne. Justinian is said to have replied, "If I spare one of them, may God drown me right here." Theophanes, *Chronographia*, pp. 520–21.

232. Theophanes, *Chronographia*, pp. 522–23; Nikephoros, *Short History*, p. 103; Bede, *Anglo-Saxonis Chronicon*, id., p. 201; Paul the Deacon, *Historia Langobardorum*, id., p. 225; Agnellus, *Liber Pontificalis Ecclesiae Ravennatis*, id., p. 367; Dölger, id., No. 265, p. 32.

233. Averil Cameron and Judith Herrin, eds., *Constantinople in the Early Eighth Century: The Parastaseis Syntomoi Chronikai* (Leiden, 1984), p. 99. Elsewhere in the same text, Justinian is referred to as αθέου or "godless." Id., p. 139.

234. Theophanes, *Chronographia*, p. 523; Nikephoros, *Short History*, p. 103. The *Liber Pontificalis* also records Justinian II's return to power, including the assistance he received from Terbelis and the Bulgarians. It relates, however, that Leontios and Tiberios II "had their throats cut in the middle of the Circus when all the people were present." *LP I*, p. 385.

235. Theophanes, *Chronographia*, p. 523; Nikephoros, *Short History*, p. 105; Georgios Monachos, *Chronicon*, p. 733; Leo Grammatikos, *Chronographia*, p. 169; Georgios Cedrenos, *Historiarum Compendium*, p. 781; Ioannes Zonaras, *Epitome Historiarum*, p. 327; Michael Glykas, *Annalium, Pars IV, PG* 158: 521–22; Bede, *Anglo Saxonis Chronicon*, p. 201; Paul the Deacon, *Historia Langobardorum*, p. 225; Ado, bishop of Vienne, *Chronicon*, *PL* 123: 118; *LP I*, p. 385.

236. Theophanes, *Chronographia*, p. 523; Nikephoros, *Short History*, p. 105.

237. Agnellus, *Liber Pontificalis Ecclesiae Ravennatis*, id., pp. 367–369; *LP I*, p. 389.

238. *LP I*, p. 389; Bede, *Anglo Saxonis Chronicon*, p. 201; Paul the Deacon, *Historia Langobardorum*, p. 225; Dölger, id., No. 266, p. 32; Jaffé, id., p. 248. The Greek chroniclers are altogether silent on Pope Constantine's visit to Constantinople. For a reevaluation of Justinian II's second reign and an effort to show that upon his return to the throne he was not "the irresponsible, power-crazed despot his detractors would have us believe," see Constance Head, "Toward a Reinterpretation of the Second Reign of Justinian II (705–711)," *Byzantion* 40 (1970): 14–32.

239. *LP* I, p. 360.

240. *LP* I, p. 363.

241. *LP* I, p. 366.

242. *LP* I, pp. 368–69.

243. *LP* I, pp. 372–74.

244. *LP* I, p. 383.

245. *LP* I, pp. 385–86.

246. Jean-Marie Sansterre, "Le Pape Constantin Ier (708–715) et la Politique Religieuse des Empereurs Justinien II et Philippikos," *Archivum Historiae Pontificae* 22 (1984): 7–29; J. M. Hussey, *The Orthodox Church in the Byzantine Empire* (Oxford, 1986), p. 28; Head, id., pp. 132–36; Luigi Magi, *La Sede Romana nella Corrispondenza degli Imperatori e Patriarchi Bizantini (VI–VII sec.)* (Louvain, 1972), p. 266; Bréhier and Aigrain, id., pp. 199–200.

247. Byzantium had treated harshly Roman pontiffs who resisted the imperial will. In 551, Pope Vigilius had been arrested and brought to Constantinople where his recalcitrance in acceding to Justinian I's demand that he condemn the Three Chapters resulted in his being seized from a church where he had fled for refuge, dragged through the streets of the capital with a rope around his neck, and finally put in jail. *LP* I, pp. 296–98; Theophanes, *Chronographia*, p. 327. Pope Martin I had also been arrested and brought to Constantinople to answer charges that he violated the *Typos* issued by the emperor Constans II prohibiting any further discussions on the issue of Christ's wills. *LP* I, pp. 336–38.

248. According to the *Liber Pontificalis*, Pope Constantine "immediately" or "on the spot" (*illico*) began making preparations for the sea voyage to Constantinople after receiving the imperial mandate. *LP* I, p. 389.

249. Theophanes, *Chronographia*, pp. 37, 46; Herrin, id., pp. 24, 33–34; Nicolas Cheetham, *A History of the Popes* (New York, 1982), p. 59; A. Alföldi, "On the Foundation of Constantinople. A Few Notes," *Journal of Roman Studies* 37 (1947): 10–16; H. G. Beck, "Konstantinopel—Das Neue Rom," *Gymnasium* 71 (1964): 166–74; Louis Bréhier, "Constantin et la fondation de Constantinople," *Revue Historique* 119 (1915): 241–72; Sabina G. MacCormack, "Roma, Constantinopolis, the Emperor and His Genius," *Classical Quarterly*, n.s., 25 (1975): 131–50; see also Gudrun Bühl, *Constantinopolis und Roma: Stadtpersonifikationen der Spätantike* (Zurich, 1995). Constantine the Great is recognized as a saint in the Eastern church, but not by the church of Rome. *Ὡρολόγιον τό Μέγα*, id., p. 285.

250. *LP* I, pp. 350, 355n5; *Mansi* XI, p. 725; *PL* 96: 399; Jaffé, No. 2118, id., p. 240.

251. *LP* I, p. 389.

252. The Easterners in the papal entourage included bishops Niketas of Silva Candida and Georgios of Portus, the priests Michael, Paulus, and Georgios, the *secundicerius* Georgios, Ioannes, chief of the *defensores*, the *sakellarios* Cosmas, the *nomenclator* Sissinius, the *scriniarius* Sergius, and a subdeacon named Dorotheos. The only Latins in the group were the deacon Gregory (the future Pope Gregory II) and a subdeacon named Julian. *LP* I, pp. 389–90; Jeffrey Richards, *The Popes and the Papacy in the Early Middle Ages, 476–752* (London, 1979), p. 275.

253. At his consecration, archbishop Felix had refused to provide Pope Constantine with the customary *cautio episcopi* in the form prescribed by the *Liber Diurnus* pursuant to which a newly consecrated bishop undertook to observe certain rules of ecclesiastical conduct, including certain professions of obedience toward the Roman church. *Liber Diurnus LXXIV*, "Cautio Episcopi," id., pp. 74–78. The document he did provide was placed in the confessio of St. Peter's and, upon being examined a few days later, was discovered to be charred as if ignited by fire. It was, according to the *Liber Pontificalis*, this act of arrogance toward Rome that Justinian II punished by his harsh treatment of Ravenna. *LP* I, pp. 389, 393n2.

254. *LP* I, pp. 392–93; Sansterre,"Le Pape Constantin Ier (708–715) et la Politique Religieuse des Empereurs Justinien II et Philippikos," id., pp. 28–29.

255. *LP* I, p. 390.

256. Sansterre, "Le Pape Constantin Ier (708–715) et la Politique Religieuse des Empereurs Justinien II et Philippikos," id., pp. 10–11.

257. *LP* I, p. 390.

258. The καμελαύκιον, or *kamelaukion*, was a diadem that, along with various other vestments, had been divinely created and sent by God through an angel to the emperor Constantine the Great with the command that they be placed above the altar of the Great Church of St. Sophia and be worn by the emperor only on great public festivals of the Lord, after which they were to be returned to the church. The misuse of this imperial apparel carried with it a curse (κατάρα) of anathema and excommunication pronounced by the emperor Constantine himself. Constantine VII Porphyrogenitos, *De Administrando Imperio*, ed. and trans., Gy. Moravcsik and R. J. H. Jenkins (Washington, D.C., 1967), pp. 66–69. For the history of the evolution of the *kamelaukion* and the oriental provenance of the papal tiara, see Michel de Waha, "Entre Byzance et l'Occident," in Hadermann-Misguich and Raepsaert, eds., *Rayonnement Grec: Hommages à Charles Delvoye*, id., pp. 405–19 and Allen Maloof, "The Eastern Origin of the Papal Tiara," *Eastern Churches Review* 1 (1966–1967): 146–49.

259. *LP* I, p. 391; Bede, *Anglo Saxonis Chronicon*, p. 202; Paul the Deacon, *Historia Langobardorum*, p. 226; Ado of Vienne, *Chronicon*, PL 123: 118. Not a single Eastern source says anything about Pope Constantine's visit to Constantinople.

260. Sansterre, "Le Pape Constantin Ier (708–715) et la Politique Religieuse des Empereurs Justinien II et Philippikos," id., pp. 12–13. The *Liber Pontificalis* consistently portrays emperors as prostrating themselves before Roman pontiffs in acts of self-abasement. See, namely, the emperor Justin I's meeting with Pope John I, and Justinian I's encounter with Pope Agapitus. *LP* I, pp. 275, 288.

261. *LP* I, p. 391; Sansterre "Le Pape Constantin Ier (708–715) et la Politique Religieuse des Empereurs Justinien II et Philippikos," id., p. 21, 21n87.

262. Gregory assumed the Papacy on May 19, 715, as Pope Gregory II. He was the first non-Eastern pope in thirty years. *LP* I, p. 396. It was not until 872 or 873, during the pontificate of Pope John VIII (872–882), that the issue of the canons of the Quinisext Council was finally resolved when the pope announced, with customary vagueness, that the Roman church agreed to adopt those canons that were not in opposition to the true faith and to the traditions and decrees of the church of Rome. *Mansi* XII, p. 982; PL 129: 196–97.

263. Apologizing to Pope Constantine for his lapse into Monothelitism during the reign of the emperor Philippikos, patriarch John VI of Constantinople made an oblique reference to the pope's own encounter with Justinian II on the issue of the Trullan canons, declaring to the pontiff, "You know from your own experience that in the face of force it is not so easy to resist with too much intensity. You need to exercise some skill and intelligence." *Mansi* XII, p. 200; PG 96: 1421–24. On the concept of *economia* in canon law, see Pierre Rai, "L'économie dans le droit canonique byzantin dès origines jusqu'au XIe siècle. Recherches historiques et canoniques," *Istina* 18 (1973): 260–326, esp. pp. 272–73 and 292–94.

264. Vittorio Peri, "Introduzione," in Nedungatt and Featherstone, id., p. 31.

Epilogue
Zacharias, Son of Polychronios
The Last of the Greek Popes

On the day of Pope Gregory III's funeral, the Romans unanimously chose Zacharias, then a deacon of the Roman church, to take his place upon the apostolic throne. Five days later he was consecrated pope. Since then, the aging septuagenarian from the heavily Hellenized region of Calabria had lived in the papal residence which over the years he had richly adorned with a portico and tower, bronze doors and railings, and a dazzling new *triclinium* with marble and mosaics, thus creating a replica upon the Lateran of the Great Palace in Constantinople.[1] Can Zacharias have known that he would be the last in the long succession of Greek popes who had presided over the church of Rome?

Although of oriental lineage and justly proud of their culture and traditions, each of those popes had been unflinchingly Roman by faith, resisting at every turn the East's proclivity to lapse into doctrinal error and ecclesiastical innovation. Had not the Greco-Palestinian Pope Theodore been a moving force behind the Lateran Council that in 649 had the temerity to ignore an imperial decree and declare Monothelitism to be heresy? Was it not the lengthy concatenation of patristic *florilegia* sent from Rome to Constantinople by the Greco-Sicilian Pope Agatho that had caused the Sixth Ecumenical Council to anathematize the Monothelite heresy once and for all? Had not the Syrian pontiff Sergius I, targeted for assassination by an imperial *spatharios*, declared that he would prefer to die rather than accede to those canons of the Quinisext Council that were contrary to the traditions of the church of Rome? Had not his own predecessor of blessed memory, the Syrian Gregory III, admonished the emperors in Constantinople to abandon the error of iconoclasm and return to the ancient customs of the Church? Had he not also sent his own *apokrisiarii* to the capital, urging the emperor Constantine V to desist from his continued attack on holy images?

Surely the popes of oriental provenance had fulfilled their duty to the Roman church as well as any Latin pontiff.

Rome spread out before Pope Zacharias. The city that had emerged from the shambles of the Gothic wars and the Justinianic reconquest of Italy had, over the course of the seventh and early eighth centuries, come to bear the unmistakable imprint of the East. The triumphal column that the emperor Phocas had erected in the Forum around 607 still stood as a reminder that it was not an isolated outpost in the West preserving a purely Latin culture. The ties that bound Rome to the East were palpable and present. The Byzantine administration of the city, headed by the duke of Rome, still occupied the old imperial palace on the Palatine. You could hear Greek spoken throughout the city, especially if you had occasion to trade in the commercial district near the Aventine. Financial obligations were still paid in coins bearing the image of the emperor reigning in Constantinople.[2] On the way to the quays along the Tiber, you could pass any number of churches dedicated to saints of Eastern provenance, served by a Greek-speaking clergy, using Greek in the liturgy, and attended by faithful of Eastern ancestry. The interiors of these churches were embellished with mosaics and paintings created by oriental iconographers, who depicted their holy subjects as gaunt, remote, and timeless figures, just as they appeared in churches in Thessalonika and Constantinople. Greek monks continued to stream into Rome in ever increasing numbers.[3] Where once they had come to escape the Persian and Arab invasions of the East, they now sought refuge from iconoclasm. Had not Zacharias himself translated Pope Gregory's *Dialogues* into Greek in order to provide this new infusion of monastics with a text from which they might appreciate that there were ascetics in the West to rival even Antony?[4] And were there not *scriptoria* in Rome where works such as the lives of Ambrose of Milan and Martin of Tours and the passions of St. Denys and St. Anastasia were being translated from Latin into Greek for the benefit of Rome's burgeoning oriental community?[5] Diaconies also—those charitable institutions whose origins lay far away in Palestine and Egypt—continued to spring up in Rome. Between 715 and 731, Pope Gregory II had founded one adjacent to the church of St. Agatha in Suburra, and generously endowed another, which he named in honor of St. Eustathios, an Eastern saint who achieved a remarkable degree of fame in Rome.[6] Gregory III had expanded the diaconie named in honor of the oriental saints Sergius and Bacchus and bestowed upon it sufficient assets so that it could always serve the city's poor.[7] In late-sixth-century Constantinople one had yearned to be a "Roman"[8]; in mid-eighth century Rome, one was practically a Constantinopolitan.

Zacharias may well have shuddered for a moment as his thoughts turned to the Lombards and the Franks. Pope Gregory II had brokered a reconciliation between King Liutprand and the exarch Eutychius, which had temporarily put an end to hostilities between the Lombards and Byzantium on the Italian peninsula.[9] But the peace between them was short lived. By the time of Gregory

III, Liutprand was again threatening Rome, pitching his tents in the Campus Neronis and plundering the Campanian countryside.[10] In utter desperation, the pope had called upon the Frankish leader Charles Martel to deliver Rome from Liutprand's oppression. His plea had been entirely ignored. The Greek proverb that if you have a Frank as a friend, you have no neighbor had not been coined without reason.[11] Since then, the Lombards had not ceased stirring up trouble for the Romans. Zacharias could not recall a single year in his pontificate when he had not somehow contended with Liutprand's aggression. The Lombard king had died two years ago. But his successor Ratchis was hardly any better, setting out to capture Perugia and other imperial cities in the Pentapolis.[12] And just recently, the Franks had surfaced once again. The Carolingian leader Pepin had audaciously dispatched his envoys to the Apostolic See hoping that by clever rhetoric he might obtain the pontiff's imprimatur for his plan to usurp the throne of Francia from the Merovingians.[13] The peoples of the West offered little solace for the Papacy. For Zacharias, the royal city along the Golden Horn was his only consolation.

Like every Roman pontiff who had come before him, Zacharias considered himself a loyal servant of the *imperium Romanum Christianum* and a dutiful subject of the emperor who occupied the throne in Constantinople. The empire was, after, all the terrestrial image of the kingdom of heaven. It was a sacred realm of which Rome and the papacy were integral components. It represented culture and civilization. It was the irrefragable chain that connected the present to the classical past and gave his beloved Rome the aura of eternity. Most of all, it was the empire that guarded and protected the holy catholic and apostolic church.[14] The emperor was God's elected representative on earth. He held the empire in the name of Christ whose instrument he was and from whom he derived his power and authority. To criticize the emperor was a sacrilege; to fail to obey and pray for him, whether he was good or bad, unthinkable impiety. Had not Pope Leo taught that to rebel against the emperor was to rebel against the Lord himself?[15]

Zacharias could not fail to remember the example of his predecessor Gregory II. When all of Italy had risen up against Leo III because of his iconoclastic edicts, the pope had restrained their plan to choose a rival emperor, hoping instead that the emperor might be converted from his error.[16] And later when the seducer Tiberius Petasius had tried to usurp the empire for himself, Pope Gregory had once again shown his loyalty to the legitimate emperor by joining forces with the exarch to strike him down.[17] Even when Leo sent the exarch to assassinate the very pontiff who had helped him, Gregory II had calmed the anger of his flock and urged them never to cease in their fidelity to the Roman empire.[18] Gregory III had followed in his predecessor's footsteps by helping the exarch recover Ravenna after Liutprand had captured it in 732.[19] Zacharias himself had done no less. In 742, he negotiated as the official agent of the duke of Rome with Liutprand for the return of four cities that the Lombad king had seized.[20]

In 743, he intervened to persuade Liutprand to cease his campaign against the exarchate.[21] Six years later in 749, he prevailed upon King Ratchis to give up his attack on Perugia and other imperial cities.[22] Although relations between Rome and Constantinople had been ambivalent and sometimes even hostile, the emperor in Constantinople was still the sole legitimate authority on earth.[23] While he might oppress his Italian subjects by onerous taxation and scandalize them by committing holy icons to the flames, he remained the exclusive object of their allegiance and they would never cease to pray that his reign might last for many years.[24] The former imperial capital on the Tiber had adopted and embraced a great deal from Byzantium and the Byzantines in the two hundred years since the reconquest of Italy by Justinian. But that was not surprising to Pope Zacharias. For after all, the Greeks had never really been strangers in Rome.

Notes

1. *LP* I, pp. 426, 432; Giorgio S. Marcou, "Zaccaria. Un Pontefice di Origine Greca," *Il Veltro* 27 (1983): 145–53; Liutprand, *Antapodosis*, ed. A. Bauer and R. Rau in *Quellen zur Geschichte der sächischen Kaiserzeit* (Darmstadt, 1971), VI, 8; Jan Kostenec, "Studies on the Great Palace in Constantinople I. The Palace of Constantine the Great," *Byzantinoslavica* 49/2 (1998): 279–96.

2. The Roman mint continued to strike gold *solidi* as late as the reigns of the emperors Leo III, Artavasdos, and Constantine V. Philip Grierson, *Byzantine Coins* (London, 1982), Plate 39, nos. 707–9, 716–17 (Leo III); no. 710 (Artavasdos); nos. 712–13, 718–20 (Constantine V).

3. In order to accommodate the increasing number of Eastern monastics who arrived in Rome during the eighth century, Latin communities were in some cases transferred to Greek monks. Sometime between 768 and 773, for example, Pope Stephen III transferred the monastery of St. Andrew, which had been founded in the late sixth century by Gregory the Great in his ancestral home on the Caelian Hill, from Latin to Greek control. *PL* 75: 229. Claiming the transfer to have occurred "by necessity more than desire," John the Deacon, in an unrestrained expression of anti-Greek sentiment, yearned for the day when it would "be returned once more, to the Latin mode of worship, the Lord willing." Id. His wish appears, however, to have remained unfulfilled, for a century later, in the time of Pope Nicholas I (858–867), St. Andrews was still ruled by a Greek abbot named (ironically) Zacharias. Id., 236.

4. *LP* I, p. 435; *PL* 75: 225; see also Ivan Havener, "The Greek Prologue to the 'Dialogues' of Gregory the Great," *Revue Bénédictine* 99 (1989): 103. The wide audience that the *Dialogues* achieved in the East as a consequence of Pope Zacharias's translation was almost certainly responsible for Gregory the Great becoming recognized as St. Gregory "Dialogos" by the eastern churches. See Viktor Matthaiou, ed., *Paulos Evergetinos: Synagoge ton theophthongon rematon kai didaskalion ton theophoron kai agion pateron*, 3 vols. (Repr. Athens, 1957–1964).

5. Cyril Mango, "La Culture Grecque et l'Occident au VIIIe Siècle," in *I Problemi dell'Occidente nel Secolo VIII*, 6–12 April 1972, Settimane di Studio del Centro Italiano

di Studi sull'Alto Medioevo, Vol. 2 (Spoleto, 1973), pp. 709–10; E. Dekkers, "Les traductions grecques des écrits patristiques latins," *Sacris Erudiri* 5 (1953): 202; H. Delehaye, "La Vie grecque de S. Martin de Tours," *Studi bizantini e neoellenici* 5 (1939): 428ff. For the passion of St. Denys, see *BHG* 554, which Mango describes as "a bad translation" of *BHL* 2178, Mango, id., p. 710n118, and R. Loenertz, "Le panégyrique de S. Denys l'Aréopagite par S. Michel le Syncelle," *Analecta Bollandiana* 68 (1950): 225ff. For the passion of St. Anastasia, see H. Delehaye, "Étude sur le légendier romain," *Subsidia hagiographica* 23 (Brussels, 1936): 155.

6. *LP* I, p. 402; Jaffé, No. 2220, p. 256. For the life and *acta* of St. Eustathios, see *AA.SS.* Sept. VI (1757), pp. 123–25, *BHG* 641–43, and Augustus Marini, *Acta graeca S. Eusthathi martyris* in *Studi Storici*, Vol. 6 (Livorno, 1897), pp. 331–41. For an encomium on St. Eustathios by Niketas Paphlagonis, see *PG* 105:376–417. St. Eustathios would become the protagonist in a popular Roman folkloristic novella composed at the turn of the eighth century. E. Follieri, "Santi Occidentali nell'Onnografia Bizantina," in *Atti del Convegno Internazionale sul Tema: L'Oriente Cristiano nella Storia della Civiltà*, 31 March–3 April 1963 (Rome, 1964): 254; H. Delehaye, "La légende de saint Eustache," in *Academie Royale de Belgique, Bulletin de la Classe des Lettres et des Sciences Morales et Politiques* (Brussels, 1919), pp. 175–210.

7. *LP* I, p. 420. et concedans omnia quae in usu diaconie existunt, statuit perpetuo tempore pro sustentatione pauperum in diaconiae ministerio deservire.

8. Gilbert Dagron, "Rome et l'Italie Vues de Byzance (IVe-VIIe siècles)," in *Bisanzio, Roma e l'Italia nell'Alto Medioevo*, 3–9 April 1986, Settimane di Studio del Centro Italiano di Studi sull'Alto Medioevo, Vol. I (Spoleto, 1988), p. 63. Dans la Constantinople du VIe siècle, on joue, en effet, à être romain.

9. *LP* I, p. 407; J. T. Hallenbeck, "The Roman-Byzantine Reconciliation of 728: Genesis and Significances," *Byzantinische Zeitschrift* 74 (1981): 34.

10. *LP* I, p. 420.

11. Benedict of Soracte, *Chronicon*, ed. Giuseppe Zuchetti, *Il Chronicon di Benedetto, Monaco di S. Andrea del Soratte* (Rome, 1920), p. 115. ΤΟΝ ΦΡΑΝΚΟΝ ΦΙΛΟΝ ΕΧΙϹ, ΙΤΟΝΑ ΟΥΚ ΕΧΙϹ.

12. *LP* I, pp. 433–34.

13. Marcou, id., p. 147.

14. François Paschoud, *Roma Aeterna* (Neuchâtel, 1967).

15. P. Stockmeier, Leo I. des Großen. *Beurteilung der kaiserlichen Religionspolitik* (Munich, 1959), pp. 48–50, 70–74, 76–78, 181–93; P. Stockmeier, "'Imperium' bei Papst Leo dem Großen," *Studia Patristica* 3 (Berlin, 1961): 413–20; John of Damascus. *Hiera, PG* 95: cols. 1121, 1292, 1573; André Guillou, "Le système de vie enseigné au VIIIe siècle dans le monde byzantin," in *I Problemi dell'Occidente nel Secolo VIII*, Settimane di Studio del Centro Italiano di Studi sull'Alto Medioevo, 6–12 April 1972 (Spoleto, 1973): 343ff.; Paschoud, id., p 317ff.

16. *LP* I, p. 405. sed conpescuit tale consilium pontifex, sperans conversionem principis.

17. *LP* I, p. 408.

18. *LP* I, p. 407. ne desisterent ab amore vel fidei Romani imperii ammonebat. See Milton V. Anastos, "Leo III's Edict against the Images in the Year 726–727 and Italo-Byzantine Relations between 726 and 730," *Byzantinische Forschungen* 3 (1968): 5–41.

19. John the Deacon, *Chronicon Venetum*, ed. G. H. Pertz, MGH Scriptores VII (Hanover, 1846), p. 12. Part of Gregory III's assistance to the exarch included writing a letter to duke Antonio of Grado enlisting his support in imperial efforts to retake Ravenna. Tellenbach contends that Gregory III did so "come membro dell'impero bizantino." Gerd Tellenbach, "L'Italia nell'Occidente Cristiano nell' Secolo VIII," in *I Problemi dell'Occidente nel Secolo VIII*, Settimane di Studio del Centro Italiano di Studi sull'Alto Medioevo, 6–12 April 1972 (Spoleto, 1973): 399–400.

20. *LP* I, p. 427.

21. *LP* I, pp. 429–31; H. Hubert, "Étude sur la formation des états de l'église. Les papes Grégoire II, Grégoire III, Zacharie, et Étienne II et leurs relations avec les empereurs iconoclastes (726-757)," *Revue historique* 79 (1899): 34–35.

22. *LP* I, pp. 433–34; *Pauli Continuatio Casinensis*, ed. G. Waitz, MGH SSrL (Hanover, 1878), pp. 198–99.

23. T. S. Brown, *Gentlemen and Officers*, id., p. 162. As with his predecessors, Zacharias had dated all documents emanating from the papal chancery by reference to the regnal year of the emperor in Constantinople. Gregory II's Roman synod of 721, for example, is dated in the "sixth year of the reign of the most pious lord Augustus Leo [III] and the second year of the reign of his son Constantine [V]. *Mansi* XII, p. 266. The marble tablets erected by Pope Gregory III in the oratory that he built in St. Peter's are dated "in the sixteenth year of the reign of the most pious lord Augustus Leo [III] and the thirteenth year of his son the emperor Constantine [V]." De Rossi, id., p. 414nn8–9. Two letters from Pope Zacharias directed respectively to bishops Witta of Burnaburg and Burchard of Würtzburg are both dated by reference to the regnal year of the emperor Constantine V. *Mansi* XII, p. 320; Jaffé, Nos. 2265 and 2266, p. 263; *PL* 89: 922. Zacharias's Roman synod of 743 as well as two letters from the pope to St. Boniface are dated by reference to the regnal years of Artabasdos, who seized the imperial throne for about two and one-half years sometime around between 741 and 743 until Constantine V finally secured it. After that, Zacharias resumed dating his documents by reference to Constantine V's regnal years. See *Mansi* XII, pp. 381–82; Jaffé, Nos. 2270 and 2271, p. 264 and p. 265ff. The papal chancery continued to date documents according to the regnal years of the Byzantine emperors until 772. Jaffé, No. 2398, p. 290.

24. Πολλά τά ετη ("May your years be many.")

~

Bibliography

Primary Sources

Texts and Collections

Acta Conciliorum Oecumenicorum, ed. E. Schwartz and J. Straub, 5 vols. in 32 parts (Berlin and Leipzig, 1914–).

Acta Sanctorum (Brussels, 1643–).

Ado, bishop of Vienne. *Vetus Romanum Martyrologium*, ed. J. Migne, *Patrologia Latina*, v. 123, cols. 130–420 (Paris, 1845–1866).

Agnellus qui et Andreas. *Liber Pontificalis Ecclesiae Ravennatis*, ed. O. Holder-Egger, *MGH Scriptores Rerum Langobardicarum et Italicarum saeculum VI–IX* (Hanover, 1878).

Alexander Monachos. *De venerandae crucis inventione*, ed. J. Migne, *Patrologia Graeca*, v. 87/3, col. 4015ff. (Paris, 1857–1866).

Anastasios the Persian. *Saint Anastase le Perse et l'histoire de la Palestine au début du VIIe siècle*, ed. Bernard Flusin, 2 vols. (Paris, 1992).

Anastasios Sinaites. *Viae dux*, ed. J. Migne, *Patrologia Graeca*, v. 89, cols. 36–309 (Paris, 1857–1866).

Andrieu, Michel, ed. *Les Ordines Romani du haut moyen age*, 3 vols. (Louvain, 1971).

Antiochos Monachos. *Epistula Antiochi monachi laurae Sabae ad Eustathium praepositum monasterii Attalinae, civitatis Ancyrae Galatiae*, ed. J. Migne, *Patrologia Graeca*, vol. 89, cols. 1421–1428 (Paris, 1857–1866).

Antiochos Monachos. *Pandects*, ed. J. Migne, *Patrologia Graeca*, vol. 89, cols. 1428–1849 (Paris, 1857–1866).

Apophthegmata Patrum. Benedicta Ward, trans. *The Sayings of the Desert Fathers* (Kalamazoo, 1975).

Athanasius. Robert C. Gregg, trans. *The Life of Antony and the Letter to Marcellinus* (New York, 1980).

Bede. *Opera Historica Minora*, ed. Joseph Stevenson (London, 1841).

Bede. *Historia Ecclesiastica Gentis Anglorum*, ed. Bertram Colgrave and R. A. B. Mynors (Oxford, 1969).

Bede. *Chronicon de sex aetatibus mundi*, ed. Th. Mommsen, *Chronica minora*, III, MGH *Auctores Antiquissimi*, 13 (Berlin, 1898).

Benedict of Soracte. *Chronicon*, ed. Giuseppe Zucchetti, *Il Chronicon di Benedetto monaco di S. Andrea del Soratte*, Fonti per la Storia d'Italia, 55 (Rome, 1920).

Bibliotheca hagiographica graeca, ed. F. Halkin, Subsidia hagiographica 8a, 3 vols. (Brussels, 1957).

Bibliotheca hagiographica latina, ed. Society of Bollandists, Subsidia hagiographica 6, 2 vols. (Brussels 1898–1901), Supplement, 2nd ed., Subsidia hagiographica 12 (Brussels, 1911).

Cameron, Averil and Judith Herrin, eds., *Constantinople in the Eighth Century: The Parastaseis Syntomoi Chronikai* (Leiden, 1984).

Cedrenos, Georgios. *Historiarum Compendium*, ed. I. Bekker, Corpus scriptorum historiae Byzantinae, 2 vols. (Bonn, 1838–1839).

Choniates, Niketas. *Historia*, ed. J. A. Van Dieten, Corpus Fontium Historiae Byzantinae, 2 vols. (Berlin and New York, 1975).

Chronica Patriarcharum Gradensium, ed. G. Waitz, MGH *Scriptores Rerum Langobardicarum* (Hanover, 1878).

Chronicle of Monemvasia, ed. I. Dujcev, *Cronaca di Monemvasia*. Istituto siciliano di studi buzantini e neoellenici, Testi 12 (Palermo, 1976).

Chronicon 724. *Chronicon miscellaneum ad AD 724 pertinens*, trans. Andrew Palmer, *The Seventh Century in the West-Syrian Chronicles* (Liverpool, 1993).

Chronicon 1234. *Chronicon anonymum ad AD 1234 pertinens*, vol. i, trans. J. B. Chabot, Corpus Scriptorum Christianorum Orientalium, Scriptores Syri, 3rd ser. 14 (Louvain, 1937); vol. ii, trans A. Abouna, ibid., vol. 154 (Louvain, 1974).

Chronicon Paschale, trans. M. Whitby and M. Whitby, *Chronicon Paschale AD 284–632* (Liverpool, 1989).

Clavis Patrum Graecorum. M. Geerard, *Clavis Patrum Graecorum*, II–IV (Turnhout, 1974–1980).

Clavis Patrum Latinorum. E. Dekkers, *Clavis Patrum Latinorum*, 2nd ed. (Sacris erudiri 3 (Steenbrugge, 1961).

Codex Iustinianus, ed. P. Krüger in *Corpus Iuris Civilis*, vol. 2, 12th ed. (Berlin, 1959).

Constantine VII Porphyrogenitos. *De ceremoniis aulae byzantinae*, ed. J. J. Reiske, Corpus scriptorum historiae Byzantinae (Bonn, 1829), partial French tr. Albert Vogt, *Le Livre des Cérémonies*, 2 vols. (Paris, 1967).

Constantine VII Porphyrogenitos. *De Thematibus*, trans. A. Pertusi, *Constantino Porfirogenito De Thematibus*, Studi e Testi 160 (Vatican City, 1952).

Constantine VII Porphyrogenitos. *De Administrando Imperio*, ed. and trans. Gy. Moravcsik and R. J. H. Jenkins, Corpus Fontium Historiae Byzantinae, 2nd ed. (Washington, D.C., 1967).

Corippus. *In Laudem Iustini Augusti minoris Libri IV*, ed., trans., and comm. Averil Cameron (London, 1976).

Cummian. *De controversia Paschali*. *Epistola Cummiani Hiberni ad segienum Huensem ab-*

batem de controversia Paschali, ed. J. Migne, *Patrologia Latina*, vol. 87, cols. 968–978 (Paris, 1845–1866).

Cyril of Scythopolis. R. M. Price, trans. *Lives of the Monks of Palestine* (Kalamazoo, 1991).

Darrouzès, Jean, *Notitiae episcopatum ecclesiae Constantinopolitanae* (Paris, 1981).

De Rossi, Giovanni Baptista, *Inscriptiones christianae urbis Romae septimo saeculo antiquiores* II, 1 (Rome, 1857–1888).

De Rossi, Giovanni Baptista, *Codices Palatini Latini Bibliothecae Vaticanae*, Vol. I (Rome, 1886).

Diehl, Charles, *Inscriptiones latinae christianae veteres*, 3 vols. (Berlin, 1925–1928). *Supplementum*, ed. J. Moreau and H. J. Marrou (Berlin, 1967).

Dionysius the Areopagite. *Pseudo-Dionysius. The Complete Works*, trans. Colum Luibheid (New York, 1987).

Doctrina Iacobi nuper baptizati, ed. V. Déroche, *Travaux et Mémoires* 11 (1991) 47–229.

Dölger, Franz, *Regesten der Kaiserurkunden des Oströmischen Reiches von 565–1453*, Vol. I (Munich and Berlin, 1924).

Eddius Stephanus. *Vita Wilfridi episcopi Eboracensis auctore Stephano*, ed. W. Levison, MGH *Scriptores Rerum Merovingicarum* VI (Hanover, 1913) and also Bertram Colgrave, trans., *The Life of Bishop Wilfrid by Eddius Stephanus* (Cambridge, 1927).

Egeria. *Itinerarium*, ed. P. Maraval, *Égerie, Journal de voyage*, Sources chrétiennes 296 (Paris, 1982).

Ephrem the Syrian. Kathleen E. McVey, trans., *Hymns* (New York, 1989).

Eusebius. *Historia Ecclesiastica*, ed. E. Schwartz, 3 vols. (Leipzig, 1903–1909) and G. A. Williamson, trans., *Eusebius: The History of the Church* (Harmondsworth, 1965).

Evagrius Scholasticus. *Ecclesiastical History*, ed. J. Bidez and L. Parmentier (London, 1898).

Fortunatus, Venantius. *Opera Poetica*, ed. F. Leo, MGH *Auctores Antiquissimi* 4, 1 (Berlin, 1881).

Gams, P. B., ed. *Series Episcoporum Ecclesiae Catholicae* (Ratisbon, 1873). Reprint. Graz, 1957.

George the Chozibite. *Vita sancti Georgii Chozibitae auctore Antonio Chozibitae*, ed. C. House, *Analecta Bollandiana* 7 (1881): 95–144.

George of Pisidia. *Bellum Avaricum*, in *Giorgio di Pisidia, Poemi, I. Panegirici Epici*, ed., tr., and comm. A. Pertusi (Ettal, 1959).

George of Pisidia. *Expeditio Persica* in *Giorgio di Pisidia, Poemi, I. Panegirici Epici*, ed., tr., and comm. A. Pertusi (Ettal, 1959).

George of Pisidia. *Heraclias* in *Giorgio di Pisidia, Poemi, I. Panegirici Epici*, ed., tr., and comm. A. Pertusi (Ettal, 1959).

George of Pisidia. *In Restitutionem S. Crucis* in *Giorgio di Pisidia, Poemi, I. Panegirici Epici*, ed., tr., and comm. A. Pertusi (Ettal, 1959).

Georgios Monachos. *Chronicon*, ed. C. deBoor (Leipzig, 1904).

Giorgi, Ignazio and Ugo Balzani, eds. *Il Regesto di Farfa*, vol. 2 (Rome, 1879).

Gregory of Tours. *Historia Francorum*, ed. B. Krusch and W. Levison, I (Hanover, 1951) and also *The History of the Franks*, trans. Lewis Thorpe (Harmondsworth, 1974).

Gregory of Tours. *Liber Vitae Patrum*, ed. B. Krtusch, *MGH Scriptores Rerum Merovingicarum*, vol. 1.2 (Hanover, 1885).

Gregory I, Pope. *Dialogi*, ed. Adalbert de Vogué (Paris, 1978).

Gregory I, Pope. *Forty Gospel Homilies*, ed. and trans. David Hurst (Kalamazoo, 1990).

Gregory I, Pope. *Homiliae in Hiezechihelem*, ed. Mark Adriaen. Corpus Christianorum Series Latina 142 (Turnhout, 1971).

Gregory I, Pope. *Registrum epistularum*, 2 vols., ed. D. Norberg. Corpus Christianorum Series Latina 140–140A (Turnhout, 1982).

Gregory I, Pope. *Moralia in Iob*, 3 vols., ed. Mark Adriaen. Corpus Christianorum Series Latina 143, 143A, and 143B (Turnhout, 1979–1985).

Gregory I, Pope. *Regula Pastoralis*, ed. Floribert Rommel, trans. Charles Morel. (Paris, 1992).

Gregory I, Pope. *XL Homiliarum in Evangelia Libri Duo*, ed. J. Migne, *Patrologia Latina*, vol. 76, cols. 1075–1312 (Paris, 1845-66).

Grumel, Venance, *Les regestes des actes du patriarcat de Constantinople. I: Les actes des patriarches. I: Les regestes de 381 à 715*, 2nd ed. (Paris, 1972).

Guenther, P. ed., *Epistulae imperatorum pontificium aliorum [367-553] … Avellana quae dicitur collectio*, Corpus Scriptorum Ecclesiae Latinae, 2 pts. in 1 vol. (Vienna, 1895–1898).

Henry, Archdeacon of Huntingdon. *Historia Anglorum*, ed. and trans. Diana Greenway (Oxford, 1996).

Jaffé, Philip, ed., *Regesta Pontificum Romanorum ab condita Ecclesia ad annum post Christum natum MCXCVIII*, Vol. I, 2nd ed. by W. Wattenbach, S. Loewenfeld, F. Kaltenbrunner, and P. Ewald (Leipzig, 1885).

John of Biclar. *Chronicle*, ed. Th. Mommsen, *MGH Auctores Antiquissimi* xi (Berlin, 1894).

John the Deacon. *Vita S. Gregorii*, ed. J. Migne, *Patrologia Latina*, vol. 75, cols. 59–242 (Paris, 1845–1866).

John of Ephesus. *Ecclesiastical History*, Part III, ed. and trans. E. W. Brooks, Corpus Scriptorum Christianorum Orientalium, Scriptores Syri 3rd ser. 3 (Louvain, 1952) and also tr. R. Payne Smith, *The Third Part of the Ecclesiastical History of John of Ephesus* (Oxford, 1860).

John Lydus. *De Magistratibus Populi Romani*, ed. R. Wuensch (Leipzig, 1903) and also ed. and trans. A. C. Bandy, *John Lydus, On Powers or The Magistracies of the Roman State* (Philadelphia, 1983).

John Moschos. *Pratum Spirituale*, ed. J. Migne, *Patrologia Graeca*, vol. 87, cols. 2852–3112 (Paris 1857-66) and also *The Spiritual Meadow*, trans. John Wortley (Kalamazoo, 1992).

John of Nikiu. *Chronicle of John, Bishop of Nikiu*, tr. R. H. Charles (London, 1916).

Justinian. *Novellae*, ed. R. Schoell and W. Kroll (Berlin, 1963).

Kehr, Paul F., *Regesta Pontificum Romanorum, Italia Pontificia*, I (Rome, 1961).

Lauchert, Friedrich, *Die Kanones der Wichtigsten Altkirchlichen Concilien* (Frankfurt, 1961).

Lemerle, Paul, ed. and trans., *Les Plus Anciens Receuils des Miracles de Saint Démétrius et la Pénétration des Slaves dans les Balkans*, Vol. I (Paris, 1979).

Leo the Deacon. *Leonis diaconi historia*, ed. C. B. Hase, Corpus Scriptorum Historiae Byzantinae (Bonn, 1828).

Leo Grammatikos. *Chronographia*, ed. I. Bekker, Corpus Scriptorum Historiae Byzantinae (Bonn, 1842).

Leontius of Naples. *Vie de Syméon le Fou et Vie de Jean de Chypre*, ed. and trans. A.-J. Festugière and L. Ryden (Paris, 1974).

Leontius of Naples. *Vita S. Gregorii Agrigentini*, ed. J. Migne, *Patrologia Graeca*, vol. 98, cols. 550-715 (Paris, 1857–1866).

Liber Diurnus Romanorum Pontificum, ed. Hans Foerster (Bern, 1958) and also ed., Theodor E. Von Sickel (Darmstadt, 1966).

Liber Pontificalis, ed. L. Duchesne, 2 vols. (Paris, 1884–1892), and also tr. Eng., Raymond Davis, *The Book of Pontiffs (Liber Pontificalis)* (Liverpool, 1989) and *The Lives of the Eighth Century Popes (Liber Pontificalis)* (Liverpool, 1992).

Mai, Angelo, *Scriptorum veterum nova collectio a Vaticanis codicibus edita*, V (Rome, 1831).

Mansi, J. D. *Sacrorum Conciliorum Nova et Amplissima Collectio*, ed. P. Labbe, P. Cossart, and J. D. Mansi, 53 vols. (Florence. 1758–1798). Reprint. Graz, 1901.

Mary, Mother and Kallistos Ware, trans. *The Festal Menaion* (Reprint. London, 1984).

Mateos, J., ed. *Le Typicon de la Grande Église*, Orientalia Christiana Periodica 165–66, 2 vols. (Paris, 1962–1963).

Mauricius, Flavius Tiberius (Emperor). *Das Strategikon des Maurikios*, ed. and trans. George T. Dennis and Ernst Gamillscheg, Corpus Fontium Historiae Byzantinae, Vol. 17 (Vienna, 1981).

Maximus Confessor. *Selected Writings*, ed. George C. Berthold (New York, 1985).

Maximus Confessor. *Disputatio cum Pyrrho*, ed. J. Migne, *Patrologia Graeca*, vol. 91, cols. 288–353 (Paris, 1857–1866).

Maximus Confessor. *S. Maximi Confessori epistolae, partim communes, partim dogmaticae et polemicae*, ed. J. Migne, *Patrologia Graeca*, vol. 91, cols. 364–649 (Paris, 1857–1866).

Maximus Confessor. *S. Maximi Confessori Opuscula theologica et polemica*, ed. J. Migne, *Patrologia Graeca*, vol. 91, cols. 9–285 (Paris, 1857–1866).

Mega Horologion (Athens, 1973).

Menander Protector. Menander Protector, Fragments, in *The History of Menander the Guardsman*, ed. and trans. R. C. Blockley (Liverpool, 1985).

Michael Glykas. *Annalium, Pars IV*, ed. J. Migne, *Patrologia Graeca*, vol. 158, cols. 520ff. (Paris, 1857–1866).

Michael the Syrian. *Chronique de Michel le Syrien, Patriarche Jacobite d'Antioche 1166–1199*, ed. and trans. J. B. Chabot, 4 vols. (Paris, 1899–1924).

Muratori, L. A., *Rerum Italicarum Scriptores*, 25 vols. (Milan, 1723–1751).

Nau, F., ed. and trans. *Martyrologes et Ménologes Orientaux. Un Martyrologe et Douze Ménologes Syriaques* (Paris, 1912).

Nikephoros, Patriarch of Constantinople. *Short History*, ed., trans., and comm. Cyril Mango, Corpus Fontium Historiae Byzantinae, (Washington, D.C., 1990) and also *Chronographikon syntomon*, ed. C. deBoor, *Nicephori opuscula historica* (Leipzig, 1880).

Nikephoros Kallistos Xanthopoulos. *Historia Ecclesiastica*, ed. J. Migne, *Patrologia Graeca*, vol. 145–47 (Paris, 1857–1866).

Patrologiae Cursus Completus, series Graeco-Latina, ed. J. P. Migne (Paris, 1857–1866; 1880–1903).

Patrologiae Cursus Completus, series Latina, ed. J. P. Migne (Paris, 1844–1974).

Paul the Deacon. Historia Langobardorum, ed. G. Waitz, MGH Scriptores Rerum Germanicarum in usum scholarum separatim editi (Hanover, 1987) and also tr. Eng. W. D. Foulke, Paul the Deacon, History of the Lombards (Philadelphia, 1974).

Paul the Deacon. S. Gregorii Magni Vita, ed. J. Migne, Patrologoa Latina, vol. 75, cols. 42–62 (Paris, 1844–1855).

Paul the Silentiary. Ἔκφρασις τοῦ ναοῦ τῆς ἉγίαςΣοφίας ed. L. Friedlaender (Leipzig and Berlin, 1912) and also trans. and comm. N. G. Garsoïan (Cambridge, MA, 1989).

Procopius. History of the Wars, ed. and trans. H. B. Dewing, 7 vols. (Cambridge, MA, 1914-40).

Riedinger, Rudolf, ed. Concilium Lateranense a. 649 celebratum, 2 vols. (Berlin, 1984).

Riedinger, Rudolf, ed. Concilium Universale Constantinopolitanum Tertium, 2 vols. (Berlin, 1990).

Schaff, Philip and Henry Wace, eds., A Select Library of the Christian Church: Nicene and Post-Nicene Fathers, Second Series. (Repr. Philadelphia, 1995).

Schreiner, Peter, ed. Die Byzantinishcen Kleinchroniken, Vol. XII, Pt. 1, Corpus Fontium Historiae Byzantinae (Vienna, 1975).

Sebeos. Histoire d'Héraclius par l'evêque Sébéos, trans. F. Macler (Paris, 1904).

Severus of Asmounein. History of the Coptic Church of Alexandria, ed. and trans. B. Evetts, Patrologia Orientalis, Tome I, Fasc. 2 (Paris, 1904).

Sophronios of Jerusalem. Anacreontica, ed. M. Gigante, Sophronii Anacreontica (Rome, 1957).

Sophronios of Jerusalem. In Nativitatem, ed. H. Usener, Rheinisches Museum, N. F., 41 (1886), pp. 500–516.

Sophronios of Jerusalem. In Theophaniam, ed. A. Papadopoulos-Kerameus, Ἀνάλεκτα Ἱεροσολυμιτικῆς Σταχυολογίας, V (Saint Petersburg, 1898), pp. 151–68.

Sophronios of Jerusalem. Laudes in Cyrum et Joannem, ed. J. Migne, Patrologia Graeca, vol. 87/3, cols. 3380–3421 (Paris, 1857–1866).

Sophronios of Jerusalem. Epistola synodica, ed. J. Migne, Patrologia Graeca, vol. 87/3, cols. 3148–3200 (Paris, 1857–1866).

Sozomen. Historia Ecclesiastica, ed. J. Bidez, Kirchengeschichte, Die griechischen christlichen Schriftsteller der ersten Jahrhunderte, vol. 50 (Berlin, 1960).

Silvagni, Angelo, Monumenta epigraphica christiana saeculo XIII antiquiora quae Italiae finibus adhuc exstant (Vatican City, 1943).

Strategios Monachos. La Prise de Jérusalem par les Perses en 614, ed. Gérard Garitte, Corpus Scriptorum Christianorum Orientalium, vol. 203 (Louvain, 1960).

Synaxarium ecclesiae Constantinopolitanae, ed. H. Delehaye, Propylaeum ad AA.SS. Novembris (Brussels, 1902).

Synodicon Vetus, ed. J. Duffy and J. Parker (Washington, D.C., 1979).

Theodoret of Cyrrhus. Historia Ecclesiastica, ed. L. Parmentier (Berlin, 1954).

Theodoret of Cyrrhus. Historia religiosa, ed. and trans. P. Canivet and A. Leroy-Molinghen, 2 vols. (Paris, 1977–1979) and also tr. Eng. R. M. Price, A History of the Monks of Syria by Theodoret of Cyrrhus (Kalamazoo, 1985).

Theodoros Anagnostes. Kirchengeschichte, ed. G. C. Hansen (Berlin, 1971).

Theodoros Synkellos. Analecta Avarica, ed. L. Sternbach (Cracow, 1900).

Theophanes Confessor. *The Chronicle of Theophanes Confessor*, trans. and comm. Cyril Mango and Roger Scott (Oxford, 1997) and also ed. C. deBoor, 2 vols. (Leipzig, 1883–1885).

Theophylact Simocatta. *History*, trans. M. Whitby and M. Whitby (Oxford, 1986) and also ed. C. deBoor, rev. P. Wirth (Stuttgart, 1972).

Zonaras, Ioannes. *Epitome historiarum*, ed. T. Büttner-Wobst, Corpus Scriptorum Historiae Byzantinae, vol. 50 (Bonn, 1897).

Secondary Sources

Dorothy deF. Abrahamse, "Rebellion, Heresy and Popular Prophecy in the Reign of Philippikos Bardanios (711–713)," *Eastern Europe Quarterly* 13 (1979): 395–408.

H. Ahrweiler, *L'ideologie politique de l'empire byzantine* (Paris, 1975).

G. Albarigo, ed., *Storia dei concili ecumenici* (Brescia, 1990).

Suzanne Alexander, "Heraclius, Byzantine Imperial Ideology, and the David Plates," *Speculum* 52 (1977): 217–37.

H. S. Alivisatos, "Les canons 13, 30 et 55 du Trullanum," *Rivista di studi bizantini e neoellenici* 5 (1939): 581–85.

Berthold Altaner, *Patrology*, trans. Hilda C. Graef (New York, 1960).

M. Amari. *Storia dei Musulmani di Sicilia*, I, 2nd ed. (Catania, 1933).

Patrick Amory, *People and Identity in Ostrogothic Italy, 489–554* (Cambridge, 1997).

Milton V. Anastos, "Leo III's Edict against Images in 726–727 and Italo-Byzantine Relations between 727 and 730," *Byzantinische Forschungen* 3 (1969): 5–41.

Milton V. Anastos, "The Transfer of Illyricum, Calabria and Sicily to the Jurisdiction of the Patriarch of Constantinople in 732-733," *Studi Bizantini e Neoellenici in Onore di S. G. Mercati* (Rome, 1957) pp. 14–31.

Michel Andrieu, "La Carrière Ecclesiastique des Papes et les documents liturgiques du Moyen Age," *Revue des sciences religieuses* 21 (1947): 90–120.

Michel Andrieu, *Les Ordines Romani du haut moyen age*, 3 vols. (Paris, 1931–1951).

F. Antonelli, "I primi monasteri di monaci orientali in Roma, *Rivista di archeologia cristiana* 5 (1928): 105–21.

G. Arnaldi, "Le origini del patrimonio di S. Pietro," in *Storia d'Italia*, VII, I (Turin, 1987).

H. Ashworth, "The Liturgical Prayers of Gregory the Great," *Traditio* 15 (1959): 107–61.

E. G. C. F. Atchley, *Ordo Romanus Primus* (London, 1905).

J. F. Baldovin, "The Urban Character of Christian Worship in Jerusalem, Rome and Constantinople from the Fourth to the Tenth Centuries: The Origins, Development and Meaning of Stational Liturgy," *Orientalia Christiana Anecdota* 228 (Rome, 1987).

Barry Baldwin, *An Anthology of Byzantine Poetry* (Amsterdam, 1985).

J.-Ch. Balty, "Un follis d'Antioche daté de 623/624 et les campagnes syriennes d'Héraclius," *Gazette numismatique suisse* 20 (1970): 4–10.

M. G. Barberini, *I Santi Quattro Coronati a Roma* (Rome, 1990).

G. Bardy, "La Latinisation de l'Eglise d'Occident," *Irénikon* 14 (1937): 1.

F. Barisic, "Le siège de Constantinople par les Avars et les Slavs en 626," *Byzantion* 24 (1954): 371.

Domenico Bartolini, *Di S. Zaccaria Papa e degli anni del suo pontificato* (Regensburg, 1879).

Giulio Battelli, "Liber Diurnus Romanorum Pontificum," in *Enciclopedia Cattolica* 7: 1262–67 (Vatican City, 1951).

P. Battifol, *L'Abbaye de Rossano* (Paris, 1891).

P. Battifol, *Grégoire le Grand* (Paris, 1928).

P. Battifol, "Inscriptions byzantines de Saint Georges-du-Velabre," *Mélanges d'archéologie et d'histoire de l'École française de Rome* 7 (1887): 419.

P. Batiffol, "Les libraires byzantines à Rome," *Mélanges d'archéologie et d'histoire de l'École française de Rome* 8 (1888): 297–308.

Carlo Battisti, "Appunti sulla storia e sulla diffusione dell'ellenismo nell'Italia meridionale," *Revue de linguistique Romane* III (1927): 1.

A. Baumstark, "Orientalisches in den Texten der abendlandischen Palmenfeier," *Jahrbuch für Liturgiewissenschaft* 7 (1927): 146–153.

A. Baumstark, "Der Orient und die Gesange der Adoratio Crucis,"*Jahrbuch für Liturgiewissenschaft* 2 (1922): 1–17.

Bernard Bavant, "Le duché byzantin de Rome. Origine, durée et extension géographique," *Mélanges de l'École française de Rome. Moyen Age-Temps Moderne* 91 (1979): 41–88.

Norman H. Baynes, "The First Campaign of Heraclius against Persia," *English Historical Review* 19 (1904): 694–702.

Norman H. Baynes, "The Restoration of the True Cross at Jerusalem, *English Historical Review* 27 (1912): 287–299.

Normam H. Baynes, "A Note on the Chronology of the Reign of the Emperor Heraclius," *Byzantinische Zeitschrift* 26 (1926): 55–56.

Norman H. Baynes, "The Supernatural Defenders of Constantinople," *Analecta Bollandiana* 67 (1949): 165–177.

H. G. Beck, *Kirche und theologische Literatur im byzantinischen Reich* (Munich, 1959).

John Beckwith, *Early Christian and Byzantine Art* (New Haven, 1993).

P. Bernadakis, "Les appels au Pape dans l'Eglise Grecque jusqu'à Photius," *Echos d'Orient* 6 (1903): 30–42, 118–25, 249–57.

P. Bernadakis, "Le culte de la croix chez les Grecs," *Echos d'Orient* 5 (1901–1902): 193–202, 257–264.

Walter Berschin, "Abendland und Byzanz. Literatur und Sprache," *Reallexikon der Byzantinistik*, Reihe A, I (1969–1970), p. 227.

Walter Berschin, *Griechisch-lateinisches Mittelalter: von Hieronymus zu Nikolaus von Kues* (Bern, 1980).

Walter Berschin, "Bonifatius Consiliarius: Ein romischer Übersetzer in der byzantinischen Epoche des Papsttums" in *Lateinische Kultur im VIII Jarrhundert. Traube-Gedenkenschrift*, ed. A. Lebner and W. Berschin (St. Ottlien, 1989).

Carlo Bertelli, "Caput Sancti Anastasii," *Parragone (Arte)* 247 (1970), pp. 12–25.

Carlo Bertelli, *La Madonna di Santa Maria in Trastevere* (Rome, 1961).

Ottorino Bertolini, "I rapporti di Zaccaria con Costantino V," *Scritti scelti di storia medioevale* II (Livorno, 1968), pp. 463–484.

Ottorino Bertolini, "Riflessi politici delle controversie religiose con Bisanzio nelle vicende del secolo VII in Italia," *Caraterri del secolo VII in Occidente, Settimane di Studio del Centro Italiano di Studi sull'Alto Medio Evo* (Spoleto, 1958), pp. 733–89.

Ottorino Bertolini, "Per la storia delle diaconie romane nell'alto Medio Evo sino alle fine del secolo VIII," *Archivio della Società Romana di Storia Patria* 70 (1947), pp. 1–145.

Ottorino Bertolini, *Roma di fronte a Bizanzio ei ai Langobardi* (Bologna, 1941).

P. Bianchi, "Martino I papa (649–653) e il suo tempo," *XXVIII Convegno Storico Internazionale*, Todi, 13–16 October 1991, in *Rivista di Storia della Chiesa in Italia* 46 (1992), pp. 262–272.

B. Bischoff, "Das griechische Element in der abendländischen Bildung des Mittelalters," *Byzantinische Zeitschrift* 44 (1951): 28.

Edmund Bishop, *Liturgica Historica: Papers on the Liturgy and Religious Life of the Western Church* (Oxford, 1918).

P. Boglioni, "Gregorio Magno, biografo di San Benedetto," in *Atti dell VII Congresso Internazionale di Studi sell'alto Medioevo*, 29 September–5 October, 1980 (Spoleto, 1982).

G. Bognati, *L'Età Longobarda*, 4 vols. (Milan, 1966–1968).

W. F. Bolton, "The Supra-Historical Sense in the Dialogues of Gregory I," *Aevum* 33 (1959).

Antoine Bon, *Le Péloponnèse byzantin jusqu'en 1204* (Paris, 1951).

S. Borsari, "Le migrazione dall'Oriente in Italia nel VII secolo," *La Parola del Passato* 6 (1951): 133.

B. Botte, "La première fête mariale dans la liturgie romaine," *Ephemerides Liturgicae* 47 (1933): 425–430.

G. Bovini, "I mosaici dell'oratorio di San Venanzio a Roma," *Arte Ravennate* 18: 141–154.

J. D. Breckenridge, "Evidence for the Nature of Relations between Pope John VII and the Byzantine Emperor Justinian II," *Byzantinische Zeitschrift* 65 (1972): 364–74.

J. D. Breckenridge, *The Numismatic Iconography of Justinian II* (New York, 1959).

L. Bréhier, "Les colonies d'Orientaux en Occident au commencement du Moyen Age," *Byzantinische Zeitschrift* 12 (1903): 1.

L. Bréhier, *Les institutions de l'empire byzantin* (Paris, 1970).

L. Bréhier and René Aigran, *Histoire de l'Église*, Vol. 5 (Paris, 1947).

Paolo Brezzi, *Studi su Roma e l'Impero Medievale* (Siena, 1984).

Sebastian Brock, "An Early Syriac Life of Maximus the Confessor," *Analecta Bollandiana* 91 (1973): 299–346.

Sebastian Brock, "Syriac Sources for Seventh-Century History," *Byzantine and Modern Greek Studies* 2 (1976): 17–36.

E. W. Brooks, "The Sicilian Expedition of Constantine IV," *Byzantinische Zeitschrift* 7 (1908): 455–59.

L. Brou, "Les chants en langue grecque dans les litirgies latines," *Sacris Erudiri* 1 (1948): 165–180 and 4 (1952): 226–238.

Peter Brown, *Religion and Society in the Age of Augustine* (London, 1972).

Peter Brown, "The Rise and Function of the Holy Man in Late Antiquity," *Journal of Roman Studies* 61 (1971): 80–101.

Peter Brown, "Eastern and Western Christendom in Late Antiquity: A Parting of the Ways," *Studies in Church History* 13 (1976): 1–24.

T. S. Brown, "The Interplay between Roman and Byzantine Traditions and Local Sentiment in the Exarchate of Ravenna," *Settimane di Studio del Centro Italiano di Studi sull'Alto Medio Evo* (Spoleto, 1988), pp. 127–60.

T. S. Brown, "The Background of Byzantine Relations with Italy in the Ninth Century: Legacis, Attachments and Antagonisms," *Byzantinische Forschungen* 13 (1988): 27–45.

T. S. Brown, *Gentlemen and Officers: Imperial Administration in Byzantine Italy 554–800* (Rome, 1984).

T. S. Brown, "The Church of Ravenna and the Imperial Administration in the Seventh Century," *English Historical Review* 94 (1979): 6.

Felix Brunet, *Les oeuvres médicales d'Alexandre de Tralles, le dernier auteur classique des grands médicins grecs de l'Antiquité* (Paris, 1933).

Antonella Bruzzone, "Sulla lingua dei 'Dialoghi' di Gregorio Magno," *Studi Latini e Italiani* 5 (1991), pp. 195–280.

Gudrun Bühe, *Constantinopolis und Roma* (Zurich, 1995).

F. Bulgarella, "Bizanzio in Sicilia," in "Il Mezzogiorno dei Bizantini a Federico II," *Storia d'Italia* III (Turin, 1983).

Thomas S. Burns, "The Alpine Frontier and Early Medieval Italy," in *The Frontier: Comparative Studies*, ed. W. W. Savage and S. I. Thompson (Norman, Oklahoma, 1979), pp. 51–68.

C. Callewaert, "La messe stationnale à Saint-Georges au lendemain du mercredi des cendres," in C. Callewaert, *Sacris Erudiri. Fragmenta liturgica collecta* (Repr. The Hague, 1962).

Alan Cameron, "The Epigrams of Sophronius," *Classical Quarterly* 33 (1983): 284.

Alan Cameron, "Cyril of Schythopolis, V. Sabae 53: A Note on Κατὰ in Late Greek," *Glotta* 56 (1978): 87–94.

Averil Cameron, *Christianity and the Rhetoric of Empire: The Development of Christian Discourse* (Berkeley, 1991).

Averil Cameron, *Procopius and the Sixth Century* (London, 1985).

Averil Cameron, "The Construction of Court Ritual: The Byzantine Book of Ceremonies," in D. Cannadine and S. R. F. Price, eds., *Rituals of Royalty* (Cambridge, 1987).

Averil Cameron, *Changing Cultures in Early Byzantium* (Aldershot, 1996).

Averil Cameron, "The Cult of the Theotokos in Sixth-Century Constantinople: A City Finds Its Symbol," *Journal of Theological Studies*, n.s. 29 (1978): 79–108.

Averil Cameron, "Images of Authority: Elites and Icons in Late Sixth-Century Byzantium," *Past and Present* 84 (1979): 3–35.

Averil Cameron, "The Virgin's Robe: an Episode in the History of Early Seventh-Century Constantinople," *Byzantion* 49 (1979): 42–56.

Averil Cameron, "A Nativity Poem of the Sixth Century," *Classical Philology* 79 (1979): 222–232.

S. I. Camporeale, "Bisanzio e Occidente latino. Interazione e acculturazione dal IV al XVII secolo," *Memorie Domenicane* 12 (1981): 287–94.

P. Canart, "Le livre grec en Italie meridionale," *Scrittura e civiltà* 2 (1978): 103–62.

Bernard Capelle, "La tradition orientale de l'assomption d'après un ouvrage récent," *Revue Bénédictine* (1958): 173–86.

Bernard Capelle, "L'Oraison 'Veneranda" à la Messe de l'Assomption," *Ephemerides Theologicae Louvanienis* 26 (1950): 354–64.

O. Capitani, "Le relazioni tra le vite di Teodoro e Martino del 'Liber Pontificalis' e gli Atti del Concilio Lateranese del 649: nuove prospettive," *Studi e Ricerche sull'Oriente Cristiano* 15 (1992): 5–14.

F. Carcione, *Sergio di Costantinopoli ed Onorio I nella controversia monotelita del VII secolo* (Rome, 1985).

A. Carile, *Storia di Ravenna II: dall'età bizantina del'età ottoniana*, 2 vols. (Venice, 1991).

Erich Caspar, *Die Geschiche des Papsttums*, 2 vols. (Tübingen, 1933).

Erich Caspar, "Die Lateran synode von 649," *Zeitschrift fur Kirchengeschiche* 51 (1932): 25–73.

P. Catry, "Amour du Monde et amour de Dieu chez Saint Grégoire le Grand," *Studia Monastica* 15 (1973): 263.

John C. Cavadini, ed., *Gregory the Great: A Symposium* (Notre Dame, 1996).

G. Cavallo, ed., *The Byzantines* (Chicago, 1997).

G. Cavallo, et al., *I Bizantini in Italia*, 2nd ed. (Milan, 1986).

G. Cavallo, "Le tipologie della cultura nel riflesso delle testimonizane scritte," *Settimane di Studio del Centro Italiano di Studi sull'Alto Medio Evo* (Spoleto, 1986), pp. 467–516.

G. Cavallo. "La cultura italo-greca nella produzione libraria," in Vera von Falkenhausen, ed., *I Bizantini in Italia* (Milan, 1982), p. 500ff.

Roberto Cessi, "La crisi dell'esarcato ravennate agli inizi dell'iconoclastia," *Atti del Reale Istituto Veneto di Scienza, Lettere ed Arti* 93 (1933–1934), pp. 1671–85.

R. H. Chabot, "Feasts in Honor of Our Lady," in J. B. Carol, *Mariology*, iii (Milwaukee, 1960).

Henry Chadwick, *The Early Church*, rev. ed. (London, 1993).

Henry Chadwick, "John Moschus and His Friend Sophronius the Sophist," *Journal of Theological Studies*, n.s. 35 (1974): 41–74.

Henry Chadwick, "Florilegium," in *Reallexikon für Antike und Christentum*, Vol. 7, ed. T. Klauser, et al. (Stuttgart, 1950), cols. 1131–1160.

Peter Charanis, "On the Question of the Hellenisation of Sicily and Southern Italy During the Middle Ages," *American Historical Review* 52 (1946): 74–86.

Peter Charanis, "On the Capture of Corinth by the Onogars and Its Recapture by the Byzantines," *Speculum* 27 (1952): 343–50.

Peter Charanis, "Ethnic Change in the Byzantine Empire in the Seventh Century," *Dumbarton Oaks Papers* 13 (1959): 25–44.

Peter Charanis, "The 'Chronicle of Monemvasia' and the Question of the Slavonic Settlements in Greece," *Dumbarton Oaks Papers* 5 (1950): 141.

Peter Charanis, "The Significance of Coins as Evidence for the History of Athens and Corinth in the Seventh and Eighth Centuries," *Historia* 4 (1955): 163–72.

A. Chavasse, "Les plus ancines types du lectionnaire et de l'antiphonaire romains de la messe," *Revue Bénédictine* 62 (1952): 3–94.

A. Chavasse, *La liturgie de la ville de Rome du V au VIII siècle* (Rome, 1993).

A. Chavasse, "Le Sermonnaire Vatican du VIIe siècle," *Sacris Erudiri* 23 (1978–1979): 225–289.

A. Chavasse, "L'organisation stationnale du Carème romain avant le VIIIe siècle. Une organisation 'pastorale'," *Revue des Sciences Religieuses* 56 (1982): 17–32.

A. Chavasse, "L'Evangeliaire romain de 645: un receuil. Sa composition (façons et materiaux)," *Revue Bénédictine* 92 (1982): 33–75.

A. Chavasse, "Les grands cadres de la celebration à Rome 'in urbe" et 'extra muros' jusqu'au VIIIe siècle," *Revue Bénédictine* 96 (1986): 7–26.

A. Chavasse, "Le sacerdotal et le temporal gregoriens, vers 680. Distribution et origine des pieces utilisées," *Ecclesia Orans* 3 (1986): 263–288.

A. Chavasse, "Amenagements liturgiques à Rome au VIIe and au VIIIe siècle," *Revue Bénédictine* 99 (1989): 75–102.

A. Chavasse, "Les quatres fêtes de la Vièrge," in *Le sacramentaire gélasien (Vaticanus Reginensis 316)* (Tournai, 1958), pp. 375–402.

Nicolas Cheetham, *Medieval Greece* (New Haven, 1981).

Derwas Chitty, *The Desert a City* (Crestwood, NY, 1995).

Francis Clark, *The Pseudo-Gregorian Dialogues*, Vol. II (Leiden, 1987).

P. Classen, "Italien zwischen Byzanz und dem Frankenreich," *Settimane di Studio del Centro Italiano di Studi sull'Alto Medio Evo* (Spoleto, 1981), pp. 919–67.

H. W. Codrington, *The Liturgy of St. Peter* (Munster, 1936).

B. Colgrave, "Pilgrimages to Rome in the Seventh and Eighth Centuries," in E. Bagby Atwood, eds., *Studies in Language, Literature and Culture of the Middle Ages and Later* (Austin, Texas, 1969).

M. Colucci, *Bonifacio IV (608–615). Monumenti e questioni di un pontificato* (Rome, 1976).

Yves Congar, *L'écclesiologie du haut moyen age de Saint Gregoire à la désunion entre Byzance et Rome* (Paris, 1968).

D. J. Constantelos, "The Moslem Conquests of the Near East as Revealed in the Greek Sources of the Seventh and Eighth Centuries," *Byzantion* 42 (1972): 325.

D. J. Constantelos, "Canon 62 of the Synod in Trullo and the Slavic Problem," *Byzantina* 2 (1970): 21–35.

P. Conte, *Chiesa e primato nelle lettere dei papi del secolo VII* (Milan, 1972).

P. Conte, "Il significato del Primato Papale nei Padri del VI Concilio Ecumenico," *Archivium Historiae Pontificae* 15 (1977): 7–111.

P. Conte, *Il Sinodo Lateranense dell'ottobre 649. La nuova edizione degli Atti a cura di Rudlof Riedinger. Rassegna critica delle fonti dei secoli VII–XII* (Vatican City, 1989).

P. Corsi, *La spedizione italiana di Costante II* (Bologna, 1983).

P. Corsi, "Costante II in Italia," *Quaderni Medievali* 5 (1978): 95.

S. Cosentino, *Prosopografia dell'Italia bizantina (493–804)* (Bologna, 1996).

P. Courcelle, *Les lettres grecques en occident de Macrobe à Cassiodore*, 2nd ed. (Paris, 1948).

P. Courcelle, *Late Latin Writers and their Greek Sources*, trans. Harry E. Wedeck (Cambridge, MA, 1969).

P. Courcelle, "S. Grégoire le Grand à l'école de Juvenal," *Studi e materiali di storia delle religioni* (1967), pp. 170–174.

Giorgio Cracco, "Uomini di Dio e uomini di chiesa nell'alto medioevo," *Ricerche di storia sociale e religiosa* 12 (1977), pp. 163–202.

Jacques Croquison, "L'iconographie chrètienne à Rome d'après le Liber Pontificalis," *Byzantion* 34 (1964): 535–606.

Jacques Croquison, "Un preciuex monument d'art byzantin de l'ancien Tresor de Saint Pierre: l'"ombelle de Jean VII," *Rivista di archeologia cristiana* 43 (1967): 49–110.

Jacques Croquison, "Une fête liturgique mystérieuse. La mémoire de sainte Euphémie de Chalcédonie à la date du 13 avril," *Echos d'Orient* 35 (1936): 168–82.

P. A. Cusack, "The Temptation of St. Benedict: An Essay at Interpretation through the Literary Sources," *American Benedictine Review* 27 (1976): 143–63.

P. A. Cusack, "Accidie in the 'Second Dialogue' of St. Gregory I," *Studia Patristica* 23: 99–102.

G. Da Costa-Louillet, "Saints de Sicile et d'Italie méridionale aux VIIIe, IXe et Xe siècles," *Byzantion* 29–30 (1959–1960): 89–95.

C. Dagens, "Grégoire le Grand avant son pontificat: Expérience politique et expérience spirituelle," in *De Tertullien aux Mozarabes. Tome I: antiquité tardive et christianisme ancien (III–VI siècles). Melanges offerts à Jacques Fontaine* (Paris, 1992).

C. Dagens, Saint Grégoire le Grand entre l'Orient et l'Occident. Les crises de l'histoire et l'universalisme de la foi," *Communio* 16 (1991): 60–67.

C. Dagens, *Saint Grégoire le Grand. Culture et expérience chrétienne* (Paris, 1977).

C. Dagens, "Grégoire le Grand et la culture," *Revue des Études anciennes* 14 (1968): 17–26.

C. Dagens, "L'Église universelle et le monde oriéntal chez saint Grégoire," *Istina* 20 (1975): 457–75.

C. Dagens, "La fin du temps et l'église selon Saint Grégoire le Grand," *Recherches de Sciences Religieuses* 58 (1970): 287.

C. Dagens, "Grégoire le Grand et le monde oriental," *Rivista di Storia e Letteratura Religiosa* 17 (1981): 243–252.

G. Dagron, et al., eds., "Evêques, moines et empereurs (610–1054)," *Histoire du christianisme des origines à nos jours*, Vol. 4 (Paris, 1993).

G. Dagron, *Constantinople imaginaire. Études sur le receuil des 'Patria'* (Paris, 1984).

G. Dagron, *Representations de l'ancienne et de la nouvelle Rome dans les sources byzantines des VII-XII siècles* (Rome), pp. 295–306.

G. Dagron, "Aux origines de la civilisation byzantine: langue de culture et langue d'état," *Revue historique* 241 (1969): 23–56.

I. Dakoronia, "O epi en etos periorismos tou papa Martinou I eis Naxon (643-654)," *Epeteris Etaireias Kykladon Meleton* 8 (Athens, 1969–1970): 395–411.

J. Declerck, "Les rescensions greques de la Passion de S. Pancrace, martyr a Rome (BHG 1408-1409)," *Analecta Bollandiana* 105 (1987): 65–85.

Éloi Dekkers, "Les traductions grecques des écrits patristiques latins," *Sacris Erudiri* 5 (1953): 202.

Éloi Dekkers, "Saint Gregoire et les moniales," *Collectanea Cisterciensia* 46 (1984): 23–36.

E. Delaruelle, "La connaissance du grec en occident du Ve au IXe siècle," *Mélanges de la Société Toulousaine d'Études Classiques* 1 (1956): 207–26.

H. Delehaye, "Passio sanctorum LX martyrum," *Analecta Bollandiana* 23 (1904): 289–307.

H. Delehaye, "La vie grecque de S. Martin de Tours," *Studi bizantini e neoellenici* V (1939): 428.

H. Delehaye, "S. Grégoire le Grand dans l'hagiographie grecque," *Analecta Bollandiana* 23 (1904): 449–54.

H. Delehaye, *Étude sur le légendaire romain* (Brussels, 1936).

H. Delehaye, *Sanctus. Essai sur le culte des saints dans l'antiquité* (Brussels, 1927).

H. Delehaye, *Les legendes hagiographiques* (Brussels, 1927).

H. Delehaye, *Les legendes greques de saints militaires* (Paris, 1909).

Th. Delforge, "Song de Scipion et vision de s. Benoit," *Revue Bénédictine* 69 (1959): 351–54.

Paolo Delogu, et al. *Longobardi e Bizantini* (Turin, 1980).

Th. E. Detorakes, "Byzantio kai Europe: agiologikes schesis (527–1453)" in *Byzantium and Europe. First International Byzantine Conference*, Delphi, 20–24 July 1985 (Athens, 1987): 85–99.

C. deBoor, "Zur Chronographie des Theophanes," *Hermes* 25 (1890): 301–7.

B. de Gaiffier, "Les Héros des Dialogues de Grégoire le Grand inscrits au nombre des Saints," *Analecta Bollandiana* 83 (1965): 53–74.

D. C. de Iongh, *Byzantine Aspects of Italy* (New York, 1967).

Placid De Meester, *Rituale-Benedizionale Bizantino* (Rome, 1930).

Domenico de Rossi, *Studio d'architettura civile di Roma* (Lexington, MA, 1972).

G. De Santis, "Il colto di s. Erasmo fra Oriente e Occidente," *Vetera Christiana* 29 (1992): 269–304.

L. de Thorey, "Histoire de messe de Gregoire le Grand a Vatican II," *L'Information Historique* 49 (Paris, 1987): 93–101.

R. Devreesse, "La vie de Saint Maxime et ses recensions," *Analecta Bollandiana* 46 (1928): 5–49.

R. Devreesse, "La fin inédite d'une lettre de saint Maxime: un baptême forcé des Juifs et de Samaritains à Carthage en 632," *Revue des sciences religieuses* 17 (1937): 23–35.

R. Devreesse, "Le fonds grec de la Bibliotheque Vaticane dès origines à Paul V," *Studi e testi* 244 (1965): 1.

R. Devreesse, "Le texte grec de l'Hypomnesticum de Théodore Spoudée. Le supplice, l'exil et la mort des victimes illustres du Monothélisme," *Analecta Bollandiana* 53 (1935): 49–80.

Charles Diehl, *Études sur l'administration byzantine dans l'exarchat de Ravenne, 568–751* (Repr. New York, 1959).

A. Diller, "The Byzantine Quadrivium," *Isis* 36 (1945–1946): 132.

Gregory Dix, *The Shape of the Liturgy* (Repr. London, 1982).

E. Donckel, *Ausserrömische Heilige in Rom von dem Anfang unter Liberius bis Leo IV* (Luxembourg, 1938).

M. Doucet, "La tentation de Saint Benoit: Relation ou creation par Saint Gregoire le Grand?" *Collectanea Cistercensia* 37 (1975): 63–71.

Pericle Ducati, *L'Arte in Roma Dalle Origini al Secolo VIII* (Bologna, 1938).

Alain Ducellier, *L'Église Byzantine: Entre Pouvoir et Esprit (313–1204)* (Paris, 1990).

L. Duchesne, "Les titres presbytereaux et les diaconies," *Mélanges d'archéologie et d'histoire de l'École française de Rome* 7 (1887): 217–43.

L. Duchesne, "Les circonscriptions écclesiastiques de Rome pendant le moyen âge," *Revue des questions historiques* 24 (1880): 217.

L. Duchesne, "Le 'Liber Diurnus' et les élections pontificales au VIIe siècle," *Bibliothèque de l'école des chartes* 52 (1891): 5–30.

L. Duchesne, "Les régions de Rome au moyen âge," *Mélanges d'archéologie et d'histoire de l'École française de Rome* 10 (1890): 126–49.

L. Duchesne, "Le sedi episcopali nell'antico ducato di Roma," *Archivio della Società Romana di Storia di Patria* 15 (1892): 478–503.

L. Duchesne, "L'Illyricum ecclesiastique," *Byzantinische Zeitschrift* 1 (1892): 531–50.

L. Duchesne, *Origines du culte chrétien* (Paris, 1949).

L. Duchesne, *Scripta Minora. Études de topographie romaine et de geographie ecclesiastique* (Rome, 1973).

L. Duchesne, "Sainte Anastasie," *Mélanges d'archéologie et d'histoire de l'École française de Rome* 7 (1887): 403.

F. Homes Dudden, *Gregory the Great. His Place in History and Thought*, 2 vols. (London, 1905).

Albert Dufourcq, *Étude sur les Gesta Martyrum romains*, 5 vols. (Repr. Paris, 1988).

Mary B. Dunn, *The Style of the Letters of Saint Gregory the Great* (Washington, D.C., 1931).

J. Durliat, "L'evêque et la cité dans l'Italie byzantine d'après la correspondence de Grégoire le Grand," *Communication 14, 10 à la VIIe Rencontre d'Histoire Religieuse* (Fontevrault, 1983).

J. Durliat, *De la ville antique à la ville byzantine* (Rome, 1990).

Marc Dykmans, *Le ceremonial papal de la fin du Moyen Age à la Renaissance* (Brussels, 1977).

Susan Elm, *Virgins of God: The Making of Asceticism in Late Antiquity* (Oxford, 1994).

Archange Emereau, "Apocrisiarius et Apocrisiariat: notion de l'apocrisiariat: ses variétés à travers l'histoire," *Echos d'Orient* 17 (1914–1915): 289–97.

F. Ermini, "La scuola in Roma nel VI secolo," in *Medio Evo Latino, Studi e Ricerche* (Modena, 1938): 55–64.

F. Ermini, "I passionari lateranensi," in *Medio Evo Latino, Studi e Ricerche* (Modena, 1938) 99–108.

Sophronios Eustratiades, Ἁγιολόγιον τῆς Ὀρθοδόξου Ἐκκλησίας (Repr. Athens,1995).

Sophronios Eustratiades, Η Θεότοκος ἐν τῇ ὑμνογραφία (Paris-Chennevières-sur-Marne, 1930).

J. A. S. Evans, *The Age of Justinian* (London, 1996).

Giorgio Falco, *The Holy Roman Republic*, trans. K. V. Kent (London, 1964).

E. Fenster, *Laudes Constantinopolitanae* (Munich, 1968).

N. Ferrante, *Santi italogreci. Il mondo bizantino in Calabria* (Rome, 1992).

Guy Ferrari, "Early Roman Monasteries: Notes for the History of the Monasteries and Convents at Rome from the 5th to the 10th Century," *Studi di antichità* (Vatican City, 1957).

A. J. Festugière, *Les Moines d'Orient*, I–IV (Paris, 1961–1965).

J.-M. Fiey, "Les Saints Serge de l'Iraq," *Analecta Bollandiana* 79 (1961): 102–14.

J. V. A. Fine Jr., *The Early Medieval Balkans. A Critical Survey from the Sixth to the Late Twelfth Century* (Ann Arbor, 1983).

J. Finley, "Corinth in the Middle Ages," *Speculum* 7 (1932): 477–99.

E. H. Fischer, "Gregor der Grosse und Byzanz. Ein Bildung zür Geschichte der päpstlichen Politik," *Zeitschrift der Savigny-Stiftung für Rechtsgeschiche, Kanonische Abteilung XXXVI* 36 (1950): 15–144.

Georges Florovsky, *The Byzantine Fathers of the Sixth to Eighth Century*, trans. R. Miller, A. Döllinger-Labriolle, and H. Schmiedel (Vaduz, 1987).

H. Foerster, "Liber Diurnus Pontificum Romanorum," in *New Catholic Encyclopedia* 8:694 (New York, 1967).

E. Follieri, "Santi occidentali nell'iconografia bizantina," in *Atti del Convegno Internazionale sul tema: L'oriente cristiano nella storia della civiltà* (Rome, 1964).

E. Follieri, "I rapporti fra Bisanzio e l'occidente nel campo dell'agiografia," in J. M. Hussey, ed., *Proceedings of the XIIIth International Congress of Byzantine Studies*, Oxford, 5–10 September 1966 (London, 1967).

Jacques Fontaine, et al., eds. *Grégoire Le Grand, Colloques Internationaux du Centre National de la Recherche Scientifique* (Chantilly, 1986).

E. Fortino, S. *Atanasio. La liturgia greca a Roma* (Grottaferrata, 1970).

Clive Foss, "The Persians in Asia Minor," *English Historical Review* 90 (1975): 721–47.

Charles Frazee, "The Popes and the Balkan Churches. Justinian to Gregory the Great, 525–604," *Byzantinische Forschungen* 20 (1994): 45–57.

A. Frolow, "La dedicace de Constantinople dans la tradition byzantine," *Revue de l'histoire des religions* 127 (1944): 61–127.

A. Frolow, "La culte de la relique de la vraie Croix à la fin du VI et au début du VII siècles," *Byzantinoslavica* 22 (1961): 320–339.

G. Garitte, "La version géorgienne du Pré spirituel," *Mélanges Eugène Tisserant*, Studi e Testi 232 (Rome, 1964): 171–85.

J.-M. Garrigues, "Le martyre de saint Maxime le Confesseur," *Revue Thomiste* 76 (1976): 410.

F. Gastaldelli, "Osservazioni per un profilo litterario di S. Gregorio Magno," *Salesianum* 26 (1964).

Amédée Gastoué, *Les origines du chant romain: l'antiphonaire grégorien* (Paris, 1907).

Jules Gay, "Quelques remarques sur les papes grecs et syriens," *Melanges offerts à M. Gustave Schlumberger* (Paris, 1924).

Jules Gay, *L'Italie meridionale et l'Empire byzantin* (Paris, 1904).

Deno J. Geanakoplos, *Interaction of the Sibling Byzantine and Western Cultures in the Middle Ages and the Italian Renaissance (330–1600)* (New Haven, 1976).

Herman Geertman, *More veterum: il Liber Pontificalis e gli edifici ecclesiastici de Roma nella tarda antichità e nell'alto medioevo* (Rome, 1975).

Stephen Gero, *Byzantine Iconoclasm during the Reign of Leo III* (Louvain, 1973).

A. Gibelli, *L'antico monastero dei SS. Andrea e Gregorio al clivo ai Scauro sul Monte Celio* (Faenza, 1892).

M. Gigante, "Per l'interpretazione della Restitutio Crucis di Giorgio di Pisidia," in F. Paschke, ed., *Überlieferungsgeschichte Untersuchungen* (Berlin, 1981), pp. 251–52.

Agnello Giuseppe, "La Sicilia sotteranea e cristiana e la Sicilia bizantina," in *Miscellanea Paolo Orsi a cura dell'Archivio Storico per la Calabria e la Lucania* (Rome, 1935), pp. 253–74.

Walter Goffart, "Byzantine Policy in the West under Tiberius II and Maurice," *Traditio* 13 (1957): 73–118.

R. Gordon, et al., "Roman Inscriptions. 1986-1990," *Journal of Roman Studies* LXXXIII (1993): 131–58.

Franz Görres, "Justinian II und das römische Papsttum", *Byzantinische Zeitschrift* 17 (1908): 432–54.

P. Goubert, "Mystique et politique à Byzance," *Revue des Études Byzantines* 19 (1961): 152–56.

P. Goubert, *Byzance avant l'Islam. Vol. II: Byzance et l'occident sous les successeurs de Justinien* (Paris, 1965).

André Grabar, *L'Iconoclasme Byzantin. Dossier Archéologique* (Paris, 1957).

André Grabar, *Byzantine Painting* (Geneva, 1953).

Hilda Graef, *Mary: A History of Doctrine and Devotion* (London and New York, 1963).

R. Gregoire, "Monaci e monasteri in Roma nei secoli VI-VII," *Archivio della Reale Società Romana di Storia Patria* 104 (1981): 5–24.

Ferdinand Gregorovius, *History of the City of Rome in the Middle Ages*, trans. Mrs. Gustavus W. Hamilton, Vol. II (London, 1902).

E. Griffe, "Le 'Liber Pontificalis' au temps du pape S. Grégoire," *Bulletin de littérature ecclésiastique* 57 (1956): 65–70.

Hartmann Grisar, *History of Rome and the Popes in the Middle Ages*, trans. Luigi Cappadelta (London, 1912).

Hans Grotz, "Beobachtungen zu den zwei Briefen Papst Gregors II an Kaiser Leo III," *Archivium Historiae Pontificae* 18 (1980): 9–40.

Erich S. Gruen, *The Hellenistic World and the Coming of Rome*, Vol. I (Berkeley, 1984).

Venance Grumel, "Recherches sur l'histoire du monothélisme," *Echos d'Orient* 27 (1928): 6–16, 257–77; 28 (1929): 272–82; 29 (1930): 16–28.

Rodolphe Guilland, *Titres et fonctions de l'Empire Byzantine* (London, 1976).

Rodolphe Guilland, "Les Logothetes. Études sur l'histoire administrative de l'Empire Byzantine," *Revue des Études Byzantines* 29 (1971): 5–115.

André Guillou, "La Sicile byzantine: état de recherches." *Byzantinische Forschungen* 5 (1977): 95–145.

André Guillou, *Il Mezzogiorno dai Bizantini a Federico II* (Turin, 1983).

André Guillou, *La Cultura nell'Italia bizantina dal VI all'VII secolo* (Rome, 1981).

André Guillou, *L'Italia Bizantina dall'esaracto di Ravenna al tema di Sicilia* (Turin, 1988).

André Guillou, "La cultura nell'Italia bizantina dal VI all'VIII secolo," *Cultura Tardo Antico* 2 (1981) 575–86.

André Guillou, *Studies on Byzantine Italy* (London, 1970).

André Guillou, "Aspects de la civilisation byzantine. Notes sur quelques travaux recents," *Annales, Economie, Société, Civilisation* 24 (Paris, 1970): 1149–60.

André Guillou, "Demography and Culture in the Exarchate of Ravenna," *Studi Medievali* 10 (1969): 201–19.

André Guillou, "Grecs d'Italie du sud et de la Sicile au moyen age," *Mélanges de l'École française de Rome* 75 (1963): 79–110.

André Guillou, *Culture et Société en Italie Byzantine (Vie–XIe siècles)* (London, 1978).

André Guillou, *Régionalisme et Indépendance dans l'Empire Byzantin au VIIe siècle* (Rome, 1969).

André Guillou, *Aspetti della civiltà bizantina in Italia* (Bari, 1977).

J. F. Haldon, *Byzantium in the Seventh Century* (Cambridge, 1990).

J. F. Haldon, *State, Army and Society in Byzantium* (Aldershot, 1995).

F. Halkin, *Légendes grecques des 'Martyres romaines'* (Brussels, 1973).

F. Halkin, "Sainte Tatiana. Légende greque d'une 'martyre romaine'," *Analecta Bollandiana* 89 (1971): 265.

F. Halkin, "Une courte vie inedite de saint Grégoire le Grand, retraduite en grec," *Mélanges Eugène Tisserant*, Vol. 4 (Vatican City, 1964).

F. Halkin, "Le pape S. Grégoire le Grand dans l'hagiographie byzantine," *Orientalia Christiana Periodica* 21 (1955): 109–14.

F. Halkin, "La Passion Ancienne de Sainte Euphémie de Chalcédonie," *Analecta Bollandiana* 83 (1965): 95–120.

J. T. Hallenbeck, *Pavia and Rome: The Lombard Monarchy and the Papacy in the Eighth Century* (Philadelphia, 1982).

J. T. Hallenbeck, "The Roman-Byzantine Reconciliation of 728: Genesis and Significances," *Byzantinische Zeitschrift* 74 (1981): 29.

Louis Halphen, *Études sur l'administration de Rome au moyen age* (Paris, 1907).

E. A. Hannawalt, "An Annotated Bibliography of Byzantine Sources in English Translation," *Byzantine Studies* 9 (1982): 68–87.

Grisar Hartmann, "Il monastero primitivo di S. Gregorio magno al Celio," *Civilità Cattolica* 6, ser. 18 (Rome, 1896).

L. M. Hartmann, *Untersuchungen zur Geschichte der Byzantinischen Verwaltung in Italien (540-750)* (Leipzig, 1889).

R. M. Hauber, *The Late Latin Vocabulary of the 'Moralia' of Saint Gregory the Great* (Washington, D.C., 1938).

Irénée Hausherr, *Penthos: la doctrine de la componction dans l'orient chrétien*, Trans. Anselm Hufstader (Kalamazoo, 1982).

Irénée Hausherr, *Direction spirituelle en Orient autrefois*, Orientalia Christiana Analecta 144 (Rome, 1955).

I. Havener, "The Greek Prologue to the 'Dialogues' of Gregory the Great," *Revue Bénédictine* 99 (1989): 103–17.

R. F. Hayburn, *Papal Legislation on Sacred Music, 95 A.D. to 1977 A.D.* (Collegeville, Minn., 1979).

Constance Head, "Toward a Reinterpretation of the Second Reign of Justinian II," *Byzantion* 40 (1970): 14–32.

Constance Head, *Justinian II of Byzantium* (Madison, 1972).

Karl J. Hefele, *A History of the Councils of the Church*, Vol. 5, trans. William R. Clark (Edinburgh, 1895).

Karl J. Hefele, *Histoire des Conciles*, Vol. III, trans. H. Leclercq (Paris, 1909).

R. Hemmerdinger, "Les lettres latines à Constantinople jusqu'à Justinien," *Byzantinische Forschungen* 1 (1966): 174–78.

F. Henizer and Christoph von Schönborn eds., *Maximus Confessor. Actes du Symposium sur Maxime le Confesseur* (Fribourg, 1982).

J. Hennig, "The Meaning of All Saints," *Medieval Studies* 10 (1948): 47–161.

Michael W. Herren and S. Brown, eds., *The Sacred Nectar of the Greeks: The Study of Greek in the West in the Early Middles Ages* (London, 1988).

Judith Herrin, *The Formation of Christendom* (London, 1987).

R. J. Hesbert, "Les trentains gregoriens sous forme de cycles liturgiques," *Revue Bénédictine* 81 (1971): 108–22.

C. Hibbert, *Rome: The Biography of a City* (New York, 1985).

M. J. Higgins, "International Relations at the Close of the Sixth Century," *Catholic His-*

torical Review 27 (1941): 279–315.

Thomas Hodgkin, Italy and Her Invaders (Oxford, 1895–1899).

Lon P. Homo, Rome medievale, 476–1420 (Paris, 1934).

Henri Hubert, "Étude sur la Formation des États de l'Église," 69 Revue Historique (1899): 1–40.

H. Hucke, "War Gregor der Grosse Musiker?," Musikforschungen 18 (1965): 390–93.

Michel Huglo, "Relations musicales entre Byzance et l'Occident," Proceedings of the XIIIth International Congress of Byzantine Studies, ed. J. M. Hussey, Oxford, 5–10 September 1966 (London, 1967), pp. 267–80.

J. M. Hussey, The Orthodox Church in the Byzantine Empire (Oxford, 1986).

J. Irigoin, "La culture grecque dans l'Occident latin du VIIe au IXe siècle," Settimane di Studio del Centro Italiano di Studi sull'Alto Medio Evo (Spoleto, 1975), pp. 425–46.

R. Janin, Constantinople byzantine. Développment urbain et répertoire topographique, 2nd ed. (Paris, 1964).

R. Janin, La géographie ecclésiastique de l'empire byzantin. Première partie, Le siège de Constantinople et le patriarcat oecumenique. Vol. III, Les églises et les monastères (Paris, 1969).

Romilly J. H. Jenkins, Byzantium: The Imperial Centuries A.D. 610–1071 (London, 1966).

J. C. Jennings, "The Origins of the 'Elements Series' of the Miracles of the Virgin," Medieval and Renaissance Studies 6 (1968): 84–93.

J. Johns, Early Medieval Sicily (London, 1995).

E. Josi, "Lectores, Schola Cantorum, Clerici," Ephemerides Liturgicae 44 (1930): 282–90.

P. Jounel, "Le culte collectif des saints à Rome du VIIe au IXe siècle," Ecclesia Orans 6 (1989): 285–300.

Martin Jugie, "Saint André de Crète et l'Immaculée Conception," Echos d'Orient 13 (1910): 129–33.

Martin Jugie, "Les homélies de saint Germain de Constantinople sur la Dormition de la Sainte Vierge," Echos d'Orient 16 (1913): 219–21.

Martin Jugie, "L'église de Chalcopratia et la culte de la ceinture de la Sainte Vierge à Constantinople," Echos d'Orient 16 (1913): 308–12.

Martin Jugie, "L'empereur Justinien a-t-il été aphthardocète," Echos d'Orient 31 (1932): 399–402.

Martin Jugie, La Mort et l'Assomption de la Sainte Vierge (Rome, 1944).

Martin Jugie, ed., "Homélies mariales byzantins, II," in Patrologia Orientalis 19, 3: 344–430.

J. A. Jungmann, Missarum Sollemnia. The mass of the Roman Rite: its origins and development (London, 1959).

Walter E. Kaegi Jr., Byzantium and the Decline of Rome (Princeton, 1968).

T. Kardong, "A New Look at Gregory's 'Dialogues,'" American Benedictine Review 36 (1985): 44–63.

J. Kästner, De imperio Constantini III (641–688) (Leipzig, 1907).

Paul Kehr, Italia Pontificia, Vol. I (Berlin, 1961).

J. N. D. Kelly, Early Christian Doctrines, rev. ed., (San Francisco, 1978).

John H. Kent, "A Byzantine Statue Base at Corinth," Speculum 25 (1950): 544–46.

A. King, The Liturgy of the Roman Church (London, 1957).

A. J. Kinnirey, The Late Latin Vocabulary of the Dialogues of St. Gregory the Great (Washington, D.C., 1935).

J. Kirchenmeyer, "Une source d'Antiochus de Saint-Sabas (Pandectes, c. 127–128)," *Orientalia Christiana Periodica* 28 (1962): 418–21.

H. Kirkby, "The Scholar and His Public," in *Boethius*, ed. M. T. Gibson (Oxford, 1981).

J. P. Kirsche, Der stadtrömische christliche Festkalendar (Münster, 1924).

J. P. Kirsche, "Origine caratteri primitivi delle stazioni liturguche di Roma," *Pontificia Accademia Romana di Archeologia* 3 (1925).

J. P. Kirsche, "Die Stationskirchen des Missale Romanum," *Ecclesia Orans* 19 (1926).

J. P. Kirsche, "Les origines des Stations Liturgiques du Missel romain," *Ephemerides Liturgicae* 41 (1927): 137–50.

Ernst Kitzinger, *Early Medieval Art*, rev. ed. (Bloomington, IN, 1983).

Ernst Kitzinger, *Byzantine Art in the Making* (Cambridge, MA, 1995).

Ernst Kitzinger, "The Cult of Images in the Period before Iconoclasm," *Dumbarton Oaks Papers* 8 (1954): 85–150.

Th. Klauser, *Das römische Capitulare evangeliorum. Texte und Untersuchungen zu seiner ältesten Geschichte. I. Typen* (Münster, 1935).

Th. Klauser, "Der Übergang der römischen Kirche von der griechischen zur lateinischen Liturgiesprachen," in *Miscellanea G. Mercati I*, *Studi e testi* 121 (Vatican City, 1946): 467.

H. W. Klewitz, "Die Krönung des Papstes," *Zeitschrift der Savigny-Stiftung für Reichsgeschicte* 61, *Kanonische Abteilung*, 30 (1941).

D. D. Kontostergios, "Ἡ Πενθέκτη Οἰκουμενική Σύνοδος τῆς Κωνσταντινουπόλεως 691/692," in Ἐπιστημονική Ἐπετηρίδα Θεολογικῆς Σχολῆς Θεσσαλονίκης 28 (1985), pp. 487–525.

Richard Krautheimer, *Rome: Profile of a City, 312–1308* (Princeton, 1980).

Richard Krautheimer, "Santa Maria Rotunda (Pantheon)," in Richard Krautheimer, *Studies in Early Christian, Medieval and Renaissance Art* (London, 1971), pp. 107–14.

Richard Krautheimer, S. Corbett, and W. Frankel, *Corpus Basilicarum Christianarum Romae. The Early Christian Basilicas of Rome (IV–IX Centuries)*, 5 vols. (Vatican City, 1937–1977).

P. F. Krypiakiewicz, "De hymni Acathisti auctore," *Byzantinische Zeitschrift* 18 (1909): 357–82.

S. Kuttner, "Am Implied Reference to the Digest in Pope Agatho's Roman Synod of 679," *Zeitschrift der Savigny-Stiftung, Romanistische Abteilung* 107 (1990): 382–84.

P. Labriola, *I SS. Cosma e Damiano, medici e martiri. Biografia, culto, leggende, arte* (Rome, 1984).

M. L. Laistner, "The Church's Attitude to Pagan Literature," *History* 20 (1935): 49–54.

M. L. Laistner, *Thought and Letters in Western Europe, A.D. 500–900* (London, 1957).

K. Lake, "The Greek Monasteries in South Italy, I," *Journal of Theological Studies* 4 (1903): 345.

Francesco Lanzoni, "I titoli presbiterali di Roma nella storia e nella leggenda," *Rivista di archeologia cristiana* 2 (1925): 195.

Francesco Lanzoni, "Le diocesi d'Italia dalle origini al secolo VII (604)," *Studi e testi* 35 (Faenza, 1937).

David Lathoud, "Le sanctuaire de la Vierge aux Chalcopratia," *Echos d'Orient* 23 (1924): 36–61.

V. Laurent, "L'oeuvre canonique du concile in Trullo (691–692) source primaire du droit de l'Église orientale," *Revue des Études byzantines* 23 (1965): 7–41.

H. Leclercq, "Hôpitaux, Hospices, Hôtelleries," in *Dictionnaire d'Archéologie Chrétienne*, VI, cols. 2748–70.

H. Leclercq, "Laures Palestiniennes," in *Dictionnaire d'Archéologie Chrétienne*, VII, 2, cols. 1961–88.

Joseph Ledit, *Marie dans la Liturgie de Byzance* (Paris, 1976).

P. Lemerle, "Les répercussions de la crise de l'empire d'Orient au VIIe siècle sur les pays d'Occident," in *Le monde de Byzance: Histoire et Institutions* IV (London, 1978) 724.

P. Lemerle, "Invasions et migrations dans les Balkans depuis la fin de l'epoque romaine jusqu'au VIIIe siècle," *Revue historique* 211 (April–June 1954): 265–08.

P. Lemerle, "La Chronique improprement dite de Monemvasie: le contexte historique et legendaire," *Revue des Études byzantines* 21 (1963): 5–49.

P. Lemerle, "Une province Byzantin. Le Péloponèse," *Byzantion* 21 (1951): 341–54.

François Lenormant, *La Grande-Grèce. Paysage et Histoire*, 3 vols. (Paris, 1883).

J. Lestocquoy, "L'Administration de Rome et Diaconies du VIIe au IXe siècle," *Rivista di archeologia cristiana* 7 (1930): 261.

R.-J. Lilie, *Die byzantinische Reaktion auf die Ausbreitung der Graber*, Miscellanea Byzantina Monacensia 22 (Munich, 1976).

P. A. B. Llewellyn, "The Names of the Roman Clergy, 401–1046," *Rivista di Storia della chiesa in Italia* 35 (1981): 355–70.

P. A. B. Llewellyn, "Constans II and the Roman Church: A Possible Example of Imperial Pressure," *Byzantion* 46 (1976): 120–26.

P. A. B. Llewellyn, "The Roman Church in the Seventh Century: The Legacy of Gregory the Great," *Journal of Ecclesiastical History* 25 (1974): 363–80.

P. A. B. Llewellyn, "'Peculiaris populus' in Two Papal Letters of the Early Eighth Century," *Archivium Latinum Medii Aevi* 42 (1982): 133–37.

P. A. B. Llewellyn, "The Popes and the Constitution in the Eighth Century," *English Historical Review* 101 (1986): 42–67.

P. A. B. Llewellyn, *Rome in the Dark Ages* (New York, 1971).

T. C. Lounghis, *Les ambassades byzantines en Occident depuis la fondation des états barbares jusqu'aux Croisades (407–1096)* (Athens, 1980).

Andrew Louth, *Maximus the Confessor* (London, 1996).

G. Low, "Ein stadtrömisches Lektionar des VII Jahrhunderts," *Römisches Quartalschrift* 37 (1929).

G. Low, "Il piu antico sermonario di S. Pietro in Vaticano," *Rivista archeologia cristiana* 19 (1942): 249.

Henri de Lubac, "S. Grégoire et la grammaire," *Recherches de Science Religieuse* 48 (1960): 185–226.

Sabine MacCormack, *Art and Ceremony in Late Antiquity* (Berkeley, 1981).

Sabine MacCormack, "Roma, Constantinopolis, the Emperor," *Classical Philology* 25 (1976): 131–50.

Sabine MacCormack, "Change and Continuity in Late Antiquity: The Ceremony of Adventus," *Historia* 21 (1972): 721–52.

Luigi Magi, *La sede Romana nella corrispondenza degli imperatori e patriarchi bizantini (VI –VII sec.)* (Rome-Louvain, 1972).

H. G. Magoulias, *Byzantine Christianity: Emperor, Church and the West* (Chicago, 1970).

M. Mahler, "Evocations bibliques et hagiographiques dans la vie de Saint Benoit par Saint Gregoire," *Revue Bénédictine* 83 (1973): 398–429.

A. Maloof, "The Eastern Origins of the Papal Tiara," *Eastern Churches Review* 1 (1966–1967): 146–49.

D. Mandic, "Dalmatia in the Exarchate of Ravenna," *Byzantion* 34 (1964): 347–74.

Cyril Mango, *Byzantium: The Empire of New Rome* (New York, 1980).

Cyril Mango, "Deux études sur Byzance et la Perse sassanide," *Travaux et mémoires* 9 (1985): 91–118.

Cyril Mango, "The Breviarium of the Patriarch Nicephorus," in *Byzance. Hommages à André N. Stratos* (Athens, 1986), pp. 539–52.

Cyril Mango, "La culture grecque et l'Occident au VIIIe siècle," *Settimane di Studio del Centro Italiano di Studi sull'Alto Medio Evo* (Spoleto, 1973), pp. 683–721.

Max Manitius, *Geschiche der christlich-lateinischen Poesie bis zur Mitte des 8. Jahrhunderts* (Stuttgart, 1891).

Horace K. Mann, *The Lives of the Popes in the Early Middle Ages, Vol. I, Part II* (London, 1925).

R. Manselli, "Gregorio Magno e la Bibbia," in "La Bibbia nell'alto medioevo," *Settimane di Studio del Centro Italiano di Studi sull'Alto Medio Evo* (Spoleto, 1963), pp. 67–101.

F. Marazzi, "Il conflitto fra Leone III Isaurico e il papato fra il 725 e il 733, e il 'definitivo' inizio del medioevo a Roma: un ipotesi in discussione," *Papers of the British School at Rome* 59 (1991): 231–57.

G. Marchetti Longhi, "Il quartiere greco-orientale di Roma nell'antichità e nel medioevo," *Atti IV Congresso Nazionale di Studi Romani I* (Rome, 1938): 183.

G. S. Marcou, "Zaccaria (679-752): l'ultimo papa greco nella storia di Roma altomedievale. Note storico-giuridiche," *Apollinaris* 50 (1977): 274–89.

G. S. Marcou, "Zaccaria, un pontefice di origine greca," *Veltro* 27 (1983): 145–53.

Italiani B. M. Margarucci, "Omaggio a San Saba," *Strenna dei Romanisti* 30 (1969): 283–89.

Gaetano Marini, *I papiri diplomatici* (Rome, 1805).

R. A. Markus, *Gregory the Great and His World* (Cambridge, 1997).

R. A. Markus, *Sacred and Secular. Studies on Augustine and Latin Christianity* (London, 1994).

R. A. Markus, "Ravenna and Rome, 554–604," *Byzantion* 51 (1981) 566–78.

H.-I. Marrou, "Autour de la bibliothèque de Pape Agapit," *Mélanges d'archeologie et d'histoire de l'Ecole francaise de Rome* 48 (1931): 125–69.

H.-I. Marrou, "L'origine orientale des diaconies romaines," *Mélanges d'archéologie et d'histoire de l'École française de Rome* 57 (1937): 95–142.

F. Martroye, *L'Occident à l'epoque Byzantine* (Paris, 1904).

Jean Mateos, ed., *Le Typicon de la Grande Église*, Orientalia Christiana Periodica, 165–66, 2 vols. (Rome, 1962–1963).

V. Matrangolo, *La venerazione a Maria nella tradizione della chiesa bizantina* (Acireale, 1990).

Otto Mazal, *Manuel d'Études Byzantines*, trans. Claude Detienne (Repr. Brepols, 1995).

Michael McCormick, *Eternal Victory: Triumphal Relationships in Late Antiquity, Byzantium and the Early Medieval West*, 2nd ed. (Cambridge, 1990).

Michael McCormick, "Byzantium's Role in the Formation of Early Medieval Civilization," *Illinois Classical Studies* 12 (1987): 207–20.

J. M. McCulloh, "The Cult of Relics in the Letters and 'Dialogues' of Pope Gregory the Great: A Lexicographical Study," *Traditio* 32 (1976): 145–84.

J. M. McCulloh, "From Antiquity to the Middle Ages: Continuity and Change in Papal Relic Policy from the 6th to the 8th Century," in *Pietas. Festschrift für Bernhard Kotting*, ed. E. Dassmann and K. S. Frank (Münster, 1980).

Robert E. McNally, "Gregory the Great (590-604) and His Declining World," *Archivium Historiae Pontificae* 16 (1978): 7–26.

G. G. Meerssman, "Der Hymnos Akathistos im Abendland," 2 vols., *Spicilegium Friburgense* 2.3 (Fribourg, Switzerland, 1958).

L.-R. Menager, "La 'Byzantinisation' religieuse de l'Italie meridionale," *Revue d'Histoire Écclesiastique* 53 (1958): 747–74.

G. Mercati, "Sull'epigramma acrostico premeso alla versione greca di S. Zaccaria papa del Liber Dialogorum di S. Gregorio Magno," *Bessarione* 35 (1919): 67–75.

John Meyendorff, *Imperial Unity and Christian Divisions* (Crestwood, NY, 1989).

A. Michel, "Die griechischen Klösterseidlungen zu Rom bis zur Mitte des 11. Jahrhundert," *Östkirchliche Studien* I (1952): 32.

F. Michetti, *San Bonifacio IV e il suo pontificato* (Avezzano, 1992).

D. H. Miller, "The Roman Revolution in the Eighth Century," *Medieval Studies* 36 (1974): 79–133.

D. H. Miller, "Byzantine-Papal Relations during the Pontificate of Paul I: Confirmation and Completion of the Roman Revolution of the Eighth Century," *Byzantinische Zeitschrift* 68 (1975): 47–62.

D. H. Miller, "The Eighth-Century Papacy: Some Considerations of Political Theory," in *Fourth Annual Byzantine Studies Conference*, University of Michigan, Ann Arbor, 3–5 November 1978.

Simon Claude Mimouni, *Dormition et Assomption de Marie* (Paris, 1995).

V. Monachino, "I tempi e la figura del papa Vitaliano (657–672)," in *Storiografia e storia. Studi in onori di Eugenio Dupre Theseider*, 2 vols. (Rome, 1974).

E. Montmasson, "Chronologie de la Vie de saint Maxime le Confesseur (580–662)," *Echos d'Orient* 13 (1910): 149.

J. Moorhead, "Italian Loyalties during Justinian's Gothic War," *Byzantion* 53 (1983): 575–96.

Umberto Moricca, "Gregorii Magni Dialogi, Libri IV," in *Fonti per la Storia d'Italia* (Rome, 1924).

Enrico Morini, "Sicilia, Roma e Italia suburbicaria nelle tradizioni del sinassario costantinopolitano," in *Sicilia e Italia suburbicaria tra IV e VIII secolo*, Atti del Convegno di Studi, Catania, 24–27 October 1989 (Rubbettino, 1991), pp. 129–84.

C. Morrisson and J.-N. Barraudon, "La trouvaille de monnaies d'argent byzantines de Rome (VII–VIII siècles): analyse et chronologie," *Revue numismatique* ser. 6, 30 (1988): 149–65.

E. Muntz, "La tiare pontificale du VIIIe au XVIe siècle," *Mémoire de l'Academie des Inscriptions et des Belles-Lettres* 36, I (1897).

J. J. Murphy, *Rhetoric in the Middle Ages* (California, 1971).

B. S. Navarra, S. *Vitaliano Papa* (Rome, 1972).

Aidan Nichols, *Rome and the Eastern Churches* (Collegeville, MN, 1992).

Aidan Nichols, *Byzantine Gospel: Maximus the Confessor in Modern Scholarship* (Edinburgh, 1993).

I. Nikolajevic, "The Redemption of Captives in Dalmatia in the 6th and 7th Century," *Balcanoslavica* 2 (1973): 73–79.

Thomas F. X. Noble, *The Republic of St. Peter* (Philadelphia, 1984).

Thomas F. X. Noble, "A New Look at the 'Liber Pontificalis'," *Archivium Historiae Pontificae* 23 (1985): 347–58.

Dag L. Norberg, *In registrum Gregorii Magni studia critica*, I, (Uppsala, 1937).

Per Jonas Nordhagen, *Studies in Byzantine and Early Medieval Painting* (London, 1990).

Per Jonas Nordhagen, *The Frescoes of John VII (A.D. 705–707) in S. Maria Antiqua in Rome* (Rome, 1968).

René Nouailhat, *Saints et Patrons: Les premiers moins de Lérins* (Paris, 1988).

Walter F. Oakeshott, *The Mosaics of Rome* (London, 1967).

Dimitri Obolensky, *The Byzantine Commonwealth: Eastern Europe 500–1453* (London, 1971).

Dimitri Obolensky, *Byzantium and the Slavs* (Crestwood, NY, 1994).

James F. O'Donnell, *The Vocabulary of the Letters of Saint Gregory the Great: A Study in Late Latin Lexicography* (Washington, D.C., 1935).

M. O'Hara, "A Find of Byzantine Silver from the Mint of Rome for the Period A.D. 641–752," *Revue suisse de numismatique* 64 (1985): 105–56.

W. Ohnsorge, *Konstantinopel und der Okzident* (Darmstadt, 1966).

W. Ohnsorge, *Abendland und Byzanz* (Darmstadt, 1958).

Paolo Orsi, "Byzantina Siciliae," *Byzantinische Zeitschrift* 19 (1910): 475.

J. Osborne, "Byzantine Influence on Roman Painting in the First Half of the Eighth Century," *Fourth Annual Byzantine Studies Conference*, University of Michigan, Ann Arbor, 3–5 November 1978.

Georges Ostrogorsky, "L'Exarchat de Ravenna et l'origine des Themes Byzantins," *VII Corso di culture sull'Arte Ravennate e Bizantini* (1960).

Georges Ostrogorsky, "The Byzantine Empire in the World of the Seventh Century," *Dumbarton Oaks Papers* 13 (1959): 47–66.

G. Ostrogorsky, *History of the Byzantine State*, rev. ed. (New Brunswick, NJ, 1969).

G. Pardi, "La popolazione dell Sicilia attraverson i secoli," *Archivio storico siciliano* LXIX (1928): 128–78.

J. Pargoire, "Apocrisiaire," in *Dictionnaire d'Archéologie Chrétienne et de Liturgie*, Vol. I, Pt. 2 (Paris, 1924) cols. 2537–55.

R. P. J. Pargoire, *L'église byzantine de 527 à 843* (Paris, 1905).

V. Paronetto, "Gregorio Magno et la cultura classica," *Studium* 74 (1978): 665–80.

V. Paronetto, "Gregorio Magno tra romani e 'barbari'," *Vetera Christianorum* 23 (1986): 183–90.

V. Paronetto, *Gregorio Magno. Profilo del vescovo* (Milan, 1983).

Peter Partner, *The Lands of St. Peter* (London, 1972).

François Paschoud, *Roma Aeterna* (Neuchâtel, 1967).

E. Patlagean, "Les moines grecs d'Italie et l'apologie des theses pontificales," *Studi medievali* 5 (1964): 579–602.

E. Patlagean, "Les Armes et la cité à Rome du VIIe au IXe siecle," *Mélanges de l'École française de Rome. Moyen Age* 86 (1974): 25–62.

Philip Pattenden, "The Text of the Pratum Spirituale," *Journal of Theological Studies* n.s. 26 (1975): 38–54.

P. Peeters, *Orient et Byzance. Les Tréfonds Oriental de l'Hagiographie Byzantine* (Brussels, 1950).

P. Peeters, "Une Vie grecque du pape S. Martin," *Analecta Bollandiana* 51 (1933): 225–62.

Jaroslav Pelikan, *The Emergence of the Catholic Tradition (100–600)*, Vol. I (Chicago, 1971).

G. Penco, *Storia della Chiesa in Italia*, Vol. 1: *Dalle origini al Concilio di Trento* (Milan, 1978).

G. Penco, *Storia del monachismo in Italia. Dalle origini alla fine del Medioevo* (Milan, 1983).

Camille Pepe, *Il Medioevo Barbarico d'Italia*, (Rome, 1945).

A. Pertusi, "L'Encomio di S. Anastasio martire Persiano," *Analecta Bollandiana* 76 (1958): 5–63.

A. Pertusi, "Bisanzio e l'irradizione della sua civiltà in occidente nell'alto medioevo," *Settimane di Studio del Centro Italiano di Studi Sull'Alto Medioevo* (Spoleto, 1964), 75–133, 159–226.

Joan M. Petersen, "'Homo omnino latinus?' The Theological and Cultural Background of Pope Gregory the Great," *Speculum* 62 (1987): 529–51.

Joan M. Petersen, "Did Gregory the Great Know Greek?" *Studies in Church History* 13 (1976): 121–34.

Joan M. Petersen, *The Dialogues of Gregory the Great in their Late Antique Cultural Background* (Toronto, 1984).

E. Petrides, "Spoudaei et Philopones," *Echos d'Orient* 7 (1904): 341–48.

E. Petrides, "Le monastère des Spoudaei à Jérusalem et les Spoudaei de Constantinople," *Echos d'Orient* 4 (1900–1901): 225–31.

J. M. Petritakis, "Interventions dynamiques de l'empereur de Byzance dans les affaires ecclesiastiques," *Byzantina* 3 (1971): 135.

G. Piccitto, "La presenza del greco bizantino nell'Italia meridionale et le sue conseguenze linguistiche," *Atti VIII Congresso internazionale di Studi Bizantini* I (Rome, 1953), p. 304.

C. Pietri and L. Pietri, "Église universelle et 'respublica christiana' selon Grégoire le Grand," in *Memoriam Sanctorum Veterantes, Miscellanea in onore di Msgr. Victor Saxer* (Vatican City, 1992).

Iacovos G. Pililis, *Titles, Offices and Ranks in the Byzantine Empire and Orthodox Christian Church* (Athens, 1985).

Giuseppe Plessi, "La biblioteca della chiesa di Roma durante il pontificato di papa Gregorio Magno," *Archiginnasio* 35 (1940): 267.

E. Plitz, *Kamelaukion et mitra. Insignes byzantins imperiaux et ecclesiastiques* (Stockholm, 1977).

Sesto Prete, ed., *Didascaliae: studies in honor of Anselm Albareda* (New York, 1961).

Ann S. Proudfoot, "The Sources of Theophanes for the Heraclian dynasty," *Byzantion* 44 (1974): 367–439.

A. Raes, "Aux origines de la fête de l'Assomption en Orient," *Orientalia Christiana Periodica* 12 (1946): 262.

P. Rasi, *Exercitus Italicus e milizie cittadine nell'alto Medio Evo* (Padua, 1937).

V. Recchia, "La visione di S. Benedetto e la 'compositio' del secondo libro dei 'Dialoghi' di Gregorio Magno," *Revue Bénédictine* 82 (1972): 140–55.

Jeffrey Richards, *The Popes and the Papacy in the Early Middle Ages, 476–752* (London, 1979).

Jeffrey Richards, *Consul of God: The Life and Times of Gregory the Great* (London, 1980).

Pierre Riché, *Education and Culture in the Barbarian West*, trans. John J. Contreni (Columbia, SC, 1976).

R. Todd Ridder, *Musical and Theological Patterns Involved in the Transmission of Mass Chants for the Five Oldest Marian Feasts* (Ann Arbor, 1993).

Rudolf Riedinger, "Die Epistula synodica des Sophronios von Jerusalem im Codex Parisinus Graecus 1115," *Byzantiaka* 2 (1982): 143–54.

Rudolf Riedinger, "Die Nachkommen der Epistula synodica des Sophronios von Jerusalem a. 634," *Römische Historische Mitteilungen* 26 (1984): 91–106.

Rudolf Riedinger, "Aus den Akten der Lateran-Synode von 649," *Byzantinische Zeitschrift* 69 (1976): 17–38.

Rudolf Riedinger, "Grammatiker-Gelehrsamkeit in den Akten der Lateran-Synode von 649," *Jahrbuch der Oesterreichischen Byzantinistik* 25 (1976): 57–61.

Rudolf Riedinger, "Sprachschichten in der lateinischen Übersetzung der Lateranakten von 649," *Zeitschrift für Kirchengeschichte* 92 (1981): 180–203.

Rudolf Riedinger, "Die Lateranakten von 649. Ein Werk der Byzantiner um Maximos Homologetes," *Byzantina* 13 (1985): 517–34.

S. Rizou-Couroupos, "Un nouveau fragment de la 'keleusis' d'Heraclius au pape Jean IV (640–642)," in J. Dummer, ed., *Texte und Textkritik. Eine Ausatzsammulung* (Berlin, 1987).

E. Rocchi, "Da Gregorio II alla morte di Zaccaria. Lotte ed eresie," *Capitolium* 49 (1974): 13–21.

Pietro Romanelli and Per Jonas Nordhagen, *S. Maria Antiqua* (Rome, 1964).

Pietro Romanelli, "Le diaconie romane," *Studium* 40 (1940): 248–50.

K. Rozemond, "Jean Mosch, Patriarche d'Jerusalem en exil (614-634)," *Vigiliae Christianae* 31 (1977): 60–67.

Rosemary R. Ruether, *Gregory of Nazianzus: Rhetor and Philosopher* (Oxford, 1969).

L. Cracco Ruggini, "La Sicilia tra Roma e Bizanzio," in *Storia della Sicilia*, Vol. 3 (Naples, 1980).

A. Rum, "Papa Giovanni VII (705–707): 'Servus Sanctae Mariae,'" in *De cultu mariano saeculis VI–IX. Acta Congressus Mariologici-Mariani Internationalis in Croatia anno 1971*, 5 vols. (Rome, 1972).

Francesco Russo, "'La peregrinatio' dei Santi italo-greci nelle tombe degli Apostoli Pietro e Paolo," *Bolletino della badia greca di Grottaferrata*, n.s. 22 (1968): 89–99.

H.-D. Saffrey, "Le Chrétien Jean Philopon et La Survivance de l'École d'Alexandrie au

VIe siècle," *Revue des études grecques* 67 (1954): 396–410.

S. Salaville, "De l'héllenisme au byzantinisme: essai de démarcation," *Echos d'Orient* 30 (1931): 28–64.

S. Salaville, "La connaissance du grec chez saint Augustin," *Echos d'Orient* 21 (1922): 387–93.

J. M. Sansterre, "Le Monachisme à Byzance et en Occident du VIIIe à Xe siècle," *Revue Bénédictine* 103, no. 1–2 (1993): 1–288.

J. M. Sansterre, "Á propos des Titres d'Empereum et de Roi dans le Haut Moyen Âge," *Byzantion* 5 (1991): 15–43.

J. M. Sansterre, "Le monachisme byzantin à Rome," *Settimane di Studio del Centro Italiano di Studi Sull'Alto Medioevo* (Spoleto, 1988): 701–750.

J. M. Sansterre, *Les moines grecs et orientaux à Rome aux epoques byzantine et carolingienne (milieu du Vie fin du IXe siècle)* (Brussels, 1983).

J. M. Sansterre, "Jean VII (705–707): ideologie pontificale et realisme politique," in *Rayonnement grec: hommages à Charles Delvoye* (Brussels, 1982).

J. M. Sansterre, "Le Pape Constantin Ier (708–715) et la politique religieuse des Empereurs Justinien II et Philippikos," *Archivium Historiae Pontificae* 22 (1984): 7–29.

J. M. Sansterre, "À propos de la signification politico-religieuse de certain fresques de Jean VII a Ste-Marie-Antique," *Byzantion* (1987): 434–40.

L. Santifaller, "Saggio di un Elenco dei funzionari, impiegati e scrittori della cancelleria Pontificia dall'inizio all'anno 1099," *Bollettino per l'Istituto Storico Italiano per il Medio Evo e Archivio Muratoriano* 56 (1940).

P. Scheffer-Boichorst, "Zur Geschichte der Syrer im Abendlande," *Mitteilungen des Instituts für oesterreichische Geschictsforschung* 6 (1885): 521–50.

R. Schieffer, "Kreta, Rom und Laon. Vier Briefe des Papstes Vitalian vom Jahre 688," in *Papsttum, Kirche und Recht im Mittelalter. Festschrift fur Horst Fuhrmann zum 65 Geburtstag*, ed. H. Mordek (Tübingen, 1991).

Bernhard Schimmelpfennig, *The Papacy*, trans. James Sievert (New York, 1992).

F. Schneider, *Rom und Romgedanke im Mittelalter* (Munich, 1926).

P. Schreiner, "La fondation de Monemvasie en 582/3," *Travaux et mémoires* 4 (1970): 471–76.

N. Scivoletto, "I limiti dell'ars grammatica' in Gregorio Magno", *Giornale italiano di filologia* 17 (1964): 210–38.

Ernesto Seston, "La Composizione Etnica della Società in Rapporto allo Svolgimento della Civiltà in Italia nel secolo VII," in *Caraterri del Secolo VII in Occidente, Settimane di Studi del Centro Italiano di Studi sull'Alto Medioevo*, Vol. 2 (Spoleto, 1958), p. 651.

Kenneth M. Setton, "The Bulgars in the Balkans and the Occupation of Corinth in the Seventh Century," *Speculum* 25 (1950): 502–43.

Kenneth M. Setton, "The Emperor Constans II and the capture of Corinth," *Speculum* 27 (1952): 351–62.

Jonathan Shepard and Simon Franklin, eds., *Byzantine Diplomacy* (Aldershot, 1992).

G. Sicari, "Monastero dei Santi Cosma e Damiano in Mica Aurea: sue proprietà in Roma," *Alma Roma* 23 (1982): 30–44.

Augusto Simonini, *Autocefalia ed Esarcato in Italia* (Ravenna, 1969).

Bernhard Sirch, *Der Ursprung der bischöflichen Mitra und päpstlichen Tiara* (St. Ottilien, 1975).

G. Sola, "Santi Bizantini a Roma," *Atti del 3 Congresso di Studi Romani*, Vol. 2–3 (Bologna, 1953), pp. 456–67.

Heikki Solin, *Die Griechische Personnamen in Rom: Ein Namenbuch*, 3 vols. (Berlin, 1988).

J. Srutwa, "The Exile and Death of Pope Martin I on Crimea," *Antiquitas* XVII (1963) 203–9.

E. Stein, *Studien zur Geschichte des byzantinischen Reiches vornehmlich unter des Kaisern Justinus II und Tiberius Constantinus* (Stuttgart, 1919).

E. Stein, "La periode byzantine de la papauté," *Catholic Historical Review* 21 (1935–1936) 129–63.

E. Stein, "La disparition de Sénat à la fin du VIe siècle," in E. Stein, *Opera Minora Selecta* (Amsterdam, 1968), pp. 386–400.

H. Steinacker, "Die römische und die griechischen Sprachkenntnisse des Fruhmittelalters," *Mitteilungen des Insitutts fur Oesterreichische Geschichtsforschung* 62 (1954): 28–66.

Andreas N. Stratos, "Expedition de l'empereur Constantin II surnomme Constant en Italie," in *Bisanzio e l'Italia. Raccolta di studi in memoria Agostino Pertusi* (Milan, 1982).

Andreas N. Stratos, *Byzantium in the Seventh Century*, trans. Marc Ogilvie-Grant, 4 vols. (Amsterdam, 1968–1978).

Andreas N. Stratos, "The Exarch Olympios and the Supposed Arab Invasion of Italy in A.D. 652," *Jahrbuch für Oesterreichische Byzantinistik* 25 (1976): 63–73.

Carole Straw, *Gregory the Great: Perfection in Imperfection* (Berkeley, 1988).

Oliver Strunk, "Byzantine Music in the Light of Recent Research and Publication," in J. M. Hussey, ed., *Proceedings of the XIIIth International Congress of Byzantine Studies*, Oxford, 5–10 September, 1966 (Oxford, 1966), pp. 245–54.

J. Szöverffy, "Venantius Fortunatus and the Earliest Hymns to the Holy Cross," *Classical Folia* 20 (1966): 107.

Robert F. Taft, *The Byzantine Rite. A Short History* (Collegeville, MN, 1992).

G. Tchalenko, *Villages antiques de la Syrie du Nord*, I (Paris, 1953), p. 430.

E. Tea, *La Basilica di Santa Maria Antiqua* (Milan, 1937).

Natalia Teterianikov, "For Whom is Theodotus Praying? An Interpretation of the Program of the Private Chapel of S. Maria Antiqua," *Cahiers Archéologiques* 41 (1993): 37–46.

Anton Thanner, *Papst Honorius I. (625–638)* (St. Ottilien, 1989).

Jean-Baptiste Thibaut, "Origines de la messe des Présanctifiés," *Echos d'Orient* 19 (1920): 36–48.

P. Tirot, "Histoire des prières d'offertoire dans la liturgie Romaine du VIIe au XVIe siècle," *Ephemerides Liturgicae* (1984): 148–97, 323–91.

L. Traube, "Chronicon Palatinum," *Byzantinische Zeitschrift* 4 (1895): 489.

F. R. Trombley, *Church and Society in Seventh-Century Byzantium* (Los Angeles, 1978).

A. Tuilier, "La chancellerie imperiale à Byzance et le titre et les fonctions de chanceliere dans l'occident medievale," *Bulletin Phililogique et Historique (jusqu'à 1600) du Comite des Travaux Historiques et Scientifiques* (Paris, 1978), pp. 283–99.

Z. V. Udal'tsova, "Le monde vu par les historiens byzantins du IV au VII siècle," Byzanti-noslavica 33 (1972): 193–213.

Walter Ullmann, A Short History of the Papacy in the Middle Ages (London, 1972).

S. Vailhe, "Jean Mosch," Echos d'Orient 5 (1901–1902): 107.

S. Vailhe, "Sophrone le Sophiste et Sophrone le Patriarche," Revue de l'Orient Chrétien 7 (1902): 360–85; 8 (1903): 32–69, 356–87.

S. Vailhe, "Le titre de patriarche oecuménique avant saint Grégoire le Grand," Echos d'Orient 11 (1908): 65–69.

S. Vailhe, "Saint Grégoire le Grand et le titre patriarche oecuménique," Echos d'Orient 11 (1908): 161–71.

S. Vailhe, "La fête de la Présentation de Marie au Temple," Echos d'Orient 5 (1901–1902): 221–24.

S. Vailhe, "Saint André de Crète," Echos d'Orient 5 (1901–1902): 378–87.

S. Vailhe, "Origines de la fête de l'Annonciation," Echos d'Orient 9 (1906): 138–45.

Roberto Valentini and Giuseppe, Codice Topografico della città di Roma (Rome, 1942).

J.-L. Van Dieten, Geschichte der Patriarchen von Sergios I. bis Iohannes VI. (610–715) (Amsterdam, 1972).

S. J. P. Van Dijk, "The Urban and Papal Rites in 7th and 8th century Rome," Sacris Erudiri 12 (1961): 411–87.

S. J. P. Van Dijk, "The Medieval Easter Vespers of the Roman Clergy," Sacris Erudiri 19 (1969–1970): 261–363.

S .J. P. Van Dijk, "Recent Developments in the Study of the Old Roman Rite," Studia Patristica 8.

M. van Esbroeck, Aux origines de la Dormition de la Vierge. Études historiques sur les traditions orientales (Aldershot, 1995).

M. van Esbroeck, "La cult de la Vierge de Jérusalem à Constantinople au 6-7 siècles," Revue des Études Byzantines 46 (1988): 181–90.

M. van Esbroeck, "Les textes litteraire sur l'Assomption avant le Xe siècle," in F. Bovon, Les acts apocryphes des apotres (Geneva, 1981).

M. van Esbroeck, "La legende romaine des Ss. Come et Damien (BHG 373d) et sa metaphrase georgienne par Jean Xiphilin. I: La legende romain," Orientalia Christiana Periodica 47 (1981): 389–425; 48 (1982): 29–64.

A. A. Vasiliev, History of the Byzantine Empire, Vol. I, 2nd ed. (Madison, 1952).

Max Vasmer, Die Slaven in Griechenland (Berlin, 1941).

Vladimir Vavrinek, ed., From Late Antiquity to Early Byzantium: Proceedings of the Byzanti-nological Symposium in the 16th International Eirene Conference (Prague, 1985).

Paul Verghese, "The Monothelite Controversey: A Historical Survey," Greek Orthodox Theological Review 13 (1968): 196–208.

A. P. Vlasto, The Entry of the Slavs into Christendom (Cambridge, 1970).

Cyrille Vogel, Medieval Liturgy: An Introduction to the Sources, trans. William G. Storey and Niels Rasmussen (Washington, D.C., 1986).

K. Voigt, Stat und Kirche von Konstantin dem Grossen bis zum Ende der Karolingerzeit (Stutt-gart, 1936).

Hans Urs von Balthasar, Liturgie Cosmique: Maxime le Confesseur, trans. L. Lhanmet and H.-A. Prentout (Paris, 1947).

Vera von Falkenhausen, "La lingua greca nella Sicilia medioevale," *Corso di Cultura sull'Arte Ravennate e Bizantina* 27 (1980): 55–58.

Vera von Falkenhausen, "Chiesa greca e chiesa latina in Sicilia," *Archivio Storico Siracusano* n.s. 5 (1978–1979): 137–55.

Vera von Falkenhausen, *La dominazione bizantina in Italia* (Bari, 1978).

Christoph von Schönborn, "La primauté romaine vue d'Orient pendant la querelle des monoénergisme et du monothélisme (VIIe siècle)," *Istina* 20 (1975): 476–90.

Christoph von Schönborn, *Sophrone de Jérusalem: Vie Monastique et Confesion Dogmatique* (Paris, 1972).

Charles Walter, *Prayer and Power in Byzantine and Papal Imagery*, Collected Studies Series, 396 (Aldershot, 1993).

Bryan Ward-Perkins, *From Classical Antiquity to the Middle Ages: Urban Public Buildings in Northern and Central Italy* A.D. *300–850* (Oxford, 1984).

Herman A. J. Wegman, *Christian Worship in East and West*, trans. Gordon W. Lathrop (New York, 1985).

E. Weigand, "Das Theodosiosklöster," *Byzantinische Zeitschrift* 23 (1914): 167–216.

K. Weitzmann, "Various Aspects of Byzantine Influence on the Latin Countries from the 6th to the 12th Centuries," *Dumbarton Oaks Papers* 20 (1966): 6–10.

Egon Wellesz, "Eastern Elements in Western Chant. Studies in the Early History of Ecclesiastical Music," *Monumenta Musicae Byzantinae, Subsidia* 2 (Oxford, 1947).

Egon Wellesz, "The Akathistos Hymn," *Dumbarton Oaks Papers* 9–10 (1955–1956): 141–74.

A. Wenger, *L'Assomption de la tres saint Vierge dans la tradition byzantine du VIe au Xe siècle* (Paris, 1955).

Mary Whitby, "Eutychius, Patriarch of Constantinople: An Epic Holy Man," in Michael Whitby, Philip Hardie, and Mary Whitby, eds., *Homo Viator: Classical Essays for John Bramble* (Bristol, 1987).

Michael Whitby, *The Emperor Maurice and His Historian: Theophylact Simocatta on Persian and Balkan Warfare* (Oxford, 1988).

Lynn T. White Jr., *Latin Monasticism in Norman Sicily* (Cambridge, MA, 1934).

Lynn T. White Jr., "Byzantinization of Sicily," *American Historical Review* 42 (1936): 1–21.

Mark Whittow, *The Making of Byzantium, 600–1025* (Berkeley, 1996).

Chris Wickham, *Early Medieval Italy: Central Power and Local Society 400–1000* (Totowa, NJ, 1981).

G. G. Willis, "The Roman Canon of the Mass at the End of the Sixth Century," *Downside Review* 98 (1980): 124–37.

F. Winkelmann, "Die Quellen zur Erforschung des monoenergitisch-monoteletischen Streites," *Klio* 69 (1987): 515–59.

H. A. Wilson, ed., *Gregorian Sacramentary* (1894).

Gerhard Wirth, Karl-Heinz Schwarte, and Johannes Heinrichs, eds., *Romanitas-Christianitas: Untersuchungen zur Geschichte und Literatur der römischen Kaiserzeit* (Berlin, 1982).

A. Wittmann, *Kosmas und Damiam. Kultausbreitung und Volksdevotion* (Berlin, 1967).

C. Wolfsgruber, *Die vorpäpstliche Lebensperiode Gregors des Großen nach seinen Briefen dargestellt* (Vienna, 1886).

W. Wolska-Conus, "Stéphanos d'Athènes et Stéphanos d'Alexandrie: essai d'identification et de biographie," *Revue des Études Bzyantines* 47 (1989): 5–89.

John Wortley, "The Sixtieth Canon of the Council 'in Trullo,'" *Studia Patristica* 15–16 (1984–1985): 255–60.

D. H. Wright, "The Shape of the Seventh Century in Byzantine Art," in *First Annual Byzantine Studies Conference*, Cleveland, 24–25 October 1995. Abstracts of Papers (Chicago, 1975).

S. Yerasimos, "Apocalypses Constantinopolitaines," *Critique* 48 (1992): 609–24.

Gaston Zananiri, *Histoire de l'Église Byzantine* (Paris, 1954).

R. Zserfass, "Die Idee der römischen Stationsfeier und Ihr Fortleben," *Liturgisches Jahrbuch* 8 (1958): 218–29.

Index

~

About the Author

Andrew J. Ekonomou was educated at Emory University where he graduated magna cum laude and Phi Beta Kappa. After receiving a law degree, he served as Assistant Attorney General for the State of Georgia and thereafter as Assistant U.S. Attorney for the Northern District of Georgia. In 1983, he entered the private practice of law in Atlanta. In 2000, he earned a Ph.D. in Medieval History from Emory, where he teaches Byzantine history and literature. He and his wife, who is a violinist and the orchestra director at a private school, reside in Atlanta.